Lecture Notes in Computer Science   **10588**

Commenced Publication in 1973
Founding and Former Series Editors:
Gerhard Goos, Juris Hartmanis, and Jan van Leeuwen

More information about this series at http://www.springer.com/series/7409

Claudia d'Amato · Miriam Fernandez
Valentina Tamma · Freddy Lecue
Philippe Cudré-Mauroux · Juan Sequeda
Christoph Lange · Jeff Heflin (Eds.)

The Semantic Web – ISWC 2017

16th International Semantic Web Conference
Vienna, Austria, October 21–25, 2017
Proceedings, Part II

 Springer

Editors
Claudia d'Amato 🆔
University of Bari
Bari
Italy

Miriam Fernandez
KMi, The Open University
Milton Keynes
UK

Valentina Tamma
University of Liverpool
Liverpool
UK

Freddy Lecue
Accenture Technology Labs
Dublin
Ireland

Philippe Cudré-Mauroux
University of Fribourg
Fribourg
Switzerland

Juan Sequeda
Capsenta, Inc.
Austin, TX
USA

Christoph Lange 🆔
Universität Bonn
Bonn
Germany

Jeff Heflin
Lehigh University
Bethlehem, PA
USA

ISSN 0302-9743   ISSN 1611-3349   (electronic)
Lecture Notes in Computer Science
ISBN 978-3-319-68203-7   ISBN 978-3-319-68204-4   (eBook)
DOI 10.1007/978-3-319-68204-4

Library of Congress Control Number: 2017955717

LNCS Sublibrary: SL3 – Information Systems and Applications, incl. Internet/Web, and HCI

Printed on acid-free paper

This Springer imprint is published by Springer Nature
The registered company is Springer International Publishing AG
The registered company address is: Gewerbestrasse 11, 6330 Cham, Switzerland

Preface

The International Semantic Web Conference (ISWC) is the premier forum for Semantic Web researchers and practitioners from around the world to gather and share ideas and discoveries. The conference continues to bring together a diverse set of individuals with skills and interests ranging from artificial intelligence to information systems and Web systems. We continue to see steadily increasing adoption of semantic technologies, although more often than not, their use is invisible to consumers.

This volume contains the proceedings of ISWC 2017 with all the papers accepted to the main conference tracks: the Research, Resources, and In-Use Tracks. In addition to the long-standing Research and In-Use Tracks, we have continued the Resources and Journal Tracks that were introduced last year. We also brought back an Industry Track and hope that this will encourage even more cross-fertilization between practitioners and researchers.

The Research Track is home to the most ground-breaking results in the field. This year, we received 197 full submissions, of which 44 were accepted for publication in this volume and presentation at the conference. A large team of reviewers, including 423 Program Committee (PC) members and 23 Senior Program Committee (SPC) members, was carefully selected to ensure a wide coverage of expertise. Each paper was assigned to five reviewers and to an SPC member. The assignment process was based on a bidding phase where PC and SPC members selected papers to review based on their expertise. PC members received a maximum of three papers to review, while SPC members received a maximum of nine papers. A specific form was designed by the Research Track chairs to facilitate the reviewing process and to ensure that all important aspects of the papers were examined. As per the usual process, we included a rebuttal period where authors could respond to the initial reviews. SPC members oversaw the reviews and discussion for each paper in order to resolve disagreements when possible and ensure constructive feedback. Discussions for the papers took place before and after the rebuttal phase to ensure that the authors could answer the key concerns highlighted by the reviewers and that the provided answers were debated, acknowledged, and considered for the final recommendation. Over the course of five days, the SPC members and Research Track chairs held discussions to assess all papers and to make a final decision on which papers to select. During this process, additional reviews were requested for controversial papers. Meta-reviews were written to summarize these discussions and the final recommendation for each paper. While the names of PC members were not visible to the authors, or to each other, during the reviewing period, PC members were given the opportunity to sign their reviews and discussions before the final decision was sent to the authors.

The purpose of the Resources Track is to share resources and best practices for developing them, as we strongly believe that this is crucial in order to consolidate research material, ensure reproducibility of results, and in general gain new scientific insights. The term "resource" can refer to: datasets, ontologies, vocabularies, workflows, evaluation benchmarks or methods, replication studies, services, APIs, and software frameworks that have contributed to the generation of novel scientific work. One of the requirements of this track is that the resources were published with a permanent URI in order to guarantee future access. This year, our publisher piloted a dedicated infrastructure for publishing snapshots of resources to facilitate this process. The track received 76 submissions and accepted 23 of them; seven of these, as well as three of the Research Track, made use of the dedicated resource publishing facility, as can be seen from the respective references in these papers. Each paper received four reviews, and an SPC member provided a meta-review. Similar to the Research Track, there was a rebuttal phase, which was then followed by further discussion among the reviewers and managed by the SPC member who summarized all views in a recommendation to the Resource Track chairs. The final decisions were determined through discussions between the track chairs and the SPC members and were based on the overall views expressed by the reviewers, the meta-reviews and the lively discussions that occurred before and after the rebuttal phase.

The In-Use Track provides a forum for the community to explore the benefits and challenges of applying semantic technologies in concrete, practical applications, in contexts ranging from industry to government and science. This year, the track required that papers provide evidence that there is use of the proposed application or tool by the target user group, preferably outside the group that conducted the development. We received 29 submissions, and accepted nine. Each submission was assigned four reviewers.

Traditionally, ISWC has a different keynote speaker to kick off each day of the main conference. This year we had three exciting keynote talks delivered by Nada Lavrac (Jozef Stefan Institute), Deborah L. McGuinness (Rensselaer Polytechnic Institute), and Jamie Taylor (Google). The titles and abstracts of these talks are included in this volume.

There were many important activities at ISWC 2017 that are not represented in these proceedings. The two days prior to the main conference involved many smaller sessions: workshops, tutorials, and the doctoral consortium. Aidan Hogan and Valentina Presutti were our workshops and tutorials chairs, and selected seven tutorials and 19 workshops for the program. The doctoral consortium was chaired by Lora Aroyo and Fabien Gandon. In all, 26 PhD students submitted papers, and after review by the PC, 13 were accepted to the event.

The Journal Track provided the authors of papers recently published in Semantic Web journals the opportunity to present their papers to the conference community. The editors of the *Journal of Web Semantics* and the *Semantic Web Journal* selected a total of 12 papers published in the previous year (but never presented at ISWC).

The first day of the main conference included an Industry Track and a Posters and Demonstrations Session. The Industry Track was chaired by Achille Fokoue and Peter Haase with the goal of presenting the state of adoption of semantic technologies in industrial applications, whether it be specific industries or as a horizontal technology. This track received 30 submissions and accepted 18 for presentation. The Posters and Demonstrations Track was chaired by Nadeschda Nikitina and Dezhao Song.

This year saw the return of a reinvigorated Semantic Web Challenge. Led by Dan Bennett, Axel Ngonga, and Heiko Paulheim, this year's challenge involved two measurable tasks, i.e., knowledge graph population and knowledge graph validation.

In recognition of the maturing of the field, we added two new events to the conference. In order to reach out to the general public, we featured an event supported by the Vienna Business Agency for the local community in the form of a combined local business lounge and Semantic Web meet-up, co-located with the Posters and Demonstration Track. In addition, this year ISWC celebrated its first Job Fair, bringing together job candidates with open positions in both industry and academia.

The success of a large conference like ISWC also depends on a number of people whose contribution is not directly reflected in the program. We would like to thank our sponsorship chairs Michel Dumontier, Sabrina Kirrane, and Harald Sack, for their efforts in securing external funding to help offset the fixed costs of the conference. We would like to thank our student coordinators Lalana Kagal and Gianluca Demartini for managing the student travel fellowships and organizing the mentoring lunch. Stefan Dietze and Davide Taibi provided the valuable service of collecting and organizing our metadata; an essential task for a community that places so much value on semantics. Our publicity chair Anna Lisa Gentile did a fantastic job of getting the word out on multiple platforms. And of course, the proceedings you are reading today (whether in "old-school" paper form or electronically) would not have been possible without the diligent efforts of our proceedings chair, Christoph Lange.

Last, but certainly not least, we would like to give a big thank you to our local chairs Axel Polleres and Elmar Kiesling. Few people realize the amount of work that goes into the logistics of a conference of this scale, and often the local chairs are invisible unless something goes horribly wrong. Axel, Elmar, and their team have worked countless hours over the course of two years to ensure that everything runs smoothly.

October 2017

Claudia d'Amato
Miriam Fernandez
Valentina Tamma
Freddy Lecue
Philippe Cudré-Mauroux
Juan Sequeda
Jeff Heflin

Organization

Organizing Committee

General Chair

Jeff Heflin — Lehigh University, USA

Local Chairs

Axel Polleres — WU Wien, Austria
Elmar Kiesling — TU Wien, Austria

Research Track Chairs

Claudia d'Amato — University of Bari, Italy
Miriam Fernandez — KMi, The Open University, UK

Resources Track Chairs

Valentina Tamma — University of Liverpool, UK
Freddy Lecue — Accenture, Dublin, Ireland/Inria, Sophia Antipolis, France

In-Use Track Chairs

Philippe Cudré-Mauroux — University of Fribourg, Switzerland
Juan Sequeda — Capsenta, Austin, USA

Workshop and Tutorial Chairs

Aidan Hogan — Universidad de Chile, Chile
Valentina Presutti — Institute of Cognitive Sciences and Technologies,
CNR, Italy

Poster and Demo Track Chairs

Nadeschda Nikitina — University of Oxford, UK
Dezhao Song — Thomson Reuters, Eagan, USA

Journal Track Chairs

Abraham Bernstein — University of Zurich, Switzerland
Pascal Hitzler — Wright State University, USA
Steffen Staab — University of Koblenz, Germany

Industry Track Chairs

Achille Fokoue — IBM Yorktown, USA
Peter Haase — metaphacts, Germany

Doctoral Consortium Chairs

Lora Aroyo	Vrije Universiteit Amsterdam, The Netherlands
Fabien Gandon	Inria Sophia Antipolis, France

Semantic Web Challenge Chairs

Dan Bennett	Thomson Reuters, Eagan, USA
Axel Ngonga	University of Paderborn, Germany
Heiko Paulheim	University of Mannheim, Germany

Proceedings Chair

Christoph Lange	University of Bonn and Fraunhofer IAIS, Germany

Metadata Chairs

Stefan Dietze	L3S, Leibniz University, Germany
Davide Taibi	Institute for Educational Technology, CNR, Italy

Sponsorship Chairs

Michel Dumontier	Maastricht University, The Netherlands
Sabrina Kirrane	WU Wien, Austria
Harald Sack	FIZ Karlsruhe, KIT Karlsruhe, Germany

Student Coordinators

Lalana Kagal	Massachusetts Institute of Technology, USA
Gianluca Demartini	University of Queensland, Australia

Publicity Chair

Anna Lisa Gentile	IBM Research Almaden, USA

Local Committee

Bettina Bauer	SBA Research, Vienna, Austria
Fajar J. Ekaputra	TU Wien, Austria
Javier D. Fernández	WU Wien, Austria
Yvonne Poul	SBA Research, Vienna, Austria
Doris Wyk	WU Wien, Austria

Program Committee

Senior Program Committee – Research Track

Harith Alani	Knowledge Media Institute, Open University, UK
Abraham Bernstein	University of Zurich, Switzerland
Kalina Bontcheva	University of Sheffield, UK
Philipp Cimiano	Bielefeld University, Germany

Oscar Corcho	Universidad Politécnica de Madrid, Spain
Mathieu D'Aquin	Insight Centre, National University of Ireland Galway, Ireland
Fabien Gandon	Inria, France
Jose Manuel Gomez-Perez	Expert System, Spain
Jorge Gracia	Universidad Politécnica de Madrid, Spain
Claudio Gutierrez	Universidad de Chile, Chile
Olaf Hartig	Linköping University, Sweden
Pascal Hitzler	Wright State University, USA
Craig Knoblock	University of Southern California, USA
Vanessa Lopez	IBM Research, USA
Thomas Lukasiewicz	University of Oxford, UK
H. Sofia Pinto	Instituto Superior Tecnico, Portugal
Uli Sattler	University of Manchester, UK
Stefan Schlobach	Vrije Universiteit Amsterdam, The Netherlands
Steffen Staab	Institut WeST, University of Koblenz-Landau, Germany and WAIS, University of Southampton, UK
Vojtěch Svátek	University of Economics, Prague, Czech Republic
Tania Tudorache	Stanford University, USA
Maria Esther Vidal	Universidad Simon Bolivar, Venezuela
Denny Vrandečić	Google, USA

Program Committee – Research Track

Maribel Acosta	Institute AIFB, Karlsruhe Institute of Technology, Germany
Alessandro Adamou	Knowledge Media Institute, The Open University, UK
Nitish Aggarwal	IBM Watson, USA
Guadalupe Aguado-De-Cea	Universidad Politécnica de Madrid, Spain
Panos Alexopoulos	Textkernel B.V., The Netherlands
Jose Julio Alferes	Universidade Nova de Lisboa, Portugal
Muhammad Intizar Ali	Insight Centre for Data Analytics, National University of Ireland, Galway
Marjan Alirezaie	Orebro University, Sweden
Faisal Alkhateeb	Yarmouk University, Jordan
Tahani Alsubait	Umm Al-Qura University, Saudi Arabia
José Luis Ambite	University of Southern California, USA
Pramod Anantharam	Bosch Research and Technology Center, USA
Renzo Angles	Universidad de Talca, Chile
Grigoris Antoniou	University of Huddersfield, UK
Kemafor Anyanwu	North Carolina State University, USA
Manuel Atencia	University of Grenoble Alpes and Inria, France
Ioannis N. Athanasiadis	Wageningen University, The Netherlands
Medha Atre	IIT Kanpur, India

Jérôme Euzenat	Inria and University of Grenoble Alpes, France
James Fan	HelloVera.ai, USA
Nicola Fanizzi	Università di Bari, Italy
Catherine Faron-Zucker	Université Nice Sophia Antipolis, France
Anna Fensel	Semantic Technology Institute (STI) – University of Innsbruck, Austria
Alberto Fernandez	University Rey Juan Carlos, Spain
Javier D. Fernández	Vienna University of Economics and Business WU Wien, Austria
Sebastien Ferre	University of Rennes 1, France
Besnik Fetahu	L3S Research Center, Germany
Tim Finin	University of Maryland Baltimore County, USA
Valeria Fionda	University of Calabria, Italy
Lorenz Fischer	Sentient Machines, UK
Fabian Flöck	GESIS Cologne, Germany
Antske Fokkens	VU University Amsterdam, The Netherlands
Muriel Foulonneau	Luxembourg Institute of Science and Technology, Luxembourg
Enrico Franconi	Free University of Bozen-Bolzano, Italy
Flavius Frasincar	Erasmus University Rotterdam, The Netherlands
Fred Freitas	Universidade Federal de Pernambuco (UFPE), Brazil
Adam Funk	University of Sheffield, UK
Aldo Gangemi	Université Paris 13 and CNR-ISTC, Italy
Shen Gao	University of Zurich, Switzerland
José Maria García	University of Seville, Spain
Raúl García Castro	Universidad Politécnica de Madrid, Spain
Andrés García-Silva	Expert System, Spain
Claire Gardent	CNRS/LORIA Nancy, France
Daniel Garijo	Information Sciences Institute, University of Southern California, USA
Anna Lisa Gentile	IBM Research Almaden, San Jose, CA, USA
Chiara Ghidini	FBK-irst, Italy
Alain Giboin	Inria Sophia Antipolis/Méditerranée, France
Rafael S. Gonçalves	Stanford University, USA
Gregory Grefenstette	Biggerpan, France
Ruediger Grimm	University of Koblenz Landau, Germany
Paul Groth	Elsevier Labs, The Netherlands
Tudor Groza	The Garvan Institute of Medical Research, Australia
Alessio Gugliotta	Innova, Italy
Cathal Gurrin	Dublin City University, Ireland
Christophe Guéret	Accenture, Ireland
Olaf Görlitz	Chefkoch GmbH, Germany
Peter Haase	metaphacts, Germany
Armin Haller	Australian National University, Australia
Harry Halpin	World Wide Web Consortium, UK
Karl Hammar	Jönköping University, Sweden

Matthias Knorr	Universidade Nova de Lisboa, Portugal
Magnus Knuth	Hasso Plattner Institute, University of Potsdam, Germany
Boris Konev	University of Liverpool, UK
Stasinos Konstantopoulos	NCSR Demokritos, Greece
Roman Kontchakov	Birkbeck, University of London, UK
Jacek Kopecky	University of Portsmouth, UK
Manolis Koubarakis	National and Kapodistrian University of Athens, Greece
Adila Krisnadhi	Wright State University, USA and Universitas Indonesia, Indonesia
Udo Kruschwitz	University of Essex, UK
Tobias Kuhn	VU University Amsterdam, The Netherlands
Benedikt Kämpgen	Empolis Information Management GmbH, Germany
Patrick Lambrix	Linköping University, Sweden
Steffen Lamparter	Siemens AG Corporate Technology, Germany
Christoph Lange	University of Bonn and Fraunhofer IAIS, Germany
David Laniado	Eurecat - Technology Centre of Catalonia, Spain
Ken Laskey	The MITRE Corporation, USA
Agnieszka Lawrynowicz	Poznan University of Technology, Poland
Danh Le Phuoc	Technische Universität Berlin, Germany
Maxime Lefrançois	MINES Saint-Etienne, France
Maurizio Lenzerini	University of Rome La Sapienza, Italy
Chengkai Li	University of Texas at Arlington, USA
Juanzi Li	Tsinghua University, China
Wenwen Li	Arizona State University, USA
Giorgia Lodi	DigitPA, Italy
Nuno Lopes	TopQuadrant Inc., Ireland
Chun Lu	Université Paris-Sorbonne and Sépage, France
Markus Luczak-Roesch	Victoria University of Wellington, New Zealand
Carsten Lutz	Universität Bremen, Germany
Ioanna Lytra	Enterprise Information Systems, Institute of Applied Computer Science, University of Bonn and Fraunhofer IAIS, Germany
Alexander Löser	Beuth Hochschule für Technik Berlin, Germany
Frederick Maier	Institute for Artificial Intelligence, USA
Maria Maleshkova	AIFB, Karlsruhe Institute of Technology, Germany
Claudia Marinica	ETIS/ENSEA UCP CNRS, France
David Martin	Nuance Communications, USA
Trevor Martin	University of Bristol, UK
Mercedes Martinez-Gonzalez	University of Valladolid, Spain
Miguel Martinez-Prieto	University of Valladolid, Spain
Wolfgang May	Universität Göttingen Germany, Germany
Diana Maynard	University of Sheffield, UK
John McCrae	National University of Ireland Galway, Ireland
Fiona McNeill	Heriot Watt University, UK

Lionel Médini	LIRIS/University of Lyon, France
Eduardo Mena	University of Zaragoza, Spain
Robert Meusel	SAP SE, Germany
Franck Michel	Université Côte d'Azur, CNRS, I3S, France
Nandana Mihindukulasooriya	Universidad Politécnica de Madrid, Spain
Peter Mika	Schibsted, Norway
Alessandra Mileo	INSIGHT Centre for Data Analytics, Dublin City University, Ireland
Daniel Miranker	Institute for Cell and Molecular Biology, The University of Texas at Austin, USA
Riichiro Mizoguchi	Japan Advanced Institute of Science and Technology, Japan
Dunja Mladenic	Jozef Stefan Institute, Slovenia
Marie-Francine Moens	KU Leuven, Belgium
Pascal Molli	University of Nantes/LS2N, France
Gabriela Montoya	Aalborg University, Denmark
Federico Morando	Nexa Center for Internet and Society, Politecnico di Torino, Italy
Luc Moreau	King's College London, UK
Yassine Mrabet	National Library of Medicine, USA
Paul Mulholland	The Open University, UK
Raghava Mutharaju	GE Global Research, USA
Ralf Möller	University of Lübeck, Germany
Claudia Müller-Birn	Freie Universität Berlin, Germany
Hubert Naacke	UPMC, France
Amedeo Napoli	LORIA Nancy (CNRS - Inria - Université de Lorraine), France
Axel-Cyrille Ngonga-Ngomo	University of Paderborn, Germany
Matthias Nickles	Digital Enterprise Research Institute, National University of Ireland Galway, Ireland
Nadeschda Nikitina	Oxford University, UK
Andriy Nikolov	metaphacts GmbH, Germany
Malvina Nissim	University of Groningen, The Netherlands
Lyndon Nixon	MODUL Technology GmbH, Austria
Andrea Giovanni Nuzzolese	STLab ISTC-CNR, Italy
Leo Obrst	MITRE, USA
Francesco Osborne	KMi, The Open University, UK
Raul Palma	Poznan Supercomputing and Networking Center, Poland
Matteo Palmonari	University of Milano-Bicocca, Italy
Jeff Pan	University of Aberdeen, UK
Rahul Parundekar	Toyota Info-Technology Center, USA
Bibek Paudel	University of Zurich, Switzerland
Heiko Paulheim	University of Mannheim, Germany

Terry Payne	University of Liverpool, UK
Tassilo Pellegrini	University of Applied Sciences St. Pölten, Austria
Laura Perez-Beltrachini	University of Edinburgh, UK
Silvio Peroni	University of Bologna, Italy
Catia Pesquita	LaSIGE, Universidade de Lisboa, Portugal
Rafael Peñaloza	Free University of Bozen-Bolzano, Italy
Reinhard Pichler	Vienna University of Technology, Austria
Emmanuel Pietriga	Inria, France
Giuseppe Pirrò	Institute for High Performance Computing and Networking (ICAR-CNR), Italy
Vassilis Plachouras	Thomson Reuters, UK
Dimitris Plexousakis	Institute of Computer Science FORTH, University of Crete, Greece
Simone Paolo Ponzetto	University of Mannheim, Germany
Mike Pool	Goldman Sachs Group, USA
Livia Predoiu	University of Oxford, UK
Laurette Pretorius	University of South Africa, South Africa
Cédric Pruski	Luxembourg Institute of Science and Technology, Luxembourg
Guilin Qi	Southeast University, China
Yuzhong Qu	Nanjing University, China
Jorge-Arnulfo Quiané-Ruiz	QCRI, Qatar
Filip Radulovic	Sépage Paris, France
Dnyanesh Rajpathak	General Motors, Operations Research R&D, USA
Ganesh Ramakrishnan	IIT Bombay, India
Maya Ramanath	IIT Delhi, India
David Ratcliffe	CSIRO Data61 and Australian National University, Australia
Dietrich Rebholz-Schuhmann	Insight Centre for Data Analytics, National University of Ireland Galway, Ireland
José Luis Redondo-García	Amazon Research, UK
Georg Rehm	DFKI, Germany
Achim Rettinger	Karlsruhe Institute of Technology, Germany
Juan Reutter	Pontificia Universidad Catòlica, Chile
Martin Rezk	Rakuten Inc., Japan
German Rigau	IXA Group – UPV/EHU, Spain
Carlos Rivero	Rochester Institute of Technology, USA
Giuseppe Rizzo	ISMB, Italy
Mariano Rodríguez Muro	IBM Research, USA
Marco Rospocher	Fondazione Bruno Kessler, Italy
Camille Roth	CNRS, Germany
Marie-Christine Rousset	University of Grenoble Alpes, France
Ana Roxin	University of Burgundy UMR CNRS, France

Sebastian Rudolph	Technische Universität Dresden, Germany
Owen Sacco	Institute of Digital Games, University of Malta, Malta
Harald Sack	FIZ Karlsruhe Leibniz Institute for Information Infrastructure and KIT Karlsruhe, Germany
Hassan Saif	KMi, The Open University, UK
Angelo Antonio Salatino	KMi, The Open University, UK
Muhammad Saleem	AKSW, University of Leizpig, Germany
Cristina Sarasua	Institute for Web Science and Technologies (WeST), Universität Koblenz-Landau, Germany
Felix Sasaki	Lambdawerk, Germany
Bahar Sateli	Concordia University, Canada
Kai-Uwe Sattler	TU Ilmenau, Germany
Vadim Savenkov	Vienna University of Economics and Business (WU), Austria
Marco Luca Sbodio	IBM Research, Ireland
Johann Schaible	GESIS, Leibniz Institute for the Social Sciences, Germany
Bernhard Schandl	mySugr GmbH, Austria
Ansgar Scherp	Kiel University and ZBW, Leibniz Information Center for Economics Kiel, Germany
Marvin Schiller	University of Ulm, Germany
Claudia Schon	Universität Koblenz-Landau, Germany
Marco Schorlemmer	Artificial Intelligence Research Institute IIIA-CSIC, Spain
Lutz Schröder	Friedrich-Alexander-Universität Erlangen-Nürnberg, Germany
Daniel Schwabe	PUC-Rio, Brazil
Erich Schweighofer	University of Vienna, Austria
Frederique Segond	Viseo Innovation, France
Giovanni Semeraro	University of Bari, Italy
Juan Sequeda	Capsenta, USA
Luciano Serafini	Fondazione Bruno Kessler, Italy
Estefania Serral	KU Leuven, Belgium
Saeedeh Shekarpour	Kno.e.sis Center, USA
Sakr Sherif	The University of New South Wales, Australia
Gerardo Simari	Universidad Nacional del Sur and CONICET, Argentina
Kiril Simov	Linguistic Modelling Department, IICT-BAS, Bulgaria
Elena Simperl	University of Southampton, UK
Hala Skaf-Molli	Nantes University, France
Sebastian Skritek	TU Wien, Austria
Monika Solanki	University of Oxford, UK
Dezhao Song	Thomson Reuters, USA
Biplav Srivastava	IBM Research, USA
Yannis Stavrakas	Institute for the Management of Information Systems, Research and Innovation Center Athena, Greece
Sławek Staworko	University of Lille 3, France
Armando Stellato	University of Rome Tor Vergata, Italy

Audun Stolpe	Norwegian Defence Research Establishment (FFI), Norway
Umberto Straccia	ISTI-CNR, Italy
Markus Strohmaier	RWTH Aachen and GESIS, Germany
Heiner Stuckenschmidt	University of Mannheim, Germany
Gerd Stumme	University of Kassel, Germany
Fabian Suchanek	Télécom ParisTech University, France
Jing Sun	The University of Auckland, New Zealand
York Sure-Vetter	Karlsruhe Institute of Technology (KIT), Germany
Marcin Sydow	PJIIT and ICS PAS Warsaw, Poland
Pedro Szekely	USC/Information Sciences Institute, USA
Mohsen Taheriyan	Google, USA
Hideaki Takeda	National Institute of Informatics, Japan
Kerry Taylor	Australian National University, Australia
Annette Ten Teije	VU University Amsterdam, The Netherlands
Andrea Tettamanzi	University of Nice Sophia Antipolis, France
Kia Teymourian	Rice University, USA
Dhavalkumar Thakker	University of Bradford, UK
Matthias Thimm	Universität Koblenz-Landau, Germany
Allan Third	The Open University, UK
Krishnaprasad Thirunarayan	Wright State University, USA
Ilaria Tiddi	KMi, The Open University, UK
Ramine Tinati	University of Southampton, UK
Thanassis Tiropanis	University of Southampton, UK
Konstantin Todorov	LIRMM/University of Montpellier, France
David Toman	University of Waterloo, Canada
Nicolas Torzec	Yahoo, USA
Farouk Toumani	Limos Blaise Pascal University Clermont-Ferrand, France
Yannick Toussaint	LORIA, France
Sebastian Tramp	eccenca GmbH, Germany
Cassia Trojahn	UT2J and IRIT, France
Raphaël Troncy	EURECOM, France
Dmitry Tsarkov	Google, Switzerland
Anni-Yasmin Turhan	Technische Universität Dresden, Germany
Jürgen Umbrich	Vienna University of Economy and Business (WU), Austria
Jörg Unbehauen	University of Leipzig, Germany
Jacopo Urbani	Vrije Universiteit Amsterdam, The Netherlands
Alejandro Vaisman	Instituto Tecnològico de Buenos Aires, Argentina
Herbert Van De Sompel	Los Alamos National Laboratory Research Library, USA
Marieke van Erp	KNAW Humanities Cluster, The Netherlands
Willem Robert van Hage	Netherlands eScience Center, The Netherlands
Jacco van Ossenbruggen	CWI and VU University Amsterdam, The Netherlands

Ruben Verborgh	Ghent University – imec, Belgium
Daniel Vila-Suero	Ontology Engineering Group UPM, Spain
Serena Villata	CNRS, Laboratoire d'Informatique Signaux et Systèmes de Sophia Antipolis, France
Marta Villegas	Barcelona Supercomputing Center, Spain
Piek Vossen	VU University Amsterdam, The Netherlands
Domagoj Vrgoc	Pontificia Universidad Catòlica de Chile, Chile
Holger Wache	University of Applied Science and Arts Northweastern Switzerland, Switzerland
Claudia Wagner	GESIS-Leibniz Institute for the Social Sciences, Germany
Simon Walk	Graz University of Technology, Austria
Haofen Wang	Shenzhen Gowild Robotics Co. Ltd., China
Kewen Wang	Griffith University, Australia
Shenghui Wang	OCLC Research, The Netherlands
Zhichun Wang	Beijing Normal University, China
Paul Warren	KMi, The Open University, UK
Grant Weddell	University of Waterloo, Canada
Rigo Wenning	W3C, France
Erik Wilde	CA Technologies, Switzerland
Cord Wiljes	CITEC, Bielefeld University, Germany
Gregory Todd Williams	Rensselaer Polytechnic Institute, USA
Jiewen Wu	Accenture Tech Labs, Ireland
Marcin Wylot	TU Berlin, Germany
Josiane Xavier Parreira	Siemens AG Österreich, Austria
Yong Yu	Shanghai Jiao Tong University, China
Fouad Zablith	American University of Beirut, Lebanon
Ondřej Zamazal	University of Economics Prague, Czech Republic
Benjamin Zapilko	GESIS, Leibniz Institute for the Social Sciences, Germany
Amrapali Zaveri	Maastricht University, The Netherlands
Sergej Zerr	L3S Research Center, Germany
Qingpeng Zhang	City University of Hong Kong, China
Ziqi Zhang	Nottingham Trent University, UK
Jun Zhao	University of Oxford, UK
Antoine Zimmermann	École des Mines de Saint-Étienne, France

Additional Reviewers – Research Track

Ahn, Jinhyun
Anelli, Vito Walter
Ara, Safina Showkat
Atencia, Manuel
Bader, Sebastian
Bakhshandegan Moghaddam, Farshad
Basile, Valerio
Batsakis, Sotiris

Binns, Reuben
Blume, Till
Bosque-Gil, Julia
Bourgaux, Camille
Brank, Janez
Calleja, Pablo
Čerāns, Kārlis
Charalambidis, Angelos

Charron, Bruno
Chen, Jiaoyan
Chernushenko, Iurii
Ciortea, Andrei
Collarana, Diego
Comerio, Marco
Dehghanzadeh, Soheila
Di Francescomarino, Chiara
Dimitrov, Dimitar
Donadello, Ivan
Feier, Cristina
Frank, Matthias
Freitas, Andre
Galkin, Mikhail
Gao, Shen
Gao, Yimei
Giboin, Alain
Giménez-García, José M.
Gottschalk, Simon
Hanika, Tom
Hildebrandt, Marcel
Janke, Daniel
Jiaoyan, Chen
Kaefer, Tobias
Kamdar, Maulik R.
Kasper, Patrick
Keppmann, Felix Leif
Keskisärkkä, Robin
Kilias, Torsten
Kling, Christoph
Kondylakis, Haridimos
Koopmann, Patrick
Laforest, Frederique
Lee Sungin
Lima, Rinaldo
Liu, Qian
Mehdi, Gulnar
Mihindukulasooriya, Nandana
Mireles, Victor
Molinari, Andrea
Moodley, Kody

Mossakowski, Till
Musto, Cataldo
Nanni, Federico
Narducci, Fedelucio
Niebler, Thomas
Nishioka, Chifumi
Novalija, Inna
Osmani, Aomar
Padia, Ankur
Patkos, Theodore
Pham, Le Thi Anh Thu
Piao, Guangyuan
Plu, Julien
Qiu, Lin
Rettig, Laura
Revenko, Artem
Ringsquandl, Martin
Rokicki, Markus
Saeef, Mohammed Samiul
Sarker, Md Kamruzzaman
Schneider, Patrik
Setty, Vinay
Shivaprabhu, Vivek
Simkus, Mantas
Smirnova, Alisa
Soru, Tommaso
Steinmetz, Nadine
Suchanek, Fabian M.
Tachmazidis, Ilias
Thoma, Steffen
Thost, Veronika
Tommasini, Riccardo
Usbeck, Ricardo
Van Harmelen, Frank
Wang, Xin
Wang, Zhe
Xiao, Guohui
Xu, Kang
Yimei, Gao
Zaraket, Fadi
Zhang, Gensheng

Senior Program Committee – Resources Track

Mauro Dragoni	Fondazione Bruno Kessler – FBK-IRST, Italy
Daniel Garijo	Information Sciences Institute, University of Southern California, USA
Alasdair Gray	Heriot-Watt University, UK
Matthew Horridge	Stanford University, USA
Ernesto Jimenez-Ruiz	University of Oslo, Norway
Bijan Parsia	University of Manchester, UK
Stefan Schulte	Vienna University of Technology, Austria

Program Committee – Resources Track

Muhammad Intizar Ali	Insight Centre for Data Analytics, National University of Ireland, Galway, Ireland
Elena Cabrio	Université Côte d'Azur, CNRS Inria I3S, France, France
Mari Carmen Suárez-Figueroa	Universidad Politécnica de Madrid, Spain
David Carral	TU Dresden, Germany
Tim Clark	Massachusetts General Hospital/Harvard Medical School, USA
Francesco Corcoglioniti	Fondazione Bruno Kessler, Italy
Daniele Dell'Aglio	University of Zurich, Switzerland
Ying Ding	Indiana University, USA
Mohnish Dubey	Computer Science Institute, University of Bonn, Germany
Fajar J. Ekaputra	Vienna University of Technology, Austria
Diego Esteves	University of Bonn, Germany
Stefano Faralli	University of Mannheim, Germany
Mariano Fernández López	Universidad San Pablo CEU, Spain
Aldo Gangemi	Université Paris 13 and CNR-ISTC, Italy
Alejandra Gonzalez-Beltran	University of Oxford, UK
Rafael S. Gonçalves	Stanford University, USA
Christophe Guéret	Accenture, Ireland
Amelie Gyrard	Ecole des Mines de Saint Etienne, France
Pascal Hitzler	Wright State University, USA
Robert Hoehndorf	King Abdullah University of Science and Technology, Saudi Arabia
Aidan Hogan	DCC, Universidad de Chile, Chile
Antoine Isaac	Europeana and VU University Amsterdam, The Netherlands
Chen Jiaoyan	GIScience, Heidelberg University, Germany
Simon Jupp	European Bioinformatics Institute, UK
Maria Keet	University of Cape Town, South Africa, South Africa
Elmar Kiesling	Vienna University of Technology, Austria

Additional Reviewers – Resources Track

Amini, Reihaneh
Atemezing, Ghislain Auguste
Bianchi, Federico
Bosque-Gil, Julia
Byamugisha, Joan
Chakraborty, Nilesh
Daquino, Marilena
Francis, Jonathan
Gracia, Jorge
Halilaj, Lavdim
Hu, Wei
Kastler, Leon
Lehrig, Sebastian
Mader, Christian
Mulligan, Natasha
Navas-Loro, María

Nayyeri, Mojtaba
Poggi, Francesco
Priyatna, Freddy
Radulovic, Filip
Sarker, Md Kamruzzaman
Sarntivijai, Sirarat
Sazonau, Viachaslau
Shimizu, Cogan
Spahiu, Blerina
Tommasi, Pierpaolo
Wadkar, Sudarshan
Warrender, Jennifer
Weller, Tobias
Wiens, Vitalis
Zhou, Lu

Program Committee – In-Use Track

Jean-Paul Calbimonte	University of Applied Sciences and Arts Western Switzerland HES-SO, Switzerland
Christophe Guéret	Accenture, Ireland
Mauro Dragoni	Fondazione Bruno Kessler, FBK-IRST, Italy
Oshani Seneviratne	Massachusetts Institute of Technology, USA
Tudor Groza	The Garvan Institute of Medical Research, Australia
Stefan Dietze	L3S Research Center, Germany
Héctor Pérez-Urbina	Google, USA
Tim Clark	Massachusetts General Hospital/Harvard Medical School, USA
Anna Lisa Gentile	IBM Research Almaden, USA
Dezhao Song	Thomson Reuters, USA
Prateek Jain	BlackRock, USA
Brian Davis	Insight Centre for Data Analytics, Galway, Ireland
Andriy Nikolov	metaphacts GmbH, Germany
Raphaël Troncy	EURECOM, France
Pedro Szekely	USC/Information Sciences Institute, USA
Harald Sack	FIZ Karlsruhe, Leibniz Institute for Information Infrastructure and KIT Karlsruhe, Germany
Daniel Garijo	Information Sciences Institute, University of Southern California, USA
Achille Fokoue	IBM Research, USA
Matthew Horridge	Stanford University, USA
Irene Celino	CEFRIEL, Italy
Jérôme Euzenat	Inria and University of Grenoble Alpes, France
Boris Motik	University of Oxford, UK

Additional Reviewers – In-Use Track

Sponsors

Platinum Sponsors

http://www.ibm.com/   http://www.elsevier.com/

Gold Sponsors

https://www.semantic-web.at/

metaphacts
http://www.metaphacts.com/

https://www.big-data-europe.eu/

http://www.oracle.com/

SIEMENS
Ingenuity for life

http://siemens.at/

https://data.world/

http://www.thomsonreuters.com/

ontotext

http://www.ontoforce.com/

http://ontotext.com/

http://www.videolectures.net/

Bronze Sponsors

https://www.inria.fr/centre/sophia/

Google

http://www.google.com/

Student Travel Award Sponsors

https://www.nsf.gov/

http://swsa.semanticweb.org/

WiFi Sponsor

https://www.kapsch.net/

Supporters

Supported by

http://swsa.semanticweb.org/

https://viennabusinessagency.at/

https://www.w3.org/

https://www.eurai.org/

http://www.iospress.nl/

http://www.springer.com/

Organizers

https://www.wu.ac.at/en/

https://www.tuwien.ac.at/en/

https://www.sba-research.org/

Abstracts of Invited Talks

From Relational to Semantic Data Mining

Nada Lavrač[1,2,3]

[1] Jožef Stefan Institute, Ljubljana, Slovenia
nada.lavrac@ijs.si
[2] Jožef Stefan International Postgraduate School, Ljubljana, Slovenia
[3] University of Nova Gorica, Nova Gorica, Slovenia

Abstract. Relational Data Mining (RDM) addresses the task of inducing models or patterns from multi-relational data. One of the established approaches to RDM is propositionalization, characterized by transforming a relational database into a single-table representation. The talk provides an overview of propositionalization algorithms, and a particular approach named wordification, all of which have been made publicly available through the web-based ClowdFlows data mining platform. The focus of this talk is on recent advances in Semantic Data Mining (SDM), characterized by exploiting relational background knowledge in the form of domain ontologies in the process of model and pattern construction. The open source SDM approaches, available through the ClowdFlows platform, enable software reuse and experiment replication. The talk concludes by presenting the recent developments, which allow to speed up SDM by data mining and network analysis approaches.

Ontologies for the Modern Age

Deborah L. McGuinness

Rensselaer Institute for Data Exploration and Applications, USA
dlm@cs.rpi.edu

Abstract. Ontologies are seeing a resurgence of interest and usage as big data proliferates, machine learning advances, and integration of data becomes more paramount. The previous models of sometimes labor-intensive, centralized ontology construction and maintenance do not mesh well in today's interdisciplinary world that is in the midst of a big data, information extraction, and machine learning explosion. In this talk, we will provide some historical perspective on ontologies and their usage, and discuss a model of building and maintaining large collaborative, interdisciplinary ontologies along with the data repositories and data services that they empower. We will give a few examples of heterogeneous semantic data resources made more interconnected and more powerful by ontology-supported infrastructures, discuss a vision for ontology-enabled future research and provide some examples in a large health empowerment joint effort between RPI and IBM Watson Health.

Applied Semantics: Beyond the Catalog

Jamie Taylor

Google, USA
jamietaylor@google.com

Abstract. A decade ago a number of semantic catalogs started appearing. These catalogs gave identifiers to things, assigned them categories and asserted facts about them. Dubbed knowledge graphs, the intent is to describe the world in a machine readable way.

These catalogs have proved incredibly useful, allowing publishers to organize their content management systems, powering machines that can win game shows and allowing search engines to guide users by interpreting their queries as being about "things not strings."

While useful, these catalogs are semantically limited. The connections entities participate in are sparse, requiring human understanding when decoding relationships and categorical membership. Entities are frequently identified by lucky linguistic matches rather than constraints against semantic intent.

If machines are to understand our world and react intelligently to requests about it, knowledge graphs need to grow beyond catalogs, encoding things which stretch the notion of "fact" and act as semantic APIs for the real world.

Contents – Part II

In-Use Track

Contents – Part I

Resource Track

Diefficiency Metrics: Measuring the Continuous Efficiency of Query Processing Approaches

Maribel Acosta[1]([⊠]), Maria-Esther Vidal[2,3], and York Sure-Vetter[1]

[1] Institute AIFB, Karlsruhe Institute of Technology, Karlsruhe, Germany
{maribel.acosta,york.sure-vetter}@kit.edu
[2] Fraunhofer Institute for Intelligent Analysis and Information Systems (IAIS),
Sankt Augustin, Germany
vidal@cs.uni-bonn.de
[3] Universidad Simón Bolívar, Caracas, Venezuela

Abstract. During empirical evaluations of query processing techniques, metrics like execution time, time for the first answer, and throughput are usually reported. Albeit informative, these metrics are unable to quantify and evaluate the efficiency of a query engine over a certain time period – or diefficiency –, thus hampering the distinction of cutting-edge engines able to exhibit high-performance gradually. We tackle this issue and devise two experimental metrics named *dief@t* and *dief@k*, which allow for measuring the diefficiency during an elapsed time period t or while k answers are produced, respectively. The *dief@t* and *dief@k* measurement methods rely on the computation of the area under the curve of answer traces, and thus capturing the answer concentration over a time interval. We report experimental results of evaluating the behavior of a generic SPARQL query engine using both metrics. Observed results suggest that *dief@t* and *dief@k* are able to measure the performance of SPARQL query engines based on both the amount of answers produced by an engine and the time required to generate these answers.

1 Introduction

Reproducibility and replicability are two important issues to be addressed in the validation of experimental results. Testbeds and benchmarks are bedrocks towards achieving these issues, and the Semantic Web community has made important contributions in this direction, e.g., in the series of workshops on Evaluation of Ontology-based Tools (EON) [4] and the activities of the Ontology Alignment Evaluation Initiative (OAEI). Moreover, testbeds and benchmarks such as LUBM [9], Feasible [15], or WatDiv [3], have become building blocks for the evaluation of existing Semantic Web technologies.

Metrics provide measurement methods for reporting and analyzing experimental results, thus representing an important premise to allow for reproducibility and replicability of experimental studies. Particularly, in the area of the Semantic Web, metrics provide measurement methods for quantifying the behavior of Semantic Web technologies, e.g., introducing semantics-aware metrics and

© Springer International Publishing AG 2017
C. d'Amato et al. (Eds.): ISWC 2017, Part II, LNCS 10588, pp. 3–19, 2017.
DOI: 10.1007/978-3-319-68204-4_1

normalization for ontologies [19], measuring link discovery approaches [12], or the performance [7,16] or scalability [6] of query engines over RDF datasets.

Specifically, to assess the performance of query processing techniques, metrics like execution time, time for the first answer, answer completeness, and throughput are usually reported. These metrics provide measurement methods to quantify the performance of a query processing technique at a given point in time, i.e., either when the first or all answers are produced. However, these metrics are unable to quantify and evaluate the efficiency of a query engine over a certain time period – or dieffiency[1]. In consequence, continuous high-performance engines cannot be clearly distinguished from those which only exhibit high-performance at certain discrete points in time or that produce answers at a slower rate.

In this paper, we tackle the problem of measuring the continuous efficiency of query processing techniques and propose two experimental metrics named *dief@t* and *dief@k*. The proposed metrics capture the dieffiency during an elapsed time period t or while k answers are produced. Specifically, the *dief@t* and *dief@k* measurement methods rely on the computation of the area under the curve of answer traces to capture the concentration of answers over a time interval.

We evaluate the effectiveness of *dief@t* and *dief@k* on different configurations of a SPARQL query engine which produces results incrementally at different rates. The observed measurements capture complementary information about the continuous behavior of the studied engine. More importantly, the reported results allow for uncovering properties of the engine. For instance, these results provide valuable insights about the engine configuration that continuously produces more answers over time or at a slower rate. None of these properties could be either detected or explained if only traditional metrics would be measured.

In summary, the contributions of this work are as follows:

– Novel experimental metrics, *dief@t* and *dief@k*, that measure the continuous efficiency of query engines.
– Formal properties and proofs that demonstrate the theoretical soundness of the proposed metrics.
– An empirical evaluation that indicates that *dief@t* and *dief@k* allow for uncovering particularities in the performance of query processing approaches that could not be captured with metrics defined in the literature.

The remainder of this paper is structured as follows: Related work is presented in Sect. 2. We motivate our work in Sect. 3 by illustrating the processing of two SPARQL queries against the DBpedia dataset using a typical query engine. In Sect. 4 we formally introduce the two new experimental metrics *dief@t* and *dief@k* for measuring the performance of incremental query processing approaches. We evaluate our approach in Sect. 5 by conducting an empirical study where we evaluate the performance of different SPARQL engines with the proposed metrics. Finally, the paper concludes in Sect. 6.

---

[1] We propose the term *dieffiency* as the combination of the Greek prefix *di(a)-* (which means "through" or "across") and *efficiency*.

2   Related Work

The Database and Semantic Web communities have actively worked on the definition of metrics to provide computational methods to measure the behavior of knowledge and data management approaches. For example, ontologies can be measured during the whole ontology life cycle, and metrics as the one proposed by Vrandecic and Sure [19] allow for semantics-aware metrics which, e.g., can be used for ontology assessment and for tracking ontology evolution. Further, metrics for evaluating the quality of ontology matching and alignment techniques have been defined by benchmarking activities of the Ontology Alignment Evaluation Initiative (OAEI)[2] which resulted in [8].

Metrics also capture the behavior of knowledge and database systems in terms of different dimensions, e.g., efficiency or effectiveness. Table 1 summarizes metrics included in existing benchmarks [3,5,9,11,14–17,20], and commonly used to evaluate one-time and continuous query processing tools [2,10,13,18], i.e., query engines over persistent datasets or against volatile data streams.

LUBM [9] is an exemplar benchmark to evaluate OWL applications with different reasoning capabilities and storage mechanisms. LUBM includes both data and query generators, as well as precise measurement methods to evaluate efficiency and effectiveness of OWL systems. Effectiveness represents the quality of the answers produced by the evaluated query processing technique, and it is measured in terms of the metric of answer completeness and soundness. LUBM also proposes to measure data processing efficiency in terms of two metrics: load time and query response time. Further, a combined metric enables to quantify the behavior of a query processing engine as the harmonic mean of query response time, and answer completeness and soundness. The Berlin Benchmark [5] (BSBM) is a benchmark generator tailored to evaluate SPARQL query engines. In addition to data and query, BSBM makes available a test driver able to execute sequences of queries over the system under test (SUT), thus simulating concurrent access of multiple clients. Additionally, BSBM presents a set of metrics to measure the SUT efficiency. The proposed measurement methods allow for quantifying queries executed per hour or second, load time, query execution time, loading time, and overall runtime. In addition, time required for a query engine to produce the first answer is commonly reported in experimental studies that evaluate the incremental behavior of the query engine [2,10].

Metrics have also been proposed to capture the behavior of query processing systems over continuous data. SRBench is a benchmark for streaming SPARQL query processing. Besides datasets and queries, SRBench proposes metrics to evaluate effectiveness in terms of correctness, and efficiency according to throughput and response time. Finally, Sharaf et al. [18] define two metrics to evaluate the performance of data stream management systems: (a) the average response time captures a system's output rate, and (b) the average slowdown is the average of the ratio of a system's response time to its ideal processing time.

---

[2] http://oaei.ontologymatching.org/.

Table 1. Characteristics of metrics. Metrics are characterized according to the type of query processing for which they have been defined, i.e., one-time or continuous, and in terms of the metric interpretation: higher is better (HB) or lower is better (LB). Different measurement methods have been proposed to calculate similar metrics, e.g., Query Response Time [9], Response Time [20], and Execution Time [10].

Metrics	Characteristics		
	One-Time Query Processing	Continuous Query Processing	Metric Interpretation
Effectiveness			
Answer Completeness and Soundness [9]	✓		HB
Correctness [20]		✓	HB
Answer Completeness [10]	✓		HB
Efficiency			
Query Response Time [9]	✓		LB
Loading Time [9]	✓		LB
Throughput [20]		✓	HB
Response Time [20]		✓	LB
Queries per Second [5]	✓		HB
Queries Mixes per Hour [5]	✓		HB
Min/Max Query Execution Time [5]	✓		LB
Overall Runtime [5]	✓		LB
Composite Query Execution Time [5]	✓		LB
Avg. Execution Time All Queries [5]	✓		LB
Average Response Time [18]		✓	LB
Average Slowdown [18]		✓	LB
Response Time of Joined Tuples [18]		✓	LB
Slowdown of Joined Tuples [18]		✓	LB
Time for the First Tuple [2]	✓		LB
Source Selection Time [10]	✓		LB
Execution Time [10]	✓		LB
Combined			
Combined Metric [9]	✓		HB

These metrics enable the evaluation of a query engine at a given point in time, e.g., either when the first or all answers are produced, as well as the quality of the produced answers. Nevertheless, none of these metrics are able to quantify the continuous behavior of either a one-time or a continuous query engine over a time period, i.e., diefficiency. The *dief@t* and *dief@k* measurement methods overcome this limitation, and provide complementary information to existing metrics that enables to quantify the answer generation rate in a time interval.

3   Motivating Example

Consider the SPARQL queries Query 1 from Listing 1.1 and Query 2 from Listing 1.2 to be executed against the DBpedia dataset using a query engine.[3] To illustrate, we selected the nLDE engine [1], and executed both queries using three different configurations of nLDE: Not Adaptive, Selective, and Random.

Listing 1.1. Query 1: Retrieve information about resources classified as DBpedia places and infrastructures.

```
SELECT * WHERE {
 ?d1 a dbo:Place .
 ?d2 a dbo:Infrastructure .
 ?d1 dbp:r2LengthF ?o .
 ?d2 dbp:lats ?o .
 ?d1 geo:point ?o1 .
 ?d2 dbp:coordinatesRegion ?o2 . }
```

Listing 1.2. Query 2: Retrieve information about resources classified as DBpedia alcohol and Yago alcohol.

```
SELECT * WHERE {
 ?d1 dc:subject dbc:Alcohols .
 ?d1 dbp:routesOfAdministration ?o .
 ?d1 dbp:smiles ?s .
 ?d2 a dbyago:Alcohols .
 ?d2 dbp:routesOfAdministration ?o .
 ?d2 dbp:molecularWeight ?w . }
```

Table 2. Query performance measured using metrics from the literature. The performance of the approaches nLDE Not Adaptive (**NA**), nLDE Selective (**Sel**), and nLDE Random (**Ran**) are compared. For each SPARQL query and metric, highlighted cells indicate the approach that exhibits the best performance in that metric.

Metrics	Query 1			Query 2		
	NA	Sel	Ran	NA	Sel	Ran
Time First Answer (sec.)	28.438	27.058	7.641	0.371	0.242	0.333
Execution Time (sec.)	300.328	300.404	300.137	10.593	12.210	9.304
Throughput (answers/sec.)	46.416	24.334	77.031	486.274	421.868	553.659
Completeness	50.31%	26.38%	83.44%	100%	100%	100%

Table 2 reports the performance achieved by the three nLDE approaches using conventional query processing metrics.[4] Based on Table 2, we can conclude the following about the performance of the approaches when executing Query 1: (1) nLDE Random clearly outperforms the other approaches in all the metrics, and (2) nLDE Selective exhibits the worst performance in this case. Regarding the performance achieved by the nLDE approaches when executing Query 2, we can conclude that: (3) nLDE Random achieves the best performance in terms of execution time and throughput, (4) nLDE Selective is able to produce the first answer faster than the other approaches, and (5) nLDE Selective, however, exhibits the worst performance when considering execution time and throughput.

In order to further inspect the behavior of the approaches, let us consider now the continuous performance achieved by the nLDE engine when executing the

---

[3] Prefixes are used as in http://prefix.cc/.

[4] For simplicity, we assume that the reported results are significantly different.

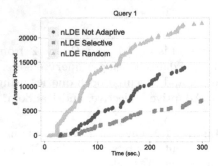 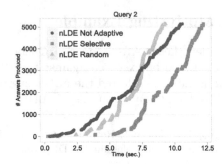

(a) **Query 1**: The approaches exhibit uniform behavior over time.

(b) **Query 2**: The approaches exhibit irregular behavior over time.

Fig. 1. Answer traces: continuous query performance. Answers produced (y-axis) as a function of time (x-axis). (a) nLDE Random continuously outperforms the other approaches. (b) The answer trace reveals that in the first 7.45 s of execution, nLDE Not Adaptive outperforms other approaches by producing more answers per time unit. However, this behavior is not captured by the metrics reported in Table 2.

SPARQL queries. Figure 1 depicts the answer trace of each approach. Answer traces (cf. Definition 1) record the progression of answers produced over time by an engine. Regarding Query 1, we observe in Fig. 1(a) that the three approaches exhibit a uniform behavior over time, i.e., one of the approaches exhibits the best performance in all the reported metrics. For instance, nLDE Random steadily outperforms the other approaches by continuously producing more answers over time. Moreover, the answer trace shows that nLDE Selective produced answers at a slower rate in comparison with the other approaches. These findings are consistent with the results (1) and (2).

Regarding the execution of Query 2, in Fig. 1(b) we can observe that the approaches exhibit an irregular behavior over time. For example, the answer trace reveals that nLDE Not Adaptive exhibits a better performance than nLDE Random during the first 7.45 s of query execution. This new result provides complementary information about the performance of nLDE Random, which was not captured by the analysis (3) using the metrics from Table 2. Furthermore, the high slope of the answer trace of nLDE Selective indicates that it produces over 1,000 answers at a higher rate than the other approaches from seconds 5 to 7.45 of execution. This finding uncovers novel properties about the behavior of nLDE Selective that were not visible with the metrics reported in Table 2 and to some extent invalidates the conclusion derived in (5).

In this section, we have presented a brief qualitative analysis of the performance of different settings of the nLDE engine over time by manually inspecting the answer trace of the engine when executing two queries. However, to enable reproducibility and replicability of experimental studies, we need quantitative methods to measure the continuous efficiency of query processing approaches.

4 The Diefficiency Metrics

Analyses of answer traces provide valuable insights about the continuous efficiency – or diefficiency – of query engines. Therefore, we devise diefficiency metrics that rely on answer traces to measure the performance of SPARQL query engines. The answer trace records the exact point in time when an engine produces a query answer and can be formally defined as follows.

Definition 1 (Answer Trace). *Let ρ be an approach, Q a query, and Ω the set of query answers produced by ρ when executing Q. The answer trace of ρ when executing Q, denoted $A_{\rho,Q}$, is defined as a sequence of pairs $(t_1, \mu_1), \ldots, (t_n, \mu_n)$ where $\mu_i \in \Omega$ is the ith answer, $t_i \in \mathcal{R}$ is the timestamp that indicates the point in time when μ_i is produced, and $t_i \leq t_{i+1}$ for all $1 \leq i < n$.*

For example, consider that the engine α executes a query Q and produces an answer μ_1 at the second 1.0 followed by another answer $\mu2$ at the second 2.0. Then, the answer trace of α is as follows: $A_{\alpha,Q} = \langle (1.0, \mu_1), (2.0, \mu_2) \rangle$. Note that when a SPARQL engine ρ produces no answers ($\Omega = \emptyset$) for a query Q, then the answer trace $A_{\rho,Q}$ correspond to the empty sequence.

Based on the answer trace, we can determine whether a SPARQL engine follows an incremental or a blocking approach during query execution. Incremental approaches are able to produce results over time, i.e., answers are produced at different points in time. In our example, $A_{\alpha,Q}$ indicates that α produces answers incrementally while executing Q. In contrast, blocking approaches produce all query answers at a single point in time – usually at the end of query execution. For instance, the answer trace $A_{\beta,Q} = \langle (2.0, \mu_1), (2.0, \mu_2) \rangle$ of an engine β indicates that β corresponds to a blocking approach while executing Q. In the following, we define incremental and blocking approaches.

Definition 2 (Incremental Approach). *Let ρ be an approach and $A_{\rho,Q}$ its answer trace when executing a query Q. ρ is an incremental approach if there exists (t_j, μ_j) in $A_{\rho,Q}$ such that $t_j < t_{j+1}$.*

Definition 3 (Blocking Approach). *Let ρ be an approach and $A_{\rho,Q}$ its answer trace when executing a query Q. If $t_j = t_{j+1}$ for all $1 \leq j < n$, then ρ is considered a non-incremental or blocking approach.*

Besides characterizing incremental and blocking approaches, answer traces allow for determining the distribution of answers over time, i.e., the answer rate of the engine in intervals of time. For instance, based on the answer traces $A_{\alpha,Q}$ and $A_{\beta,Q}$ from the running example, Fig. 2 depicts the answer distribution for the engines α (incremental) and β (blocking): at $t = 1$, α has produced one answer while β has produced no answers until that point.

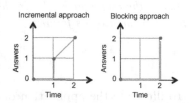

Fig. 2. Answer distribution

The answer distribution corresponds to the number of answers produced in function of time. In the case of incremental approaches, the answer distribution function is computed by applying a linear interpolation between the time points recorded in the answer trace. For blocking approaches, the answer distribution function corresponds to the maximum of number of answers produced at a point in time. Formally, the answer distribution function is defined as follows.

Definition 4 (Answer Distribution Function). *Let ρ be a SPARQL query engine and $A_{\rho,Q} = \langle (t_1, \mu_1), \ldots, (t_n, \mu_n) \rangle$ its answer trace when executing a query Q. The answer distribution function of ρ when executing Q, denoted $X_{\rho,Q}$, is defined as a function $X_{\rho,Q} : [0; t_n] \to \mathcal{N}$. For a given $t \in [0; t_n]$, with $0 \leq t < t_1$, $X_{\rho,Q}(t) = 0$. For t such that $t_i \leq t \leq t_{i+1}$, with $1 \leq i \leq n$, $X_{\rho,Q}(t)$ is as follows:*

$$X_{\rho,Q}(t) = \begin{cases} i + \frac{t - t_i}{t_{i+1} - t_i} & , t_i \neq t_{i+1} \\ max(\{j \mid (t_j, \mu_j) \in A_{\rho,Q}, t_j = t_i\}) & , t_i = t_{i+1} \end{cases}$$

In order to measure the continuous efficiency of engines while producing query answers over time, we propose metrics that rely on the answer distribution function. The proposed metrics comprise two novel measurement methods, *dief@t* and *dief@k*. Both *dief@t* and *dief@k* compute the area under the curve of the answer distribution function, which allows for measuring the diefficiency achieved by engines during query execution. Furthermore, in the following sections we will show that *dief@t* and *dief@k* capture the irregular behavior of incremental approaches, such as the one reported in Fig. 1(b).

4.1   *dief@t*: Diefficiency at Time t

The measurement method *dief@t* measures the diefficiency of an engine in the first t time units of query execution. To do so, *dief@t* computes the area under the curve of the answer distribution function until t. Formally, this area can be defined as the definite integral of the answer distribution function from the moment the engine starts executing a query until the time t.

Definition 5 (*dief@t*). *Let ρ be an approach, Q a query, and $X_{\rho,Q}$ the answer distribution function when ρ executes Q. Consider that ρ produces n answers, i.e., $X_{\rho,Q}$ is defined for the interval $[0; t_n]$. Given $t \in \mathcal{R}$ a point in time such that $t \in [0; t_n]$, the diefficiency of ρ in the first t time units of execution, denominated dief@t, is computed as follows:*

$$dief_{\rho,Q}@t := \int_0^t X_{\rho,Q}(x) \; dx$$

To illustrate the application of *dief@t* in diefficiency analysis, consider the answer traces of the nLDE variants from the motivating example. Figure 3 depicts the computation of *dief@t* at $t = 7.45$ s. Intuitively, approaches that produce answers at a higher rate in a certain period of time must exhibit high diefficiency values. Figure 3 indicates that nLDE Not Adaptive achieves the

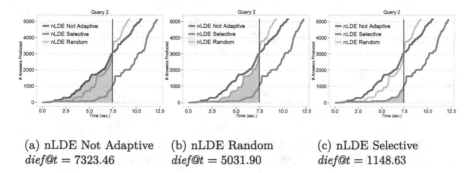

(a) nLDE Not Adaptive   (b) nLDE Random   (c) nLDE Selective
$dief@t = 7323.46$ $dief@t = 5031.90$ $dief@t = 1148.63$

Fig. 3. *dief@t* of the nLDE engine for **Query 2** at $t = 7.45$. (a), (b), and (c) highlight the area under the curve of the answer distribution function that is computed for measuring the diefficiency of the approaches at the given t. nLDE Not Adaptive exhibits the best performance for the given interval, followed by nLDE Random and lastly nLDE Selective. The reported *dief@t* values are congruent with these observations.

best performance among the other approaches. The *dief@t* values reported in Figs. 3(a)–3(c) confirm that nLDE Adaptive exhibits the highest diefficiency followed by nLDE Random, while nLDE Selective is the least efficient approach. In the following property, we formally state the interpretation of *dief@t*.

Property 1. Let $\rho 1$ and $\rho 2$ be approaches that execute a query Q. Given $t \in \mathcal{R}$ for which $X_{\rho 1, Q}$ and $X_{\rho 2, Q}$ are defined. If $dief_{\rho 1, Q}@t > dief_{\rho 2, Q}@t$ then $\rho 1$ exhibits a better performance than $\rho 2$ until t in terms of diefficiency.

> *dief@t* interpretation: Higher is better.

Lastly, it is important to note that *dief@t* and throughput are not the same metrics. For example, until $t = 7.45$, nLDE Not Adaptive and nLDE Random have produced nearly the same amount of answers,[5] in consequence, the throughput values of both approaches are also almost the same.[6] However, we can observe that nLDE Not Adaptive continuously produced more answers than nLDE Random and this is captured by *dief@t*. In contrast to throughput that considers the total number of answers produced at a single point in time, *dief@t* accounts for the progression of answers over an entire time interval.

4.2   *dief@k*: Diefficiency at k Answers

The metric *dief@k* measures the diefficiency of an engine while producing the first k answers of a query, after the first answer was produced. *dief@k* computes the area under the curve of the answer distribution until the point in time t_k when

---

[5] Until $t = 7.45$, nLDE Not Adaptive produced 3075 answers and nLDE Random 3067.
[6] The throughput values achieved by nLDE Not Adaptive and nLDE Random are 410 and 408.93 (answers/sec.), respectively.

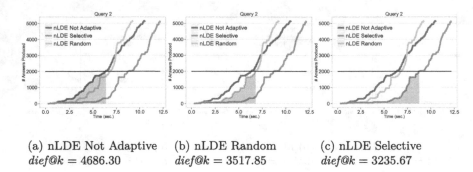

(a) nLDE Not Adaptive   (b) nLDE Random   (c) nLDE Selective
$dief@k = 4686.30$ $dief@k = 3517.85$ $dief@k = 3235.67$

Fig. 4. *dief@k* of the nLDE engine for Query 2 at $k = 2000$. (a), (b), and (c) highlight the area under the curve of the answer distribution function that is computed for measuring the dieﬃciency of the approaches while producing the first k answers. The slope of the answer distributions indicate that nLDE Selective produces the first 2000 answers at a higher rate, followed by nLDE Random and then by nLDE Not Adaptive. The reported *dief@k* values are congruent with these observations.

the engine produces the kth answer, as recorded in the answer trace. Formally, this area corresponds to the definite integral of the answer distribution function from the moment the engine starts the query execution until t_k.

Definition 6 (*dief@k*). *Let ρ be an approach, Q a query, and $A_{\rho,Q}$ and $X_{\rho,Q}$ the answer trace and answer distribution function when ρ executes Q, respectively. Consider that ρ produces n answers. Given $k \in \mathcal{N}$ such that $0 < k \leq n$, the dieﬃciency of ρ while producing the first k answers, denominated dief@k, is computed as follows:*

$$dief_{\rho,Q}@k := \int_0^{t_k} X_{\rho,Q}(x) \ dx$$

where $t_k \in \mathcal{R}$ is the point in time when ρ produces the kth answer of Q, i.e., $(t_k, \mu_k) \in A_{\rho,Q}$.

In Fig. 4, we illustrate the application of *dief@k* based on the answer traces of nLDE. Intuitively, engines that require a short amount of time to produce k answers are considered more efficient. In consequence, the lower the value of *dief@k*, the higher the continuous efficiency (or dieﬃciency) of the engine. Figure 4 indicates that nLDE Selective achieves the best performance among the other approaches when producing the first 2000 answers. Figures 4(a) to (c) report the values of *dief@k*, which confirm that nLDE Selective achieves the highest dieﬃciency, while nLDE Not Adaptive is the least efficient approach in terms of the rate while producing the first 2000 answers. In the following property, we formally state the interpretation of *dief@k*.

Property 2. Let $\rho 1$, $\rho 2$ be approaches, and Q a query. Let $n1$, $n2$ be the number of answers produced by $\rho 1$ and $\rho 2$ when executing Q, respectively. Given $k \in \mathcal{N}$,

$k \leq n1$ and $k \leq n2$, if $dief_{\rho 1,Q}@k < dief_{\rho 2,Q}@k$ then $\rho 1$ exhibits a better performance than $\rho 2$ in terms of dieffiency while producing the first k answers.

$dief@k$ interpretation: Lower is better.

4.3   Extensions and Properties of $dief@t$ and $dief@k$

Measuring Dieffieny at Any Time Interval. So far, we have defined metrics to measure the dieffiency since the approach starts the execution of a query until the last answer is produced. Nonetheless, the metric $dief@t$ can be extended to measure the dieffiency of a querying approach at any given time interval $[t_a; t_b]$ defined in the answer trace. Intuitively, the dieffiency in $[t_a; t_b]$ corresponds to the area under the curve of the answer distribution in that interval. By applying the additive property of integration on intervals, this area can be computed with the metric $dief@t$ at t_a and t_b as follows:

$$\int_0^{t_a} X_{\rho,Q}(x)\, dx + \int_{t_a}^{t_b} X_{\rho,Q}(x)\, dx = \int_0^{t_b} X_{\rho,Q}(x)\, dx$$
$$\int_{t_a}^{t_b} X_{\rho,Q}(x)\, dx = \int_0^{t_b} X_{\rho,Q}(x)\, dx - \int_0^{t_a} X_{\rho,Q}(x)\, dx \qquad (1)$$
$$\int_{t_a}^{t_b} X_{\rho,Q}(x)\, dx = dief_{\rho,Q}@t_b - dief_{\rho,Q}@t_a$$

The dieffieny of an approach in the interval $[t_a; t_b]$ is $dief@t_b - dief@t_a$.

Measuring Dieffieny Between the $k_a th$ and the $k_b th$ Answers. The metric $dief@k$ can also be used to measure the dieffiency of a query engine during the production of the k_ath and the k_bth answers, with $k_a \leq k_b$. From the answer trace of the approach, it is possible to obtain t_{ka} and t_{kb}, the points in time when the k_ath and the k_bth answers are produced, respectively. By definition of the answer trace (cf. Definition 1), it holds that $t_{ka} \leq t_{kb}$. In this case, the dieffiency of the engine corresponds to the area under the curve of the answer distribution in the interval $[t_{ka}; t_{kb}]$. By applying the additive property of integration on intervals, this area can be computed with $dief@k$ as follows:

$$\int_0^{t_{ka}} X_{\rho,Q}(x)\, dx + \int_{t_{ka}}^{t_{kb}} X_{\rho,Q}(x)\, dx = \int_0^{t_{kb}} X_{\rho,Q}(x)\, dx$$
$$\int_{t_{ka}}^{t_{kb}} X_{\rho,Q}(x)\, dx = \int_0^{t_{kb}} X_{\rho,Q}(x)\, dx - \int_0^{t_{ka}} X_{\rho,Q}(x)\, dx \qquad (2)$$
$$\int_{t_{ka}}^{t_{kb}} X_{\rho,Q}(x)\, dx = dief_{\rho,Q}@k_b - dief_{\rho,Q}@k_a$$

The dieffieny of an approach while producing the k_ath and the k_bth answers is $dief@k_b - dief@k_a$.

Based on the definitions of $dief@t$ and $dief@k$, it is possible to establish: the analytical relationship between the proposed metrics (Proposition 1), the dieffiency of blocking approaches at any point in time (Theorem 1), and the total dieffiency – from the moment the approach starts the query execution until it produces the last answer – of incremental approaches (Theorem 2).

Proposition 1 (Analytical Relationship Between *dief@t* and *dief@k*).
*Let ρ be an approach, Q a query, and $X_{\rho,Q}$ the answer distribution function
when ρ executes Q. Consider that $X_{\rho,Q}$ is defined for the interval $[0;t_n]$. The
following condition holds for all k such that $1 \leq k \leq n$:*

$$dief_{\rho,Q}@t_k = dief_{\rho,Q}@k$$

Theorem 1. *The diefficiency of blocking approaches is always zero.*

Proof. Consider β a blocking approach and $X_{\beta,Q}$ its answer distribution function
when executing a query Q. Assume that $X_{\beta,Q}$ is defined for the interval $[0;t_n]$.
Without loss of generality, assume that diefficiency is measured with *dief@t*.
We will show that the $dief_{\beta,Q}@t'$ is zero for all t' in the interval $[0;t_n]$. By
definition of blocking approach (cf. Definition 2), it holds that $t_i = t_n$ with
$1 \leq i \leq n$. With Definition 4, we obtain that $X_{\beta,Q}(t) = 0$, for all $0 \leq t < t_n$,
then $\int_0^t X_{\beta,Q}(x)\ dx = 0$, i.e., $dief_{\beta,Q}@t' = 0$. Lastly, $X_{\beta,Q}$ is greater than zero
only for $t' = t_n$, for which we obtain that $\int_{t_n}^{t_n} X_{\beta,Q}(x) = 0$, i.e., $dief_{\beta,Q}@t_n = 0$.

Theorem 2. *In queries where the number of answers is higher than one, the
total diefficiency of incremental approaches is higher than zero.*

Proof. Consider α an incremental approach, $X_{\alpha,Q}$ its answer distribution and
$n \in \mathcal{N}$ the number of answers when executing a query Q. By hypothesis, $n > 1$.
By contradiction, assume that the total diefficiency of α is zero. Without loss of
generality, assume that the diefficiency of α is measured with *dief@k*, therefore,
$dief_{\alpha,Q}@n = 0$. Since $n > 1$ and α is incremental, there exists an answer μ_j
produced by α, such that $1 \leq j < n$ and $t_j < t_n$. Without loss of generality,
lets assume that $j = n - 1$. The diefficiency of α between the n-1th and the
nth answer can be measured as $dief_{\alpha,Q}@n - dief_{\alpha,Q}@n\text{-}1$. Since $X_{\alpha,Q}$ is non-
decreasing, it holds that $dief_{\alpha,Q}@n \geq dief_{\alpha,Q}@n\text{-}1$. By hypothesis $dief_{\alpha,Q}@n = 0$,
therefore $dief_{\alpha,Q}@n\text{-}1 = 0$. Applying Eq. (2) we obtain that $\int_{t_{n-1}}^{t_n} X_{\alpha,Q}(x)\ dx = 0$.
Note that, by Definition 4, $X_{\alpha,Q}(x) > 0$ for all x with $t_1 \leq t_{n\text{-}1} \leq x \leq t_n$. In
consequence, if $\int_{t_{n-1}}^{t_n} X_{\alpha,Q}(x)\ dx = 0$ then $t_{n\text{-}1} = t_n$. However, this contradicts
the hypothesis that α is incremental.

5   Empirical Study

We empirically assess the effectiveness of our metrics *dief@t* and *dief@k* to measure the performance of SPARQL query engines. Experimental results are available at https://doi.org/10.6084/m9.figshare.5255686 under CC BY 4.0.

Approaches and Implementations: We compare the performance of three
configurations of the nLDE engine [1] to execute SPARQL queries, i.e., Not
Adaptive, Random, and Selective. nLDE is implemented in Python 2.7.6. Experiments were run on a Debian Wheezy 64 bit machine with CPU: 2x Intel(R)
Xeon(R) CPU E5-2670 2.60 GHz (16 physical cores), and 256 GB RAM. We set
the query evaluation timeout to 300 s. with random delays as specified in [1].

Dataset and Query Benchmark: We use the nLDE Benchmark 1 [1] that comprises 20 queries executed against the DBpedia dataset (v. 2015). Benchmark queries are composed of basic graph patterns of between 4 and 14 triple patterns; these queries are non-selective and produce a large number of intermediate results. We selected 16 queries for which all the approaches produce more than one answer to compute the area under curve of the answer distribution.

5.1 Measuring the Performance of SPARQL Query Processing Approaches with Metrics from the Literature and *dief@t*

In this evaluation, we report on the performance achieved by the nLDE approaches when executing the benchmark queries using metrics defined in the literature (cf. Sect. 2) and our proposed metric *dief@t*. The values for each metric are defined and measured/computed as follows:

- Execution time (**ET**): Elapsed time spent by the approach to complete the execution of a query. ET is measured as the absolute wall-clock system time as reported by the Python `time.time()` function.
- Time for the first tuple (**TFFT**): Elapsed time spent by the approach to produce the first query answer. TFFT is measured as the absolute wall-clock system time as reported by the Python `time.time()` function.
- Completeness (**Comp**): Percentage of the total number of answers produced by the approach after executing a query.
- Throughput (**T**): Number of total answers produced by the approach after evaluating a query divided by its execution time (ET).
- *dief@t:* As in Definition 5, where t is the minimum execution time registered by one of the tested approaches when executing a query; *dief@t* is computed with the function `auc` from the `flux` package in R.

In Fig. 5, we report on the results of the performance achieved by the nLDE configurations per query using radar plots. Radar plots allow for comparing the performance of the studied approaches in multiple dimensions, in this case, in several metrics. For the sake of readability, we transformed the axes of the plots such that all the metrics have the same interpretation: higher is better.

Figure 5(a) comprises the queries where the performance of the nLDE approaches is consistent in all the metrics, i.e., the approaches display a "uniform" behavior over time. The consistent performance can be easily observed when the polygon of an approach encloses the ones of the other approaches. For example, according to the plotted results in **Q16**, the approach nLDE Random exhibits the best performance in all the dimensions, followed by nLDE Not Adaptive, and then by nLDE Selective. In cases like these, the metrics defined in the literature accurately capture the overall performance of the approaches. It is important to note that, for these queries, *dief@t* is consonant with the other metrics, thus, corroborating the steady outperformance of one approach.

Figure 5(b) groups the queries in which the approaches exhibit a fluctuating performance among the metrics. In **Q2**, for instance, the values of the metrics

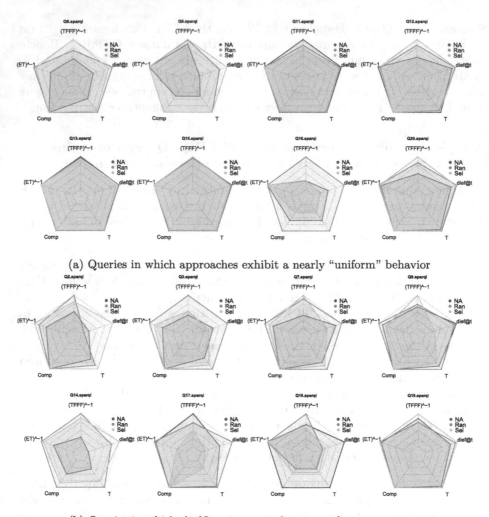

(a) Queries in which approaches exhibit a nearly "uniform" behavior

(b) Queries in which *dief@t* uncovers unknown performance patterns

Fig. 5. Performance per benchmark query of SPARQL query processing approaches: nLDE Not Adaptive (NA), nLDE Random (Ran), nLDE Selective (Sel). Axes correspond to the following experimental metrics: Inverse of execution time (ET^{-1}), inverse of time for the first tuple ($TFFT^{-1}$), completeness (Comp), throughput (T), and *dief@t*. Interpretation of all metrics (axes): higher is better.

from the literature indicate that nLDE Random and nLDE Selective are competitive approaches. Yet, *dief@t* allows for uncovering that nLDE Selective is able to continuously produce answers at a faster rate than nLDE Random for this query. Conversely, in **Q7**, conventional metrics indicate that nLDE Not Adaptive is outperformed by the other approaches. Nonetheless, *dief@t* suggests that nLDE Not Adaptive is rather competitive in terms of diefficiency. In summary, *dief@t* allows for more comprehensive analyses of approaches, while characterizing the entire engine performance during query execution.

5.2 Measuring the Continuous Answer Rate of SPARQL Query Processing Approaches with *dief@k*

We now analyze the diefficiency achieved by the nLDE approaches while producing the first k answers for queries from Fig. 5(b).[7] We compute *dief@k* as in Definition 6, and we set k to the minimum amount of answers produced among all the nLDE variants in each query. Figure 6 reports on the *dief@k* values of nLDE while producing the first 25%, 50%, 75%, and 100% of the query answers. We can observe that, in most of the cases, nLDE Not Adaptive maintains a steady answer rate over time (except for Q7 and Q9). Furthermore, *dief@k* values show that the behavior of nLDE Selective and nLDE Random fluctuates[8], even producing the first 25% of the answers up to 3 times slower than nLDE Not Adaptive (in Q7); this fluctuating behavior can be a consequence of the adaptive heuristics implemented by nLDE Random and nLDE Selective during query processing. With this study, we show how the metric *dief@k* can be used to explain and quantify continuous answer rates of query engines.

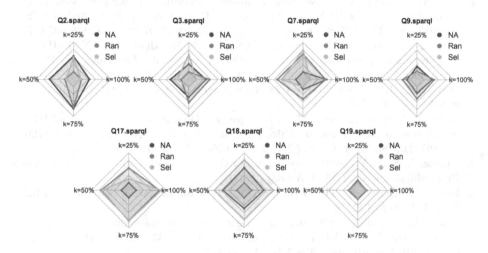

Fig. 6. Diefficiency while producing a portion k of the answers, per benchmark query and SPARQL query processing approaches: nLDE Not Adaptive (NA), nLDE Random (Ran), nLDE Selective (Sel). Performance is measured with *dief@k*, with $k = 25\%$, $k = 50\%$, $k = 75\%$, $k = 100\%$. Interpretation of the axes: lower is better.

---

[7] Q14 was discarded since it produces only four answers.
[8] This can be observed when the polygons in the plot are not perfect diamonds.

6   Conclusions and Future Work

In this paper, we tackled the problem of quantifying the continuous behavior of a query engine, and define two novel experimental metrics, *dief@t* and *dief@k*. Formal properties of these metrics demonstrate the analytical characteristics of the proposed measurement methods, as well as stating lower bounds according to the characteristics of the assessed query engine. Additionally, *dief@t* and *dief@k* were empirically evaluated, and observed results allow for uncovering patterns in the performance of the evaluated engines that could not be quantified with existing metrics. As proof of concept, *dief@t* and *dief@k* were used to evaluate SPARQL query approaches, however, both metrics will be able to capture and quantify the behavior of any method that produces results incrementally.

In the future, we plan to use *dief@t* and *dief@k* to evaluate state-of-the-art SPARQL query engines, and compare observed patterns with the ones quantified by metrics proposed by existing benchmarks. We hypothesize that *dief@t* and *dief@k* will allow for uncovering unknown characteristics of these engines.

References

1. Acosta, M., Vidal, M.-E.: Networks of linked data eddies: an adaptive web query processing engine for RDF data. In: Arenas, M., et al. (eds.) ISWC 2015. LNCS, vol. 9366, pp. 111–127. Springer, Cham (2015). doi:10.1007/978-3-319-25007-6_7
2. Acosta, M., Vidal, M.-E., Lampo, T., Castillo, J., Ruckhaus, E.: ANAPSID: an adaptive query processing engine for SPARQL endpoints. In: Aroyo, L., Welty, C., Alani, H., Taylor, J., Bernstein, A., Kagal, L., Noy, N., Blomqvist, E. (eds.) ISWC 2011. LNCS, vol. 7031, pp. 18–34. Springer, Heidelberg (2011). doi:10.1007/978-3-642-25073-6_2
3. Aluç, G., Hartig, O., Özsu, M.T., Daudjee, K.: Diversified stress testing of RDF data management systems. In: Mika, P., et al. (eds.) ISWC 2014. LNCS, vol. 8796, pp. 197–212. Springer, Cham (2014). doi:10.1007/978-3-319-11964-9_13
4. Angele, J., Sure, Y., (eds).: Proceedings of the EON Workshop, CEUR Workshop Proceedings, vol. 62, CEUR-WS.org (2002)
5. Bizer, C., Schultz, A.: The Berlin SPARQL benchmark. Int. J. Semant. Web Inf. Syst. **5**(2), 1–24 (2009)
6. Cheng, L., Kotoulas, S.: Efficient large outer joins over mapreduce. In: Dutot, P.-F., Trystram, D. (eds.) Euro-Par 2016. LNCS, vol. 9833, pp. 334–346. Springer, Cham (2016). doi:10.1007/978-3-319-43659-3_25
7. Duan, S., Kementsietsidis, A., Srinivas, K., Udrea, O.: Apples and oranges: a comparison of RDF benchmarks and real RDF datasets. In: SIGMOD, pp. 145–156 (2011)
8. Euzenat, J., Shvaiko, P.: Ontology Matching, 2nd edn. Springer, Heidelberg (2013)
9. Guo, Y., Pan, Z., Heflin, J.: LUBM: a benchmark for OWL knowledge base systems. Web Semant. **3**(2–3), 158–182 (2005)
10. Montoya, G., Vidal, M.-E., Corcho, O., Ruckhaus, E., Buil-Aranda, C.: Benchmarking federated SPARQL query engines: are existing testbeds enough? In: Cudré-Mauroux, P., et al. (eds.) ISWC 2012. LNCS, vol. 7650, pp. 313–324. Springer, Heidelberg (2012). doi:10.1007/978-3-642-35173-0_21

11. Morsey, M., Lehmann, J., Auer, S., Ngonga Ngomo, A.-C.: DBpedia SPARQL benchmark – performance assessment with real queries on real data. In: Aroyo, L., Welty, C., Alani, H., Taylor, J., Bernstein, A., Kagal, L., Noy, N., Blomqvist, E. (eds.) ISWC 2011. LNCS, vol. 7031, pp. 454–469. Springer, Heidelberg (2011). doi:10.1007/978-3-642-25073-6_29
12. Nentwig, M., Hartung, M., Ngomo, A.N., Rahm, E.: A survey of current link discovery frameworks. Semant. Web **8**(3), 419–436 (2017)
13. Le-Phuoc, D., Dao-Tran, M., Xavier Parreira, J., Hauswirth, M.: A native and adaptive approach for unified processing of linked streams and linked data. In: Aroyo, L., Welty, C., Alani, H., Taylor, J., Bernstein, A., Kagal, L., Noy, N., Blomqvist, E. (eds.) ISWC 2011. LNCS, vol. 7031, pp. 370–388. Springer, Heidelberg (2011). doi:10.1007/978-3-642-25073-6_24
14. Rakhmawati, N. A., Saleem, M., Lalithsena, S., Decker, S.: QFed: query set for federated SPARQL query benchmark. In: iiWAS, pp. 207–211 (2014)
15. Saleem, M., Mehmood, Q., Ngonga Ngomo, A.C.: FEASIBLE: a feature-based SPARQL benchmark generation framework. In: Arenas, M., et al. (eds.) ISWC 2015. LNCS, vol. 9366, pp. 52–69. Springer, Cham (2015). doi:10.1007/978-3-319-25007-6_4
16. Schmidt, M., Görlitz, O., Haase, P., Ladwig, G., Schwarte, A., Tran, T.: FedBench: a benchmark suite for federated semantic data query processing. In: Aroyo, L., Welty, C., Alani, H., Taylor, J., Bernstein, A., Kagal, L., Noy, N., Blomqvist, E. (eds.) ISWC 2011. LNCS, vol. 7031, pp. 585–600. Springer, Heidelberg (2011). doi:10.1007/978-3-642-25073-6_37
17. Schmidt, M., Hornung, T., Lausen, G., Pinkel, C.: SP^{2}Bench: a SPARQL performance benchmark. In: ICDE, pp. 222–233 (2009)
18. Sharaf, M.A., Chrysanthis, P.K., Labrinidis, A., Pruhs, K.: Algorithms and metrics for processing multiple heterogeneous continuous queries. ACM Trans. Database Syst. **33**(1), 5:1–5:44 (2008)
19. Vrandečić, D., Sure, Y.: How to design better ontology metrics. In: Franconi, E., Kifer, M., May, W. (eds.) ESWC 2007. LNCS, vol. 4519, pp. 311–325. Springer, Heidelberg (2007). doi:10.1007/978-3-540-72667-8_23
20. Zhang, Y., Duc, P.M., Corcho, O., Calbimonte, J.-P.: SRBench: a streaming RDF/SPARQL benchmark. In: Cudré-Mauroux, P., et al. (eds.) ISWC 2012. LNCS, vol. 7649, pp. 641–657. Springer, Heidelberg (2012). doi:10.1007/978-3-642-35176-1_40

CodeOntology: RDF-ization of Source Code

Mattia Atzeni and Maurizio Atzori[✉]

Math/CS Department, University of Cagliari,
Via Ospedale 72, 09124 Cagliari (CA), Italy
ma.atzeni12@studenti.unica.it, atzori@unica.it

Abstract. In this paper, we leverage advances in the Semantic Web area, including data modeling (RDF), data management and querying (JENA and SPARQL), to develop *CodeOntology*, a community-shared software framework supporting expressive queries over source code. The project consists of two main contributions: an ontology that provides a formal representation of object-oriented programming languages, and a parser that is able to analyze Java source code and serialize it into RDF triples. The parser has been successfully applied to the source code of OpenJDK 8, gathering a structured dataset consisting of more than 2 million RDF triples. CodeOntology allows to generate Linked Data from any Java project, thereby enabling the execution of highly expressive queries over source code, by means of a powerful language like SPARQL.

Keywords: Ontology · SPARQL · RDF · OWL · Programming languages

1 Introduction

Nowadays, the online availability of an increasingly large amount of source code is dramatically changing the way programmers approach the development of large software systems. The possibility of reusing existing code allows developers to focus on the added value of their products, speed up the development process and easily explore new possibilities and solutions, while keeping high quality components at the foundations of the system. Several studies have been conducted to understand the general attitude of developers towards the comprehension of large code bases. For instance, in [1] questions asked by programmers during software evolution tasks are analyzed and classified in 44 different categories. The study also highlights the lack of specific methods to answer these questions. Hence, in this paper, we introduce *CodeOntology*, as a resource aimed at supporting the adoption of Semantic Web technologies, in the domain of software development and software engineering. The project has been conceived as an approach to leverage the Semantic Web technology stack and the impressive amount of code available online, to extract structured information from source code, thereby allowing to publish it on the Web in the form of Linked Open Data, as well as enabling the execution of highly expressive queries over source code by means of a powerful language like SPARQL. Thus, CodeOntology is of

© Springer International Publishing AG 2017
C. d'Amato et al. (Eds.): ISWC 2017, Part II, LNCS 10588, pp. 20–28, 2017.
DOI: 10.1007/978-3-319-68204-4_2

particular interest not only to the Semantic Web community, but also to software developers and engineers.

CodeOntology consists of two contributions: an ontology to represent the domain of programming languages and a parser that allows to parse Java source code or bytecode, to serialize it into RDF triples. The ontology is mainly focused towards the Java programming language, but it has been designed with flexibility in mind, thereby being suitable to be reused to represent more languages. On the other hand, the parser is able to extract structural information common to all object-oriented programming languages, like class hierarchy, methods and constructors. Optionally, it can also serialize into RDF triples all the statements and expressions, thereby providing a complete RDF-ization of source code. We then apply semantic techniques like Named Entity Disambiguation, to analyze the comments available within the code and link entities extracted from source code to specific DBpedia [2] resources. This way, it is possible to take advantage of SPARQL to run semantic queries over source code for different purposes, including computer-aided programming, static code analysis, component search and reuse, question answering over source code.

2   Related Work

Querying source code is a critical task in software engineering. Most of the research in software engineering, indeed, is focused towards the development of tools to enhance the maintenance and understanding of extremely large and old software systems. This need has underpinned the development of several source code querying systems, such as OMEGA [3] and CIA (The C Information Abstraction System) [4], which are based on the relational model. More powerful systems, such as Software Refinery [5] are based on graphs and abstract syntax trees. These systems are more sophisticated than tools based on the relational model, but they lack a well-defined query language.

More recently, the online availability of large amounts of open source code has motivated the development of tools to enable programmers to take advantage of this otherwise unstructured information. As an example, Sourcerer [6] allows to collect source code from open repositories and automatically leverage structural information extracted from arbitrary Java projects. The data used by this system, however, are not published on the Web as Linked Open Data, with obvious limitations. Such limitations are partially addressed in [7], where a system to automatically generate an ontology from source code is introduced. This system does not use a unique ontology to describe the entities belonging the programming languages domain, but it generates a different ontology for each input project.

An approach that is more similar to CodeOntology is represented by SCRO (Source Code Representation Ontology) [8]. However, SCRO does not allow to represent some features of modern object-oriented programming languages, such as parameterized types and exceptions handling. Furthermore, the project lacks a system to serialize source code into RDF triples. CodeOntology, unlike other state-of-the-art systems, makes full use of all the resources made available by the Semantic Web technology stack. Data are extracted from source code according to an appropriate ontology and are published using the RDF data model. The collected information is then available to be queried by means of a highly expressive language like SPARQL. Furthermore, CodeOntology allows to analyze documentation comments and link entities extracted from source code to appropriate DBpedia resources that are semantically associated with these entities.

3   The Ontology

The ontology is written in OWL 2 and has been designed using the Protégé tool [9], according to the design principles of clarity, coherence, extensibility, minimum encoding bias and minimum ontological commitment, introduced in [10]. It consists of 65 classes, 86 object properties and 11 data properties and it has been checked for satisfiability, incoherence and inconsistencies using the HermiT reasoner [11]. The modelling process underlying the creation of the ontology has been guided by common competency questions that usually arise during software process and has been inspired by a re-engineering of the Java abstract syntax, as specified in [12]. However, the ontology is sufficiently general to be extended in order to meet future requirements. For instance, it is possible to reuse the ontology to better represent other programming languages, apart from Java. The IRI associated with the ontology is http://rdf.webofcode.org/woc/, abbreviated as woc. The ontology represents structural entities common to all object-oriented programming languages, such as classes, methods, variables, statements and expressions, in a hierarchy of disjoint classes. The root of this hierarchy is the *CodeElement* class, that is the common superclass of all the elements extracted from source code. Since the parser is also able to serialize into RDF triples the structure of Java projects and to analyze libraries such as JAR files, two other classes, namely *Project* and *Library*, have been defined to represent these entities.

The design of the ontology has been conducted according to well-known Ontology Design Patterns, best practices and naming conventions. As an example, the domain of object-oriented programming languages involves large part-whole relations. For instance, a statement may be part of a method, which in turn is part of a class, that is contained in a specified package. In order to represent this partitive relations, the ontology employs a common Content OP and reuses the XKOS vocabulary [13], more precisely the terms xkos:hasPart and xkos:isPartOf. According to the Transitive Reduction pattern, only the most general property is transitive. Thus, transitivity is delegated to the XKOS vocabulary, which in turn gets transitivity from SKOS[1] and DCMI Metadata Terms[2]. We make use of XKOS because it allows to represent both partitive

---

[1] https://www.w3.org/TR/skos-reference/.
[2] http://dublincore.org/documents/dcmi-terms/.

(part-whole) and generic (generic-specific) relations. The domain of programming languages, indeed, includes also generic relations between entities. For instance, inheritance in object-oriented programming turns into generic-specific relations between classes. CodeOntology also makes use of other common Ontology Design Patterns and best practices, such as the N-ary relation pattern[3] and the SV (Specified Values) pattern[4] originally introduced by the W3C SWBPD (Semantic Web Best Practices and Deployment) Working Group. They are used in the ontology to model both access modifiers and primitive data types.

The ontology is available at http://doi.org/10.5281/zenodo.577939, under CC BY 4.0 license. Each entity in the ontology has been annotated by means of the `rdfs:comment` and `rdfs:label` properties. A documentation of the ontology, generated using Parrot [14], is available at http://codeontology.org.

4   The Parser

The RDF triple extraction process is managed by the parser, that is the module of CodeOntology that analyzes and parses Java source code to serialize it into RDF triples. As shown in Fig. 1, the RDF serialization of a Java project acts in three steps: first the project is analyzed to download all of its dependencies and load them in class path, then an abstract syntax tree of the source code and its dependencies is built and processed to extract a set of RDF triples.

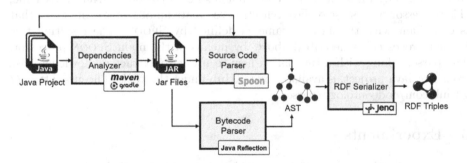

Fig. 1. The RDF serialization process.

CodeOntology currently supports both Maven and Gradle projects. When analyzing a project, the parser first looks at its structure to recognize whether it is built with Maven or Gradle and download the dependencies of the project. JAR files downloaded in this step can optionally be processed and serialized into RDF triples, as well.

Next, the parser builds the abstract syntax tree of the whole input project. This step is handled by SPOON [15], an AST-based source code analysis and

---

[3] https://www.w3.org/TR/swbp-n-aryRelations/.
[4] https://www.w3.org/TR/swbp-specified-values/.

transformation library, that provides a Java metamodel designed to be easy to understand, query and manipulate. This library is used by CodeOntology to build a model containing information about packages, classes, interfaces, methods, as well as statements, expressions, comments and so on. SPOON allows to define processors to be launched over the abstract syntax tree. The RDF triple extraction is managed by a SPOON processor invoked for every package in the input project. From a particular package, the control flow moves to the types contained in that package, such as classes and interfaces, up to the fields, constructors and methods declared within a specified class. CodeOntology looks then inside the body of each method, to take note of all the referenced types, fields, constructors, methods and variables. The RDF serialization process is handled using Apache Jena[5] and it can optionally involve also all the statements and expressions. The parser also allows to keep track of unstructured information such as comments. We then use TagMe [16] to analyze these comments and automatically link entities extracted from source code to pertinent DBpedia resources.

Beside the processor aimed at walking the abstract syntax tree created by SPOON, CodeOntology actually has three more processors. One of these processors is used to analyze the structure of the input project and serialize it into RDF triples. The second one is used to parse comments and detect Javadoc tags, to extract useful information about parameters and method return values. The last processor is used to analyze JAR files, thereby enabling CodeOntology to run not only on Java source code, but also on bytecode. Given a JAR file, this processor makes use of Java reflection to create an abstract syntax tree that is compliant with the Java metamodel defined by SPOON. The resulting tree is then processed as described above, by means of the main SPOON processor. The parser, along with a tutorial on how to use it to extract a knowledge base from any Java project, is available on GitHub under the GPLv3 license: https:// github.com/codeontology/parser.

5   Experiments

The parser has been successfully applied to extract a knowledge base from the OpenJDK 8 source code[6]. These data can be queried through a remote SPARQL endpoint at: http://codeontology.org/sparql. Moreover, the dataset is available at https://doi.org/10.5281/zenodo.818116 and on figshare [17]. The analysis has been conducted on about 1.5 million lines of code, retrieving a total of almost 2M RDF triples falling into 4 categories: structural information on source code (1.9M triples), DBpedia links (309k triples), actual source code as literals (134k triples) and literal comments (105k triples). Quality assessments have been conducted on a sample of methods and classes. Figure 2 shows a small subset of the triples produced by the parser from a simple "hello world" class. This representation allows to run expressive queries over source code, some of which are shown in

---

[5] https://jena.apache.org/.
[6] http://openjdk.java.net/.

```
package org.codeontology;

public class Example {
  /** Prints a "hello world" message to the standard output */
  public static void main(String[] args) {
    System.out.println("Hello CodeOntology!");
  }
}
```

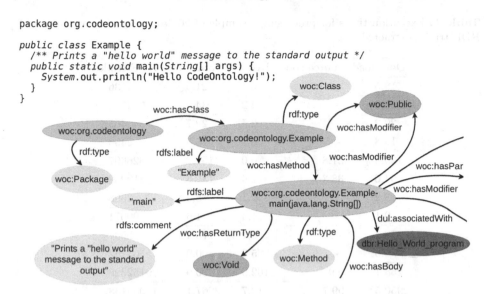

Fig. 2. An excerpt of the RDF serialization produced for a simple "hello world" code.

[18]. As an example, since the output of the parser is a graph, we can easily apply to software not only metrics specifically designed for software engineering tasks, but also metrics borrowed from other fields, such as Social Network Analysis. Suppose we want to rank classes in OpenJDK, to select only the most important ones, according to a specified metric. For instance, we can select the three classes that turn out to be the most referenced by the methods of the other classes. When a method m references a specific class c, then the parser is able to serialize this information into a triple of the form: m *woc:references* c. Thus, we can rank the classes in OpenJDK according to this metric and retrieve the most referenced ones, by means of a simple SPARQL query[7]. Unsurprisingly, the most referenced class in OpenJDK is the `java.lang.String` class, followed by the classes `java.lang.Object` and `java.io.IOException`. In order to compute such a metric efficiently, a graph-based representation of software systems is needed.

Moreover, the extracted DBpedia links can be used to run highly expressive semantic queries over source code. For instance, we can retrieve all the methods for computing the cube root of a real number, by selecting the resources associated with the entity `dbpedia:Cube_root`.

Besides OpenJDK, the system has also been tested on a sample of 20 Java repositories randomly collected from GitHub. Table 1 shows the execution times required to download the dependencies, in the form of JAR files, analyze the source code and process the JAR files previously downloaded. All the times are expressed in seconds. Table 1 also shows the total number of RDF triples extracted from each project.

---

[7] see http://codeontology.org/examples.

Table 1. Execution times for processing a sample of 20 Java projects and number of RDF triples extracted.

Download	Source code	JAR	Total time	RDF triples
18.5	3.0	0.1	21.6	4336
30.3	–	4.2	34.4	544744
20.2	–	2.5	22.7	344465
15.3	–	0.2	15.5	2496
129.3	21.8	6.0	157.2	626607
94.6	38.3	2.4	135.3	212258
18.2	–	0.1	18.3	2598
0.1	–	1.4	1.6	90071
78.4	–	0.1	78.4	2597
95.6	–	5.3	100.9	505262
258.1	9.9	162.9	430.9	9152328
2950.5	99.7	216.7	3267.1	17059138
171.8	–	0.2	172.0	2499
53.8	–	0.2	54.0	2496
47.0	–	6.9	54.0	561580
121.1	–	2.4	123.4	95376
140.8	93.9	3.5	238.1	171267
78.3	–	0.1	78.6	4992
34.2	–	10.9	45.2	1101273
26.4	–	1.2	27.6	26212
4382.5	266.6	427.3	5076.8	30512595

In some cases, it was not possible to analyze source code because SPOON failed building the Abstract Syntax Tree for different reasons, such as missing dependencies that were not automatically downloaded. However, the parser has been able to extract a knowledge base consisting of more than 30.5 million RDF triples, from only 20 repositories.

6   Conclusions and Future Work

CodeOntology is a project that consists of two contributions: an ontology describing structural entities common to all object-oriented programming languages and a parser capable of serializing Java source code and bytecode into RDF triples. In this paper, we have described the core ideas underlying the design of the ontology and we have analyzed the architecture of the parser. Furthermore, CodeOntology allows to analyze Java comments, in order to link entities extracted from source code to DBpedia resources. This way, it is possible to precisely search specific software components using expressive semantic queries. In the future, we plan to develop a Question Answering system to hide the complexity of SPARQL queries and allow retrieving software components by means of questions in natural language. Moreover, it will be possible to dereference and execute the source code of the methods in the datasets, using the *Web of Functions* technology [19].

Acknowledgments. This work was supported in part by a 2015 Google Faculty Research Award and Sardegna Ricerche (*project OKgraph*, CRP 120). The authors wish to thank the anonymous reviewers for their insightful comments.

References

1. Sillito, J., Murphy, G.C., De Volder, K.: Questions programmers ask during software evolution tasks. In: Proceedings of the 14th ACM SIGSOFT 2006/FSE-14, pp. 23–34. ACM, New York (2006)
2. Lehmann, J., Isele, R., Jakob, M., Jentzsch, A., Kontokostas, D., Mendes, P.N., Hellmann, S., Morsey, M., van Kleef, P., Auer, S., Bizer, C.: DBpedia - a large-scale, multilingual knowledge base extracted from Wikipedia. Semant. Web J. **6**(2), 167–195 (2015)
3. Linton, M.A.: Implementing relational views of programs. SIGSOFT Softw. Eng. Notes **9**(3), 132–140 (1984)
4. Chen, Y.F., Nishimoto, M.Y., Ramamoorthy, C.V.: The C information abstraction system. IEEE Trans. Softw. Eng. **16**(3), 325–334 (1990)
5. Reasoning Systems: Refine user's guide (1992)
6. Bajracharya, S., Ossher, J., Lopes, C.: Sourcerer: an infrastructure for large-scale collection and analysis of open-source code. Sci. Comput. Program. **79**, 241–259 (2014)
7. Ganapathy, G., Sagayaraj, S.: To generate the ontology from Java source code OWL creation. Int. J. Adv. Comput. Sci. Appl. **2**(2), 111–116 (2011)
8. Alnusair, A., Zhao, T.: Component search and reuse: an ontology-based approach. In: IRI, IEEE Systems, Man, and Cybernetics Society, pp. 258–261 (2010)
9. Musen, M.A.: The protégé project: a look back and a look forward. AI Matters **1**(4), 4–12 (2015)
10. Gruber, T.R.: Toward principles for the design of ontologies used for knowledge sharing. Int. J. Hum.-Comput. Stud. **43**(5–6), 907–928 (1995)
11. Shearer, R., Motik, B., Horrocks, I.: Hermit: a highly-efficient OWL reasoner. In: OWLED, CEUR Workshop Proceedings, vol. 432, CEUR-WS.org (2008)
12. Gosling, J., Joy, B., Steele, G., Bracha, G., Buckley, A.: The Java Language Specification, Java SE 8 edn. Oracle (2015)
13. Gillman, D., Cotton, F., Jaques, Y.: XKOS: extending SKOS for describing statistical classifications. In: The 12th International Semantic Web Conference (2013)
14. Tejo-Alonso, C., Berrueta, D., Polo, L., Fernández, S.: Metadata for web ontologies and rules: current practices and perspectives. In: García-Barriocanal, E., Cebeci, Z., Okur, M.C., Öztürk, A. (eds.) MTSR 2011. CCIS, vol. 240, pp. 56–67. Springer, Heidelberg (2011). doi:10.1007/978-3-642-24731-6_6
15. Pawlak, R., Monperrus, M., Petitprez, N., Noguera, C., Seinturier, L.: SPOON: a library for implementing analyses and transformations of Java source code. Softw.: Pract. Exp. **46**, 1155–1179 (2016). http://onlinelibrary.wiley.com/doi/10.1002/spe.2346/full

16. Ferragina, P., Scaiella, U.: Fast and accurate annotation of short texts with Wikipedia pages. IEEE Softw. **29**(1), 70–75 (2012)
17. Atzeni, M., Atzori, M.: CodeOntology OpenJDK8 dataset. figshare (2017). https://doi.org/10.6084/m9.figshare.5234878
18. Atzeni, M., Atzori, M.: CodeOntology: querying source code in a semantic framework. In: Proceedings of the ISWC 2017 Posters & Demonstrations Track co-located with 16th International Semantic Web Conference (ISWC 2017)
19. Atzori, M.: Toward the web of functions: interoperable higher-order functions in SPARQL. In: Mika, P., et al. (eds.) ISWC 2014. LNCS, vol. 8797, pp. 406–421. Springer, Cham (2014). doi:10.1007/978-3-319-11915-1_26

Linked Data Publication of Live Music Archives and Analyses

Sean Bechhofer[1](✉), Kevin Page[2], David M. Weigl[2], György Fazekas[3],
and Thomas Wilmering[3]

[1] School of Computer Science, University of Manchester, Manchester, England
sean.bechhofer@mancheseter.ac.uk
[2] Oxford e-Research Centre, University of Oxford, Oxford, England
{kevin.page,david.weigl}@oerc.ox.ac.uk
[3] Centre for Digital Music, Queen Mary University of London, London, England
{g.fazekas,t.wilmering}@qmul.ac.uk

Abstract. We describe the publication of a linked data set exposing metadata from the Internet Archive Live Music Archive along with detailed feature analysis data of the audio files contained in the archive. The collection is linked to existing musical and geographical resources allowing for the extraction of useful or nteresting subsets of data using additional metadata.

The collection is published using a 'layered' approach, aggregating the original information with links and specialised analyses, and forms a valuable resource for those investigating or developing audio analysis tools and workflows.

1 Introduction and Context

The Internet Archive Live Music Archive[1] (further referred to here as LMA) is an online resource providing access to a large community-contributed collection of live recordings. Covering nearly 5,000 artists, chiefly in rock genres, the archive contains over 130,000 live recordings made openly available with the permission of the artists concerned. Audio files are available in a variety of formats (and with varying levels of quality), and each recording is accompanied by metadata describing information about dates, venues, set lists, the provenance of the audio files and so on.

From a musicological perspective, the collection is valuable for a number of reasons. First of all, it provides access to the underlying audio files. Thus the LMA provides a corpus that can be used for Music Information Retrieval (MIR) [3] tasks such as genre detection, key detection, segmentation as exemplified by the MIREX series of workshops [7]. It provides multiple recordings by individual artists[2] allowing comparisons across performances. It provides multiple recordings of single events, allowing for enhanced user experience through

---

[1] http://archive.org/details/etree.
[2] In the case of the Grateful Dead, an act that for many years encouraged audience taping of performances, the LMA contains over 8,000 recorded performances.

© Springer International Publishing AG 2017
C. d'Amato et al. (Eds.): ISWC 2017, Part II, LNCS 10588, pp. 29–37, 2017.
DOI: 10.1007/978-3-319-68204-4_3

Layer	Details
Feature Metadata	Feature summary/provenance LD Service
Computational Analysis	Sonic Annotator feature analysis
Collection Metadata	etree LD Service
Collection	Internet Archive Live Music Archive

Fig. 1. Layers in the etree/CALMA dataset

combinations of recordings [13]. Furthermore, in live situations artists will frequently play works by other artists ("covers"), providing source content for cover detection algorithms. The collection is not without challenges, however. Recordings in the LMA range in source from handheld tape recorders, through smart phones in the audience, to a feed from the mixing deck. A poorly tuned instrument or late entry constitute a 'truth' in live performances that would more likely trigger a re-take in the studio. The signals themselves can be noisy, with crowd chatter, on-stage banter and improvisation.

Semantic Web technologies have been previously applied in the context of digital music collections [1,6,8] and successfully applied to other projects under the auspices of *Transforming Musicology* [5,11].

In CALMA[3] we have built a layered Music Digital Library using Semantic Web technologies to combine and interpret metadata and content-based analyses (see Fig. 1). The data set builds on the source audio and (largely free-text) metadata, introducing consistent structure and links to external sources.

The original, community contributed, metadata has been converted to RDF and published as linked data [2] (the *etree* dataset). The data set has been enhanced with connections and links to a number of external data sources providing additional information about the entities in the data – sources such as MusicBrainz[4], GeoNames[5] and last.fm[6]. In addition to the contributed metadata, audio analysis is being performed on the underlying audio files in the collection, resulting in a corpus of feature data, analysis results and provenance. This data has again been published [12] (the *CALMA* dataset), exposing the computational results as "blobs" with accompanying feature and provenance data in RDF. The original data sources are published "as is", with collection metadata, computational analysis results and feature metadata layered on top of this substrate. This allows a clear separation between the source and enhancements, with corresponding provenance information. This is particularly important in a context such as musicology, where findings may be contingent or speculative. The results of analyses performed using different tools and algorithms may have varying results or quality given the context (e.g. noise in the recording), therefore the provenance data we publish can be crucial in establishing trust.

---

[3] Computational Analysis of the Live Music Archive.
[4] http://musicbrainz.org.
[5] http://www.geonames.org.
[6] http://www.lastfm.org.

2   The Collection

The LMA is largely focused on recordings of live performances, concerts or events. Each of these will include a number of songs or tracks, with each song associated with an uploaded audio file. These files are in a variety of formats, and have been produced using a variety of techniques, from hand held microphones in the crowd, through to high quality digital feeds taken directly from a mixing desk. Audio files have often been post-processed by the uploader before addition. As a result, the audio files vary not just in format, but in quality and may also contain artifacts due to the recording or processing techniques used. For example, many recordings contain crowd noise or on-stage banter. Metadata contributed by the uploader describes information about the event such as the location and date along with lineage or source information that describes, for example, the signal processing chain used for post-processing. Note that this information is not structured or controlled.

The LMA is typical of many collections in its metadata being the most comprehensive means for indexing and accessing what is clearly a valuable cultural resource. This metadata is, however, gathered using free text fields entered by the audio uploader, so is potentially prone to errors (e.g. in set list order) or typographic mistakes (e.g. misspelling of artists, track titles, or venues). Given one potential value of the LMA for study lies in comparing recordings of the same track, artist, or venue, correcting – or accepting – metadata imperfections within analyses must be addressed for scholarly adoption.

The initial motivation for this work was to enable investigations such as the following examples: (1) Identify the same song performed by the same artist, but at multiple venues over multiple dates, analysing the audio for tempo. If an artist performs with a faster tempo at a venue, do other artists do the same at that venue? Is there a correlation between tempo differences and performance date, line up, weather etc.? (2) Finding performances by artists in their home towns, does audience reaction (between songs) differ from other venues? (3) Metadata from the LMA can be incomplete, with missing or erroneous labels. Can we cross-validate with audio analyses?

We note that investigations into the first two questions require additional information which is held outside of the LMA, for example geo-location data, membership or history of bands or meteorological data. The use of a Linked Data approach (See Sect. 3) offers promise in providing this additional contextual information.

We also recognise that an investigation of any one of these topics alone does not *require* this data publication; it is also plausible that software focused on a single investigation might be achieved at lower cost in time and code. We argue that investment in our approach is returned when layers can be re-used, extended, and adapted; when one can re-use and extend the layers of others; and in their transparency for peer-review and validation.

The etree and CALMA datasets have differing, but complementary purposes. Considering them together illustrates benefits descended from our use of Linked Data: the consistent application of two distinct dataset motivations within each dataset (one bibliographic; the other audio analytic); the ability to build a new second dataset (CALMA) upon the foundation of the first (etree), where the former postdates the latter by several years and was achieved through the addition of new institutions and expertise into the collaboration; and the easy retrofitting of CALMA links back into etree/LMA referencing once the analyses were completed.

3   Modelling, Ontologies and Vocabularies

Lynch [9] proposes that digital collections should be exposed as databases of raw cultural heritage materials along with layers of interpretation and presentation built upon these databases and making reference to the objects within them. This is the approach taken here. As discussed in [12], the original metadata is preserved and made available. Our publication process introduces a set of uniform identifiers for the entities represented in the data (artists, events, songs, venues etc.) along with links, both within the dataset and to resources outside.

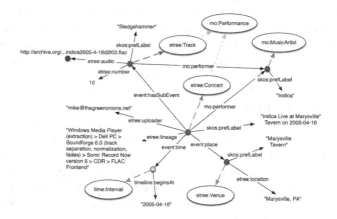

Fig. 2. Basic data model

The basic modelling pattern used in the dataset is shown in Fig. 2. In the figures, green, dashed, unlabelled links are `rdf:type`. Blue, dotted, unlabelled links are `rdfs:subClassOf`. The ontology used to describe the collection is relatively inexpressive, essentially providing classes for performances and venues and properties for the assertion of values and relationships. Where possible, existing ontologies and vocabularies have been used in the descriptions of entities. These include:

Music The Music Ontology or MO[7] provides terms that describe performances, artists and the relationships between them.

---

[7] http://musicontology.com/.

Events The Event Ontology or EO[8] provides terms for describing events.

Similarity The Similarity Ontology[9] provides terms for asserting associations between entities. This is used to associate entities in the collection such as artists or locations with external entities from e.g. MusicBrainz and GeoNames. A key design decision is to provide explicit resources modelling similarities in order to allow for the recording of provenance information on these similarities. The Similarity Ontology was chosen due to its existing usage within the computational musicology community.

SKOS SKOS[10] labelling properties are used to label entities.

PROV-O The W3C provenance ontology[11].

VoID The W3C dataset metadata ontology[12].

VAMP A vocabulary describing VAMP[13] audio analysis plugins[14].

In addition to the vocabularies listed above, bespoke ontologies[15,16] define subclasses of Music Ontology classes and specific properties used in the etree metadata.

The collection offers possibilities for record linkage with external datasets. In particular, music artists and geographical locations are entities that are described in a number of external data sources (many of which are also published as Linked Data).

Artist Alignment MusicBrainz[17] is an "open music encyclopedia" providing identifiers for a large number of music artists and is a clear candidate for linking from a collection like LMA. Alignments between etree artists and MusicBrainz use a combination of string matching on artist names and song titles. In keeping with the strategy outlined above, the relationships between the artists and MusicBrainz are asserted using the Similarity Ontology as shown in Fig. 3.

The Music Ontology considers mo:MusicArtist to encapsulate "A person or a group of people [...], whose musical creative work shows sensitivity and imagination" and the current dataset makes no distinction between solo artists and bands/groups of musicians. There is no information in the source corpus that distinguishes between solo artist and group or identifies relationships between, for example, a singer and a band. For our initial purposes, identifying "artist" is sufficient. Mappings to MusicBrainz may allow for further identification of groups or solo artists and a refinement of the types applied (for example asserting that

---

[8] http://motools.sourceforge.net/event/event.html.
[9] http://purl.org/ontology/similarity/.
[10] http://www.w3.org/TR/skos-reference.
[11] http://www.w3.org/TR/prov-o/.
[12] http://www.w3.org/TR/void/.
[13] http://vamp-plugins.org/.
[14] http://purl.org/ontology/vamp/.
[15] http://etree.linkedmusic.org/vocab.
[16] http://calma.linkedmusic.org/vocab.
[17] http://musicbrainz.org.

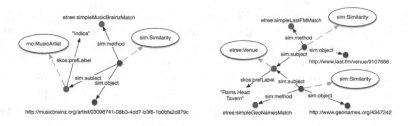

Fig. 3. Similarities with MusicBrainz (left) and Lolcations (right)

a resource is in fact a `mo:MusicGroup`). Artists are aligned in a similar way with last.fm[18].

Geographical Alignment Performances occur at a particular place[19] and can thus potentially be mapped to geographical locations in collection such as GeoNames. Concert performances also tend to take place in specific venues (theatres, concert halls etc.) which are described in data sources such as last.fm. Information about venues and general locations is given in the source metadata, with variable granularity and consistency, using the *venue* and *coverage* tags, where venue describes the name of the venue where the performance was recorded e.g. *The 9:30 Club* and coverage gives the larger geographical area for the location, e.g. *Washington, DC.*

The raw location information suffers from inconsistencies in presentation (*Chicago, IL*; *Chicago, Il*; *Chicago, Illinois*; *Chicago* etc.). Location information may in some cases also be ambiguous, with only city or town name being given (e.g. *Amsterdam* or *Springfield*). As discussed above, our approach in the collection is to expose the underlying source data and layer additional mappings on top. Thus each performance is associated with a *unique* venue entity with a name and location. A description that refers to the venue *Academy* in *Manchester* could refer to one of at least four distinct venues and, since there is insufficient information in the raw LMA data to reliably disambiguate, collapsing them is undesirable.

Two external data sources provide additional information about venues and geographical locations which is of use here. *GeoNames* provides identifiers for over eight million place names, while *last.fm* provides a comprehensive list of music venues. For a performance with a given venue and coverage, candidates for mappings are obtained through queries to the GeoNames and last.fm APIs. If potential candidates are returned from both collections, the geographical locations are cross-compared (both GeoNames and last.fm provide latitude/longitude information). Geographical co-location (up to a threshold of 10

---

[18] http://last.fm.

[19] To the best of our knowledge, the collection does not contain examples of performances recorded by artists collaborating virtually in geographically distributed locations.

miles) then gives us further confidence in the potential alignment. Mapping candidates are associated with venues again using an explicit Similarity Ontology relationship. Note that these geographical alignments are *not* necessarily asserting that the entities are the same. For example, a venue entity in LMA may be associated with a GeoNames district. As yet, no formal evaluation of the quality of the alignments has been done.

Provenance The use of the Similarity Ontology (see Fig. 3) provides objects that represent associations between objects and thus allow us to attach additional metadata to those objects asserting the provenance of the relationship. In the current dataset, this includes a link to a URI describing the method that was used to derive the alignment. We do not (as yet) provide explicit links to the *code* that was run in order to produce the alignments, but such an approach may be the topic of further work. Relationships from the W3C's PROV-O ontology are used to assert additional information about the provenance of these mappings. PROV-O vocabulary is also used to record provenance of audio feature extraction, including information about the VAMP plugins used, parameters, etc.

The basic metadata collection (excluding audio feature metadata) contains over 12 million RDF triples concerning over 135,000 distinct performances and nearly 5,000 artists with at least one performance. The analysis feature data currently covers 300,000 individual tracks and comprises approx 1.1TB of (compressed) data.

4   Usage and Access

Audio feature extraction (and analysis) is resource-intensive. The original harmonised metadata proved invaluable in supporting the selection of "interesting" events to initially target. Our initial question was to consider how performances of songs might possibly change over time, thus we focused on artists with multiple events where particular songs or pieces have multiple performances. A workset was established using a SPARQL query against the catalogue metadata layer, selecting those artists in etree with more than 200 but less than 1,000 performances, constrained to those who performed at least one song title in more than 100 distinct performance recordings[20].

Although this *would* have been possibly via queries over the original metadata, the SPARQL endpoint made it simple. As discussed in [12], the workflow for analysis involves retrieving audio from the Internet Archive[21] and running Python scripts built around the Sonic Annotator platform for audio feature extraction [4]. The computational results are themselves stored as an RDF blob (although this may not always be an appropriate format hence our treatment of the results as a blob) with the feature metadata and provenance information regarding the execution of the workflow added to our data set. This metadata

---

[20] The SPARQL query can be found on the dataset descriptive web pages.
[21] Our collection contains only the metadata, not the audio files.

again uses existing published vocabularies as described earlier (MO and PROV-O).

An investigation into "typicality" summarising feature value distributions within multi-performance, same-song collections is reported in [12]. Metadata from LMA and CALMA feature analysis (accessed via the data set) has also been used to develop an immersive experience through alignment and clustering of recordings [13]. Discussions are ongoing with the Internet Archive, with the hope that information may be re-ingested into the IA collections. We also believe that the metadata could support musicological analyses and new music discovery tools (e.g. MusicWeb [10]).

The collection can be accessed via two persistent URLs http://purl.org/etree and http://purl.org/calma. The PURLs resolve to resources that provide VoID metadata about the respective collections. The LMA metadata is accessible via a SPARQL endpoint and a browsable (pubby) front end is also provided. Currently, the CALMA metadata and feature extraction results are available via direct download. Metadata and analysis results are made available under Creative Commons CC0.

The data in LMA is largely static, in that the audio and metadata are not usually edited once they have been deposited. Annotations may be added – for example alignments to other data sources – but as these use the layered approach described here, this is additive. Thus, to date, we have not been troubled with issues relating to versioning. Update of our translated resource is not, as yet, automated – the LMA is updated with additional recordings daily. The workflow supporting inclusion of additional performances into the collection is clear, however, and for the purposes of many investigations, historical recordings are sufficient.

5   Conclusions and Future Work

We have presented a layered digital library providing multimedia access to audio, user-provided metadata, and audio-derived feature metadata of the Live Music Archive, in turn allowing novel exploratory analyses across and within its layers. The dataset provides access to a large open data collection in the Digital Humanities, supporting musicological scholarship at scale, and representing an augmentation and enrichment of a valuable public resource for fans and listeners. We also envisage applications that go beyond musicological analyses and support further services that are built on such "enhanced archives".

Acknowledgments. This work was supported through a subaward of the Semantic Media Network (EPSRC EP/J010375/1); the FAST IMPACt project (EPSRC EP/L019981/1); and the EU Commission H2020 grant AudioCommons (688382). We thank the Internet Archive and Brewster Kahle for encouragement, support and access to the dataset.

References

1. Bainbridge, D., Hu, X., Downie, J.S.: A Musical progression with greenstone: how music content analysis and linked data is helping redefine the boundaries to a music digital library. In: Proceedings of 1st International Workshop on Digital Libraries for Musicology, pp. 1–8. ACM (2014)
2. Bechhofer, S., Page, K., De Roure, D.: Hello cleveland! linked data publication of live music archives. In: 14th International Workshop on Image and Audio Analysis for Multimedia Interactive Services. IEEE (2013)
3. Byrd, D., Crawford, T.: Problems of music information retrieval in the real world. Inf. Process. Manag. **38**, 249–272 (2002)
4. Cannam, C., Sandler, M., Jewell, M.O., Rhodes, C., d'Inverno, M.: Linked data and you: bringing music research software into the semantic web. J. New Music Res. **39**(4), 313–325 (2010)
5. Crawford, T., Fields, B., Lewis, D., Page, K.: Explorations in linked data practice for early music corpora. In: Digital Libraries (JCDL), pp. 309–312. IEEE (2014)
6. De Roure, D., Klyne, G., Page, K.R., Pybus, J.P.N., Weigl, D.M.: Music and science: parallels in production. In: Proceedings of 2nd International Workshop on Digital Libraries for Musicology, pp. 17–20. ACM (2015)
7. Downie, J.S.: The music information retrieval evaluation eXchange (MIREX). D-Lib Magazine, vol. 12, no. 12, December 2006
8. Fazekas, G., Raimond, Y., Jacobson, K., Sandler, M.: An overview of semantic web activities in the OMRAS2 project. J. New Music Res. **39**(4), 295–311 (2010)
9. Lynch, C.: Digital collections, digital libraries and the digitization of cultural heritage information. First Monday **7**(5) (2002)
10. Mora-Mcginity, M., Allik, A., Fazekas, G., Sandler, M.: MusicWeb: music discovery with open linked semantic metadata. In: Garoufallou, E., Subirats Coll, I., Stellato, A., Greenberg, J. (eds.) MTSR 2016. CCIS, vol. 672, pp. 291–296. Springer, Cham (2016). doi:10.1007/978-3-319-49157-8_25
11. Nurmikko-Fuller, T., Dix, A., Weigl, D.M., Page, K.R.: In collaboration with in concert: reflecting a digital library as linked data for performance ephemera. In: Proceedings of 3rd International Workshop on Digital Libraries for Musicology, pp. 17–24. ACM (2016)
12. Page, K.R., Bechhofer, S., Fazekas, G., Weigl, D.M. Wilmering, T.: Realising a layered digital library: exploration and analysis of the live music archive through linked data. In: ACM/IEEE-CS Joint Conference on Digital Libraries (JCDL) (2017)
13. Wilmering, T., Thalmann, F., Sandler, M.B.: Grateful live: mixing multiple recordings of a dead performance into an immersive experience. In: AES Convention 141 (2016)

The MedRed Ontology for Representing Clinical Data Acquisition Metadata

Jean-Paul Calbimonte[1(✉)], Fabien Dubosson[1], Roger Hilfiker[2],
Alexandre Cotting[1], and Michael Schumacher[1]

[1] Institute of Information Systems, University of Applied Sciences and Arts Western
Switzerland, HES-SO Valais-Wallis, Sierre, Switzerland
{jean-paul.calbimonte,fabien.dubosson,alexandre.cotting,
michael.schumacher}@hevs.ch
[2] Institute of Health Sciences, University of Applied Sciences and Arts Western
Switzerland, HES-SO Valais-Wallis, Leukerbad, Switzerland
roger.hilfiker@hevs.ch

Abstract. Electronic Data Capture (EDC) software solutions are progressively being adopted for conducting clinical trials and studies, carried out by biomedical, pharmaceutical and health-care research teams. In this paper we present the MedRed Ontology, whose goal is to represent the metadata of these studies, using well-established standards, and reusing related vocabularies to describe essential aspects, such as validation rules, composability, or provenance. The paper describes the design principles behind the ontology and how it relates to existing models and formats used in the industry. We also reuse well-known vocabularies and W3C recommendations. Furthermore, we have validated the ontology with existing clinical studies in the context of the MedRed project, as well as a collection of metadata of well-known studies. Finally, we have made the ontology available publicly following best practices and vocabulary sharing guidelines.

1 Introduction

Clinical research activities require the involvement of heterogeneous individuals of a given population, needed to assess and validate biomedical hypotheses concerning behavior, treatments, interventions and other studies. Clinical trials and other such studies can be complex and span long periods of time, and the data acquisition process requires careful management and accuracy. Although in the past, manually filled forms were the norm for acquiring data in this context, nowadays the use of Electronic Data Capture (EDC) solutions has shown to improve the efficiency of the process, while maintaining quality and accuracy standards [3,19]. In particular, EDC helps reducing and/or eliminating data transcription and transmission times, providing data validation and input enforcement, or helping scheduling the site visits [5,7]. Furthermore, EDC provides faster access to data in running studies, which can help to perform live-analytics over the acquired datasets. Due to these benefits, clinical research

C. d'Amato et al. (Eds.): ISWC 2017, Part II, LNCS 10588, pp. 38–47, 2017.
DOI: 10.1007/978-3-319-68204-4_4

organizations, pharmaceutical companies, and university hospitals, among others, make use of EDC and related systems such as OpenClinica, REDCap, TrialDB, InForm, Medidata Rave or Datatrak [16].

As an example, consider an osteoarthritis study performed by the Physiotherapy Lab at HES-SO Valais-Wallis, on the local population. The implementation of this study may include the usage of several *instruments*, such as questionnaires over a selected group of patients, each of which contains several *sections, questions*, and *variables* to be annotated and recorded. The study can be divided in different *arms* where diverse methods are applied for comparison purposes; and furthermore, it can be split in repeated *events* over time, using similar instruments for evolution tracking. Such study could reuse well known and validated instruments, such as the HOOS Hip survey [14], or extend it with additional instruments, sections, and variables.

Given the large number of clinical studies that are performed worldwide, and their complexity, it has become a need to share their results, as well as their structure and metadata. This would enable: validating existing protocols, reusing and refining clinical research instruments, extending previous studies, performing surveys and systematic analytics of clinical trials, etc. However, to achieve this, it is first necessary to tackle the heterogeneity issues regarding the description and representation of these studies. The most used format for representing studies in EDC software, ODM (Operational Data Model) [9], lacks a semantically-rich model able to address the aforementioned challenges, and is therefore insufficient as a foundational model for achieving semantic interoperability for clinical studies and trials.

In this paper we present the MedRed Ontology, a semantically-rich model designed to represent the metadata of clinical studies, including the definition of its constituting instruments, the different steps of each one, their organization in arms and events, as well as the data variables captured using them. Thanks to its integration with existing vocabularies (PROV-O [11] and P-Plan [6]), the MedRed ontology can also capture complex relationships among instruments and studies, including composition, derivation, authoring, and versioning. These features make it possible to track changes of a study across time, or to indicate that a study was designed based on an existing one. MedRed also includes the representation of validation conditions on the clinical instruments, using the SHACL language [8] for representing constraints. The MedRed Ontology has been validated using pilot studies led by the Institute of Health of HES-SO Valais-Wallis, in the context of the MedRed data lifecycle project[1]. It has also been applied to a heterogeneous collection of study metadata descriptions extracted from the REDCap [7] library of health studies and instruments. Finally, MedRed has been made publicly available under standard formats, on a permanent URL, and following ontology publication guidelines.

---

[1] MedRed Project: http://w3id.org/medred/project.

2   Related Work

Ontologies for clinical studies have been developed in recent years, typically focusing on the description of different types of studies, including taxonomies and classifications [17]. The OBO Foundry [18] contains several biomedical ontologies, some of which are related to the description of studies. Examples include the Ontology for Biomedical Investigations, Clinical Measurement Ontology, and the Informed Consent Ontology. However, these are more specific to biomedical document descriptions, measurements, and consent information, respectively. The Bioportal repository also contains relevant ontologies, e.g. Clinical Trials Ontology, which contains a large vocabulary of clinical trial types. Other ontologies in Bioportal (e.g. MESH, SNOMED, HL7) include general references to clinical study concepts, but do not provide detailed descriptions of them.

Clinical Data capture software are widely used today as a backbone technology for data acquisition in research studies. Professional tools include OpenClinica, REDCap, CancerGrid, InForm, Datatrak, Medidata Rave, etc. [4,7]. Significant efforts have been made to agree on standards for clinical studies, and the ODM (Operational Data Model) [9] proposed by CDISC[2] has been adopted by several regulating bodies and also EDC software tools. Based on XML, ODM serves as a communication interface of clinical study data, but it lacks a semantically-rich model able to capture the different relationships among the different components of a clinical study, as well as linking with other standard vocabularies. Recent works [12] developed approaches for semantic annotation of ODM XML export files, using extensions to the RDF DataCube vocabulary. Other efforts [13] have also tried to achieve semantic integration of clinical data management systems, by integrating ODM and the HL7 FHIR standard. Up to now, the ODM specifications are regarded as the reference for data interchange for these systems, although they lack several features as explained in Sect. 3. Even if there were some attempts to provide semantic annotations for ODM [3,10], there is yet no comprehensive ontology that incorporate the aspects covered in this work.

3   Design Principles

The MedRed Ontology design is founded on the representation of a generic clinical study, understood as a collection of data acquisition instruments. In the following we present the design principles behind the ontology, namely the structure of the *core model*, and the fundamental features of *composition*, *derivation*, *provenance*, and *validation*.

Core Model. According to the ODM model of CDISC [9], a *Study* has a *metadata version* element in which the different definitions of its sub-elements are contained, i.e. a *Form*, *Item*, and *Item Group* definition. These commonly materialize as instrument, question and section definitions, respectively, in a questionnaire-based instrument. Taking this model as a starting point, the MedRed ontology

---

[2] CDISC (Clinical Data Interchange Standards Consortium): http://cdisc.org.

Fig. 1. Composition and derivation in MedRed. Left: a sample instrument including its organization in sections and items. Right: a study may incorporate instruments created previously (e.g. Hip survey) or create new instruments reusing items from others (e.g. the eating disorder questionnaire).

first separates the metadata versioning aspects out of the core model, as this is a cross-cutting consideration. A MedRed *Study* is indeed composed of one or more *Instruments*, each of which has an ordered sequence of steps, modeled as *Item* elements. Different kinds of *Items* exist, such as *Question, Information,* or *Operation* items. Different sub-classes of *Instrument* may exist, such as a questionnaire, or case form, etc. *Items* may be grouped in *Sections*, providing a logical and nestable organization to the items of the instrument. Each *Item* identifies its previous item in the sequence, and they may be subject to conditional activation to allow branching logic in a sequence of steps. For each *Item* a corresponding *Variable* can be specified, which represents the data that will be captured (e.g. via a question or form entry). *Variables* are associated to data types, and constraints can be defined upon them, e.g. allowed values, rules, etc. Moreover, a *Study* can be organized in different *Arms*, or branches that focus on a particular characteristic for comparison or testing purposes (e.g. different arms for testing different drugs in parallel). MedRed also allows defining events that can help representing longitudinal studies, where different instruments are used over longer periods of time (e.g. demographics at the beginning of the study, a first set of instruments after 3 months, another set 2 months later, etc.).

Composition. The ability to compose studies and instruments using other items and elements is crucial for the MedRed metadata model. For instance, it is possible to combine different existing instruments from other studies in a new one. Similarly, it is possible to combine questions and items of several instruments to elaborate a new sequence of input items for an instrument. This should allow the reuse of existing metadata and studies that have already been successfully implemented, preventing from reinventing the wheel. A generic model that was created with the purpose of representing a sequence of scientific activities in a plan is the P-Plan ontology [6]. Introducing the basic concepts of *Plan* and *Step*, it allows nesting and constructing different structures of planned items. For this reason, it was chosen as a basis for structuring items and instruments in MedRed, allowing very flexible composition designs.

Derivation. Reusing instruments and items from existing studies also implies that one can be derived from others. One instrument can be amended or extended according to the needs of a different context (e.g. a new study on a different population), by adding new questions or modifying their validation rules, possible values, etc. The representation of this information helps keeping trace of these relationships, as exemplified in Fig. 1.

Fig. 2. Provenance examples in the MedRed ontology.

Provenance. As all studies, instruments, and items can bee seen as traceable resources (or entities according to the PROV model [11]), MedRed allows keeping record of provenance information, including attribution, versioning, authorship, etc. The PROV-O ontology [11] has precisely been defined for this purpose, and as such, we have chosen to align the MedRed core concepts with this model, so that this type of information can be recorded accordingly. For instance, as shown in Fig. 2, this allows indicating specialization, revision, source, attribution, and other related information.

Validation. In the context of clinical data capture, it is essential to guarantee certain data quality standards, and validation is crucial for defining effective instruments. MedRed opts for reusing existing constraint representation languages in order to incorporate notions of validation into the model. These validation rules should allow flexible definitions, from simple value ranges, to complex pattern matching and combinations of complex rules (e.g. answer to a cholesterol question should be a double value lower than 300 mg/dl.). For this reason, we opted for integrating shape properties, from the SHACL W3C recommendation language [8] for constraints.

4   Implementation

Following the design principles stated above, the MedRed ontology was implemented in the OWL language, using the Protégé development environment (19 classes, 12 object and 5 datatype properties). As specified in Sect. 3, the core model includes the fundamental concepts behind a clinical study: the Study itself, the definition of the Instrument items that compose it, at its inner sub-elements: Section, Item, Operation, as well as other elements as a study Arm and StudyEvent. It has been necessary to cover at least those concepts described in the ODM metamodel to guarantee a minimal compliance with that standard. Furthermore, MedRed goes beyond ODM, as it extends the P-Plan ontology [6] to incorporate nesting and composing of items in a given instrument (Step and MultiStep in P-Plan).

Given that P-Plan extends the PROV-O model, each instrument and item definition is itself a traceable entity, which can be annotated according to the PROV model, including versions, derivative instruments, etc., which are indeed common for studies that evolve with time and that reuse previous instruments.

Fig. 3. MedRed ontology network: relationship with external vocabularies.

MedRed also aligns to the DDI-RDF vocabulary [2] for describing scientific metadata, as it includes concepts such as Instrument and Questionnaire. Also, for the validation of data acquisition items, MedRed reuses property paths from the SHACL vocabulary [8], which are specifically designed to represent this type of constraints. These dependencies are depicted in Fig. 3.

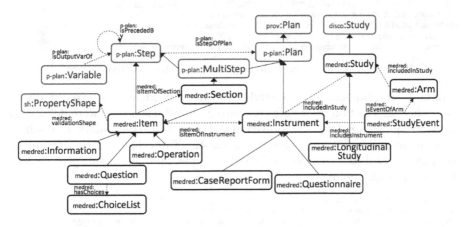

Fig. 4. MedRed ontology: an overview of the central concepts.

The central concepts in MedRed (see Fig. 4), as explained above, surround those of an Instrument and Item. Subclasses of these allow for a further specialization of the type of study (e.g. based on questionnaires, entry forms, etc.), or other extensions for more specific uses. The unique identification of each of these items is a fundamental principle for allowing referencing and composing new instruments based on existing ones, therefore meeting the design principles of Sect. 3. Moreover, the inclusion of the Section concepts allows an unrestricted number of levels and nesting of instrument items, which allows a modular organization of the clinical study.

The salient points of the implementation can be explained through the following examples[3]. The example in Listing 1 shows a 3-month follow-up study definition, including six instruments: one for collecting demographics, another for base line data, 3 monthly questionnaires and a final completion instrument.

---

[3] Prefixes are used as defined in http://prefix.cc. medred is used for the MedRed Ontology.

```
ex:3MonthFollowUpStudy  a medred:Study ;
  dcterms:description "General health conditions of a patient study ..." ;
  dcterms:identifier  "3MonthFollowUpStudy" ;
  dcterms:title       "3-Month follow up study" ;
  medred:hasInstruments (ex:demographics ex:baseline_data ex:month_1_data ex:month_2_data ex:
      month_3_data ex:completion_data).
```

Listing 1. Study following the MedRed ontology.

Each of these instruments can also be fully described, e.g. in terms of their constituent Item elements, as in Listing 2. The instrument is organized in different sections and may include provenance information including authoring, related publications, revisions, etc.

```
ex:expanded_prostate_cancer_index_composite_epic_v2 a  medred:Instrument ;
  medred:items ( ex:epic2200_section1 ex:epic2200_section2 ex:epic2200_section3
               ex:epic2200_section4 ex:epic2200_section5 ex:epic2200_section6) ;
  dcterms:identifier   "expanded_prostate_cancer_index_composite_epic_2200" ;
  prov:wasAttributedTo  ex:wei, ex:dunn, ex:litwin, ex:sandler;
  prov:generatedAtTime  "2011-07-16T01:52:02Z"^^xsd:dateTime;
  prov:hadPrimarySource ex:epic_article_Urology_56_2000;
  prov:wasRevisionOf    :ex:expanded_prostate_cancer_index_composite_epic_v1;
```

Listing 2. An Instrument description using the MedRed ontology

In fact, all components of the study (and instrument) can be annotated with provenance information in order to capture how and when they were defined. In the following examples we omit provenance due to space constraints. In Listing 3 a specific item is described, in this case a question from the previous instrument. The question and its text, the associated variable, and possible display choices, are defined at this point.

```
ex:epic_q48 a medred:Question ;
  medred:isItemofSection ex:section3 ; dcterms:identifier  "epic_q48" ;
  dcterms:title       "14. How often have you had crampy pain in your abdomen, pelvis or rectum?" ;
  medred:choices      ( ex:Morethanonceaday_1 ex:Aboutonceaday_2 ex:Morethanonceaweek_3
                      ex:Aboutonceaweek_4 ex:Rarelyornever_5 ) ;
  pplan:hasOutputVar  ex:epic_q48_var .
```

Listing 3. A Question item described with the MedRed ontology

Furthermore, the variable associated to a question (or any Item) can be specified, along with validation rules expressed using SHACL, as in Listing 4. A Cholesterol value is specified, and minimal and maximal values are indicated using a SHACL shape.

```
ex:chol_3 a medred:Question ;
  dcterms:identifier "chol_3" ; dcterms:title "Cholesterol (mg/dL)" ;
  pplan:hasOutputVar ex:chol_3_var ;
  medred:isItemOfSection ex:month_3_datasection\,1 ;
  medred:validationShape ex:chol_3_shape .
ex:chol_3_shape a sh:PropertyShape ; sh:path medred:dataValue ;
  sh:maxInclusive "300.0" ;  sh:minInclusive "100.0" .
ex:chol_3_var a pplan:Variable ; medred:dataType xsd:double ; medred:varName  "chol_3" .
```

Listing 4. Item validation using the MedRed ontology and SHACL.

5 Exploitation and Discussion

The MedRed Ontology is currently used to represent the metadata of real instruments used in several pilot projects carried out at HES-SO Valais-Wallis, led by the Institute of Health Sciences, and in the scope of the MedRed project. The MedRed project aims at providing an institutional data acquisition platform, mainly targeting clinical data capture. All studies' metadata and their corresponding instruments will be represented in RDF using the ontology, including the entire description of its elements, branching logic, validation, variables, data types, etc. Furthermore, to show the applicability of the ontology to a wider range of clinical data instruments, we have taken a sample of more than thirty instruments from the shared library of REDCap[4], collected by the REDCap project for research purposes from studies all over the world. The full list of instruments used for this experiments can be found in the project source page[5]. A summary, including three of the finished MedRed pilot projects is illustrated in the table of Fig. 5. It showcases the heterogeneity of the studies and the features that we covered with the MedRed ontology.

Concerning the availability of the ontology, it has been published through a permanent URI: http://w3id.org/medred/medred, under a CC-BY 4.0 license. The ontology is also referenced through Zenodo, with a DOI assigned to it[6]. The documentation for the ontology has been prepared using the Ontoology [1] framework, and it has also been checked using the OOPS! pitfall scanner service [15]. The latter has only reported minor issues, mainly for the imported ontologies (Oops! report available in the Github repository). The ontology has been made

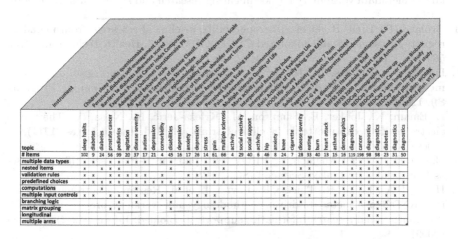

Fig. 5. Summary of the clinical instruments used to showcase the usage of the MedRed ontology.

---

[4] https://projectredcap.org/resources/library/.

[5] Instruments used to validate the MedRed ontology: https://github.com/jpcik/medred.

[6] MedRed Zendoo DOI:https://doi.org/10.5281/zenodo.819875.

available and discoverable through the Linked Open Vocabularies (LOV) repository , widely used as a reference site for finding vocabularies. Regarding the sustainability of the ontology, it is maintained in an initial phase by the MedRed project. Afterwards, the MedRed platform is expected to function under a business plan similar to that of a Clinical Trial unit, which would consequently guarantee support for the ontology and other related information resources.

6 Conclusion

We presented the MedRed ontology for capturing metadata of clinical studies, following a set of design principles, and extending well-known recommendations. We made it available publicly following best practices and we have shown it fits well for a heterogeneous set of existing instruments. The ontology will be maintained by the MedRed data acquisition project, and in the long term, its growing community.

Acknowledgements. MedRed is supported by the Swissuniversities CUS-P2 program.

References

1. Alobaid, A., Garijo, D., Poveda-Villalón, M., Pérez, I.S., Corcho, O.: OnToology, a tool for collaborative development of ontologies. In: ICBO (2015)
2. Bosch, T., Cyganiak, R., Gregory, A., Wackerow, J.: DDI-RDF discovery vocabulary: a metadata vocabulary for documenting research and survey data. In: LDOW (2013)
3. Bruland, P., Breil, B., et al.: Interoperability in clinical research: from metadata registries to semantically annotated CDISC ODM. Stud. Health Technol. Inf. **180**, 564–568 (2012)
4. Davies, J., Gibbons, J., Harris, S., Crichton, C.: The cancergrid experience: metadata-based model-driven engineering for clinical trials. Sci. Comput. Program. **89**, 126–143 (2014)
5. El Emam, K., Jonker, E., Sampson, M., Krleža-Jerić, K., Neisa, A.: The use of electronic data capture tools in clinical trials. J. Med. Internet Res. **11**(1), e8 (2009)
6. Garijo, D., Gil, Y.: Augmenting PROV with plans in P-Plan: scientific processes as linked data. In: Linked Science LISC (2012)
7. Harris, P.A., Taylor, R., Thielke, R., Payne, J., et al.: Research electronic data capture REDCap–a metadata-driven methodology and workflow process for providing translational research informatics support. J. Biomed. Inform. **42**(2), 377–381 (2009)
8. Knublauch, H., Kontokostas, D.: Shapes constraint language (SHACL). W3C Candidate Recommendation (2017)
9. Kuchinke, W., Aerts, J., Semler, S., Ohmann, C., et al.: CDISC standard-based electronic archiving of clinical trials. Methods Inf. Med. **48**(5), 408–413 (2009)
10. Laleci, G.B., Yuksel, M., Dogac, A.: Providing semantic interoperability between clinical care and clinical research domains. J. Biomed. Health Inform. **17**(2), 356–369 (2013)

11. Lebo, T., Sahoo, S., McGuinness, D., Belhajjame, K., Cheney, J., Corsar, D., Garijo, D., Soiland-Reyes, S., Zednik, S., Zhao, J.: PROV-O: the PROV ontology. W3C recomm. (2013). https://www.w3.org/TR/prov-o/
12. Leroux, H., Lefort, L.: Semantic enrichment of longitudinal clinical study data using the CDISC standards and the semantic statistics vocabularies. J. Biomed. seman. **6**(1), 16 (2015)
13. Leroux, H., Metke, A., Lawley, M.J.: ODM on FHIR: towards achieving semantic interoperability of clinical study data. In: SWAT4LS, pp. 59–68 (2015)
14. Nilsdotter, A., et al.: Hip disability and osteoarthritis outcome score (HOOS)-validity and responsiveness in total hip replacement. BMC Musculoskelet. Disord. **4**(1), 10 (2003)
15. Poveda-Villalón, M., Gómez-Pérez, A., Suárez-Figueroa, M.C.: Oops!(ontology pitfall scanner!): an on-line tool for ontology evaluation. IJSWIS **10**(2), 7–34 (2014)
16. Shah, J., et al.: Electronic data capture for registries and clinical trials in orthopaedic surgery: open source versus commercial systems. Clin. Orthop. Relat. Res.® **468**(10), 2664–2671 (2010)
17. Sim, I., et al.: The ontology of clinical research (OCRe): an informatics foundation for the science of clinical research. J. Biomed. Inform. **52**, 78–91 (2014)
18. Smith, B., et al.: The OBO foundry: coordinated evolution of ontologies to support biomedical data integration. Nat. Biotechnol. **25**(11), 1251 (2007)
19. Souza, T., Kush, R., Evans, J.P.: Global clinical data interchange standards are here! Drug Discovery Today **12**(3), 174–181 (2007)

Iguana: A Generic Framework for Benchmarking the Read-Write Performance of Triple Stores

Felix Conrads[1], Jens Lehmann[2], Muhammad Saleem[1], Mohamed Morsey[3],
and Axel-Cyrille Ngonga Ngomo[1,4(✉)]

[1] University of Leipzig, AKSW, Leipzig, Germany
{conrads,saleem,ngomo}@informatik.uni-leipzig.de
[2] University of Bonn and Fraunhofer IAIS, Bonn, Germany
jens.lehmann@cs.uni-bonn.de, jens.lehmann@iais.fraunhofer.de
[3] System and Network Engineering Group, University of Amsterdam, Amsterdam,
Netherlands
m.morsey@uva.nl
[4] Department of Computer Science, University of Paderborn, Paderborn, Germany

Abstract. The performance of triples stores is crucial for applications driven by RDF. Several benchmarks have been proposed that assess the performance of triple stores. However, no integrated benchmark-independent execution framework for these benchmarks has yet been provided. We propose a novel SPARQL benchmark execution framework called Iguana. Our framework complements benchmarks by providing an execution environment which can measure the performance of triple stores during data loading, data updates as well as under different loads and parallel requests. Moreover, it allows a uniform comparison of results on different benchmarks. We execute the FEASIBLE and DBPSB benchmarks using the Iguana framework and measure the performance of popular triple stores under updates and parallel user requests. We compare our results (See https://doi.org/10.6084/m9.figshare.c.3767501.v1) with state-of-the-art benchmarking results and show that our benchmark execution framework can unveil new insights pertaining to the performance of triple stores.

Keywords: Benchmarking · Triple stores · SPARQL · RDF · Log analysis

Type: Benchmarking paper
Permanent URL: http://github.com/AKSW/Iguana
Permanent URL for results: https://figshare.com/collections/Iguana_-_Benchmark_2016/3767501/1
Website and documentation: http://iguana-benchmark.eu/

1 Introduction

The size of the Linked Open Data cloud has grown considerably over the last decade. We are now faced with a compendium of more than 10,000 data sets

C. d'Amato et al. (Eds.): ISWC 2017, Part II, LNCS 10588, pp. 48–65, 2017.
DOI: 10.1007/978-3-319-68204-4_5

and more than 150 billion triples.[1] These data sets cover domains as diverse as geography, media and life sciences. Many Linked Data applications that consume and manipulate data rely on triple stores for persisting data, which hold one or more of these data sets [7,10,11]. It is thus evident that the performance of triple stores plays a vital role for the deployment and use of Linked-Data-driven applications. This leads to the need for robust benchmarking, which is (1) able to pinpoint the strengths and weaknesses of the triple store under test. This in turn allows, (2) the evaluation of the suitability of a specific triple store to the application under which it is to operate, and the proposal of the best candidate triple stores for that application. In addition, benchmarking triple stores can also help (3) identifying the best running conditions for each triple store (e.g., the best memory configuration) as well as (4) providing developers with insights pertaining to how to improve their frameworks.

While many benchmarks (e.g., [1,2,5,7,11,14]) have resulted from these considerations, the comparability of benchmarking results remains problematic as each benchmark usually provides its own execution environment, thus making the results across different evaluations difficult if not impossible to compare. For example, while some of the benchmarks above provide dedicated execution scripts, these cannot always be ported easily to other benchmarks. In this replication and benchmark paper, we address this gap by proposing a novel SPARQL benchmark execution framework called IGUANA (Integrated Suite for Benchmarking SPARQL). IGUANA is a *benchmarking suite* that takes a benchmark, a dataset and possible updates as input. The suite is able to test the behavior of triple stores in a holistic manner, i.e., it can test for load times as well as concurrent query execution and data updates with different user configurations. The suite is thus *complementary to benchmarks* (which most commonly provide data or queries) and can execute both synthetic benchmarks and benchmarks based on real data and real queries to give more complete insights into the behavior of a triple store. Note that thanks to its flexible configuration of benchmark execution, the suite allows the assessment of endpoints which serve multiple agents (users, software systems, etc.) of different types (e.g., query and update) concurrently (e.g., the DBpedia endpoint with approximately 860k queries per day). The methodology implemented by IGUANA follows the four key requirements for domain-specific benchmarks that are postulated in the Benchmark Handbook [4], i.e., it is

1. *relevant*, as it allows the testing of typical operations within the specific domain,
2. *portable* as it can be executed on different platforms and using different benchmarks and datasets,
3. *scalable* as it is possible to run benchmarks on both small and large data sets with variable rates of updates and concurrent users and
4. *understandable* as it returns results using standard measures that have been used across literature for more than a decade.

---

[1] http://lodstats.aksw.org.

Our contributions are as follows:

- We present the first (to the best of our knowledge) integrated and extensible benchmarks execution suite for SPARQL that can uniformly execute state-of-the-art triple store benchmarks under realistic loads such as concurrent requests and updates.
- We provide the first (to the best of our knowledge) realistic evaluation of triple stores with concurrent queries and updates. We evaluate commonly used triple stores under real loads from DBpedia Live and Semantic Web Dog Food (SWDF) and present novel insights pertaining to their behavior.
- As an example showcase, we integrate FEASIBLE [11] and DBPSB [6] real SPARQL benchmarks generators and evaluate state-of-the-art triple stores on four datasets.
- Our results show that while the triple stores we evaluated seem to scale up well to concurrent queries and updates, they are all affected significantly by the size of the datasets.

This paper is organized as follows. We begin by presenting the core of IGUANA. We then present an evaluation of state-of-the-art triple stores on standard server hardware under different loads. Thereafter, we give an overview of the state of the art in benchmarking triple store. Finally, we detail future work and conclude. The code can be found at https://github.com/AKSW/IGUANA Links to all information pertaining to IGUANA (including its source code, GPLv3) can be found at http://iguana-benchmark.eu. A guide on how to get started is at http://iguana-benchmark.eu/gettingstarted.html.

2   The Iguana Framework

This section describes IGUANA. We begin by presenting the components of the framework. We then present the main necessary and optional parameters through which it can be configured. Finally, we give an overview of the core functionality of the framework.

2.1   Overview

Figure 1 shows the core components of the IGUANA framework. The input for the framework is a *configuration file* (short: config file), which contains (1) the configuration parameters (see Sect. 2.2), (2) instructions that orchestrate how queries are to be processed and issued as well as (3) a specification of the benchmarking process and (4) the external data sources to be used during this process. A representation of the parsed config file is stored internally in a *configuration object* (short: config object). If the config object points to a query log, then the *analyzer processor* analyzes this query log file and generates benchmark queries (e.g., using the FEASIBLE [11] approach). IGUANA also supports the benchmark queries being directly provided to the framework. The *dataset generator process* creates a fraction (e.g., 10% of DBpedia) of dataset, thus enabling it to test the scalability of the triple stores with varying sizes of the same dataset. Note that this generator is an interface which can be used to integrate data generators (e.g., the DBPSB [7] generator) that can create datasets of varying size. The *warmup processor* allows the execution of a set of test queries before the start of the actual stress testing. The *testcase processor* then performs the benchmarking by means of stress tests according to the parameters specified in the config file. Finally, the *result processor* generates the results which can be emailed by the *email processor*. In the following, we describe the core components of IGUANA in more detail.

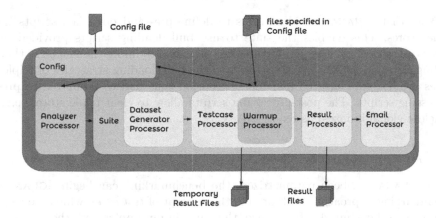

Fig. 1. Overview of the IGUANA benchmarking components.

2.2 Input Parameters

The IGUANA framework (see Fig. 1 for an overview) requires the following input parameters:

1. An *input dataset* (necessary). This is the dataset upon which the SPARQL queries are to be executed. The dataset is part of the input because the framework also measures the time necessary for triple stores to load data.
2. *A set of change sets* (optional). The change sets are triples that are added or deleted from the triple store at runtime. In real applications, it is common to write and read from a triple store while queries are executed. This behavior is emulated by means of the change sets contained in this portion of the input.
3. *Benchmark queries to use* (necessary). This is the set of queries that are to be executed to assess the performance of the triple store to benchmark. Note that we support both query templates (see [7]) and query sets (see, e.g., [11]) as provided by most of the existing benchmarks.
4. *Number and type of workers* (necessary). IGUANA supports two main types of workers: Update workers perform SPARQL INSERT queries to inject new triples into a triple store. Query workers can perform SELECT, ASK, DESCRIBE and CONSTRUCT queries to gather information from the triple

store. The workers are parametrized by the frequency at which they carry out queries. This frequency can either be static (e.g., every 500 ms) or abide by a statistical distribution such as a Gaussian (e.g., mean = 500 ms, standard deviation = 100 ms).

5. *Amount of data to load into the triple store* (optional). With this parameter, benchmarks on a fraction of a dataset (e.g., 10% of DBpedia) are made possible.

6. *Warmup parameters* (optional). An *optional set of warm up queries*, i.e., queries used by the systems that are to be benchmarked to fill the triple store caches, as well as an *optional warm up time* can be set.

Note that IGUANA provides means to define pre- and post-shell scripts for triple stores. This enables the suite to use bulk loading scripts provided by some triple stores as these scripts are often significantly more time-efficient than loading data via INSERT queries. However, the bulk loading strategies of triples stores are not standardized and their execution thus had to be moved to pre-processing scripts. The post-processing scripts allow to clear triple stores (e.g., to delete global indexes) as requested.

2.3   Anatomy of a Test Case

Once IGUANA has been parametrized, the benchmarking can begin. IGUANA's benchmarking approach is built around the concept of *test cases*, which are basically runs of benchmarks. In essence, the core simply implements the methods and interfaces necessary to execute these test cases. First, the core *pre-processes* all the data necessary to carry out a given test case. The pre-processing begins with the gathering the endpoints which should be tested on particular datasets, the details about the configuration of the benchmark data as well the properties of the test case. Thereafter, a *reference connection* is created if necessary. This connection is used during the configuration of query templates into queries for the benchmark. The reference connection links the benchmark to an auxiliary data source that contains the same data as the triple store to benchmark. Note that this connection should not point to the triple store we aim to benchmark as the queries sent through the auxiliary connection could falsify the results at runtime. As an example, if we aim to benchmark a triple store containing DBpedia data, we can set http://dbpedia.org/sparql as the auxiliary connection. Note that the reference connection is only needed for the purpose of generating queries from query templates. Consequently, if IGUANA is provided with queries (not templates), it does not require this connection. IGUANA completes this first step by setting up all the data necessary to carry out the test case at hand. For example, it converts query patterns into complete SPARQL queries with the help of the auxiliary connection.

After the pre-processing stage, IGUANA tests every given dataset described in the config file. To this end, our framework runs the test cases in the order stated in the config file. For example, if the user declares a *pre-shell script*, IGUANA will firstly execute this script, therewith enabling users to configure the triple store to benchmark at will before the beginning of the benchmark. Typically (and in our evaluation as well), these scripts are used to stop and start the current triple store as well as copy a dataset dump to triple store. Note that IGUANA measures how long the pre-shell script takes to be executed. Hence, our framework can measure how long a framework needs for bulk loading data. For the sake of completeness, IGUANA provides the possibility to benchmark the upload via SPARQL INSERT queries. While this test is not recommended when loading a large amount of data, as most frameworks provide bulk loading scripts, IGUANA will check for the existence of upload tests, the corresponding dataset and upload it to the triple store that is currently being tested by means of INSERT queries.

IGUANA then starts the *warm-up phase* (if the user defined one), during which a set of user-defined SPARQL queries and updates are sent to the triple store for a pre-defined period of time (default = 20 min). After the warm-up phase has been completed, the stress test begins (see Sect. 3). The completion of the stress test also marks the completion of the test case. The core gathers the results and adds them to the results which were gathered in previous steps of the test case (if any). If the user defined a *post-shell script* (e.g., to free resources on the server, backup data, clean out a dump, send a message marking the end of the stress test) the core will executes it and proceed to the next testcase. Once every dataset has been tested with every triple store and every test case, IGUANA saves the final results and exits.

3 Anatomy of a Stress Test

The main objective of this strategy is to simulate the operation of a live triple store which is updated continuously, while many users send queries at the same time. IGUANA's default stress test aims to simulate such real workloads of triple stores. Hence, it implements a situation in which several users belonging concurrently access the triple store. In general, there are two types of users querying the triple store: The *first type of user* queries the triple store using SELECT, ASK, DESCRIBE or CONSTRUCT queries while the *second type* updates the same triple store by sending INSERT queries. Consequently, our default stress test consists of two main components, namely the *query component*, and the *update component* as shown in Fig. 2. The query component issues all queries from the first type of users to the triple store while the update component inserts and deletes triples from the test triple store.

3.1 Query Component

To initialize the query component, the stress test needs query templates or queries that are to be posed to the system. Given that having static queries is a special case of having query templates, we describe how the system deals with query templates. Query templates are modelled as parameterized SPARQL queries (i.e., ASK, SELECT, CONSTRUCT or DESCRIBE queries) which can contain several template variables. Each template variable abides by the syntax %%v[0–9]*%%. For example a template can look as follows:

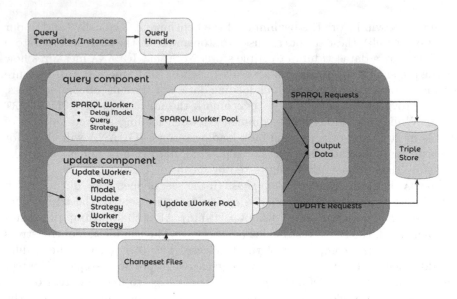

Fig. 2. Overview of the IGUANA stress test

```
1  PREFIX dct:<http://purl.org/dc/terms/>
2  SELECT ?s ?p FROM <http://dbpedia.org>
3  WHERE
4  {    ?s ?p %%v1%% .
5       %%v1%% dct:creator %%v2%% }
6  LIMIT 10
```

The template variables serve as slots to be replaced by resources, literals or blank nodes that lead to a query that can be executed on the data contained in the triple store to benchmark. The large number of valid queries that can be generated from such a template attenuates, if not circumvents, the effect of naïve caching in the triple stores to evaluate. The maximum number of instances of each template generated out of the data is set by the user. Note here that it can happen that the user requires more instances than query solutions available in the triple store, in which case IGUANA selects all solutions to generate query instances. Instead of querying the triple store to benchmark for relevant replacements of the variables, the *query component* uses the *reference connection* (see Sect. 2.3) provided by the user to obtain valid replacements for the variables. In the example, it will try to get instances for %%v1%% and %%v2%%. To achieve this goal, the query generator transforms the input query to the following:

```
1    PREFIX dct:<http://purl.org/dc/terms/>
2    SELECT ?v1 ?v2 FROM <http://dbpedia.org>
3    WHERE
4    {?s ?p ?v1 .
5    ?v1 dct:creator ?v2}
6    LIMIT K
```

where K is the number of queries per template set by the user.

This query is now sent to the reference connection. The results are stored in a table of key-value pairs for each of the query templates. With this approach, we ensure that the instantiations of the template that we generate return (non-empty) results. In a final step, the variables in the query templates are replaced with all key-value pairs in the table and the results are stored in one reference file per query. This whole process is carried out once during the complete test case. The approach ensures that all triple stores that are to be compared are confronted with exactly the same queries.

Now that the queries to be sent to the triple store are available, a *pool of query workers* is created. For the given test case, the workers are assigned a seed number. This number is used to seed a pseudo-random number generator. This generator then computes the index of the query template as well as the index of the instantiation of the said query template that is to be used. Note that as the seeds are generated for each stress test, all triple stores are confronted with the same query load. Each worker sends the query that the generator selected, waits for results and sends the next query after a preset delay according to a delay strategy (constant delay, Gaussian delay, etc.) specified by the user. Each of the workers sends queries to the endpoint until the *benchmark runtime* (which is shared across all workers) has elapsed.

3.2   Update Component

The update component relies on a predefined set of triple additions and deletions that are to be carried out during the stress test. The update component relies on a pool of a pre-defined number of *update workers* and an overall update strategy. The *update strategy* defines whether the update workers are to (1) first carry out every insert and then every deletion, (2) execute first every deletion and then every insert, (3) insert then delete in an alternating fashion or (4) alternatively first delete then insert. Each worker of the update component is also assigned a *worker strategy*, which defines whether it is only to carry out additions, deletions or both. Moreover, a *delay model* is assigned to each worker, which determines how long the worker is to wait between two update queries. The user can set a fixed time or assign a variable time with the seed value s. In case of a variable time, a pool of numbers between $s - \sqrt{s}$ and $s + \sqrt{s}$ is created. Every time a new update is needed the corresponding worker will draw a random time out of the interval to wait until it generates the next update. Again, all random values are pseudo-random and thus the same across all experiments.

Once the stress test has been completed, the results are saved. Through the whole stress test, the runtime of each query as well as the number of failed and successful queries for each and every template is saved for every user. The framework also computes (1) the number of queries per time, (2) the number of queries per second for every user and (3) the mean and sums over all users for all measurements.

4   Evaluation

The motivation behind our evaluation was to check whether the IGUANA approach reveals new insights across several benchmarks. In this section, we describe how we went about addressing this question. We begin by presenting our experimental setup and subsequently present the results of our evaluation in detail.

4.1   Experimental Setup

All experiments were performed on a desktop machine with an Intel i7-3770 CPU with 3.4 GHz, 32 GB RAM, 4 TB HDD running Ubuntu 14.04 and Java 1.7. The benchmark program and the test triple stores were executed on the same machine to avoid any network delay. We used the following criteria to select triple stores for the benchmark: (1) The triple store had to be able to load and process the DBpedia dataset which currently has 391,020,690 triples.[2] (2) The triple store had to be able deal with the characteristics of DBpedia, e.g., its high number of properties (this rules out stores such as 4Store, which is optimised for a low number of properties). (3) The triple store had to have no benchmarking restrictions or the maintainers had to approve the inclusion of their system in the benchmark, and the publication of the results to the public. After selecting the candidate systems and contacting the maintainers for approval when required, the following systems were included in the benchmark: OpenLink Virtuoso,[3] Blazegraph®,[4] and Apache Jena TDB.[5]

For all stores, we selected the standard configuration except for an adjustment of their memory limits. We chose this configuration because it is the configuration most commonly used by lay users. Still, we are aware that the configurations can be tuned and that the results we present are thus to be taken with the corresponding grain of salt.

The configuration of each triple store was as follows:

1. *Virtuoso* Open-Source Edition version 7.0.0: We set the following memory-related parameters: NumberOfBuffers = 1360000, MaxDirtyBuffers = 1000000.

---

[2] The W3C wiki at http://www.w3.org/wiki/LargeTripleStores lists triple stores that are used commonly and the number of triples they can store.
[3] http://virtuoso.openlinksw.com.
[4] http://www.blazegraph.com.
[5] http://jena.apache.org/documentation/tdb.

2. *Blazegraph* Version 1.5.3, with Jetty as HTTP interface: We set the Java heap size to 16 GB.
3. *Jena TDB* Version 2.3.0 with Fuseki2 as HTTP interface: We also set the Java heap size to 16 GB.

We used the DBpedia Live dataset for the experiments on DBpedia.[6] For Semantic Web Dog Food[7] we computed the difference between the provided dump[8] and a dump generated by the SPARQL endpoint[9] from March 1st, 2016. This difference was separated into three files which contained (1) the triples in both the dump and the endpoint, (2) the triples available only in the dump and (3) the triples present only in the endpoint. The triples in (2) were split into 5 files, which were used to delete data from the triple store. File (3) was split into 140 files, which were used to add data to the triple store. An overview of the data sets can be found in Table 1.

We configured IGUANA as follows: The warm-up phase was set to 20 min. The hot run phase was set to 60 min. The number of workers that update the system was varied between 0 and 1, while the number of workers that query the system was set to 1, 4, or 16. As queries, we used 250 real queries benchmark generated by FEASIBLE [11] and the 20 query templates of DBPSBv2 [7]. We selected these benchmark generation frameworks because they generate benchmarks from the real query logs, thus allowing us to test the triple stores under a more realistic evaluation environment.

Table 1. Overview of the data sets used in our experiments

	SWDF	DBpedia 10%	DBpedia 50%	DBpedia 100%
No. of triples	307, 787	40, 234, 659	197, 951, 941	391, 020, 690
No. of classes	149	715	752	778
No. of properties	301	27, 337	47, 310	61, 707
No. of subjects	32, 111	2, 100, 802	12, 637, 791	26, 557, 064

4.2   Results and Discussion

The aim of our evaluation was to show how IGUANA can be used to address the following research questions:

Q1: Baseline: How do triple stores scale for static data sets of different sizes?
Q2: How do triple stores scale under parallel load?
Q3: How do triple stores scale under updates?
Q4: How do triple stores scale under parallel load and updates?
Q5: Are some benchmarks more demanding than others?

---

[6] The dump can be found here https://doi.org/10.6084/m9.figshare.4954598.v1.
[7] http://semanticweb.org/.
[8] http://data.semanticweb.org/dumps/.
[9] http://data.semanticweb.org/sparql.

The configuration as well as the complete results are available for download.[10] To test the scalability of the selected triple stores on static data sets of different sizes, we created two additional subsets of DBpedia, namely DBpedia 10% and DBpedia 50% (see Table 1). The partitioning was carried out by truncating the dump. Note IGUANA also support the dataset slicing introduced in DBPSB and DAW [12]. The goal of the partitioning was to check how the triple stores perform with the increasing size of the datasets.

Figure 3 shows the performance of the selected triple stores in terms of the number of queries executed per hour for the different sizes of the DBpedia and SWDF benchmarks generated by FEASIBLE framework (Q1). As expected, the performance of Virtuoso decreases by *80.62%* while going from DBpedia 10% to DBpedia 50% and decreases further by *53.26%* while going from DBpedia 50% to DBpedia 100%. Similarly, the performance of Blazegraph decreases by *30.91%* while going from 10% to 50% and decreases by *73.68%* while going from 50% to 100%. Surprisingly, the performance of Fuseki is not greatly affected by the size of the data set, which seems to suggest that the store scales better. However in reality, the reason for this behavior is seen in the absolute number of queries that Fuseki can answer per hour. The triple store is unable to complete one query mix (i.e., 250 queries) within the time set, while Virtuoso achieves more than 40 and is thus more than 100 times faster. Fuseki's behavior is however superior to that of BlazeGraph, which has the same performance issues with DBpedia 10% and whose performance decreases further with the dataset size. The performance of the triple stores being greatly influenced by the dataset size is further confirmed by the results on the small control dataset SWDF, where Blazegraph performs as well as Virtuoso. This clearly answers Q1: while triple stores can work well with small datasets, their performance is significantly affected when it comes to dealing with large datasets. Devising scalable triple stores is an important research direction to be considered in the future.

Figure 4 shows the effect of parallel query users on the performance of the selected triple stores on the FEASIBLE queries (Q2). As an overall performance evaluation, the number of queries executed per hour increases with the number of simultaneous querying users. This is simply due to all triple stores making use of parallel answer threads. When transitioning from 1 to 4 parallel query workers on DBpedia 10%, the performance of Virtuoso increases by *222.75%*. Blazegraph is *69.09%* better and Fuseki is *3.2 times faster*. The transition from 4 to 16 parallel users leads to a further improvement of Virtuoso by *220.5%* while Blazegraph improves by *527.27%* and Fuseki by *1480.85%*.

On DBpedia 50%, we also see an increase of performance when comparing the behavior of the systems with 1 and 4 users. Only Blazegraph's performance decreases by *35.29%* when it is confronted with 16 users. The other systems keep on improving. On DBpedia 100%, the performance of Virtuoso increases by *157.02%*, Blazegraph improves by *170%* and Fuseki is *1.1 times faster* with

[10] See https://doi.org/10.6084/m9.figshare.c.3767501.v1. Note that due to space restrictions, we cannot present all results in detail. Instead, we focus on the highlights of our findings.

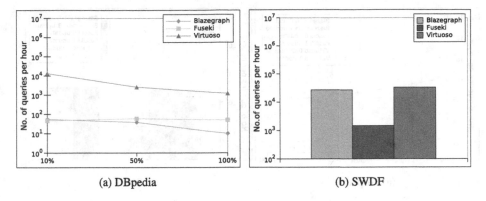

Fig. 3. Scalability test of triple stores based on single querying user and no updates using FEASIBLE. The y-axis is in logarithmic scale.

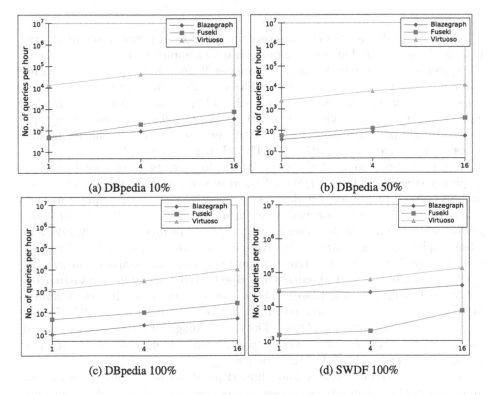

Fig. 4. Effect of parallel requests using the FEASIBLE queries. The x-axis shows the number of simultaneous querying users

4 parallel users. The improvements are even larger when moving from 4 to 16 users, where Virtuoso is *784.19%* faster while Blazegraph and Fuseki improve by *440%* resp. *460%*.

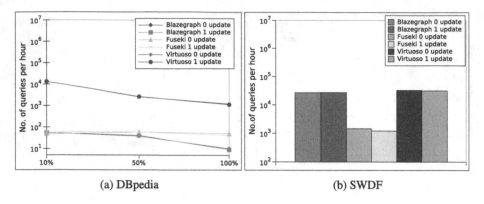

(a) DBpedia   (b) SWDF

Fig. 5. Scalability test of triple stores based on a single querying user and a single update user for FEASIBLE. The y-axis is in logarithmic scale.

Our control dataset SWDF confirms the increase in performance of all systems with more users but also points to an upper bound for the performance of the systems. For example, Virtuoso can answer 92.39% more queries when transitioning from 1 to 4 users. However, Blazegraph's performance remains quasi constant (-1.23%) while Fuseki improves by 33.54%. Virtuoso improves further when comparing its behavior with 4 and 16 users (309.37%) while Blazegraph increases only moderately (55.62%). Fuseki profits the most of the 16 parallel users on a relative scale $(+424.56\%)$. This clearly answers Q2.

Figures 5 shows some of the most interesting results of this work as they display (to the best of knowledge) the first results of systems with parallel queries and updates (1 query user, 1 update user). For FEASIBLE, the triple stores are barely affected by the update workers in most cases (Q3). On DBpedia 10%, the performance of Virtuoso decreases by $0.24\ \%$, Fuseki's increases by 29.79%, and Blazegraph's remains constant. On DBpedia 50%, the performance of Virtuoso increases by $2.59\ \%$, Fuseki's remains constant, and Blazegraph's improves by $7.89\ \%$ with single worker updates. On DBpedia 100%, small losses (Virtuoso = $-6.98\ \%$, Fuseki = -16%, Blazegraph = $-10\ \%$) can be monitored. A similar picture can be derived from the results on SWDF (Virtuoso = -4.02%), Fuseki = -16.6%, Blazegraph = $-1.14\ \%$). The results suggest that a single query and update worker duo does not significantly affect the overall performance of triple stores when faced with FEASIBLE queries.

We were hence interested to know how triple stores scale under parallel load and updates (Q4). Figure 6 shows that the performance of all triple stores only decreases slightly on DBpedia 10% with parallel loads and updates, as compared to only parallel loads and no updates (ref. Fig. 4). Here, no system has more than 20% performance loss (Virtuoso = -2.32%, Blazegraph = constant, Fuseki = 3.03% with 4 parallel users; Virtuoso = -0.42%, Blazegraph = -16.23%, Fuseki = -6.59% with 16 parallel users; a similar picture). On DBpedia 50%, more drastic performance changes occur, with Blazegraph's performance decreasing

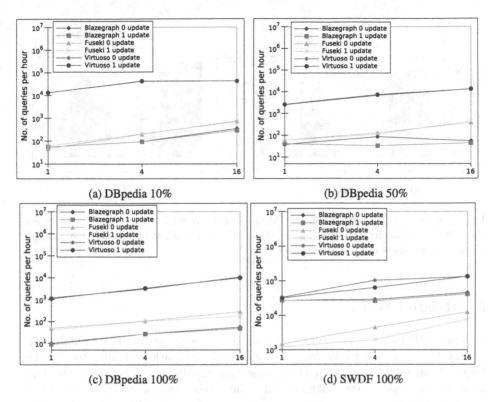

Fig. 6. Effect of parallel requests with and without updates, X-axis shows the number of simultaneous querying users

by *61.18%* with 4 parallel users and decreasing further by *20%* with 16 parallel users. In combination with Fig. 7, IGUANA allows for the first unified comparison of benchmark results (FEASIBLE vs. DBPSBv2). The clear decrease in performance of Fuseki on DBPSBv2 (more than 1 order of magnitude, see Fig. 7) demonstrates that (1) FEASIBLE pushes most of the systems closer to the edge than DBPSBv2, leading to the systems not being able to carry out a lot of queries (Q5) and (2) Virtuoso clearly scales up to heavy load better than the other solutions.

Overall, these results suggest that all systems can deal well with parallel updates and queries. However, their performance is significantly affected by the dataset sizes. Virtuoso is clearly the fastest system in all experiments while Fuseki is most commonly faster than Blazegraph. The systems all implement efficient parallel query handling and can thus be used for multiple concurrent requests. While Fuseki seems to scale up well with the number of concurrent users, its performance with 16 users still remains significantly poorer than Virtuoso's.

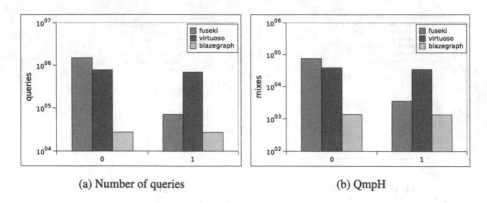

(a) Number of queries   (b) QmpH

Fig. 7. Queries per Hour and Query Mixes Per Hour with 16 querying workers for the DBPSBv2 benchmark on DBpedia 100%. The x-axis shows the number of update users. The y-axis is in logarithmic scale.

5   Related Work

Several RDF benchmarks were developed over recent years. The Lehigh University Benchmark (LUBM) [5] is a synthetic benchmark that aims to test the triple stores and reasoner for their reasoning capabilities. The synthetic data is about universities, their departments, the professors, etc. SP^{2}Bench [14] is a synthetic benchmark for testing the query processing capabilities of triple stores. The synthetic data is based on the DBLP [11] bibliographic database. The Berlin SPARQL Benchmark (BSBM) [2] is a synthetic triple stores benchmark based on an e-commerce use case in which a set of products is provided by a set of vendors and consumers post reviews regarding those products. Since v3.1 it uses synthetic updates. It tries to mimic a real user operation, i.e., it orders the queries in a sequence to resemble the real operation sequence performed by a human user. The SRBench [16] is a RDF benchmark designed for the benchmarking of streaming RDF/SPARQL engines. The streaming data arrives as a continuous stream at a high rate. It uses real RDF data sets and 17 synthetic queries. The main advantage of that benchmark is that it addresses the various features of SPARQL 1.1 and reasoning. In [8], the authors propose a synthetic benchmark based on `Last.fm`, which can benchmark systems w.r.t. various SPARQL 1.1, e.g., property paths, and subqueries. [15] proposes a SPARQL benchmark based on electronic publishing scenario. It uses 8 different data set sizes, and 19 queries covering various SPARQL constructs. Although the data used is real, the queries are still synthetic. *The Waterloo SPARQL Diversity Test Suite* (WatDiv) [1] provides synthetic data and query generator to generate large numbers of queries from a total of 125 queries templates. The queries cover both simple and complex categories with a varying number of features such as result set sizes, total number

---

[11] http://www.informatik.uni-trier.de/~ley/db/.

of query triple patterns, join vertices and mean join vertices degree. However, this benchmark is restricted to conjunctive SELECT queries (single BGPs).

The DBpedia SPARQL Benchmark (DBPSB) [7] is a SPARQL benchmark that uses both real data, i.e., DBpedia, and real queries, i.e., the query log of the DBpedia endpoint, for benchmarking. An important feature of DBPSB is that it selects the queries based on their frequency, i.e., it does not only selects the queries that cover certain SPARQL features, but it also picks the query with the highest frequency among those queries of the query log. However, this benchmark does not consider key query features (i.e., number of join vertices, mean join vertices degree, mean triple pattern selectivities, the query result size and overall query runtimes) while selecting query templates. Previous works [1,3] have however pointed out that these query features greatly affect the triple stores performance and thus should be considered while designing SPARQL benchmarks. Some of the drawbacks of DBPSB are addressed by the FEASIBLE benchmark [11], a real benchmark generation framework which can generate customized benchmarks out of query logs. The approach underlying the benchmark takes SPARQL features as well as SPARQL query types into consideration while deriving prototypical queries and can easily be ported to any query log. Finally FedBench [13] and LargeRDFBench [9] are benchmarks for federated SPARQL query processing. To the best of our knowledge, IGUANA is the first unified benchmark execution platform for SPARQL queries. This framework is orthogonal to the current state of art as it allows the execution of all of the benchmarks above and the comparison of their results with and without data updates and parallel requests. In addition, IGUANA is also able to execute federated SPARQL queries benchmarks.

6   Conclusions and Future Work

We presented IGUANA, an execution framework for SPARQL query benchmarks. We evaluated 3 triples stores on 4 datasets under 6 different settings using FEASIBLE and DBPSBv2. Our results unveiled that the triple stores perform well on small amounts of data and scale well with the number of reading users. Moreover, they are also able to deal well with 1 update user. However, systems such as Blazegraph struggle with large datasets such as DBpedia 100%. For the first time, we were able to compare two benchmarks within an identical environment and revealed that the FEASIBLE queries stress triple stores significantly more than the DBPSBv2 queries. Overall, we showed that IGUANA can be used for benchmarking triple stores in a variety of settings and that this flexibility gives new insights into the behavior of triple stores. In future works, we will extend of our framework to streaming RDF data. The sustainability of the framework will be ensured by making it one of the key assets of the HOBBIT association, which will emerge from the EU-funded project HOBBIT (http://project-hobbit. eu) and already has 9 funding members.

Acknowledgements. This work was supported by the project HOBBIT, which has received funding from the European Union's H2020 research and innovation action program (GA number 688227), and by the SAKE project (GA 01MD15006E) financed by the BMWI.

References

1. Aluç, G., Hartig, O., Özsu, M.T., Daudjee, K.: Diversified stress testing of RDF data management systems. In: Mika, P., et al. (eds.) ISWC 2014. LNCS, vol. 8796, pp. 197–212. Springer, Cham (2014). doi:10.1007/978-3-319-11964-9_13
2. Bizer, C., Schultz, A.: The Berlin SPARQL benchmark. Int. J. Semant. Web Inf. Syst. **5**(2), 1–24 (2009)
3. Görlitz, O., Thimm, M., Staab, S.: SPLODGE: systematic generation of SPARQL benchmark queries for linked open data. In: Cudré-Mauroux, P., et al. (eds.) ISWC 2012. LNCS, vol. 7649, pp. 116–132. Springer, Heidelberg (2012). doi:10.1007/978-3-642-35176-1_8
4. Gray, J. (ed.): The Benchmark Handbook for Database and Transaction Systems, 1st edn. Morgan Kaufmann, Burlington (1991)
5. Guo, Y., Pan, Z., Heflin, J.: LUBM: a benchmark for OWL knowledge base systems. J. Web Semant. **3**(2–3), 158–182 (2005)
6. Morsey, M., Lehmann, J., Auer, S., Ngonga Ngomo, A.-C.: DBpedia SPARQL benchmark – performance assessment with real queries on real data. In: Aroyo, L., Welty, C., Alani, H., Taylor, J., Bernstein, A., Kagal, L., Noy, N., Blomqvist, E. (eds.) ISWC 2011. LNCS, vol. 7031, pp. 454–469. Springer, Heidelberg (2011). doi:10.1007/978-3-642-25073-6_29
7. Morsey, M., Lehmann, J., Auer, S., Ngonga Ngomo, A.-C.: Usage-centric benchmarking of RDF triple stores. In: Proceedings of the 26th AAAI Conference on Artificial Intelligence (AAAI 2012) (2012)
8. Przyjaciel-Zablocki, M., Schätzle, A., Hornung, T., Taxidou, I.: Towards a SPARQL 1.1 feature benchmark on real-world social network data. In: Proceedings of the First International Workshop on Benchmarking RDF Systems (2013)
9. Saleem, M., Hasnain, A., Ngomo, A.-C.N.: Largerdfbench: a billion triples benchmark for sparql endpoint federation. Web Semantics: Science, Services and Agents on the World Wide Web (2017). Elsevier
10. Saleem, M., Kamdar, M.R., Iqbal, A., Sampath, S., Deus, H.F., Ngonga Ngomo, A.-C.: Big linked cancer data: integrating linked TCGA and pubmed. JWS (2014)
11. Saleem, M., Mehmood, Q., Ngonga Ngomo, A.-C.: FEASIBLE: a feature-based SPARQL benchmark generation framework. In: Arenas, M., et al. (eds.) ISWC 2015. LNCS, vol. 9366, pp. 52–69. Springer, Cham (2015). doi:10.1007/978-3-319-25007-6_4
12. Saleem, M., Ngonga Ngomo, A.-C., Xavier Parreira, J., Deus, H.F., Hauswirth, M.: DAW: duplicate-aware federated query processing over the web of data. In: Alani, H., et al. (eds.) ISWC 2013. LNCS, vol. 8218, pp. 574–590. Springer, Heidelberg (2013). doi:10.1007/978-3-642-41335-3_36
13. Schmidt, M., Görlitz, O., Haase, P., Ladwig, G., Schwarte, A., Tran, T.: FedBench: a benchmark suite for federated semantic data query processing. In: Aroyo, L., Welty, C., Alani, H., Taylor, J., Bernstein, A., Kagal, L., Noy, N., Blomqvist, E. (eds.) ISWC 2011. LNCS, vol. 7031, pp. 585–600. Springer, Heidelberg (2011). doi:10.1007/978-3-642-25073-6_37

14. Schmidt, M., Hornung, T., Lausen, G., Pinkel, C.: SP2Bench: a SPARQL performance benchmark. In: International Conference on Data Engineering (ICDE), pp. 222–233. IEEE (2009)
15. Tarasova, T., Marx, M.: ParlBench: a SPARQL benchmark for electronic publishing applications. In: Cimiano, P., Fernández, M., Lopez, V., Schlobach, S., Völker, J. (eds.) ESWC 2013. LNCS, vol. 7955, pp. 5–21. Springer, Heidelberg (2013). doi:10.1007/978-3-642-41242-4_2
16. Zhang, Y., Duc, P.M., Corcho, O., Calbimonte, J.-P.: SRBench: a streaming RDF/SPARQL benchmark. In: Cudré-Mauroux, P., et al. (eds.) ISWC 2012. LNCS, vol. 7649, pp. 641–657. Springer, Heidelberg (2012). doi:10.1007/978-3-642-35176-1_40

Ireland's Authoritative Geospatial Linked Data

Christophe Debruyne[1(✉)], Alan Meehan[1], Éamonn Clinton[2],
Lorraine McNerney[2], Atul Nautiyal[1], Peter Lavin[1],
and Declan O'Sullivan[1]

[1] ADAPT Centre, Trinity College Dublin, Dublin 2, Ireland
{christophe.debruyne,alan.meehan,atul.nautiyal,
peter.lavin,declan.osullivan}@adaptcentre.ie
[2] Ordnance Survey Ireland, Phoenix Park, Dublin 8, Ireland
{eamonn.clinton,lorraine.mcNerney}@osi.ie

Abstract. Data.geohive.ie aims to provide an authoritative service for serving Ireland's national geospatial data as Linked Data. The service currently provides information on Irish administrative boundaries and the boundaries used for the Irish 2011 census. The service is designed to support two use cases: serving boundary data of geographic features at various level of detail and capturing the evolution of administrative boundaries. In this paper, we report on the development of the service and elaborate on some of the informed decisions concerned with the URI strategy and use of named graphs for the support of aforementioned use cases – relating those with similar initiatives. While clear insights on how the data is being used are still being gathered, we provide examples of how and where this geospatial Linked Data dataset is used.

Keywords: Geospatial linked data · Ordnance survey Ireland

Resource type: Dataset
Permanent URL: http://purl.org/geohive

1 Introduction

The Ordnance Survey Ireland (OSi), Ireland's national mapping agency, aims to adopt Linked Data to enable third parties to explore and consume some of OSi's authoritative datasets. In [5], we reported on how the OSi's object-centric relational database, called Prime2 [1], was used to publish administrative boundary datasets according to best practices and guidelines for geospatial Linked Data. The service was developed to support two use cases: (i) providing the boundary detail in varying levels of detail and (ii) capturing the evolution of boundaries. In this paper, we provide more details on the dataset [4], and its value and potential impact in the context of Ireland.

© Springer International Publishing AG 2017
C. d'Amato et al. (Eds.): ISWC 2017, Part II, LNCS 10588, pp. 66–74, 2017.
DOI: 10.1007/978-3-319-68204-4_6

2 Related Work

Shadbolt et al. highlighted the importance of location in data and its role in interlinking and aligning datasets [18]. This is certainly the case for government data, which often reports numbers that are related to certain territories (administrative units, jurisdictions, etc.). The Linked Data Web has numerous geographic datasets; GeoNames and LinkedGeoData[1] (which cover a vast part of the world) and Ordnance Survey Linked Data[2] (for the UK), just to name a few. Except for the latter, many of these geographic datasets are not authoritative in nature, nor are they necessarily accurate. LinkedGeoData, for example, uses the information collected by the OpenStreetMap[3] project, which itself is an open environment in which volunteers collaboratively create a geospatial knowledge base. Though OpenStreetMap is quite accurate compared to official sources [9], its coverage has been shown to be incomplete [14]. Though the data provided by LinkedGeoData might be good for a lot of applications; one may wish or need to avail of authoritative datasets with legal weight. One can thus see the potential and added value of publishing and linking with *authoritative* geospatial data.

The Ordnance Survey of Great Britain was one of the first to publish some of their geospatial data on the Web [8]. While this is a great example of publishing authoritative geospatial Linked Data, in our opinion, it is unfortunate that they have not adopted a standard for representing features, spatial relations, and representation of geometries. Instead, they rely on a bespoke ontology. Reasoning over their geospatial data either requires relying on rules for that bespoke schema, or mapping the data onto standardized vocabularies such as OGC GeoSPARQL [17], for which implementations exists.

Other countries are looking at publishing their authoritative geospatial information on the Web as well. One such example is the Cadaster[4] in The Netherlands, which is driven by the public administration. [2] proposed vocabularies and an approach for serving geographic reference data for the French national mapping agency. In the EU, the INSPIRE directive (Infrastructure for Spatial Information in Europe) aims to standardize Spatial Data Infrastructures across Europe. In order for one to discover, access and visualize geospatial information in a homogenous manner across Europe, the directive prescribes metadata formats, services, etc. that each member state has to comply with. [16] proposed to map INSPIRE onto GeoSPARQL to provide an RDF perspective on such data and applied their method in the context of Greece.

3 Approach

In this section we elaborate on how the OSi's geospatial information has been organized and how this has been delivered to agents.

---

[1] http://www.geonames.org/ and http://linkedgeodata.org/

[2] http://data.ordnancesurvey.co.uk/

[3] https://www.openstreetmap.org/

[4] http://www.pilod.nl/, and http://almere.pilod.nl/sparql

3.1 URI Strategy

Coming up with adequate URI strategies for publishing 5-star Linked Open Government Data on the Web is challenging, especially when one has to take into account the difference in governance practices, heterogeneity, etc. across different government bodies. A URI strategy for geospatial data has been proposed in [19], which was based on a more generic URI strategy for The Netherlands [15].

In the case of the OSi, the term "dataset" in "boundaries dataset" is actually a misnomer when referring to administrative boundaries in Ireland. This particular dataset is a dynamic dataset that evolves over time, unlike datasets that are created at a particular point in time such as census data. While progress has been made since the start of this project on drafting a URI strategy for the Irish Government's open data initiative [11, 12], early discussions encouraged the inclusion of attributes such as creation date in the HTTP URIs. This approach would not have suited the OSi as this necessitated the creation of datasets for each change. This in turn would have complicated the governance of links between these datasets, and also the governance of links to the OSi datasets by 3rd parties. In conjunction with the Department of Public Expenditure and Reform (DPER) and the Central Statistics Office (CSO), we have decided to use a subset of the recommended attributes, allowing us to still be in line with most of the recommendations that were then put forward.

Currently, URIs, for the resources that the OSi are the custodians of, follow the following pattern: http://data.geohive.ie/{**type**}/{**concept**}/{**GUID**}, where:

- The *domain* follows the two recommendations formulated by [15]: solely be used for the publication of OSi's geospatial information and not include the name of any organization, as they may evolve over time.[5]
- *Type* can take any of the following values: "resource" for the HTTP URI of a resource, and "page" and "data" for that resource's HTML and RDF documents respectively.
- *Concept* and *GUID*: with Prime2, all features are assigned a *GUID*. Therefore, although we would have been able to create fully opaque URIs by only providing the GUID, we have chosen to provide a hint of what this resource is about by providing a label referring to that resource's class in *concept*.

Concerning the GUIDs, we note that Prime2 provides governance rules that prescribe how features may evolve over time. One of these rules prescribes that features do not change in nature. When a hospital is transformed into an apartment building, for example, it is considered a new feature (and therefore has a different GUID) that happens to have the same geometric representation.

Finally, one important decision that we have made concerning our URI strategy was not to provide URIs for the geometries. A clear distinction is made between a geographical feature (such as a county), and its geometry (such as its boundary

---

[5] GeoHive is an initiative by OSi to provide easy access to publicly available authoritative spatial data. The same top-level domain was used for the publication of their Linked Data. We have not chosen to adopt a sub-domain under osi.ie as by 2017, several government bodies including the OSi will be merged and change (domain) names. GeoHive will remain.

represented by a polygon). When adopting ontologies such as GeoSPARQL (see the next section), two distinct classes reflect this distinction. This means that instances of these classes can be identified with a URI. In practice, we notice that users abuse the boundaries and use them as the identifier of the feature. In other words, they would refer to the county's boundary as the county, rather than referring to the resource representing the county. To avoid this problem for OSi's Linked Data, we have decided not to provide URIs to geometries and publish them as blank nodes.

3.2   Knowledge Organization: Different Representations

The distinction between a geographic feature and its geometry (or even geometries) is argued to be important [3]. The geometry of a feature can evolve over time – e.g., due to coastal erosion, and these changes do not have an impact on the feature. In other words, the geometry of a feature is "merely" an attribute.

Since we have not found suitable ontologies for appropriately annotating the different administrative boundaries (e.g., Counties and Electoral Divisions) in an Irish context, we decided to create a new ontology[6] that *extends* GeoSPARQL.[7] GeoSPARQL is an ontology for describing geographical features and their geometries. It also defines predicates for spatial queries in SPARQL, making it a suitable candidate for our service. Subclasses of the concept geo:Feature were introduced for each type of administrative boundary we serve.

Finally, OSi's bespoke information system captures the geometries using the Irish Transverse Mercator (ITM) coordinate system. At an international level, however, World Geodetic System 84 (or WGS 84) is the standard used in cartography and navigation. As OSi also wishes to encourage the uptake of WGS 84 within Ireland, a decision was made to serve the geometries in WGS 84 only; third parties can themselves rely on services to transform the data between coordinate systems. We use the Well-known Text (WKT) markup language for representing the geometries.

Our first use case was to provide boundary data with different levels of detail (or "resolutions"). The polygons are generalized up to 20, 50 and 100 m. Higher resolutions provide more detail but require more data transfer. Different resolutions are used for different purposes; the Irish census uses 20 m resolutions and 100 m resolutions for information exchange at a European level, for instance

We generate instances of geo:Geometry for each resolution and store them in dedicated graphs (one for each resolution). The feature and its resolutions are related with geo:hasGeometry. A geo:defaultGeometry predicate is also declared between the feature and its 20 m boundary data, as per best practice. Moreover, if two features happen to have geometries which are identical polygons, we do not reuse that geometry. Instead, we create two geometries that happen to have the same polygon (WKT literal). We then attach provenance information to each of these geometries. This is necessary as each feature (and its geometry) may have a different change history

---

[6] http://ontologies.geohive.ie/osi.

[7] We note that we did not consider reusing vocabularies that were not built on standards (e.g., [8]) or that were developed for another context (e.g., see [2] for France).

(see Sect. 3.3). Finally, links from features to resources in external Linked Data datasets are stored in a separate named graph.

3.3 Knowledge Organization: Evolution of Geometries

Our second use case was to support capturing the evolution of boundaries. Though they are rare for administrative boundaries, they are ordered by so called Statutory Instruments. Statutory Instruments are available on the Web and are accessible via a URI, making it possible to relate the evolution of boundaries with these instruments. To capture the evolution of boundaries, we have chosen to extend PROV-O [13] with a new prov:Activity called "Boundary Change", which is informed by a new prov:Entity called "Statutory Instrument".[8] Prior versions of features and their geometries are captured in separate graphs.

At the present time, OSi's database only contains current versions of administrative boundary data and does not contain any historical record of versions that may have existed in the past (i.e., prior to the release of Prime2 in 2014). OSi's database has not yet started ingesting prior (versions of) administrative boundary data before its release in 2014. We therefore have to rely on simulations, using geometries related to buildings, to demonstrate the feasibility of this approach. Geometries that are related to buildings have a much higher churn, but are not part of OSi's open data.

One can argue that capturing all provenance information related to boundary changes into one graph (per resolution) results in – over time – very large graphs. Indeed, another approach would have been to capture each change in dedicated graphs, which is the approach adopted by the Dutch public administration (see Sect. 4). The latter, however, would require the formulation of queries over different named graphs. Our approach was informed by the fact that use cases for retrieving the history of geometries are specific (e.g., of interest to building planners), which makes us believe that simpler queries will be favored at the expense of query execution time.

4 Discussion

In this section, we discuss the evaluation criteria as outlined by the ISWC 2017 call for resources track papers [10].

On Potential Impact. The resource is sufficiently general to be applied in many domains and scenarios, and this supports the arguments which will be made about its reusability (see "On Reusability"). The resource provides an authoritative source for use when adding a geospatial dimension to other datasets. The resource can be used by, inter alia, other Linked Data initiatives that are ongoing or emerging in government entities across Ireland. Therefore, its impact is more societal in nature.

The design and approach used in developing the resource has been compared to the state of the art. It has also been presented (at a seminar,) to representatives of other public administrations who have started similar initiatives (e.g. The Netherlands and

---

[8] http://ontologies.geohive.ie/osiprov.

Flanders, Belgium).[9] Ireland and The Netherlands have adopted different approaches to organizing the history of features and geometries using PROV-O, and we hope, over time, to inform each other of insights gained.

On Reusability. Shadbolt et al. [18] have already provided the motivation for, and established the usefulness of geospatial data for aligning, exploring and analyzing data in many domains and scenarios. Furthermore, Ireland's Department of Public Expenditure and Reform has funded two projects via their Open Data Engagement Fund. The first project was to inform the public on how to add an authoritative geospatial dimension to CSV files on their open data portal [7]. The second project organized seminars on publishing and interlinking Linked Data with the resource. Data.cso.ie – an initiative between the CSO and the Insight Centre for Data Analytics – is a Linked Data Service for the census 2011 (and soon 2016) results. We have sent to data.cso.ie a set of links between their boundary identifiers and our administrative units. It is hoped they will deploy those links at the same time as they publish the 2016 results. With regard to the 2016 census boundaries; the ontology is straightforward to extend and we will adopt a similar approach for generating Linked Data for those boundaries as soon as the census 2016 polygons have been approved for publication. We have anecdotal evidence that various groups are using the resource. As an example, the Chronic Disease Informatics Group (CDIG) in Trinity College Dublin is using the datasets to relate observations (weather, pollution, etc.) to particular administrative boundaries in an effort to identify triggers for particular diseases.

On Design and Technical Quality. In the previous section, we provided details on our URI strategy, adoptions and extensions of standardized vocabularies, as well as informed decisions on knowledge organization. All of these are informed by best practices in other public administrations and provide for both the evolution of geometries as well as multiple representations thereof. The reuse of those standardized vocabularies allow agents, both human and computer-based, to avail of those predicates with existing tools; especially using the spatial predicate provided by GeoSPARQL. We furthermore like to stress our informed decision not to provide HTTP URIs to the geometries, as they are "merely" attributes of a feature that can evolve over time and to encourage users to link to entities rather than their "shapes".

Metadata in VoID about the boundaries dataset has been generated for the whole dataset, but also for specific subsets (e.g., County Councils of Ireland) that can be found on the resource's website. The whole dataset and its VoID dataset description have been made available on DataHub.

Both the URIs of resources and our ontologies resolve to human and machine-readable representations via content negotiation. In addition, the HTML pages of the resources even plot the geometries on OSi's basemaps.

On Availability. The dataset is available on http://data.geohive.ie/, on DataHub.io, and on figshare [21], all of which provide links to dumps. Data is provided under a Create Commons Attribution 4.0 International license (CC BY 4.0) which is documented in both the HTML and in the dataset description using VoID. URIs resolve to

---

[9] http://www.pilod.nl/wiki/Linked_Data_Seminar_-_December_2,_2016.

either HTML pages or RDF serialization by means of content negotiation. The OSi has decided not to provide access to a GeoSPARQL endpoint, but instead refers to a Triple Pattern Fragments (TPF) [20] Server and Client are provided. We also provide a TPF client that has been extended with GeoSPARQL functions to allow users to query over the geometries [6]. The resource has furthermore been published on DataHub (with appropriate license information) and uses and extends standardized vocabularies such as GeoSPARQL and PROV-O. This enhances its reusability in other contexts.

Organizations are subject to changes and this impacts on web domain names used; OSi is no exception. At the end of 2017, OSi will merge with the Property Registration Authority of Ireland (PRA) and the Valuation Office (VO) to create Tailte Éireann, a new government body. Following this, mapping services, Prime2 and GeoHive will be under the remit of Tailte Éireann. Such a merging of bodies validates the decision to dedicate the domain name `data.geohive.ie` to the resource, a name not tied to any of those bodies, facilitating the sustainability of the resource.

5   Conclusions and Future Work

In this paper, we presented the authoritative boundaries dataset that has been made available as Linked Open Data with a CC BY 4.0 license. The data and ontologies developed for this dataset extend standardized vocabularies such a PROV-O and GeoSPARQL, facilitating its interoperability. Future work consists of extending the dataset with the boundaries used for the 2016 census and other (administrative) boundaries not yet included in this dataset. We aim to gather further insights into our approach for capturing the evolution of boundaries in a provenance graph and compare those with similar initiatives elsewhere (e.g., in The Netherlands).

Acknowledgements. The ADAPT Centre for Digital Content Technology is funded under the SFI Research Centres Programme (Grant 13/RC/2106) and is co-funded under the European Regional Development Fund.

References

1. Prime2: Data concepts and data model overview. Technical report, Ordnance Survey Ireland (2014). http://www.osi.ie/wp-content/uploads/2015/04/Prime2-V-2.pdf
2. Atemezing, G.A., Abadie, N., Troncy, R., Bucher, B.: Publishing reference geodata on the web: opportunities and challenges for IGN France. In: Kyzirakos, K., Grütter, R., Kolas, D., Perry, M., Compton, M., Janowicz, K., Taylor, K. (eds.) Joint Proceedings of the 6th International Workshop on the Foundations, Technologies and Applications of the Geospatial Web, TC 2014, and 7th International Workshop on Semantic Sensor Networks, SSN 2014, Co-located with 13th International Semantic Web Conference (ISWC 2014), Riva del Garda, October 20, 2014. CEUR Workshop Proceedings, vol. 1401, pp. 9–20. CEUR-WS.org (2014)
3. Battle, R., Kolas, D.: Enabling the geospatial semantic web with Parliament and GeoSPARQL. Semant. Web **3**(4), 355–370 (2012). doi:10.3233/SW-2012-0065

4. Debruyne, C., Meehan, A., Clinton, E., McNerney, L., Nautiyal, A., Lavin, P., O'Sullivan, D.: GeoHive Administrative Boundaries Dataset. figshare (2017). https://doi.org/10.6084/m9.figshare.5235961
5. Debruyne, C., Clinton, E., McNerney, L., Nautiyal, A., O'Sullivan, D.: Serving Ireland's geospatial information as linked data. In: Kawamura, T., Paulheim, H. (eds.) Proceedings of the ISWC 2016 Posters & Demonstrations Track co-located with 15th International Semantic Web Conference (ISWC 2016), Kobe, October 19, 2016. CEUR Workshop Proceedings, vol. 1690. CEUR-WS.org (2016)
6. Debruyne, C., Clinton, E., O'Sullivan, D.: Client-side processing of GeoSPARQL functions with triple pattern fragments. In: Auer, S., Berners-Lee, T., Bizer, C., Capadisli, S., Heath, T., Janowicz, K., Lehmann, J. (eds.) Workshop on Linked Data on the Web co-located with 26th International World Wide Web Conference (WWW 2017). CEUR Workshop Proceedings, CEUR-WS.org (2017)
7. Debruyne, C., McGlinn, K., McNerney, L., O'Sullivan, D.: A lightweight approach to explore, enrich and use data with a geospatial dimension with semantic web technologies. In: Proceedings of the Fourth International ACM Workshop on Managing and Mining Enriched Geo-Spatial Data. pp. 1:1–1:6. GeoRich 2017, ACM, New York (2017). http://doi.acm.org/10.1145/3080546.3080548
8. Goodwin, J., Dolbear, C., Hart, G.: Geographical linked data: the administrative geography of Great Britain on the semantic web. Trans. GIS **12**(s1), 19–30 (2008)
9. Haklay, M.: How good is volunteered geographical information? A comparative study of OpenStreetMap and ordnance survey datasets. Environ. planning B: Planning des. **37**(4), 682–703 (2010)
10. Lecue, F., Tamma, V.: ISWC 2017 resources track: author and reviewer instructions (2017). http://dx.doi.org/10.6084/m9.figshare.4679152
11. Lee, D., Cyganiak, R., Decker, S.: Open data Ireland: best practice handbook. Technical report, Insight Centre for Data Analytics, NUI Galway (2014). http://per.gov.ie/wp-content/uploads/Best-Practice-Handbook.pdf
12. Lee, D., Cyganiak, R., Decker, S.: Open data Ireland: open data Publication Handbook. Technical report, Insight Centre for Data Analytics, NUI Galway (2014). http://per.gov.ie/wp-content/uploads/Open-Data-Publication-Handbook.pdf
13. McGuinness, D., Lebo, T., Sahoo, S.: PROV-O: the PROV ontology. W3C Recommendation, W3C (Apr 2013). http://www.w3.org/TR/2013/REC-prov-o-20130430/
14. Mooney, P., Corcoran, P., Winstanley, A.C.: Towards quality metrics for OpenStreetMap. In: Agrawal, D., Zhang, P., Abbadi, A.E., Mokbel, M.F. (eds.) 18th ACM SIGSPATIAL International Symposium on Advances in Geographic Information Systems, ACM-GIS 2010, November 3–5, 2010, San Jose, Proceedings. pp. 514–517. ACM (2010). http://doi.acm.org/10.1145/1869790.1869875
15. Overbeek, H., van den Brink, L.: Towards a national URI-Strategy for linked data of the Dutch public sector. Technical report, Kennis- en Exploitatiecentrum Officiële Overheidspublicaties & Geonovum (2013). http://www.pilod.nl/w/images/a/aa/D1-2013-09-19_Towards_a_NL_URI_Strategy.pdf
16. Patroumpas, K., Georgomanolis, N., Stratiotis, T., Alexakis, M., Athanasiou, S.: Exposing INSPIRE on the semantic web. J. Web Sem. **35**, 53–62 (2015). doi:10.1016/j.websem.2015.09.003
17. Perry, M., Herring, J.: GeoSPARQL - A geographic query language for RDF data, OGC (2012). http://opengeospatial.org/standards/geosparql
18. Shadbolt, N., O'Hara, K., Berners-Lee, T., Gibbins, N., Glaser, H., Hall, W., schraefel, M.C.: Linked open government data: lessons from data.gov.uk. IEEE Intell. Syst. **27**(3), 16–24 (2012). doi:10.1109/MIS.2012.23

19. van den Brink, L., Janssen, P., Quak, W., Stoter, J.: Linking spatial data: semi-automated conversion of geo-information models and GML data to RDF. Int. J. Spat. Data Infrastruct. Res. **9**, 59–85 (2014)
20. Verborgh, R., Vander Sande, M., Hartig, O., Van Herwegen, J., De Vocht, L., De Meester, B., Haesendonck, G., Colpaert, P.: Triple pattern fragments: a low-cost knowledge graph interface for the web. J. Web Sem. **37–38**, 184–206 (2016). doi:10.1016/j.websem.2016.03.003
21. Meehan, A., McNerney, L., Clinton, E., O'Sullivan, D., Nautiyal, A., Lavin, P.: GeoHive Administrative Boundaries Dataset. Figshare (2017). https://doi.org/10.6084/m9.figshare.5235961

LOD-a-lot

A Queryable Dump of the LOD Cloud

Javier D. Fernández[1,2(✉)], Wouter Beek[3], Miguel A. Martínez-Prieto[4],
and Mario Arias[5]

[1] Vienna University of Economics and Business, Vienna, Austria
`javier.fernandez@wu.ac.at`
[2] Complexity Science Hub Vienna, Vienna, Austria
[3] Department of Computer Science, VU University Amsterdam,
Amsterdam, Netherlands
`w.g.j.beek@vu.nl`
[4] Department of Computer Science, Universidad de Valladolid, Segovia, Spain
`migumar2@infor.uva.es`
[5] Mario Arias Software, London, UK
`mario.arias@gmail.com`

Abstract. LOD-a-lot democratizes access to the Linked Open Data
(LOD) Cloud by serving more than 28 billion unique triples from 650 K
datasets over a single self-indexed file. This corpus can be queried online
with a sustainable Linked Data Fragments interface, or downloaded and
consumed locally: LOD-a-lot is easy to deploy and demands affordable
resources (524 GB of disk space and 15.7 GB of RAM), enabling Web-
scale repeatable experimentation and research even by standard laptops.

1 Introduction

The last decade has seen an impressive growth of the Linked Open Data (LOD)
community, which promotes to use the Resource Description Framework (RDF)
to publicly share semi-structured data on the Web and to connect different
data items by reusing HTTP International Resource Identifiers (IRIs) across
data sources [3]. Besides HTTP access to RDF data, publishers also provide
RDF dataset dumps (for download), and query endpoints that expose various
capabilities, ranging from basic queries in RESTful APIs, such as Linked Data
Fragments (LDF) [22], to SQL-like structured queries using SPARQL [9].

Although the LOD paradigm should provide access to a huge distributed
knowledge base that can be browsed and queried online, efficient web-scale consumption of LOD has proven problematic in practice. Consider, for example,
retrieving all entities with the label *"Tim Berners-Lee"*, which can be formulated
in SPARQL as follows: `select distinct ?x { ?x owl:sameAs*/rdfs:label
"Tim Berners-Lee" }`. Given the distributed nature of Linked Open Data, the
resolution of this simple query would require one of the following approaches:

- *Download, index and query datasets locally.* This approach is costly for the
  data consumer, who is likely to run into scalability issues.

© Springer International Publishing AG 2017
C. d'Amato et al. (Eds.): ISWC 2017, Part II, LNCS 10588, pp. 75–83, 2017.
DOI: 10.1007/978-3-319-68204-4_7

– *Run a federated query against all known sources* [5]. This approach is as good as the query endpoints that it relies on. Unfortunately, SPARQL endpoints are known to have low availability [7,21], and federated queries are difficult to optimize beyond a limited number of sources [17].
– *Browse online sources in a "follow-your-nose" way* [11]. This requires on-the-fly traversal of the universally distributed RDF graph. In practice, many IRIs do not dereference, and since our particular query does not contain an IRI at all (only a literal), it is not clear where graph traversal should start.

Thus, the three main approaches for querying LOD all have significant drawbacks, making it unfeasible to evaluate even simple queries on the Semantic Web [12]. Some of these issues are partially solved by services like Datahub[1] and LOD Laundromat[2] [2], which provide central catalogs for discovering and accessing cached versions of Linked Open Datasets. However, data consumers still need to navigate and process large corpora, consisting of thousands of dumps or endpoints, in order to evaluate queries or conduct large-scale experiments.

In this paper, we propose the **LOD-a-lot dataset** which offers low-cost consumption of a large portion of the LOD Cloud. We integrate 650 K datasets that are crawled by LOD Laundromat [2] into a single, self-indexed HDT [8] file. This HDT file is conveniently small and can be directly queried by data consumers with a limited memory footprint. LOD-a-lot contains 28 billion unique triples and, to the best of our knowledge, is the first approach to provide *an indexed and ready-to-consume crawl of a large portion of the LOD Cloud that can be used offline*. In addition, an online LDF interface to LOD-a-lot is provided.

The paper is organized as follows. Section 2 presents LOD-a-lot and its main benefits. Section 3 describes the available interfaces and tools to work with LOD-a-lot. We summarize LOD-a-lot statistics in Sect. 4, and describe potential use cases for it in Sect. 5. Section 6 concludes and devises future work.

2   LOD-a-lot: Concepts and Benefits

LOD-a-lot proposes an effective way of packaging a standards-compliant subset of the LOD Cloud into a ready-to-use file format.

LOD Laundromat [2] is a service that crawls, cleans and republishes Linked Open Datasets from Open Data portals like Datahub. As illustrated in Fig. 1, each dataset is cleaned to improve data quality: (i) syntax errors are detected and heuristics are used to recover from them; (ii) duplicate statements within datasets are removed; (iii) *Skolemization* is performed to replace blank nodes with well-known IRIs[3]; and (iv) the cleaned dataset is lexicographically sorted. The current version (May 2015) is composed of 657,902 datasets and contains over 38 billion triples (including between-dataset duplicates). For each dataset a *gzipped* Canonical N-Triples file, an HDT file, and an LDF [22] endpoint are published.

---

[1] See https://datahub.io/.
[2] See http://lodlaundromat.org/.
[3] See https://www.w3.org/TR/rdf11-concepts/#section-skolemization.

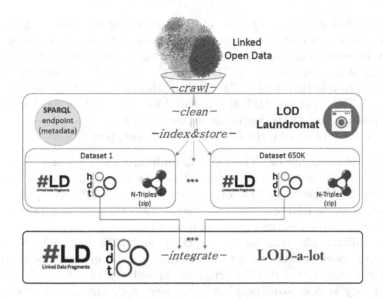

Fig. 1. LOD-a-lot overview and data flow.

Header-Dictionary-Triples (HDT) [8] is a binary compression format and – at the same time – a self-contained and queryable data store for RDF. HDT represents its main components (Dictionary and Triples) with compact data structures that enable storing, parsing and loading Big Semantic Data in compressed space. HDT data are indexed by subject, and therefore can be used to efficiently resolve subject-bounded *Triple Pattern* (TP) as well as unbounded queries [8]. *HDT-Focused on Querying* (HDT-FoQ) [15] extends HDT with two indexes (enabling predicate and object-based access, respectively) than can be created by the HDT consumer in order to speed up all TP queries. HDT can be used as a storage backend for large-scale graph data that achieves competitive query performance [15].

Linked Data Fragments (LDF) [22] is aimed at improving the scalability and availability of SPARQL endpoints by minimizing server-side processing and moving intelligence to the client. LDF allows simple Triple Patterns to be queried, where results are retrieved incrementally through pagination. Each of these pages (referred to as *fragments*) includes the estimated results and hypermedia controls (using the Hydra Vocabulary [14]), such that clients can perform query planning, retrieve all fragments, and join sub-query results locally. As such, server load is minimized and large data collections can be exposed with high availability. Given that HDT provides fast, low-cost TP resolution, LDF has been traditionally used in combination with HDT.

In spite of the inherent benefits of LOD Laundromat to conduct large-scale experiments, consumers still need to access each dataset or endpoint independently over HTTP, which results in additional overheads when analyzing the corpus as a whole. LOD-a-lot tackles this issue and provides a unified view of all the data crawled and cleaned by the LOD Laundromat into one big knowledge graph. To do so, we carefully integrate the 650 K HDT datasets into a single HDT file. In order to improve the scalability of this process, we perform parallel and incrementally large merges of HDT files, integrating Dictionary and Triples components. In addition to the HDT file, we also create and expose the HDT-FoQ index[4]. The resulting HDT file is offered for download for local use and is exposed through an LDF endpoint for online use (Fig. 1).

The resultant LOD-a-lot dataset has the following properties:

- **Standards-compliance.** The LOD Laundromat cleaning process and the HDT conversion guarantee that the indexed data is standards-compliant [2].
- **Volume & Variety.** LOD-a-lot consists of over 28 billion triples (one of the largest single RDF dataset) and merges more than 650 K datasets, which cover a large subset of the topic domains in LOD.
- **Accessibility.** The combination of HDT and LDF in LOD-a-lot allows users to perform structured queries through a uniform access point that is standards-compliant and self-descriptive through Hydra [14].
- **Scalability & Availability.** Most LOD query endpoints are either exposing a small dataset, have low availability, or are too expensive to maintain. LOD-a-lot alleviates these problems for online and offline data consumption: HDT is highly compressed and can resolve triple pattern queries at rest, with limited memory footprint (in practice, 3% of the total dataset size). In turn, LDF deploys such functionality online and minimizes the server burden, pushing the composition of more complex queries to the client.
- **Ease of (re)use.** Because LOD-a-lot is just one file, it can be downloaded, copied, or linked to easily.
- **Cost-effectiveness.** Due to the HDT compression technique, the hardware footprint of LOD-a-lot is relatively small, requiring 524 GB of (solid-state) disk space and (when queried) 15.7 GB of RAM. At the time of writing the combined cost of these two hardware resources is approximately 305 euros.

3   Availability and Sustainability

LOD-a-lot is available at http://purl.org/HDT/lod-a-lot and listed in the datahub.io catalog[5], where we provide the following access to the dataset:

- **HDT Dump** + HDT-FoQ index, released under the ODC PDDL[6] license.
- **LDF interface**, to serve online SPARQL resolution using LDF clients.
- **VoID description** of the dataset to aid automatic discovery services.

Because LOD-a-lot integrates 650 K+ datasets into one integrated RDF graph, it does not store the locations from which particular statements originate. This provenance information can be retrieved from LOD Laundromat,

---

[4] HDT creation took 64h & 170 GB RAM. HDT-FoQ took 8h & 250 GB RAM.
[5] See https://datahub.io/dataset/lod-a-lot.
[6] See https://opendatacommons.org/licenses/pddl/1-0/.

which stores the original source location, crawling metadata, and dataset metrics [20].

The sustainability of LOD-a-lot is supported by the joint effort of the LOD Laundromat and HDT projects. These projects, together with LDF, have been running for the last 3–6 years and are now well-established. We are creating an update policy for LOD-a-lot, to run in tandem with new LOD Laundromat crawls. The LOD-a-lot file can be used with a wealth of available HDT tools, including libraries for C++, Java, Node.js and SWI-Prolog. HDT tools are easily deployed using Docker and integrations with other open source projects (Apache Jena, Tinkerpop) exist.[7]

The canonical citation for LOD-a-lot is *"Fernández, J. D., Beek, W., Martínez-Prieto, M.A., and Arias, M. LOD-a-lot: A Queryable Dump of the LOD cloud (2017).* http://purl.org/HDT/lod-a-lot."

4 LOD-a-lot Statistics Summary

A simple analysis of LOD-a-lot reports some interesting statistics. Table 1 compares the number of unique triples, and different subjects, predicates, and objects in our dataset. The two-rightmost columns also report the number of *common* subjects and objects, i.e. those terms playing both roles in the dataset, and the total number of literal objects. Results are in line with the widespread perception that the number of predicates is very limited w.r.t the number of triples (in this case, 1M distinct predicates in 28B triples. i.e. less than 0.004%) due to vocabulary reuse. A more elaborated analysis (Fig. 2, middle) shows that predicates follow a *power-law* distribution, where a long-tail of predicates is barely used while a limited set of predicates appears in a great number of triples.

Interestingly, almost the same number of subjects and objects (3B terms) are used in LOD-a-lot. The high proportion w.r.t the number of triples (11%) shows a low reuse of such terms. Figure 2 further elaborates on this and depicts subject (left) and object (right) distributions. Power-laws are reported in both cases, but a longer tail is drawn for objects with massive (up to 1B) repetitions. Finally, note two interesting numbers to understand the underlying dataset structure: (i) around 40% of subjects and objects play both roles, which means that it is easy to find chain paths of, at least, two connected triples; and (ii) more than 1.3B of objects are literals, so 41% of object nodes have no output links.

Table 1. LOD-a-lot summary statistics.

#Triples	#Subjects	#Predicates	#Objects	#Common SO	#Literals
28,362,198,927	3,214,347,198	1,168,932	3,178,409,386	1,298,808,567	1,302,285,394

---

[7] See https://github.com/rdfhdt.

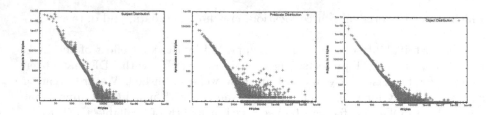

Fig. 2. Distribution of subjects, predicates, and objects in LOD-a-lot (log-log scale).

A *space complexity* analysis shows that the HDT LOD-a-lot dump encodes 28B triples in 304 GB: 133 GB are used for compressing the Dictionary, and 171 GB for the Triples component. HDT-FoQ indexes are also built to speed up all TP queries over the queryable dump: these additional structures use 220 GB.

Finally, we performed a deployment test (using the HDT-C++ library) on a modest computer[8], resulting in a load time of only 144 s and a memory footprint of 15.7 GB of RAM ($\approx$ 3% of the total dataset size). Furthermore, LDF queries (with 100 results as page size) are resolved at the level of milliseconds. This shows the LOD-a-lot affordable cost to manage and query 28B triples.

5   Relevance of the Dataset

This section describes three focused use cases for LOD-a-lot.

Query resolution at Web scale (UC1) is still an open challenge. Besides the aforementioned drawbacks of query federation [17,18]) and follow-your-nose traversal querying [12], pioneer centralized approaches, such as Sindice [19], are already discontinued. The OpenLink Software's LOD Cloud Cache[9] maintains a SPARQL endpoint of a portion of the LOD Cloud, but it only reports 4B triples and the system suffers from the traditional size/time restrictions of SPARQL endpoints and simple unbounded queries (e.g. the query in Sect. 1) incurs in timeouts. LOD-a-lot promotes query resolution at Web scale not only by actually serving such service for the indexed 28B triples, but it also shows the feasibility, scalability and efficiency of a centralized approach based on HDT and LDF.

Evaluation and benchmarking (UC2) have increasingly gained attention in the Semantic Web community [4]. However, Semantic Web evaluations still lack in terms of volume and variety. The Billion Triple Challenge (BTC) [13], the WebDataCommons Microdata, RDFa and Microformats dataset series [16] assist in this context by crawling RDF data from the Web and providing a single integrated dataset. However, BTC is limited to 4B triples[10] and uses a minimum sample of each crawled data source, which provides an incomplete view

---

[8] 8 cores (2.6 GHz), RAM 32 GB and a SATA HDD on Ubuntu 14.04.5 LTS.
[9] See http://lod.openlinksw.com/.
[10] See http://km.aifb.kit.edu/projects/btc-2014/.

of the data. In turn, the WebDataCommons dataset scales in size (44B triples[11]) but the focus is on Microdata and thus its variety and general application is very limited in practice. LOD Laundromat addresses this issue and republishes heterogeneous RDF datasets, but these have to be managed independently, which can result in a pain point for consumers. Thus, LOD-a-lot integrates the main advantages of all these proposals in terms of size (28B triples), variety (650K datasets) and single access point. LOD-a-lot is extremely easy and efficient to deploy in a local environment (via HDT), which allows Semantic Web academics and practitioners to run experiments over the largest and most heterogeneous, indexed and ready-to-consume RDF dataset.

RDF metrics and analytics (UC3) are widely adopted for SPARQL query optimization techniques [10] in order to find the optimal query plan. However, few studies inspect structural properties of real-world RDF data at Web scale [6] and, even those, only involve few million triples. More recently, the potential of LOD Laundromat has been exploited to characterize the quality of the data [1]. LOD-a-lot characteristics (see Sect. 2) democratize the computation of RDF metrics and analytics at Web scale (see the degrees in Fig. 2 as a practical example). Furthermore, particular metrics can take advantage of the HDT components in isolation, e.g. knowing the average length of URIs and literals would only scan the Dictionary (collecting all terms), whereas computing the in-degrees of object would only access the Triples (indexing the graph).

In addition, we also envision further practical applications for entity linking and data enrichment (e.g. leveraging in-links and `owl:sameAs` related entities), ranking of entities and vocabularies (e.g. analyzing their use), data summarization and other data mining techniques (e.g. finding commonalities in the data).

6 Conclusions and Future Work

The steady adoption of Linked Open Data (LOD) in recent years has led to a significant increase in the number and volume of RDF datasets. Today, problems such as data discovery and structured querying at web scale remain open challenges given the distributed nature of LOD.

This paper has presented LOD-a-lot, a simple and cost-effective way to query and study a large copy of the LOD Cloud. LOD-a-lot recollects all data gathered from the LOD Laundromat service and exposes a single HDT file, which can be queried online for free, and that can be downloaded locally and queried over commodity hardware. Requiring 524 GB of disk space and 15.7 GB of RAM, LOD-a-lot allows more than 28 billion unique triples to be queried using hardware costing – at the time of writing – 305 euro.

We plan to update LOD-a-lot regularly and include further datasets from the LOD Cloud. We are also working on a novel HDT variation to index quad information and thus keep track of the the input sources contributing to LOD-a-lot. Altogether, we expect LOD-a-lot to democratize the access to LOD and be one of the references for low-cost Web-scale evaluations.

---

[11] See http://webdatacommons.org/structureddata/2016-10/stats/stats.html.

Acknowledgments. Partly funded by Austrian Science Fund: M1720-G11, European Union's Horizon 2020 research and innovation programme under grant 731601, WU Post-doc Research Contracts, and MINECO, Spain: TIN2013-46238-C4-3-R, and TIN2016-78011-C4-1-R. We also thank the KEYSTONE COST Action IC1302.

References

1. Beek, W., Ilievski, F., Debattista, J., Schlobach, S., Wielemaker, J.: Literally better: analyzing and improving the quality of literals. Semant. Web J. (2017). http://www.semantic-web-journal.net/content/literally-better-analyzing-and-improving-quality-literals-1
2. Beek, W., Rietveld, L., Bazoobandi, H.R., Wielemaker, J., Schlobach, S.: LOD laundromat: a uniform way of publishing other people's dirty data. In: Mika, P., Tudorache, T., Bernstein, A., Welty, C., Knoblock, C., Vrandečić, D., Groth, P., Noy, N., Janowicz, K., Goble, C. (eds.) ISWC 2014. LNCS, vol. 8796, pp. 213–228. Springer, Cham (2014). doi:10.1007/978-3-319-11964-9_14
3. Bizer, C., Heath, T., Berners-Lee, T.: Linked data: the story so far. Int. J. Semant. Web Inf. Syst. **5**(3), 1–22 (2009)
4. Boncz, P., Fundulaki, I., Gubichev, A., Larriba-Pey, J., Neumann, T.: The linked data benchmark council project. Datenbank-Spektrum **13**(2), 121–129 (2013)
5. Buil-Aranda, C., Arenas, M., Corcho, O., Polleres, A.: Federating queries in SPARQL 1.1: syntax, semantics and evaluation. JWS **18**(1), 1–17 (2013)
6. Ding, L., Finin, T.: Characterizing the semantic web on the web. In: Cruz, I., Decker, S., Allemang, D., Preist, C., Schwabe, D., Mika, P., Uschold, M., Aroyo, L.M. (eds.) ISWC 2006. LNCS, vol. 4273, pp. 242–257. Springer, Heidelberg (2006). doi:10.1007/11926078_18
7. Ermilov, I., Lehmann, J., Martin, M., Auer, S.: LODStats: the data web census dataset. In: Groth, P., Simperl, E., Gray, A., Sabou, M., Krötzsch, M., Lecue, F., Flöck, F., Gil, Y. (eds.) ISWC 2016. LNCS, vol. 9982, pp. 38–46. Springer, Cham (2016). doi:10.1007/978-3-319-46547-0_5
8. Fernández, J.D., Martínez-Prieto, M.A., Gutiérrez, C., Polleres, A., Arias, M.: Binary RDF representation for publication and exchange (HDT). JWS **19**, 22–41 (2013)
9. Garlik, S.H., Seaborne, A., Prud'hommeaux, E.: SPARQL 1.1 query language. W3C Recommendation (2013). https://www.w3.org/TR/sparql11-query/
10. Gubichev, A., Neumann, T.: Exploiting the query structure for efficient join ordering in SPARQL queries. In: Proceedings of EDBT, pp. 439–450 (2014)
11. Hartig, O.: SQUIN: a traversal based query execution system for the web of linked data. In: Proceedings of SIGMOD, pp. 1081–1084 (2013)
12. Hartig, O., Pirró, G.: A context-based semantics for SPARQL property paths over the web. In: Gandon, F., Sabou, M., Sack, H., d'Amato, C., Cudré-Mauroux, P., Zimmermann, A. (eds.) ESWC 2015. LNCS, vol. 9088, pp. 71–87. Springer, Cham (2015). doi:10.1007/978-3-319-18818-8_5
13. Käfer, T., Harth, A.: Billion Triples Challenge Data Set (2014). http://km.aifb.kit.edu/projects/btc-2014/
14. Lanthaler, M., Gütl, C.: Hydra: A Vocabulary for Hypermedia-Driven Web APIs. In: CEUR, vol. 996 (2013)

15. Martínez-Prieto, M.A., Arias Gallego, M., Fernández, J.D.: Exchange and consumption of huge RDF data. In: Simperl, E., Cimiano, P., Polleres, A., Corcho, O., Presutti, V. (eds.) ESWC 2012. LNCS, vol. 7295, pp. 437–452. Springer, Heidelberg (2012). doi:10.1007/978-3-642-30284-8_36
16. Meusel, R., Petrovski, P., Bizer, C.: The webdatacommons microdata, RDFa and microformat dataset series. In: Mika, P., Tudorache, T., Bernstein, A., Welty, C., Knoblock, C., Vrandečić, D., Groth, P., Noy, N., Janowicz, K., Goble, C. (eds.) ISWC 2014. LNCS, vol. 8796, pp. 277–292. Springer, Cham (2014). doi:10.1007/978-3-319-11964-9_18
17. Millard, I.C., Glaser, H., Salvadores, M., Shadbolt, N.: Consuming multiple linked data sources: challenges and experiences. In: Proceedings of COLD, vol. 665, pp. 37–48. CEUR (2010)
18. Oguz, D., Ergenc, B., Yin, S., Dikenelli, O., Hameurlain, A.: Federated query processing on linked data: a qualitative survey and open challenges. Knowl. Eng. Rev. 30(5), 545–563 (2015)
19. Oren, E., Delbru, R., Catasta, M., Cyganiak, R., Stenzhorn, H., Tummarello, G.: Sindice.com: a document-oriented lookup index for open linked data. Int. J. Metadata Semant. Ontol 3(1), 37–52 (2008)
20. Rietveld, L., Beek, W., Hoekstra, R., Schlobach, S.: Meta-data for a lot of LOD. Semantic Web J. 8(6), 1067–1080 (2017)
21. Vandenbussche, P.Y., Umbrich, J., Matteis, L., Hogan, A., Buil-Aranda, C.: SPARQLES: Monitoring public SPARQL endpoints. Semantic Web J. 8(6), 1049–1065 (2017)
22. Verborgh, R., Vander Sande, M., Hartig, O., Van Herwegen, J., De Vocht, L., De Meester, B., Haesendonck, G., Colpaert, P.: Triple pattern fragments: a low-cost knowledge graph interface for the web. JWS 37–38, 184–206 (2016)

IMGpedia: A Linked Dataset with Content-Based Analysis of Wikimedia Images

Sebastián Ferrada[✉], Benjamin Bustos, and Aidan Hogan

Department of Computer Science, Center for Semantic Web Research,
Universidad de Chile, Santiago, Chile
{sferrada,bebustos,ahogan}@dcc.uchile.cl

Abstract. IMGPEDIA is a large-scale linked dataset that incorporates visual information of the images from the WIKIMEDIA COMMONS dataset: it brings together descriptors of the visual content of 15 million images, 450 million visual-similarity relations between those images, links to image metadata from DBPEDIA COMMONS, and links to the DBPEDIA resources associated with individual images. In this paper we describe the creation of the IMGPEDIA dataset, provide an overview of its schema and statistics of its contents, offer example queries that combine semantic and visual information of images, and discuss other envisaged use-cases for the dataset.

Resource type: Dataset
Permanent URL: https://dx.doi.org/10.6084/m9.figshare.4991099.v2

1 Introduction

Many datasets have been published on the Web following Semantic Web standards and Linked Data principles. At the core of the resulting "Web of Data", we can find linked datasets such as DBPEDIA [6], which contains structured data automatically extracted from WIKIPEDIA; and WIKIDATA [10], where users can directly add and curate data in a structured format. We can also find various datasets relating to multimedia, such as LINKEDMDB describing movies, BBC MUSIC describing music bands and genres, and so forth. More recently, DBPE-DIA COMMONS [9] was released, publishing metadata extracted from WIKIMEDIA COMMONS[1]: a rich source of multimedia containing 38 million freely usable media files (image, audio and video).

Related Work. Amongst the available datasets describing multimedia, the emphasis has been on capturing the high-level metadata of the multimedia files (e.g., author, date created, file size, width, duration) rather than audio or visual features of the multimedia content itself. However, as mentioned in previous

---

[1] http://commons.wikimedia.org.

© Springer International Publishing AG 2017
C. d'Amato et al. (Eds.): ISWC 2017, Part II, LNCS 10588, pp. 84–93, 2017.
DOI: 10.1007/978-3-319-68204-4_8

works (e.g., [1,4,8]), merging structured metadata with multimedia content-based descriptors could lead to a variety of applications, such as semantically-enhanced multimedia publishing, retrieval, preservation, etc. While such works have proposed methods to describe the audio or visual content of multimedia files in Semantic Web formats, we are not aware of any public linked dataset incorporating content-based descriptors of multimedia files. For example, DBPEDIA COMMONS [9] does not extract any audio/visual features directly from the multimedia files of WIKIMEDIA COMMONS, but rather only captures metadata from the documents describing the files.

Contribution. Along these lines, we have created IMGPEDIA: a linked dataset incorporating visual descriptors and visual similarity relations for the images of WIKIMEDIA COMMONS, linked with both the DBPEDIA COMMONS dataset (which provides metadata for the images, such as author, license, etc.) and the DBPEDIA dataset (which provides metadata about resources associated with the image). The initial use-case we are exploring for IMGPEDIA is to perform *visuo-semantic* queries over the images, where, for example, using SPARQL federation over IMGPEDIA and DBPEDIA, we could request: *given a picture of the Cusco Cathedral, retrieve the top-k most similar cathedrals in Europe.* More generally, as discussed later, we foresee a number of potential use-cases for the dataset as a test-bed for research in the potentially fruitful intersection of the Multimedia and Semantic Web areas.

Outline. In this paper, we describe the IMGPEDIA dataset[2]. We first introduce the image analysis used to extract visual descriptors and similarity relations from the images of WIKIMEDIA COMMONS. Next we give an overview of the lightweight ontology used to represent the resulting visual information as RDF. We then provide some high-level statistics of the resulting dataset and the best-practices used in its publication. Thereafter, we provide some example visuo-semantic queries and their results. Finally we conclude with discussion of other use-cases we envisage as well as our future plans to improve upon and extend the IMGPEDIA dataset.

2   Image Analysis

WIKIMEDIA COMMONS is a dataset of 38 million freely-usable media files contributed and maintained collaboratively by users. Around 16 million of these media files are images, which are hosted on a mirror server accessible via rsync[3]. We downloaded the images, with a total size of 21 TB, in order to be able to process them offline. The download took 40 days with a bandwidth of

---

[2] In a previous short paper, we proposed the idea of the project and gave details of initial progress [3]; this paper describes the dataset resulting from that initial work.

[3] rsync://ftpmirror.your.org/wikimedia-images/.

500 GB/day. In order to facilitate later image processing tasks, we only consider images with (commonly supported) JPG or PNG encodings, equivalent to 92% of the images.

After the acquisition of the images, we proceeded to compute different *visual descriptors*, which are high-dimensional vectors that capture different elements of the content of the images (such as color distribution or shape/texture information); later we will use these descriptors to compute visual similarity between images, where we say that two images are visually similar if the distance between their descriptors is low. The descriptors computed are the following:

- **Gray Histogram Descriptor:** We transform the image from color to grayscale and divide it into a fixed number of blocks. A histogram of 8-bit gray intensities is then calculated for each block. The concatenation of all histograms is used to generate a description vector with 256 dimensions.
- **Histogram of Oriented Gradients Descriptor:** We extract edges of the grayscale image by computing its gradient (using Sobel kernels), applying a threshold, and computing the orientation of the gradient. Finally, a histogram of the orientations is made and used as a description vector with 288 dimensions.
- **Color Layout Descriptor:** We divide the image into blocks and for each block we compute the mean (YCbCr) color. Afterwards the Discrete Cosine Transform is computed for each color channel. Finally the concatenation of the transforms is used as the descriptor vector, with 192 dimensions.

Computing the descriptors was performed on a machine with Debian 4.1.1, a 2.2 GHz 24-core Intel® Xeon® processor, and 120 GB of RAM. With multi-threading, computing GHD took 43 h, HOG took 107 h, while CLD took 127 h. We have made implementations to compute these visual descriptors available in multiple programming languages under a GNU GPL license [3][4].

The next task is to use these descriptors to compute the visual similarity between pairs of images. Given the scale of the dataset, in order to keep a manageable upper-bound on the resulting data (we selected ~4 billion triples as a reasonable limit), we decided to compute the 10 nearest neighbors for each image according to each visual descriptor. To avoid $\binom{n}{2}$ brute-force comparisons, we use approximate search methods where we selected the Fast Library for Approximated Nearest Neighbors (FLANN) since it has been proven to scale for large datasets [7][5]. In order to facilitate multi-threading, we divide the images into 16 buckets, where for each image, we initialize 16 threads to search for the 10 nearest neighbors in each bucket. At the end of the execution we have 160 candidates

---

[4] https://github.com/scferrada/imgpedia.

[5] We configured FLANN with a goal precision of 90% and tested it on a brute-forced gold standard of 20,000 images. FLANN achieved an actual precision of 79% on this dataset. However, while the gold standard took 3.5 days to compute with 16 threads, FLANN finished in 13 min with 1 thread. We concluded that FLANN offers a good precision/efficiency trade-off for a large-scale collection of images such as ours.

to be the global 10 nearest neighbors so we choose the 10 with the minimum distances among them to obtain the final result. This process took about 13 h with the machine previously described. In Fig. 1 we show an example of the results of the similarity search based on the HOG descriptor, which captures information about edges in the image.

Fig. 1. 10 nearest neighbors of an image of Hopsten Marktplatz using HOG

3   Ontology and Data

The visual descriptors and similarity relations of the images form the core of the IMGPEDIA dataset. To represent this information as RDF, we create a custom lightweight IMGPEDIA ontology. All IMGPEDIA resources are identified under the http://imgpedia.dcc.uchile.cl/resource/ namespace. The vocabulary is described in RDFS/OWL at http://imgpedia.dcc.uchile.cl/ontology; this vocabulary (authoritatively) extends related terms from the DBpedia Ontology, schema.org and the Open Graph Protocol where appropriate, and has been submitted to the Linked Open Vocabularies (LOV) service. In Fig. 2, we show the classes, datatype- and object-properties available for representing images, their visual descriptors and the similarity links between them.

An imo:Image is an abstract resource representing an image of the WIKI-MEDIA COMMONS dataset, describing the dimensions of the image (height and width), the image URL in WIKIMEDIA COMMONS, and an owl:sameAs link to the complementary resource in DBPEDIA COMMONS. In Listing 1 we see an example of the RDF for the imo:Image representation of Hopsten Marktplatz.

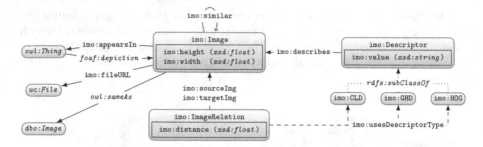

Fig. 2. IMGPEDIA ontology overview: classes are shown in boxes; solid edges denote relations between instances of both classes, dotted lines are between the classes themselves, while dashed lines are from instances to classes; external terms are italicized; datatype properties are listed inside the class boxes for conciseness.

Listing 1. RDF example of a visual entity

```
@prefix imo: <http://imgpedia.dcc.uchile.cl/ontology#>
@prefix im: <http://imgpedia.dcc.uchile.cl/resource/>
@prefix dbcr: <http://commons.dbpedia.org/resource/File:>
im:Hopsten_Marktplatz_3.jpg a imo:Image ;
 owl:sameAs dbcr:Hopsten_Marktplatz_3.jpg;
 imo:width 400 ; imo:height 300 ;
 imo:fileURL <http://commons.wikimedia.org/wiki/File:Hopsten_Marktplatz_3.jpg>.
```

An `imo:Descriptor` respresents a visual descriptor of an image and is linked to it through the `imo:describes` relation. An `imo:Descriptor` can be of type `imo:GHD`, `imo:HOG`, or `imo:CLD` corresponding to the three types of descriptors previously discussed. In Listing 2 we show an example of a visual descriptor in RDF. To keep the number of output triples manageable, we store the vector of the descriptor as a string; storing individual dimensions as (192–288) individual objects would inflate the output triples to an unmanageable volume; in addition, we do not currently anticipate SPARQL queries over individual values of the descriptor.

Listing 2. RDF example of a descriptor

```
im:Hopsten_Marktplatz_3.jpg.HOG a imo:HOG ;
   imo:describes im: Hopsten_Marktplatz_3.jpg ;
   imo:value "[0.34418711, 0.10582313, 0.05867421, ...]".
```

An `imo:ImageRelation` is a resource that contains the similarity links between two images; it also contains the type of descriptor that was used and the Manhattan distance between the descriptors of both images. Although Manhattan distance is symmetric, these relations are materialized based on a k-nearest-neighbors (k-nn) search, where image a being in the k-nn of b does not imply the inverse relation; hence the image relation captures a source and target image where the target is in the k-nn of the source. We also add a `imo:similar` relation from the source image to the target k-nn image. Listing 3 shows an example of a k-nn relation in RDF.

Listing 3. RDF example of a visual similarity relation

```
im:176147ac95660a47d5d58c57d5260572cdce11f98ad4.HOG a imo:ImageRelation;
    imo:sourceImage im:Hopsten_Marktplatz_3.jpg ;
    imo:targetImage im:Boze_Cialo-glowny.JPG ;
    imo:distance 1.219660e+01 ; imo:usesDescriptor imo:HOG .

im:Hopsten_Marktplatz_3.jpg imo:similar im:Boze_Cialo-glowny.JPG .
```

Finally, aside from the links to DBPEDIA COMMONS, we also provide links
to DBPEDIA, which provides a context for the images. To create these links,
we use an SQL dump of English WIKIPEDIA and perform a join between
the table of all images and the table of all articles, so we can have pairs
(image_name,article_name) if the image appears in the article. In Listing 4 we
give some example links for DBPEDIA. Such links are not provided by DBPEDIA
COMMONS.

Listing 4. RDF example of DBPEDIA links

```
im:Chamomile_original_size.jpg imo:appearsIn dbr:Nephelium_hypoleucum .
im:Rose_Amber_Flush_20070601.jpg imo:appearsIn dbr:Nephelium_hypoleucum .
im:Rose_Amber_Flush_20070601.jpg imo:appearsIn dbr:Acer_shirasawanum .
im:HondaS2000-004.png imo:appearsIn dbr:Alfa_Romeo_Scighera .
```

4   Dataset

The dataset of IMGPEDIA contains information about 14.7 million images of
WIKIMEDIA COMMONS, the description of their content, links to their most
similar images and to the DBPEDIA resources that form part of their context. A
general overview of the size and data of IMGPEDIA can be seen in Table 2. There
we can see that for each visual entity we computed three different descriptors
and for each descriptor we computed 10 similarity links using the 10 nearest
neighbors, defining a similarity graph with 14.7 million vertices and 442 million
edges.

Accessibility and Best Practices. IMGPEDIA is available as a Linked Dataset
(with dereferenceable IRIs), as a SPARQL endpoint (using Virtuoso), and as a
dump. Locations are provided in Table 1. As aforementioned, we provide a lightweight RDFS/OWL Ontology that extends well-known vocabularies as appropriate. We also provide a VoID description of the dataset, which includes metadata
from DC-terms as well as brief provenance statement using the PROV ontology
and licensing information. With respect to the license, the most restrictive licensing clauses allowed for images on WIKIPEDIA COMMONS are attribution and
share-alike[6]; non-derivative or non-commercial clauses are not permitted. Hence
we release IMGPEDIA under an Open Database License (ODC-ODbL) license[7],
which is an attribution/share-alike license specifically intended for databases.
According to the 5-star model for Linked Open Data [2], IMGPEDIA is a 5-star

---

[6] https://commons.wikimedia.org/wiki/Commons:Licensing.
[7] http://www.opendatacommons.org/licenses/odbl/.

Table 1. Locations of IMGPEDIA resources

Resource	Location
LD IRI (example)	http://imgpedia.dcc.uchile.cl/resource/ Rose_Amber_Flush_20070601.jpg
SPARQL endpoint	http://imgpedia.dcc.uchile.cl/sparql
Dump	http://imgpedia.dcc.uchile.cl/dumps/20170506/
VoID	http://imgpedia.dcc.uchile.cl/dumps/20170506/void.nt
Ontology	http://imgpedia.dcc.uchile.cl/ontology#
Issue tracker	http://github.com/scferrada/imgpedia/issues
Datahub	http://datahub.io/dataset/imgpedia

Table 2. High-level statistics for IMGPEDIA

Name	Count	Description
Visual entities	14,765,300	Entities about the images
Links to DBPEDIA COMMONS	14,765,300	Links to additional image metadata
Descriptors	44,295,900	Visual descriptors of the images
Similarity links	442,959,000	Nearest neighbor relations between images
IRIs	502,020,200	Unique resource names
Links to DBPEDIA	12,683,423	Links to the resource about the article of the image
Triples	3,119,207,705	Number of triples present in the graph

dataset since it is an RDF graph that uses IRIs to identify its resources and provides links to other data sources (DBPEDIA and DBPEDIA COMMONS) to provide context. IMGPEDIA also has an issue tracker on GitHub, so users and collaborators can request features for future versions and report any problems they may find. The dataset is also registered at DataHub so researchers and other public can easily find and use it.

With respect to sustainability, given the large sizes of the dumps, we have yet to find a mirror host to replicate the data. However, internally, data are replicated on NAS storage and the source code is provided to replicate the dataset from the source WIKIMEDIA COMMONS images. The first author has also secured funding to pursue a PhD on the topic, which will start this year; hence the dataset will be in active maintenance and development. With respect to updating the dataset, while building the original dataset was costly, we are planning to implement an incremental update where rsync is used to fetch new images; the descriptors for these images can then be computed, while only the k-nn similarity relations involving new images (potentially pruning old relations) need to be computed.

5 Use-Cases

We first provide some examples of queries that IMGPEDIA can answer.

First, we can query the visual similarity relations to find images that are similar by color, edges and/or intensity according to the nearest neighbor computation. In Listing 5 we show such a query, requesting the nearest neighbors of the image of Hopsten Marktplatz using the HOG descriptor (capturing visual similarity of edges). The results of this query are the images shown previously in Fig. 1.

Listing 5. SPARQL Query for similar images to Hopsten Marktplatz

```
SELECT DISTINCT ?Target ?Distance WHERE {
        ?rel imo:sourceImage im:Hopsten_Marktplatz_3.jpg ;
        imo:usesDescriptorType imo:HOG ;
        imo:targetImage ?Target ;
        imo:distance ?Distance . }
ORDER BY ?Distance
```

Second, we can use federated SPARQL queries to perform visuo-semantic retrieval of images, combining visual similarity of images with semantic metadata through links to DBPEDIA. In Listing 6, we show an example federated SPARQL query using the DBPEDIA SPARQL endpoint that takes the images from articles categorized as *"Roman Catholic cathedrals in Europe"* and looks for similar images from articles categorized as *"Museum"*. In Fig. 3, we show the retrieved images. To obtain more accurate results, SPARQL property paths can be used in order to include hierarchical categorizations, e.g. dcterms:subject/skos:broader* can be used in the first **SERVICE** clause to obtain all cathedrals that are labeled as a subcategory of European cathedral, such as French cathedral.

Listing 6. Query for images of museums similar to European Catholic cathedrals

```
SELECT DISTINCT ?urls ?urlt WHERE{
    SERVICE <http://dbpedia.org/sparql>{
        ?sres dcterms:subject dbc:Roman_Catholic_cathedrals_in_Europe . }
    ?source imo:appearsIn ?sres ;
            imo:similar ?target ;
            imo:fileURL ?urls .
    ?target imo:appearsIn ?tres ;
            imo:fileURL ?urlt .
    SERVICE <http://dbpedia.org/sparql>{
        ?tres dcterms:subject ?sub
        FILTER(CONTAINS(STR(?sub), "Museum"))}}
```

With regards to *usage*, we released IMGPEDIA to the public on May 6th, 2017 and we keep a log of the SPARQL queries asked through the query endpoint, which at the time of writing (11 weeks later) contains 588 queries. However, we emphasize that IMGPEDIA was recently published. Our current plan is to further explore the potential of semantically-enhanced image retrieval that IMGPEDIA

Cathedral of St. Mary and Museum of Fine Arts   Basilica of St. John L. and Nat. Hist. Museum of Helsinki   Cathedral of St. Mary and Dumbarton House Museum

Fig. 3. Results of Listing 6 query

offers. The dataset also opens up a number of other use-cases. For example, one could consider combining the semantic information from DBPEDIA and the visual similarity information of IMGPEDIA to create a labeled dataset along the lines of IMAGENET[8], but with variable levels of granularity (e.g., Catholic cathedral, cathedral, religious building, etc.). Another use-case would be to develop a clustering technique for images based both on visual similarity and semantic context. We also believe that IMGPEDIA can compliment existing research works in the intersection of the Semantic Web and Multimedia, where it could provide a test-bed for works on media fragments [4,8], or on combining SPARQL with multimedia retrieval [5], etc.

6   Conclusions and Future Work

In this paper we have presented IMGPEDIA: a linked dataset that offers visual descriptors and similarity relations for the images of WIKIMEDIA COMMONS; this dataset is also linked with DBPEDIA and DBPEDIA COMMONS to provide semantic context and further metadata. We described the construction of the dataset, the structure and provenance of the data, statistics of the dataset, and the supporting resources made available. Finally, we showed some examples of *visuo-semantic* queries enabled by the dataset and discussed potential use-cases.

There are many things that can be improved and added to IMGPEDIA. We will develop a web application to make IMGPEDIA more user-friendly, where users can ask queries intuitively (without needing SPARQL) and browse through results where images are displayed. We also plan to explore more modern visual descriptors that can help us to improve the current similarity relations between images, as well as defining similarity relations that combine descriptors.

Acknowledgments. This work was supported by the Millennium Nucleus Center for Semantic Web Research, Grant № NC120004 and Fondecyt, Grant № 11140900. We would also like to thank Camila Faúndez for her assistance.

References

1. Addis, M., Allasia, W., Bailer, W., Boch, L., Gallo, F., Wright, R.: 100 million hours of audiovisual content: digital preservation and access in the PrestoPRIME project. In: INTL- DPIF. ACM (2010)

---

[8] http://www.image-net.org/.

2. Berners-Lee, T.: Linked Data. In: W3C Design Issues, July 2006 (2010)
3. Ferrada, S., Bustos, B., Hogan, A.: IMGpedia: enriching the web of data with image content analysis. In: AMW. CEUR (2016)
4. Kurz, T., Kosch, H.: Lifting media fragment uris to the next level. In: Linked Media Workshop (LIME-SemDev) at ESWC (2016)
5. Kurz, T., Schlegel, K., Kosch, H.: Enabling access to linked media with SPARQL-MM. In: World Wide Web (WWW), pp. 721–726 (2015)
6. Lehmann, J., Isele, R., Jakob, M., Jentzsch, A., Kontokostas, D., Mendes, P.N., Hellmann, S., Morsey, M., van Kleef, P., Auer, S., Bizer, C.: DBpedia - a large-scale, multilingual knowledge base extracted from wikipedia. Semant. Web J. **6**, 167–195 (2014)
7. Muja, M., Lowe, D.G.: Fast approximate nearest neighbors with automatic algorithm configuration. In: VISSApp, pp. 331–340. INSTICC Press (2009)
8. Troncy, R., Mannens, E., Pfeiffer, S., Deursen, D.V.: Media fragments URI 1.0. In: W3C Recommendation (2012)
9. Vaidya, G., Kontokostas, D., Knuth, M., Lehmann, J., Hellmann, S.: DBpedia commons: structured multimedia metadata from the wikimedia commons. In: Arenas, M., et al. (eds.) ISWC 2015. LNCS, vol. 9367, pp. 281–289. Springer, Cham (2015). doi:10.1007/978-3-319-25010-6_17
10. Vrandečić, D., Krötzsch, M.: Wikidata: a free collaborative knowledgebase. Comm. ACM **57**, 78–85 (2014)

WIDOCO: A Wizard for Documenting Ontologies

Daniel Garijo[✉]

Information Sciences Institute, University of Southern California,
4676 Admiralty Way, Marina del Rey, CA 90292, USA
dgarijo@isi.edu

Abstract. In this paper we describe WIDOCO, a *WIzard for DOCumenting Ontologies* that guides users through the documentation process of their vocabularies. Given an RDF vocabulary, WIDOCO detects missing vocabulary metadata and creates a documentation with diagrams, human readable descriptions of the ontology terms and a summary of changes with respect to previous versions of the ontology. The documentation consists on a set of linked enriched HTML pages that can be further extended by end users. WIDOCO is open source and builds on well established Semantic Web tools. So far, WIDOCO has been used to document more than one hundred ontologies in different domains.

Keywords: Ontology documentation · Ontology evolution · Ontology understanding · OWL ontologies

Resource Type: Software
Permanent URL: https://w3id.org/widoco
Software DOI: https://doi.org/10.5281/zenodo.591294

1 Introduction

Ontology engineering methodologies acknowledge *reuse of existing vocabularies* as a crucial step when developing a new ontology [11]. Therefore, ontology authors often provide a human-readable documentation of their vocabularies, in order to facilitate their understanding and adoption by other researchers [9].

There are three main aspects related to ontology documentation. The first one is creating a human-readable representation of the content of the ontology: metadata, definition of classes and properties, visualization (e.g., diagrams relating the different concepts) and versioning (explanation of the difference between versions of the ontologies). The second aspect is creating machine-readable annotations of documentation metadata (e.g., provenance, snippets for facilitating vocabulary discovery by search engines) and the third aspect is preparing the documentation files to be accessed as a web resource (doing content negotiation).

Related work has been proposed to facilitate some of these aspects. For example, ontology editors like Protégé [8], have plugins for automatically creating an HTML documentation with the definition of classes and properties.[1] Similarly,

---

[1] https://protegewiki.stanford.edu/wiki/OWLDoc.

© Springer International Publishing AG 2017
C. d'Amato et al. (Eds.): ISWC 2017, Part II, LNCS 10588, pp. 94–102, 2017.
DOI: 10.1007/978-3-319-68204-4_9

approaches like LODE [9] or Parrot [12] provide drag-and-drop services to automatically document ontology terms. However, most approaches are typically designed for Semantic Web experts, presenting some of the following issues:

1. *Lack of guidelines and best practices for ontology documentation*: users developing ontologies may not know which are the common terms used to describe the metadata of their ontologies. These metadata are important, because they are used by existing tools to create human readable descriptions of an ontology.
2. *Lack of ontology metadata completion*: Current efforts do not indicate which key information may be missing when documenting an ontology.
3. *Lack of an ecosystem for ontology documentation and customization*: most existing approaches focus on specific aspects of ontology documentation. On the one hand, approaches like LODE [9] generate a human readable description of the classes and properties of a given ontology, but neglect the generation of diagrams. On the other hand, tools like WebVowl [5] create dynamic visualizations of ontologies, but do not deal with the generation of text. Integrating the outcome of these and other tools and customizing them according to user preferences takes time, especially to non programmers.

In this paper we describe WIDOCO, a wizard for documenting ontologies designed to tackle these issues in an automated way. WIDOCO takes as input an annotated RDF vocabulary (e.g., an OWL file with labels and definitions for its concepts) and generates a set of linked HTML pages containing a human readable description of the ontology.[2] WIDOCO *guides users through the steps to be followed* when documenting an ontology, relying on common best practices and *indicating missing metadata that should be included*. WIDOCO also *facilitates customizing the produced documentation*, enabling users to select which aspects they want to include in their document (e.g., sections, diagrams, provenance information, etc.). WIDOCO integrates and extends well established tools, like LODE [9] for term documentation, WebVowl [5] for interactive diagram creation, Bubastis [6] for adding automated change logs between versions and web services like Licensius[3] for completing ontology metadata. In addition, WIDOCO enriches the documentation with snippets discoverable by search engines, prepares content negotiation files for an ontology using W3C best practices, exposes the documentation in multiple languages and exports provenance information of the creation process. We consider that these features make WIDOCO a useful resource for documenting ontologies, and so far we have received positive feedback from the community.

The rest of the paper is structured as follows: a description of the main features of WIDOCO in shown in Sect. 2. Section 3 discusses the community adoption of the proposed resource, followed by a brief overview of related work describing approaches for ontology documentation in Sect. 4. Finally, Sect. 5 points out future directions of work.

---

[2] An overview with examples can be accessed online: https://w3id.org/widoco/gallery.
[3] http://licensius.com/.

2   WIDOCO: A Wizard for Documenting Ontologies

WIDOCO is a standalone java application developed to help users documenting their ontologies. Given an ontology file or URL as input, WIDOCO guides the user through a wizard that generates a customized enriched HTML documentation of the ontology. In this section we describe the main features of WIDOCO in Sect. 2.1, explaining the steps to be followed by users on WIDOCO's wizard in Sect. 2.2 and how users may extend the generated documentation on Sect. 2.3.

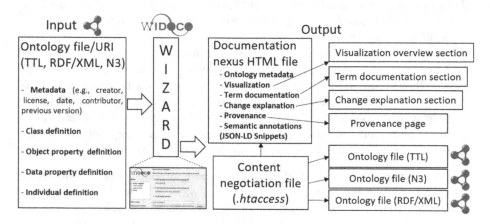

Fig. 1. Overview of WIDOCO: given an ontology file with metadata and definitions for its ontology terms, WIDOCO generates a set of linked HTML files (linked through a nexus file) with definitions of terms, an interactive diagram, an explanation of changes from previous versions and annotations of the ontology document itself (provenance file). In addition, the system generates a file for facilitating documentation publication through content negotiation (*.htaccess*).

2.1   WIDOCO Overview

Figure 1 shows an overview of the different aspects of the documentation process tackled by WIDOCO. Users provide as input to the system a URI or file with metadata annotations (e.g., creators, title, contributors, license, etc.) and definitions for the different ontology terms. After following the steps of the wizard, WIDOCO generates a customized documentation with the most relevant metadata of the ontology. The documentation is composed by a set of linked HTML files, including a main *nexus* file and several *section* files. Each section file describes the content of part of the documentation (e.g., abstract, definition of ontology terms, overview diagrams, etc.) while the nexus file links all the sections together. In addition, WIDOCO generates separate provenance records about the ontology documentation and annotates the nexus file with JSON-LD snippets,[4] which help search engines discovering the ontology metadata. Finally,

---

[4] https://www.w3.org/TR/json-ld/.

WIDOCO prepares a content negotiation file and serializations of the ontology to facilitate serving the documentation and ontology in different formats. WIDOCO's features are further described below:

Documenting Relevant Ontology Metadata: WIDOCO uses the OWL API [4] to process and recognize over forty properties for ontology metadata description from common vocabularies and standards. These terms have been grouped in metadata categories and collected in a best practices document,[5] including a rationale of their importance when describing a vocabulary. Some examples of metadata categories are *vocabulary access* (e.g., namespace URI that should be used to dereference the vocabulary), *attribution* (e.g., creators, contributors or publishers), *provenance* (e.g., creation date, sources, previous versions) or *citation* (e.g., DOI of the vocabulary, how to cite it) among others.

Ontology Visualization: We have reused WebVowl [5] to add an interactive diagram to the documentation. The diagram is a useful aid, as it simplifies the visualization in bigger ontologies (automatically filtering loosely connected terms) and helps having an overview of the main properties and classes. WIDOCO transforms the ontology into the format required by WebVowl and saves the result as a separated HTML file.

Ontology Terms Documentation: WIDOCO builds on top of LODE [9], an open source tool designed to generate an HTML file with the definition of classes, properties, data properties and individuals of an ontology, based on the annotations made by the user. WIDOCO extends LODE by expanding the properties a user may use to qualify a term in the ontology. For example, LODE uses *rdfs:label* to represent the names of ontology terms, and *rdfs:comment* to describe their definition in the HTML documentation. However, users may use other similar properties for this purpose, such as *skos:label* and *skos:definition*. WIDOCO includes these properties and recognizes new properties to qualify ontology terms, such as examples of concepts or their rationale for inclusion in the ontology. These properties are also part of the list of best practices for ontology metadata description mentioned above (See footnote 5).

Explaining Changes from Previous Versions: Ontologies are likely to evolve, being released in different versions. In these cases, part of the documentation is targeted towards explaining the differences from the last version of the ontology. WIDOCO expands Bubastis [6], a software for capturing differences between classes in ontologies automatically, adding also which are the object properties, data properties and annotations that have changed from version to version.

Provenance: WIDOCO produces a separate page, linked to the nexus file of the documentation, with the statements that refer to the provenance of the documentation itself (sources, previous versions, authors, etc.). The page is captured both in a human readable and machine readable way, following the PROV-O standard [7].

---

[5] https://w3id.org/widoco/bestPractices.

Semantic annotations: WIDOCO includes JSON-LD snippets on the nexus HTML file with a description of the ontology metadata annotated according to Schema.org.[6] These snippets are useful for search engines to find and explore the metadata of the ontology documentation automatically.

Ontology Serialization and Content Negotiation: WIDOCO automatically creates an *.htaccess* file to access the documentation through its URI once it is published online. We have adopted the W3C best practices for vocabulary publishing on the Web,[7] adapting content negotiation to the vocabulary URI (hash versus slash vocabularies) and preparing the *.htaccess* file to serve (by default) the RDF/XML, TTL and N3 serializations.

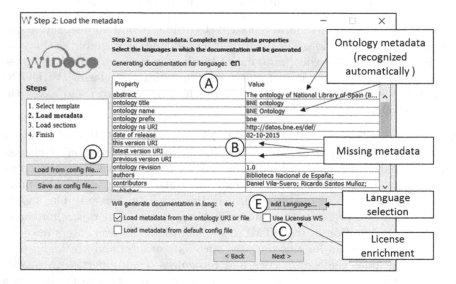

Fig. 2. Snapshot of the wizard for gathering ontology metadata: WIDOCO will automatically extract all available metadata from the ontology, showing missing properties that may be included in the documentation.

2.2 Guiding Users Through the Documentation Process

WIDOCO consists on a wizard that helps users create, customize and enrich a documentation for their ontologies automatically. The main steps are:

1. *Metadata collection:* After selecting an ontology, WIDOCO will load it and fill a table of recommended metadata values, as shown in Fig. 2(A). If a metadata field is not found in the ontology, the corresponding value will appear blank in the table (B), so users can complete it if desired. Users may also choose

---

[6] http://schema.org/.
[7] https://www.w3.org/TR/swbp-vocab-pub/.

Fig. 3. An overview of the options for customizing the documentation of a vocabulary.

to let WIDOCO look for the license name and URL used in the ontology (C) by querying the Licensius web service and license dataset.[8]

Alternatively, ontology metadata may be loaded from a file using a key value pair (D). This option is useful when several ontologies share common metadata but do not have their ontology files annotated.

Finally, this step of the wizard also lets the user select the languages in which the documentation will be generated (E). Metadata loaded in the table is customized to the selected language, which is useful when generating a documentation in multiple languages.

2. *Customization:* In this step a user can select whether to include or not each of the features of WIDOCO in the final documentation. Figure 3 shows an overview of the different options: include default sections (i.e., introduction, overview, description and references) or load them from existing files, include annotation properties or individuals as part of the ontology documentation; export the provenance of the vocabulary as a separated page, create an .htaccess file to handle content negotiation for the ontology, include an interactive diagram and show the changes with respect to the last version of the ontology. In addition, users may choose between two different CSS styles for the documentation.

3. *Ontology browsing:* the final step of the wizard shows up after the documentation has been generated successfully, allowing opening it on a local web browser. This step also enables users to produce evaluation reports of the ontology, facilitating checking whether the ontology has any design flaws or not. WIDOCO produces these reports by using the OOPS! web service [10], which evaluates ontologies against a catalog of pitfalls.

2.3   Extending the Generated Documentation

WIDOCO organizes its output to be easily modified, allowing users to expand their documentation with additional narratives and diagrams. Each of the sections included in the documentation (e.g., abstract, introduction, description, cross reference, etc.) are separated in individual HTML files, which can be edited

---

[8] http://licensius.com/apidoc/index.html.

individually. If new sections or subsections are added to any existing page, all section numbers and table of contents will be updated consistently. Furthermore, WIDOCO supports Markdown,[9] which is generally easier to edit than HTML.

3   Usage and Community Adoption

WIDOCO started as a simple wizard to help non-programmers documenting their ontologies. Due to the uptake and suggestions by users, we have progressively added new functionality (e.g., supporting new types of metadata, creating diagrams, etc.) and expanded the user base. To date, WIDOCO has been used to document more than a hundred ontologies in different domains,[10] ranging from earth sciences to bio-informatics. WIDOCO has also been adopted by tools for supporting ontology engineering such as OnToology [1] and VoCol [3].

Thanks to our interactions with the community, we have developed a benchmark of vocabularies to test and validate WIDOCO.[11] The benchmark aggregates 35 real-world ontologies with different characteristics for generating documentation, such as incomplete metadata, availability in different formats, sizes or languages, unavailability of imported ontologies, etc.

WIDOCO is available in GitHub,[12] where users can download it, open issues or ask for help. WIDOCO is released under an Apache-2.0 license.[13]

4   Related Work

Many approaches have been developed to help create human readable description of ontologies. These often focus on concrete aspects of ontology documentation, including human-readable definitions (e.g., LODE [9], Parrot [12], etc.), differences between versions of ontologies (e.g., Bubastis [6]) or diagram creation (e.g., WebVowl [5]). Other efforts describe end-to-end frameworks for publishing and versioning ontologies, such as Neologism [2], VoCol [3] or OnToology [1]. To our knowledge, WIDOCO is the only approach that includes guidance for users during the documentation process, helping them to complete and enrich their metadata while customizing their final documentation.

5   Conclusions and Future Work

In this paper we have described WIDOCO, a wizard for documenting and customizing ontologies which (a) guides users through the documentation process;

---

[9] https://learn.getgrav.org/content/markdown.
[10] https://w3id.org/widoco/usage.
[11] https://w3id.org/widoco/benchmark.
[12] https://github.com/dgarijo/Widoco/.
[13] https://www.apache.org/licenses/LICENSE-2.0.

(b) helps identifying missing metadata in the ontology and (c) extends and integrates existing work for documenting ontology terms, diagram visualizations and ontology revisions. WIDOCO has been used to document more than one hundred ontologies across different domains, and has been adopted by other existing efforts like OnToology and VoCol.

WIDOCO is an ongoing effort, and we are open to suggestions proposed by the community. In fact, we have already addressed several issues raised by adopters of the tool. Our future work aims to facilitate filtering and enrichment of ontology terms to be included in the documentation with external metadata.

Acknowledgements. We would like to acknowledge support from the US National Science Foundation with grants ICER-1541029 and ICER-1440323, and from the National Institutes of Health with grant 1R01GM117097-01. We also thank Yolanda Gil for her feedback.

References

1. Alobaid, A., Garijo, D., Poveda-Villalón, M., Pérez, I.S., Corcho, O.: OnToology, a tool for collaborative development of ontologies. In: ICBO (2015)
2. Basca, C., Corlosquet, S., Cyganiak, R., Fernández, S., Sch, T.: Neologism: Easy Vocabulary Publishing (2012)
3. Halilaj, L., Petersen, N., Grangel-González, I., Lange, C., Auer, S., Coskun, G., Lohmann, S.: VoCol: an integrated environment to support version-controlled vocabulary development. In: Blomqvist, E., Ciancarini, P., Poggi, F., Vitali, F. (eds.) EKAW 2016. LNCS (LNAI), vol. 10024, pp. 303–319. Springer, Cham (2016). doi:10.1007/978-3-319-49004-5_20
4. Horridge, M., Bechhofer, S.: The OWL API: a Java API for OWL ontologies. Semant. Web **2**(1), 11–21 (2011)
5. Lohmann, S., Link, V., Marbach, E., Negru, S.: WebVOWL: web-based visualization of ontologies. In: Lambrix, P., Hyvönen, E., Blomqvist, E., Presutti, V., Qi, G., Sattler, U., Ding, Y., Ghidini, C. (eds.) EKAW 2014. LNCS, vol. 8982, pp. 154–158. Springer, Cham (2015). doi:10.1007/978-3-319-17966-7_21
6. Malone, J., Holloway, E., Adamusiak, T., Kapushesky, M., Zheng, J., Kolesnikov, N., Zhukova, A., Brazma, A., Parkinson, H.: Modeling sample variables with an experimental factor ontology. Bioinformatics **26**(8), 1112 (2010)
7. McGuinness, D., Lebo, T., Sahoo, S., Belhajjame, K., Cheney, J., Corsar, D., Garijo, D., Soiland-Reyes, S., Zednick, S., Zhao, J.: PROV-O: the PROV ontology. W3C Recommendation, W3C (2013)
8. Musen, M.A.: The protégé project: a look back and a look forward. AI Matters **1**(4), 4–12 (2015). http://doi.acm.org/10.1145/2757001.2757003
9. Peroni, S., Shotton, D., Vitali, F.: The live OWL documentation environment: a tool for the automatic generation of ontology documentation. In: ten Teije, A., Völker, J., Handschuh, S., Stuckenschmidt, H., d'Acquin, M., Nikolov, A., Aussenac-Gilles, N., Hernandez, N. (eds.) EKAW 2012. LNCS, vol. 7603, pp. 398–412. Springer, Heidelberg (2012). doi:10.1007/978-3-642-33876-2_35
10. Poveda-Villalón, M., Suárez-Figueroa, M.C., Gómez-Pérez, A.: OOPS! (OntOlogy Pitfall Scanner!): an on-line tool for ontology evaluation. Int. J. Semant. Web Inf. Syst. (IJSWIS) **10**(2), 7–34 (2014)

11. Suárez-Figueroa, M.C., Gómez-Pérez, A., Fernández-López, M.: The NeOn methodology framework: a scenario-based methodology for ontology development. Appl. Ontol. **10**(2), 107–145 (2015)
12. Tejo-Alonso, C., Berrueta, D., Polo, L., Fernández, S.: Metadata for web ontologies and rules: current practices and perspectives. In: García-Barriocanal, E., Cebeci, Z., Okur, M.C., Öztürk, A. (eds.) MTSR 2011. CCIS, vol. 240, pp. 56–67. Springer, Heidelberg (2011). doi:10.1007/978-3-642-24731-6_6

The CEDAR Workbench:
An Ontology-Assisted Environment
for Authoring Metadata that Describe
Scientific Experiments

Rafael S. Gonçalves$^{(\boxtimes)}$ ⓘ, Martin J. O'Connor,
Marcos Martínez-Romero, Attila L. Egyedi, Debra Willrett,
John Graybeal, and Mark A. Musen

Stanford Center for Biomedical Informatics Research, Stanford University,
Stanford, CA, USA
`rafael.goncalves@stanford.edu`

Abstract. The Center for Expanded Data Annotation and Retrieval (CEDAR) aims to revolutionize the way that metadata describing scientific experiments are authored. The software we have developed—the CEDAR Workbench—is a suite of Web-based tools and REST APIs that allows users to construct metadata templates, to fill in templates to generate high-quality metadata, and to share and manage these resources. The CEDAR Workbench provides a versatile, REST-based environment for authoring metadata that are enriched with terms from ontologies. The metadata are available as JSON, JSON-LD, or RDF for easy integration in scientific applications and reusability on the Web. Users can leverage our APIs for validating and submitting metadata to external repositories. The CEDAR Workbench is freely available and open-source.

Keywords: Metadata · Metadata authoring · Metadata repository · Ontologies

1 State of Metadata in Scientific Repositories

There are vast amounts of scientific data hosted in a multitude of public repositories. These repositories are either discipline-specific, such as the Gene Expression Omnibus (GEO) for functional genomics data [1], or generic, such as the Zenodo repository for any type of data [2]. Despite the different types of content, these repositories share a common need for submitted data to be accompanied with precise, machine-interpretable descriptions of what the data represent—that is, *metadata*. Consider BioSample [3], a repository of metadata about samples used in biomedical experiments, maintained by the U.S. National Center for Biotechnology Information (NCBI). The data about these biological samples are typically associated with experimental data that are submitted elsewhere (e.g., GEO). For a better chance at understanding the associated experiment, or reusing the data to replicate that experiment, these resources should be appropriately linked by using agreed-upon terms, ideally from ontologies or other controlled term sources. A variety of studies have demonstrated that this linkage and rigorous typing rarely occur [4–6]. As a consequence, metadata in public

© Springer International Publishing AG 2017
C. d'Amato et al. (Eds.): ISWC 2017, Part II, LNCS 10588, pp. 103–110, 2017.
DOI: 10.1007/978-3-319-68204-4_10

repositories are typically weak. This lack of high-quality metadata hinders advancements in science, as the scientific community has difficulties reproducing findings or using existing data for new analyses [7]. To address this problem, the biomedical community developed dozens of metadata guidelines, which researchers can use to annotate experiment results. The so-called "minimal information" metadata guidelines specify the minimum information about experimental data that are necessary to ensure that the associated experiments can be reproduced. BioSharing [8]—a curated Web-based collection of data standards, databases, and policies in the life, environmental, and biomedical sciences—serves about a hundred of these "minimal information" guidelines and formats, such as the Minimal Information About a Microarray Experiment (MIAME) guideline [9]. However, such guidelines are typically loosely-defined and lack semantic linkage. For instance, GEO requests that investigators submit their datasets together with metadata that conform to the MIAME guideline. While MIAME specifies that submitters must include information for specified fields, it does not define how these values should be specified. As a result, typical GEO field values are unstructured free text. It is difficult to make an efficient use of these metadata when performing subsequent analyses.

The poor quality of metadata in scientific repositories is partly explained by the lack of appropriate tooling for producing high-quality metadata. Metadata repositories typically require spreadsheet-based submissions and specify a variety of *ad hoc* formats. To describe even a simple metadata submission using such formats demands significant effort on the author's part. Various tools exist to ease the burden of constructing metadata formats. The ISA Tools [10] provide a desktop application that allows users to construct spreadsheet-based submissions for metadata repositories, although there is no support for ontologies. The linkedISA software [11] adds mechanisms to annotate the spreadsheet-templates with controlled terms. Rightfield [12] is an Excel plugin that allows users to embed ontology-derived values in spreadsheets, and to restrict cell values to terms from ontologies. Annotare [13] is a desktop application similar to ISA Tools, although with support for using ontology terms. These tools all rely on spreadsheet-based representations, which are limited in their expressivity and difficult to extend. There is a need for software infrastructure based on an open format that is compliant with Web standards. The FAIR data principles [14] specify desirable criteria that metadata should meet. These data principles provide desiderata for a format and associated tooling for metadata authoring, which CEDAR [15] is developing.

2   CEDAR Workbench

With the goal of drastically improving the metadata that annotate datasets in public repositories, we built the CEDAR Workbench—a set of open-source, Web-based tools for the acquisition, storage, search, and reuse of metadata templates. The CEDAR Workbench offers its users the ability to construct metadata-acquisition forms or *templates*. The metadata produced using CEDAR templates are designed to be adherent to the FAIR data principles, and to be interoperable with Linked Open Data. CEDAR metadata is retrievable in JSON, JSON-LD, and RDF formats.

The CEDAR Workbench is used for generating metadata that describe scientific experiments. Users have access to metadata and associated metadata-authoring functionality using CEDAR's Web front-end or REST services. We host a public instance of the CEDAR Workbench at http://cedar.metadatacenter.net. The software is available on GitHub (http://github.com/metadatacenter) and released under the open-source 2-Clause BSD license. The project is described in full detail at http://metadatacenter.org.

2.1 System Architecture

The CEDAR Workbench is a highly modular system, designed to allow its users to employ individual services in their applications or workflows. Figure 1 shows the CEDAR Workbench architecture. The primary goal of CEDAR is to generate high-quality metadata describing scientific data that are semantically enriched with terms from ontologies. To that end, we developed a model that serves as a common, standards-based format for describing templates, fields, and metadata [16]. For interoperability on the Web, it is crucial that all resources be represented using an open model that can be serialized to widely accepted formats such as JSON-LD or any RDF

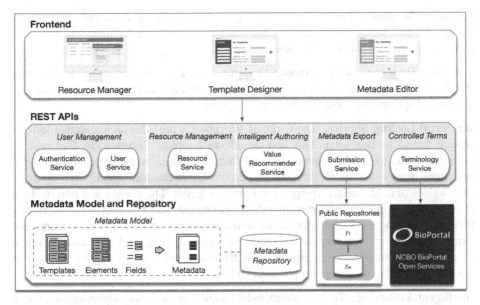

Fig. 1. Primary components of the CEDAR Workbench. Our software follows a microservice-based architecture. The system is built from a collection of loosely-couple services that provide self-contained functionality (e.g., User Service for user management). The CEDAR Workbench is composed of front-end components featuring a Resource Manager tool for managing and organizing resources into folders, a Template Designer for assembling templates, and a Metadata Editor for entering metadata. The Submission Service allows users to upload metadata to external, public repositories. The Terminology Service bridges CEDAR technology with BioPortal ontologies. All resources adhere to the CEDAR Metadata Model, and are stored in the Metadata Repository.

syntax. We used JSON Schema and JSON-LD to encode the model. The model provides mechanisms for template composition to promote the reuse of templates.[1]

The resources in the CEDAR Workbench—templates, fields, and metadata—are represented as JSON-LD documents that conform to our model. Templates and fields can be annotated with terms from ontologies [17] in the NCBO BioPortal—an online repository that serves as one of the primary platforms for hosting and sharing over 500 biomedical ontologies [18]. Because JSON-LD is a concrete syntax for RDF, all CEDAR metadata instances are RDF documents as well. All resources are stored in our Metadata Repository, which scientists can use to search for and browse templates in a faceted way.

The CEDAR Workbench microservices are implemented in Java using the Dropwizard framework (http://www.dropwizard.io), while the front-end is implemented in AngularJS (http://angularjs.org).

2.2   Main Features

The overarching objective of the CEDAR Workbench is to make it easier and faster for users to annotate datasets with metadata. We target this goal by allowing users to build modular, customized metadata templates that can be filled out to create metadata.

Resource Manager. The Resource Manager is the primary front-end component. Using this tool, users can create templates and folders, search for metadata and templates, populate templates, and share resources.

Template Designer. In the Template Designer (Fig. 2), users can assemble metadata templates from other templates or fields. There are numerous field types and template formatting options available to template designers.

BioPortal Lookup Service. The CEDAR Workbench provides an interactive lookup service linked to BioPortal. This service allows template designers to find sets of ontology terms to annotate templates and fields—that is, to add type and property assertions using ontology classes and properties. Users can also specify that the possible values of fields must correspond to ontology terms. The classes and object, data, or annotation properties for performing these annotations can be selected from terms in BioPortal ontologies. When appropriate terms to do not exist, users can create new terms and value sets dynamically at template design-time (Fig. 2). Upon creating a new term, users can map it to existing terms in BioPortal ontologies using SKOS (http://www.w3.org/TR/skos-reference) properties [19].

Intelligent Authoring. To decrease metadata authoring time, we implemented a value recommendation feature that provides context-sensitive suggestions for input field values [20]. The value recommender learns associations between data values in metadata submissions, computes suggestions based on these associations, and presents the suggestions to metadata authors. The suggestions are ranked according to their

---

[1] Further details at: https://metadatacenter.org/tools-training/outreach/cedar-template-model.

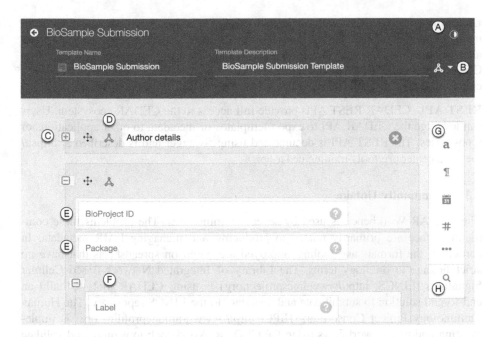

Fig. 2. Screenshot of the Template Designer loaded with a CEDAR template for a BioSample metadata submission. The annotated items in the screenshot are: (A) button to visualize the JSON Schema code corresponding to the template; (B) button to add terms from ontologies to annotate the template; (C) template element, which is collapsed and named; (D) button to add properties from ontologies to annotate the element; (E) fields that compose elements and templates; (F) element nested within an element; (G) field type options (in sight: text, paragraph, date, number, and a trigger for more options); (H) button to search for template elements to add.

applicability for each specific field. During metadata entry, users are prompted with drop-down lists and auto-complete suggestions given by the value recommender.

Metadata Editor. The Metadata Editor is designed to facilitate rapid entry of metadata. This tool generates a streamlined, form-based acquisition interface based on a metadata template definition. Filling in metadata using the Metadata Editor is made easy with suggestions provided by the value recommender. When field values are constrained to a set of ontology terms, users select a term from the generated list of possible values with minimal effort.

Validation. With better metadata quality in mind, we designed validation features to improve the output of our tools. Metadata entered through CEDAR templates are automatically validated against the corresponding template's JSON Schema model to get immediate feedback regarding structural errors (e.g., a user enters a numeric value in a field where an ontology term is expected). Additionally, metadata can be validated against some existing, external validation service (such as a REST endpoint) that is provided as a parameter to CEDAR at template design-time. For example, the NCBI BioSample Validator [3], which validates the format and content of metadata submissions to BioSample, can be used with the BioSample template shown in Fig. 2.

Collaboration. The CEDAR Workbench provides a highly-collaborative environment, where users can create groups composed of their team members. Users can share all types of resources with individual users, among groups of users, or with the entire CEDAR community. When sharing resources, users can restrict access to these with common read/write permissions.

REST API. CEDAR REST APIs provide full access to the CEDAR ecosystem. Users can leverage the CEDAR API to export templates or metadata to other applications or repositories. The REST API is documented using Swagger and is described at https://metadatacenter.org/tools-training/cedar-api.

2.3 Community Uptake

The CEDAR Workbench is used by several communities. The problems these communities face are primarily related to producing and managing FAIR metadata. In particular, the formats and tooling employed are based on spreadsheets that have no strict linkage to ontology terms. The Library of Integrated Network-Based Cellular Signatures (LINCS, http://www.lincsproject.org) is using CEDAR tools to build an end-to-end solution to submit data and metadata to the LINCS repository. The Human Immunology Project Consortium (HIPC, http://www.immuneprofiling.org) is implementing end-to-end workflows using the CEDAR Workbench to acquire and validate precisely-defined metadata entered by their users, which are then submitted to the BioSample or ImmPort repositories [21]. The Stanford Digital Repository (http://sdr.stanford.edu) in the Stanford University Libraries is testing the use of CEDAR templates for authoring metadata in several of their projects. These groups have encoded minimum information models as CEDAR templates, which they use in their submission pipelines. Note that none of these communities used ontology terms at all when authoring metadata. CEDAR helped to introduce semantics to the work that these groups carry out.

The AIRR community (http://airr-community.org) is developing standards for describing datasets acquired using sequencing technologies. The AIRR submission process involves submitting the generated metadata to the public NCBI BioSample repository. We built a submission pipeline to upload metadata to BioSample, which the AIRR community is successfully using. Based on our experience with the NCBI BioSample repository, we intend to generalize our submission infrastructure to other NCBI repositories.

These projects have succeeded in setting-up CEDAR-based metadata submission pipelines. The feedback from users in these communities is very positive—they find that working with CEDAR tools is straightforward, and that the metadata generated through CEDAR are of significantly higher quality than what they produced before. Our expectation is that progressively more communities will realize the potential that the CEDAR Workbench has for producing high-quality metadata.

3 Summary

We developed the CEDAR Workbench to improve the quality of metadata submitted to public repositories. CEDAR provides a freely-available suite of tools to build metadata templates, to fill them in with metadata, to submit the metadata to external repositories, and to store, search, and manage templates and metadata.

The novelty of our approach lies in the use of a principled, open format for the description of metadata resources, the ability to fill in metadata with guidance from intelligent authoring features, and finally, the ability to annotate templates and to restrict template field values to terms from ontologies. The CEDAR Workbench provides modular, highly-reusable components via a microservice-based architecture, allowing users to employ individual services for specific tasks, such as the BioPortal-linked Terminology Service. The metadata produced using CEDAR templates are FAIR-adherent by design, and are available in JSON, JSON-LD, and RDF formats for interoperability with Linked Open Data and Semantic Web applications.

Currently we use JSON Schema for imposing constraints on template input data. The SHACL candidate recommendation (http://www.w3.org/TR/shacl) may provide a more appropriate solution for constraining input data. However, SHACL is not yet standardized, and has limited tool support.

We are working toward allowing our users to submit metadata from CEDAR to an increasing number of external repositories. The submission pipelines we created are the first of many that will serve an increasing number of users, and help bring a semantic foundation to future metadata submission efforts.

Acknowledgements. CEDAR is supported by grant U54 AI117925 awarded by the National Institute of Allergy and Infectious Diseases through funds provided by the trans-NIH Big Data to Knowledge (BD2K) initiative (http://www.bd2k.nih.gov). NCBO is supported by the NIH Common Fund under grant U54HG004028.

References

1. Edgar, R., Domrachev, M., Lash, A.E.: Gene expression omnibus: NCBI gene expression and hybridization array data repository. Nucleic Acids Res. **30**(1), 207–210 (2002)
2. OpenAIRE and CERN: Zenodo. http://zenodo.org. Accessed 13 May 2017
3. Barrett, T., et al.: BioProject and BioSample databases at NCBI: facilitating capture and organization of metadata. Nucleic Acids Res. **40**, D57–D63 (2012)
4. Park, T.-R.: Semantic interoperability and metadata quality: an analysis of metadata item records of digital image collections. Knowl. Organ. **33**, 20–34 (2006)
5. Park, J.-R., Tosaka, Y.: Metadata quality control in digital repositories and collections: criteria, semantics, and mechanisms. Cat. Classif. Q. **48**(8), 696–715 (2010)
6. Zaveri, A., Dumontier, M.: MetaCrowd: crowdsourcing biomedical metadata quality assessment. In: Proceedings of Bio-Ontologies (2017)
7. Vasilevsky, N.A., et al.: On the reproducibility of science: unique identification of research resources in the biomedical literature. PeerJ **1**, e148 (2013)

8. McQuilton, P., et al.: BioSharing: curated and crowd-sourced metadata standards, databases and data policies in the life sciences. Database J. Biol. Databases Curation **2016** (2016). doi:10.1093/database/baw075

9. Brazma, A., et al.: Minimum information about a microarray experiment (MIAME)—toward standards for microarray data. Nat. Genet. **29**(4), 365–371 (2001)

10. Rocca-Serra, P., et al.: ISA software suite: supporting standards-compliant experimental annotation and enabling curation at the community level. Bioinformatics **26**(18), 2354–2356 (2010)

11. González-Beltrán, A., Maguire, E., Sansone, S.-A., Rocca-Serra, P.: linkedISA: semantic representation of ISA-Tab experimental metadata. BMC Bioinform. **15**, S4 (2014)

12. Wolstencroft, K., et al.: RightField: embedding ontology annotation in spreadsheets. Bioinformatics **27**(14), 2021–2022 (2011)

13. Shankar, R., et al.: Annotare—a tool for annotating high-throughput biomedical investigations and resulting data. Bioinformatics **26**(19), 2470–2471 (2010)

14. Wilkinson, M.D., et al.: The FAIR guiding principles for scientific data management and stewardship. Sci. Data **3**, 160018 (2016)

15. Musen, M.A., et al.: The center for expanded data annotation and retrieval. J. Am. Med. Inform. Assoc. **22**(6), 1148–1152 (2015)

16. O'Connor, M.J., Martínez-Romero, M., Egyedi, A.L., Willrett, D., Graybeal, J., Musen, M.A.: An open repository model for acquiring knowledge about scientific experiments. In: Blomqvist, E., Ciancarini, P., Poggi, F., Vitali, F. (eds.) EKAW 2016. LNCS, vol. 10024, pp. 762–777. Springer, Cham (2016). doi:10.1007/978-3-319-49004-5_49

17. Martínez-Romero, M., et al.: Supporting ontology-based standardization of biomedical metadata in the CEDAR workbench. In: Proceedings of International Conference on Biomedical Ontology (ICBO) (2017, in press)

18. Noy, N.F., et al.: BioPortal: ontologies and integrated data resources at the click of a mouse. Nucleic Acids Res. **37**, W170–W173 (2009)

19. Miles, A., Matthews, B., Wilson, M.: SKOS core: simple knowledge organisation for the web. In: Proceedings of International Conference on Dublin Core and Metadata Applications (2005)

20. Martínez-Romero, M., et al.: Fast and accurate metadata authoring using ontology-based recommendations. In: Proceedings of AMIA Annual Symposium (2017, in press)

21. Bhattacharya, S., et al.: ImmPort: disseminating data to the public for the future of immunology. Immunol. Res. **58**(2–3), 234–239 (2014)

WebIsALOD: Providing Hypernymy Relations Extracted from the Web as Linked Open Data

Sven Hertling[(✉)] and Heiko Paulheim[(✉)]

Data and Web Science Group, University of Mannheim, Mannheim, Germany
{sven,heiko}@informatik.uni-mannheim.de

Abstract. Hypernymy relations are an important asset in many applications, and a central ingredient to Semantic Web ontologies. The IsA database is a large collection of such hypernymy relations extracted from the Common Crawl. In this paper, we introduce WebIsALOD, a Linked Open Data release of the IsA database, containing 400M hypernymy relations, each provided with rich provenance information. As the original dataset contained more than 80% wrong, noisy extractions, we run a machine learning algorithm to assign confidence scores to the individual statements. Furthermore, 2.5M links to DBpedia and 23.7k links to the YAGO class hierarchy were created at a precision of 97%. In total, the dataset contains 5.4B triples.

Keywords: Hypernyms · Hearst patterns · Linked dataset

1 Introduction

Hypernymy relations are an important asset in many applications, and a central ingredient to Semantic Web ontologies. They can be used in various applications – for example in named entity recognition and disambiguation tools, or as background knowledge to improve the performance of data mining tasks [9]. Often the approaches rely on knowledge bases like Wikidata, DBpedia or YAGO, which are good at head entities, but lack coverage and level of detail for tail entities. While hypernymy datasets have been created, such as LHD [6], they rely on entities which are contained as instances in Wikipedia, and hence expose the same bias towards head entities [10]. To fill that gap, Seitner et al. created a large database of hypernymy relations extracted from the Web [12], the IsADB.

The main idea of the IsADB is to extract hypernymy relations from a huge and fixed web crawl called CommonCrawl[1]. The extraction method is based on 58 Hearst-like lexico-syntactic patterns which are frequent patterns to describe type relations. For example, the sentence *Still, people use Gmail and other Web services* implies the hypernymy relation between *Gmail* and *Web service*, which can be captured by the pattern *NP and other NP*.[2]

---

[1] https://commoncrawl.org.
[2] *NP* stands for *noun phrase*.

© Springer International Publishing AG 2017
C. d'Amato et al. (Eds.): ISWC 2017, Part II, LNCS 10588, pp. 111–119, 2017.
DOI: 10.1007/978-3-319-68204-4_11

In this work, we present a Linked Data endpoint to the IsADB, following the best practices for Linked Open Data [11]. The dataset provides access via HTTP URIs and a SPARQL endpoint, and it is interlinked to DBpedia [7] and YAGO [13]. Furthermore, it provides rich provenance information for each hypernymy relation, which capture

- the pre modifier, post modifier, and head noun for both the hypernym and the hyponym. In the example above, *service* is the head noun of the hypernym, and *Web* is its pre-modifier;
- the set of pattern ids (PIDs) matching the hypernymy relation;
- the set of sentences which was used for the extraction;
- the set of pay-level domains (PLDs) on which the sentences appear; and
- the absolute number of hyponym-hypernym pair occurrences (frequency).

That information is also used to apply machine learning for computing confidence scores for all relations. Hence, the provided dataset also allows for quality-based filtering on the provided information.

The rest of this paper is structured as follows. Section 2 analyses the original (non-LOD) IsADB dataset. Section 3 introduces the model used for providing WebIsALOD. Section 4 describes the interlinking to DBpedia and YAGO, and Sect. 5 describes the method applied for computing confidence scores. Section 6 provides a first content profile of the resulting dataset.

2   The Original IsADB Dataset

The original dataset contains 400,533,808 relations, 120,992,255 unique hyponyms, and 107,691,822 unique hypernyms collected with 58 different patterns. To assess the quality of the dataset i.e. how many relations are actually valid, a crowdsourced survey via Amazon Mechanical Turk (MTurk)[3] was conducted.

The participants of the survey were presented sentences in the form *hyponym is a hypernym*, constructed from random pairs of hyponyms and hypernyms from the database. For each of those sentences, they could answer "Yes", "Uncertain", or "No".[4]

In order to gain stable results, each sentence was rated by nine different workers. The final label ("true", "false", "uncertain") was assigned by majority voting.

For estimating the fraction of correct axioms, 500 randomly sampled hypernymy relations from the original dataset were presented to the participants. Additionally, we estimated the quality of the dataset at different lower thresholds of two key figures: (1) the amount of patterns which are used for the extraction and (2) the amount of pay-level domains. Both can be understood as (weak)

---

[3] https://www.mturk.com.

[4] We restricted the workers to have a 95% approval rate and a minimum of 100 approved HITs (human intelligence tasks), following the recommendations by [3,5], and restricted their location to the US to attract a large fraction of native speakers.

indicators for the correctness of a relation. A dataset with the given threshold t is defined by

$$dataset(t) = \{r \in R \mid \mid r.pld \mid > t \wedge \mid r.pid \mid > t\}$$

Seven thresholds were chosen for evaluation: $0, 1, 2, 3, 5, 10, 20$, where 0 corresponds to the full dataset. Figure 1 shows the amount of relations in the corresponding set as well as the percentage of the majority vote. It shows that there is a steep quality increase when stepping from a threshold 0 to a threshold of 1, while there is only moderate gain for lower thresholds of 10 and 20. On the other hand, increasing the threshold drastically decreases the number of relations from 400M to little more than 10k. When utilizing all the data (i.e., imposing a threshold of 0), 7.4% of 400,533,808 relations are correct. Extrapolating these values results in 29,639,501 true relations.

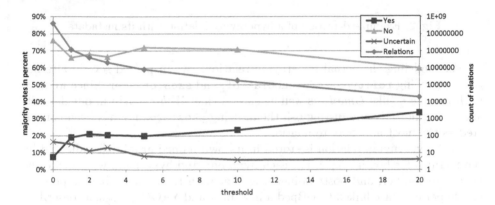

Fig. 1. Quality ratings and overall count of relations for different thresholds of pattern and PLD spread.

These figures show simply applying a lower threshold on $|r.pld|$ and $|r.pid|$ would remove a large amount of noise, it also reduces the dataset size drastically, limiting its utility. Hence, we chose a different approach: we train a machine learning model to assign confidence scores to the relations. This model is applied to the full dataset, allowing users of the dataset to impose a quality threshold and trade off coverage and accuracy indivdually given their task at hand.

3 Dataset Modeling and Provision

A major goal of providing the WebIsALOD dataset is to not only provide access to the hypernymy relations as such, but also to rich metadata for those relations.

Figure 2 shows an excerpt of the hypernymy relation used above (*Web service* is a hypernym of *GMail*), together with a subset of its metadata.

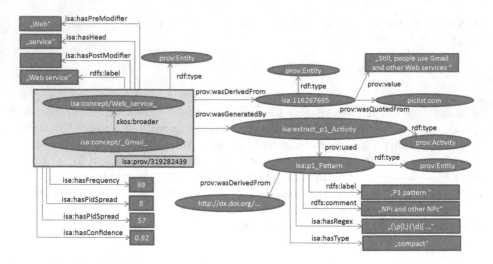

Fig. 2. Example depiction of a hypernymy relation with its metadata

For modeling the actual hypernymy relations, we inspected several alternatives, including `rdf:type`, `rdfs:subClassOf`, and `skos:broader`. Since we have both instances (like *Gmail*) as well as classes (like *Web service*) in our dataset, and we cannot trivially distinguish them, using `skos:broader` has been considered as the most appropriate relation.

Each hypernymy relation is stored in its own named graph [2], indicated by the rectangular box in Fig. 2. For each hyponym and hypernym, we provide the head, premodifier, and postmodifier, together with the actual label. Hyponyms and hypernyms are linked to DBpedia instances and YAGO classes, as described in Sect. 4. Statements about the provenance of the hypernymy relation are then made about that named graph, including

- the originating sentence from which the relation was extracted, and the Web page on which the sentence was found,
- the pattern which was used to extract the relation, together with a description, a regular expression formulation, and a link to the literature source in which the pattern was proposed, and
- statistical metadata, such as the global frequency, the PID and PLD spread ($|r.pid|$ and $|r.pld|$), and the confidence score computed (see Sect. 5).

The data is provided as Linked Open Data, using dereferencable URIs, as a dump for download, as well as through a SPARQL endpoint.[5] The latter also allows the user for filtering by a specific confidence threshold in order to control the quality of the returned information, and trade off coverage against precision per use case. The source code as well as the templates and results of the crowdsourced survey is available at github.[6]

---

[5] http://webisa.webdatacommons.org/.
[6] https://github.com/sven-h/webisalod.

4 Linking to DBpedia and YAGO

In order to follow the Linked Data best practices and provide interlinks to other datasets, we chose two different datasets as link targets: DBpedia for instances, as it is the de facto interlinking hub of the Linked Open Data cloud [11], and YAGO for classes, as it provides one of the richest general purpose class hierarchies.

For performing the interlinking of instances, three approaches were tried:

- Using plain string matching on lower cased strings
- Using the DBpedia surface forms [1]
- Using DBpedia Spotlight [8] on the original sentences

To evaluate the different strategies, we created another Amazon MTurk survey, where we asked the annotators to provide Wikipedia pages and categories for both the hyponym and the hypernym of a relation. The Wikipedia pages were then translated to DBpedia URIs as a gold standard to test the interlinking of instances. The plain string matching clearly outperformed the other two with an F1 score of 0.97 (precision 0.97, recall 0.97, compared to an F1 score of 0.59 for surface forms and 0.54 for DBpedia Spotlight). Hence, we used this approach to create in total 2,593,181 instance interlinks.

Since the results were satisfying for instance matching, and neither the surface forms approach nor DBpedia Spotlight can produce links to YAGO classes (or Wikipedia categories), we also use this approach to create links to YAGO classes. Since those are derived from Wikipedia categories, we use the MTurk gold standard for evaluation. We achieve an F1 score of 0.72 (precision 0.93, recall 0.59), and create a total of 23,771 links to YAGO classes.

5 Computing Confidence Scores

For computing the confidence scores, we trained a machine learning classifier on the labels ("correct", "incorrect", "uncertain") assigned in the initial Amazon MTurk evaluation on dataset(1). In total, the dataset contains 95 correct and 330 incorrect instances; the 75 instances with a majority of "uncertain" or an equal share of "correct" and "incorrect" were discarded. By classifying the relations as correct or incorrect, the classifier's confidence score for the label *correct* can be used as a confidence score for the relation itself.

We used six different classifiers and performed parameter tuning in 10-fold cross validation:

- Decision Trees optimized by minimum leaf size and maximum depth of tree (1–20)
- Gradient Boosted Trees optimized by maximum depth (1,5,9,12,16,20) and number of trees (20,40,60,80,100)
- RandomForest optimized by number of trees (1–100 with 10 steps) and minimum leaf size (1–10)
- Naive Bayes (without specific parameter tuning)

- SVM with Radial Base Function kernel, and C and gamma tuned according to [4]
- Neural Network with one hidden layer in two different sizes $F/2 + 2, sqrt(F)$, and two hidden layers of $F/2$ and $sqrt(F)$, where F denotes the number of features

Table 1 lists the results of all machine learning approaches together with three different feature sets:

- FS1 consists of frequency, amount of patterns, amount of pay-level domains for the relation itself as well as for the relation without pre and post modifier, and a binary value for each pattern indicating if it is extracting the relation or not.
- FS2 adds features derived from the hypernym and hyponym itself, i.e., amount of tokens, average token length, and the existence of a pre and a post modifier.
- FS3 adds features derived from the originating sentences, in particular the token distance between the hyponym and the hypernym. We use the minimum, maximum, and average across all sentences, as well as the number of sentences a pattern spans.

We used the gold standard crowd sources for dataset(1) (i.e., the dataset with a minimum threshold of 1 for $|r.pid|$ and $|r.pld|$) for training, and tested it both in cross validation and on the gold standard for dataset(0) (i.e., the full dataset). Table 1 shows the results for the area under the ROC curve (AUC). We chose an optimization towards ROC AUC because this is an indicator of the quality of confidence scores, and hence the selection criterion for a classification algorithm. Based on those results, we chose the RandomForest classifier utilizing the full set of features trained on the gold standard for dataset(1) to create confidence scores for the full dataset.[7]

Table 1. Results of different classifiers and feature sets using 10-fold cross validation on the gold standard of dataset(1) (AUC 1), and evaluated on the gold standard of dataset(0) (AUC 0)

ML approach	FS 1		FS 1+2		FS 1+2+3	
	AUC 1	AUC 0	AUC 1	AUC 0	AUC 1	AUC 0
Decision Tree	0.7572	0.6063	0.7801	0.6544	0.7547	0.6742
GBT	0.8032	0.6490	0.8176	0.6783	0.8086	0.6954
RandomForest	0.8287	0.7020	**0.8446**	0.6427	0.8377	**0.7246**
Naive Bayes	0.5782	0.5080	0.5782	0.5080	0.6338	0.5183
SVM	0.8194	0.6444	0.8410	0.6994	0.8411	0.6863
Neural Net	0.7783	0.6080	0.7753	0.6684	0.7757	0.5988

---

[7] The reason why we did not use the gold standard of the full dataset for training is its imbalance (cf. Sect. 2), i.e., the number of positive examples (only 37 out of 500) is too low for learning a meaningful model.

6   Analysis of Resulting Dataset

The final resulting dataset consists of 400.5M hypernymy relations, together with a confidence score and metadata, as well as 2,593,181 instance links to DBpedia and 23,771 class links to YAGO. All in all, the dataset consists of 5.4B triples.

In order to obtain a first content profile, we analyzed the fraction of instances which are linked to and typed in DBpedia, and analyzed the type hierarchy in DBpedia to estimate the distribution of those entities. That resulting distribution is depicted in Fig. 3.

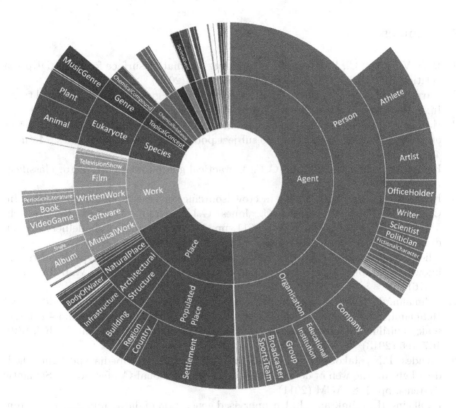

Fig. 3. Type breakdown of the instances linked to DBpedia

We can observe that about half of the information is about persons and organizations. Places, works, and species make up for 18%, 12%, and 5%, respectively, while the rest is a mix of other types.

7   Conclusion and Outlook

In this paper, we have introduced a new dataset of hypernymy relations extracted from the Web, provided as Linked Data with provenance information and interlinks to DBpedia and YAGO.

The dataset has room for improvement in various directions. Examples of ongoing and future work include the learning of better scoring models and the induction of a type hierarchy, where the latter also includes the subtask of automatically distinguishing *subclass of* and *instance of* relations.

Another crucial issue is the identification of homonyms in the dataset. Given the two assertions *Bauhaus is a goth band* and *Bauhaus is a German school*, it is clear that the subjects are two disjoint instances, while *Bauhaus is a goth band* and *Bauhaus is a post-punk band* are not. Identifying such homonyms, e.g., by exploiting upper ontologies, is an ongoing effort.

References

1. Bryl, V., Bizer, C., Paulheim, H.: Gathering alternative surface forms for DBpedia entities. In: NLP-DBPEDIA@ISWC, pp. 13–24 (2015)
2. Carroll, J.J., Bizer, C., Hayes, P., Stickler, P.: Named graphs, provenance and trust. In: International Conference on World Wide Web, pp. 613–622. ACM (2005)
3. Hauser, D.J., Schwarz, N.: Attentive Turkers: MTurk participants perform better on online attention checks than do subject pool participants. Behav. Res. Methods **48**(1), 400–407 (2016)
4. Hsu, C.W., Chang, C.C., Lin, C.J.: A practical guide to support vector classification (2003)
5. Kazai, G.: In search of quality in crowdsourcing for search engine evaluation. In: Clough, P., Foley, C., Gurrin, C., Jones, G.J.F., Kraaij, W., Lee, H., Mudoch, V. (eds.) ECIR 2011. LNCS, vol. 6611, pp. 165–176. Springer, Heidelberg (2011). doi:10.1007/978-3-642-20161-5_17
6. Kliegr, T., Zamazal, O.: LHD 2.0: a text mining approach to typing entities in knowledge graphs. Web Semant.: Sci. Serv. Agents World Wide Web **39**, 47–61 (2016)
7. Lehmann, J., Isele, R., Jakob, M., Jentzsch, A., Kontokostas, D., Mendes, P.N., Hellmann, S., Morsey, M., van Kleef, P., Auer, S., Bizer, C.: DBpedia - a large-scale, multilingual knowledge base extracted from wikipedia. Semant. Web J. **6**(2), 167–195 (2013)
8. Mendes, P.N., Jakob, M., García-Silva, A., Bizer, C.: DBpedia spotlight: shedding light on the web of documents. In: 7th International Conference on Semantic Systems, pp. 1–8. ACM (2011)
9. Paulheim, H., Fümkranz, J.: Unsupervised generation of data mining features from linked open data. In: 2nd International Conference on Web Intelligence, Mining and Semantics, p. 31. ACM (2012)
10. Ringler, D., Paulheim, H.: One knowledge graph to rule them all? Analyzing the differences between DBpedia, Yago, Wikidata & Co. In: 40th German Conference on Artificial Intelligence (2017)
11. Schmachtenberg, M., Bizer, C., Paulheim, H.: Adoption of the linked data best practices in different topical domains. In: Mika, P., Tudorache, T., Bernstein, A., Welty, C., Knoblock, C., Vrandečić, D., Groth, P., Noy, N., Janowicz, K., Goble, C. (eds.) ISWC 2014. LNCS, vol. 8796, pp. 245–260. Springer, Cham (2014). doi:10.1007/978-3-319-11964-9_16

12. Seitner, J., Bizer, C., Eckert, K., Faralli, S., Meusel, R., Paulheim, H., Ponzetto, S.: A large database of hypernymy relations extracted from the web. In: Language Resources and Evaluation Conference, Portoroz, Slovenia (2016)
13. Suchanek, F.M., Kasneci, G., Weikum, G.: YAGO: a core of semantic knowledge unifying wordnet and wikipedia. In: 16th International Conference on World Wide Web, pp. 697–706 (2007)

Ontology-Based Data Access to Slegge

Dag Hovland[1], Roman Kontchakov[2]($\boxtimes$), Martin G. Skjæveland[1],
Arild Waaler[1], and M. Zakharyaschev[2]

[1] Department of Informatics, University of Oslo, Oslo, Norway
{hovland,martige,arild}@ifi.uio.no
[2] Department of Computer Science and Information Systems,
Birkbeck, University of London, London, UK
{roman,michael}@dcs.bbk.ac.uk

Abstract. We report on our experience in ontology-based data access to the Slegge database at Statoil and share the resources employed in this use case: end-user information needs (in natural language), their translations into SPARQL, the Subsurface Exploration Ontology, the schema of the Slegge database with integrity constraints, and the mappings connecting the ontology and the schema.

1 Introduction

We present the resources developed for ontology-based data access (OBDA) to the Slegge database at the international oil and gas company Statoil using the OBDA system Optique platform [7]. In the OBDA paradigm based on query rewriting [9], the data remains stored in the original DBMS, while user queries are formulated in terms of an OWL 2 QL ontology designed specifically for the end-users—rather than directly over the database, which presupposes detailed knowledge of the database schema and requires an assistance of an IT expert. The OBDA system makes use of the mappings that relate the ontology vocabulary to the database schema to transform the ontology-mediated queries into standard SQL queries, which are then executed by the DBMS.

OBDA has been an active research area since the mid 2000s, with OBDA systems used in a variety of projects within both academia and industry, e.g., [1–4,6,11,13]. However, full details of an industrial use case have never been made publicly available. The main aim of this paper is to fill this gap by publishing the following complete set of OBDA specifications for the Slegge use case:

- the Subsurface Exploration OWL Ontology specifically designed to capture the terms used by the geologists at Statoil when querying subsurface exploration data;
- the typical information needs (in natural language) and respective SPARQL queries;
- the SQL schema of the Slegge database;
- the R2RML mappings connecting the ontology vocabulary to the schema;
- statistics on the Slegge data (the data is private and cannot be made public).

© Springer International Publishing AG 2017
C. d'Amato et al. (Eds.): ISWC 2017, Part II, LNCS 10588, pp. 120–129, 2017.
DOI: 10.1007/978-3-319-68204-4_12

The Slegge schema demonstrates the intrinsic complexity of industrial databases, which is reflected in the mappings that encode the semantics of the data using, in particular, multiple joins. The large body of queries are collected from domain experts at Statoil, totalling 73 natural language information needs and 96 corresponding SPARQL queries. The ontology captures the vocabulary of the SPARQL queries and describes parts of the petroleum subsurface exploration domain represented in Slegge. Since the resources we publish include all the intricacies and peculiarities of a large industrial setup, we believe they will be useful to the developers of OBDA technologies and to the wider semantic technologies and information systems communities. In particular, the resources could be used for benchmarking query rewriting and optimising engines and for development of methods and tools for ontology and mapping construction and analysis. The Slegge resources and an extended version of this paper are available at http://purl.org/slegge under the CC Attribution 4.0 International Public License.

The main feature distinguishing the Slegge resources from other available OBDA specifications is that Slegge straddles the long distance between two industrial artefacts. Our starting points were the Statoil geologists' information needs (Sect. 3) and the large industrial database with hundreds of tables (Sect. 4). We designed the ontology capturing the vocabulary of the needs in the context of oil and gas exploration (Sect. 3) and the complex mappings bridging the substantial conceptual gap between the ontology and the data (Sect. 5). Other publicly available OBDA specifications for databases with real data include FishMark [2], IMDb OBDA [11] and NPD FactPages [14]. Their ontologies, however, are quite similar to their database schemas, and so the mappings are almost direct (with very few joins). The NPD FactPages comes with simple queries generic for the oil and gas domain, while FishMark and IMDb OBDA only contain queries stemming from existing SQL queries or invented by the authors. The Texas benchmark [12] and the OBDA extensions of the Berlin SPARQL Benchmark (BSBM) [12] and LUBM [11] are all examples with synthetic data based on existing non-OBDA benchmarks, where the mappings are also almost direct.

2 Data Gathering at Statoil

The task of the exploration department at Statoil is to find exploitable deposits of oil and gas. Geoscientists model the subsurface geography by classifying rock layers according to multiple stratigraphic hierarchies using information from various sources. This model largely determines the location of new wellbores for direct exploration and possible exploitation of the hydrocarbon resource. Since wellbore drilling is a major expense, the quality of the model, which depends on the availability of and the ease of accessing the relevant data, becomes a crucial factor for efficiency of the exploration process.

We illustrate the current workflow with a typical domain expert *information need*, which is an informal natural language description of a user question:

(001) In my area of interest, return the wellbores penetrating a given chronostratigraphic unit X and return information about the lithostratigraphy and the hydrocarbon content in the wellbore interval that penetrates X. Also return information about other wellbore intervals with hydrocarbon content in the wellbores with hydrocarbon in X.

To find answers, the geologist will use pre-defined SQL queries covering parts of the information need and then integrate their results, often with primitive data management tools such as spreadsheets. This process is onerous and error-prone: for example, the comparison of depths in a wellbore can easily go wrong as there are multiple units, reference points and types of depth measurements. An alternative solution would be to ask the IT department to construct a custom SQL query. However, employing IT personnel for the task generally takes days (or even weeks) because there are very few people with the rare combination of intimate knowledge of the geological domain *and* database structure required to translate the information needs into database queries.

The OBDA paradigm [9] offers a third alternative, where an *ontology* describes the geologists' vocabulary. For example, given an ontology in the W3C standard language OWL 2 QL containing classes such as Wellbore, StratigraphicUnit, MeasuredDepth, and properties such as name, hasUnit, hasWellboreInterval, valueInStandardUnit, the geologist can recast information need **(001)** more formally in the following way:

(001/02′) Give me the names of the available wellbores with the chronostratigraphic units and the top depths of the intervals they were found in; the depths should be in the standard units and from standard reference points (metres along the drill string). Also, return all lithostratigraphic units from depths overlapping the depths at which the chronostratigraphic units were found.

And, following the structure of the ontology, the geologist can easily formalise such a query with, e.g., the visual query interface OptiqueVQS [15] of the Optique platform:

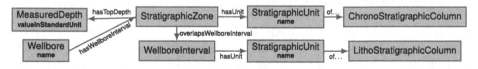

The formalised query **(001/02′)** is automatically translated into a SPARQL query, and an OBDA tool such as Ontop [5,11] will use the *mappings* to 'rewrite' the *ontology-mediated query* into an SQL query over the database, optimise and execute it, returning

?wellbore	?chronostrat_unit	?lithostrat_unit	?top_md_m
"NO 1/2-1"	"Jurassic"	"Fisk"	"1234.5"

So, in the OBDA paradigm, the geologist does not need to know the structure of the database to create new queries. And, instead of supporting geologists directly (by translating their information needs into SQL), the IT expert has an easier task of constructing and maintaining mappings that populate the ontology classes and properties with data from the database. Thus, mappings explicate the IT expert's knowledge of the database. The reader can find the rewritten SQL query in the full paper and appreciate the knowledge required from the IT expert to produce an SQL query over Slegge by hand.

3   From Information Needs to Ontology and SPARQL Queries

The starting point of the Slegge use case was a list of 73 **information needs** collected from end-users at Statoil over a period of four years. It turned out that 39 information needs are beyond the scope of the Slegge database: they concern user interface configuration, data entry processes or require data unavailable in Slegge. The remaining 34 information needs provided the basic *competency questions* for creating the Subsurface Exploration Ontology, which gives the vocabulary (ontology classes and properties) for translating the information needs into SPARQL queries. We publish all 73 information needs as they can be useful for the research in natural language processing and for the future work on other data sources at Statoil.

The **Subsurface Exploration Ontology** describes parts of the petroleum subsurface exploration domain and captures the classes and properties from the user information needs. Class `Wellbore` represents a path drilled through the Earth crust. Rock samples (class `Core`) are normally extracted from the wellbore during drilling. Smaller samples (`CoreSample`) are drilled out of the core and used for direct visual and experimental observations. A `WellboreInterval` is a depth interval along a wellbore, defined by its top and bottom depths. It has two natural subclasses: `Reservoir` and `StratigraphicZone`.

Numerous measurements taken from wellbores are modelled by the taxonomy under the class `Measurement`, with subclasses such as `TrueVerticalDepth`, `Permeability` and `FormationPressure`. Each measurement provides a value in the *standard* and in the *original* units because translation from a variety of units in the database to the standard ones may mask suspicious values, e.g., depth 9999 ft. Since wellbores are not necessarily vertical, there are two types of depth for relating points along them: `MeasuredDepth` refers to the length along the wellbore or drill string, while `TrueVerticalDepth` is the length of the normal to the reference surface, usually the mean sea level.

To represent geographical objects and connect Slegge to other Statoil data sources, we imported class `SpatialObject` (with its subclasses) from GeoSPARQL 1.1.

The resulting Subsurface Exploration Ontology has 71 classes, 46 object properties and 34 data properties. The depth of the class hierarchy (without `SpatialObject`) is 5, and the depth of the property hierarchy is 4. The existential depth, which measures the length of chains of labelled nulls (caused by existential quantifiers in the ontology), is 5: for instance, every `Permeability` must be related by the inverse of property `hasPermeability` to some `CoreSample`, which in turn is related by the inverse of `hasCoreSample` to a `Core`; every `Core` is `extractedFrom` some `WellboreInterval` linked by the inverse of `hasWellboreInterval` to a `Wellbore` and then to a `Well` via the inverse of `hasWellbore`. Note, however, that the structure of the mappings and database integrity constraints make sure that wherever there is a `Permeability`, the data itself contains the required chain of length 5 as above, and so the corresponding labelled nulls in the chase are not needed. This fact substantially simplifies query rewriting.

We incorporated some background knowledge in the ontology even if it required constructs unavailable in OWL 2 QL such as functionality of properties and local range constraints of the form `DrillingOperation` $\sqsubseteq$ $\forall$`hasActivityPart.WellboreDrilling`. Fortunately, the structure of the mappings and database imply most of the non-OWL 2 QL axioms, while the remaining ones are not relevant for the mappings. The smallest standard description logic capable of representing the ontology is Horn-$\mathcal{ALCHIQ}(\mathcal{D})$.

Each of the 34 information needs in the scope of Slegge was recast in SPARQL. The resulting 96 **SPARQL queries** (some information needs are vague and can be interpreted in SPARQL in different ways) were constructed manually, either by hand or using OptiqueVQS. These queries have an average of 13 triple patterns, ranging from 3 to 30; 16 queries use OPTIONAL and 3 use FILTER NOT EXISTS. Most queries capture only part of the corresponding information need, often because some data is not available in Slegge. There is also a considerable overlap among the SPARQL queries because the information needs overlap too; these mainly include different features of wellbores and their surroundings. Many information needs, e.g., (**001**), contain the expression 'for my area of interest', which could be interpreted as 'restrict the query to the geographical area I am interested in'. There is no general translation of such needs into SPARQL, but many queries such as (**001/02′**) in the query catalogue use concrete geographical areas in the North Sea identified by coordinates (in the example in Sect. 2, we omitted the coordinates for simplicity).

4   Slegge Database

Slegge is an Oracle database with about 700 GB of data. Its schema was initially constructed in the late 1990s on the basis of Epicentre v2.2. The Epicentre data model had been developed by the Petrotechnical Open Standards Consortium (POSC) since the early 1990s, and its latest v3.0 is maintained by Energistics [10]. It defines the object-oriented logical database model and its standard projection to the physical model in an Oracle database. The main features of Epicentre and its implementation in Slegge are:

- extensive inheritance hierarchies are projected by two methods: (a) a table per subtype and (b) a single table for all subtypes with a discriminating column;

– denormalisation: many columns are duplicated to avoid joins when querying;
– lack of foreign keys: many relationships involve multiple tables for subtypes, and so foreign keys would have to be *conditional*, which is not supported by the DBMS.

Entities well and wellbore are subtypes of facility. Abstract entities such as facility have no database tables, but each of the non-abstract entities is represented by a table: e.g., WELL for entity well. These tables contain columns for the normal attributes of the entity: WELLBORE has a COMPLETION_DATE column for the date when the wellbore was available for service. Tables for subtypes 'inherit' columns from supertypes: e.g., tables for all sorts of facilities inherit column R_EXISTENCE_KD_NM to specify whether the facility is actual, planned, etc. Instances of entities (objects) are identified by their unique IDs, which are surrogate primary keys in the tables: e.g., column WELL_S in table WELL. On the other hand, the (user-friendly) well identifiers (attribute identifier of the supertype entity facility) are represented in column WELL_ID.

Epicentre also follows an alternative approach to hierarchies, where all subtypes of an entity are projected to the same table, and a *discriminating column* specifies the object's subtype: e.g., the four subtypes of stratigraphic_marker are mapped to the same table, STRAT_MRK, with column ENTITY_TYPE_NM containing the subtype name.

For composite attributes (such as quantities with units of measure), Epicentre uses *properties*, which, like entities, have instances and are arranged in an extensive hierarchy. Properties are normally projected to tables. However, many attributes in Slegge are *denormalised*: e.g., table WELL_SURFACE_PT for the well_surface_point entity has columns WATER_DEPTH and WATER_DEPTH_U to store the value and the unit of measure of the water depth property pty_water_depth. So, values are stored directly in the 'entity' table rather than in the property table P_WATER_DEPTH, which is empty in the database. Only 20 (out of 543) property tables are non-empty in Slegge: e.g., coordinates of wells' surface points are stored in the table P_LOCATION_2D for property pty_location_2d.

Reference entities collect standard values: e.g., ref_unit_of_measure is projected to table R_UOM with information about 974 units of measure (others are much smaller). The primary key in such a table is often referenced by foreign keys of entity and property tables: e.g., WATER_DEPTH_U is one of 814 columns referencing ACRONYM in R_UOM.

In the Epicentre data model, relationships are in fact attributes of entities: both end-points of a relationship have an attribute—one for the relationship, the other for its inverse. *One-to-many relationships* are normally projected as columns in the tables. For example, column WELL_S in WELLBORE specifies the identifier of the well containing this wellbore. In this exceptional case, the database contains a *foreign key*: WELL_S of WELLBORE references WELL_S of WELL. However, most of such foreign keys are missing because the subtypes are distributed over tables. For example, the relationship between activity and facility is represented by column FACILITY_S in ACTIVITY. Since facilities are covered in a number of tables, there is no foreign key. Instead, ACTIVITY has another column, FACILITY_T, to specify the facility subtype it refers to ('WELLBORE' or 'WELL'), and so the pair FACILITY_T/_S identifies the referenced table and the row in it.

Denormalised attributes are quite common in Slegge—they reduce the number of joins in queries: e.g., table WELLBORE, along with the reference to the primary key WELL_S of WELL, contains a column duplicating WELL_ID from WELL.

Many-to-many relationships in Epicentre use association entities, which are then projected to tables: e.g., topological relationships such as 'inside' between instances of topological_object (and its subtypes field, core and facility) are modelled by the topological_relationship association entity in the table TOPOLOGICAL_REL.

The Slegge Oracle database has 6 schemas. The SLEGGE_EPI schema is a dated implementation of the Epicentre data model and consists of 1545 tables with 19 719 columns: 1141 tables are empty because large portions of the data model are not used by the tools; 221 tables contain only 1–100 rows (mostly for reference entities), but 9 tables have more than a million rows each. Schemas SLEGGE_SNP, MDS_COORD and SIS_CATALOG are much smaller (21, 14 and 1 table, respectively) and related to other applications; ENTITLED has two tables modelling user privileges. The main SLEGGE schema integrates the other five schemas and defines 1722 views to their tables. However, most of them (1632) contain no joins and no WHERE clauses—they simply rename tables and columns; two views additionally limit access in accordance with the user privileges from ENTITLED. The remaining 88 views vary from two-table joins to 31-way joins with additional WHERE and GROUP BY clauses; many also contain ORDER BY clauses, which suggests their primary use for reporting and user interfaces. In addition, SLEGGE contains 102 tables for various purposes. Finally, there are five *materialised views*, two of which are joins of 12 and 15 tables, respectively, while the other three use calls to stored procedures (with more queries and even Java code inside).

5   Mapping Ontology to Slegge Database

One of the main challenges in the project was to map the classes and properties of the ontology to database objects, which required detailed knowledge of both components. Unfortunately, the Slegge implementation does not fully comply with any version of Epicentre, and the documentation on Slegge has become either unavailable or hard to obtain at Statoil. The lack of integrity constraints (foreign keys)[1] and abundance of denormalisation made any initial attempts at automated schema analysis inefficient. The sheer size of the database (1727 views and 1685 tables) only exacerbated the problem. Our main source of information about the schema was the 2996 queries found in the configuration files of

---

[1] Even though SLEGGE_EPI has 3112 foreign keys, 2727 of them refer to just 18 reference tables such as R_UOM; in fact, most of the remaining 385 foreign keys refer to 'single-purpose' reference tables such as R_OBJECT_NTRS listing topological relations.

ProSource, a proprietary tool developed in-house and the *de facto* way of accessing Slegge. It turned out, however, that a significant number of these queries, in particular, the most useful ones for mappings were quite large (up to 91 joins). The distribution of the number of tables and views per query is illustrated below:

# tables/views	1	2	3	4–10	11–20	21–30	31–40	41–50	51–92
# ProSource queries	1801	545	327	228	51	18	7	10	9

Such large queries are necessary to provide the geologist users with all the information about complex domain objects such as wellbores and their litho- and chronostratigraphic columns. However, the ontology 'decomposes' such objects into a number of classes linked by object properties, with data properties providing 'scalar' attributes such as names, measured values, etc. The user will then be able, in a SPARQL query, to assemble triple patterns featuring classes and properties into required complex objects.

We used the query catalogue and ontology vocabulary to identify relevant ProSource queries. These were carefully analysed and split into subqueries that match classes and properties of the ontology. The integrity constraints (both declared in the database and implied by the Epicentre model) were used to validate and simplify joins in the queries.

As a result, we obtained an R2RML specification with 62 logical tables and 180 mapping assertions (combinations of subject, predicate and object maps); the ontology-saturated mappings have 324 assertions. The logical tables vary from base tables to 6-way joins with up to 5 additional filter expression in the WHERE clause:

# tables/views	1	2	3	4	5	6		# filters	0	1	2	3	4	5
# mappings	32	8	13	2	2	5		# mappings	10	24	15	8	3	2

Also, two SQL queries have GROUP BY and 8 contain stored procedure calls.

For testing the OBDA specification outside Statoil, we identified a small fragment of the database schema that supports the mappings. It consists of tables, views and materialised views occurring in the mappings and/or relevant integrity constraints (with only necessary columns). The result consists of schemas SLEGGE and SLEGGE_EPI and contains 66 tables with 379 columns, 55 views, 5 materialised views and 4 stored procedures (functions). It also has 47 foreign keys, with only *three* referring to entity tables.

6   Conclusions and Future Work

The application of OBDA technologies at Statoil dramatically reduces the amount of time for information gathering by allowing the geologists to express their needs as ontology-mediated queries and efficiently execute them over the database [8]. This paper presents the *complete OBDA specification* of the Statoil use case and includes the geologists' queries, the Subsurface Exploration Ontology, the schema of the Slegge database, and the mappings between the ontology and the database. We are planning to develop a synthetic data generator for the OBDA specification, where the main challenge will be the faithful modelling of implicit domain constraints.

Our work on the mappings revealed a lack of tools to support the following tasks (taking account of the database integrity constraints):

– checking whether a mapping assertion is implied by the ontology and other mapping assertions (e.g., as the property `:overlapsWellboreInterval` is symmetric, the mapping assertions obtained by swapping the object and subject are redundant);
– checking whether a mapping assertion for a property generates all the triples of the assertions for the subclasses of its domain/range; a negative answer (even though is not an error) may indicate incorrect modelling if similar SQL queries are used.

Routine tasks such as checking whether IRI templates of classes/properties match could also be automated: for example, a Protégé plugin could list all IRI templates for the currently selected class or property (with ontology inferences taken into account). Developing tool support for such reasoning tasks is an important direction of future work.

Acknowledgements. This work was supported by EU IP Optique FP7-318338 and UK EPSRC project iTract EP/M012670. We are grateful to Statoil for allowing publication of the resources, and to everyone's help, especially Toralv Nordtveit and Hallstein Lie.

References

1. Antonioli, N., Castanò, F., Coletta, S., Grossi, S., Lembo, D., Lenzerini, M., Poggi, A., Virardi, E., Castracane, P.: Ontology-based data management for the Italian public debt. In: Proceedings of FOIS 2014, FAIA, vol. 267, pp. 372–385. IOS Press (2014)
2. Bail, S., Alkiviadous, S., Parsia, B., Workman, D., van Harmelen, M., Goncalves, R.S., Garilao, C.: Fishmark: a linked data application benchmark. In: Proceedings of SSWS+HPCSW (2012)
3. Brandt, S., Güzel Kalaycı, E., Kontchakov, R., Ryzhikov, V., Xiao, G., Zakharyaschev, M.: Ontology-based data access with a Horn fragment of metric temporal logic. In: AAAI, pp. 1070–1076. AAAI Press (2017)
4. Calvanese, D., De Giacomo, G., Lembo, D., Lenzerini, M., Poggi, A., Rodriguez-Muro, M., Rosati, R., Ruzzi, M., Savo, D.F.: The MASTRO system for ontology-based data access. Semant. Web **2**(1), 43–53 (2011)
5. Calvanese, D., Cogrel, B., Komla-Ebri, S., Kontchakov, R., Lanti, D., Rezk, M., Rodriguez-Muro, M., Xiao, G.: Ontop: answering SPARQL queries over relational databases. Semant. Web **8**(3), 471–487 (2017)
6. Calvanese, D., Liuzzo, P., Mosca, A., Remesal, J., Rezk, M., Rull, G.: Ontology-based data integration in EPNet: production and distribution of food during the Roman Empire. Eng. Appl. Artif. Intell. **51**, 212–229 (2016)

7. Giese, M., Soylu, A., Vega-Gorgojo, G., Waaler, A., Haase, P., Jiménez-Ruiz, E., Lanti, D., Rezk, M., Xiao, G., Özçep, Ö.L., Rosati, R.: Optique: zooming in on big data. IEEE Comput. **48**(3), 60–67 (2015)

8. Kharlamov, E., et al.: Ontology based access to exploration data at Statoil. In: Arenas, M., et al. (eds.) ISWC 2015. LNCS, vol. 9367, pp. 93–112. Springer, Cham (2015). doi:10.1007/978-3-319-25010-6_6

9. Poggi, A., Lembo, D., Calvanese, D., De Giacomo, G., Lenzerini, M., Rosati, R.: Linking data to ontologies. J. Data Semant. **10**, 133–173 (2008)

10. POSC Epicentre v3.0. http://w3.energistics.org/archive/Epicentre/Epicentre_v3.0

11. Rodríguez-Muro, M., Kontchakov, R., Zakharyaschev, M.: Ontology-based data access: *ontop* of databases. In: Alani, H., et al. (eds.) ISWC 2013. LNCS, vol. 8218, pp. 558–573. Springer, Heidelberg (2013). doi:10.1007/978-3-642-41335-3_35

12. Sequeda, J.F., Arenas, M., Miranker, D.P.: OBDA: query rewriting or materialization? In practice, both! In: Mika, P., et al. (eds.) ISWC 2014. LNCS, vol. 8796, pp. 535–551. Springer, Cham (2014). doi:10.1007/978-3-319-11964-9_34

13. Sequeda, J.F., Miranker, D.P.: A pay-as-you-go methodology for ontology-based data access. IEEE Internet Comput. **21**(2), 92–96 (2017)

14. Skjæveland, M.G., Lian, E.H., Horrocks, I.: Publishing the Norwegian Petroleum Directorate's FactPages as semantic web data. In: Alani, H., et al. (eds.) ISWC 2013. LNCS, vol. 8219, pp. 162–177. Springer, Heidelberg (2013). doi:10.1007/978-3-642-41338-4_11

15. Soylu, A., Giese, M., Jiménez-Ruiz, E., Vega-Gorgojo, G., Horrocks, I.: Experiencing OptiqueVQS: a multi-paradigm and ontology-based visual query system for end users. Univ. Access Inf. Soc. **15**(1), 129–152 (2016)

BiOnIC: A Catalog of User Interactions with Biomedical Ontologies

Maulik R. Kamdar[(✉)], Simon Walk, Tania Tudorache, and Mark A. Musen

Stanford Center for Biomedical Informatics Research,
Stanford University, Stanford, USA
{maulikrk,walk,tudorache,musen}@stanford.edu

Abstract. BiOnIC is a catalog of aggregated statistics of user clicks, queries, and reuse counts for access to over 200 biomedical ontologies. BiOnIC also provides anonymized sequences of classes accessed by users over a period of four years. To generate the statistics, we processed the access logs of BioPortal, a large open biomedical ontology repository. We publish the BiOnIC data using DCAT and SKOS metadata standards. The BiOnIC catalog has a wide range of applicability, which we demonstrate through its use in three different types of applications. To our knowledge, this type of interaction data stemming from a real-world, large-scale application has not been published before. We expect that the catalog will become an important resource for researchers and developers in the Semantic Web community by providing novel insights into how ontologies are explored, queried and reused. The BiOnIC catalog may ultimately assist in the more informed development of intelligent user interfaces for semantic resources through interface customization, prediction of user browsing and querying behavior, and ontology summarization. The BiOnIC catalog is available at: http://onto-apps.stanford. edu/bionic.

Keywords: Ontology exploration · Reuse · User behavior · Log analysis

1 Understanding User Behavior by Analyzing Access Logs

Over the past decade, ontologies have proliferated in the biomedical domain. Bio-Portal[1]—an open online repository of biomedical ontologies [7]—hosts over 550 ontologies to date. Biomedical researchers use these ontologies to drive a wide-range of biomedical applications [2]. In the first half of 2016 alone, more than 215,000 unique IP addresses submitted 2.52 million requests to access ontologies hosted on BioPortal. Biomedical ontologies often contain thousands of entities, are highly specialized, and they are very expensive to develop. To better serve the ontology development and consumer communities, it is crucial for Semantic

---

[1] http://bioportal.bioontology.org/.

© Springer International Publishing AG 2017
C. d'Amato et al. (Eds.): ISWC 2017, Part II, LNCS 10588, pp. 130–138, 2017.
DOI: 10.1007/978-3-319-68204-4_13

Web researchers to gain insights into how these ontologies are explored, queried and reused.

Users may access the content of BioPortal ontologies in two ways: *(i)* the BioPortal Web interface (further referred to as *WebUI*) to explore the ontologies, and *(ii)* the REST API[2] to query the ontology content programmatically. All access to BioPortal, either via the WebUI or through the API, is captured in the BioPortal Apache access logs, which record the request URL, the time of request, and the IP address of the requestor. We have previously used the information stored in these access logs to identify categories of users accessing ontologies in BioPortal [6], to study ontology reuse [4], and to visualize ontology exploration and query patterns [5].

In this resource paper, we present BiOnIC–the Catalog of User Interactions with Biomedical Ontologies. The catalog contains two types of datasets— *(i)* aggregated statistics of user clicks, queries and reuse counts for all classes in BioPortal ontologies, and *(ii)* anonymized sequences of user interactions with BioPortal ontologies. The catalog currently contains the anonymized data for access to 255 BioPortal ontologies collected between 2013–2016. The BiOnIC catalog is freely available under the Creative Commons (CC) BY-NC-SA license at: http://onto-apps.stanford.edu/bionic.

In the following sections, we describe the vocabulary schema (Sect. 3), the VisIOn Web application for visualizing the catalog datasets (Sect. 4), and three applications that rely on the BiOnIC catalog, as well as further application types that would benefit from the BiOnIC catalog (Sect. 6).

2 BiOnIC Datasets Generation

Filtering the BioPortal Logs. We collected all WebUI and API calls from the BioPortal Apache access logs submitted between January 2013–June 2016. To obtain a list of actual user actions, we filtered these logs (e.g., removing robot calls, removing invalid calls) using the filtering methods we developed previously [6]. After the filtering, we obtained 5.4 million WebUI clicks and 67.2 million API queries. For every single request we extracted a valid BioPortal ontology identifier and a class IRI.

Filtering the Ontologies. We identified a set of 255 BioPortal ontologies from these logs whose classes were reused in other ontologies. To extract statistics about classes in each of these ontologies (e.g., reuse and sibling count), we pre-processed the ontologies using the methods described in Kamdar et al. [4].

Computing Class Counts. For each class in each ontology, we aggregated the total and the unique number of users that clicked or queried the class using the WebUI or the API, respectively. We also computed the number of ontologies that reuse each class, and other structural characteristics, such as, the number

---

[2] http://data.bioontology.org/documentation.

of sibling classes, direct super-classes, direct sub-classes, and maximum depth of the class in the class hierarchy.

Computing the Sequence of User Actions. For each ontology, we generated ordered sequences of classes accessed by each user, as well as their associated relative timestamps. While it is possible that a group of users may have used the same IP address to access a set of classes in an ontology, or one user may explore or query classes present in two or more BioPortal ontologies simultaneously, publishing a unique sequence dataset for each ontology facilitates a simple organizational structure for these sequences.

Anonymizing the User Data. We converted all logged IP addresses to unique user identifiers, consisting of a randomized string and an integer, encoded with the SHA-224 hashing algorithm [3]. We also converted all absolute timestamps to a value relative to the start timestamp, when the user visited BioPortal for the first time ever.

3   BiOnIC Schema

To define the BiOnIC RDF dataset schema (shown in Fig. 1), we used SKOS, the Data Catalog vocabulary (DCAT), and the Provenance Ontology (PROV-O). BiOnIC contains two types of datasets: (1) Class Statistics Datasets, and (2) User Interaction Sequences Datasets. Each dataset contains data for a specific BioPortal ontology.

Class Statistics Datasets. The `bionic:StatDataset` class represents datasets that publish the aggregated statistics for each ontology class. The `bionic:ClassInfo` captures the structural characteristics of the class (e.g., number of subclasses, siblings, depth). The `bionic:ReuseCount` represents the number of ontologies that reuse a specific ontology class and the type of reuse (reuse by IRI or reuse by CUI [4]). The `bionic:RequestCount` represents the total and unique counts of clicks and queries for each ontology class. For additional content, these RDF datasets can be queried in conjunction with the ontologies and ontology mappings in BioPortal [7].

User Interaction Sequences Datasets. The `bionic:SeqDataset` class represents datasets of user interactions sequences for a particular ontology for both the BioPortal WebUI or the BioPortal API (indicated via the `bionic:accessType` property). The anonymized user identifiers are represented as `prov:Agent` instances. We decided to use `prov:Agent` over `prov:Person`, since the underlying IP addresses may indicate an individual user or an organization. A sequence of user interactions—captured as an instance of `bionic:Sequence`—is represented as a list of `bionic:SeqEntity` instances linked via the `bionic:nextEntity` properties.

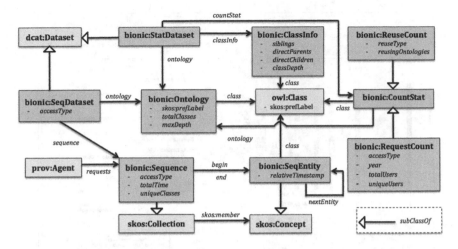

Fig. 1. BiOnIC Schema. BiOnIC facilitates the publishing of two different types of datasets for each ontology in the catalog: *(i)* Class Statistics Datasets, which capture the total number of users that explored or queried a particular class, the total number of reusing ontologies, and other class characteristics, and *(ii)* User Interaction Sequences Datasets, which capture interaction sequences extracted from BioPortal access logs.

A BiOnIC dataset is associated with one ontology in the BioPortal repository. Users who want to use BiOnIC to perform cross-ontology research (e.g., set of ontologies browsed together, sequence of classes in different ontologies) can easily reconcile these datasets using the `prov:Agent` instances and the `bionic:relativeTimestamp` attributes of the sequence entities. The BiOnIC RDF datasets can be deployed to a SPARQL endpoint, and queries can be formulated in federation with the BioPortal SPARQL endpoint.[3] Example queries include: *(i) How many agents click on the subclasses after exploring the parent class in Gene Ontology?*, or *(ii) What is the average time spent browsing the Gene Ontology in the BioPortal WebUI?*.

4   VisIOn Web Application

We developed an interactive Web application, VisIOn (<u>Vis</u>ualizing <u>On</u>tology <u>I</u>nteractions), to help users explore the two types of datasets (class statistics and user interaction sequences) available in the BiOnIC catalog. VisIOn can visualize a dataset in 4 different perspectives: *(i)* scatter plot, *(ii)* volcano plot, *(iii)* word cloud, and *(iv)* PolygOnto visualizations [5]. The scatter plot perspective allows the user to select the features to display on the X- and Y-axes, and then visualizes the aggregate statistics along with the structural features of the classes (Fig. 2).

The volcano plot perspective is a special kind of scatter plot that visualizes the statistical significance of changes in large datasets. We execute a Fisher's

---

[3] http://sparql.bioontology.org/.

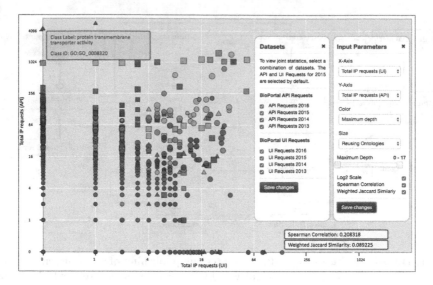

Fig. 2. VisIOn Web Application. An example scatter plot perspective that visualizes the total number of API requests against the WebUI requests for the Gene Ontology [1] between 2013–2016. The user can interactively select the different statistics for visualization, and also use structural features to change the node shape, color and size.

exact test by keeping either the time period or the access mode constant. To correct for multiple hypothesis testing, we use FDR-adjusted (False Discovery Rate) p-values and odds ratios. The Log-10 p-values are plotted against the Log-2 transformed odds ratios for the volcano plot, creating a volcano-shaped scatter plot. The volcano plot helps a user determine if a particular class in a selected ontology is significantly accessed through a particular access mode (e.g., API vs WebUI) or during a particular time period (e.g., 2014 vs 2015). For example, we found that *protein transmembrane transporter activity* and other related classes in the Gene Ontology were significantly accessed during 2015 (Log-10 p-value ≈ −7, Log-2 odds ratio ≈ −4), compared to 2016.

The word cloud perspective visualizes the labels (`skos:prefLabel`) for the classes that are significantly accessed over different periods of time. The size of these labels is determined from the odd ratios computed from the Fisher's exact test. Finally, in the PolygOnto perspective (Fig. 3), we visualize the ontology as a graphical polygon shape, and we visualize the different sequences as smaller blue-colored polygons overlaid on the ontology polygon (red polygon). The height of the polygon represents the number of hierarchical layers in the ontology, whereas the width represents the number of classes in each layer. We developed the method to generate the PolygOnto visualization for an ontology and its sequence datasets in our prior work [5].

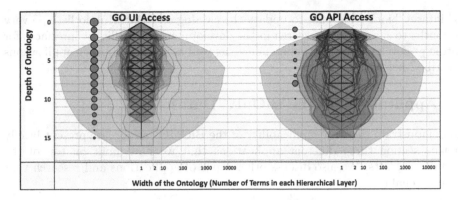

Fig. 3. PolygOnto Visualization. This example PolygOnto visualization displays the user interactions with the Gene Ontology [1] using through the BioPortal WebUI and the API. The underlying red polygon depicts the class hierarchy, whereas each smaller blue polygon represents the set of ontology classes accessed. The width represents the number of classes at a given depth in the hierarchy. Lower levels of the ontological hierarchy are rarely explored or queried. (Color figure online)

5 Dataset Characteristics and Availability

BiOnIC publishes the aggregate class statistics and interaction sequences for 255 biomedical ontologies and 515,456 total users. Table 1 lists the summary statistics (maximum, median, standard deviation) for the user-level features (total and unique entities in a sequence, total time of interaction) and ontology-level features (% of classes accessed, number of unique users) for the two modes of accessing BioPortal (WebUI and API).

The BiOnIC vocabulary, the RDF and the Tab Separated Values (TSV) files for the datasets can be downloaded from: http://onto-apps.stanford.edu/bionic. The VisIOn Web application is publicly available at: http://onto-apps.stanford. edu/vision. The BiOnIC datasets are also listed at DataHub https://datahub.

Table 1. Characteristics of the BiOnIC datasets

Feature	WebUI			API		
	Max	Median	Std. dev.	Max	Median	Std. dev.
Total time of interaction (sec.)	88,644,234	4,738	16,168,783	89,816,694	5	7,087,630
Total sequence classes	217,938	3	576	14,062,502	13	42,051
Unique sequence classes	52,813	3	153	299,391	2	1,456
% of classes accessed	100	22	26	100	18	26
Unique users	202,163	185	14,888	55,339	153	4,019

io/dataset/bionic. We plan to update the catalog and DataHub.io listing every 6 months to support the research in the development of intelligent interfaces for ontology development and maintenance, as well as for use in other applications described below.

6   Applications of the BiOnIC Datasets

To demonstrate the wide applicability of the BiOnIC catalog, we present briefly in this section three different applications that we have built on top of the BiOnIC datasets. We also discuss other types of applications and research that BiOnIC enables.

6.1   Application 1: Characterizing User Behaviors

BioPortal is a very important resource for the biomedical community. Millions of users have accessed it to drive a wide range of biomedical applications. However, we did not have any insights into how different types of users are accessing BioPortal features. Thus, we used the BiOnIC sequence datasets consisting of both the WebUI and API requests to model the browsing behavior of BioPortal users using memoryless Markov chains [6]. We represented the user behavior as a vector, and we clustered these vectors using k-means. We were able to categorize BioPortal users into seven distinct categories (e.g., class explorers, search users). We will use these results to customize the BioPortal user interface to better suit the navigation patterns of the users.

6.2   Application 2: Identifying Exploration and Querying Patterns in Ontologies

Ontology reuse is an important guideline in developing ontologies. We investigated if classes that are more heavily accessed through the BioPortal WebUI and API inform the reuse of these classes in other ontologies. For this study, we used the BiOnIC statistics on user clicks, queries and reuse counts for each class in every ontology. We did not find a significant Spearman correlation between class access and reuse.

We also investigated if user browsing behaviors through the BioPortal WebUI and the API correlate with each other. For this reason, we developed the PolygOnto visualization [5] (Fig. 3) that exploits the class hierarchy to reveal regions in an ontology where users tend to explore and query more. Classes are arranged in different layers based on the maximum depth from the root class in the ontology. The height of a polygon is indicative of the number of layers, and the width at each layer is proportional to the number of classes in that layer. The underlying red polygon depicts the ontological hierarchy. The smaller blue polygons represent the set of ontology classes accessed by a user. We observe two types of exploration patterns: *(i) Triangles:* 1 parent → 2 child classes, and *(ii) Inverted Triangles:* 1 child → 2 parent classes. We also observe that classes in the lower levels of the class hierarchy are rarely explored or queried by users.

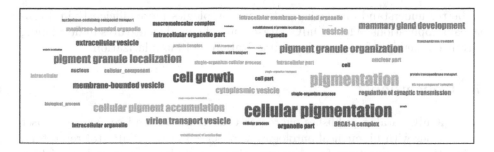

Fig. 4. Word Cloud Perspective. Gene Ontology classes significantly accessed using the BioPortal API in 2015, when compared to 2016.

6.3 Application 3: Comparing BioPortal Access Modes and Temporal Influences

Understanding how users access different parts of an ontology in BioPortal (through WebUI or API) can reveal trends into the evolution of an ontology. We use Fisher's exact test over the BiOnIC aggregative statistics, and multiple hypotheses testing, to investigate if users access certain ontology classes significantly more when compared between different access modes and different time periods. The VisIOn Web application (see Sect. 4) provides fascinating insights in the influence of access modes and time on information retrieval in ontologies. For example, as seen in the word cloud perspective of VisIOn (Fig. 4), more users queried the Gene Ontology using the BioPortal API for classes related to *pigmentation* in 2015, when compared to 2016. Fig. 2 shows that certain classes (e.g., *protein transmembrane transporter activity*) are requested multiple times using the BioPortal API, but are never requested using the BioPortal WebUI. Moreover, by observing the VisIOn word cloud and the volcano plot perspectives, we can observe the rise of queries for certain classes related to *Zika virus* and *Ebolavirus* in several disease ontologies. These discrepancies may be due to temporal influences or other reasons, which can be ascertained by domain experts.

6.4 Applications and Areas of Research Enabled by BiOnIC

The BiOnIC catalog can enable further applications and areas of research. For example, our study to categorize user browsing behaviors can be extended to incorporate the structural features of the ontology classes. The insights gathered from such a study will support the development of personalized user interfaces for ontology navigation, which will take into account the user type and the predictions of the next class that a user is likely to access. These insights may be generalizable to other ontology repositories that feature similar interfaces for user browsing. Ontology summarization and modularization are active research areas that aim to reduce the size and complexity of large ontologies to enable users to better understand ontologies and to use ontologies more efficiently in downstream applications. The BiOnIC datasets may be used as features in developing advanced methods for ontology summarization and modularization.

7   Conclusion

The BiOnIC catalog publishes aggregate class statistics and sequences of user interactions with biomedical ontologies as observed in the BioPortal repository. Using the best practices for anonymization, vocabulary reuse and publishing Linked Data, we made these datasets available as RDF files. We also presented the VisIOn Web-based visualization application that offers different perspectives of these datasets to biomedical researchers, practitioners and ontology developers. We showcase three applications that are built on top of the BiOnIC catalog to demonstrate how this resource will be valuable to ontology developers, repository maintainers and domain users. To the best of our knowledge, this is the first attempt to publish user interactions data from a widely-used semantic application. Semantic Web researchers can analyze these datasets to gain more insights into the interaction and behavior of users when browsing, querying and reusing ontologies. We envision, that the analysis of the BiOnIC datasets will spur the development of a variety of novel applications, such as, intelligent and intuitive interfaces for ontology browsing and editing.

Acknowledgments. This work is supported in part by grants U54-HG004028 and GM086587 from the US National Institutes of Health.

References

1. Ashburner, M., et al.: Gene Ontology: tool for the unification of biology. Nat. Genet. **25**(1), 25–29 (2000). doi:10.1038/75556
2. Bodenreider, O.: Biomedical ontologies in action: role in knowledge management, data integration and decision support. Yearb. Med. Inf., 67–79 (2008). https://imia.schattauer.de/en/contents/archive/issue/2256/manuscript/9821.html
3. Housley, R.: A 224-bit one-way hash function: SHA-224 (2004)
4. Kamdar, M.R., et al.: A systematic analysis of term reuse and term overlap across biomedical ontologies. Semant. Web **8**(6), 853–871 (2017)
5. Kamdar, M.R., et al.: Analyzing user interactions with biomedical ontologies: a visual perspective. J. Web Semant. (2017, under review). https://goo.gl/qmQBLE
6. Walk, S., et al.: How users explore ontologies on the web: a study of NCBO's bioportal usage logs. In: Proceedings of the 26th International Conference on World Wide Web, WWW 2017, pp. 775–784 (2017)
7. Whetzel, P.L., et al.: BioPortal: enhanced functionality via new web services from the national center for biomedical ontology to access and use ontologies in software applications. Nucleic Acids Res. **39**(suppl 2), W541–W545 (2011)

Neural Embeddings for Populated Geonames Locations

Mayank Kejriwal[✉] and Pedro Szekely

Information Sciences Institute, Marina del Rey, USA
{kejriwal,pszekely}@isi.edu

Abstract. The application of neural embedding algorithms (based on architectures like skip-grams) to large knowledge bases like Wikipedia and the Google News Corpus has tremendously benefited multiple communities in applications as diverse as sentiment analysis, named entity recognition and text classification. In this paper, we present a similar resource for geospatial applications. We systematically construct a weighted network that spans all populated places in Geonames. Using a network embedding algorithm that was recently found to achieve excellent results and is based on the skip-gram model, we embed each populated place into a 100-dimensional vector space, in a similar vein as the GloVe embeddings released for Wikipedia. We demonstrate potential applications of this dataset resource, which we release under a public license.

Keywords: Geonames · Geospatial applications · DeepWalk · Neural embeddings · Skip-gram · Word2vec · Deep learning

Resource Type. Datasets generated using novel methods/algorithms.
Github. https://github.com/mayankkejriwal/Geonames-embeddings
Figshare/DOI. https://doi.org/10.6084/m9.figshare.5248120
License. MIT License

1 Introduction

In recent years, embedding architectures based on neural networks (i.e. skip-grams and continuous bag of words) and matrix optimization have been successfully applied to a variety of large natural language datasets [7,8]. Once released publicly, 'word embeddings' on common corpora like Wikipedia and the Google News Corpus have found widespread use in many independent applications, especially in Natural Language Processing (NLP) [3].

In the Semantic Web, RDF is the prevalent data model for publishing facts as triples. Similar to Wikipedia in the NLP community, some RDF datasets, such as DBpedia and Geonames [1,12], cover large domains and are useful for a variety of distant supervision applications [4]. For example, Geonames, which is a large, comprehensive knowledge base of geographical locations, both populated and unpopulated, and at different administrative levels (e.g., city, country), is useful both in information extraction and entity linking. With the advent of high-performance graph embedding and network embedding algorithms [9], there is an opportunity to use these algorithms to embed useful knowledge bases into a vector space. For example, the RDF2Vec system was used to embed nodes in Wikidata and DBpedia; these embeddings were subsequently used in node classification problems and were also independently released [10]. The general method in RDF2Vec is to first convert the knowledge graph into an unweighted network by ignoring all property label information, such that nodes are URIs (literals are ignored). An embedding algorithm designed for networks, for which there are several candidates in the literature [9,10], is then used on this unweighted network.

While RDF2Vec and other algorithms like it have been shown to work well for cross-domain data with rich contexts, their application to domain-specific, and more specifically, geolocation datasets has not been shown. There are two problems with a straightforward embedding approach, along the lines of what was described in the previous paragraph. First, not all nodes in Geonames are equally important. Many applications are concerned with extracting locations (e.g., from Twitter) where people reside. This class of locations is special enough that Geonames has dedicated a special 'feature code' to distinguish between populated and unpopulated geolocations. A second, more serious, problem is that the literals in Geonames are extremely useful, and should not be ignored, as in RDF2Vec. Latitudes and longitudes are available in Geonames, and can be used for tasks such as visualization and spatial indexing. Since latitudes and longitudes are real-valued and have specific geolocation semantics, simply using them as nodes (similar to URI nodes) is also problematic. Hypothetically, such a network would have two places that lie on opposite sides of the globe (but share the latitude) separated by a path of 2 edges and 1 node (the shared latitude). Clearly, we have to use the latitude *and* longitude both during network construction, as well as during network embedding, for meaningful (i.e. in the sense of preserving spatial proximity in the vector space) *contexts* to be used as inputs in the neural embedding algorithm.

In this paper, we present a methodology for constructing a *directed, weighted, almost weakly connected graph* where the nodes are populated locations and the edge weight between two nodes (if the edge exists) approximates the *geodesic distance* between the two nodes. We embed the nodes into a unit hypersphere in a latent space such that a simple dot product similarity approximates the spatial proximity between the nodes (Fig. 1). We train the embeddings by adapting an unweighted network embedding algorithm, DeepWalk, that utilizes the skip-gram neural architecture and has yielded excellent performance in recent years. Embeddings are independently trained for latent spaces with 100-dimensions, and all embeddings are publicly released under an open license. To maximize utility, we serialize our files in an exchangeable, rather than software-dependent, format (JSON lines). Our vectors can be used without any knowledge of embedding algorithms and software packages. We illustrate at least two applications for which these vectors may be employed.

Fig. 1. An illustration of model results given a collective query of three cities (in red); the result (the town of Regan; name not shown on map) returned by the embedding model is the black pin. The embeddings reflect spatial proximity and can be used as feature vectors for the corresponding location entities in a machine learning pipeline. (Color figure online)

Table 1. Datasets and resources released in this work.

Dataset	Description
Weighted directed network	Represented as adjacency list (described in Sect. 2)
Random walk corpus	Set of random walks on which weighted DeepWalk is executed (described in Sect. 3)
Embeddings	split into multiple JSON lines files to facilitate easy access and download (described in Sect. 3)
Samples	for easy viewing in browser

Motivations. The primary purpose for neural embeddings (on graph data) is *automatic context-based* construction of *feature vectors* in a dense *latent* space. These feature vectors can then be used in a variety of tasks, especially those concerning distant supervision [4], usually in combination with external data. In Sect. 4, we briefly mention at least two such applications, including toponym resolution and anomaly detection [2,4]. More generally, any application that seeks to use Geonames via distant supervision, and there are several such applications in the literature, can potentially avail of our dataset for improved machine learning performance (through feature enrichment). It is also possible to use the method and constructed graph in this paper for embedding 'higher' order geolocations like states and countries, which are not amenable to simple 'coordinate' embeddings in a geographical space, as they are not describable as points at any reasonable granularity. Finally, although we do not explore it herein, the embeddings can be adapted for spatial reasoning tasks using only efficient dot product computations in the latent vector space. We argue that all of these are good motivations for formally publishing the datasets as citeable resources for public use. Table 1 enumerates the datasets being released with this paper. All resources are publicly published in Github under a friendly license (MIT). We expect to keep improving, adding to, and maintaining, the embeddings in the near future.

2 Constructing Weighted Geonames Graph

A principled approach to embeddings requires a principled approach to graph construction. For reasons explained earlier in the introduction, a naive embedding of the Geonames graph (i.e. not taking latitude-longitude information into account, or taking them into account only trivially) has several associated problems. We propose a novel method for constructing a weighted, *almost* weakly connected Geonames graph from the raw Geonames knowledge base. The 4.4 million nodes in this graph comprise the set of geolocations in the Geonames knowledge base with an ID and that are identified by the following Geonames *feature codes*: ['PPL', 'PPLA', 'PPLA2', 'PPLA3', 'PPLA4', 'PPLC', 'PPLCH', 'PPLF', 'PPLG', 'PPLH', 'PPLL', 'PPLQ', 'PPLR', 'PPLS', 'PPLW', 'PPLX', 'STLMT']. Each of these feature codes is fully documented on the following Geonames page[1]; for example, PPL stands for populated place and is described in Geonames as 'a city, town, village, or other agglomeration of buildings where people live and work'.

The next step in the construction concerns the edges and also the edge weights. For the graph to be spatially meaningful, we calculate edge weights using the following principle: given that a directed edge $e = (u, v)$ between two nodes u and v exists, the weight $w(e)$ of e is given by the *geodesic distance*[2] between u and v.

There is a well-known formula, called the *haversine equation*, in the geospatial and spherical trigonometry literature for calculating such a great-circle distance between two locations, using only the latitudes and longitudes of the locations [11]. We state the formula as follows:

$$a = sin^2(\Delta\phi/2) + cos\phi_1.\phi_2.sin^2(\Delta\lambda/2) \tag{1}$$

$$c = 2.atan2(\sqrt{a}, \sqrt{(1-a)}) \tag{2}$$

$$dist = R.c \tag{3}$$

where ϕ is latitude, λ is longitude, R is earth's radius (mean radius = 6,371 km), *dist* is the requested distance (in units of R), and all angles are in radians.

An efficiency concern immediately arises if we attempt to construct the complete graph with 4.4 million × 4.4 million ≈19 trillion edges, and call a function calculating *dist* trillions of times. For the purposes of the subsequent neural

---

[1] http://www.geonames.org/export/codes.html.

[2] This is the shortest ('as-the-crow-flies') distance between the locations on the physical (i.e. curved) surface of the planet.

embedding, we devised a reasonable, much sparser approximation as follows. First, we compiled two sorted lists of locations, where one list is sorted according to latitude and one list, according to longitude. We slide a window of size 50 over each of these sorted lists, and construct a weighted directed edge between the first entity and all other entities in this window, if an edge doesn't already exist. Furthermore, to ensure that all embeddings represent meaningful and relevant locations, we perform an extra round of pruning by checking the *population* of each of the two locations incident on the edge, and only keeping those edges where the populations of both edges are non-zero (precluding the inclusion of towns or cities that do not *currently* exist). This results in a graph with 357,550 nodes[3], each of which has a non-zero population and also has a latitude-longitude annotation.

The reason why we construct a directed, not undirected, network is to ensure that random walks (described subsequently) do not oscillate back and forth. That is, a random walk initiated from a given node will always be forced to move in a north-south or east-west direction at each step of the walk.

The final graph G_W is stored as a weighted adjacency list, and comprises of 357,550 nodes and 8,997,845 edges. There are three important advantages that the construction above confers, in addition to preventing localized random walk oscillations. First, it yields an *almost weakly connected*[4] graph because of the sliding window methodology and a large window size of 50. Second, the graph is almost regular: neither the in-degree nor out-degree of a node varies by much and tends to be well below 50 (the original window size) because of the outsize presence of nodes with population 0. Third, we ensure that the weights play a meaningful role in determining the latent space embedding, as we next describe.

3 Latent Space Embedding of Weighted Graph

One of the early (though not the first) successful algorithms to use neural networks for latent space embeddings was word2vec [7]. Word2vec can be trained using two different neural models (and both models admit a range of sub-configurations), namely, continuous bag of words (CBOW) and skip-gram. The latter has emerged as the more powerful model, especially with negative sampling. The model takes as input a set of sequences (typically, of words) and embeds each item in the sequence in a d-dimensional vector space, with d specified as a model hyperparameter. Trained on large corpora like Wikipedia, skip-gram word2vec was found to yield remarkably intuitive results, especially in role analogy tasks e.g., *vec(king) − vec(man) + vec(woman)* was found to be close to the vector representation for *queen* [7].

Because of the success of the basic model, originally conceived only for natural language sentence sequences, researchers were quick to apply it to graphs.

---

[3] This is less than 10% of the almost weakly connected graph originally constructed from the raw Geonames knowledge base (described in the first paragraph).

[4] The graph is not *guaranteed* to be weakly connected because of the zero-population pruning.

The DeepWalk embedding model is one example of this approach [9]. Given an unweighted network, DeepWalk initiates a set of truncated random walks from each node. Since each random walk is a sequence, it is analogous to a sentence in natural language. The union of all sets of random walks is akin to a corpus of sequences, and each element in each sequence corresponds to a node. Thus, the result of running DeepWalk on a network (whether directed or undirected) is a *node embedding* in the skip-gram latent space.

3.1   Weighted DeepWalk

In its original formulation, DeepWalk was designed for unweighted networks. Namely, for each node, a set of p k-step random walks were initiated, k and p both being constants. That is, every neighbor of node n had equal probability of being the next step in a random walk initiated from n. Each random walk sequence, being like a sentence in natural language, is input to the skip-gram word2vec neural model either in batch or incremental mode.

In contrast, since we would like to ensure that spatially proximate nodes in our weighted network are over-sampled when doing a random walk (thus all edges and neighbors should *not* be equal), we sample the steps according to the *local edge probability distribution*, which may not be uniform any longer due to the weights. We derive a valid probability distribution over the neighbors of node n as follows. For a node m that is a neighbor of n, let the weight of the edge (n, m) be denoted by w. We compute a new *dampened weight* $w' = max(1.0/ln(w), e)$ where ln is the natural log. We $l1$-normalize (divide by the sum) the dampened weight distribution to achieve a valid probability distribution. Note that all probabilities in the distribution are guaranteed to be non-zero due to the soft lower bound.

More generally, the dampened weight formula is designed with two principles in mind: (1) it is inversely proportional to the dampened distance, ensuring that sampling during the random walks is not overwhelmed by only the closest locations; (2) it prevents *underflow* numerical computations both by setting a lower bound and through the natural log (we always divide by a number that grows much slower than linearly). Because of the soft lower bound and the almost-weak connectivity, we also increase the chances that a random walk starting from a random node, if executed long enough, will eventually reach 'the other side of the planet'. This last property is important statistically, as it (stochastically) ensures broad coverage.

Although the distributions are not necessarily uniform, the sampling process for each random walk is Markovian, similar to ordinary random walks. That is, the history of each walk does not factor into the sampling of the next node from a given node. We set p to 5 and k to 10. Other parameters can also be tried using our original data files; in the context of an actual application, the parameter values will differ depending on application performance on a held-out validation dataset. However, as the case study in Fig. 1 illustrates, even with such minimal sampling, spatial proximity is maintained in the vector space. Furthermore, because the sampling rate is low, the process of generating the random walk corpora is extremely efficient, and could be accomplished in memory on a serial machine. Once a corpus of random walks has been sampled, we embed all nodes into a latent 100-dimensional vector space using skip-gram. Each vector is l2-normalized and lies on the unit-radius 100-dimensional hypersphere. We serialize the output in JSON lines, such that each JSON is a simple key-value pair, where the key represents a node in the graph, and the value is a 100-dimensional real-valued vector. Rather than use the Geonames ID for representing each key, we compose a mnemonic representation of the form {human-readable-name} − {Geonames-ID}, so that a human can manually inspect results.

It is important to note the rationale between having 100-dimensional embeddings, since the latitude-longitude embeddings are only 2-dimensional. The reason for setting the dimensionality parameter so high is that we are 'compressing' each vector into a unit hypersphere (a *dense* latent space), and expect the cosine similarity to approximate the role of the haversine similarity in the lat-long embedding space. While we set the dimensionality to be 100, lower (or higher) values can also be tried by retraining the embeddings on the files we have published in the GitHub repository. In previous work, setting the dimensionality between 20–200 was found to generally achieve optimal results, with minor variance.

Finally, because each line in the JSON lines format is a vector, vectors (i.e. JSONs) can be sampled independently of each other; also, a per-line iterator can be used for reading vectors into memory (hence, iterator parallelism, amenable to both shared-nothing and shared-memory architectures, can be used). Furthermore, because of the mnemonics we have used, in addition to using the explicit ID in identifying a location, a human can inspect results without necessarily having to always do ID lookups.

4   Applications and Extensions

As described earlier as motivation, the primary application of geolocation embeddings is in expressing a location as a feature vector e.g., in a downstream machine learning system. One application where we are exploring these embeddings is *toponym resolution* [4]. For example, when geotagging Web documents, one needs to extract geolocations from the Web document [6]. At least two problems tend to arise, especially in difficult domains (like human trafficking) that are of investigative importance: first, geolocations can be extremely ambiguous. For example, a geo-extraction 'Melbourne' can refer to the city in Australia, but may also be referring to the city in Florida. However, if there is some other clue (e.g., phrases like 'sunshine state' or 'down under'), the resolution can still be effected by combining such phrasal features (e.g., using bag-of-words) with each candidate geolocation embedding and picking the location with the higher posterior probability. A machine learning model, in a training phase, would learn to associate certain words (like 'sunshine' and 'Florida') more strongly with Florida geolocation embeddings than otherwise.

Another application is *anomaly detection* [2], which arises when some other entity type (e.g., a name like Charlotte) gets extracted as a geolocation (the city in North Carolina). Assuming that a true set of geolocations also got extracted (e.g., locations in California), the embeddings can be used to detect the 'anomalous' location, in this case, Charlotte. We have already published the collective power of geolocation extractions in a recent work [5].

We are also exploring extensions of the embeddings, mainly via alternate constructions of the weighted graph. For example, one could forge an edge between two nodes if they have textual similarity between their Wikipedia pages. This would ensure that locations that are described in similar ways would have strong edge connections. One could even combine vectors derived from several such graphs for expressive geoenrichment.

References

1. Bizer, C., Lehmann, J., Kobilarov, G., Auer, S., Becker, C., Cyganiak, R., Hellmann, S.: Dbpedia-a crystallization point for the web of data. Web Semant.: Sci. Serv. Agents World Wide Web **7**(3), 154–165 (2009)
2. Chandola, V., Banerjee, A., Kumar, V.: Anomaly detection: a survey. ACM Comput. Surv. (CSUR) **41**(3), 15 (2009)
3. Collobert, R., Weston, J., Bottou, L., Karlen, M., Kavukcuoglu, K., Kuksa, P.: Natural language processing (almost) from scratch. J. Mach. Learn. Res. **12**(Aug), 2493–2537 (2011)
4. DeLozier, G., Baldridge, J., London, L.: Gazetteer-independent toponym resolution using geographic word profiles. In: AAAI, pp. 2382–2388 (2015)
5. Kapoor, R., Kejriwal, M., Szekely, P.: Using contexts and constraints for improved geotagging of human trafficking webpages. arXiv preprint arXiv:1704.05569 (2017)
6. Kejriwal, M., Szekely, P.: Information extraction in illicit web domains. In: Proceedings of the 26th International Conference on World Wide Web, pp. 997–1006. International World Wide Web Conferences Steering Committee (2017)
7. Mikolov, T., Sutskever, I., Chen, K., Corrado, G.S., Dean, J.: Distributed representations of words and phrases and their compositionality. In: Advances in Neural Information Processing Systems, pp. 3111–3119 (2013)
8. Pennington, J., Socher, R., Manning, C.D.: Glove: global vectors for word representation. EMNLP **14**, 1532–1543 (2014)
9. Perozzi, B., Al-Rfou, R., Skiena, S.: Deepwalk: online learning of social representations. In: Proceedings of the 20th ACM SIGKDD International Conference on Knowledge Discovery and Data Mining, pp. 701–710. ACM (2014)
10. Ristoski, P., Paulheim, H.: RDF2Vec: RDF graph embeddings for data mining. In: Groth, P., Simperl, E., Gray, A., Sabou, M., Krötzsch, M., Lecue, F., Flöck, F., Gil, Y. (eds.) ISWC 2016. LNCS, vol. 9981, pp. 498–514. Springer, Cham (2016). doi:10.1007/978-3-319-46523-4_30
11. Robusto, C.C.: The cosine-haversine formula. Am. Math. Mon. **64**(1), 38–40 (1957)
12. Wick, M.: GeoNames Geographical Database (2011)

Distributed Semantic Analytics Using the SANSA Stack

Jens Lehmann[1,2(✉)], Gezim Sejdiu[1], Lorenz Bühmann[3], Patrick Westphal[3],
Claus Stadler[3], Ivan Ermilov[3], Simon Bin[3], Nilesh Chakraborty[1],
Muhammad Saleem[3], Axel-Cyrille Ngonga Ngomo[3,4], and Hajira Jabeen[1]

[1] University of Bonn, Bonn, Germany
{jens.lehmann,sejdiu,chakrabo,jabeen}@cs.uni-bonn.de,
jens.lehmann@iais.fraunhofer.de
[2] Fraunhofer IAIS, Bonn, Germany
[3] Institute for Applied Informatics (InfAI), University of Leipzig, Leipzig, Germany
{buehmann,patrick.westphal,cstadler,iermilov,sbin,
saleemm}@informatik.uni-leipzig.de
[4] Data Science Group, Paderborn University, Paderborn, Germany
axel.ngonga@uni-paderborn.de

Abstract. A major research challenge is to perform scalable analysis of large-scale knowledge graphs to facilitate applications like link prediction, knowledge base completion and reasoning. Analytics methods which exploit expressive structures usually do not scale well to very large knowledge bases, and most analytics approaches which do scale horizontally (i.e., can be executed in a distributed environment) work on simple feature-vector-based input. This software framework paper describes the ongoing Semantic Analytics Stack (SANSA) project, which supports expressive and scalable semantic analytics by providing functionality for distributed computing on RDF data.

Resource type: Software Framework
Website: http://sansa-stack.net
Permanent URL: https://figshare.com/projects/SANSA/21410

1 Introduction

In this paper, we introduce SANSA[1], an open-source[2] *structured data processing engine* for performing distributed computation over large-scale RDF datasets. It provides data distribution, scalability, and fault tolerance for manipulating large RDF datasets, and facilitates analytics on the data at scale by making use of cluster-based big data processing engines. It comes with: (i) specialised serialisation mechanisms and partitioning schemata for RDF, using vertical partitioning

---

[1] http://sansa-stack.net/.
[2] https://github.com/SANSA-Stack.

© Springer International Publishing AG 2017
C. d'Amato et al. (Eds.): ISWC 2017, Part II, LNCS 10588, pp. 147–155, 2017.
DOI: 10.1007/978-3-319-68204-4_15

strategies, (ii) a scalable query engine for large RDF datasets and different distributed representation formats for RDF, namely graphs, tables and tensors, (iii) an adaptive reasoning engine which derives an efficient execution and evaluation plan from a given set of inference rules, (iv) several distributed structured machine learning algorithms that can be applied on large-scale RDF data, and (v) a framework with a unified API that aims to combine distributed in-memory computation technology with semantic technologies.

To achieve the goal of storing and manipulating large RDF datasets, we leverage existing big data frameworks like Apache Spark[3] and Apache Flink[4], which have matured over the years and offer a proven and reliable method for general-purpose processing of large-scale data.

The remainder of the paper is structured as follows: Sect. 2 depicts a new vision of combining distributed computing frameworks with the semantic technology stack and an overview of the SANSA architecture. We present some of the use cases demonstrating a variety of applications of the SANSA framework in detail in Sect. 3. We discuss related work in Sect. 4 and conclude in Sect. 5 along with directions for future work.

2   Vision and Architecture

Research efforts in the areas of distributed analytics and semantic technologies have so far been mostly isolated. As illustrated in Fig. 1, we see several core aspects in which both areas have complementary strengths and weaknesses.

State-of-the-art distributed in-memory analytics frameworks, such as Apache Spark and Apache Flink, provide graph-based analytics [1] but do not support semantic technology standards. The application of these approaches on heterogeneous data sources faces many limitations, in particular due to non-standardised input formats and the need for manual data integration. This can lead to large amounts of time and effort being spent on pre-processing data rather than performing the actual data analytics task. Semantic technologies are W3C-standardised and have the potential to significantly alleviate the pre-processing overhead: although the initial effort for modelling input data in RDF may be higher, the repeated reuse of the datasets in various analytics tasks can lead to a reduction of overall effort. Moreover, there are many connectors from existing data sources to RDF (e.g. via the R2RML standard) and they provide sophisticated data integration, e.g. via link discovery and fusion approaches for RDF. We want to go a step further and use this modelling standard as a basis for machine learning and data analytics. The layered architecture of SANSA is a direct consequence of this vision and is depicted at the top of Fig. 1. We will now discuss the different layers and currently implemented functionality in SANSA.

---

[3] http://spark.apache.org/.
[4] http://flink.apache.org/.

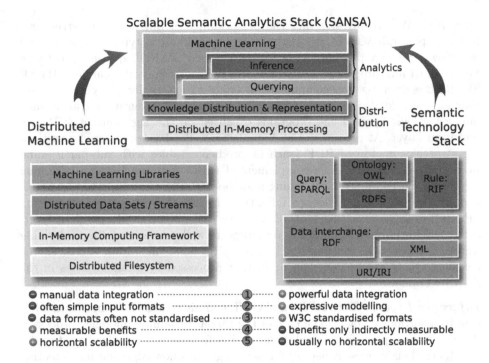

Fig. 1. The SANSA framework combines distributed analytics (left) and semantic technologies (right) into a scalable semantic analytics stack (top). The colours encode what part of the two original stacks influence which part of the SANSA stack. A main vision of SANSA is the belief that the the characteristics of each technology stack (bottom) can be combined and retain the respective advantages. (Color figure online)

Knowledge Distribution & Representation Layer.[5,6] This is the lowest layer on top of the existing distributed frameworks (Apache Spark or Apache Flink). It provides APIs to load/store native RDF or OWL data from HDFS or a local drive into the framework-specific data structures, and provides the functionality to perform simple and distributed manipulations on the data. Moreover, it allows the users to compute RDF statistics described in [7] in a distributed manner. For the representation of OWL axioms, we are also investigating data structures that allow an efficient, distributed computation of light-weight reasoning tasks like inferring the closure w.r.t. sub class relations.

Query Layer.[7] Querying an RDF graph is the primary method for searching, exploring, and extracting information from the underlying RDF data. SPARQL[8] is the W3C standard for querying RDF graphs. Our aim is to have cross-representational transformations and partitioning strategies for efficient query

---

[5] https://github.com/SANSA-Stack/SANSA-RDF.
[6] https://github.com/SANSA-Stack/SANSA-OWL.
[7] https://github.com/SANSA-Stack/SANSA-Query.
[8] https://www.w3.org/TR/rdf-sparql-query/.

answering. We are investigating the performance of different data structures (e.g., graphs, tables, tensors) in the context of different types of queries and workflows. SANSA provides APIs for performing SPARQL queries directly in Spark and Flink programs. It also features a W3C standard compliant HTTP SPARQL endpoint server component for enabling externally querying the data that has been loaded using its APIs. These queries are eventually transformed into lower-level Spark/Flink programs executed on the Distribution & Representation Layer. At present, SANSA implements flexible triple-based partitioning strategies on top of RDF (such as predicate tables with sub-partitioning by datatypes), which will be complemented with sub-graph based partitioning strategies. Based on the partitioning and the SQL dialects supported by Spark and Flink, SANSA provides an infrastructure for the integration of existing SPARQL-to-SQL rewriting tools. This bears the potential advantage of leveraging the optimizers of both the rewriters as well as those of the underlying frameworks for SQL. Currently, the Sparqlify[9] implementation serves as the baseline. Query results can then be further processed by other modules in the SANSA Framework.

Inference Layer.[10] Both RDFS and OWL contain schema information in addition to assertions or facts. The core of the forward chaining inference process is to iteratively apply inference rules on existing facts in a knowledge base to infer new facts. This process is helpful for deriving new knowledge and for detecting inconsistencies. Currently, SANSA supports efficient algorithms for the well-known reasoning profiles RDFS (with different subsets) and OWL-Horst, future releases will contain others like OWL-EL, OWL-RL and OWL-LD. In addition, SANSA contains a preliminary version of an adaptive rule engine that can derive an efficient execution plan from a given set of inference rules by generating, analysing and transformation of a rule-dependency graph. By using SANSA, applications will be able to fine tune the rules they require and – in case of scalability problems – adjust them accordingly.

Machine Learning Layer.[11] While the majority of machine learning algorithms use feature vectors as input, the machine learning algorithms in SANSA exploit the graph structure and semantics of the background knowledge specified using the RDF and OWL standards. Similar to Markov Logic Networks [16], this enables the algorithms to exploit the expressivity of semantic knowledge structures and potentially attain better performance or more human-understandable results. At the moment, the machine learning layer contains distributed implementations of link prediction algorithms based on two knowledge graph embedding models, namely Bilinear-Diag [24] and TransE [3], and scalable algorithms for RDF data clustering and association rule mining. Effectively and efficiently distributing data structures in potentially complex machine learning approaches is a major challenge in this layer.

---

[9] https://github.com/AKSW/Sparqlify.
[10] https://github.com/SANSA-Stack/SANSA-Inference.
[11] https://github.com/SANSA-Stack/SANSA-ML.

3   Use Cases

The main goal of the SANSA framework is to build a generic stack which can work with large amounts of linked data, offering algorithms for scalable, i.e. horizontally distributed, semantic data analysis. To validate this, we are developing use case implementations in several domains and projects.

Life Sciences – Open PHACTS. The Open Pharmacological Concepts Triple Store (Open PHACTS)[12] discovery platform provides open access to pharmaceutical data which is gathered and structured through multiple efforts, e.g. Uniprot, GOA, ChEMBL, OPS Chemical Registry, DisGeNET, OPS Identity Mappings, WikiPathways, Drugbank, ConceptWiki and ChEBI, with 2.8 billion triples [18]. Even though this data can potentially fit into the memory of a server (efficient compression techniques in triple stores can compress it to 100 GB), intermediate results of query joins, inference and machine learning algorithms do not fit into memory. For example, our initial experiments have shown that even light-weight inference and analysis for a subset of the used data sources (specifically UniProt, EggNOG, StringDB) cannot be efficiently performed on single machines even with 1 TB of main memory. For this reason, distributed approaches are relevant for Open PHACTS. Specifically, they have developed workflows for key questions on the platform [5] which are then used to elaborate API calls that need to be executed. Open PHACTS is currently investigating SANSA as a scalable alternative to perform these workflows over their continuously growing datasets. For example, to answer Question(Q) 6 – "For a specific target family, retrieve all compounds in specific assays" – the task is to look for a particular target family (from the ChEMBL protein classification) and retrieve compounds acting on members of that family (from ChEMBL). SANSA aims to optimise this and similar queries by making use of efficient distributed indexing/querying techniques. SANSA is also under consideration to help in answering complex questions for Open PHACTS, which do not even have a workflow e.g. Q2- "For a given compound, what is its predicted secondary pharmacology?". Tasks like this can be solved by using predictive machine learning models integrated with knowledge graph models, i.e. to search for the primary pharmacology and predicting the associated secondary pharmacologies.

Big Data Platform – BDE. Big Data Europe (BDE)[13] [2] is a large Horizon2020 funded EU project which offers an open source big data processing platform allowing users to install numerous big data processing tools and frameworks. The platform is being tested and used by the 17 different partners of the project scattered across Europe and its 7 different use cases cover a variety of societal challenges like climate, health, weather etc. As a specific example, SANSA can be used for log analysis in the context of the BDE platform. The mu.semte.ch micro service in BDE transforms docker events to RDF and stores them in a triple store. Work is also being done in order to translate HTTP network traffic to RDF. The data from these logs (events and HTTP traffic) can

---

[12] https://www.openphacts.org.
[13] https://github.com/big-data-europe.

be then combined with the data for a particular micro service and its relevant load (CPU/memory usage) on the server. SANSA can then build a predictive cost model for the micro service calls. This can further be extended for efficient resource allocation, monitoring and creation of common user profiles.

Publishing Sector – Elsevier. Semantic technologies are very useful in the publishing industry. For example, with in-depth medical knowledge and more than 400 000 scientific articles published per year, annotated with more than 8 million entities and mappings to the Elsevier Merged Medical Taxonomy (EMMeT), Elsevier is building up and testing a large-scale knowledge graph. Elsevier is currently applying (and approaching the limits of) state-of-the-art matrix and tensor factorisation methods, which will be distributed and enhanced in SANSA. There are at least three critical application areas for the methods developed in SANSA: (1) entity resolution (of author profiles, organisation profiles, etc.), (2) semantic querying in complex databases (e.g. Clinical Key) and (3) taxonomy construction. At present publishers, and Elsevier specifically, have to resort to methods which are less accurate than the state of the art due to scalability problems.

Education Sector – University of Bonn. While not an external use case, the university labs [14] in which we use SANSA have also further progressed and we now have 12 students divided into 7 groups using the framework and implementing different scenarios using SANSA functionalities. There are also at least seven students conducting their master thesis on top of the SANSA framework.

Proprietary Data Analytics – Ten Force. Ten Force is using SANSA for the clustering of the ESCO[15], and their proprietary data to analyse the grouping of skills and occupations. Tenforce is also in the process of using association rule mining on their proprietary data to analyse the shopping baskets.

4   Related Work

We give a brief and incomplete account of existing work in distributed RDF querying, inference and machine learning focusing on approaches available as software frameworks.

Querying: SparkRDF [23] and H2RDF+ [15] use RDF dataset statistics to find best merge-join orders for efficient querying. Huang et al. [12] present a hybrid system using in-memory retrieval and map-reduce. TriAD [11] is a specialised shared nothing system that was later [13] improved by using dynamic data exchange for join evaluation. SPARQLGX [9] is an approach for a distributed RDF querying which translates SPARQL to Spark operations. SANSA partially includes the Spark-based S2RDF [17] querying engine which rewrites SPARQL

---

[14] http://sda.cs.uni-bonn.de/teaching/sose2017dbda/.
[15] https://ec.europa.eu/esco/portal/escopedia.

queries to SQL. SANSA facilitates the integration of existing engines under a uniform set of APIs and extends the state of the art in querying through new distributed indexing and partitioning strategies.

Inference: Different distributed rule-based approaches, optimised for one of the many language profiles for the semantic web, have been developed in the past. A scalable distributed reasoning for RDFS entailment rules introduced by Urbani et al. [20], uses optimal execution ordering of the rules to reduce computation time. The WebPIE [19] forward chaining reasoner uses a MapReduce approach. QueryPie [21], uses backward chaining and distributes the schema triples. Cichlid [10] is a distributed reasoning engine, using the Apache Spark framework. The above systems only support (fragments of) the OWL RL language profile. SANSA provides a general rule-based reasoning engine that optimises executions plans for an arbitrary set of rules by taking into account the logical dependencies between rules, the distribution of the data w.r.t. the rules, and the technical features of the underlying distributed processing framework.

Machine Learning: There are numerous centralised machine learning frameworks and algorithms for RDF data. DL Learner [4] is a framework for inductive learning for the Semantic Web. AMIE [8] learns association rules from RDF data. ProPPR [22] and TensorLog [6] are recent frameworks for efficient probabilistic inference in first order logic. Nickel et al. provide a review of statistical relational learning techniques for knowledge graphs [14]. Scaling up structured machine learning algorithms, which are mostly iterative convergent in nature, using Bulk Synchronous Parallel frameworks (e.g. Spark, Flink) is a challenging task.

General: Previous approaches demonstrate specialised efforts related to specific layers of the SANSA stack. In contrast to this, SANSA provides a unified platform for distributed machine learning over large-scale knowledge graphs, combined with querying and rule-based inference. This makes it easier for developers to access its functionality, move between different implementations and assemble existing functionality into larger workflows. To the best of our knowledge, SANSA is the only holistic framework for distributed analytics on large-scale RDF data.

5 Conclusions and Future Work

We presented the SANSA framework, which combines the advantages of distributed in-memory computing and semantic technologies. Its holistic layered approach leverages data integration and modelling capabilities provided by semantic technologies with machine learning functionality and improved horizontal scalability provided by distributed in-memory frameworks. We believe that SANSA is an important framework for the semantic technology community as well as those parts of the distributed in-memory development community which require more sophisticated data modelling capabilities. In the future, we will enrich SANSA with algorithms for inference-aware knowledge graph embeddings, distributed approximate reasoning and further data partitioning strategies.

Acknowledgements. This work was partly supported by the grant from the European Union's Horizon 2020 research Europe flag and innovation programme for the project Big Data Europe (GA no. 644564) and a research grant from the German Ministry BMWI under the SAKE project (Grant No. 01MD15006E).

References

1. Andersen, J.S., Zukunft, O.: Evaluating the scaling of graph-algorithms for big data using GraphX. In: International Conference on Open and Big Data (OBD), pp. 1–8. IEEE (2016)
2. Auer, S., et al.: The BigDataEurope platform – supporting the variety dimension of big data. In: Cabot, J., De Virgilio, R., Torlone, R. (eds.) ICWE 2017. LNCS, vol. 10360, pp. 41–59. Springer, Cham (2017). doi:10.1007/978-3-319-60131-1_3
3. Bordes, A., Usunier, N., Garcia-Duran, A., Weston, J., Yakhnenko, O.: Translating embeddings for modeling multi-relational data. In: Advances in Neural Information Processing Systems, pp. 2787–2795 (2013)
4. Bühmann, L., Lehmann, J., Westphal, P.: DL-Learner-a framework for inductive learning on the semantic web. Web Semant.: Sci. Serv. Agents World Wide Web **39**, 15–24 (2016)
5. Chichester, C., Digles, D., Siebes, R., Loizou, A., Groth, P., Harland, L.: Drug discovery FAQs: workflows for answering multidomain drug discovery questions. Drug Discov. Today **20**(4), 399–405 (2015)
6. Cohen, W.W.: TensorLog: a differentiable deductive database. arXiv preprint arXiv:1605.06523 (2016)
7. Ermilov, I., Lehmann, J., Martin, M., Auer, S.: LODStats: the data web census dataset. In: Groth, P., Simperl, E., Gray, A., Sabou, M., Krötzsch, M., Lecue, F., Flöck, F., Gil, Y. (eds.) ISWC 2016 Part II. LNCS, vol. 9982, pp. 38–46. Springer, Cham (2016). doi:10.1007/978-3-319-46547-0_5
8. Galárraga, L., Teflioudi, C., Hose, K., Suchanek, F.M.: Fast rule mining in ontological knowledge bases with AMIE+. Very Large Databases J. **24**, 707–730 (2015)
9. Graux, D., Jachiet, L., Genevès, P., Layaïda, N.: SPARQLGX: efficient distributed evaluation of SPARQL with apache spark. In: Groth, P., Simperl, E., Gray, A., Sabou, M., Krötzsch, M., Lecue, F., Flöck, F., Gil, Y. (eds.) ISWC 2016 Part II. LNCS, vol. 9982, pp. 80–87. Springer, Cham (2016). doi:10.1007/978-3-319-46547-0_9
10. Gu, R., Wang, S., Wang, F., Yuan, C., Huang, Y.: Cichlid: efficient large scale RDFS/OWL reasoning with spark. In: 2015 IEEE International Parallel and Distributed Processing Symposium (IPDPS), pp. 700–709. IEEE (2015)
11. Gurajada, S., Seufert, S., Miliaraki, I., Theobald, M.: TriAD: a distributed shared-nothing RDF engine based on asynchronous message passing. In: Proceedings of the 2014 ACM SIGMOD International Conference on Management of Data, SIGMOD 2014, pp. 289–300. ACM, New York (2014)
12. Huang, J., Abadi, D.J., Ren, K.: Scalable SPARQL querying of large RDF graphs. PVLDB **4**(11), 1123–1134 (2011)
13. Nenov, Y., Piro, R., Motik, B., Horrocks, I., Wu, Z., Banerjee, J.: RDFox: a highly-scalable RDF store. In: Arenas, M., et al. (eds.) ISWC 2015 Part II. LNCS, vol. 9367, pp. 3–20. Springer, Cham (2015). doi:10.1007/978-3-319-25010-6_1

14. Nickel, M., Murphy, K., Tresp, V., Gabrilovich, E.: A review of relational machine learning for knowledge graphs. Proc. IEEE **104**(1), 11–33 (2016)
15. Papailiou, N., Konstantinou, I., Tsoumakos, D., Koziris, N.: H2RDF: adaptive query processing on RDF data in the cloud. In: Proceedings of the 21st International Conference on World Wide Web, pp. 397–400. ACM (2012)
16. Richardson, M., Domingos, P.: Markov logic networks. Mach. Learn. **62**(1–2), 107–136 (2006)
17. Schuetzle, A., Przyjaciel-Zablocki, M., Skilevic, S., Lausen, G.: S2RDF: RDF querying with SPARQL on spark. PVLDB **9**(10), 804–815 (2016)
18. Troumpoukis, A. Charalambidis, A., Mouchakis, G., Konstantopoulos, S., Siebes, R., de Boer, V., Soiland-Reyes, R., Digles, D.: Developing a benchmark suite for semantic web data from existing workflows. In: BLINK@ISWC (2016)
19. Urbani, J., Kotoulas, S., Maassen, J., van Harmelen, F., Bal, H.: OWL reasoning with WebPIE: calculating the closure of 100 billion triples. In: Aroyo, L., Antoniou, G., Hyvönen, E., ten Teije, A., Stuckenschmidt, H., Cabral, L., Tudorache, T. (eds.) ESWC 2010 Part I. LNCS, vol. 6088, pp. 213–227. Springer, Heidelberg (2010). doi:10.1007/978-3-642-13486-9_15
20. Urbani, J., Kotoulas, S., Oren, E., van Harmelen, F.: Scalable distributed reasoning using mapreduce. In: Bernstein, A., Karger, D.R., Heath, T., Feigenbaum, L., Maynard, D., Motta, E., Thirunarayan, K. (eds.) ISWC 2009. LNCS, vol. 5823, pp. 634–649. Springer, Heidelberg (2009). doi:10.1007/978-3-642-04930-9_40
21. Urbani, J., van Harmelen, F., Schlobach, S., Bal, H.: QueryPIE: backward reasoning for OWL horst over very large knowledge bases. In: Aroyo, L., Welty, C., Alani, H., Taylor, J., Bernstein, A., Kagal, L., Noy, N., Blomqvist, E. (eds.) ISWC 2011 Part I. LNCS, vol. 7031, pp. 730–745. Springer, Heidelberg (2011). doi:10.1007/978-3-642-25073-6_46
22. Wang, W.Y., Mazaitis, K., Cohen, W.W.: Structure learning via parameter learning. In: Proceedings of the 23rd ACM International Conference on Conference on Information and Knowledge Management, pp. 1199–1208. ACM (2014)
23. Xu, Z., Chen, W., Gai, L., Wang, T.: SparkRDF: in-memory distributed RDF management framework for large-scale social data. In: Dong, X.L., Yu, X., Li, J., Sun, Y. (eds.) WAIM 2015. LNCS, vol. 9098, pp. 337–349. Springer, Cham (2015). doi:10.1007/978-3-319-21042-1_27
24. Yang, B., Yih, W., He, X., Gao, J., Deng, L.: Embedding entities and relations for learning and inference in knowledge bases. arXiv preprint arXiv:1412.6575 (2014)

The MIDI Linked Data Cloud

Albert Meroño-Peñuela[1(✉)], Rinke Hoekstra[1,6], Aldo Gangemi[2,8,9],
Peter Bloem[1], Reinier de Valk[5], Bas Stringer[1], Berit Janssen[3],
Victor de Boer[1], Alo Allik[4], Stefan Schlobach[1], and Kevin Page[7]

[1] Department of Computer Science, Vrije Universiteit Amsterdam,
Amsterdam, Netherlands
`albert.merono@vu.nl`
[2] ISCT-CNR, Consiglio Nazionale Delle Ricerche, Rome, Italy
[3] Meertens Instituut, KNAW, Amsterdam, Netherlands
[4] Queen Mary University of London, London, UK
[5] Data Archiving and Networked Services, KNAW, Hague, Netherlands
[6] Faculty of Law, University of Amsterdam, Amsterdam, Netherlands
[7] Oxford e-Research Centre, Oxford, UK
[8] University of Bologna, Bologna, Italy
[9] Paris Nord University, Villetaneuse, France

Abstract. The study of music is highly interdisciplinary, and thus requires the combination of datasets from multiple musical domains, such as catalog metadata (authors, song titles, dates), industrial records (labels, producers, sales), and music notation (scores). While today an abundance of music metadata exists on the Linked Open Data cloud, linked datasets containing interoperable symbolic descriptions of music itself, i.e. music notation with note and instrument level information, are scarce. In this paper, we describe the MIDI Linked Data Cloud dataset, which represents multiple collections of digital music in the MIDI standard format as Linked Data using the novel `midi2rdf` algorithm. At the time of writing, our proposed dataset comprises 10,215,557,355 triples of 308,443 interconnected MIDI files, and provides Web-compatible descriptions of their MIDI events. We provide a comprehensive description of the dataset, and reflect on its applications for research in the Semantic Web and Music Information Retrieval communities.

Keywords: MIDI · Linked data · Music interoperability

1 Introduction

Musicology is the scholarly study of *music* [2]. Most of its subdisciplines are highly interdisciplinary, and require combinations of datasets from different domains in order to succeed. For example, a musicologist studying the popularity of a dance style may need to combine audio, video, notation, and market sales datasets. This depicts an ideal scenario for the deployment of Linked Data. However, only certain types of musical *metadata* are available as Linked Data. DBpedia contains general metadata about popular bands, albums and songs,

© Springer International Publishing AG 2017
C. d'Amato et al. (Eds.): ISWC 2017, Part II, LNCS 10588, pp. 156–164, 2017.
DOI: 10.1007/978-3-319-68204-4_16

but not about their musical characteristics. MusicBrainz [10] offers more fine-grained descriptions for albums, songwriters, versions and recordings, linking those to AcoustID,[1] which assigns unique fingerprints to audio files based on their content. AccousticBrainz[2] describes "acoustic characteristics of music and includes low-level spectral information".

Despite these successful initiatives, our community has given little attention to musical *notation*, traditionally the source of musical knowledge. Current formats for musical notation are diverse, and not directly interoperable. MusicXML [1], and the Notation Interchange File Format[3] (NIFF) represent Western musical notation and are used in various scorewriting applications. The Music Encoding Initiative[4] (MEI) formalizes notation using a core set of rules. The Musical Instrument Digital Interface (MIDI) [11] standard allows electronic musical devices to communicate by exchanging messages that can be interpreted as music notation. However, the mutual compatibility of these formats is burdened by different adoptions across applications and different features [7].

Linked Data can potentially benefit music notation in at least two important aspects: *notation interoperability*, since current notation formats would use RDF to encode musical information; and *entity interlinking*, since musically related entities (groups of notes linked to a motif; instruments linked to DBpedia) could easily be connected. In previous work, we have shown that the MIDI format can be losslessly represented as Linked Data , using `midi2rdf` [5]. In this paper, we describe the *MIDI Linked Data Cloud*, a first step towards interoperable, and interconnected music notation knowledge on the Web. By following best practices within the Semantic Web community, we publish a dataset of 10,215,557,355 triples, representing 308,443 interconnected MIDI scores. We argue that this dataset opens up new research challenges, and can be used to support specific evaluation tasks associated to these challenges in the Semantic Web and Music Information Retrieval communities (Sect. 3).

2 MIDI Linked Data

The MIDI Linked Data Cloud is published at http://purl.org/midi-ld, and provides access to the community, documentation, source code, and dataset. All relevant dataset links and namespaces are shown in Table 1. A GitHub organization hosts all project repositories, including documentation and tutorials, source MIDI collections, and the dataset generation code. The dataset is the result of applying this code to the source MIDI collections, and adding the resources described in this Section. It is accessible as a full dump download, via a SPARQL endpoint, and via a RESTful API. This API is built using SPARQL queries that we publish on GitHub. The dataset includes a VoID description and is registered at Figshare, Datahub, and Zenodo; released under the CC0 1.0 Universal (CC0 1.0) license; and compliant with the FAIR principles [14].

---

[1] See https://acoustid.org/.

[2] See https://acousticbrainz.org/.

[3] See http://www.music-notation.info/en/formats/NIFF.html.

[4] See http://music-encoding.org/.

Table 1. Links to key resources of the MIDI Linked Data Cloud dataset.

Meroño-Peñuela, A. et al. (2017). *The MIDI Linked Data Cloud.*
doi:10.5281/zenodo.579603

Resource	Link
MIDI Linked Data Cloud dataset	http://purl.org/midi-ld
Portal page	https://midi-ld.github.io/
midi2rdf-as-a-Service	http://purl.org/midi-ld/midi2rdf
MIDI Vocabulary namespace	http://purl.org/midi-ld/midi# (prefix midi)
MIDI Resource namespace	http://purl.org/midi-ld/ (prefix midi-r)
MIDI Notes namespace	http://purl.org/midi-ld/notes/ (prefix midi-note)
MIDI Programs namespace	http://purl.org/midi-ld/programs/ (prefix midi-prog)
MIDI Chords namespace	http://purl.org/midi-ld/chords/ (prefix midi-chord)
MIDI Pieces namespace	http://purl.org/midi-ld/piece/ (prefix midi-p)
GitHub organization & code	https://github.com/midi-ld/
Dataset generation code	https://github.com/midi-ld/midi2rdf
Documentation and tutorials	https://github.com/midi-ld/documentation
Source MIDI collections	https://github.com/midi-ld/sources
Sample SPARQL queries	https://github.com/midi-ld/queries
VoID description	http://purl.org/midi-ld/void
Full dump downloads	http://midi-ld.amp.ops.labs.vu.nl/
SPARQL endopint	http://virtuoso-midi.amp.ops.labs.vu.nl/sparql
RESTful API	http://grlc.io/api/midi-ld/queries/
Figshare	https://figshare.com/articles/ The_MIDI_Linked_Data_Cloud/4990415
Zenodo	https://zenodo.org/record/579603#.WRluUXV97MU
Datahub	https://datahub.io/dataset/the-midi-linked-data-cloud

Generation, Model, and IRI Strategy. To generate the MIDI Linked Data Cloud dataset we use midi2rdf [5]. This algorithm reads MIDI events from a file, and generates an equivalent representation in RDF by mapping MIDI events into the lightweight MIDI ontology shown in Fig. 1 (the complete event hierarchy is included in the documentation). The top MIDI container is midi:Piece, which contains all MIDI data organized in midi:Tracks, each containing a number of midi:Events. midi:Event is an abstract class around all possible musical events in MIDI, for example start playing a note (midi:NoteOnEvent), stop playing it (midi:NoteOffEvent), or changing the instrument (midi:ProgramChangeEvent). Concrete events have their own attributes (e.g. a midi:NoteOnEvent has a note pitch and veloc-

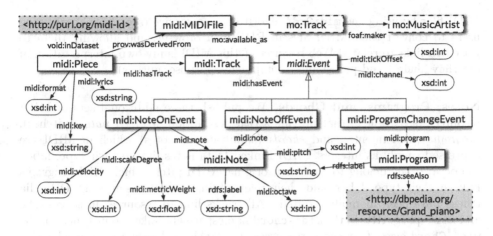

Fig. 1. Excerpt of the MIDI ontology: pieces, tracks, events, and their attributes.

```
1   midi-p:cb87a5bb1a44fa72e10d519605a117c4 a midi:Piece ;
2       midi:format 1 ;
3       midi:key"E minor" ;
4       midi:hasTrack midi-p:cb87a5bb1a44fa72e10d519605a117c4/track00,
5              midi-p:cb87a5bb1a44fa72e10d519605a117c4/track01, ... .
6   midi-p:cb87a5bb1a44fa72e10d519605a117c4/track01 a midi:Track ;
7       midi:hasEvent midi-p:cb87a5bb1a44fa72e10d519605a117c4/track01/event0000,
8              midi-p:cb87a5bb1a44fa72e10d519605a117c4/track01/event0001, ... .
9   midi-p:cb87a5bb1a44fa72e10d519605a117c4/track01/event0006 a midi:NoteOnEvent ;
10      midi:channel 9 ;
11      midi:note midi-note:36 ;
12      midi:scaleDegree 6 ;
13      midi:tick 0 ;
14      midi:velocity 115 ;
15      midi:metricWeight 1.0 .
```

Listing 1.1. Excerpt of Black Sabbath's *War Pigs* as MIDI Linked Data.

ity), but all event types have a `midi:tickOffset` locating them temporally within the track. Instances of `midi:Track` are linked to the original file (an instance of `midi:MIDIFile`) they were derived from through `prov:wasDerivedFrom`. To enable interoperability and reuse with other datasets, and future extensions, we link the class `mo:Track` of the Music Ontology [8] to the class `midi:MIDIFile` through the property `mo:available_as`. An excerpt of a MIDI file is shown as Turtle in Listing 1.1. IRIs of `midi:Piece` instances have the form midi-r:piece/<hash>/, where <hash> is the unique MD5 hash of the original MIDI. Instances of `midi:Track` and `midi:Event` get IRIs of the form midi-r:piece/<hash>/track<tid> and midi-r:piece/<hash>/track<tid>/event<eid>, where <tid> and <eid> their respective IDs.

MIDI Sources. The MIDI files in our dataset come from two different sources. The first is a manually curated list of well-known MIDI collections maintained in our GitHub organization. The second is users, who can contribute their own

MIDI files by using the `midi2rdf` algorithm as a service (see Table 1), allowing users to convert their MIDI files to RDF in a browser, and allowing them to get extra links to related Web resources ("this MIDI is my own interpretation of `dbr:Hey_Jude`") and provenance (equipment, purpose, author).

Notes, Programs, and Chords. We publish three additional sets of MIDI resources (see Table 1) that provide a rich description of *MIDI notes* (pitches), *programs* (instruments), and *chords* (simultaneous notes) which in MIDI are expressed simply as integers. MIDI Linked Data notes link to their type, label, the octave they belong to, and their original MIDI pitch value. MIDI programs link to their type, label, and their relevant instrument resource in DBpedia (these have been manually crafted). All tracks link to resources in `midi-note` and `midi-prog`. IRIs in the `midi-chord` namespace are linked to instances of the `midi:Chord` class. Our chord resources (see Table 1) describe a comprehensive set of chords, each of them with a label, quality, the number of pitch classes the chord spans, and one or more intervals –the number of half-steps each pitch class is above the chord's tonic.

Enriching MIDI Files. We enrich the resulting Linked Data with additional features that are not present in the original MIDI files: *provenance*, integrated *lyrics*, and *key-scale-metric* information. To generate provenance, we link the extracted `midi:Piece` with the files they were generated from, the conversion activity that used them, and the agent (`midi2rdf`) associated with such activity. 8,391 MIDI files contained lyrics that were split by syllables, to be used mainly in karaoke software; we join these syllables into an integrated literal, using the `midi:lyrics` property, to facilitate lyrics-based search. Finally, we use the music analysis library `music21`[5] to further enrich the data: the *key* is extracted directly from the MIDI file or automatically detected via e.g. the Krumhansl-Schmuckler algorithm [4]; every note event is represented as the *scale degree* in relation to that key; and we detect and attach *metric* accents for each note (see Listing 1.1).

3 Applications

3.1 Semantic Web Research

Data Integration. The interoperable representation of MIDI as Linked Data can help data integration across music notation databases. Their current formats are incompatible (MIDI, MusicXML, NIFF, MEI, etc.). We envision the study and development of notation *converters*, *vocabularies* and *ontologies* that explicitly specify shared conceptualizations and aid integration. For instance, a simple OWL vocabulary for MusicXML, a format supported by over 210 notation programs,[6] together with a chord structure example[7] can steer integration

---

[5] http://web.mit.edu/music21.

[6] http://www.ontologydesignpatterns.org/ont/musicml/musicml.owl.

[7] http://www.ontologydesignpatterns.org/ont/musicml/confirmation.ttl.

of MusicXML and MIDI databases. This allows for extended querying in non-proprietary tools and formats, helping to close the gap between produced music signal, song structures, and music metadata. Music notation could also be integrated with related artistic notations such as *dance notation*, for which various machine-readable formats have been proposed, notably LabanXML [3] as RDF. The MIDI Linked Data Cloud can provide a common dataspace for these notations to be linked and integrated, opening up new possibilities for archiving and retrieval, analysis, and choreography and accompanying music generation.

Entity Linking. The MIDI Linked Data Cloud represents musical knowledge with a great level of detail. Concepts such as notes, melodies, chords, and motifs make their appearance as new Semantic Web resources. We must therefore consider the general task of automatically finding new and interesting links among these new entities, and between them and other related entities in the Semantic Web. This has the potential for new challenges in methods for entity linking and link discovery. The novelty our proposed dataset brings to these methods is the potential combination of music *metadata* with *musical content*. A first important task is to generate *quality links between notation and metadata*. For example: how to find relevant links between the score of the Beatles' *Hey Jude* and other Linked Data resources describing this song (e.g. http://dbpedia.org/resource/Hey_Jude)? Relevant metadata for this task, such as the artist name and the song title, can often be extracted from MIDI embedded text[8], further harmonised with the Music Ontology (see Sect. 2), and used to generate links to e.g. MusicBrainz services and the DBpedia musical information graph. Furthermore, through MusicBrainz it becomes possible to retrieve content-based audio features from the AcousticBrainz service, such as its key, tempo or timbre. Such linkage will provide unprecedented queries that combine the full spectrum of musical metadata, features, and notation.

Another group of important links to discover is between *elements of the symbolic notations*, like groups of notes, and other *external symbolic resources*, like chord repositories (see Sect. 3.2). Using our proposed Linked Data chord classification, we devise an algorithm that uses the interval notation to generate links between groups of notes and chords. The results could be used for recognizing chord schemas, representing them in different ways, performing chord substitution adaptation, analysing chord patterns, and consequently searching, mining, matching, and composing them. Linking *notation to audio* is generally more difficult; approaches that map audio to scores [12] are relevant, but could be improved if the target scores are augmented with features correlated to signal. Links in the opposite direction, i.e. from scores to audio, could be generated by using Fast Fourier Transform fingerprinting on sampled MIDI files, but this needs the individual parts (voices) in a piece stored in different MIDI tracks, for which *voice separation* systems are relevant [13]. Finally, an exciting possibility using link prediction would be an *entity classification* task, where we could

---

[8] See a preliminary algorithm at https://github.com/midi-ld/ner-midi.

remove all `dbr:genre` relations and attempt to predict them, as performed in [9] with predicting critical response to an album in DBpedia.

Semantics and Ontologies. Publishing music notation as Linked Data poses also challenges for semantics and ontologies. Although some of these have been previously addressed (e.g. by the Music, Chord and Timeline ontologies[9]), the *semantics* of musical concepts are still underspecified. For instance, different compositional devices can be used to convey feelings of happiness, sadness, darkness, nostalgia, etc. Similarly, scales, improvisations and motifs transmit different messages based on temporality and interpretation. Explicit, formal specifications of emotions based on musical features could lead to a new generation of creative systems.

3.2   Musicology and Music Information Retrieval (MIR)

Analyses of Chords, Patterns, and Melodies. The MIDI Linked Data Cloud enables a novel, data-driven approach to investigate music in its wider historical, geographical, cultural, economic, and stylistic context. Such combined queries can help musicologists to study influences between composers, investigate the popularity of certain melodic or rhythmic patterns, or understand the use of basic musical building blocks across cultures. It is of obvious musical interest to study the occurrences of resources in the existing vast amount of music repositories, including melody patterns, song collections, chords, and melodies, in music scores. For example, iReal Pro is an open-Web repository of user-contributed chords from thousands of songs, allowing to adapt the key, tempo, and style from these chords. Other repositories contain song melodies, but these are not freely available due to copyright, yet existing MIDI encoding of those melodies could be linked to chords for more functionalities. Another obstacle in reusing these is the lack of established vocabularies for encoding chords, melodies, and their metadata. The MIDI Linked Data Cloud points at addressing these traditional problems of symbolic music analysis: spread and disconnected repositories, incompatible encoding standards, heavily copyrighted databases, and unmanageable high volumes of raw audio data.

Recommender Systems. Analysis of MIDI content as Linked Data could enhance current music discovery and recommendation platforms. Existing systems frequently model similarities between artists as measures for music discovery and recommendation. Similarity models typically rely on collaborative filtering, content-based feature extraction, or a combination of both. Known limitations of these methods (including limited exposure of a collection and lack of high-level descriptions) can be alleviated by adopting Linked Data practices and semantic representations of musical concepts [6], including symbolic analysis of MIDI files. Such analysis could be integrated with other methods, which

---

[9] http://motools.sourceforge.net/timeline/timeline.html.

take advantage of Linked Data best practices and can enable the identification of musical entities and the discovery of valuable connections between them.

Machine Learning and Music Generation. The most ambitious application of the dataset for machine learning is to learn a *generative model* over knowledge graphs representing music. A generative model represents a class of instances as a probability distribution, allowing us to produce convincing samples of classes of images, natural language, or sound. For knowledge graphs, this task is complicated by our inability to recognize what constitutes a convincing sample. The MIDI Linked Data Cloud presents a solution: a good generative model should produce data that sounds realistic when translated to MIDI samples. This is no simple task: the model should learn that certain triples in the graph represent elements of a stream, and that this stream contains harmonies, a meter and so on. The included metadata should help the model make stylistic choices: a fugue by Bach should not contain tracks with distorted guitars, and a pop song is unlikely to contain more than 8 different tracks.

Linked-Data DJ. Maybe the most simple, though powerful, potential usage of the MIDI Linked Data Cloud is to use formal querying as a language for music mixing. Based on the previously described analytics, a language such as SPARQL can directly be used to filter datasets according to musical properties, such as keys, styles, harmonies, tempo, etc. This provides previously unknown opportunities for mixing and composing new music.

Audiolisation. Visualisations are often very powerful means to help people understand properties of data. Audiolisation, the attempt to use music and sounds to convey meaning, has been applied to algorithms previously but not to data. In order to map audio-expressible features to datasets, the MIDI Linked Data Cloud provides an exciting source for a systematic comparison of both audio and structural features of datasets.

4   Conclusions

This paper presents the MIDI Linked Data Cloud, a linked dataset of more than 10 billion MIDI RDF statements, as a foundation for a common dataspace where musical notation, metadata, and structured music repositories can be linked together on the Web. We have identified its potential for being used in diverse research areas and new challenges in the Semantic Web and Music Information Retrieval communities. We plan to extend the integration, linkage, and ontological methods sustaining this work with in-progress applications for Dutch grants and European funding.

Acknowledgements. We want to express our gratitude to the reviewers for their useful comments; to Frank van Harmelen for his support and motivation; and to Paul Groth for his valuable advice.

References

1. MusicXML 3.0 Specification. Technical report, MakeMusic, Inc. (2015). http://www.musicxml.com/
2. Duckles, V., et al.: "Musicology." Grove Music Online. Oxford Music Online. http://www.oxfordmusiconline.com/subscriber/article/grove/music/46710pg1
3. El Raheb, K., Ioannidis, Y.: A labanotation based ontology for representing dance movement. In: Efthimiou, E., Kouroupetroglou, G., Fotinea, S.-E. (eds.) GW 2011. LNCS, vol. 7206, pp. 106–117. Springer, Heidelberg (2012). doi:10.1007/978-3-642-34182-3_10
4. Krumhansl, C.L.: Cognitive Foundations of Musical Pitch. Oxford University Press, New York (1990)
5. Meroño-Peñuela, A., Hoekstra, R.: The song remains the same: lossless conversion and streaming of MIDI to RDF and back. In: Sack, H., Rizzo, G., Steinmetz, N., Mladenić, D., Auer, S., Lange, C. (eds.) ESWC 2016. LNCS, vol. 9989, pp. 194–199. Springer, Cham (2016). doi:10.1007/978-3-319-47602-5_38
6. Mora-Mcginity, M., Allik, A., Fazekas, G., Sandler, M.: MusicWeb: music discovery with open linked semantic metadata. In: Garoufallou, E., Subirats Coll, I., Stellato, A., Greenberg, J. (eds.) MTSR 2016. CCIS, vol. 672, pp. 291–296. Springer, Cham (2016). doi:10.1007/978-3-319-49157-8_25
7. Raffel, C., Ellis, D.P.W.: Extracting ground truth information from MIDI files: a MIDIfesto. In: ISMIR 2016 (2016)
8. Raimond, Y., Abdallah, S., Sandler, M., Giasson, F.: The music ontology. In: Proceedings of the 8th International Conference on Music Information Retrieval, ISMIR 2007, Vienna, Austria, 23–27 September 2007
9. Ristoski, P., Vries, G.K.D., Paulheim, H.: A collection of benchmark datasets for systematic evaluations of machine learning on the semantic web. In: Groth, P., Simperl, E., Gray, A., Sabou, M., Krötzsch, M., Lecue, F., Flöck, F., Gil, Y. (eds.) ISWC 2016. LNCS, vol. 9982, pp. 186–194. Springer, Cham (2016). doi:10.1007/978-3-319-46547-0_20
10. Swartz, A.: MusicBrainz: a semantic web service. IEEE Intell. Syst. **17**, 76–77 (2002). https://doi.org/10.1109%2F5254.988466
11. The MIDI Manufacturers Association: MIDI 1.0 detailed specification. Technical report, Los Angeles, CA (1996–2014). https://www.midi.org/specifications
12. Thickstun, J., Harchaoui, Z., Kakade, S.: Learning features of music from scratch. arXiv.org Statistics, Machine Learning. https://arxiv.org/abs/1611.09827
13. de Valk, R.: Structuring lute tablature and MIDI data: Machine learning models for voice separation in symbolic music representations. Ph.D. thesis, City University, London (2015)
14. Wilkinson, M.D., et al.: The FAIR guiding principles for scientific data management and stewardship. Nat. Sci. Data **3**(160018) (2016) doi:10.1038/sdata.2016.18

SocialLink: Linking DBpedia Entities to Corresponding Twitter Accounts

Yaroslav Nechaev[1,2], Francesco Corcoglioniti[1(✉)], and Claudio Giuliano[1]

[1] Fondazione Bruno Kessler, Via Sommarive 18, 38123 Trento, Italy
{nechaev,corcoglio,giuliano}@fbk.eu
[2] University of Trento, Via Sommarive 14, 38123 Trento, Italy

Abstract. We present SocialLink, a publicly available Linked Open Data dataset that matches social media accounts on Twitter to the corresponding entities in multiple language chapters of DBpedia. By effectively bridging the Twitter social media world and the Linked Open Data cloud, SocialLink enables knowledge transfer between the two: on the one hand, it supports Semantic Web practitioners in better harvesting the vast amounts of valuable, up-to-date information available in Twitter; on the other hand, it permits Social Media researchers to leverage DBpedia data when processing the noisy, semi-structured data of Twitter. SocialLink is automatically updated with periodic releases and the code along with the gold standard dataset used for its training are made available as an open source project.

Keywords: Social media · Linked open data · Machine learning

Resource Type: Dataset
Persistent URL: http://w3id.org/sociallink/

1 Introduction

Today it is hard to imagine a public person or an organisation that does not have a social media account. Such entities typically have a rich presence in the social media, sharing content, engaging with their audience, and maintaining and expanding their popularity. They typically keep all the information in their profiles and posts as relevant and precise as possible, so that a potential consumer or a fan can be informed about the latest developments in no time. Thus, social media have become a primary source of information providing up-to-date knowledge on a wide variety of topics, from major events to the opening hours of stores or what books or songs a particular celebrity likes.

Coincidentally, such people and organisations often have dedicated Wikipedia pages, and thus corresponding entries in knowledge bases (KB) related to Wikipedia, such as DBpedia, YAGO, or Wikidata. Data in social media and KBs present opposite characteristics. On the one hand, KBs provide high-quality, structured, and easily accessible information, while data from social

© Springer International Publishing AG 2017
C. d'Amato et al. (Eds.): ISWC 2017, Part II, LNCS 10588, pp. 165–174, 2017.
DOI: 10.1007/978-3-319-68204-4_17

media accounts is often noisy, unstructured, and hidden behind restrictive APIs. To extract from social media as much information as typically contained in a KB entry, sophisticated pipelines have to be built implementing tasks like event detection, user profiling, and entity linking. These tasks exploit supervised machine learning requiring large training sets that are scarcely available and expensive to create manually. On the other hand, social media provide up-to-date information, while contents in KBs may lag behind from hours to months, depending on how many people care about those topics; such delays may prevent using these KBs in some areas. In light of these differences, an integration of KBs and social media may be beneficial to address the shortcomings of one leveraging the strengths of the other.

In this paper, we present SocialLink[1], a publicly available Linked Open Data (LOD) dataset that matches social media accounts on Twitter, a popular social network providing up-to-date publicly available contents, to their corresponding entities in DBpedia. This resource creates a bridge between the highly structured LOD cloud and the vibrant and up-to-date social media world. By aligning around 271 K DBpedia persons and organisations to their Twitter profiles, SocialLink serves two purposes. On the one hand, it aims at facilitating social media processing by leveraging DBpedia data, e.g., as a source of ground truth properties for training supervised systems for user profiling, or as contextual data in natural language understanding tasks (e.g., Named Entity Linking) operating on social media contents [2,6]. On the other hand, SocialLink gives Semantic Web practitioners the ability to populate KBs with up-to-date data from social media accounts of DBpedia entities, such as structured attributes, images, connections, user locations, and descriptions. To the best of our knowledge, SocialLink is unique in the alignment task it addresses. This task shares some similarities with the *profile matching* task on (different) social media [5], but KBs do not contain attributes that are vital for that task, such as usernames, user-generated content, and social graph, meaning that techniques for profile matching cannot be directly applied in our context.

SocialLink was introduced in mid 2016 using the supervised alignment approach described in [7]. Since then, we have significantly expanded its scope and alleviated some of the restrictions of the original system. To name a few, the approach is no longer restricted by the limits of Twitter REST API and is now able to use entity data from 128 DBpedia chapters, allowing us to align DBpedia entities present only in localized DBpedia chapters, and to provide more context to our matching algorithm, improving its performances and increasing the amount of processed entities by a factor of three. The SocialLink pipeline generating the dataset is available open source[2] along with the revised gold standard dataset used to train and evaluate the system. SocialLink is repopulated periodically in an automatic way to insure that alignments are always up-to-date.

---

[1] http://sociallink.futuro.media/—Creative Commons Attribution license (CC BY 4.0).

[2] http://github.com/Remper/sociallink.

In the remainder of the paper, Sects. 2 and 3 present respectively the SocialLink pipeline and the latest version of the SocialLink dataset. Section 4 discusses some example use cases where SocialLink has been or can be used, while Sect. 5 concludes.

2 SocialLink Pipeline

Figure 1 highlights the three phases of the SocialLink pipeline used to generate the dataset. Processing starts with the *data acquisition* phase, where the required Twitter and DBpedia data, including preexisting gold standard alignments from DBpedia, are gathered, prepared, and indexed locally for further processing. Next, in the *candidate acquisition* phase, for each DBpedia entity a list of candidate matching Twitter profiles is obtained by querying the indexes. Finally, the *candidate selection* phase uses the gold standard alignments to train a Deep Neural Network (DNN) that scores and selects the best matching candidate. The system may abstain if there is no suitable candidate. After an entity passes through this pipeline it is ready to be added to the SocialLink dataset. More details on the candidate acquisition and selection phases are available in [7].

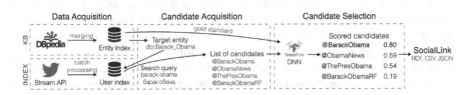

Fig. 1. Principal software components

Data Acquisition. We consider person and organisation entities[3] from all the 128 language chapters of DBpedia (version 2016-04). To speed up processing, we build a local entity index consisting of a Virtuoso triplestore populated with data from multiple DBpedia chapters. We use a *merging* component based on RDFpro [3], which downloads the required DBpedia data, filters out unwanted triples, and merges the remaining ones along owl:sameAs links ('smushing'), so that each entity is assigned a *canonical* URI used in its triples and linked to the entity owl:sameAs aliases. Overall, the merging component downloads 87 GB of compressed RDF corresponding to 7.3 B triples, and populates the index with 1.4 B triples, including 58745 gold standard alignments.[4]

From the social media side, SocialLink requires access to either the Twitter Streaming API or the Twitter Search API in order to populate the list of

---

[3] These types account for the majority of the DBpedia–Twitter alignments in DBpedia.

[4] Gold alignments derive from selected foaf:isPrimaryTopicOf and wikidata:P2002 triples of entities assumed living based on presence/values of selected properties (full details on website).

candidates. The latter option was used in the original paper and was the main bottleneck of the approach due to strict API rate limits. To avoid this bottleneck, the Twitter Streaming API is now accessed to download a (sampled) stream of tweets from which user accounts and text are extracted and indexed locally according to a continuous process, allowing the system to perform hundreds of queries per second on a single machine and enabling frequent, reliable, and fully automatic population and update of the resource. Additionally, this index provides much more user-related data, thus increasing alignment performances. We currently gathered three years of raw Twitter data, out of which 450 GB of indexed and accessible user data were produced. Processing is implemented using Apache Flink,[5] a framework providing reliability (via automatic checkpoints) and scalability (via automatic horizontal scaling). PostgreSQL is used as a backend for the Twitter user index.

Candidate Acquisition. The introduction of the custom user index allows a great degree of flexibility in acquiring the candidate accounts possibly matching a given DBpedia entity, as different query strategies can be implemented. In this release we employ the strategy that combines all known names of an entity deduplicated and sorted by frequency. Names consisting only of a first or a last name (from foaf:givenName and foaf:surname properties) are filtered out to prevent noisy results. Additionally, the approach now modifies the query (if possible) and performs additional requests in case the original query produces no results or is too broad (i.e., it results in too many candidates). Our index and query strategies are currently based on simple multi-language stemming and tokenisation techniques that perform well on Western languages but weak on Asian and Arabic languages. Despite this, we could further increase the recall of this phase (i.e., the amount of entities with a Twitter account for which some candidate is returned) from 56.5% reported in [7] to 59.2% of the current dataset release.

Candidate Selection. The scoring procedure for each ⟨candidate, entity⟩ pair, used to select the matching candidate given a DBpedia entity (if any), is straightforward. A DNN is trained using the gold standard to perform a binary classification task: to align or not to align. Five kinds of features and all their pairwise combinations are used [7]: (i) name-based features (edit distances); (ii) profile metrics ('is verified' flag, followers/friends/listed/statuses counts); (iii) cosine similarities between profile descriptions, tweets content and DBpedia descriptions; (iv) entity type (person/organisation/other); (v) homepage-related features (e.g., if foaf:homepage property contains a unique reference to the Twitter account). The result is a confidence value representing the probability of a ⟨candidate, entity⟩ pair being a correct alignment. The scoring subsystem has then to decide whether there is a correct alignment for a given entity using two predefined thresholds: *minimum score* required to consider an alignment correct and *minimum improvement* over the second best pick. The latter ensures that the algorithm can abstain if two or more candidates are indistinguishable, even

---

[5] http://flink.apache.org/.

if they pass the minimum score requirement. We include raw scores for each ⟨candidate, entity⟩ pair in SocialLink to allow tuning thresholds for a desired precision/recall balance. The thresholds for this dataset release are optimized for precision and are set to 0.4 minimum score and 0.4 minimum improvement, leading to 90% precision and 41% recall of generated alignments (vs. 85% precision, 52% recall in [7] where we optimized for F1). Candidate selection alone has 89.4% precision and 69.2% recall, assuming candidate acquisition succeeds in including the correct candidate. Alignments are more reliable for entities having rich Twitter accounts, as amount and relatedness of Twitter content play a key role in our feature set. Up-to-date performance figures are reported on the website.

The SocialLink pipeline is implemented as an open source project that we have been constantly contributing to since the original version described in [7]. The majority of the system is written in Java. Along with the code of the SocialLink pipeline, we are also releasing a complementary web-based test bench called *Social Media Toolkit*. It provides a convenient way to query the SocialLink dataset via the REST API, as well as additional social media-related functionalities that leverage SocialLink, such as a custom Named Entity Linking pipeline that links entities in a free text to social media profiles.

3   SocialLink Dataset

The result of running the SocialLink pipeline is the SocialLink dataset, that we generate periodically to account for updates in DBpedia and Twitter. The SocialLink dataset is distributed in different formats, with RDF being the main one that also includes all the intermediate candidate data. We describe here the modeling choices behind the RDF format of the SocialLink dataset, summarizing the statistics of its latest release and discussing how the dataset is made available online and kept up-to-date.

RDF Format. We encode our alignments in RDF using terms from FOAF, Dublin Core Terms, and our custom SocialLink vocabulary (prefix sl), as exemplified in Fig. 2.

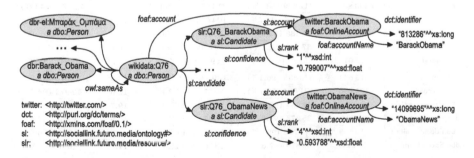

Fig. 2. Representation of alignments in RDF.

DBpedia entities are referenced using canonical URIs possibly taken from Wikidata, like wikidata:Q76 for entity Barack Obama in Fig. 2. Each canonical URI has owl:sameAs links to itself and to corresponding URIs in other DBpedia chapters (based on gathered DBpedia data), allowing querying the dataset using localized entity URIs.

Twitter accounts, like twitter:BarackObama in Fig. 2, are modeled as foaf:OnlineAccount individuals, using properties foaf:accountName and dct:identifier to respectively encode the account screen name and numeric identifier (useful in applications).

The alignment between a DBpedia entity and the corresponding Twitter account is expressed using property foaf:account. In addition, individuals of type sl:Candidate (e.g., slr:Q76_BarackObama in Fig. 2) reify the many-to-many relation between DBpedia entities and candidate Twitter accounts, linked via properties sl:candidate and sl:account. This reified relation is enriched with properties sl:confidence and sl:rank encoding the candidate confidence score (i.e., estimated correctness probability) and its rank among the candidates for the entity, to simplify querying for the top candidate.

Based on this modeling, the following SPARQL query retrieves the Twitter account (if any) aligned to an entity identified by any of its localized DBpedia URIs <E>:

```
SELECT ?account
WHERE {?e owl:sameAs <E>; foaf:onlineAccount ?account}
```

Dataset Statistics. Table 1 reports relevant statistics for the latest release of the SocialLink dataset. For the considered dbo:Person and dbo:Organisation DBpedia entity types, and their top five subtypes with the largest number of alignments, we report: (i) the total number of entities of that type in DBpedia (after merging all chapters); (ii) the number of *living* entities that may be

Table 1. Dataset statistics by DBpedia entity type.

Entity type	Entities in DBpedia	Living entities in DBpedia	Entities with candidates	Candidates / entity	Entities aligned
dbo:Person	2 975 645	2 035 590 (68.4%)	737 017 (24.8%)	12.6	234 450 (7.9%)
dbo:Athlete	493 867	412 629 (83.6%)	214 070 (43.3%)	15.1	71 935 (14.6%)
dbo:Artist	269 745	188 095 (69.7%)	104 614 (38.8%)	12.3	41 740 (15.5%)
dbo:Politician	123 460	65 135 (52.8%)	28 554 (23.1%)	11.7	12 400 (10.0%)
dbo:Writer	69 753	37 744 (54.1%)	16 630 (23.8%)	9.6	5 195 (7.4%)
dbo:Model	7 601	7 470 (98.3%)	4 915 (64.7%)	8.4	2 164 (28.5%)
dbo:Organisation	575 644	553 433 (96.1%)	169 332 (29.4%)	13.3	37 374 (6.5%)
dbo:Company	131 056	121 554 (92.7%)	50 778 (38.7%)	12.0	12 972 (9.9%)
dbo:Group	66 868	62 087 (92.9%)	39 472 (59.0%)	19.7	11 198 (16.7%)
dbo:Broadcaster	35 394	35 373 (99.9%)	18 674 (52.8%)	10.9	3 263 (9.2%)
dbo:EducationalInst.	116 139	115 722 (99.6%)	13 515 (11.6%)	5.7	2 366 (2.0%)
dbo:SportsTeam	62 221	60 870 (97.8%)	18 767 (30.2%)	11.5	2 067 (3.3%)
All entities	3 551 289	2 589 023 (72.9%)	906 349 (25.5%)	12.7	271 824 (7.7%)

aligned to Twitter; (iii) the number of living entities for which at least a candidate account was matched in the candidate acquisition phase; (iv) the average number of candidates per living entity (when matches were found); and, (v) the number of entities aligned to Twitter accounts for that type. The percentages in parenthesis refer to the total number of entities of a type. Due to chosen thresholds, the system *abstains* producing an alignment for about 2/3 of all entities having candidates (906 349), corresponding either to ambiguity cases (e.g., cannot distinguish between fake and real Twitter accounts) or to cases where the correct account is not among the produced candidates (e.g., Twitter name not occurring in DBpedia).

Availability and Sustainability. The SocialLink dataset is indexed on DataHub[6] and is available for download on SocialLink website, together with VOID statistics, old dataset releases, the gold standard (encoded using the same RDF representation), and non-RDF versions of alignments (JSON, TSV, no intermediate candidate data). Canonical citations (DOIs) for the dataset are available via Springer Nature [9] (this release) and Zenodo [8] (all releases) digital repositories. Alignment data is also available and queryable by end users and applications via a publicly accessible SPARQL endpoint[7] using Virtuoso. The SocialLink vocabulary is published according to LOD best practices, and both vocabulary and data URIs are dereferenceable with support of content negotiation.

Extensive documentation is available via the website, covering: (i) dataset scope, format, statistics, and access mechanisms; (ii) instructions for deploying and running the SocialLink pipeline to recreate the resource; (iii) example applications using the dataset; and, (iv) links to external resources like the GitHub repository and issue tracker.

The main requirement for generating the SocialLink dataset is the collection of (at least) some months of raw data from the Twitter Streaming API, e.g., via our data acquisition components. We run a SocialLink pipeline on our premises to continuously collect this data and sustain the periodic update of the dataset. No code modifications are foreseen unless breaking changes occurs in formats and APIs of Twitter and DBpedia.

4   Using SocialLink

As stated in Sect. 1, SocialLink establishes a link between DBpedia and Twitter, centered on popular entities occurring in both of them, which enables transferring knowledge from one resource to another and back, as well as comparing and jointly analysing the DBpedia graph and Twitter network. In the following, we describe three example use cases where these capabilities can be leveraged.

DBpedia to Twitter: User Profiling. The task of inferring users attributes based on their digital footprint is typically referred to as *user profiling*. Prediction of various attributes based on a person's social graph, posted content, or

---

[6] http://datahub.io/dataset/sociallink.
[7] http://sociallink.futuro.media/sparql.

other attributes is popular among researchers and companies. However, in most setups, namely supervised machine learning-based ones, user profiling requires significant amounts of manual labour to construct training sets. This both limits the possible attributes that can be inferred and the applicability of approaches operating on large amounts of training data, such as DNNs. Recently, researchers focused on automatic crawling of user profiling datasets from social media. However, even the largest datasets only contain few thousands examples per property [4] and are limited to properties explicitly present in social media.

SocialLink helps tackling user profiling by providing accurate machine-readable descriptions for hundreds of thousands of social media profiles. Any attribute present in DBpedia can now be modeled without relying on expensive manual annotation, and SocialLink can be used both to train and evaluate any proposed attribute classifiers.

Another example is inferring user interests based on social graph. Consider a user following, mentioning, or otherwise interacting with accounts aligned in SocialLink. By using this information, one can try to model interests, location, and language of the user by just looking at the DBpedia properties of these accounts [1]. For instance, following dbr:SpaceX and dbr:NASA can point on a dbr:Aerospace_engineering industry fan, while many dbr:Donald_Trump-related tweets can reveal a dbr:GOP supporter.

DBpedia to Twitter: Entity Linking. Another use case is the Named Entity Linking (NEL) task, whose goal is to link mentions of named entities in a text to their corresponding entities in a KB such as DBpedia. Challenging on its own, the NEL task presents additional unique challenges when applied to social media posts due to noisiness, lack of sufficient textual context, and informal nature of posts (e.g., use of slang).

Social media posts typically contain explicit mentions of social media accounts in the form of @username snippets. When referring to Twitter, some of these mentions (especially the ones referring to popular accounts) may be aligned in SocialLink, and thus can be directly disambiguated to DBpedia with high precision using our resource. Apart being part of the NEL result, these links provide additional contextual information (injected from DBpedia) that can be leveraged for disambiguating other named entities occurring in the post being processed. SocialLink was used in this capacity by two teams [2,6] participating to a NEL challenge on Italian tweets (NEEL-IT task) as part of the EVALITA 2016 campaign, allowing both of them to improve their results.

It is worth noting that the two-step approach of the SocialLink pipeline can be adapted to directly disambiguate named entities in texts against the social media. Such functionality is present in the Social Media Toolkit available on SocialLink website.

Twitter to DBpedia: Extracting FOAF Profiles. Up-to-date information about DBpedia persons and organisations can be extracted from Twitter after an alignment is established through SocialLink. Focusing on persons, different profile properties expressible with FOAF may be extracted from a DBpedia person's Twitter account, including:

- basic properties like foaf:name, foaf:surname, foaf:gender, foaf:birthday, and foaf:depiction linking to user images scarce in DBpedia but available in Twitter profiles;
- acquaintances (foaf:knows), extracted from friends, followers and Twitter accounts a user interacted with that are aligned to DBpedia entities in SocialLink;
- links to homepages (foaf:homepage and similar) and other web resources from a Twitter user description and posts, that can be matched to external links in DBpedia to mine relations with other DBpedia entities (e.g., affiliation, authorship, participation, all expressible in FOAF).

While a basic FOAF profile can be extracted from any Twitter account, the links to DBpedia provided by SocialLink allow grounding the extracted data and disambiguating the values of object properties with respect to a larger KB, this way increasing the usefulness of extracted FOAF profiles.

5   Conclusions and Future Work

In this paper we presented SocialLink, a Linked Open Data dataset that links Twitter profiles to corresponding DBpedia entities in multiple language chapters. By improving our initial approach described in [7], we have made SocialLink a valuable resource for the Semantic Web community and Social Media researchers alike. Use cases of SocialLink include, but are not limited to, user profiling, entity linking, and knowledge base enrichment. Our resource is automatically populated using an open source software allowing reproducibility and welcoming contributions from the community.

We will continue to gradually update SocialLink by both improving the approach and expanding the scope to accommodate a larger subset of Linked Open Data entities. A significant goal in our current roadmap consists in the expansion of our approach to other social networks, such as Facebook and Instagram. By introducing more social media to SocialLink we will be able to not only improve coverage but also exploit cross-network information to validate our alignments.

References

1. Besel, C., Schlötterer, J., Granitzer, M.: Inferring semantic interest profiles from Twitter followees: does Twitter know better than your friends?. In: ACM SAC, pp. 1152–1157 (2016)
2. Corcoglioniti, F., Palmero Aprosio, A., Nechaev, Y., Giuliano, C.: MicroNeel: combining NLP tools to perform named entity detection and linking on microposts. In: EVALITA (2016)
3. Corcoglioniti, F., Rospocher, M., Mostarda, M., Amadori, M.: Processing billions of RDF triples on a single machine using streaming and sorting. In: ACM SAC, pp. 368–375 (2015)
4. Farseev, A., Nie, L., Akbari, M., Chua, T.S.: Harvesting multiple sources for user profile learning: a big data study. In: ACM ICMR, pp. 235–242 (2015)

5. Goga, O.: Matching user accounts across online social networks: methods and applications. Ph.D. thesis, LIP6-Laboratoire d'Informatique de Paris 6 (2014)
6. Minard, A., Qwaider, M.R.H., Magnini, B.: FBK-NLP at NEEL-IT: active learning for domain adaptation. In: EVALITA (2016)
7. Nechaev, Y., Corcoglioniti, F., Giuliano, C.: Linking knowledge bases to social media profiles. In: ACM SAC, pp. 145–150 (2017)
8. Nechaev, Y., Corcoglioniti, F., Giuliano, C.: SocialLink dataset. Zenodo (2017). https://doi.org/10.5281/zenodo.820160
9. Nechaev, Y., Giuliano, C., Corcoglioniti, F.: SocialLink: knowledge transfer between social media and linked open data. Figshare (2017). https://doi.org/10.6084/m9.figshare.5235823

UNDO: The United Nations System Document Ontology

Silvio Peroni[1](✉), Monica Palmirani[2], and Fabio Vitali[1]

[1] DASPLab, DISI, University of Bologna, Bologna, Italy
{silvio.peroni,fabio.vitali}@unibo.it
[2] CIRSFID, University of Bologna, Bologna, Italy
monica.palmirani@unibo.it

Abstract. Akoma Ntoso is an OASIS Committee Specification Draft standard for the electronic representations of parliamentary, normative and judicial documents in XML. Recently, it has been officially adopted by the United Nations (UN) as the main electronic format for making UN documents machine-processable. However, Akoma Ntoso does not force nor define any formal ontology for allowing the description of real-world objects, concepts and relations mentioned in documents. In order to address this gap, in this paper we introduce the United Nations System Document Ontology (UNDO), i.e. an OWL 2 DL ontology developed and adopted by the United Nations that aims at providing a framework for the formal description of all these entities.

Keywords: Akoma Ntoso · Judicial documents · Normative documents · OWL 2 DL · Parliamentary documents · UNDO · United Nations

1 Introduction

The parliamentary, normative and judicial documents published by the United Nations System of organizations are full of references to real-world objects and concepts, such as other documents, people, organizations, legal terms, roles and deliberation steps. The United Nations has recently started to adopt Akoma Ntoso [2], an XML language that is in the process of becoming an OASIS standard, for providing an electronic representations of all UN Documents and the entities they contain. While it is not defined formally, Akoma Ntoso introduce a sort of informal ontological structure for all the entities it allows one to describe, according to two kinds of classes:

– document classes focus on representing the different aspects of a document as intellectual creation, the forms (versions, translations, etc.), its physical embodiment (e.g. PDF, XML, HTML, paper, etc.);
– non-document classes focus on representing the responsible for the production of the content and what the content is about (e.g. concept, object, event, locations, roles, deliberation steps, etc.).

C. d'Amato et al. (Eds.): ISWC 2017, Part II, LNCS 10588, pp. 175–183, 2017.
DOI: 10.1007/978-3-319-68204-4_18

While the informal definition of document classes is based on the Functional Requirements for Bibliographic Records (FRBR) standard [6] of the International Federation of Library Associations (IFLA), in the Akoma Ntoso specification there is no explicit mention of a possible adoption of a certain model for addressing the description of non-document entities.

As one of the outcomes of the work that the High-Level Committee on Management (HLCM) Working Group on Document Standards of the United Nations has done in the past year, in this paper we introduce the United Nations System Document Ontology (UNDO), i.e. an OWL 2 DL ontology developed and adopted by the United Nations that aims at providing a framework for the formal description of all entities and the relations that can exist among them in UN Documents. The idea behind the development of this model is to have a mechanism for sharing data about any legal/legislative/parliamentary document and its content in RDF format in an interchangeable way and, eventually, to allow the various agencies of the United Nations to extend it so as to meet their own domain specific requirements. In addition, UNDO follows the FAIR principles: it is identified with a w3id.org persistent identifier, it has been made available in different formats accessible by means of the classic content negotiation mechanism, it reuses several existing ontologies so as to increase interoperability, and it has been made available with a CC-BY license for enabling its reuse.

The rest of the document is organized as follows. In Sect. 2 we introduce all the methods and existing models that have been adopted and reused for the development of UNDO. In Sect. 3 we provide a brief introduction of UNDO, highlighting its main intended coverage and features. In Sect. 4 we address some possible applications of the ontology for modelling the documents published by the United Nations. Finally, in Sect. 5, we conclude the paper sketching out some future works.

2   Methods and Material

Akoma Ntoso and ALLOT. Akoma Ntoso [2] is an XML vocabulary for legal and legislative documents whose primary objective is to provide semantic information on top of a received legal text. Akoma Ntoso does not prescribe the use of a particular ontology. However, Akoma Ntoso defines a minimal and loose ontology based on FRBR and other eight *Top Level Classes* (TLCs) informally defining generic concepts such as person, role, event, etc. ALLOT (https://w3id.org/akn/ontology/allot) is an implementation of such TLCs as a formal OWL 2 DL ontology. It has been aligned to two important foundational ontologies, i.e. BFO [1] and DOLCE [4], so as to enable the reusability of the model in different contexts and domains (e.g. BFO is already used in several models adopted by the United Nations) and to provide a methodological organization of all the TLCs and their relations. The adoption of ALLOT as starting point for the development of UNDO is crucial for guaranteeing the best interoperability with Akoma Ntoso documents.

Development Tools. SAMOD [8] is a novel agile methodology for the development of ontologies that is organised in three simple steps within an iterative process that focuses on creating well-developed and documented models. It has been used to develop UNDO since the beginning, in combination with LODE, Graffoo, and DiTTO. LODE [9] is a service that renders entities defined in an OWL ontology in a human-readable HTML page designed for browsing and navigation by means of embedded links. Graffoo [3] is an open source tool that can be used to present the classes, properties and restrictions within OWL ontologies, or sub-sections of them, as clear and easy-to-understand diagrams. DiTTO [5] is a Web application that is able to translate diagrams expressed in Graffoo into OWL ontologies. In the context of the development of UNDO, LODE has been used to produce its HTML documentation, Graffoo has been used to create draft diagrams during the development of UNDO and the final diagram summarising the ontology, while DiTTO has been used to convert the Graffoo diagrams of the draft of the ontology into OWL automatically.

Other Ontologies Reused. For describing a domain concerning documents, and the entities they describe, other ontologies are relevant and, therefore, have been directly reused in UNDO. Time-indexed Value in Context (TVC) [7] is an ontology pattern that allows one to describe scenarios in which someone (e.g., a person) has a value (e.g., a particular role) during a particular time and for a particular context. Time Interval (http://www.ontologydesignpatterns.org/cp/owl/timeinterval.owl) is an ontology pattern that enables the description of period of times characterised by a starting date and an ending date. Web Annotation Ontology (http://w3.org/ns/oa) is a set of RDF classes, predicates and named entities that are used by the Web Annotation Data Model for creating annotations in RDF. DC Terms (http://purl.org/dc/terms/) is an ontology implementing all the metadata terms maintained by the Dublin Core Metadata Initiative, including properties, vocabulary encoding schemes, syntax encoding schemes, and classes. FOAF (http://xmlns.com/foaf/0.1/) is an ontology for describing people and their relations with other people, documents, and other information objects. ISO 639-1 (http://id.loc.gov/vocabulary/iso639-1) is a vocabulary describing the first part of the ISO 639 international-standard language-code family. LKIF Core (http://www.estrellaproject.org/lkif-core/lkif-core.owl) is a library of ontologies relevant for describing concepts from both legal and common-sense domains. SKOS (http://www.w3.org/2004/02/skos/core) is a common data model for sharing and linking knowledge organization systems via the Web. Finally, several ontological modules included in the SPAR Ontologies [7] have been used as well, since they have been developed to deal with several aspects of the document and publishing domain at large, such as document metadata, document statuses, publishing agent's roles, and publishing workflow processes.

3   Describing United Nations Documents

The United Nations System Document Ontology (UNDO), available at https://w3id.org/un/ontology/undo, is an OWL 2 DL ontologies that enables the description of UN Documents (and the entities they mention) in RDF. While UNDO has been developed from scratch by using SAMOD (after three iterations of the process, as documented in the GitHub repository of the ontology, i.e. https://w3id.org/un/repository/undo, in the directory "development"), we have also reused existing and well-known models (briefly introduced in Sect. 2) so as to make the ontology interoperable in different context. In particular, UNDO does not redefine properties that have been already defined elsewhere. For instance, all the data properties for describing the title (`dcterms:title`), the year of publication (`fabio:hasPublicationYear`), and other similar metadata, are already available in the FRBR-aligned Bibliographic Ontology (FaBiO, http://purl.org/spar/fabio) [7] to which UNDO is explicitly aligning with, and thus, in these cases, such properties should be preferred and used.

So as to regulate the way the entities defined in such external models have been reused, we have applied the following guidelines:

– some of these ontologies (e.g. ALLOT, TVC, and Web Annotation Ontology) have been imported as a whole (by means of the property `owl:imports`), since some of them have entities that are directly reused in UNDO for providing a description of the domain in consideration (e.g. we use `allot:hasRealization` to link a document to its version in a specific language);
– some ontological entities defined in external models (e.g. DCTerms, FOAF, and ISO 639-1, referred via `rdfs:isDefinedBy`) have been reused in UNDO (e.g. `dcterms:language`) without importing the original models since they have not been defined formally as OWL 2 DL ontologies;
– other ontological entities defined in external models (e.g. FaBiO, LKIF Core, and SKOS, referred via `rdfs:isDefinedBy`), which are proper OWL 2 DL ontologies, have been included for the sake of aligning UNDO with other relevant and existing models.

However, since UNDO should be intended as a domain ontology that could be extend by any party (e.g. a United Nations agency) for specific purposes, it is also possible to develop or reuse a different set of ontological entities for describing the part of the domain that are not explicitly defined in UNDO – being care of keeping the ontology consistent with the underlying description logic of OWL 2. Currently, UNDO is able to describe the entities introduced in the following subsections, summarised in Fig. 1.

3.1   Documents, Versions, and Mentioned Entities

By means of the Functional Requirements for Bibliographic Records (FRBR) [6], UNDO separates documents (e.g. UN resolution A/RES/50/100) and versions (e.g. language versions) in two specific and distinct layers, characterized by two classes: `undo:Document` (which has several subclasses defining specific types such as `undo:Resolution`, `undo:Constitution`, and `undo:Standard`) and `undo:DocumentVersion`. It is worth mentioning that, in case it is needed, the

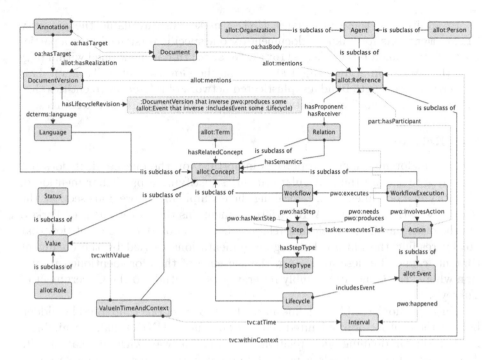

Fig. 1. The Graffoo diagram of UNDO, summarising its main classes and properties.

characterisation of the document components (paragraphs, sections, figures, tables, etc.) should be handled by means of the Document Components Ontology (DoCO, http://purl.org/spar/doco) [7].

There are four properties available in UNDO that can be used for defining relations among these classes:

- property `allot:hasRealization`, which links a document with its versions;
- property `frbr:revision`, which links a specific version to another version of it (e.g. a draft that has been amended and revised) – it is possible to add appropriate information concerning which document produced the revision, when the new revision is effective, and the list of the revisions produced by means of some of the models that have been aligned/imported by UNDO, i.e. PWO and FaBiO [7];
- property `dcterms:language`, which allows one to specify the language associated to the specific version in consideration – translations in different languages can be linked by means of the property `frbr:translation` defined in FRBR DL (http://purl.org/spar/frbr) to which UNDO aligns;
- property `frbr:transformation`, used for describing documents that are transformed somehow in another original document (even of another type) in a sufficient degree to warrant to be considered as new works (e.g. when the General Assembly publish a new resolution from a draft provided by someone).

In addition to these properties, UNDO makes also available the property `allot:mentions` for linking a document (or one specific version of it) to a particular entity (defined by the class `allot:Reference`) that is mentioned within (e.g. that the resolution A/RES/50/100 mentions the Government of Turkey). This property allows one to build a sophisticated network of references to entities that enables the cross-navigation between documents and other related resources.

3.2   Relations

While the aforementioned property is important, on the one hand, it does not allow one to specify the particular semantics justifying a particular mention of an entity in a document – e.g., recalling the example in the previous section, the reasons why the resolution A/RES/50/100 mentions the Government of Turkey. On the other hand, other relevant relations between non-document entities, that are by reading the natural language argumentations carried by the document content, cannot be described – e.g. the sentence of the aforementioned resolution where "the General Assembly reiterates its gratitude to the Government of Turkey".

Since it is not possible to define all the kinds of relations that could be hidden behind the content of any United Nations document, UNDO makes available a mechanism for defining such relations in a flexible way without changing its Tbox every time one needs a new relation. In fact, we have chosen to define relations between entities by means of a particular class, i.e. `undo:Relation`, so as to enable their specification by means of the following properties:

- `undo:hasProponent`, which is used for identifying the subject entity of a relation (e.g. the "General Assembly" described in the sentence "the General Assembly reiterates its gratitude to the Government of Turkey");
- `undo:hasReceiver`, which is used for identifying the object entity of a relation (e.g. the "Government of Turkey", in the previous example);
- `undo:hasSemantics`, which is used for specifying the particular concept defining the semantics of the relation (e.g. "reiterates its gratitude", in the previous example).

3.3   Annotations to documents

By reading a document content, several people can derive different (even contrasting) interpretations upon the same text. For instance, the same sentence, e.g. "Encourages all relevant non-governmental organizations [...] to participate in and contribute to the Conference" can be read as an invitation or as a reproach for having not doing any action yet. Therefore, it is important to have some mechanism for allowing the existence of all these different interpretations in a way that is understandable and still consistent from an ontological perspective.

For this reason, UNDO reuses the framework defined in the Web Annotation Ontology that allows one to annotate documents (or even portions of them) by means of another entity, such as a relation as introduced in the previous subsection. In particular, every annotation in UNDO is defined as an individual of the class `undo:Annotation`, and the following properties are used to link an entity to the document (or one of its parts) it annotates:

- the property `oa:hasBody` is used to specify the body of the annotation to be attached to the document;
- the property `oa:hasTarget` is used to indicate the particular document to which the annotation is specified.

3.4   Terms and their semantics

Broadly speaking, terms are words or groups of words whose meanings are defined in a formal and precise manner by means of specific concepts. Thus, terms can refer to nouns (e.g. "computer keyboard"), verbs (e.g. "decide"), persons (e.g. "John"), cities (e.g. "New York"), etc., they can share the same textual content while being polysemous (e.g. the city "Paris" and the person "Paris"), they can refer to the same meaning (e.g. the third person verb "decides" in English and its related in Spanish, "decide"), and so on.

In UNDO the class `allot:Term` is used to define terms, while the property `undo:hasRelatedConcept` enables to link a term to the concept (introduced by the class `allot:Concept`) defining the meaning of the term in consideration.

3.5   Values, time and context

Several kinds of objects can be involved in situations describing them as holding a certain value associated for a specific interval or according to a specific context. For instance, agents having a particular role (e.g. being the President of the United Nations General Assembly for the whole 2016) or documents holding particular status (e.g. a document that has been under-review from September 2016 to October 2016) in a specific time and/or related to a particular context are examples for these situations.

In UNDO these situations can be described by means of the class `undo:ValueInTimeAndContext`, which introduces the framework defined by the TVC ontology pattern introduced in Sect. 2. In particular, it allows one to specify:

- the entity holding such value (e.g. an agent or a document) by means of the property `tvc:hasValue`;
- the value held (e.g. a role or a status) by means of the property `tvc:withValue`;
- the time defining when such value is held (e.g. from 2006 to 2015) using the property `tvc:atTime`;
- the context to which the scenario applies (e.g. the United Nations General Assembly) using the property `tvc:withinContext`.

3.6   Workflows and their executions

Keeping track of the processes concerning the creation and modification of documents is a crucial task to address in the legal and legislative domain. Each of these processes, commonly called workflow, is actually composed by a sequence of steps. Each step is responsible to produce some outputs (e.g. a review) starting from some inputs (e.g. a document).

In UNDO, workflows can be described from two different points of view, by reusing the framework implemented included in the SPAR Ontologies, i.e. the Publishing Workflow Ontology (PWO, http://purl.org/spar/pwo) [7]. On the one hand, there is the declaration of the workflow schema, or simply the workflow (`undo:Workflow`), which is how a specific process (e.g. the publication of a document, the deliberative process) is organized in sequential steps (`undo:Step`). On the other hand, each particular execution of a workflow (`undo:WorkflowExecution`) is a specific entity per se and it is usually composed by sets of actions (`undo:Action`), and each action is executed within a particular interval (`pwo:happened`). It is worth mentioning that this module of UNDO is able to describe the full characterisation that Akoma Ntoso provides in its specification about document workflows and lifecycles – the latter by means of the class `undo:Lifecycle`.

4   Uses of UNDO in the United Nations

The development of UNDO is the result of a joint effort of some of the United Nations agencies for producing a Semantic Interoperability Framework (UNSIF) for normative and parliamentary documents (http://www.unsceb.org/content/akn4un) – it is worth mentioning that all the authors of this paper have been involved as external experts by the UN in the UNSIF. This framework includes UNDO and a particular customization of Akoma Ntoso for the United Nations System (AKN4UN), which defines the guidelines for the localisation of the Akoma Ntoso XML standard to the specific requirements of UN parliamentary and normative documents.

As result of this work, the United Nations have already started to adopt the first version of the AKN4UN Guidelines (https://www.w3id.org/un/schema/akn4un/) for the markup of UN normative and parliamentary documents and UNDO as the main reference for the implementation of UNSIF (http://www.unsystem.org/content/akn4un). Both AKN4UN and UNDO are considered living documents by the UN, since they can evolve in the future so as to address and incorporate new developments and requirements. However, even if these resources are living standards, their adoption has put the foundations for marking UN documents with machine-readable data, so as to foster collaboration and to reduce costs in information management across the system. The aim is to transform the information inclosed within word-processor documents into a Linked Open Data that can be navigated and interpreted by machines to create innovative services.

Thus, while the sustainability of UNDO is guaranteed by the United Nations, as it is one of its assets, there is no explicit evidence of its broad adoption worldwide so far, since it is has been released recently. However, it is the basic ontology that the United Nations and their agencies will use for describing their documents and their relations in RDF.

5 Conclusions

In this document we have provided an overview of the United Nations Document Ontology (UNDO), i.e. an OWL 2 DL ontology that aims at providing a framework for the description of all the entities mentioned in United Nations documents stored in Akoma Ntoso, and the relations that can exists among them. The idea behind the development of this model is to provide a common framework to be used and, eventually, extended by the various agencies of the United Nations for sharing data about documents and their content in RDF format in an interchangeable way. There are several works that can be done in the future in the context of UNDO and related entities, so as to guarantee its broad usage within the United Nations. The most urgent one is to study and implement an algorithm (e.g. based on XSLT) that takes Akoma Ntoso documents as input and returns a set of RDF statements compliant with UNDO, so as to foster the adoption of the ontology.

References

1. Arp, R., Smith, B., Spear, A.D.: Building Ontologies with Basic Formal Ontology. MIT Press, Cambridge (2015). ISBN 978-0262527811
2. Barabucci, G., Cervone, L., Di Iorio, A., Palmirani, M., Peroni, S., Vitali, F.: Managing semantics in XML vocabularies: an experience in the legal and legislative domain. In: Proceedings of Balisage 2009 (2010). doi:10.4242/BalisageVol5. Barabucci01
3. Falco, R., Gangemi, A., Peroni, S., Vitali, F.: Modelling OWL ontologies with Graffoo. In: Proceedings of ESWC 2014 Satellite Events (2014). doi:10.1007/978-3-319-11955-7_42
4. Gangemi, A., Guarino, N., Masolo, C., Oltramari, A., Schneider, L.: Sweetening ontologies with DOLCE. In: Proceedings of EKAW 2002 (2002). doi:10.1007/3-540-45810-7_18
5. Gangemi, A., Peroni, S.: DiTTO: diagrams transformation into OWL. In: Proceedings of the ISWC 2013 Posters & Demonstrations Track. (2013). http://ceur-ws.org/Vol-1035/iswc2013_demo_2.pdf
6. IFLA Study Group on the FRBR.: Functional requirements for bibliographic records (2009). http://www.ifla.org/publications/functional-requirements-for-bibliographic-records. Accessed 7 May 2017
7. Peroni, S.: The Semantic publishing and referencing ontologies. In: Semantic Web Technologies and Legal Scholarly Publishing. Springer, Cham (2014). doi:10.1007/978-3-319-04777-5_5
8. Peroni, S.: A simplified agile methodology for ontology development. In Proceedings of the OWLED-ORE 2016 (2017). doi:10.1007/978-3-319-54627-8_5
9. Peroni, S., Shotton, D., Vitali, F.: The live OWL documentation environment: a tool for the automatic generation of ontology documentation. In: Proceedings of EKAW 2012 (2012). doi:10.1007/978-3-642-33876-2_35

One Year of the OpenCitations Corpus
Releasing RDF-Based Scholarly Citation Data into the Public Domain

Silvio Peroni[1(✉)], David Shotton[2], and Fabio Vitali[1]

[1] DASPLab, DISI, University of Bologna, Bologna, Italy
{silvio.peroni,fabio.vitali}@unibo.it
[2] Oxford e-Research Centre, University of Oxford, Oxford, UK
david.shotton@oerc.ox.ac.uk

Abstract. Reference lists from academic articles are core elements of scholarly communication that permit the attribution of credit and integrate our independent research endeavours. Hitherto, however, they have not been freely available in an appropriate machine-readable format such as RDF and in aggregate for use by scholars. To address this issue, one year ago we started ingesting citation data from the Open Access literature into the OpenCitations Corpus (OCC), creating an RDF dataset of scholarly citation data that is open to all. In this paper we introduce the OCC and we discuss its outcomes and uses after the first year of life.

Keywords: OCC · Open citation data · OpenCitations · OpenCitations corpus · Public domain · SPAR ontologies

1 Introduction

The availability of open citation data has been recently recognised as an important objective for the scholarly community at large. One of the most important movements in this direction has been the recently launched Initiative for Open Citations (I4OC, https://i4oc.org). The premise of this initiative has been the fact that, while citations are unanimously recognised as crucial for knitting together our scientific and cultural knowledge, regrettably they are mostly not freely accessible. Rather, the best citation databases charge high subscription rates, and are oriented towards human readability rather than machine readability and data re-use. In response to this situation, I4OC has established a collaboration between scholarly publishers, researchers, and other interested parties to promote the unrestricted availability of scholarly citation data, initially by encouraging scholarly publishers to make open the article reference lists they already deposit to Crossref. This initiative has achieved massive initial success, with almost all the major scientific publishers now opening their reference lists in this way.

Among the I4OC founders, one specific organization, OpenCitations [9,13], has the objective of employing Semantic Web technologies to create an open

© Springer International Publishing AG 2017
C. d'Amato et al. (Eds.): ISWC 2017, Part II, LNCS 10588, pp. 184–192, 2017.
DOI: 10.1007/978-3-319-68204-4_19

repository of the citation data that publishers have made available. In this paper, we introduce the main service developed by that organization, namely the OpenCitations Corpus (OCC), an open repository of RDF-based scholarly citation data (obtained by parsing the articles included in the PubMed Central Open Access subset[1]), made freely available so that others may use and build upon them. All the resources published by OpenCitations – namely the data within the OCC, the ontologies describing the data, and the software developed to build the OCC – are available to the public with open licenses. In particular, the OCC strictly follows the FAIR principles for data-intensive science, namely that the data should be findable, accessible, interoperable, and re-usable [14], and employs the three basic criteria promoted by I4OC, namely that the citation data must be structured, separable, and open (https://i4oc.org/#goals).

The rest of this paper is structured as follows. In Sect. 2, we introduce some of the most important related works in the area. In Sect. 3, we briefly introduce the models and tools used to create the OCC, explain which data it contains, and summarize the nature of the services used for the automatic ingestion of citation data. In Sect. 4, we present descriptive statistics about the OpenCitations Corpus almost one year since its launch, to show its impact to the scholarly community at large. Finally, in Sect. 5, we summarize and outline future developments.

2   Related Works

In recent years we have seen a growing interest within the Semantic Web community for creating and making available RDF datasets concerning the bibliographic metadata of scholarly documents.

Semantic Lancet [2] aims at building a Linked Open Data (LOD) dataset of scholarly publication metadata starting from articles published by Elsevier. In particular, the current dataset contains SPAR-based [8] metadata about several papers published in the Journal of Web Semantics, including citation links marked with the motivations justifying them using CiTO properties[2].

WikiCite[3] is a proposal, with a related series of workshops, which aims at building a bibliographic database in Wikidata to serve all Wikimedia projects. As of 30 April 2017, Wikidata contains around 3,000,000 citation links between bibliographic resources.

The Springer Nature SciGraph[4] is a new (LOD) platform aggregating data sources from Springer Nature and other partners, and it contains data about funders, research projects, conferences, affiliations and publications.

Springer LOD [3] is an RDF dataset made available by Springer Nature that publishes Springer metadata about conferences as LOD. Its main focus is on proceedings volumes and the related conferences, but it does not contain metadata describing the individual articles within such proceedings.

---

[1] https://www.ncbi.nlm.nih.gov/pmc/tools/openftlist/.

[2] http://purl.org/spar/cito.

[3] https://meta.wikimedia.org/wiki/WikiCite.

[4] http://www.springernature.com/scigraph.

OpenAIRE [1] is an Horizon 2020 open data project which publishes metadata of more than 14,000,000 of publications and thousands of datasets, but does not include their citations. It makes available a mechanism for searching, discovering and monitoring scientific outputs.

Finally, Scholarly Data [5] is a project that refactors the Semantic Web Dog Food so as to keep the dataset growing in good health, and that has adopted a new ontology (aligned with other existing models, including the SPAR Ontologies [8]) for describing the data.

3   Building the OpenCitations Corpus

OpenCitations (http://opencitations.net) [9] formally started in 2010 as a one-year Open Citations Project at the University of Oxford, that was funded by JISC[5] and subsequently extended for an additional half year. The main goal of the project was the creation of a collection of open citation data called the OpenCitations Corpus (OCC), harvested from the open access literature in PubMed Central and made available in RDF. To our knowledge, it was the first RDF-based dataset of open citation data. At the end of 2015, a formal collaboration between the University of Oxford and the University of Bologna was initiated to build from that initial Oxford prototype by setting up a new instantiation of the OCC based on a revised metadata schema and employing several new technologies to automate the daily ingestion of fresh citation metadata from authoritative sources. The OCC is now the largest truly open collection of RDF-based citation data available on the Web.

This new instantiation of the OCC holds accurate scholarly citation data derived from bibliographic references harvested from the scholarly literature, and makes them available under a Creative Commons public domain dedication (CC0)[6]. These are described using the SPAR Ontologies [8] and other standard vocabularies according to the OCC metadata document [10] that is briefly summarized in Fig. 1, and are implemented by means of the OpenCitations Ontology (OCO, https://w3id.org/oc/ontology). OCO is not yet another bibliographic ontology, but rather simply a mechanism for grouping together existing complementary ontological entities from several other ontologies, for the purpose of providing descriptive metadata for the OCC all in one place. Specifically, it provides a way to describe the citing/cited bibliographic resources (conference papers, book chapters, journal articles, etc.) and their containers (academic proceedings, books, journals, etc.), the formats in which they have been embodied (digital vs. print, first and ending pages, etc.), the roles of relevant bibliographic agents (author, editor, publisher, etc.) related to the bibliographic resources, the textual content of each reference in the reference list of a citing bibliographic resource, all the identifiers (e.g. DOI, PubMed ID, PubMed Central ID, ORCID, ISSN, etc.) for the bibliographic resources and the agents involved, and the names

---

[5] http://www.jisc.ac.uk/whatwedo/programmes/inf11/jiscexpo/jiscopencitation.aspx.
[6] https://creativecommons.org/publicdomain/zero/1.0/legalcode.

of those agents such as their given and family names. A detailed description of the whole model is given in [12].

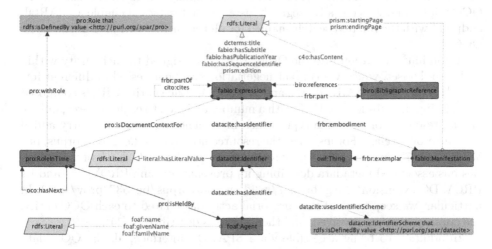

Fig. 1. The Graffoo diagram [4] of the main ontological entities described by the OCC metadata model – all the prefix declarations are defined in OCO.

The OCC stores all the aforementioned metadata in RDF. The corpus URL (https://w3id.org/oc/corpus/) identifies the entire OCC, which is composed of several sub-datasets, one for each of the following kinds of bibliographic entities included in the corpus: bibliographic resources ("br", identified by the class `fabio:Expression`), resource embodiments ("re", class `fabio:Manifestation`), bibliographic entries ("be", class `fabio:BibliographicReference`), responsible agents ("ra", class `foaf:Agent`), agent roles ("ar", class `pro:RoleInTime`), and identifiers ("id", class `datacite:Identifier`). Each of these has a URL composed by suffixing the corpus URL with the two-letter short name for the class of entity (e.g. "be" for a bibliographic entry) followed by an oblique slash (e.g. https://w3id.org/oc/corpus/be/). Each dataset is described appropriately by means of the Data Catalog Vocabulary[7] and the VoID Vocabulary[8].

The ingestion of new data into the OCC is curated by two Python scripts, the *Bibliographic Entries Extractor*, a.k.a. *BEE*, and the *SPAR Citation Indexer*, a.k.a. *SPACIN*. Both of these are available on the OpenCitations GitHub repository (https://github.com/essepuntato/opencitations) and are released as open source code according to the ISC Licence[9]. BEE is responsible for the creation of JSON files[10] containing reference lists from articles in the OA subset of PubMed Central (retrieved by using the Europe PubMed Central API[11]).

---

[7] https://www.w3.org/TR/vocab-dcat/.

[8] https://www.w3.org/TR/void/.

[9] https://opensource.org/licenses/ISC.

[10] An example of these JSON files is introduced at http://opencitations.net/corpus.

[11] https://europepmc.org/RestfulWebService.

SPACIN processes each JSON file created by BEE, retrieves additional meta-data information about all the citing/cited articles described in it by querying the Crossref API[12] and the ORCID API[13], and finally stores all the data in the OCC triplestore, which is a Blazegraph instance that makes available a SPARQL endpoint with the full text search enabled for all the entities included in the entire OCC.

Upon initial curation into the OCC, a URL is assigned to each entity within each sub-dataset, which via content negotiation can be accessed in different for-mats (HTML, RDF/XML, Turtle, and JSON-LD). Each entity URL is composed by suffixing the sub-dataset URL with a number assigned to each resource, unique among resources of the same type, which increments for each new entry added to that resource class. For instance, the resource https://w3id.org/oc/corpus/be/537 is the 537th bibliographic entry recorded within the OCC. Each of these enti-ties has associated metadata describing its provenance using PROV-O[14] and its PROV-DC extension[15] (e.g. https://w3id.org/oc/corpus/be/537/prov/se/1). In particular, we keep track of the curatorial activities related to each OCC entity, the curatorial agents involved, and their roles, as described in [11].

In addition to being accessible via a SPARQL interface, all the OCC data are also made available as data dumps, which are created monthly and are stored online by means of the support of Figshare[16]. Each dump is composed of several zip archives, each containing either data or provenance information, stored in JSON-LD, relating to a particular sub-dataset within the OCC. We decided to use JSON-LD as storing format in order to make the OCC data easily comprehensible also to Web-developers and researchers with no expertise in Semantic Web technologies and formats. In addition, one of these archives includes the whole triplestore for easy reuse (e.g. the April 2017 dump of the entire OCC triplestore – approx. 16 Gbytes of zipped data – is available at [7]). As introduced by an appropriate README file included in each archive, after unzipping it, one needs to use Disk ARchive (DAR) – a multi-platform archive tool for managing huge amounts of data – to recreate the entire OCC structure. It has been also produced a single n-quad file of the whole OCC of the April 2017 dump (approx. 12 Gbytes of zipped data) that is available at [6].

4   Community Uptake and Statistics

The intended goal of the new instantiation of the OCC, which started data acquisition in early July 2016, was to ingest around five hundred thousand new citation links per month, so as to reach the goal of 6,000,000 citation links after one year of processing, as anticipated in [12]. As of 15 May 2017, the OCC has

---

[12] https://api.crossref.org/.
[13] http://members.orcid.org/api/.
[14] https://www.w3.org/TR/prov-o/.
[15] https://www.w3.org/TR/prov-dc/.
[16] https://figshare.com/authors/OpenCitations_Project/3068259.

ingested the references from 150,000 citing bibliographic resources, and it contains information about 6,500,000 citation links to more than 4,000,000 cited resources – thus achieving our original goal in only ten months. Since May 2016, the OpenCitations website has been accessed more than 540,000 times[17] (as of 8 May 2017) by users from several countries (identified by IP address of the request), as shown in Fig. 2. It is worth mentioning that the pages related to the data available and the services for querying them (i.e. "corpus" and "sparql" portions of the right-most pie chart in Fig. 2) have together gained a very high percentage of the overall accesses (i.e. 88%), showing that the main reason people access the OpenCitations website is to explore and use the data in the OCC. These statistics provide clear evidence of the interest that the scholarly communication community is showing in OpenCitations.

Fig. 2. The page accesses the OpenCitations website has received in the past year, grouped by month, by country, and by each of the nine OC website pages, as of 8 May 2017.

In Fig. 3, we show the statistics (as of 8 May 2017) concerning the OCC data dumps that have been made available on Figshare. With the exception of the first dump we released on 24 September 2016, where the archive containing the entire triplestore has been downloaded over 2,500 times (probably by several software agents via the Figshare APIs), the absolute numbers of downloads show an increasing trend with time, while the percentage of the users visiting the OCC data dumps on Figshare who also download the datasets is also increasing for the most recent dumps.

We have also analysed the statistics related to the OpenCitations social web resources, namely the OpenCitations Twitter account (https://twitter.com/opencitations) and the OpenCitations Blog on Wordpress (https://opencitations.wordpress.com). As shown in Fig. 4, there is a clear increase in usage following the 6 April 2017 launch of the Initiative for Open Citations, of which OpenCitations is a founding member.

In addition to the aforementioned evidences of interest in OpenCitations within the global scholarly community, the citation data provided by the OCC are being used by a number of independent international projects, among which

---

[17] We have excluded from this list the hits done by well-known spiders and crawlers – e.g. Google crawlers.

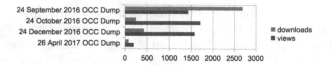

Fig. 3. The number of times the OCC data dumps released on Figshare have been visited and downloaded (as of 8 May 2017). The low numbers for the 26 April 2017 dump is because only twelve days had elapsed since data deposit when the counts were made. Note that dumps were not made in November 2016, nor in January, February and March 2017, for technical reasons that have now been resolved.

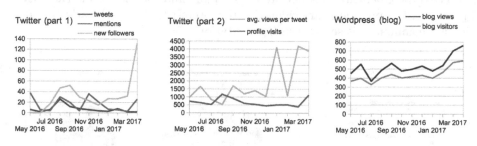

Fig. 4. The number of interactions that the OpenCitations social media accounts have had over the past year.

are Wikidata, OpenAIRE, and LOC-DB[18]. In particular, the first includes the property OpenCitations bibliographic resource ID[19] when linking Wikidata resources to those included in the OCC; the second is in the process of re-publishing within their database all the article metadata included in the December 2016 dump of the OCC; while the third is using the OpenCitations data model [10] for modelling their citation data. This demonstrates reuse by those projects of the metadata structures developed for OpenCitations and the citation data produced by the OpenCitations ingestion workflow. It is worth mentioning that the OCC resources have been made available and accessible in different ways, so as to facilitate their reuse in different contexts: as monthly dumps (http://opencitations.net/download), via the SPARQL endpoint (https://w3id.org/oc/sparql), and by accessing them directly by means of the HTTP URIs of the stored resources (via content negotiation, e.g. https://w3id.org/oc/corpus/br/1).

The data collected by the new instantiation of the OCC since its start in July 2016, and available in the dump made on 26 April 2017, are summarized in Table 1.

---

[18] https://locdb.bib.uni-mannheim.de/.
[19] https://www.wikidata.org/wiki/Property:P3181.

Table 1. The number of different bibliographic entity types presently described within the OCC dump made on 26 April 2017.

Entity type	Number of entities in the OCC
Bibliographic resource (br)	5.4 millions
Resource embodiment (re)	3.1 millions
Bibliographic entries (be)	6.5 millions
Responsible agents (ra)	16.7 millions
Agent roles (ar)	21.2 millions
Identifiers (id)	11 millions

5 Conclusions

In this paper we have introduced the OpenCitations Corpus (OCC), which is an open repository of RDF-based scholarly citation data. All the data included in the OCC are made available under a Creative Commons CC0 Public Domain dedication, while the other resources used for building the OCC (software, documentation, etc.) are also made available to the public with appropriate open licenses. The initial sustainability of this new instantiation of the OCC was made possible using the IT services of the Department of Computer Science and Engineering of the University of Bologna, to whom we are most grateful. We have now received funding from the Alfred P. Sloan Foundation[20], which will enable us substantially to extend the current infrastructure and the rate of data ingest. Our immediate goal is to increment the daily ingestion of citation data from 500,000 citations per month to 500,000 *per day*. In addition, we plan to extend the scripts developed so as to add links to external datasets, to analyse the OCC so as to understand the quality of its current data, and to develop new user interfaces that will expand the means whereby users can interact with the OpenCitations data.

Acknowledgements. We would like to thank all the reviewers for having provided useful comments and desiderata to include in OpenCitations Corpus. Their suggestions have been already added as issues in the GitHub repository (see issues 11–19) and they will be taken into consideration as future developments of the resource.

References

1. Alexiou, G., Vahdati, S., Lange, C., Papastefanatos, G., Lohmann, S.: OpenAIRE LOD services: scholarly communication data as linked data. In: González-Beltrán, A., Osborne, F., Peroni, S. (eds.) SAVE-SD 2016. LNCS, vol. 9792, pp. 45–50. Springer, Cham (2016). doi:10.1007/978-3-319-53637-8_6

---

[20] https://sloan.org/.

2. Bagnacani, A., Ciancarini, P., Di Iorio, A., Nuzzolese, A.G., Peroni, S., Vitali, F.: The semantic lancet project: a linked open dataset for scholarly publishing. In: Lambrix, P., Hyvönen, E., Blomqvist, E., Presutti, V., Qi, G., Sattler, U., Ding, Y., Ghidini, C. (eds.) EKAW 2014. LNCS, vol. 8982, pp. 101–105. Springer, Cham (2015). doi:10.1007/978-3-319-17966-7_10

3. Bryl, V., Birukou, A., Eckert, K., Kessler, M.: What's in the proceedings? Combining publisher's and researcher's perspectives. In: Proceedings of SePublica 2014 (2014). http://ceur-ws.org/Vol-1155/paper-01.pdf

4. Falco, R., Gangemi, A., Peroni, S., Shotton, D., Vitali, F.: Modelling OWL ontologies with graffoo. In: Presutti, V., Blomqvist, E., Troncy, R., Sack, H., Papadakis, I., Tordai, A. (eds.) ESWC 2014. LNCS, vol. 8798, pp. 320–325. Springer, Cham (2014). doi:10.1007/978-3-319-11955-7_42

5. Nuzzolese, A.G., Gentile, A.L., Presutti, V., Gangemi, A.: Conference linked data: the scholarlydata project. In: Groth, P., Simperl, E., Gray, A., Sabou, M., Krötzsch, M., Lecue, F., Flöck, F., Gil, Y. (eds.) ISWC 2016. LNCS, vol. 9982, pp. 150–158. Springer, Cham (2016). doi:10.1007/978-3-319-46547-0_16

6. OpenCitations: the entire OCC n-quads data dump, made on 26 April 2017. figshare (2017). doi:10.6084/m9.figshare.5147068

7. OpenCitations: the entire OCC triplestore data dump, made on 26 April 2017. figshare (2017). doi:10.6084/m9.figshare.4959869

8. Peroni, S.: The semantic publishing and referencing ontologies. Semantic Web Technologies and Legal Scholarly Publishing. LGTS, vol. 15, pp. 121–193. Springer, Cham (2014). doi:10.1007/978-3-319-04777-5_5

9. Peroni, S., Dutton, A., Gray, T., Shotton, D.: Setting our bibliographic references free: towards open citation data. J. Doc. **71**(2), 253–277 (2015). doi:10.1108/JD-12-2013-0166

10. Peroni, S., Shotton, D.: Metadata for the OpenCitations corpus. Figshare (2016). doi:10.6084/m9.figshare.3443876

11. Peroni, S., Shotton, D., Vitali, F.: A document-inspired way for tracking changes of RDF data – The case of the opencitations corpus. In: Proceedings of Drift-a-LOD 2016, pp. 26–33 (2016). http://ceur-ws.org/Vol-1799/Drift-a-LOD2016_paper_4.pdf

12. Peroni, S., Shotton, D., Vitali, F.: Freedom for bibliographic references: opencitations arise. In Proceedings of LD4IE 2016, pp. 32–43 (2016). http://ceur-ws.org/Vol-1699/paper-05.pdf

13. Shotton, D.: Open citations. Nature **502**(7471), 295–297 (2013). doi:10.1038/502295a

14. Wilkinson, M.D., Dumontier, M., Aalbersberg, I.J., Appleton, G., et al.: The fair Guiding Principles for scientific data management and stewardship. Sci. Data **3**, 160018 (2016). doi:10.1038/sdata.2016.18

An Entity Relatedness Test Dataset

José Eduardo Talavera Herrera[1]([✉]), Marco Antonio Casanova[1],
Bernardo Pereira Nunes[1,2], Luiz André P. Paes Leme[3],
and Giseli Rabello Lopes[4]

[1] Department of Informatics, Pontifical Catholic University of Rio de Janeiro,
Rio de Janeiro, RJ, Brazil
{jherrera, casanova, bnunes}@inf.puc-rio.br
[2] Federal University of the State of Rio de Janeiro, Rio de Janeiro, RJ, Brazil
[3] Fluminense Federal University, Niterói, RJ, Brazil
lapaesleme@ic.uff.br
[4] Federal University of Rio de Janeiro, Rio de Janeiro, RJ, Brazil
giseli@dcc.ufrj.br

Abstract. A knowledge base stores descriptions of entities and their relationships, often in the form of a very large RDF graph, such as DBpedia or Wikidata. The entity relatedness problem refers to the question of computing the relationship paths that better capture the connectivity between a given entity pair. This paper describes a dataset created to support the evaluation of approaches that address the entity relatedness problem. The dataset covers two familiar domains, music and movies, and uses data available in IMDb and last. fm, which are popular reference datasets in these domains. The paper describes in detail how sets of entity pairs from each of these domains were selected and, for each entity pair, how a ranked list of relationship paths was obtained.

Keywords: Entity relatedness · Relationship path · Path ranking · Linked data · Knowledge bases

1 Introduction

A Knowledge Base (KB) stores descriptions of entities and their relationships, often in the form of a very large RDF graph, such as DBpedia or Wikidata. A *relationship path* between an entity pair is a path in an RDF graph that connects the nodes that represent the entities. The *entity relatedness problem* refers to the question of computing the relationship paths that better describe the connectivity between a given entity pair.

Several approaches [1–6] have been proposed to address the entity relatedness problem. They apply a simple strategy: (1) search for relationship paths between the given entity pair – the larger the number of paths found, the stronger the connectivity between the entities is likely to be; and (2) sort the paths found and select the relevant ones. However, there currently is no adequate benchmarks to measure the effectiveness of such approaches. In some cases, expert users evaluate the results, and an apparently reliable method to judge the effectiveness of the approach is introduced. In others, a *ground truth* is created, which is a difficult and time-consuming task, and hardly the

© Springer International Publishing AG 2017
C. d'Amato et al. (Eds.): ISWC 2017, Part II, LNCS 10588, pp. 193–201, 2017.
DOI: 10.1007/978-3-319-68204-4_20

authors make the resources available. Thus, an open challenge is: *How to evaluate and compare approaches that address the entity relatedness problem?*

The major contribution of this paper is a dataset created to support the evaluation of approaches that address the entity relatedness problem, which we refer to as the *Entity Relatedness Test Dataset*. The dataset contains entities and relationship paths extracted from DBpedia that pertain to two familiar domains, music and movies, and additional data extracted from the Internet Movie Database – IMDb and last.fm, which are popular reference datasets in these domains. The dataset and resources are available at [17–21].

The paper describes in detail the major steps and design decisions behind the construction of the dataset. The first design decision was to select DBpedia as the reference knowledge base, from which we extracted relationships paths. The second design decision was to select the movies and music domains, which are backed up by two well-known datasets, IMDb and last.fm, from which we extracted reliable domain-specific knowledge. The dataset construction process involved three major steps. The first step consisted in the selection of a set of entity pairs from the music and movies domains. The second step referred to the extraction of a set of relationship paths from DBpedia, for each entity pair. The final step was to rank the paths, based on information extracted from IMDb and last.fm, and to select the top-k ones.

This paper is structured as follows. Section 2 summarizes related work. Section 3 introduces a generic strategy to find and rank relationship paths. Section 4 describes the construction of the dataset. Finally, Sect. 5 presents the conclusions.

2   Related Work

Finding and Ranking Relationship Paths Between a Given Entity Pair in a Knowledge Base. RECAP [3], EXPLASS [4] and DBpedia Profiler [6] implemented path finding processes in an RDF knowledge base with the help of SPARQL queries [9]. REX [2] used two breadth-first searches on the RDF graph to enumerate relationship paths between two entities, and considered the degree of a node as an activation criterion to prioritize nodes. Likewise, the work in [15] used the Jaccard similarity to compute an approximated minimal distance between the start and the end nodes, and to discover meaningful connection between the nodes.

Evaluating Relationship-Path Ranking in a Knowledge Base. Path-ranking measures were proposed in [3, 6, 8] to rank relationship paths in knowledge databases. Some approaches [3, 4, 6] evaluated relationship path rankings with the help of user experiments. However, the evaluation methods did not clearly define the capabilities of the approaches analyzed. The work proposed in [10] argued that entity similarity heuristics increase the relevance of the links between nodes. The authors compared and measured the effectiveness of different search strategies through user experiments.

In this paper, we describe a dataset containing entity pairs and relationship paths in two entertainment domains, music and movies, to compare approaches that address the entity relatedness problem.

3   A Generic Relationship Path Finding and Ranking Process

An RDF graph G is a set of RDF triples of the form $G = \{(s, p, o)\} = (V, E)$, where the subject is an entity $s \in V$, and it has property $p \in E$ whose value is an object $o \in V$, which is either another entity. Particularly, p is seen as the edge that link the entities s and o in an RDF Graph. We will use the terms *entity* and *node* of G interchangeably.

A *relationship path* in G between nodes w_0 and w_k in G is an expression of the form $(w_0, p_1, w_1, p_2, w_2, ..., p_{k-1}, w_{k-1}, p_k, w_k)$, where: k is the *length* of the path; w_i is a node of G such that w_i and w_j are different, for $0 \le i \ne j \le k$; and either (w_i, w_{i+1}) or (w_{i+1}, w_i) are edges of G labeled with p_{i+1}, for $0 \le i < k$. Note that, since a relationship path is an undirected path, but G is a directed graph, we allow either (w_i, w_{i+1}) or (w_{i+1}, w_i) to participate in the path. Alternatively, one may assume that each property p has an inverse, denoted "$\hat{p}$", using SPARQL notation.

To construct the dataset, we adopt a generic path finding and ranking process, briefly described as follow.

The path finding algorithm receives an RDF graph G, two *target entities*, v_{start} and v_{end}, a *maximum distance* k, and an *activation function* τ. It implements two breadth first searches (BFS), executed in parallel, to find paths in G between the target entities [7, 10, 14]. A BFS is started from each target entity (line 6). Subpaths are generated in the expansion step, and full paths are created when one of the target entities is reached, or the subpaths S_{left} or S_{right} share a common entity (line 7). An activation function τ optimizes the traversal of G; only entities that comply with the activation criteria are considered. The output of the algorithm is a set of RDF paths between v_{start} and v_{end}.

The path ranking algorithm receives a set of paths *Paths* and a *path ranking function f*, and outputs a ranked subset of *Paths*.

The final algorithm calls the path finding algorithm and then the path ranking algorithm. It outputs a ranked list of paths.

PathFinding(G, v_{start}, v_{end}, k, τ): *Paths*
Input: an entity pair v_{start} and v_{end}
    a maximum distance k
    an activation function τ
Output: a set of paths *Paths* that link
    the given pair of entities

1: *expanding* ← 0, *Paths* ←∅
2: *side* ← 0, *left* ← 0 , *right* ← 1
3: S_{left} ← {*subpath*(v_{start}, null, null)}
4: S_{right} ← { *subpath*(v_{end}, null, null)}
5: **repeat**
6:    S_{side} ←*expand*(S_{side}, τ)
7:    *Paths* ←*Join*(S_{left}, S_{right}, v_{start}, v_{end})
8:    *expanding* ← *expanding* + 1
9:    *side* = (*side* +1) *mod* 2
10: **until** *expanding* <= k
11: **return** *Paths*

ReferencePathList(G, v_{start}, v_{end}, k, τ, f): *Paths*
Input: an entity pair v_{start} and v_{end}
    a maximum distance k
    an activation function τ
    a path ranking measure f
Output: a set of paths *Paths* sorted

1: *Paths* ← **PathFinding**(G, v_{start}, v_{end}, k, τ)
2: *Paths* ← **PathRanking**(*Paths*, f)
3: **return** *Paths*

4   Constructing the Entity Relatedness Test Dataset

The construction of the Entity Relatedness Test Dataset poses three major challenges: (1) how to select entity pairs; (2) how to find relationship paths for the entity pairs selected; and (3) how to rank the relationship paths. We addressed these challenges in the movies and music domains.

The dataset and resource are available at [17–21]. Examples and a more detailed evaluation of how use this dataset can be found in [16].

4.1   Selecting Entity Pairs

We focused on best-selling music artists[1], in the music domain, and on famous classic actors and actresses[2], in the movies domain. We considered the box office sales and the actor's fame as relevance criteria for the music and movies domains.

After selecting a list of entities from each of these two domains, we submitted each entity to Google Search to select a set of related entities. Then, for the possible entity pair, we computed their semantic connectivity score[3] [11] in DBpedia, with maximum length 4, to discover entity pairs with high connectivity. The maximum path length between two entities was set to 4, since it is a value backed up by the small world [12] phenomenon, which says that a pair of nodes is separated by a small number of connections, and since it was confirmed in previous experiments [15].

4.2   Finding Relationship Paths

For each of the 40 entity pairs of our dataset, we used the path finding algorithm, described in Sect. 3 (and introduced in [16]), to create 40 sets, each with 50 relationship paths. We applied the algorithm to the RDF graph of DBpedia, and used an activation function that prioritizes entities which are instances of classes of the DBpedia ontology that pertain to the domain in question. The classes or types of an entity in DBpedia are defined through the rdf:type property. The classes of the DBpedia ontology in music and movie domains are defined in Tables 7 and 8 in Sect. 5 at [16]. The entities that belong to previous classes are considered in the generations of relationship paths in DBpedia. The path finding algorithm uses as single activation function the classes of the DBpedia ontology in the domain concerned, the expansion process analyses the types of each entity, if an entity belongs to a class of the ontology domain, then it is prioritized to generate relationship paths.

To define which classes of the DBpedia ontology pertain to each of the domains in question, we adopted as reference the Music Ontology, for the music domain, and the Movie Ontology, for the movies domain. Then, we manually selected classes of the DBpedia ontology that could be paired with the major classes of each reference ontology.

---

[1] https://en.wikipedia.org/wiki/List_of_best-selling_music_artists.

[2] http://www.IMDb.com/list/ls000035399/.

[3] http://lod2.inf.puc-rio.br/scs/SemConnectivities.

4.3 Mapping Entities

As a preparation to the path ranking process, we mapped entities in DBpedia to entities in the reference datasets, as explained in this section.

Music Domain. To map DBpedia entities to last.fm, we used the keyword search API of last.fm[4]: `api:artist.getInfo`, `api:album.getInfo` and `api:track. getInfo`.

We first determined whether the entity represented an artist or a musical content by analyzing the `rdf:type` property, as in [6]. For example, the entity `dbr: Michael_Jackson` has type `dbo:Artist`. If the entity represented an artist, we extracted keywords from its URI (such as "`Michael + Jackson`") and submitted them to `api:artist.getInfo`[5] to search for the entity. If the search was successful, we had an exact mapping, otherwise we used other keywords. It the entity represented musical content (an album, song or single), we had to identify its main artist in DBpedia, through the property `dbp:artist`. For example, the main artist of `dbr:Thriller_(album)` is `dbr:Michael_Jackson`. If the entity represented a musical album, we called `api:album.getInfo`[6] to search for the entity. Similarly, it the entity represented a song or a single, we called `api:track.getInfo`.

Movies Domain. In DBpedia, we used the property `rdf:type` to decide if an entity was a movie. In any other case, we considered the entity as a participant of a movie. We identified the immediate type of an entity using the method proposed in [6].

To map DBpedia entities to IMDb, we imported the IMDb[7] database to a local PostgreSQL database and re-created data about names, movies and casts (people who worked in a movie). Usually, the entities in DBpedia have an auto description in the URI. For example, the URL `dbr:Cleopatra_(1963_film)` indicates the name of a movie, "`Cleopatra`", and its release year, "`1963`". We used this basic description to find the same entity in IMDb through classic SQL queries. For those cases where the queries returned more than one result, we used the Levenshtein Distance [13] to choose the IMDb entity most similar to the DBpedia entity.

4.4 Ranking the Relationship Paths

We ranked the paths in each of the 40 sets using semantic information extracted from IMDb and last.fm to compute entity ratings, and information extracted from DBpedia to compute property relevance scores.

To obtain the ranked lists, we first computed the *score* of each path π as the average of the *rating* of the entities involved in the path. Recall that π is a path in the DBpedia graph. Each entity e used in π was first mapped to an equivalent entity e' in IMDb or

---

[4] http://www.last.fm/api.

[5] http://ws.audioscrobbler.com/2.0/?api_key=YOUR_API_KEY&method=artist.getinfo&artist= Michael+Jackson.

[6] http://ws.audioscrobbler.com/2.0/?api_key=YOUR_API_KEY&method=album.getInfo&artist= Michael+Jackson&album=Thriller.

[7] http://www.imdb.com/interfaces.

last.fm, as explained in Sect. 4.3; the rating of e' was computed from data in IMDb or last.fm, as described below, and assigned to e. Finally, the score of π was computed as the average of the ratings of the entities that occur in π.

For each entity pair, we ranked the paths using their scores and retained the top 50 paths. However, since the path score ignores the relevance of the properties, paths that involve the same entities will have the same score. As a further step, we inspected each ranked list and used the *relevance scores* of the properties, computed in DBpedia, to help rank the paths with the same entities.

This ranking process is justified for two basic reasons. On one hand, we intended to create a dataset that would help evaluate approaches that address the entity relatedness problem, which typically involve a path ranking measure. Therefore, it would not be reasonable to adopt a path ranking measure from the literature (which would create ranked lists biased to that measure). On the other hand, it would be infeasible to manually rank the relationship paths that connect two entities (in DBpedia), whose number is typically very high [16]. Hence, we opted to: (1) select two domains – music and movies – for which specialized data were available; (2) filter the paths in DBpedia so that they traverse only entities in each of these domains; (3) use specialized domain data to pre-rank the paths found; (4) manually inspect and sanction the pre-ranking, which proved to be a feasible task. The computation of entity ratings and property relevance scores is detailed below.

Entity Rating in the Music Domain. In last.fm, each artist and musical content has two relevance scores: the listeners score and the play count score. This information can be accessed through the search API of last.fm. The listeners score represents the number of different users who listen a song, and the play count score is the number of times a person listens to a song. An album, depending on the number of songs, receives as play count score (or listener score) the sum of the play count scores (or listeners scores) of the songs in the album. Similarly, an artist receives a play count score and a listener score. We used the play count score to create an entity rating in the music domain; if the entity is not identified in the mapping, we assigned a zero score.

Entity Rating in the Movies Domain. IMDb publishes user-generated ratings for movies; an IMDb registered user can cast a vote (from 1 to 10) for every released movie in the database. Users can vote as many times as they want, but each vote will overwrite the previous one. In the case of people (actors, directors, writers) involved in a movie, we computed the average rating of the movies where the person participated to generate his/her rating. We imported the movies ratings to our local database and, with the table Cast, we related movies and actors to compute the artist rating. Again, if the entity is not identified in the mapping, we assign a zero score.

Property Relevance Score in DBpedia. We used the *inverse triple frequency* (ITF) [3] as the property relevance score, defined as $itf(p, G) = log \frac{|G|}{|G_p|}$, where $|G|$ is the number of triples in a knowledge base and $|G_p|$ is the number of triples in G whose property is p.

Example: Consider the following paths of the DBpedia RDF graph:

P_1. **Elizabeth_Taylor** ^producer **The_Taming_of_the_Shrew** starring **Richard_Burton**

P_2. **Elizabeth_Taylor** ^starring **The_Taming_of_the_Shrew** starring **Richard_Burton**

where "**Elizabeth_Taylor**", "**Richard_Burton**" and "**The_Taming_of_the_Shrew**" actually are abbreviations for the URIs of these DBpedia entities, and likewise for the properties.

The first step is to compute the entity rating of these entities using information from IMDb, which involves finding these DBpedia entities in IMDb. The path scores are computed as the average of the rating of the entities in the path. Since these two paths involve the same entities, they will have the same score. The second step is then to compute the ITF in DBpedia of the properties "^starring" and "^producer" to help disambiguate the ranking. Since "^producer" is less frequent in DBpedia than "^starring", it has a higher ITF. Path P_1 should then be ranked before P_2. However, this is subjected to manual inspection to confirm the preference of P_1 over P_2, which was the final decision in this case, on the grounds that P_1 is perhaps more informative to the user than P_2.

5   Conclusions and Future Work

In this paper, we described a dataset created to support the evaluation of approaches that address the entity relatedness problem. The dataset contains entity pairs in the movies and music domains, and lists of relationship paths in DBpedia, ranked based on information about their entities found in IMDb and last.fm, and on information about their properties computed from DBpedia.

The dataset can be used to test activation functions, based on entity similarity measures, and path ranking measures directly on the DBpedia graph. To use the dataset in the context of another knowledge base K, one should remap the entities and properties used in our reference dataset to K, much as we described in Sect. 4.

The construction process can be replicated to other domains where, intuitively: (1) entities with high reputation help select "meaningful" paths; (2) less frequent properties, or more discriminatory properties, also help select "meaningful" paths. In fact, the construction process described in Sect. 4 is as interesting as the resulting dataset. Therefore, as future work, we plan to focus on other domains, such as Sports, Video Games and Academic Publication, to increase the size of the Entity Relatedness Test Dataset described in the paper.

Acknowledgments. This work was partly funded by CNPq under grants 444976/2014-0, 303332/2013-1, 442338/2014-7 and 248743/2013-9 and by FAPERJ under grant E-26/201.337/2014 and E-26/010.000794/2016.

References

1. Heim, P., Hellmann, S., Lehmann, J., Lohmann, S., Stegemann, T.: RelFinder: revealing relationships in RDF knowledge bases. In: Chua, T.-S., Kompatsiaris, Y., Mérialdo, B., Haas, W., Thallinger, G., Bailer, W. (eds.) SAMT 2009. LNCS, vol. 5887, pp. 182–187. Springer, Heidelberg (2009). doi:10.1007/978-3-642-10543-2_21
2. Fang, L., Sarma, A.D., Yu, C., Bohannon, P.: REX: explaining relationships between entity pairs. PVLDB 5(3), 241–252 (2011)
3. Pirrò, G.: Explaining and suggesting relatedness in knowledge graphs. In: Arenas, M., et al. (eds.) ISWC 2015. LNCS, vol. 9366, pp. 622–639. Springer, Cham (2015). doi:10.1007/978-3-319-25007-6_36
4. Cheng, G., Zhang, Y., Qu, Y.: Explass: exploring associations between entities via top-K ontological patterns and facets. In: Mika, P., et al. (eds.) ISWC 2014. LNCS, vol. 8797, pp. 422–437. Springer, Cham (2014). doi:10.1007/978-3-319-11915-1_27
5. Mohan, Y., Bolin, D., Surajit, C., Chakrabarti, K.: Finding patterns in a knowledge base using keywords to compose table answers. PVLDB 7(14), 1809–1820 (2014)
6. Herrera, J., Casanova, M.A., Nunes, B.P., Lopes, G.R., Leme, L.A.: DBpedia profiler tool: profiling the connectivity of entity pairs in DBpedia. In: IESD 2016 (2016)
7. Le, W., Li, F., Kementsietsidis, A., Duan, S.: Scalable keyword search on large RDF data. IEEE TKDE 26(11), 2774–2788 (2014)
8. Hulpuş, I., Prangnawarat, N., Hayes, C.: Path-based semantic relatedness on linked data and its use to word and entity disambiguation. In: Arenas, M., et al. (eds.) ISWC 2015. LNCS, vol. 9366, pp. 442–457. Springer, Cham (2015). doi:10.1007/978-3-319-25007-6_26
9. Färber, M., Ell, B., Menne, C., Rettinger, A.: A comparative survey of DBpedia, freebase, OpenCyc, Wikidata and YAGO. Semant. Web J. (1), 1–5 (2015)
10. De Vocht, L., Beecks, C., Verborgh, R., Mannens, E., Seidl, T., Van de Walle, R.: Effect of heuristics on serendipity in path-based storytelling with linked data. In: Yamamoto, S. (ed.) HIMI 2016. LNCS, vol. 9734, pp. 238–251. Springer, Cham (2016). doi:10.1007/978-3-319-40349-6_23
11. Nunes, B.P., Herrera, J., Taibi, D., Lopes, G.R., Casanova, M.A., Dietze, S.: SCS connector - quantifying and visualising semantic paths between entity pairs. In: Presutti, V., Blomqvist, E., Troncy, R., Sack, H., Papadakis, I., Tordai, A. (eds.) ESWC 2014. LNCS, vol. 8798, pp. 461–466. Springer, Cham (2014). doi:10.1007/978-3-319-11955-7_67
12. Watts, D.J., Strogatz, S.H.: Collective dynamics of 'small-world' networks. Nature 393(6684), 440–442 (1998)
13. Levenshtein, V.: Binary codes capable of correcting deletions, insertions and reversals. In: Soviet Physics Doklady, vol. 10, p. 707 (1966)
14. De Vocht, L., Coppens, S., Verborgh, R., Sande, M., Mannens, E., de Walle, R.: Discovering meaningful connections between resources in the web of data. In: LDOW CEUR-WS.org, vol. 996 (2013)
15. Nunes, B.P., Dietze, S., Casanova, M.A., Kawase, R., Fetahu, B., Nejdl, W.: Combining a co-occurrence-based and a semantic measure for entity linking. In: Cimiano, P., Corcho, O., Presutti, V., Hollink, L., Rudolph, S. (eds.) ESWC 2013. LNCS, vol. 7882, pp. 548–562. Springer, Heidelberg (2013). doi:10.1007/978-3-642-38288-8_37
16. Herrera, J.: On the connectivity of entity pairs in knowledge bases. Ph.D. thesis, Department of Informatics, Pontifical Catholic University of Rio de Janeiro (2017). http://www-di.inf.puc-rio.br/~casanova/Publications/Dissertations-Theses/2017-Jose-Talavera.pdf
17. Herrera, J., Casanova, M.A., Nunes, B.P., Lopes, G.R., Leme, L.A.: Entity Relatedness Test Dataset.figshare (2017). https://doi.org/10.6084/m9.figshare.5234701

18. Herrera, J., Casanova, M.A., Nunes, B.P., Lopes, G.R., Leme, L.A.: RDF Version of the Entity Relatedness Test Dataset. GitHub (2017). https://github.com/lapaesleme/EntityRelatednessTestData
19. Herrera, J., Casanova, M.A., Nunes, B.P., Lopes, G.R., Leme, L.A.: SPARQL Endpoint of the Entity Relatedness Test Dataset (2017). http://swlab.ic.uff.br/fuseki/DatasetDescriptions/sparql
20. Herrera, J., Casanova, M.A., Nunes, B.P., Lopes, G.R., Leme, L.A.: Root Resources of the Entity Relatedness Test Dataset (2017). http://swlab.ic.uff.br/void.ttl#EntityrelatednessTestData_v3
21. Herrera, J., Casanova, M.A., Nunes, B.P., Lopes, G.R., Leme, L.A.: Source Code of the Entity Relatedness Test Dataset. GitHub (2017). https://github.com/jtherrera1/EntityRelatedness

RSPLab: RDF Stream Processing Benchmarking Made Easy

Riccardo Tommasini, Emanuele Della Valle, Andrea Mauri$^{(\boxtimes)}$,
and Marco Brambilla

DEIB, Politecnico di Milano, Milan, Italy
{riccardo.tommasini,emanuele.dellavalle,andrea.mauri,
marco.brambilla}@polimi.it

Abstract. In Stream Reasoning (SR), empirical research on RDF Stream Processing (RSP) is attracting a growing attention. The SR community proposed methodologies and benchmarks to investigate the RSP solution space and improve existing approaches. In this paper, we present RSPLab, an infrastructure that reduces the effort required to design and execute reproducible experiments as well as share their results. RSPLab integrates two existing RSP benchmarks (LSBench and CityBench) and two RSP engines (C-SPARQL engine and CQELS). It provides a programmatic environment to: deploy in the cloud RDF Streams and RSP engines, interact with them using TripleWave and RSP Services, and continuously monitor their performances and collect statistics. RSPLab is released as open-source under an Apache 2.0 license.

Keywords: Semantic Web · Stream Reasoning · RDF Stream Processing · Benchmarking

1 Introduction

In the recent years, research about Semantic Web and streaming data – Stream Reasoning (SR) – constantly grew. The community has been investigating foundational research on algorithms for RDF Stream Processing (RSP) [6], applied research with systems architectures [3,10] and, recently, empirical research on benchmarks [1,5,8,11,15] and evaluation methodologies [12,14,17].

Focusing on the latter two, the state of the art comprehends RSP engines prototypes [3,10] and benchmarks that address the different challenges the community investigated: query language expressive power [15], performance [11], correctness of results [5,8], memory load and latency [1,8]. This heterogeneity of benchmarks helps to explore the solution space, but hinders the systematic evaluation of RSP engines. Therefore, [14] proposed a requirement analysis for benchmarks and ranked existing benchmark accordingly; [17] proposed a framework for systematic and comparative RSP research. Beside the aforementioned community efforts, the evaluation of RSP engines is still not systematic.

In this paper, we propose RSPLab [18] a cloud-ready open-source test driver to support empirical research for SR/RSP. RSPLab offers a programmatic environment design and execute experiments. It uses linked data principle to publish RDF streams [9] and a set of REST APIs [2] to interact with RSP engines.

© Springer International Publishing AG 2017
C. d'Amato et al. (Eds.): ISWC 2017, Part II, LNCS 10588, pp. 202–209, 2017.
DOI: 10.1007/978-3-319-68204-4_21

RSPLab continuously monitors memory consumption and CPU load of the deployed RSP engines and it persists the measurements on a time-series database. It allows to estimate results correctness and max throughput post-hoc by collecting query results on a reliable file storage. RSPLab provides real-time assisted data visualization by the means of a dashboard. Finally, it allows to publish experimental reports as linked data.

2   RSPLab

In this section, we present the requirements for a RSP test driver, we describe the test driver architecture and how RSPLab currently implements it.

Requirements. We elicit the requirements for a test driver considering the existing research on benchmarking of RSP systems. We focused on the different engines involved, the data used and the applied methodologies. Therefore, our requirements analysis comprises:

(R.1) *Benchmarks Independence.* RSPLab must allow its users to integrate any benchmark, i.e. ontologies, streams, dataset and queries.
(R.2) *Engine Independence.* RSPLab must be agnostic to the RSP engine under test and it must not be bounded to any specific query language (QL).
(R.3) *Minimal yet Extensible KPI set.* According to the state of the art [1, 14, 17], the KPI set must include at least query result correctness and throughput. However, the KPI set must be extensible to include KPIs that are measurable in specific implementation and deployment.
(R.4) *Continuous Monitoring.* RSPLab must enable the observation of the RSP engine dynamics under the whole experiment execution.
(R.5) *Error Minimization.* RSPLab must minimize the experimental error, isolating each module to avoid resource contention.
(R.6) *Ease of Deployment.* RSPLab must be easy-to-deploy and it must simplify the deployment of the experiments modules, e.g. streams and engines.
(R.7) *Ease of Execution.* RSPLab must simplify the access to the available resource, e.g. reuse existing benchmarks, and the execution of experiments.
(R.8) *Repeatability.* RSPLab must guarantee experiment repeatability under the specific settings.
(R.9) *Data Analysis.* RSPLab must render simple data analyses about the collected statistics and allow its users to perform custom ones.
(R.10) *Data Publishing.* RSPLab must simplify the publications of performance statistics, query results and experiment design using linked data principles.

Architecture. Figure 1 presents RSPLab architecture that comprises four independent tiers: *Streamer, Consumer, Collector* and *Controller.* For each tier, it shows its logical submodules, e.g., a timeseries database in the Collector, and it refers to the technologies involved in the current implementation, e.g. InfluxDB.

The *Streamer,* the data provisioning tier, publishes RDF streams from existing benchmarks (R.1). The *Streamer* can stream any (virtual) RDF dataset that has a temporal dimension. Published RDF streams are accessible from the web.

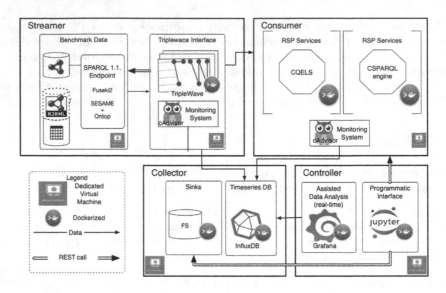

Fig. 1. RSPLab architecture and implementation

The *Consumer*, the data processing tier, exposes the RSP engines on the web by the mean of REST APIs (R.2). The minimal required method comprise source, query and sinks registration (R.1).

The *Collector*, the monitoring tier, comprises two submodules: (1) a *monitoring system* that, during the executions of experiments, continuously measures the performance statistics of any deployed module (R.4), (2) a time-series database to save the statistics and a persistent storage to save the query results. (R.3).

The *Controller*, the control and analysis tier, allows the RSPLab user to control the other tiers. It allows to design and execute the experiments programmatically (R.7). It enable the verification of the results (R.8). through an assisted and customized real time data analysis dashboard (R.9).

Implementation Experience. To develop RSPLab, we used Docker, i.e. a lightweight virtualization framework[1]. Docker simplifies the deployment process, it reduces the biases and foster the reproducibility of experiments [4]. As any virtualization theniques, it grants full control to the available resources, allowing to scale the virtual infrastructure (R.6). It minimizes the experimental error (R.5) by guaranteeing components isolation. Moreover, it fosters reproducibility by making the execution hardware-independent (R.8). Figure 1 illustrates how we deployed RSPLab's components in independent virtual machines. It also shows how the dockerization is done and it references the used technologies. RSPLab is natively deployable on AWS[2] and Azure[3] infrastructures (R.6).

---

[1] https://www.docker.com/.

[2] https://aws.amazon.com.

[3] https://azure.microsoft.com.

Streamer. This tier is implemented using a modified version of TripleWave [9][4,5] that includes methods to registers and start streams remotely. It includes synthetic RDF data from LSBench. We used the included data generator and we loaded them into a SPARQL endpoint to stream with TripleWave. It also includes data from CityBench. We exploited R2RML mappings and to convert CSV data into RDF on-demand. This tier is not limited to them. Streams from other benchmarks can be added following TripleWave principles.

Consumer. This tier uses the RSP Services [2], i.e. a set of REST methods that abstract from the RSP engine's query language syntax and semantics. The RSP services generalize the processing model enabling streams registration, queries registration and results consumption. This tier includes, but it not limited to, CQELS [10] and C-SPARQL [3] engine. Using the RSP Services, new RSP engines can be added to RSPLab.

Collector. This tiers includes (1) a distributed continuous monitoring system, called cAdvisor[6], that collects statistics about memory consumption, CPU load every 100 ms (R.3) for Docker containers. We target those running RSP engines but any of RSPLab's component can be observed. (2) A time-series database, called InfluxDB,[7] where we write the collected statistics. (3) A python daemon, called RSPSink, that persists query results on a cloud file systems (e.g., Amazon S3 or Azure Blob Storage), allowing to verify correctness and estimate the system's maximum throughput post-hoc.

Controller. This tier is implemented using iPython Notebooks[8]. We developed an ad-hoc python library [16] that allows to interact with the whole environment. It includes wrappers to RSP services, TripleWave APIs and sinks. Thanks to this programmatic APIs the RSPLab user can run TripleWave and RSP engine instances, execute experiment over them and analyze the results in a programmatic way (R.7). Moreover, with Grafana[9] it provides an assisted data visualization dashboard that reads data from InfluxDB enabling real-time monitoring (R.9). Last, but not least, the included library automatically generates experiments reports using the VOID vocabulary (R.10).

3   RSPLab In-Use

In this section, we show how to design and execute experiments and how to publish the results as linked using RSPLab.

Experiment Design. For this process, we consider the following experiment definition from [17]. An RSP experiment is a tuple $\langle \mathcal{E}, \mathcal{K}, \mathcal{Q}, \mathcal{S}, \mathcal{T}, \mathcal{D} \rangle$ where $\mathcal{E}$ is the RSP engine subject of the evaluation, $\mathcal{K}$

	Citybench
$\mathcal{E}$	CSPARQL engine
$\mathcal{K}$	Memory & CPU
$\mathcal{T}$	Citybench ontology
$\mathcal{D}$	SensorRepository
$\mathcal{S}$	Aarhus Traffic Data 182955 & 158505
$\mathcal{Q}$	Q1

Table 1. The running experiment.

---

4 https://github.com/streamreasoning/triplewave/tree/rsplab.
5 https://hub.docker.co/r/streamreasoning/triplewave/.
6 https://github.com/google/cadvisor.
7 https://www.influxdata.com/.
8 https://ipython.org/notebook.html.
9 https://grafana.com/.

is the set of KPIs measured in the experiment, i.e., those included in RSPLab. $\mathcal{Q}$ is the set of continuous queries that the engine has to answer. $\mathcal{S}$ is the set of RDF streams required to the queries in $\mathcal{Q}$. Finally, $\mathcal{T}$, $\mathcal{D}$ are, respectively, the static set of terminological axioms (TBox), and the static RDF datasets.

```
1  _Q1 = rsp.BenchmarkQueries.CityBench.Q1
2  e = rsp.new_experiment()
3  e.add_engine("http://cqles.rsp-lab.org", 80, rsp.Dialects.CQELS)
4  e.add_KPIs(rsp.KPI.Memory_Consumption, rsp.KPI.CPU_Load)
5  e.add_query("CB.Q1", rsp.QueryType.Query, _Q1, rsp.Dialects.CQELS)
6  e.add_tbox("CB.Q1", name="citytraffic.owl", base="rsp-lab.org")
7  e.add_graph("CB.Q1", name="SensorRepository.rdf", base="rsp-lab.org")
8  e.add_stream("CB.Q1","AarhusTrafficData158505", base="rsp-lab.org")
9  e.add_stream("CB.Q1","AarhusTrafficData182955", base="rsp-lab.org")
```

Listing 1.1. RSP Experiment Design RSPLab

Table 1 shows an example of an experiment that can be defined within RSPLab. We took this example from the Citybench benchmark. The engine used is C-SPARQL, the observed measures are Memory and CPU load, the TBox is the *citybench* ontology and the RDF dataset involved is *SensorRepository*. The query-set consists of the only query *Q1* which utilizes data coming from two traffic streams (e.g., *AarhusTrafficData182955* and *AarhusTrafficData158505*). Listing 1.1 shows how to create the experiment with the included python library. All the static data, streams and queries are available at on GitHub[10].

```
1   #WARM-UP
2   rsp = RSPEngine(ehost, eport);
3
4   for d in experiment.graphs():
5     rsp.register_graph(d)
6   for s in experiment.streams():
7     rsp.register_stream(s)
8   for q in experiment.queries():
9     rsp.register_query(q)
10    rsp.new_observer(query,'
         default')
11  spawn_sinks(experiment)
12
13  # OBSERVE
14  wait(experiment.duration())
15
16  for q in engine.queries():
17    for o in engine.observers(q):
18        rsp.unregister_observer(o)
19    rsp.unregister_query(q)
20  for s in engine.streams():
21    rsp.unregister_stream(s)
22  rsp.report.publish(experiment)
```

Listing 1.2. Execution with RSPLab.

```
@prefix:<http://rsp-lab.org/vocab/>

:RSPLab a foaf:Organization;
:exp1 a void:Dataset;
  dcterms:subject <:CSPARQL_Engine>;
  dcterms:contributor :RSPLab;
  dcterms:created "2017/05/08";
  dcterms:license <http://..cc/>;
  void:subset :exp, :results, :cpu .

:exp a void:Dataset;
  void:dataDump <exp1.jsonld>
  dcterms:subject <:Experiment> .

:cpu a void:Dataset;
  void:dataDump <exp1-cpu.csv>;
  dcterms:subject <rsplab:CPULoad> .

:results a void:Dataset;
  void:subset [
    dcterms:subject <:Results>;
    void:feature <format:Turtle>;
    void:dataDump <Q1.ttl> .]
```

Listing 1.3. Experimental Report with VoID.

Experiment Execution. In RSP, the experimental workflow has a warm-up phase followed by an observation phase because most of the transient behaviors occur during the engine warm-up and they should not bias the performance measures [1,11,12].

WARM-UP. In this phase, RSPLab deploys engine and RDF streams. It registers the streams, the queries and the observers on the RSP engine subject of the evaluation. It sets up the sinks to persists the queries results. Observing the engine's dynamics using the assisted dashboard (Grafana) and it possible

---

[10] https://github.com/streamreasoning/rsplab, at rsplab/streamer/citybench/setup/.

to determinate when the RSP engine is steady. Listing 1.2, lines 1 to 14, shows how this phase looks like in RSPLab. Figure 2 shows how this phase impacts the system dynamics approximatively until 15.16.

OBSERVE. In this phase, which usually has a fixed duration, the RSP engine is stable. It consumes the streams and answers the queries. The results and the performance statistics are persisted. When time expires, everything is shut down. Listing 1.2, lines 15 to 24 shows how this phase looks like in RSPLab. RSPLab makes possible to define more complex workflows, simulate real scenarios, e.g. add/remove queries or tune stream rates while observing the engine response.

Report and Analysis. RSPLab automatically collects performance statistics and enable experiment reporting using linked data principles. An example of data visualization using the integrated dashboard is in Fig. 2. Listing 1.3 shows an example of experimental done with RSPLab that uses VOID vocabulary to publish experiment design, CPU performance metrics and query results.

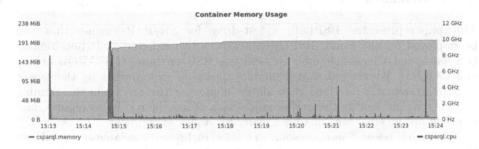

Fig. 2. C-SPARQL engine CPU and memory usage.

4   Related Work

In this section, we compare RSPLab with existing research solutions from SR/RSP, Linked Data, and database.

LSBench's and Citybench [1,11] proposed two test-drivers that push RDF Stream to the RSP engine subject of the evaluation. Differently from RSPLab, they are not benchmark-independent (R.1). The test drivers are designed to work with the benchmark queries and stream the benchmark data and do not guarantee error minimization by the means of module isolation(R.5).

Heaven [17] includes a test-bed proof of concept, with an architecture similar to RSPLab. However, Heaven does not include a programmatic environment that simplifies experiment execution (R.7), is not engine-independent (R.2), and its scope is limited to window-based, single-thread RSP engines. Like RSPLab, Heaven treats RSP engines as black box, but communication happens using Java Facade rather than a RESTful interface. Therefore, Heaven constrains the RSP engine's processing model. It enables analysis of performance dynamics but it does not offer assisted data visualization (R.9) nor automated reporting (R.10).

LOD Lab [13] aims at reducing the human cost of approach evaluation. It also supports data cleaning and simplifies dataset selections using metadata. However, RDF Streams and RSP engine testing are not in its scope. LOD Lab does not offer a continuous monitoring system, but only addresses the problem of data provisioning. It provides a command line interface to interact with it (R.6), but not a programmatic environment to control the experimental workflow (R.7).

OLTP-Bench [7] is a universal benchmarking infrastructure for relational databases. Similarly to RSPLab it supports the deployment in a distributed environment (R.6) and it comes with assisted statistics visualization (R.9). However, it does not offer a programmatic environment to interact with the platform, execute experiments (R.7) and publish reports (R.10). OLTP-Bench includes a workload manager, but does not consider RDF Streams. Moreover, it provides an SQL dialect translation module, which is flexible enough in the SQL area but not in the SR/RSP one (R.2).

5   Conclusion

This paper presented RSPLab, a test-drive for SR/RSP engines that can be deployed on the cloud. RSPLab integrates two existing RSP benchmarks (LSBench and CityBench) and two exiting RSP engines (C-SPARQL engine and CQELS). We showed that it enables design of experiments by the means of a programmatic interface that allows deploying the environment, running experiments, measuring the performance, visualizing the results as reports, and cleaning up the environment to get ready for a new experiment.

RSPLab is released as open-source citable [16,18] and available at rsp-lab.org Examples, documentation and deployment guides are available on GitHub hosted by the Stream Reasoning organization.

Future work on RSPLab comprise (i) the integration of all the existing RSP benchmarks datasets and queries, i.e. SRBench and YaBench, (ii) the integration of CSRBench's and YABench's oracles for correctness checking (iii) the execution of existing benchmark experiments at scale and systematically. Last, but not least, (iv) the extension of RSPLab APIs towards a RSP Library.

References

1. Ali, M.I., Gao, F., Mileo, A.: CityBench: a configurable benchmark to evaluate RSP engines using smart city datasets. In: Arenas, M., et al. (eds.) ISWC 2015. LNCS, vol. 9367, pp. 374–389. Springer, Cham (2015). doi:10.1007/978-3-319-25010-6_25
2. Balduini, M., Della Valle, E.: A restful interface for RDF stream processors. In: Proceedings of the ISWC 2013 Posters and Demonstrations Track, Sydney, pp. 209–212, 23 October 2013
3. Barbieri, D.F., Braga, D., Ceri, S., Della Valle, E., Grossniklaus, M.: C-SPARQL: a continuous query language for RDF data streams. Int. J. Semant. Comput. 4(1), 3–25 (2010)
4. Boettiger, C.: An introduction to Docker for reproducible research. Oper. Syst. Rev. 49(1), pp. 71–79 (2015).http://doi.acm.org/10.1145/2723872.2723882

5. Dell'Aglio, D., Calbimonte, J.-P., Balduini, M., Corcho, O., Della Valle, E.: On correctness in RDF stream processor benchmarking. In: Alani, H., Kagal, L., Fokoue, A., Groth, P., Biemann, C., Parreira, J.X., Aroyo, L., Noy, N., Welty, C., Janowicz, K. (eds.) ISWC 2013. LNCS, vol. 8219, pp. 326–342. Springer, Heidelberg (2013). doi:10.1007/978-3-642-41338-4_21
6. Dell'Aglio, D., Della Valle, E., Calbimonte, J., Corcho, Ó.: RSP-QL semantics: a unifying query model to explain heterogeneity of RDF stream processing systems. Int. J. Semant. Web Inf. Syst. **10**(4), 17–44 (2014)
7. Difallah, D.E., Pavlo, A., Curino, C., Cudré-Mauroux, P.: Oltp-bench: an extensible testbed for benchmarking relational databases. PVLDB **7**(4), 277–288 (2013)
8. Kolchin, M., Wetz, P., Kiesling, E., Tjoa, A.M.: YABench: a comprehensive framework for RDF stream processor correctness and performance assessment. In: Bozzon, A., Cudre-Maroux, P., Pautasso, C. (eds.) ICWE 2016. LNCS, vol. 9671, pp. 280–298. Springer, Cham (2016). doi:10.1007/978-3-319-38791-8_16
9. Mauri, A., Calbimonte, J.-P., Dell'Aglio, D., Balduini, M., Brambilla, M., Della Valle, E., Aberer, K.: TripleWave: spreading RDF streams on the web. In: Groth, P., Simperl, E., Gray, A., Sabou, M., Krötzsch, M., Lecue, F., Flöck, F., Gil, Y. (eds.) ISWC 2016. LNCS, vol. 9982, pp. 140–149. Springer, Cham (2016). doi:10.1007/978-3-319-46547-0_15
10. Le-Phuoc, D., Dao-Tran, M., Xavier Parreira, J., Hauswirth, M.: A native and adaptive approach for unified processing of linked streams and linked data. In: Aroyo, L., Welty, C., Alani, H., Taylor, J., Bernstein, A., Kagal, L., Noy, N., Blomqvist, E. (eds.) ISWC 2011. LNCS, vol. 7031, pp. 370–388. Springer, Heidelberg (2011). doi:10.1007/978-3-642-25073-6_24
11. Le-Phuoc, D., Dao-Tran, M., Pham, M.-D., Boncz, P., Eiter, T., Fink, M.: Linked stream data processing engines: facts and figures. In: Cudré-Mauroux, P., Heflin, J., Sirin, E., Tudorache, T., Euzenat, J., Hauswirth, M., Parreira, J.X., Hendler, J., Schreiber, G., Bernstein, A., Blomqvist, E. (eds.) ISWC 2012. LNCS, vol. 7650, pp. 300–312. Springer, Heidelberg (2012). doi:10.1007/978-3-642-35173-0_20
12. Ren, X., Khrouf, H., Kazi-Aoul, Z., Chabchoub, Y., Curé, O.: On measuring performances of C-SPARQL and CQELS. CoRR abs/1611.08269
13. Rietveld, L., Beek, W., Schlobach, S.: LOD lab: experiments at LOD scale. In: Arenas, M., Corcho, O., Simperl, E., Strohmaier, M., d'Aquin, M., Srinivas, K., Groth, P., Dumontier, M., Heflin, J., Thirunarayan, K., Staab, S. (eds.) ISWC 2015. LNCS, vol. 9367, pp. 339–355. Springer, Cham (2015). doi:10.1007/978-3-319-25010-6_23
14. Scharrenbach, T., Urbani, J., Margara, A., Della Valle, E., Bernstein, A.: Seven commandments for benchmarking semantic flow processing systems. In: Cimiano, P., Corcho, O., Presutti, V., Hollink, L., Rudolph, S. (eds.) ESWC 2013. LNCS, vol. 7882, pp. 305–319. Springer, Heidelberg (2013). doi:10.1007/978-3-642-38288-8_21
15. Stupar, A., Michel, S.: Srbench-a benchmark for soundtrack recommendation systems. In: 22nd ACM International Conference on Information and Knowledge Management, CIKM 2013, San Francisco, pp. 2285–2290 October 27 - November 1, (2013)
16. Tommasini, R.: streamreasoning/rsplib: Rsplib beta v0.2.4. https://doi.org/10.5281/zenodo.579659
17. Tommasini, R., Della Valle, E., Balduini, M., Dell'Aglio, D.: Heaven: a framework for systematic comparative research approach for RSP engines. In: Sack, H., Blomqvist, E., d'Aquin, M., Ghidini, C., Ponzetto, S.P., Lange, C. (eds.) ESWC 2016. LNCS, vol. 9678, pp. 250–265. Springer, Cham (2016). doi:10.1007/978-3-319-34129-3_16
18. Tommasini, R., Mauri, A.: streamreasoning/rsplab: Rsplab v0.9. https://doi.org/10.5281/zenodo.572320

LC-QuAD: A Corpus for Complex Question Answering over Knowledge Graphs

Priyansh Trivedi[1(✉)], Gaurav Maheshwari[1], Mohnish Dubey[1],
and Jens Lehmann[1,2]

[1] University of Bonn, Bonn, Germany
{priyansh.trivedi,gaurav.maheshwari}@uni-bonn.de,
{dubey,jens.lehmann}@cs.uni-bonn.de
[2] Fraunhofer IAIS, Bonn, Germany
jens.lehmann@iais.fraunhofer.de

Abstract. Being able to access knowledge bases in an intuitive way
has been an active area of research over the past years. In particular,
several question answering (QA) approaches which allow to query RDF
datasets in natural language have been developed as they allow end users
to access knowledge without needing to learn the schema of a knowledge
base and learn a formal query language. To foster this research area,
several training datasets have been created, e.g. in the QALD (Question
Answering over Linked Data) initiative. However, existing datasets are
insufficient in terms of size, variety or complexity to apply and evaluate
a range of machine learning based QA approaches for learning complex
SPARQL queries. With the provision of the Large-Scale Complex Question Answering Dataset (LC-QuAD), we close this gap by providing a
dataset with 5000 questions and their corresponding SPARQL queries
over the DBpedia dataset. In this article, we describe the dataset creation process and how we ensure a high variety of questions, which should
enable to assess the robustness and accuracy of the next generation of
QA systems for knowledge graphs.

Resource Type: Dataset
Website and documentation: http://lc-quad.sda.tech/
Permanent URL: https://figshare.com/projects/LC-QuAD/21812

1 Introduction

With the advent of large scale knowledge bases (KBs), such as DBpedia [7],
Freebase [1], and Wikidata [12], Question Answering (QA) over structured data
has become a major research topic (see [6] for a survey on QA systems). QA
systems over structured data, as defined in [6] is users asking questions in natural language in their own terminology and receiving a concise answer from the
system. Using structured data as their background knowledge, these systems

P. Trivedi, G. Maheshwari and M. Dubey—These three authors contributed equally.

© Springer International Publishing AG 2017
C. d'Amato et al. (Eds.): ISWC 2017, Part II, LNCS 10588, pp. 210–218, 2017.
DOI: 10.1007/978-3-319-68204-4_22

frequently model the QA problem as that of conversion of natural language questions (NLQ) to a formal query language expression, such as SPARQL or λ-Calculus expressions.

One of the pivotal requirements to evaluate and solve the QA problem, as we will discuss in detail in Sect. 2, is the availability of a large dataset comprising of varied questions and their logical forms. In this direction, we introduce the LC-QuAD (Large-Scale Complex Question Answering Dataset) dataset. LC-QuAD consists of 5000 questions along with the intended SPARQL queries required to answer questions over DBpedia. The dataset includes complex questions, i.e. questions in which the intended SPARQL query does not consist of a single triple pattern. We use the term "complex" to distinguish the dataset from the simple questions corpus described in SimpleQuestions [2]. To the best of our knowledge, this is the largest QA dataset including complex questions with the next largest being Free917 [3] with 917 questions and QALD-6 [11] with 450 training questions and 100 test questions, respectively.

We frame our question generation problem as a transduction problem, similar to [10], in which KB *subgraphs* generated by the *seed entity* are fitted into a set of *SPARQL* templates which are then converted into a Normalized Natural Question Template (NNQT). This acts as a canonical structure which is then manually transformed into an NLQ having lexical and syntactic variations. Finally, a review is performed to increase the quality of the dataset.

The main contributions are as follows:

1. A dataset of 5000 questions with their intended SPARQL queries for DBpedia. The questions exhibit large syntactic and structural variations.
2. A framework for generating NLQs and their SPARQL queries which reduces the need for manual intervention.

The article is organized into the following sections: (2) Relevance, where the importance of the resource is discussed; (3) Dataset Creation Workflow, where the approach of creating the dataset is discussed; (4) Dataset Characteristics; in which various statistics about the dataset are discussed; (5) Availability & Sustainability, describing the accessibility and long term preservation of the dataset; and (6) Conclusion & Future Work, summarizing and describing future possibilities.

2 Relevance

Relevance for Question Answering Research: Question answering approaches over structured data typically fall into two categories (as described in [14]): (i) *semantic parsing* based methods where the focus is to construct a semantic parser which can convert NLQs to an intermediate form, and then convert the intermediate form into a logical form, and (ii) *information retrieval* based techniques, which convert NLQs to a formal query language expression or directly to an answer, usually without any explicit intermediary form.

Approaches in the first category (semantic parsing based methods), frequently rely on handmade rules [4,6]. Naturally, a goal of current research is to automate these manual steps. However, the size of the currently available training datasets is limited. The maximum size of the SPARQL-based QA dataset is 450 queries [11] and for λ-Calculus, the maximum size is 917 queries [3]. Due to these size limitations, it is currently unknown to what extent can these manual steps be automated. In particular, the relation between the size of a dataset, and the improvement in accuracy of employed ML techniques is unknown. The provision of LC-QuAD will allow to address these research questions in the future publication of semantic parsing based approaches.

Recent approaches in the second category (information retrieval based) are based on neural networks and have achieved promising results [2,8]. However, these techniques are currently limited to answering simple questions, i.e. those which can be answered using a SPARQL query with a single triple pattern. Many queries are not simple: Comparative questions (e.g. "Was John Oliver born before Jon Stewart?"), boolean questions (e.g. "Is Poland a part of Eurozone?"), questions involving fact aggregation (e.g. "Who has won the most Grammy awards?"), or even logically composite question (e.g. "In which university did both Christopher Manning and Sebastian Thrun teach?") cannot be answered by a system restricted to simple questions. We believe that it would be very interesting to explore neural network based approaches also for answering these complex questions. LC-QuAD provides initial foundations for exploring this research direction. While 5000 questions are likely insufficient in the long term, it should also be noted that the dataset size can be increased substantially by entity replacement (see Sect. 6). This dataset may enable neural networks based QA system to process a much larger variety of questions, and may lead to a substantial increase in their F-score.

Relevance for Other Research Areas

- **Entity and Predicate Linking:** During the expert intervention part of the workflow (see Sect. 3), the tokens referring to entities and predicates in the SPARQL query were edited as well. As a result, our dataset can be treated as a set of questions, along with a corresponding list of entities and predicates present in it. There are 5000 total questions, 615 predicates and 5042 entites in the dataset. In future work, we will release a version of the dataset where the questions are annotated with RDF entities.
- **SPARQL Verbalization:** This dataset can also assist the task of SPARQL verbalization, which has attracted research interest in the Semantic Web community [5,9].

Relevance of and for the Semantic Web Community. A significant portion of research in question answering over structured data has been done on non-RDF knowledge graphs [8,13]. This could be attributed in part to the absence of large-scale QA datasets which use semantic technologies. By closing this gap via LC-QuAD, we believe that there can be a two fold benefit: On the one hand, researchers in question answering outside of the Semantic Web community can benefit from existing W3C standards, such as SPARQL, as a framework for formalizing and approaching the QA problem. While, on the other hand, the Semantic Web community itself will be more centrally positioned in the area of question answering.

3   Dataset Generation Workflow

The primary objective while designing the framework for question generation was to generate a high quality large dataset with low domain expert intervention. In both QALD-6 [11], and Free917 [3], the logical forms of the questions were generated manually. This process of writing formal expressions needs domain experts with a deep understanding of the underlying KB schema, and syntaxes of the logical form. Secondly, following this approach makes the data more susceptible to human errors, as unlike natural language, formal languages are not fault tolerant.

To avoid these aforementioned shortcomings, instead of starting with NLQs and manually writing their corresponding logical forms, we invert the process. Figure 1 provides a outline of our dataset generation framework. It begins by creating a set of SPARQL templates[1], a list of seed entities[2], and a predicate whitelist[3]. Then, for each entity in the list of seed entities, we extract subgraphs from DBpedia. Here, each subgraph contains triples within a 2-hop distance from

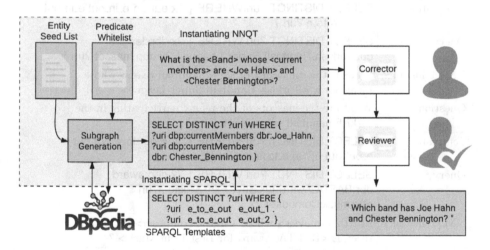

Fig. 1. Using a list of seed entities, and filtering by a predicate whitelist, we generate subgraphs of DBpedia to insantiate SPARQL templates, thereby generating valid SPARQL queries. These SPARQL queries are then used to instantiate NNQTs and generate questions (which are often grammatically incorrect). These questions are manually corrected and paraphrased by reviewers.

---

[1] https://figshare.com/articles/Templates/5242027.

[2] https://figshare.com/articles/Seed_Entities/5008286.

[3] https://figshare.com/articles/White_List_Relations/5008283.

the seed entity in the RDF graph. We then interpret the templates to create valid SPARQL queries using the triples in the subgraph. It is to be noted that while we use DBpedia resources to create these lists, this framework can be generalized to any target knowledge base.

The previously described approach generates SPARQL queries with non-empty results over the target knowledge base. However, as human intervention is required to paraphrase each query into a question, we avoid generating similar questions. Herein, we define two questions to be similar if they have same SPARQL template, same predicates, and entities of same RDF class, which, when verbalized would also have a *similar* syntactic structure. For instance, Q1: *What is the capital of Germany?* has the following logical expression: **SELECT ?uri WHERE** {dbr:Germany dbo:capital ?uri .}. This question is similar to Q2: *What is the capital of France?* whose logical form is **SELECT ?uri WHERE** {dbr:France dbo:capital ?uri .}. Thus, in order to achieve more variations in our dataset with the same amount of human work, we prune the subgraphs to avoid generation of similar questions. In the future, we aim to automatically increase the size of our dataset by replacing entities (e.g. Germany in Q1) with entities of the same class (e.g. France in Q2) (Table 1).

Table 1. Some examples from LC-QuAD

Template	SELECT DISTINCT ?uri WHERE { ?x e_in_to_e_in_out e_in_out . ?x e_in_to_e ?uri }
Query	SELECT DISTINCT ?uri WHERE { ?x dbp:league dbr:Turkish_Handball_Super_League . ?x dbp:mascot ?uri }
NNQT instance	What is the <mascot> of the <handball team> whose <league> is <Turkish Handball Super League>?
Question	What arc the mascots of the teams participating in the turkish handball super league?
Template	SELECT DISTINCT ?uri WHERE { ?x e_out_to_e_out_out e_out_out . ?uri e_to_e_out ?x }
Query	SELECT DISTINCT ?uri WHERE { ?x dbo:award dbr:BAFTA_Award_for_Best_Film_Music . ?uri dbo:musicComposer ?x }
NNQT instance	List the <movies> whose <music composer>'s <honorary title> is <BAFTA Award for Best Film Music>.?
Question	List down the movies whose music composers have won the BAFTA Award for Best Film Music ?

Our dataset is characteristic of the target KB, i.e. DBpedia. Thus, inconsistencies or semantically invalid triples in the KB can percolate into the dataset in the form of nonsensical questions. Since DBpedia has a lot of predicates which are used for metadata purposes, and are not of immediate semantic information[4], those should be avoided in the question generation process. To avoid these triples, we create a whitelist of 615 DBpedia predicates, and trim all the triples in the subgraph whose predicate is not in the whitelist.

Thereafter, we create an equivalent natural language template for every SPARQL template, called Normalized Natural Question Templates (NNQT). These are then instantiated to generate NLQs corresponding to every SPARQL query. The generated NLQs are often grammatically incorrect, but can be used by humans as a base for manual paraphrasing. The grammatical errors are due to fact that surface forms of DBpedia predicates correspond to varying parts of speech. For instance, while *president* is a noun, *largest city* is a modified noun, *bought* is a verb, whereas *born in* a prepositional phrase. These variations, along with complex entity surface forms (e.g. *2009 FIFA Club World Cup squads*) create a need for manual intervention to correct the grammar and paraphrase the questions. This task can be done by fluent english speakers, who are not required to understand formal query languages, or the underlying schema of the KB. In this manner, using NNQT, we transduce the task of interpreting and verbalizing SPARQL queries, to a simpler task of grammar correction and paraphrasing, and thereby reduce the domain expertise required for our dataset generation process.

Finally, every question is reviewed by an independent reviewer. This second iteration ensures a higher quality of data, since the reviewer is also allowed to edit the questions in case any errors are found.

4   Dataset Characteristics

Table 2 compares some statistics of QA Datasets over structured data. While QALD has 450 questions and Free917 has 917, LC-QuAD has 5000 questions. As mentioned in Sect. 2, QALD is the only dataset based on DBpedia, therefore, in this section we describe the characteristics of our dataset in contrast to it. Although LC-QuAD is tenfold in size compared to it, questions in QALD dataset are more complex and colloquial as they have been created directly by domain experts. Since the questions in our dataset are not extracted out of some external source, they are not an accurate representative of actual questions asked, but are characteristic of the knowledge base on which they were made. Nevertheless, due to human paraphrasing of both syntactic structure of the questions as well as the surface forms of entities and predicates, the questions in our dataset resemble questions actually asked by humans.

On an average, every question in our dataset has 12.29 tokens. The manual paraphrasing process was done by the first three authors who are native English speakers. Although the time taken to paraphrase a question varies significantly depending on the SPARQL template it is based on, it took about 48 s on average to correct each question. After this, the final reviewer took about 20 s to complete

---

[4] For e.g., dbo:abstract, dbo:soundRecording, dbo:thumbnail, dbo:wikiPageExternal Link, dbo:filename etc.

verification and, if needed, further editing. On the other hand, when a randomly sampled set of 100 SPARQL queries from our dataset was given to the same people (without instantiated NNQTs), it took them about 94 s to verbalize a query. This indicates that our framework reduces the workload of creating QA datasets.[5]

Table 2. A comparison of datasets having questions and their corresponding logical forms

Data set	Size	Entities	Predicates	Formal lang
QALD-6	450	383	378	SPARQL
Free917	917	733	852	λ-Calculus
LC-QuAD	5000	5042	615	SPARQL

Our dataset has 5042 entities and 615 predicates over 38 unique SPARQL templates. The SPARQL queries have been generated based on the most recent (2016-04) DBpedia release[6]. Among the 5000 verbalized SPARQL queries, only 18% are simple questions, and the remaining queries either involve more than one triple, or COUNT/ASK keyword, or both. Moreover, we have 18.06% queries with a COUNT based aggregate, and 9.57% boolean queries. As of now, we do not have queries with OPTIONAL, or UNION keyword in our dataset. Also, we do not have conditional aggregates in the query head.

5   Availability and Sustainability

In this section, we describe the interfaces to access the dataset as well as how we plan to support sustainability. We have published our dataset on figshare[7] under CC BY 4.0[8] license. Figshare promises data persistence and public availability, thereby ensuring that the dataset should always be accessible regardless of the running status of our servers. The figshare project of LC-QuAD includes following files

- **LC-QuAD** - A JSON dump of Question Answering Dataset.
- **VoID description** - A machine readable description of the dataset in RDF.
- **Tertiary resources** - These include numerous resources, such as SPARQL templates, NNQTs, predicate whitelists etc. mentioned throughout the article.

---

[5] Naturally, the time required to start completely from scratch and think of a typical query and formalise it in SPARQL would be substantially higher and also lead to a low diversity from previous experience in the QALD challenge.
[6] http://wiki.dbpedia.org/downloads-2016-04.
[7] https://figshare.com/projects/LC-QuAD/21812.
[8] https://creativecommons.org/licenses/by/4.0/.

Regarding sustainability, the dataset will be integrated into the QALD challenge – specifically in QALD-8 and beyond. QALD is running since 2011 and recently the HOBBIT EU project has taken over its maintenance. From 2019 on, the HOBBIT association will run the challenge.

Our framework is available as an open source repository[9], under a GPL 3.0[10] License. The documentation of the framework, and its user manual have been published on the repository's Wiki as well. We intend to actively use Github issues to track feature requests and bug reports. Lastly, we will also announce all the new updates of the framework and dataset on all public Semantic Web lists.

6   Conclusion and Future Work

In this article, we described a framework for generating QA dataset having questions and their equivalent logical forms. This framework aims to reduce human intervention thereby enabling creation of larger datasets with fewer errors. We used it to create a dataset, LC-QuAD, having 5000 questions and their corresponding SPARQLs. Although we used DBpedia as the target KB for our dataset, the framework is KB agnostic. We compared the characteristics of the dataset with pre-existing datasets and also described its shortcomings.

In the future, we aim to increase the number of SPARQL templates covered, thus increasing its syntactic variety. Moreover, to increase the size of the dataset by a certain factor, we can replace the entities in the questions with similar entities to synthetically add new questions. The software for this is already available and has been applied to create 2.1 million questions from 150 seed questions in QALD[11]. Increasing the dataset size in this way will likely benefit neural network based approaches for question answering as they learn the regularities in human language from scratch. However, this effect will diminish and estimating a factor up to which accuracy gains can be observed is subject for future work. Additionally, we plan to explore machine translation based techniques to reduce the need of manual grammar correction. As mentioned in Sect. 2, *in the upcoming version of LC-QuAD*, we will annotate the entities in every question, thereby enabling the dataset to be used for the entity linking task as well as exploring advanced techniques such as jointly trained entity linker and semantic parser.

Acknowledgements. This work was partly supported by the grant from the European Union's Horizon 2020 research Europe flag and innovation programme for the projects Big Data Europe (GA no. 644564), HOBBIT (GA no. 688227) and WDAqua (GA no. 642795).

---

[9] https://github.com/AskNowQA/LC-QuAD.
[10] https://www.gnu.org/licenses/gpl.html.
[11] https://github.com/hobbit-project/QuestionAnsweringBenchmark.

References

1. Bollacker, K., Evans, C., Paritosh, P., Sturge, T., Taylor, J.: Freebase: a collaboratively created graph database for structuring human knowledge. In: Proceedings of the 2008 ACM SIGMOD Conference on Management of Data, pp. 1247–1250 (2008)
2. Bordes, A., Usunier, N., Chopra, S., Weston, J.: Large-scale simple question answering with memory networks. CoRR, abs/1506.02075 (2015)
3. Cai, Q., Yates, A.: Large-scale semantic parsing via schema matching and lexicon extension. In: ACL, pp. 423–433 (2013)
4. Dubey, M., Dasgupta, S., Sharma, A., Höffner, K., Lehmann, J.: AskNow: a framework for natural language query formalization in SPARQL. In: Sack, H., Blomqvist, E., d'Aquin, M., Ghidini, C., Ponzetto, S.P., Lange, C. (eds.) ESWC 2016. LNCS, vol. 9678, pp. 300–316. Springer, Cham (2016). doi:10.1007/978-3-319-34129-3_19
5. Ell, B., Vrandečić, D., Simperl, E.: SPARTIQULATION: verbalizing SPARQL queries. In: Simperl, E., Norton, B., Mladenic, D., Della Valle, E., Fundulaki, I., Passant, A., Troncy, R. (eds.) ESWC 2012. LNCS, vol. 7540, pp. 117–131. Springer, Heidelberg (2015). doi:10.1007/978-3-662-46641-4_9
6. Höffner, K., Walter, S., Marx, E., Usbeck, R., Lehmann, J., Ngonga Ngomo, A.-C.: Survey on challenges of question answering in the semantic web. Seman. Web 1–26 (2016)
7. Lehmann, J., Isele, R., Jakob, M., Jentzsch, A., Kontokostas, D., Mendes, P.N., Hellmann, S., Morsey, M., Van Kleef, P., Auer, S., Bizer, C.: DBpedia-a large-scale, multilingual knowledge base extracted from wikipedia. Seman. Web 6(2), 167–195 (2015)
8. Lukovnikov, D., Fischer, A., Lehmann, J., Auer, S.: Neural network-based question answering over knowledge graphs on word and character level. In: Proceedings of the 26th International World Wide Web Conference, pp. 1211–1220 (2017)
9. Ngonga Ngomo, A.-C., Bühmann, L., Unger, C., Lehmann, J., Gerber, D.: Sorry, i don't speak SPARQL: translating SPARQL queries into natural language. In: Proceedings of the 22nd International World Wide Web Conference, pp. 977–988 (2013)
10. Serban, I.V., García-Durán, A., Gülçehre, Ç., Ahn, S., Chandar, S., Courville, A., Bengio, Y.: Generating factoid questions with recurrent neural networks: the 30m factoid question-answer corpus. In: 54th Annual Meeting of the Association for Computational Linguistics, p. 588 (2016)
11. Unger, C., Ngomo, A.-C.N., Cabrio, E.: 6th open challenge on question answering over linked data (QALD-6). In: Sack, H., Dietze, S., Tordai, A., Lange, C. (eds.) SemWebEval 2016. CCIS, vol. 641, pp. 171–177. Springer, Cham (2016). doi:10.1007/978-3-319-46565-4_13
12. Vrandečić, D.: Wikidata: a new platform for collaborative data collection. In: Proceedings of the 21st International World Wide Web Conference, pp. 1063–1064 (2012)
13. Yih, W.-T., Chang, M.-W., He, X., Gao, J.: Semantic parsing via staged query graph generation: question answering with knowledge base. In: Proceedings of the 53rd Annual Meeting of the ACL and the 7th International Joint Conference on NLP (2015)
14. Zhang, Y., Liu, K., He, S., Ji, G., Liu, Z., Wu, H., Zhao, J.: Question answering over knowledge base with neural attention combining global knowledge information. arXiv preprint arXiv:1606.00979 (2016)

PDD Graph: Bridging Electronic Medical Records and Biomedical Knowledge Graphs via Entity Linking

Meng Wang[1], Jiaheng Zhang[1], Jun Liu[1(✉)], Wei Hu[2], Sen Wang[3], Xue Li[4], and Wenqiang Liu[1]

[1] MOEKLINNS Lab, Xi'an Jiaotong University, Xi'an, China
wangmengsd@stu.xjtu.edu.cn, liukeen@xjtu.edu.cn
[2] State Key Laboratory for Novel Software Technology,
Nanjing University, Nanjing, China
[3] Griffith University, Gold Coast, Australia
[4] The Universtiy of Queensland, Brisbane, Australia

Abstract. Electronic medical records contain multi-format electronic medical data that consist of an abundance of medical knowledge. Facing with patient's symptoms, experienced caregivers make right medical decisions based on their professional knowledge that accurately grasps relationships between symptoms, diagnosis, and corresponding treatments. In this paper, we aim to capture these relationships by constructing a large and high-quality heterogeneous graph linking patients, diseases, and drugs (PDD) in EMRs. Specifically, we propose a novel framework to extract important medical entities from MIMIC-III (Medical Information Mart for Intensive Care III) and automatically link them with the existing biomedical knowledge graphs, including ICD-9 ontology and DrugBank. The PDD graph presented in this paper is accessible on the Web via the SPARQL endpoint, and provides a pathway for medical discovery and applications, such as effective treatment recommendations.

Keywords: Linked data · MIMIC-III · EMR · Drug · Disease

Resource type: Dataset
Permanent URL: http://kmap.xjtudlc.com/pdd

1 Introduction

Big data vendors collect and store large number of electronic medical records (EMRs) in hospital, with the goal of instantly accessing to comprehensive medical patient histories for caregivers at a lower cost. Public availability of EMRs collections has attracted much attention for different research purposes, including clinical research [14], mortality risk prediction [7], disease diagnosis [15], etc. An EMR database is normally a rich source of multi-format electronic data but remains limitations in scope and content. For example, MIMIC-III

C. d'Amato et al. (Eds.): ISWC 2017, Part II, LNCS 10588, pp. 219–227, 2017.
DOI: 10.1007/978-3-319-68204-4_23

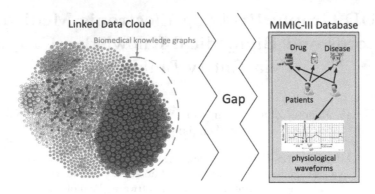

Fig. 1. Left part is the Linked Data Cloud[1], which contains interlinked biomedical knowledge graphs. Right part is the MIMIC-III database.

(Medical Information Mart for Intensive Care III) [8] collected bedside monitor trends, electronic medical notes, laboratory test results and waveforms from the ICUs (Intensive Care Units) of Beth Israel Deaconess Medical Center between 2001 and 2012. Abundant medical entities (symptoms, drugs and diseases) can be extracted from EMRs (clinical notes, prescriptions, and disease diagnoses). Most of the existing studies only focus on a specific entity, ignoring the relationship between entities. Given clinical data in MIMIC-III, discovering relationship between extracted entities (e.g. sepsis symptoms, pneumonia diagnosis, glucocorticoid drug and aspirin medicine) in wider scope can empower caregivers to make better decisions. Obviously, only focusing on EMR data is far from adequate to fully unveil entity relationships due to the limited scope of EMRs.

Meanwhile, many biomedical knowledge graphs (KGs) are published as Linked Data [1] on the Web using the Resource Description Framework (RDF) [4], such as DrugBank [9] and ICD-9 ontology [13]. Linked Data is about using the Web to set RDF links between entities in different KGs, thereby forming a large heterogeneous graph[1], where the nodes are entities (drugs, diseases, protein targets, side effects, pathways, etc.), and the edges (or links) represent various relations between entities such as drug-drug interactions. Unfortunately, such biomedical KGs only cover the basic medical facts, and contain little information about clinical outcomes. For instance, there is a relationship "adverse interaction" between glucocorticoid and aspirin in DrugBank, but no further information about how the adverse interaction affect the treatment of the patient who took both of the drugs in the same period. Clinical data can practically offer an opportunity to provide the missing relationship between KGs and clinical outcomes.

As mentioned above, biomedical KGs focus on the medical facts, whereas MIMIC-III only provides clinical data and physiological waveforms. There exists a gap between clinical data and biomedical KGs prohibiting further exploring medical entity relationship on ether side (see Fig. 1). To solve this problem, we

---

[1] Linking Open Data cloud diagram 2017. http://lod-cloud.net/.

proposed a novel framework to construct a patient-drug-disease graph dataset (called PDD) in this paper. We summarize contributions of this paper as follows:

- To our best knowledge, we are the first to bridge EMRs and biomedical KGs together. The result is a big and high-quality PDD graph dataset, which provides a salient opportunity to uncover associations of biomedical interest in wider scope.
- We propose a novel framework to construct the PDD graph. The process starts by extracting medical entities from prescriptions, clinical notes and diagnoses respectively. RDF links are then set between the extracted medical entities and the corresponding entities in DrugBank and ICD-9 ontology.
- We publish the PDD graph as an open resource[2], and provide a SPARQL query endpoint using Apache Jena Fuseki[3]. Researchers can retrieve data distributed over biomedical KGs and MIMIC-III, ranging from drug-drug interactions, to the outcomes of drugs in clinical trials.

It is necessary to mention that MIMIC-III contains clinical information of patients. Although the protected health information was de-identified, researchers who seek to use more clinical data should complete an on-line training course and then apply for the permission to download the complete MIMIC-III dataset[4].

The rest of this paper is organized as follows. Section 2 describes the proposed framework and details. The statistics and evaluation is reported in Sect. 3. Section 4 describes related work and finally, Sect. 5 concludes the paper and identifies topics for further work.

2   PDD Construction

We first follow the RDF model [4] and introduce the PDD definition.

PDD Definition: PDD is an RDF graph consisting of PDD facts, where a PDD fact is represented by an RDF triple to indicate that a patient takes a drug or a patient is diagnosed with a disease. For instance,

$$\langle pdd^5{:}274671,\ pdd{:}diagnosed,\ sepsis \rangle.$$

Figure 2 illustrates the general process of the PDD dataset generation, mainly includes two steps: PDD facts generation (described in Sect. 2.1), and linking PDD to biomedical KGs (described in Sect. 2.2).

---

[2] See figshare [16] and http://kmap.xjtudlc.com/pdd.
[3] https://jena.apache.org/documentation/fuseki2/index.html.
[4] https://mimic.physionet.org/.
[5] *pdd* is the IRI prefix http://kmap.xjtudlc.com/pdd_data/.

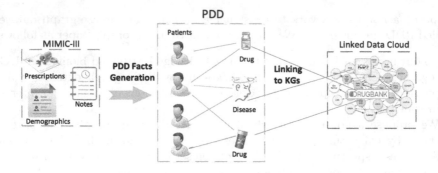

Fig. 2. Overview of PDD bridging MIMIC-III and biomedical knowledge graphs.

2.1 PDD Facts Generation

According to the PDD definition, we need to extract three types of entities from MIMIC-III (patients, drugs, and diseases), and generate RDF triples of the prescription/diagnosis facts.

Patients IRI Creation: MIMIC-III contains 46,520 distinct patients, and each patient is attached with a unique ID. We add IRI prefix to each patient ID to form a patient entity in PDD.

Prescription Triple Generation: In MIMIC-III, the prescriptions table contains all the prescribed drugs for the treatments of patients. Each prescription record contains the patient's unique ID, the drug's name, the duration, and the dosage. We extracted all distinct drug names as the drug entities in PDD. Then we added a prescription triple in to PDD. An example is

$$\langle pdd\text{:}18740, \ pdd\text{:prescribed, aspirin}\rangle,$$

where pdd:18740 is a patient entity, and aspirin is the drug's name.

Diagnosis Triple Generation: MIMIC-III provides a diagnosed table that contains ICD-9 diagnosis codes for patients. There is an average of 13.9 ICD-9 codes per patient, but with a highly skewed distribution, as shown in Fig. 3. Beyond that, each patient has a set of clinical notes. These notes contain the diagnosis information. We use the named entity recognition (NER) tool C-TAKES [12] to extract diseases from clinical notes. C-TAKES is the most commonly used NER tool in the clinical domain. Then we use the model [15] (our previous work) to assign ICD-9 codes for extracted diseases. We extracted all ICD-9 diagnosis codes as the disease entities in PDD. Then we added a diagnosis triple into PDD. An example is

$$\langle pdd\text{:}18740, \ pdd\text{:diagnosed, icd99592}\rangle,$$

where pdd:18740 is a patient entity, and icd99592 is the ICD-9 code of sepsis.

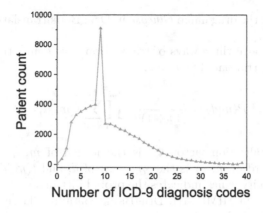

Fig. 3. The distribution of assigned ICD-9 codes per patient.

2.2 Linking PDD to Biomedical Knowledge Graphs

After extracting entities, we need to tackle the task of finding *sameAs* links [5] between the entities in PDD and other biomedical KGs. For drugs, we focused on linking drugs of PDD to the DrugBank of Bio2RDF [6] version, as the project Bio2RDF provides a gateway to other biomedical KGs. Following the analogous reason, we interlinked diseases of PDD with the ICD-9 ontology in Bio2RDF.

Drug Entity Linking: In MIMIC-III, drug names are various and often contain some insignificant words (10%, 200 mg, glass bottle, etc.), which challenges the drug entity linking if the label matching method is directly used. In order to overcome this problem, we proposed an entity name model (ENM) based on [2] to link MIMIC-III drugs to DrugBank. The ENM is a statistical translation model which can capture the variations of a drug's name.

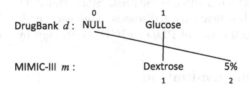

Fig. 4. The translation from *Glucose* to *Dextrose 5%*.

Given a drug's name m in MIMIC-III, the ENM model assumes that it is a translation of the drug's name d in DrugBank, and each word of the drug name could be translated through three ways:

(1) Retained (translated into itself);
(2) Omitted (translated into the word NULL);
(3) Converted (translated into its alias).

Figure 4 shows how the drug name *Glucose* in DrugBank translated into *Dextrose* 5% in MIMIC-III.

Based on the above three ways of translations, we define the probability of drug name d being translated to m as follows:

$$P(m|d) = \frac{\varepsilon}{(1_d + 1)^{l_m}} \prod_{j=1}^{l_m} \sum_{i=0}^{l_d} t(m_i|d_j) \tag{1}$$

where ε is a normalization factor, l_m is the length of m, l_d is the length of d, m_i is the i_{th} word of m, d_j is the j_{th} word of d, and $t(m_i|d_j)$ is the lexical translation probability which indicates the probability of a word d_j in DrugBank being written as m_i in MIMIC-III. DrugBank contains a large amount of drug aliases information, which can be used as training sets to compute the translation probability $t(m_i|d_j)$. After training the ENM from sample data, a drug name in MIMIC-III will be more likely to be translated to itself or aliases in DrugBank, whereas the insignificant words tend to be translated to NULL. Hence, our ENM can reduce the effects of insignificant words for drugs entity linking.

In addition, we propose two constraint rules when selecting candidate drugs for m, and discard those at odds with the rules.

Rule 1: One of the drug indications in DrugBank must be in accordance with one of the diagnoses of the patients who took the corresponding drug in MIMIC-III at least.

Rule 2: The dosage of a drug that patients took in MIMIC-III must be in accordance with one of the standard dosages listed in DrugBank.

Finally, we will choose the drug name d in DrugBank for the given drug m in MIMIC-III with maximal $P(m|d)$, and d satisfies the two constraint rules.

Disease IRI Resolution: In our previous work [15], we have assigned ICD-9 disease codes for extracted disease entities. Since the ICD-9 code is the international standard classification of diseases, and each code is unique. We can directly link the ICD-9 codes of PDD to ICD-9 ontology by string matching.

3   Statistics and Evaluation

In this section, we report the statistics of PDD and make the evaluation on its accuracy. At present PDD includes 58,030 entities and 2.3 million RDF triples.

Table 1 shows the result of entities linked to the DrugBank and ICD-9 ontology. For drugs in PDD, 3,449 drugs are linked to 972 distinct drugs in DrugBank. For diseases in PDD, 6,983 diseases are connected to ICD-9 ontology. The only two failures of matching ICD-9 codes in MIMIC-III are '71970' and 'NULL', which are not included in ICD-9 ontology. Table 2 shows the result of RDF triples in PDD. In particular, 1,259,702 RDF triples contain drugs that have *sameAs* links to DrugBank, and 650,939 RDF triples have ICD-9 diseases

Table 1. Statistics of entities

	#Overall	#Drug/disease linked to KG
Patient	46,520	
Drug	4,525	3,449
Disease	6,985	6,983

Table 2. Statistics of RDF triples

	#Overall	#Drug/disease linked to KG
Demographics	165,526	
Patients-drugs	1,517,702	1,259,702
Patients-diseases	650,987	650,939

codes. It indicates 83.4% drug-taken records in MIMIC-III can find corresponding entity in DrugBank, and 99.9% diagnosed information can link to ICD-9 ontology. A subgraph of PDD is illustrated in Fig. 5 to better understand the PDD graph.

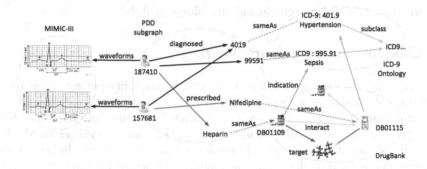

Fig. 5. An annotated subgraph of PDD.

To evaluate the ENM model, 500 samples are randomly selected, manually verified and adjusted. The ratio of positive samples to negative samples is 4:1, where positive means the entity can be linked to DrugBank. The precision is 94% and the recall is 85%. For linked entities in PDD we randomly chose 200 of them and manually evaluated the correctness of them, and the precision of entity links is 93% which is in an accordance with the result of our examples. The overall accuracy of entity linking will be affected by the performance of the entity recognition tool. No entity recognition tools so far can achieve 100% accuracy. The average accuracy of C-TAKES (we used in this paper) is 94%. Therefore, the overall precision and recall may be lower.

In order to find out why those 1,076 drugs have not been linked to DrugBank yet, we extract 100 of them that hold the highest usage frequency. The observation shows that most of them are not just contained in DrugBank. For instance, DrugBank does not consider NS (normal saline) as a drug, but PDD contains several expressions of NS (NS, 1/2 NS, NS (Mini Bag Plus), NS (Glass Bottle), etc.). For drugs wrongly linked to DrugBank, the names of those drugs are too short, e.g. 'N' i.e. nitrogen. These short names provide little information and affect the performance of ENM directly. Also, the training data from DrugBank does not include the usage frequency of each drug name. That might lead to some inconsistence with applications in MIMIC-III and cause linking errors.

4   Related Work

In order to bring the advantages of Semantic Web to the life science community, a number of biomedical KGs have been constructed over the last years, such as Bio2RDF [6] and Chem2Bio2RDF [3]. These datasets make the interconnection and exploration of different biomedical data sources possible. However, there is little patients clinical information within these biomedical KGs. STRIDE2RDF [10] and MCLSS2RDF [11] apply Linked Data Principles to represent patient's electronic health records, but the interlinks from clinical data to existing biomedical KGs are still very limited. Hence, none of the existing linked datasets are bridging the gap between clinical and biomedical data.

5   Conclusion and Future Work

This paper presents the process to construct a high-quality patient-drug-disease (PDD) graph linking entities in MIMIC-III to Linked Data Cloud, which satisfies the demand to provide information of clinical outcomes in biomedical KGs, when previous no relationship exists between the medical entities in MIMIC-III. With abundant clinical data of over forty thousand patients linked to open datasets, our work provides more convenient data access for further researches based on clinical outcomes, such as personalized medication and disease correlation analysis. The PDD dataset is currently accessible on the Web via the SPARQL endpoint. In future work, our plan is to improve the linking accuracy of ENM model by feeding more data into its training system.

Acknowledgment. This work is sponsored by The Fundamental Theory and Applications of Big Data with Knowledge Engineering under the National Key Research and Development Program of China with grant number 2016YFB1000903; National Science Foundation of China under Grant Nos. 61672419, 61370019, 61532004, 61672420, and 61532015; MOE Research Center for Online Education Funds under Grant No. 2016YB165; Ministry of Education Innovation Research Team No. IRT17R86.

References

1. Bizer, C., Heath, T., Berners-Lee, T.: Linked data-the story so far. In: Semantic Services, Interoperability and Web Applications: Emerging Concepts, pp. 205–227 (2009)
2. Brown, P.F., Pietra, V.J.D., Pietra, S.A.D., Mercer, R.L.: The mathematics of statistical machine translation: parameter estimation. Comput. Linguist. **19**(2), 263–311 (1993)

3. Chen, B., Dong, X., Jiao, D., Wang, H., Zhu, Q., Ding, Y., Wild, D.J.: Chem2Bio2RDF: a semantic framework for linking and data mining chemogenomic and systems chemical biology data. BMC Bioinform. **11**(1), 255 (2010)
4. World Wide Web Consortium: RDF 1.1 Concepts and Abstract Syntax (2014)
5. Ding, L., Shinavier, J., Shangguan, Z., McGuinness, D.L.: SameAs networks and beyond: analyzing deployment status and implications of owl:sameas in linked data. In: Patel-Schneider, P.F., Pan, Y., Hitzler, P., Mika, P., Zhang, L., Pan, J.Z., Horrocks, I., Glimm, B. (eds.) ISWC 2010. LNCS, vol. 6496, pp. 145–160. Springer, Heidelberg (2010). doi:10.1007/978-3-642-17746-0_10
6. Dumontier, M., Callahan, A., Cruz-Toledo, J., Ansell, P., Emonet, V., Belleau, F., Droit, A.: Bio2RDF release 3: a larger connected network of linked data for the life sciences. In: Proceedings of the 2014 International Conference on Posters & Demonstrations Track-Volume 1272, pp. 401–404. CEUR-WS.org (2014)
7. Ghassemi, M., Naumann, T., Doshi-Velez, F., Brimmer, N., Joshi, R., Rumshisky, A., Szolovits, P.: Unfolding physiological state: mortality modelling in intensive care units. In: Proceedings of the 20th ACM SIGKDD International Conference on Knowledge Discovery and Data Mining, pp. 75–84. ACM (2014)
8. Johnson, A.E., Pollard, T.J., Shen, L., Lehman, L.W.H., Feng, M., Ghassemi, M., Moody, B., Szolovits, P., Celi, L.A., Mark, R.G.: MIMIC-III, a freely accessible critical care database. Sci. Data **3** (2016)
9. Law, V., Knox, C., Djoumbou, Y., Jewison, T., Guo, A.C., Liu, Y., Maciejewski, A., Arndt, D., Wilson, M., Neveu, V., et al.: DrugBank 4.0: shedding new light on drug metabolism. Nucleic Acids Res. **42**(D1), D1091–D1097 (2014)
10. Odgers, D.J., Dumontier, M.: Mining electronic health records using linked data. AMIA Summits Trans. Sci. Proc. **2015**, 217 (2015)
11. Pathak, J., Kiefer, R.C., Chute, C.G.: Applying linked data principles to represent patient's electronic health records at mayo clinic: a case report. In: Proceedings of the 2nd ACM SIGHIT International Health Informatics Symposium, pp. 455–464. ACM (2012)
12. Savova, G.K., Masanz, J.J., Ogren, P.V., Zheng, J., Sohn, S., Kipper-Schuler, K.C., Chute, C.G.: Mayo clinical text analysis and knowledge extraction system (cTAKES): architecture, component evaluation and applications. J. Am. Med. Inform. Assoc. **17**(5), 507–513 (2010)
13. Schriml, L.M., Arze, C., Nadendla, S., Chang, Y.W.W., Mazaitis, M., Felix, V., Feng, G., Kibbe, W.A.: Disease ontology: a backbone for disease semantic integration. Nucleic Acids Res. **40**(D1), D940–D946 (2012)
14. Wang, S.J., Middleton, B., Prosser, L.A., Bardon, C.G., Spurr, C.D., Carchidi, P.J., Kittler, A.F., Goldszer, R.C., Fairchild, D.G., Sussman, A.J., et al.: A cost-benefit analysis of electronic medical records in primary care. Am. J. Med. **114**(5), 397–403 (2003)
15. Wang, S., Chang, X., Li, X., Long, G., Yao, L., Sheng, Q.Z.: Diagnosis code assignment using sparsity-based disease correlation embedding. IEEE Trans. Knowl. Data Eng. **28**(12), 3191–3202 (2016)
16. Wang, M., Zhang, J., Liu, J., Hu, W., Wang, S., Li, X., Liu, W.: PDD graph: bridging electronic medical records and biomedical knowledge graphs via entity linking. figshare (2017). https://doi.org/10.6084/m9.figshare.5242138

In-Use Track

A Controlled Crowdsourcing Approach for Practical Ontology Extensions and Metadata Annotations

Yolanda Gil[1(✉)], Daniel Garijo[1], Varun Ratnakar[1], Deborah Khider[2], Julien Emile-Geay[2], and Nicholas McKay[3]

[1] Information Sciences Institute, University of Southern California, Los Angeles, USA
{gil,dgarijo,varunr}@isi.edu
[2] Department of Earth Sciences, University of Southern California, Los Angeles, USA
{khider,julieneg}@usc.edu
[3] School of Earth Sciences and Environmental Sustainability, North Arizona University, Flagstaff, USA
Nicholas.McKay@nau.edu

Abstract. Traditional approaches to ontology development have a large lapse between the time when a user using the ontology has found a need to extend it and the time when it does get extended. For scientists, this delay can be weeks or months and can be a significant barrier for adoption. We present a new approach to ontology development and data annotation enabling users to add new metadata properties on the fly as they describe their datasets, creating terms that can be immediately adopted by others and eventually become standardized. This approach combines a traditional, consensus-based approach to ontology development, and a crowdsourced approach where expert users (the crowd) can dynamically add terms as needed to support their work. We have implemented this approach as a socio-technical system that includes: (1) a crowdsourcing platform to support metadata annotation and addition of new terms, (2) a range of social editorial processes to make standardization decisions for those new terms, and (3) a framework for ontology revision and updates to the metadata created with the previous version of the ontology. We present a prototype implementation for the Paleoclimate community, the Linked Earth Framework, currently containing 700 datasets and engaging over 50 active contributors. Users exploit the platform to do science while extending the metadata vocabulary, thereby producing useful and practical metadata.

Keywords: Metadata · Crowdsourcing · Semantic wiki · Collaborative ontology engineering · Semantic science · Incremental vocabulary development

1 Introduction

Existing frameworks for collaborative ontology development assume a clearly phased separation between ontology creation, release of the ontology, and use of the ontology [8, 12, 25]. These frameworks do not fit many areas of science, notably field-based

© Springer International Publishing AG 2017
C. d'Amato et al. (Eds.): ISWC 2017, Part II, LNCS 10588, pp. 231–246, 2017.
DOI: 10.1007/978-3-319-68204-4_24

sciences like ecology, Earth, and environmental sciences. These areas are extremely diverse, with data collected by many individual scientists each with idiosyncratic instruments, methodologies, representations, and requirements. As soon as an ontology is put to the test through practical use, we can anticipate the need for many additions and extensions to accommodate that diversity. Therefore, an ontology would need to be part of a framework that supports constant change while being used. Moreover, the involvement of diverse experts in the community would be needed, raising challenges about incentives and more importantly about coordination of requirements.

Our goal is to support the paleoclimate community, which studies past climate based on the imprint on various systems like trees, glacier ice, or lake sediments. This community employs such a diverse array of data collection and analytical techniques that it has been very challenging to develop shared ontologies. As a result, it is hard to find and aggregate datasets contributed by diverse scientists to paint a global picture of past climate change. Many other scientific communities face similar challenges, as do any organizations with highly heterogeneous or dynamic knowledge environments.

We propose a new approach to ontology development based on *controlled crowdsourcing*. Users (the crowd, who are experts in the domain rather than generic workers) concurrently create new terms as needed to describe their data, making the terms immediately available to others. Once the new terms are agreed upon, they can become part of the next version of the ontology. To coordinate the growth of the ontology and to create necessary incentives, we organize the community so that proper editorial control is exercised. We have implemented this approach in the Linked Earth Framework and deployed it for the paleoclimate community. The Linked Earth Framework is a socio-technical system that includes a crowdsource annotation platform to create metadata and propose new terms as needed, editorial processes to make standardization decisions for new terms and adding them to a core ontology, and a framework for ontology revision and updates. The system contains about 700 datasets and over 50 active contributors organized into 12 working groups.

The paper is structured as follows. Section 2 describes the challenges through a motivating scenario for the field sciences. Section 3 describes our new approach for controlled crowdsourcing of metadata and ontology extensions, followed by a description of our implementation in the Linked Earth Framework in Sect. 4. Section 5 describes the uptake by the paleoclimate community. The paper concludes with related work and a discussion of current limitations and plans for future work.

2 Motivation: Metadata Diversity in Ecology and Environmental Sciences

Data integration is particularly challenging in ecology and environmental sciences, where data are collected piecemeal by individual investigators with idiosyncratic organization and notation. This makes it very hard to create standards, in contrast with other sciences where there is more uniformity in the collection process such as genomics and astrophysics. Our focus is Paleoclimatology, whose goal is to reconstruct the climate in past times based on indicators such as the chemical composition of glacier ice or the width and density of tree rings. These indicators, called *climate proxies*, are obtained from various physical samples including ocean and lake sediments, ice, cave deposits, corals, and wood. There are many kinds of physical samples, hundreds of types of measurements that can be obtained from them, and hundreds of approaches to use those measurements to reconstruct *climate variables* such as temperature or rainfall. Only by integrating all this incredibly diverse data at planetary scales can we develop an understanding of climate evolution across space and time. Global climate reconstruction efforts are very valuable, for example the Past Global Changes (PAGES) 2k worldwide collaboration, devoted to the study of the climate in the last 2,000 years, published the most cited paper to date in Nature Geoscience [17]. Yet such studies require significant manual integration, and use only a fraction of the available data which is very hard to find and aggregate (e.g., [18]).

Tackling such diversity is a formidable task. The community has developed some basic standards, such as Pangaea's interoperability scheme [19] and the common variable properties in the Linked PaleoData (LiPD) format [14]. These provide a strong substrate for building community databases and integration efforts, but most scientifically relevant properties of the data still have to be found through text searches. Separately collected datasets still have to be aggregated painstakingly by hand. Additional standardization could be pursued, but it would require involving hundreds of scientists in diverse areas who study all types of samples, measurements, reconstruction methods, and variables. For example, a scientist who studies corals would compare isotopic variations among different coral species, whereas a glaciologist would care about the consistency of the methods to measure water isotopes and the composition of ancient gas in air bubbles trapped in ice. Creating standards for such a diversity of data is daunting, and yet crucial for our understanding of past climate fluctuations [4].

The metadata diversity in ecology and environmental sciences poses new requirements to support scientific metadata standardization:

1. **The creation of metadata properties should always be open to new contributors,** so that any scientist is able to suggest new properties based on their expertise and the kinds of samples and measurements that they study.
2. **A community repository should have frequently updated metadata standards,** so that it always offers users the most recent extensions.
3. **Community engagement is crucial.** There must be mechanisms for scientists to see value in the metadata properties being created in terms of enabling them to do research, that is, to find, aggregate, or analyze datasets.
4. **New metadata properties created by contributors must be coordinated and integrated with existing ones in a principled manner.** Any new distinctions that a scientist wishes to make must be related to other proposals, and must be considered in the context of the emerging standard.

There are many important challenges. Could scientists extend a metadata ontology on the fly without receiving training in ontology engineering? Could an ever-evolving ontology be used to annotate data when those annotations will need to be updated in future versions? How can we engage a scientific community that has little interest in participating in standards development (though there may be a strong interest in seeing a standard emerge and using it in their work)? How could we ensure that the extensions proposed by dozens of contributors are principled and capture the complexities involved in sophisticated scientific data, and are useful to do science? How could we avoid redundancies and inconsistencies as new metadata properties are added? These challenges involve important aspects of community engagement and incentives in addition to technical aspects of usability, collaboration, and knowledge management.

Although these requirements and challenges are motivated by our work in scientific metadata, they arise more broadly in organizations outside of science with diverse and rapidly evolving knowledge.

3   A Socio-Technical Approach for Controlled Crowdsourcing of Ontology Extensions and Metadata Annotations

We propose a novel approach that combines social and technical elements for controlled crowdsourcing of ontology extensions and metadata annotation. Note that crowdsourcing in our case means a large amount of users who are domain experts [16], rather than untrained workers. Our approach has several important features:

- A *metadata crowdsourcing platform*, where any registered user can add metadata for a dataset. In doing so, users can easily create new metadata properties as needed. These activities would be done in the platform as follows:
  - Users are first guided to choose among existing metadata properties. If none suits their needs, then they are invited to create new ones.
  - The creation of a new metadata property is as simple as adding a term and some documentation for it, so that any newcomer can easily do it and it does not get in the way of their work.
  - New properties are created because they are needed by a user to describe the dataset that they are working with. That creates a context and justification for the new metadata property, and in that sense they are practical and useful metadata.
- A *controlled standardization process*, consisting of a social structure of editor roles and working groups. The standardization process manages the community activities to consider the addition to the ontology of new properties suggested by the crowd. This way we ensure that the standard metadata ontology grows in a consistent and principled manner while being driven by the practical needs of the community. The process includes:
  - Quick turnaround decisions for clearly useful and uncontroversial new properties to be incorporated into the standard.
  - Mechanisms for escalating discussions and facilitating decision making for integrating new properties with the existing ontology.
  - Explicit reporting of changes to the ontology in new versions.
  - An initial standard upper ontology that is designed with solid principles, to be extended through crowdsourcing with more specific terms.
- A *metadata catalog evolution framework*, which supports the community to describe datasets using the ontology, use new properties as they are added, and easily transition to new versions of the ontology as they become available.

- The metadata properties that are part of the standard must co-exist with the ones that are newly created by the crowd.
- Metadata annotations should be updated with new ontology releases.

Figure 1 highlights the main aspects of the proposed controlled crowdsourcing process. There are three major components of the process: (1) annotation and vocabulary crowdsourcing, shown at the top; (2) editorial revision for ontology extensions, shown at the bottom; and (3) updates to the metadata repository, shown on the right.

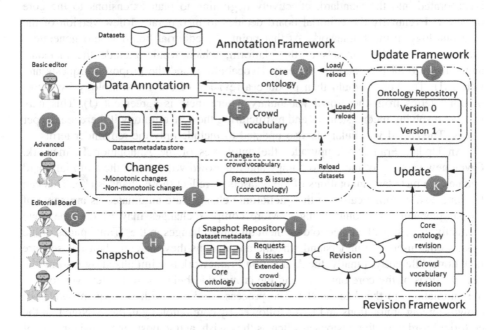

Fig. 1. Overview of our approach for controlled crowdsourcing.

An Annotation Framework supports the annotation and crowdsourcing process, shown in the top left of Fig. 1. The framework is initialized with a *core ontology* (A). The core ontology represents a standard that the community has agreed to use. Users, which form the crowd (B), interact with a metadata annotation system (C) to select terms from the core ontology for annotating datasets (D). For example, a term such as "archive type" from the core ontology could be used to express that a dataset contains coral. If a term they want to specify is missing, users may propose extensions by simply adding the term, which becomes a property in the *crowd vocabulary* (E), that new term is immediately available to other users when they are annotating their datasets. Users may also have requests and issues (F), such as requests for changes to the core ontology, comments to discuss new proposed terms, and other issues. There are two main types of changes to the core ontology that users may request:

(a) *Monotonic changes*: these are proposed new terms for the core ontology that do not affect any prior metadata descriptions made by others. For example, a user may extend the ontology for coral and add the property "species name".

(b) *Non-monotonic changes*: these concern existing terms in the core ontology or the crowd vocabulary that have already been used to describe datasets. For example, a request to rename an existing property or change its domain/range.

A Revision Framework supports the ontology revision process, shown at the bottom of Fig. 1. A select group of users form an *editorial board* (G) that is continuously reviewing the requests to extend or change the core ontology with crowd vocabulary terms. The editorial board discusses these proposals and determines if they should be incorporated into the standard, effectively beginning to plan extensions to the core ontology. Eventually the editorial board decides to incorporate a new version of the core ontology in the framework. At that point, the editorial board would generate a snapshot (H) of the contents of the platform, which would include the metadata annotations to all the datasets, the crowd vocabulary, and the proposed requests and issues (I). The board would then produce a revision of the core ontology by incorporating terms from the crowd vocabulary where there is agreement (J). This may involve resolving inconsistencies and restructuring the core ontology if there are deeper issues. The crowd vocabulary is also updated to include only the remainder terms.

An Update Framework upgrades the ontologies of the Annotation Framework. Given new versions of the core ontology and the crowd vocabulary, the editorial board updates the metadata annotations of the datasets to reflect those changes (K). This can be done semi-automatically, so that monotonic changes are automated as are some of the simpler non-monotonic changes. More complex changes may need to be done manually. Care must be taken to document all these changes in the "Talk" pages of the wiki, so that users can understand why the annotations they made to their datasets are now done differently. Finally, the Annotation Framework is reinitialized by loading the new versions of the core ontology and the crowd vocabulary and the new versions of the annotations to the datasets (L). The process continues with subsequent waves of crowdsourcing annotations and terms followed by core ontology updates. Note that the editorial board may do revisions as often as they wish, and to postpone consideration of some changes until more information is obtained from the crowd.

Appropriate community engagement is a non-trivial aspect of this approach. The metadata annotation interface must be easy to use by an average user in order to keep them involved. Users must see immediate reward for their annotations in order to continue to be engaged. Editorial board members must be selected so they are representative of the different expertise areas and able to understand the broader implications of each extension. Decisions about the standard must incorporate broad community input to be accepted and adopted in practice. The overall process must be transparent and inclusive so it is trusted as a community effort. Therefore, to implement this approach we must consider a socio-technical system that addresses both community and the technology aspects. The next section describes our work with a scientific community to investigate our approach.

4   The Linked Earth Framework

We are using our controlled crowdsourcing approach in the Linked Earth project to support the paleoclimatology community. As described earlier, the variety of samples, measurements, and analysis methods requires the involvement of a large community with diverse expertise and research goals. This section describes major components of the Linked Earth Platform that is currently supporting this community.

4.1   Annotation Framework: The Linked Earth Platform

The Linked Earth Platform [21] implements the Annotation Framework as an extension of the Organic Data Science framework [9], which is built on MediaWiki [15] and Semantic MediaWiki [13]. There are several reasons for this. First, a wiki provides a collaborative environment where multiple users can edit pages, and where the history of edits is automatically tracked. Second, MediaWiki is easily extensible, allowing us to easily create special types of pages, generate dynamic user input forms, and create many other extensions. Third, because MediaWiki is well maintained and has a strong community, there are numerous plug-ins available. Finally, the Semantic MediaWiki API makes it easy to export content and interoperate with other systems.

Each dataset is a page in the Linked Earth Platform. "Dataset" is a special class, or category in wiki parlance. When a user creates a new page for a dataset, all the properties that apply are shown in a table where the user can fill their values. For each variable they indicate if it is observed or inferred, its value, uncertainty, and how it was measured. The order of the variables as columns in the data file is also specified.

Figure 2 shows the metadata annotation interface for a lake sediment dataset. The user has provided some of the values of the metadata properties, others have not been filled out yet. The core ontology properties are shown at the top, and the crowd vocabulary properties are shown near the bottom (under "Extra Information"). The user can also specify a new subcategory for this dataset, as shown at the bottom.

When annotating metadata, the system offers in a pull-down menu the possible completions of what the user is typing based on similar terms proposed by other users. This helps avoid proliferation of unnecessary terms and helps normalize the new terms created. If none represents what the user wants to specify, then a new property will be added. The property becomes part of the crowd vocabulary, and a new wiki page is created for it. The user, or perhaps others, can edit that page to add documentation. As a result, users build the crowd vocabulary while curating their own datasets.

Figure 3 highlights the main features of the Linked Earth Platform. The map-based visualizations show datasets already annotated with location metadata. Author pages show their contributions, which help track credit and create incentives. Other pages are devoted to foster community discussions and take polls. The annotation interface is designed to be intuitive, and provides detailed documentation with examples[1].

---

[1] http://wiki.linked.earth/Best_Practices.

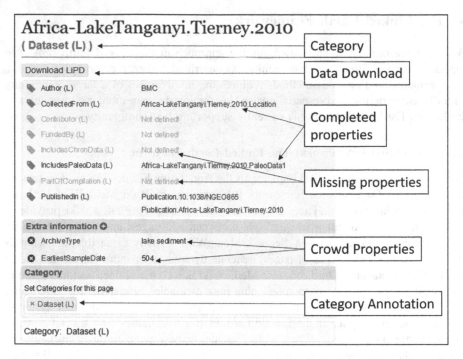

Fig. 2. Overview of the metadata annotation interface, with core ontology terms marked with an "L". The properties under "Extra Information" are part of the crowd vocabulary.

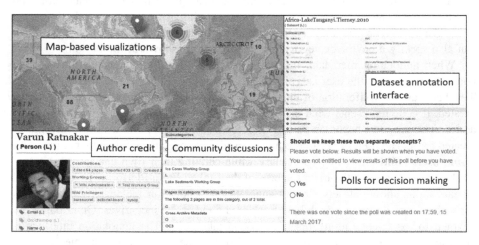

Fig. 3. Overview of the main features of the Linked Earth Platform.

4.2 Initial Core Ontology

To ensure that most changes would be crowd extensions that would not cause major redesigns of the core ontology, the initial core ontology was carefully designed.

First, the ontology was developed using a traditional methodology for ontology engineering [23]. We started by collecting terms to be included by the ontology in collaboration with a select group of domain scientists. These terms where extracted from examples provided by the community[2], and from previous workshops where the community had discussed dataset annotation [4]. The ontology development process was also informed by previous efforts to represent basic paleoclimate metadata [14], and by prior community proposals to unify terminology in the Paleo-climate domain [5].

We also took into account relevant standards and widely used models. We used several vocabularies[3]: Schema.org and Dublin Core Terms (DC) for representing the basic metadata of a dataset and its associated publications (e.g., title, description, authors, contributors, license, etc.), the wgs_84 and GeoSparql specifications for representing locations where samples are collected, the Semantic Sensor Network (SSN) to represent observation-related metadata, the FOAF vocabulary to represent basic information about contributors, and PROV-O to represent the derivation of models from raw datasets.

Figure 4 shows an overview of the ontology, which is layered and has a modular structure. The existing standards just mentioned provide an upper ontology for basic terms. We used the LiPD format, mentioned in Sect. 2, to develop the LiPD ontology[4] which contains the main terms useful to describe any paleoclimate dataset (e.g., data tables, variables, instrument used to measure them, calibration, uncertainty, etc.). A set of extensions of LiPD cover more specific aspects of the domain. The **Proxy Archive** extension defines the types of medium in which measurements are taken, such as marine sediments or coral. The **Proxy Observation** extension describes the types of observations (e.g., tree ring width, trace metal ratio, etc.) that can be measured. The **Proxy Sensor** extension describes the types of biological or non-biological components that react to environmental conditions and reflect the climate at the time. The **Instrument** extension enumerates the instruments used for taking measurements, such as a mass spectrometer. The **Inferred Variable** extension describes the types of climate variables that can be inferred from measurements or from other inferred variables (e.g. temperature). The crowd vocabulary builds on these extensions.

The core ontology and the crowd vocabulary share a common namespace for all the extensions (http://linked.earth/ontology/), in order to simplify querying as well as imports and exports of the ontology as a whole. Each extension has its own *base URI* e.g., http://linked.earth/ontology/instrument/), so they can be independently accessed

---

[2] https://github.com/LinkedEarth/Ontology/tree/master/Example.

[3] http://schema.org/, http://dublincore.org/documents/dcmi-terms/, https://www.w3.org/2003/01/geo/wgs84_pos, http://schemas.opengis.net/geosparql/1.0/geosparql_vocab_all.rdf, https://www.w3.org/2005/Incubator/ssn/ssnx/ssn#, https://www.w3.org/2005/Incubator/ssn/ssnx/ssn#, http://xmlns.com/foaf/spec/, http://www.w3.org/TR/prov-o/.

[4] http://wiki.linked.earth/Linked_Paleo_Data.

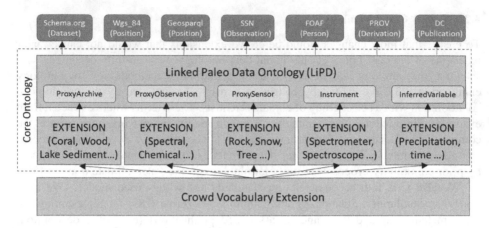

Fig. 4. An overview of the core Linked Earth Ontology and its extensions.

The Linked Earth ontology, as well as all the extensions, are accessible online[5] with content negotiation for HTML, RDF/XML and Turtle.

4.3 Community Organization and Support

The social aspects of the platform are equally important to the technical aspects. To organize the contributors' activities, we have created several mechanisms that are well documented and transparent to everyone. Our editorial processes were inspired by those of the Gene Ontology, Wikipedia, and our prior work on analyzing dozens of semantic wiki communities [10].

We have introduced four different user roles for crowd contributors. A *visitor* is any user who just wants to explore the content of the wiki. Visitors cannot change any of the contents of the wiki. By default, every user has a visitor role. A *basic editor* is a user with basic understanding on how to annotate a dataset with the Linked Earth Framework by creating a new page and adding new metadata, or by adding to a dataset created by someone else. Basic editors may also contribute to the textual documentation of existing terms from the crowd vocabulary, and may propose changes to the terms added by others. However, they cannot edit the semantics of the properties (e.g., domain and range). An *advanced editor* is a user with a more sophisticated understanding of the Linked Earth Framework and basic knowledge about ontologies. In addition to the basic editor privileges, advanced editors can add definitions for new properties, specify their semantics (e.g., domain and range, subclassing, etc.), suggest changes to existing properties proposed by others and reorganize the categories of the crowd vocabulary. Finally, an *editorial board member* is a user with extensive experience with the Linked Earth Platform, a deep understanding of the core ontology, and knowledge of the history of previous changes and issues discussed. Editorial board members are responsible for new versions of the core ontology, taking into account the

---

[5] http://linked.earth/ontology/.

possible ramifications of proposed changes by the crowd before incorporating them into the core ontology.

Users start as basic editors and then progress to advanced editors and in some cases may become an editorial board member. These user roles extend the default role functionality of MediaWiki, and are used extensively in collaborative content creation platforms such as Wikipedia [26].

In addition, we have set up *working groups* to organize activities by users with similar expertise. Led by advanced editors, working groups build use cases and examples and discuss problems raised by extensions to the crowd vocabulary. Agreements by a working group have more possibilities to convince the editorial board to accept their suggestions, as they represent the consensus of a set of experts in a particular domain instead of individual opinions. A working group is assigned a special page (of category Working Group) as a nexus for their activities. These include discussions and polls prompted by working group leaders with very specific questions and choices for community voting. Polls are implemented through a MediaWiki plug-in[6], and advertised to the community through social media.

4.4 Ontology Revision and Update Framework

Once the editorial board agrees to create a new version of the core ontology, they start by generating a snapshot of the contents of the Linked Earth Platform. Then one person does the actual edits and updates using Protégé [24] for editing the core ontology, manually updating existing dataset descriptions, creating a new version of the wiki and using WIDOCO [7] and w3id.org[7] to document and do the content negotiation on the ontology. The new version of the core ontology is published online. Each ontology extension has a different version IRI, following the convention BaseURI/ExtensionName/Version Number (for example the Instrument ex, http://linked.earth/ontology/instrument/1.0.0), so they can be independently accessed. Finally, the editorial board updates the metadata annotations for datasets and the content of wiki pages through a semi-automated process.

4.5 Incentives

An important incentive for users is getting credit for all their contributions. Each of the contributions done by a user is tracked and shown in their profile page, summarizing how many pages the user created or edited, how many terms they have proposed, as well as the working groups where the user contributes. Details on the specific contributions are accessible on every user page. This is important for recognition of the work of different individuals, as well as to acknowledge contributions in publications.

Another key feature that we have incorporated to the platform is allowing scientists to upload entire metadata specifications along with datasets already created as LiPD files [14], rather than using the annotation interface. This is important because the LiPD format is supported by a research software ecosystem that help users manipulate and

---

[6] https://www.mediawiki.org/wiki/Extension:AJAXPoll.

[7] http://w3id.org/.

analyze paleoclimate data (e.g., GeoChronR[8], Pyleoclim[9]), and as a result, some scientists store their data in the LiPD format. We support batch import of LiPD files through a web interface[10], which assists users by ensuring that the data conforms to the LiPD descriptions, and then creates metadata and adds it to the Linked Earth Platform. The LiPD format is fully aligned with the core ontology,[11] so that downloading a LiPD file from any dataset in the wiki will contain the most recent updates done to its metadata.

5 The Linked Earth Community Uptake

The Linked Earth Platform has been announced in several paleoclimate forums, receiving positive feedback from the community. The Linked Earth Platform is accessible online[12]. To date, the wiki has been populated with 692 datasets (mostly from the global PAGES 2k [18] collection[13]). We soon expect to increase this number with more than 150 additional records from a benthic oxygen isotope stack collection [1]. It is important to seed the platform with these datasets as a motivation for scientists to use the site, as well as a baseline for users to explore the capabilities of the system for querying and visualizing datasets.

Regarding user contribution, there are 150 registered users of the Linked Earth Platform (excluding the authors of this paper), with more than 50 contributors since the platform was first released. Users participate in one (or several) of the 12 available working groups, which tackle subjects in specialized topics such as how to unify cross-archive metadata and how to describe archive-specific metadata such as the storage conditions for an ice core or the coring technology used to obtain a sediment core. In order to facilitate decisions, working group members can respond to polls with specific questions. Previous votes for a particular decision are always recorded.

Figure 5 shows on the left the distribution of the main types of pages created to date. The total number of pages is more than 14,000. The right side of the figure shows the collaboration network of the main contributors of working groups. Each node represents a user, and each link between two users represents their collaboration on a given working group page (thicker lines signify several pages). The central nodes of this network are two of the authors of this paper (Jeg and Khider nodes), both editorial board members who help coordinate among the different working groups.

The vast majority of the edits to date have been annotations to the datasets using existing ontologies; a much smaller proportion has involved adding new terms. We have not deprecated terms so far, but they will be handled using current approaches: the term remains in the ontology and a warning to suggest what new related terms are

---

[8] https://github.com/nickmckay/GeoChronR.
[9] https://pypi.python.org/pypi/pyleoclim.
[10] http://lipd.net/create.
[11] https://github.com/LinkedEarth/Ontology/blob/master/draftDiscussion/MappingLiPD-Le.xlsx.
[12] http://wiki.linked.earth/.
[13] http://wiki.linked.earth/PAGES2k.

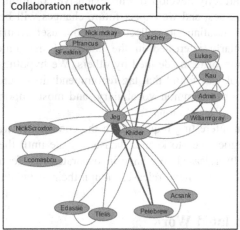

Page Distribution	
Datasets	659
ProxyAcrhive	207
ProxyObservation	76
ProxySensor	63
Instrument	45
InferredVariable	1207
MeasuredVariable	3348
Working Group	12
Location	659
Person	524
Publication	875

Fig. 5. Use of the Linked Earth Platform. On the left we show the distribution of types of pages, while on the right we show the collaboration network of select users in working groups.

recommended. We have only gone through two core ontology update cycles so far. The editors plan to do updates every six months, and will do them more often in periods of significant crowd vocabulary growth.

We are constantly working towards attracting more users to use the wiki framework. We have developed guidelines, tutorials and demos[14] on how to create content and add metadata. We have also showcased[15] how to query the datasets in the wiki through their metadata in order to analyze them with paleoclimate tools such as the Pyleoclim and the GeoChronR software mentioned earlier. We expect that these materials will help us increase the user base of the system.

In a new project, we are adapting the Linked Earth Framework for a large international neuroimaging genomics collaboration to organize datasets and experiments from hundreds of different institutions worldwide.

6   Discussion

Linked Earth is still a young project. We have iterated once through the crowdsourced annotation and controlled revision cycle (current version is 1.2.0), creating new versions of the core ontology and the crowd vocabulary and updating the metadata of datasets accordingly. Working groups are already in the next cycle, discussing and voting on new terms to be added.

One could argue that having an editorial board to approve changes introduces delays in the updating process. However, we made sure that the initial core ontology

---

[14] http://wiki.linked.earth/Best_Practices.

[15] https://goo.gl/IGldxH.

was carefully developed with extensive community feedback to address major modeling issues, and we expect future changes will be relatively uncontroversial.

We continue to collect data about user contributions to the framework. We are particularly interested in the ability of the annotation interface to encourage the adoption of terms defined by others. We hypothesize the same effect reported in [6], where it was found that tag recommendation increases reuse across users, helps converge on a common vocabulary, and most importantly, promotes an increase in the quality of annotations.

An interesting request from the community was the ability to support publication embargoes, i.e., to keep a dataset private until the associated scientific publication is officially released. We have incorporated this feature so that selected datasets remain private until official release, though their metadata is always accessible to other users.

7 Related Work

Several collaborative frameworks have been proposed for knowledge engineering and ontology development, with a focus on either handling curation and enrichment of instances or refining the definitions of ontology concepts.

Several semantic wiki platforms support different forms of collaborative editing [3]. OntoWiki [2] is a collaborative wiki framework for editing and curating instances. The goal of OntoWiki is to help users editing the contents of a knowledge base using different views like maps and forms. OntoWiki is targeted toward the curation of instances, rather than describing an ontology.

Other wiki approaches focus on ontology development, with different features and in different domains. LexWiki [11] aims for a collaborative creation and categorization of taxonomies. Similarly, CSHARE [12] proposed to build an ontology to represent studies and experimentations. MoKi [8] aims to capture more complex ontologies in the business processes domain. None of these approaches combines ontology editing with annotation of instances.

Collaborative ontology editors target users with expertise on the Semantic Web. As an example, Collaborative Protégé [24] is a full ontology editor, which includes features for enabling discussion, comments and annotations of ontologies in a distributed manner. These features also appear in Web Protégé [25], a lightweight ontology editor for the Web. Both versions can be used for defining instances of the ontology classes (e.g., through forms). SOBOLEO [27] is a collaborative vocabulary editor designed for organizing lightweight SKOS taxonomies that can annotate external web pages with the concepts in the taxonomy. PoolParty [22] is a wiki editor designed to edit and augment SKOS thesauri combined with the ability to process documents and look in external datasets for new concepts to add. However, none of these editors support the fast-paced cycle for ontology extension and immediate use for annotation in our approach.

The Diligent methodology [20] allows users to create individual extensions of a common core ontology, and these separate extensions are then merged by ontology engineers. In our work, all users work with the same extension to the core ontology, working collaboratively to create new terms.

8 Conclusions

We have presented a novel socio-technical approach for ontology development and data annotation based on controlled crowdsourcing. Key aspects of this approach are: (1) a crowdsourcing annotation process that allows users to add new terms as they use a standard ontology to do data annotation; (2) an editorial revision process that incorporates new terms into the next version of the ontology; and (3) a framework for updating the annotations according to that new version. We have implemented this approach in the Linked Earth Platform for the paleoclimate community. Seeded with an initial core ontology, the platform is being used to extend that ontology as needed by scientists as they annotate their datasets to create a crowd vocabulary. Although it is still early on in the project, the community is actively engaged in proposing terms and revising the core ontology. Future work includes facilitating ontology convergence, formalizing types of ontology changes to facilitate automation of updates to the repository, and improving update documentation and tracking.

Acknowledgements. We gratefully acknowledge funding from the US National Science Foundation under EarthCube grant ICER-1541029 and under grant IIS-1344272. We would like to thank the paleoclimate scientists who are participating in this community effort. We also thank Chris Duffy, Paul Hanson, Jie Ji, Tejal Patted, and Neha Suvarna for their contributions to the project.

References

1. Ahn, S., Khider, D., Lisiecki, L., Lawrence, C.E.: A probabilistic Pliocene-Pleistocene stack of benthic $\delta18O$ using a profile hidden Markov model. Dyn. Stat. Clim. Syst. (2017). doi:10.1093/climsys/dzx002
2. Auer, S., Dietzold, S., Riechert, T.: OntoWiki – a tool for social, semantic collaboration. In: Proceedings of International Semantic Web Conference (2006)
3. Bry, F., Schaffert, S., Vrandečić, D., Weiand, K.: Semantic Wikis: approaches, applications, and perspectives. In: Eiter, T., Krennwallner, T. (eds.) Reasoning Web 2012. LNCS, vol. 7487, pp. 329–369. Springer, Heidelberg (2012). doi:10.1007/978-3-642-33158-9_9
4. Emile-Geay, J., McKay, N.P.: Paleoclimate data standards. Pages Mag. **24**, 1 (2016). doi:10.22498/pages.24.1.47
5. Evans, M.N., Tolwinski-Ward, S.E., Thompson, D.M., Anchukaitis, K.J.: Applications of proxy system modeling in high resolution paleoclimatology. Quatern. Sci. Rev. **76**, 16–28 (2013). doi:10.1016/j.quascirev.2013.05.024
6. Font, F., Serrà, J., Serra, X.: Analysis of the impact of a tag recommendation system in a real-world Folksonomy. ACM Trans. Intell. Syst. Technol. **7**(1), 6 (2016)
7. Garijo, D.: WIDOCO: a wizard for documenting ontologies. In: Proceedings of 16th International Semantic Web Conference (ISWC) (2017)
8. Ghidini, C., Kump, B., Lindstaedt, S., Mabhub, N., Pammer, V., Rospocher, M., Serafini, L.: MoKi: the enterprise modelling Wiki. In: Proceedings of 6th Annual European Semantic Web Conference (ESWC) (2009)
9. Gil, Y., Michel, F., Ratnakar, V., Hauder, M.: Organic data science: a task-centered interface to on-line collaboration in science. In: Proceedings of ACM International Conference on Intelligent User Interfaces (IUI) (2015)

10. Gil, Y., Ratnakar, V.: Knowledge capture in the wild: a perspective from semantic Wiki communities. In: Proceedings of 7th ACM International Conference on Knowledge Capture (K-CAP) (2013)

11. Jiang, G., Solbrig, H.R.: Lex Wiki framework and use cases. In: First Meeting of Semantic Media Wiki Users, 22–23 November 2008, Boston, MA, USA (2008)

12. Jiang, G., Solbrig, H.R., Iberson-Hurst, D., Kush, R.D., Chute, C.G.: A collaborative framework for representation and harmonization of clinical study data elements using semantic MediaWiki. Summit Transl. Bioinform. **2010**, 11–15 (2010)

13. Krötzsch, M., Vrandečić, D.: Semantic MediaWiki. In: Fensel, D. (ed.) Foundations for the Web of Information and Services, pp. 311–326. Springer, Heidelberg (2011). doi:10.1007/978-3-642-19797-0_16

14. McKay, N.P., Emile-Geay, J.: Technical note: the linked Paleo data framework – a common tongue for paleoclimatology. Clim. Past **12**(4), 1093–1100 (2016). doi:10.5194/cp-12-1093-2016

15. MediaWiki: The Free Wiki Engine (2017). https://www.mediawiki.org

16. Nielsen, M.: Reinventing Discovery. Princeton University Press, Princeton (2011)

17. PAGES 2k Consortium: Continental-scale temperature variability during the past two millennia. Nat. Geosci. **6**(5), 339–346 (2013). doi:10.1038/ngeo1797

18. PAGES 2k Consortium: A global multiproxy database for temperature reconstructions of the Common Era. Sci. Data **4**, 170,088 EP (2017). doi:10.1038/sdata.2017.88

19. Pangaea Interoperability and Services (2017). https://pangaea.de/about/services.php

20. Pinto, H.S., Tempich, C., Staab, S., Sure, Y.: Distributed engineering of ontologies (DILIGENT). In: Staab, S., Stuckenschmidt, H. (eds.) Semantic Web and Peer-to-Peer. Springer, Heidelberg (2005). doi:10.1007/3-540-28347-1_16

21. Ratnakar, V.: The Linked Earth Wiki [Dataset]. Zenodo. http://doi.org/10.5281/zenodo.579646

22. Schandl, T., Blumauer, A.: PoolParty: SKOS thesaurus management utilizing linked data. In: Proceedings of 7th International Conference on the Semantic Web: Research and Applications (ESWC) (2010)

23. Suárez-Figueroa, M.-C., Gómez-Pérez, A., Motta, E., Gangemi, A.: Ontology Engineering in a Networked World. Springer, Berlin (2012). doi:10.1007/978-3-642-24794-1

24. Tudorache, T., Noy, N.F., Tu, S., Musen, M.A.: Supporting collaborative ontology development in Protégé. In: Proceedings of International Semantic Web Conference (ISWC) (2008)

25. Tudorache, T., Nyulas, C., Noy, N.F., Musen, M.A.: WebProtégé: a collaborative ontology editor and knowledge acquisition tool for the web. Semant. Web **4**(1), 89–99 (2013)

26. Wikipedia: The Free Encyclopedia (2017). https://en.wikipedia.org/

27. Zacharias, V., Braun, S.: SOBOLEO - social bookmarking and lightweight ontology engineering. In: 16th International World Wide Web Conference on Workshop on Social and Collaborative Construction of Structured Knowledge (2007)

An Investigative Search Engine for the Human Trafficking Domain

Mayank Kejriwal$^{(\boxtimes)}$ and Pedro Szekely

Information Sciences Institute, Marina del Rey, USA
{kejriwal,pszekely}@isi.edu

Abstract. Enabling intelligent search systems that can navigate and facet on entities, classes and relationships, rather than plain text, to answer questions in complex domains is a longstanding aspect of the Semantic Web vision. This paper presents an investigative search engine that meets some of these challenges, at scale, for a variety of complex queries in the human trafficking domain. The engine provides a real-world case study of synergy between technology derived from research communities as diverse as Semantic Web (investigative ontologies, SPARQL-inspired querying, Linked Data), Natural Language Processing (knowledge graph construction, word embeddings) and Information Retrieval (fast, user-driven relevance querying). The search engine has been rigorously prototyped as part of the DARPA MEMEX program and has been integrated into the latest version of the Domain-specific Insight Graph (DIG) architecture, currently used by hundreds of US law enforcement agencies for investigating human trafficking. Over a hundred millions ads have been indexed. The engine is also being extended to other challenging illicit domains, such as securities and penny stock fraud, illegal firearm sales, and patent trolling, with promising results.

Keywords: Knowledge graphs · Investigative search · Human trafficking · Illicit domains · Knowledge graph construction

1 Introduction

Recent studies confirm a formidable reach of illicit players both online and offline. For example, data from the National Human Trafficking Resource Center shows that human trafficking (HT) is not only on the rise in the United States, but is a problem of international proportions [12,21]. The advent of the Web has made the problem worse [10]. Human trafficking victims are advertised both on the Open and Dark Web, with estimates of the number of (not necessarily unique) published advertisements being in the hundreds of millions [22].

In recent years, various agencies in the US have turned to technology to assist them in combating this problem through the suggestion of leads, evidence and HT indicators. An important goal is to answer *entity-centric questions* over noisy Web corpora crawled from a subset of Web domains known for HT-related

© Springer International Publishing AG 2017
C. d'Amato et al. (Eds.): ISWC 2017, Part II, LNCS 10588, pp. 247–262, 2017.
DOI: 10.1007/978-3-319-68204-4_25

activity. Entities are typically HT victims, such as *escorts*, but could also be latent entities such as *vendors*, who organize the activity.

As a running example, consider the following real-world investigative request[1] (in natural language): *Find the average price per hour charged by escorts associated directly, or via shared phone/email links, with phone number 123-456-7890.* In the context of investigative querying, we refer to such a query as a *cluster aggregate query,* as correctly executing the query representation of such a question on a hypothetically *perfect* (sound and complete) database of instances can be achieved by the following two-step approach: first, *cluster* escort ads based on the seed phone (123-456-7890) in a well-defined manner that is described in Sect. 4.1, and then *aggregate* (in this case, average) all prices per hour in the clustered ads.

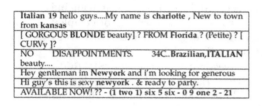

(a) Text fragments scraped from real-world human trafficking webpages, with relevant extractions in bold.

(b) An interpolated semi-log curve illustrating the long tail distribution of the number of pages (y-axis) against each of the 4,354 Web domains (e.g., backpage.com), ordered by frequency on the x-axis

Fig. 1. Illustration of obfuscations (a) and the long-tail effect (b) in illicit domains like human trafficking.

Even assuming such a machine-understandable query representation (e.g., using a SPARQL subset), achieving good performance on real-world data is challenging. First, *information extraction* (IE) is not a solved problem, even in well-studied domains like social media, news corpora or even Wikipedia [3]. The cluster aggregate query above requires both phone numbers and prices per hour to be correctly extracted from scraped websites. The quality of extractions, even coarse extractions like the main content text from the HTML of escort ads, is much worse in illicit domains, especially when the source is a messy webpage that has been downloaded by semi-automatic crawlers. We also note that the *language model* in such illicit domains is highly irregular, impeding the use of standard tools from the NLP literature (Fig. 1a). Second, illicit domains have been empirically observed to exhibit the *long-tail* effect (Fig. 1b), meaning that optimizing for, or expending manual effort on, a few of the biggest Web domains has limited utility. In many cases, investigators are explicitly interested in the long tail as a source of leads and evidence. Third, from a systems-level standpoint, integration of the different components is a difficult issue, as is the very

---

[1] Identifying information has been replaced in all examples used in this paper.

real problem of scale, since the corpora often comprise millions of webpages residing in a distributed file system (DFS). Challenges and motivations are further detailed in Sect. 3.

In this paper, we present an in-use investigative search engine that utilizes interdisciplinary research from both within and beyond the Semantic Web to satisfy a motivated set of investigative information needs (Sect. 3). A high-level overview of both the architecture as well as the dataflow is provided in Sect. 4. Our search engine has been integrated into the Domain-specific Insight Graph (DIG) architecture, which is currently used by hundreds of law enforcement agencies to combat human trafficking (Sect. 5), and is accessible via a GUI. DIG provides analysis and search capabilities over more than a hundred million webpages collected by crawlers over two years. In addition to the search engine, the DIG GUI also supports advanced facilities such as entity-centric page views over unusual entities such as phones, aggregations, temporal and geolocation analytics, and image similarity search. The search engine has been evaluated by DARPA in a competitive setting, and the engine is currently being extended to other illicit domains of vital investigative importance, notable examples being securities fraud and illegal firearm sales.

2 Related Work

The contributions in this work rely on several different research areas. Rather than attempt a comprehensive survey, we only provide pointers to overviews of these areas. *Knowledge Graph Construction* (KGC) is an important component of the DIG architecture. KGC draws on advances from a number of different research areas, including information *extraction* [3], information *integration* [6], and inferential tasks such as entity resolution [7]. In addition to DIG, another example of a principled KGC architecture is DeepDive [18].

Entity-centric Search (ECS) is another broad area of research that has influenced DIG, and was defined by Dalvi et al. as creating a 'semantically rich aggregate view' of concept instances on the Web [5]. Entity-centric search has led to novel insights about the search process itself, two examples being search as an action broker [17], knowledge base *acceleration* and filtering [8], interactive search and visualization [19], and search tailored for the Semantic Web [14]. An early entity-centric search prototype that is similar to our own effort is SWSE, which first crawls Web data and converts it to RDF [14]. The overarching principles of SWSE are similar to our own system, in that the engine is designed to be domain-specific and both database and IR technology are leveraged for representation and querying; however, SWSE is designed to be schema-independent and to support keyword-style queries. In contrast, the system herein accommodates *precise, information-rich* queries that cannot be expressed using keywords, and that are designed to support both factoid and analytical (i.e. involving aggregations and clustering) needs at scale. This also distinguishes our approach from other similar research that fuses Semantic Web research with IR research on tasks such as *ad-hoc object retrieval* (AOR) [9,23]. Despite the differences, important elements of our query prototype are inspired by the success demonstrated by these systems using *hybrid* (instead of purely structured or unstructured) search techniques for entity-centric search tasks.

Another related branch of research is *question answering*; however, unlike *question answering* systems [13], our approach is specifically optimized for investigative needs which allows us to restrain the scope of the questions and express them as *controlled-schema* queries in a language amenable to NoSQL executions. By controlled-schema, we mean that the attributes that can be queried are defined upfront, but the actual values retrieved by a search system are largely open-world i.e. do not obey strong normalization or format constraints. As is common in IR, the utility of such an answer is defined in terms of *relevance*, rather than 'correctness' as in database semantics. The queries also enable users to express aggregations, and retrieve clusters. In that sense, our system is more similar to structured query (e.g. SQL) prototypes on unstructured data [16]; however, the knowledge graph constructed by our system is more unorthodox, containing a mix of textual, numerical, pseudo-numerical and structured fields.

One of the most important aspects that separate this work from prior work is its focus on a *non-traditional* domain that has an outsize presence on the Web, and by some estimates is a multi-billion dollar industry, but due to technical and social reasons, has largely been ignored by the computational, knowledge management and IR research communities till quite recently [2,15]. We also note that, although the research described herein is specifically designed to investigate and combat human trafficking, the core elements of the overall problem and solution can be extended to other domains (e.g. from the Dark Web [4]) that are highly heterogeneous, dynamic and that deliberately obfuscate key information. Very recently, for example, the described system was extended to answering expressive queries in the securities fraud domain.

The technology described in this paper is implemented within the Domain-specific Insight Graph (DIG) architecture. The basic *knowledge graph-centric principles* of the DIG architecture (DIGv1.0) were published in an earlier work [22]. The earlier work did not include semantic search technology (only basic keyword search) or the advanced GUI capabilities that are the primary contributions of the architecture described herein and that are currently being used by law enforcement.

3   Motivation

To illustrate the motivation behind an investigative search engine, we start with a set of *information needs* that investigative experts are interested in exploring further. For example, given a seed phone number, investigators may want to find the (1) pages directly containing this phone number, (2) the average of all prices mentioned in those pages, (3) the time-series profile of the phone number, (4) the locations mentioned in the ads, plotted on a map, and (5) phone number recommendations, with corresponding pages, relevant to the current inquiry (i.e. the provided phone number). More generally, there may be multiple constraints and attributes[2] (e.g., instead of a query phone number, we are given a date range and a city), and the request may require us to retrieve tuples of attributes, ranked in order of relevance, or conduct different kinds of aggregations (e.g., max, average) on an attribute of the retrieved pages.

The rationale for the requests above are strongly influenced by real-world considerations. In illicit domains, investigative officials must commit limited resources to field investigations of leads. Usually, the initial lead comes from an on-the-ground source like a tip-off. If a system can provide useful (even if partial) solutions to (1)–(5), and a means of verifying the solutions, resource allocation can be significantly optimized. The consequence is that many more cases can be initiated and prosecuted, and the search for evidence becomes more efficient. A long-term consequence is that the *barrier-for-entry* to such illicit activities is significantly strengthened.

For present purposes, we make the closed-world assumption that the request must be facilitated over a pre-crawled Web corpus. The main reason why such an assumption is not only reasonable, but necessary, is that investigators are often interested, not just in what escort ads are *presently* on the Web, but also in escort ads published in the past and that may have been taken offline subsequently. Many ads are published for a few days only. Building cases against trafficking requires establishing a pattern of behavior over time, so it is important to retain pages that may not be available at the moment of search.

Another problem that precludes live search (e.g. on Google) is obfuscation. Some examples were provided earlier in Fig. 1a. It is not obvious how keyword-based search engines can solve complex query types such as clustering and aggregation in a purely online fashion, using only a keyword index. Finally, traditional Web search principles, which rely on hyperlinks for the robust functioning of ranking algorithms like PageRank, do not hold in the HT domain, where relevant hyperlinks present in the HTML of an escort ad tend to be sparse. We observed that most links are inserted by publishers to promote other content and may, in fact, cause traditional search crawlers to behave unexpectedly. The investigative search engine presented herein is designed to address these challenges, and be especially useful for the related purposes of *gathering evidence* and *minimizing investigative effort*, which is directly relevant to the motivation of using the system for evidence-based social good.

4 Architectural Overview

Figure 2 illustrates the architecture of the investigative search engine in DIGv3.0 (henceforth referred to as DIG). Prior to invoking DIG, a *domain-discovery system* is used to crawl large corpora from the Web based on a *relevance model* that depends, among other things, on a few seed links to relevant websites and a set of descriptive keywords. For example, in the human trafficking domain, the keywords could be 'escort', 'incall' etc. and links could include escort ads on Web

---

[2] As described subsequently, attributes are not open-world, but bound by a shallow ontology called an *investigative schema* (Sect. 4.1).

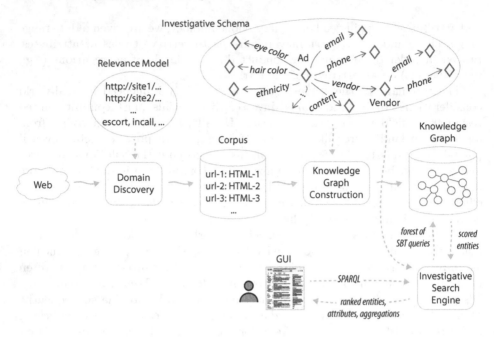

Fig. 2. An architectural overview of Domain-specific Insight Graph (DIG).

domains like backpage.com. The output of domain discovery typically results in corpora that contain at least a few million pages, and when fine-tuned for good recall on a particular illicit domain like human trafficking (that becomes better understood over time) can eventually yield hundreds of millions of webpages.

Once a Web corpus has been acquired, knowledge graph construction (KGC) is used in an offline phase to populate the DIG knowledge graph (KG) according to an *investigative schema* (IS) that was collaboratively developed over multiple weeks. The is a shallow ontology (inspired by schema.org) that contains important domain-specific classes and attributes either derived directly from schema.org (if it exists e.g., *date*) or added to the schema upon request (e.g., *hair-color*). While we expect the IS to be periodically refined based on user studies and feedback, the KGC process assumes a fixed IS in terms of which the knowledge graph is *semantically typed* using tools like Karma [11]. We also note that the DIG KGC is designed to be necessarily *query-centric* i.e. the KG is constructed with the explicit goal of supporting investigative search and not with optimizing KG quality (in terms of precision of facts in the KG) *per se*.

Once a KG is semi-automatically constructed from a raw Web corpus, it is stored and indexed in a NoSQL database (Elasticsearch). The indexed KG, and the basic key-value query engine provided by Elasticsearch, interface with the investigative search engine that is used to power the GUI. In subsequent sections, we detail all of these steps further. In the interest of space, we focus on the relevant design principles, rather than technical or algorithmic details. Core Semantic Web technologies that have prominent employment in DIG include the use of SPARQL for internal query representation, investigative schemas largely inspired by shallow ontologies like schema.org, and the use of Linked Data sources like Geonames for facilitating knowledge graph construction.

4.1 Knowledge Graph Construction (KGC)

For the purposes of this paper, we define KGC as a process that takes as input a raw corpus of Web documents, and constructs a (potentially noisy) knowledge graph (KG) of labeled nodes and labeled edges. Nodes and edge labels are semantically typed in terms of classes and properties in an investigative schema (IS), as mentioned earlier. Semantic typing is necessary because the set of extractions in the knowledge graph may not coincide with the IS, and in some cases, the type of an extraction may not even be known in advance. For example, a wrapper-based tool could extract structured fields from a webpage, but may not be able to automatically determine the type of each field. In other cases, the problem can be trivial; e.g., a regular expression program designed only to extract phone numbers will always have its extractions semantically typed as class *Phone Number* in the IS. We used the Karma tool for semantic typing [11]. Note that, from the search engine's (and hence user's) perspective, the KG can only be accessed and faceted on classes and properties from the IS.

Information Extraction (IE). To accommodate the requirements of quality, recall and robustness, we designed a *query-centric IE architecture* that considers a diverse *battery* of IE modules inspired by research in multiple research communities [3]. Included among the modules are NLP algorithms like Conditional Random Field (CRF)-based Named Entity Recognizers (for schema attributes like hair color, eye color and ethnicity), rule-based algorithms like regular expressions (for attributes like phone numbers and email addresses), and entity sets, dictionaries, lexicons and external knowledge bases (a good example being Geonames) for relatively closed-world attributes like services, names and locations. In a few cases, the extractors are *hybrid*: for example, we combine rule-based and NLP-based techniques for extracting street addresses. Finally, we also use a state-of-the-art semi-automatic wrapper-based tool, Inferlink [1], which can robustly extract structured fields on a per-domain basis with only 10 min of manual effort per Web domain. Because of the long tail distribution of human trafficking Web domains, we restricted Inferlink to a few of the largest Web domains, a notable example being backpage.com.

Each IE algorithm requires different types and levels of manual supervision. In the case of regular expressions and lexicons, for example, the extractor runs automatically once constructed, but is *non-adaptive*. On the other hand, CRFs achieve higher performance and can adapt more easily to complex domains but require high quantities of manually annotated data. For this reason, we only use CRFs for a few attributes like *hair color*, *eye color* and *ethnicity*.

An important aspect about our IE modules is that, while some are (either by design, or through parameter configuration) constructed to deliver high expected precision, others are designed to deliver high expected recall. This is one of the key innovations of DIG, as we subsequently describe. Even when the knowledge graph is extremely noisy, queries can still be answered reliably by implementing *investigative search strategies* that jointly consider high-precision and high-recall extractions in the ranking algorithm.

Phone-Email Clustering. In traditional KGC architectures, all extracted entities tend to be explicitly present in the text[3]. However, investigators are also often interested in *latent* entities that are not mentioned explicitly in the text, but need to be inferred from multiple entity extractions. Such inference relies heavily on sociological and domain-specific factors, and cannot be obviously automated without knowledge of these factors[4].

For example, in the human trafficking domain, it is well known that phones and emails serve as *pseudo-identifiers* for clustering escorts together and thereby discovering *vendors* that traffic these individuals. To facilitate phone-email clustering for the purpose of vendor discovery, we construct a weighted network where the nodes are entity (i.e. ad) IDs, and two nodes are connected by an edge iff they share a phone number or email extraction. Next, we use a clustering algorithm based on random walks to discover latent cluster entities (of a special type *Vendor* in our investigative schema). We found random walk-based clustering to be extremely scalable, executable on millions of nodes and edges without parallel programming, and to successfully account for the issue of data skew. Skew issues are very common with respect to phone extractions, even when the extraction is correct. For example, webpages often contain customer service phone numbers that can lead to significant distortions if a classic (i.e. non-stochastic) connected components algorithm is used for discovering vendors.

It is important to note that our clusters are *explainable*, and make intuitive sense. This is in contrast to, for example, deep learning and latent space algorithms, which yield higher performance but at significant cost to human-centric explainability. As we show in Sect. 5.2, domain experts cite explainability as a significant barrier to trusting advanced AI and semantic technology for expensive field investigations.

4.2   Storage, Representation and Indexing

Once the domain-specific knowledge graph has been constructed, it needs to be successfully queried by investigators. Since both efficiency and robustness are important, the knowledge graph needs to be stored, represented and indexed in a way that supports fast, expressive query execution. Furthermore, since we rely on open-source components, and can only achieve scale in cloud infrastructure, we only availed of technology that is both well-documented, released under a permissive license, and actively maintained by a technical community.

---

[3] In more advanced knowledge graph *completion* systems, additional links can be inferred, such as in entity resolution. However, nodes are still explicitly extracted.

[4] An additional problem with using powerful machine learning tools here is the lack of training data, and the uniqueness of each case.

Detailed empirical and systems-level comparisons between the viability of triplestores, and those of NoSQL key-value databases like MongoDB and Elasticsearch, illustrated considerable advantages enjoyed by the latter. In recent years, MongoDB and Elasticsearch have both continued to enjoy widespread success in domains well beyond traditional databases and IR: they have been used to power expressive GUI applications, process terabytes of data, and are amenable to easy (i.e. by default, without expert programming) horizontal scalability in machines provisioned by cloud service providers like Amazon Web Services and Microsoft Azure. REST APIs for interfacing with, and retrieving data from, Elasticsearch in established data exchange formats like JSON are available in all major programming languages and paradigms (including Apache Spark) with full documentation and error handling facilities. Triplestores were not found to enjoy the same level of support and are not natively offered or uniformly supported by the major cloud service providers.

4.3   Search and Querying

Soft Boolean Tree Queries. The investigative search engine is a customized ranking and retrieval engine that receives input directly from the DIG GUI as queries with multiple constraints. We use SPARQL for expressing the constraints (OPTIONAL and FILTER clauses, as well as aggregations) supported by DIG. Keyword queries are also supported given that the IS includes attributes such as *title* and *content*, which can be used as constraints. The search engine in Fig. 2 takes the SPARQL query as input and uses a set of semantic reformulation strategies to convert the SPARQL query into a forest of *soft boolean tree* (SBT) queries that can be executed on the Elasticsearch database.

Detailing the formal syntax of SBT queries is beyond the scope of this paper. Intuitively, an SBT query is defined recursively as a labeled tree, where a leaf node is always a qualified key-value pair (denoted as a *leaf query*, with the key denoting an IS attribute, and the value denoting a literal value. An edge label must always be selected from the set {*must, must not, should, filter*}. *Must* and *must not* have and NOT semantics, *should* has OR semantics and *filter* is a hard constraint, similar to FILTER clauses in SPARQL. In this respect, an SBT query is like a propositional formula with an additional FILTER operator. However, because the tree is soft, each leaf query is first scored by Elasticsearch using measures like tf-idf. Scores are propagated upwards to the root node using intuitive combination rules. For example, if a FILTER clause is violated, the parent node along that branch automatically receives a score of 0. For more details on the Elasticsearch query language, we refer the reader to the documentation[5].

There are two reasons why SBT queries were found to be extremely expedient in the search architecture. First, Elasticsearch can execute even large, complicated tree queries (and more generally forest queries, which are sets of weighted trees) extremely fast owing to judicious use of inverted indices that are compiled during

---

[5] https://www.elastic.co/guide/en/elasticsearch/reference/current/query-dsl.html.

the knowledge graph indexing phase. Second, SBT queries are robust to noise in the knowledge graph *if* the SPARQL query is *appropriately reformulated*.

For example, consider the (intuitively expressed) query: find all the escorts that have phone number *123-456-7890* and that have hair color *brunette*. This is a difficult query for several reasons. First, due to imperfections in extraction technology, either the phone number or the hair color did not get extracted, even though they are present in the text. Second, the extraction may not even have been present explicitly in the text. For example, there may be an escort ad that has the phone number 123-456-7890 and that has hair color *brown* in the text. Unless the system knows that *brunette* is the same as *brown* in this context, an *exact* interpretation of the original SPARQL query (which does not encase either of the two constraints in OPTIONAL) will be brittle.

To make query execution more robust without sacrificing the quality of the ranking (e.g., completely ignoring the original query semantics by naively encasing all constraints in OPTIONAL) we make use of three equally weighted *semantic reformulation strategies*. Each strategy separately processes a SPARQL query to yield an SBT query. In the current system, a combination of three strategies was found to yield good results:

Semantics-Preserving Strategy: This strategy is designed to preserve the semantics of the original SPARQL query in the following sense: an entity that should not get retrieved under strict SPARQL semantics (assuming execution against a triplestore) will get a score of 0 and not get retrieved by the search engine. Thus, this strategy respects the original user preferences, as stated.

Optional-Semantics Strategy: This strategy encodes the naive strategy mentioned earlier. All constraints are now qualified as OPTIONAL, even if they were not explicitly declared as such. This 'weaker' SPARQL query is now reformulated using the semantics-preserving strategy.

Keyword Strategy: This strategy treats each entity as a text-only document, and collates the literal values in the facets (the constraints in the SPARQL query) as a set of keywords. We search these keywords against the union of the text attributes (e.g. title, description, body etc.) of the entity. This strategy is similar to those in classic Information Retrieval search systems.

The result reformulation is a forest query comprising three equally weighted SBT trees, which is subsequently executed against the indexed KG. In addition to the strategies mentioned above, we also include domain-specific functions for (1) value expansion using entity-sets to improve recall e.g., expanding emerald to green, or japanese to asian; (2) weighting pseudo-identifier constraints like phone and email higher so that they get boosted in the final ranking, if found. All of these functions are easily customized, as they are self-contained and static.

Given the forest query, Elasticsearch executes it against the KG and, in real time, returns a set of scored entities, which we rank and display to the user on the GUI in descending order of scores. Using the GUI, the user can further explore each entity, or use facilities like facets to narrow search even further in an exploratory fashion.

Implementation. To ease integration, almost all the code in DIG is implemented in Python, including the investigative search engine. The toolkit encapsulating the battery of information extractors is publicly available as a Github project[6]. DIG also makes use of the parallelism in Apache Spark to efficiently process millions of webpages crawled by the domain discovery systems. The indexed knowledge graph is stored in the Elasticsearch NoSQL database, which is used to power the interface.

5   Real-World Usage

DIG is currently being used by over 200 law enforcement agencies, and its permanent transition to at least one state agency (the District Attorney of New York) is currently underway. We illustrate real-world usage and impact of DIG from three different viewpoints, including a case study involving a potential real-world victim soliciting as an escort online, and user studies involving actual domain experts and investigators in the human trafficking domain.

We also note that the investigative search engine has been evaluated on at least two different manually annotated, real-world human trafficking corpora, and four categories of complex queries, prepared by DARPA under the MEMEX program[7]. Specifically, the search engine was last evaluated by DARPA on 102 point fact (PF) questions, and 200 compound HT questions involving clustering and/or aggregations, against two competitive baselines (one from academia and one from industry) participating in the MEMEX program. The KG on which system retrieval performance was tested was constructed from 90,000 HT webpages collected and annotated by DARPA. Scalability was tested by executing the system for all 302 questions on multiple domain discovery corpora, with the largest being a multi-terabyte dataset containing 53.7 million webpages. On average, our system could reformulate and answer each query in less than 12 s on the largest corpus, using a regular Internet connection.

The evaluations were blind, and conducted by both NIST and DARPA: the teams building their respective search engines were not exposed to any ground-truth before final submission of results. In the first controlled evaluation (conducted in the summer of 2016), our system performed the best out of all submitted systems, achieving non-zero scores on all query categories. In the second evaluation (conducted in November, 2016), DIG achieved the best results on two of the four categories, and was competitive on the other categories.

More importantly, the absolute performance of DIG suggested that the system was ready to be deployed for detailed investigative search to law enforcement. For example, on the *point fact* query category, which resembles *factoid* questions in the question answering literature, our performance was close to 70% on a key *mean average precision* metric[8].

---

[6] https://github.com/usc-isi-i2/etk.

[7] An example of a category (cluster aggregate) was provided earlier in the introduction.

[8] This is also why it was possible to conduct user studies on actual investigative domain experts in the first place, since the technology has to meet a minimum standard before it can be presented to real-world users.

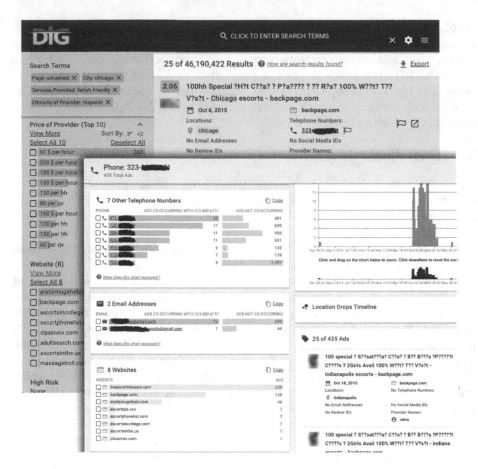

Fig. 3. A case-study illustrating complex investigative search in DIG. Details are provided in the text.

5.1   Case Study

In Fig. 3, we illustrate (using a specific case study) how the DIG interface, search engine and knowledge graph can be used to answer an actual investigative question that requires profiling and identifying a potential *vendor*[9], also referred to as a *ring* or a *stable* in the online sex trafficking literature.

First, a hypothetical investigator searches on the leads that she has, namely that an escort who is potentially in the ring is in Chicago, is of hispanic ethnicity and often uses words like *fetish friendly* and *unrushed* in her ads to describe the services she offers. In the top left corner of the underlaid image in Fig. 3, these search terms, as they are input to the search engine, are displayed. DIG returns

---

[9] Recall that vendors cannot be 'extracted' (since they do not explicitly advertise) and must be inferred through phone-email extractions and clustering.

a diverse set of results with *facets*; among the facets shown on the interface, for example, are *price* facets and *Web domain* facets.

Because the search is under-defined (many escorts meet the search conditions posed by the investigator), as it often is in investigative search scenarios, an investigator browses through the GUI, possibly exploring a few ads, and finds an ad that looks promising for eliciting further investigative leads. On this ad page (not shown in the figure), which contains such details as the extracted information from the ad, as well as activity timelines and images, the investigator clicks on a *phone number* associated with the escort in question. The search engine now displays an entity-centric page, where the entity is a phone number. This is a facility that is uniquely associated with investigative domains, and to the best of our knowledge, DIG is the only known system that has achieved it at scales of millions of phone numbers, and hundreds of millions of pages, in the human trafficking domain.

On the phone-centric page, the investigator finds information that would potentially take her months to discover, assuming the relevant pages were still online while the investigations were being conducted. The most important leads are a list of phone numbers that are *connected*, through a strong co-occurrence chain, to the phone under investigation. There are also email addresses, as well as a characterization of the levels of activity. Finally, to facilitate detailed investigations, we also list ads where these phone numbers occur. All of these ads are permanently retained in our back-end DFS. Ultimately, these ads and phone numbers can be used both to acquire evidence (possibly in retrospect) to support an ongoing prosecution, as well as to make the case for initiating a prosecution in the first place. We are aware of real-world cases in recent times that have used DIG for both purposes.

5.2   User Studies: Protocol and Observations

The GUI was evaluated by conducting controlled usability studies on 8 subject matter experts (SMEs) from 4 different US states. Due to confidentiality reasons, and because the results of the usability study are still being analyzed by NIST at the time of writing, we cannot release the affiliations of any of these experts other than that they are real-world users, and are affiliated with offices in the US that prosecute or investigate offenses like human trafficking in some capacity. Although we cannot release actual quantitative data concerning the GUI evaluations, we summarize the protocol and some observations.

Each SME was tasked with answering a set of 8 *lead generation* and 8 *lead investigation* questions, with 30 and 15 min allocated per question respectively. Each study (involving a single participant) was conducted in blocks of 2 h, over a period of a week. Both DIG, and a second search system developed by a private enterprise, were evaluated in controlled settings. Both teams were allowed to hold a 45 min training session to demonstrate the features of the GUI to the SMEs. No team had access to any of the test questions.

Lead generation questions are important for locating potential vendors (the latent entities) through careful scrutiny of published entities (especially locations and pseudo-identifiers, like phones) and their corresponding activity, while lead investigation questions have more explicit information needs. Each question requires significant exploration of the information space in the GUI.

The System Usability Scale (SUS) metric was used by NIST for assessing usability [20]. The DIG SUS mean score was higher than that[10] the second system, and within the margin of error, the DIG SUS score crossed the threshold of 70, widely believed to match real-world usability criteria.

We close this section with two important observations that emerged from the study, but that we believe are underestimated in the AI literature. First, *source retention* (in this case, the HTML page) was considered vital; even if the precision and the recall are above 90%, investigators still want an option to verify directly with the source to foster system trust. DIG offers this option. Second, it is important to *explain* why an algorithm produces an output that it does. In this sense, deep neural networks should be treated with caution, as their outputs are not obviously explainable. In current work, we are actively exploring methods for automatically annotating our extractions and outputs with feasible explanations, using techniques developed in recent research on explainable AI.

6   Future Work and Conclusion

The search engine was last evaluated by DARPA on 102 point fact (PF) questions, and 200 compound HT questions involving clustering and/or aggregations, against two competitive baselines participating in the MEMEX program. The KG on which system retrieval performance was tested was constructed from 90,000 HT webpages collected and annotated by DARPA. Scalability was tested by executing the system for all 302 questions on multiple domain discovery corpora, with the largest being a multi-terabyte dataset containing 53.7 million webpages. On average, our system could reformulate and answer each query in less than 12 s on the largest corpus, using a regular internet connection.

The success of the Web has had the unfortunate consequence of lowering the barrier-to-entry for players in illicit domains. With judicious use of semantic technology, this trend can not only be reversed, but vendors in illicit domains can be located, investigated and prosecuted in a timely manner by resource-strapped agencies. In this paper, we presented and described an investigative search system that uses knowledge graph construction and multi-interface querying to support these goals. Semantic Web components that played an important role include (1) the SPARQL language for internal query representation, (2) shallow ontologies inspired by the likes of schema.org for representing investigative domains, and (3) external Linked Data knowledge bases like Geonames for information extraction. The system is currently in use by hundreds of law enforcement agencies to combat human trafficking, has undergone rigorous usability studies that employed actual domain experts, and is extensible.

---

[10] Significance testing of this claim is currently under way.

Acknowledgements. We gratefully acknowledge our collaborators and all (former and current) members of our team who contributed their efforts and expertise to DIG, particularly during the dry and final evaluation runs: Amandeep Singh, Linhong Zhu, Lingzhe Teng, Nimesh Jain, Rahul Kapoor, Muthu Rajendran R. Gurumoorthy, Sanjay Singh, Majid Ghasemi Gol, Brian Amanatullah, Craig Knoblock and Steve Minton. This research is supported by the Defense Advanced Research Projects Agency (DARPA) and the Air Force Research Laboratory (AFRL) under contract number FA8750- 14-C-0240. The views and conclusions contained herein are those of the authors and should not be interpreted as necessarily representing the official policies or endorsements, either expressed or implied, of DARPA, AFRL, or the U.S. Government.

References

1. Inferlink r&d capabilities. http://www.inferlink.com/our-work#research-capabilities-section. Accessed 28 Apr 2017
2. Alvari, H., Shakarian, P., Snyder, J.K.: A non-parametric learning approach to identify online human trafficking. In: 2016 IEEE Conference on Intelligence and Security Informatics (ISI), pp. 133–138. IEEE (2016)
3. Chang, C.-H., Kayed, M., Girgis, M.R., Shaalan, K.F.: A survey of web information extraction systems. IEEE Trans. Knowl. Data Eng. **18**(10), 1411–1428 (2006)
4. Chen, H.: Dark Web: Exploring and Data Mining the Dark Side of the Web, vol. 30. Springer Science & Business Media, Berlin (2011)
5. Dalvi, N., Kumar, R., Pang, B., Ramakrishnan, R., Tomkins, A., Bohannon, P., Keerthi, S., Merugu, S.: A web of concepts. In: Proceedings of the Twenty-Eighth ACM SIGMOD-SIGACT-SIGART Symposium on Principles of Database Systems, pp. 1–12. ACM (2009)
6. Doan, A., Halevy, A., Ives, Z.: Principles of Data Integration. Elsevier, Amsterdam (2012)
7. Elmagarmid, A.K., Ipeirotis, P.G., Verykios, V.S.: Duplicate record detection: a survey. IEEE Trans. Knowl. Data Eng. **19**(1), 1–16 (2007)
8. Frank, J.R., Kleiman-Weiner, M., Roberts, D.A., Niu, F., Zhang, C., Ré, C., Soboroff, I.: Building an entity-centric stream filtering test collection for trec2012. Technical report, DTIC Document (2012)
9. Freitas, A., Curry, E., Oliveira, J.G., O'Riain, S.: Querying heterogeneous datasets on the linked data web: challenges, approaches, and trends. IEEE Internet Comput. **16**(1), 24–33 (2012)
10. Greiman, V., Bain, C.: The emergence of cyber activity as a gateway to human trafficking. In: Proceedings of the 8th International Conference on Information Warfare and Security, ICIW 2013, p. 90. Academic Conferences Limited (2013)
11. Gupta, S., Szekely, P., Knoblock, C.A., Goel, A., Taheriyan, M., Muslea, M.: Karma: a system for mapping structured sources into the semantic web. In: Simperl, E., Norton, B., Mladenic, D., Della Valle, E., Fundulaki, I., Passant, A., Troncy, R. (eds.) ESWC 2012. LNCS, vol. 7540, pp. 430–434. Springer, Heidelberg (2015). doi:10.1007/978-3-662-46641-4_40
12. Harrendorf, S., Heiskanen, M., Malby, S.: International statistics on crime and justice. European Institute for Crime Prevention and Control, affiliated with the United Nations, HEUNI (2010)
13. Hirschman, L., Gaizauskas, R.: Natural language question answering: the view from here. Nat. Lang. Eng. **7**(04), 275–300 (2001)

14. Hogan, A., Harth, A., Umrich, J., Decker, S.: Towards a scalable search and query engine for the web. In: Proceedings of the 16th International Conference on World Wide Web, pp. 1301–1302. ACM (2007)
15. Hultgren, M., Jennex, M.E., Persano, J., Ornatowski, C.: Using knowledge management to assist in identifying human sex trafficking. In: 2016 49th Hawaii International Conference on System Sciences (HICSS), pp. 4344–4353. IEEE (2016)
16. Jain, A., Doan, A., Gravano, L.: SQL queries over unstructured text databases. In: 2007 IEEE 23rd International Conference on Data Engineering, pp. 1255–1257. IEEE (2007)
17. Lin, T., Pantel, P., Gamon, M., Kannan, A., Fuxman, A.: Active objects: actions for entity-centric search. In: Proceedings of the 21st International Conference on World Wide Web, pp. 589–598. ACM (2012)
18. Niu, F., Zhang, C., Ré, C., Shavlik, J.W.: Deepdive: web-scale knowledge-base construction using statistical learning and inference. VLDS **12**, 25–28 (2012)
19. Saleiro, P., Teixeira, J., Soares, C., Oliveira, E.: TimeMachine: entity-centric search and visualization of news archives. In: Ferro, N., Crestani, F., Moens, M.-F., Mothe, J., Silvestri, F., Di Nunzio, G.M., Hauff, C., Silvello, G. (eds.) ECIR 2016. LNCS, vol. 9626, pp. 845–848. Springer, Cham (2016). doi:10.1007/978-3-319-30671-1_78
20. Sauro, J.: Measuring usability with the system usability scale (SUS) (2011)
21. Savona, E.U., Stefanizzi, S.: Measuring Human Trafficking. Springer, New York (2007)
22. Szekely, P., et al.: Building and using a knowledge graph to combat human trafficking. In: Arenas, M., et al. (eds.) ISWC 2015. LNCS, vol. 9367, pp. 205–221. Springer, Cham (2015). doi:10.1007/978-3-319-25010-6_12
23. Tonon, A., Demartini, G., Cudré-Mauroux, P.: Combining inverted indices and structured search for ad-hoc object retrieval. In: Proceedings of the 35th International ACM SIGIR Conference on Research and Development in Information Retrieval, pp. 125–134. ACM (2012)

Lessons Learned in Building Linked Data
for the American Art Collaborative

Craig A. Knoblock[1]([✉]), Pedro Szekely[1], Eleanor Fink[2], Duane Degler[3],
David Newbury[4], Robert Sanderson[4], Kate Blanch[5], Sara Snyder[6],
Nilay Chheda[1], Nimesh Jain[1], Ravi Raju Krishna[1], Nikhila Begur Sreekanth[1],
and Yixiang Yao[1]

[1] University of Southern California, Marina del Rey, CA, USA
knoblock@isi.edu
[2] American Art Collaborative, Washington, D.C., USA
[3] Design for Context, Bethesda, MD, USA
[4] J. Paul Getty Trust, Los Angeles, CA, USA
[5] The Walters Art Museum, Baltimore, MD, USA
[6] Smithsonian American Art Museum, Washington, D.C., USA

Abstract. Linked Data has emerged as the preferred method for publishing and sharing cultural heritage data. One of the main challenges for museums is that the defacto standard ontology (CIDOC CRM) is complex and museums lack expertise in semantic web technologies. In this paper we describe the methodology and tools we used to create 5-star Linked Data for 14 American art museums with a team of 12 computer science students and 30 representatives from the museums who mostly lacked expertise in Semantic Web technologies. The project was completed over a period of 18 months and generated 99 mapping files and 9,357 artist links, producing a total of 2,714 R2RML rules and 9.7M triples. More importantly, the project produced a number of open source tools for generating high-quality linked data and resulted in a set of lessons learned that can be applied in future projects.

Keywords: Linked Data · Data mapping · Linking · Lessons learned

1 Introduction

There is growing interest in Linked Open Data (LOD) among museums and the cultural heritage sector. In recent years it has gained traction because most museums are interested in using technology to reach new audiences, collaborate with other museums, deepen research, and help audiences of all ages experience, learn about, appreciate, and enjoy art. In fact, these concepts and others that characterize features of LOD inspired 14 art museums to form a collaborative to learn about and implement LOD within their respective museums and set the stage for the broader art-museum community to explore LOD.

The goals of the American Art Collaborative (AAC)[1] are to learn about LOD; create and publish a critical mass of LOD drawn from the collections of the 14

---

[1] http://americanartcollaborative.org/.

© Springer International Publishing AG 2017
C. d'Amato et al. (Eds.): ISWC 2017, Part II, LNCS 10588, pp. 263–279, 2017.
DOI: 10.1007/978-3-319-68204-4_26

museums that will be made available on the Internet for researchers, educators, developers, and the general public; test LOD reconciliation methods; develop open-source production and reconciliation tools; demonstrate the value of LOD through a prototype browse application; and publish good practices guidelines to help the broader museum community learn about and implement LOD.

Towards these goals, we built 5-star Linked Data (actually, we built 7-star linked data [1], which is 5-star data with an explicit meta-data schema and data validation) for 13 museums[2] by applying existing tools and developing new tools where needed to map and link the data. The project involved a number of different communities of users: about 30 representatives from the various museums, very knowledgeable about art, but inexperienced in Linked Data or ontologies, 5 Semantic Web experts who provided guidance and direction on the project, 12 USC students, inexperienced in art and the Semantic Web, who both helped develop new tools and applied the tools to the provided data, and 3 experts in the CIDOC CRM ontology who reviewed the data mappings at various stages of the project. In every stage of the project, all of these different communities were engaged in one way or another.

The three main thrusts of the project are mapping the data to a common cultural heritage ontology, linking the data to other resources, and then using the results to allow users to explore the data. For mapping the data, the AAC chose the CIDOC Conceptual Reference Model (CRM)[3] as its ontology. The CRM (ISO 21127:2006) is an extensive cultural heritage ontology containing 82 classes and 263 properties, including classes to represent a wide variety of events, concepts, and physical properties. The USC students used Karma [2] to align the museum data to the ontology. Given the complexity of the CRM ontology, the AAC project developed a Mapping Validation tool to guide the students in performing the mapping and validating them using queries to the actual data. For linking, the project focused on linking the artists to the Getty Union List of Artist Names (ULAN), a widely-used knowledge base of artists. To ensure high-quality links, we developed a link review tool that allowed museum representatives to review candidate links to make a final decision about whether each entity was the same as an entity listed in ULAN. To use the data, we developed an application that allows a user to explore the data by museum, artist, or artwork.

In the remainder of this paper, we will present the details of each thrust of the project (mapping, linking, and using) along with the lessons learned. We also compare the project to other related work and conclude with a discussion of the results, impact, and future work.

2   Mapping the Data

Managing the Data: The first step in the project was to map the data from each museum to the CRM ontology. Since each museum had as many as 14 data

---

[2] The Yale Center for British Art had already mapped and linked their data, so we only needed to build Linked Data for 13 of the 14 museums in the AAC.

[3] http://www.cidoc-crm.org/.

files, all in different formats, just managing the data from the 13 museums was a challenge. We addressed the data management problem by using the GitHub source control system to manage all project data. We set up one repository for each museum and taught the museums how to upload their data. In addition, each GitHub repository organizes and stores all the resources associated with each data set: the mappings that specify how each data set is mapped to the CRM ontology; visualizations of the mappings that enable non-technical museum personnel to review the mappings; the resulting RDF data that is then loaded into the triplestore; and the issues identified by CRM experts, and discussions that led to their resolution.

Table 1 provides the details of the use of GitHub for the data that we received from the museums, including the format of the data provided, the number of files (we only counted the ones we actually mapped), the number of mappings (each file can have more than one mapping to different classes), the number of people involved in creating and refining the mappings, the total number of GitHub commits, and the number of issues identified and discussed on the GitHub issue tracker. Note that all of this information is available online.[4]

Table 1. The AAC mapping process

Museum	Format	Files	Mappings	People	Commits	Issues
Archives of American Art	xls	5	5	5	67	17
Amon Carter Museum	xml	2	3	7	195	17
Autry Museum	xlsx	6	6	9	309	68
Crystal Bridges Museum	csv	8	14	7	572	76
Colby College Museum of Art	json	1	2	7	345	31
Dallas Museum of Art	csv	2	2	3	250	11
Gilcrease Museum	xlsx	9	12	5	447	24
Indianapolis Museum of Art	json	3	3	6	214	16
National Museum of Wildlife Art	csv	2	3	6	196	9
National Portrait Gallery	xlsx	11	12	7	334	75
Princeton University Art Museum	json	10	11	7	421	53
Smithsonian American Art Museum	csv	11	14	4	408	49
Walters Art Museum	xml	6	12	6	878	28
Total		4	76	99		4,636	474

Mapping the Data: After the raw data was uploaded to GitHub, the next and most difficult challenge, was mapping the data to the CRM domain ontology. This was challenging for several reasons. First, there was a lot of data, much more than we originally expected since it included data about artists, artwork,

---

[4] http://github.com/american-art.

exhibitions and bibliographies, as well as collection data from the Smithsonian Archives of American Art. Second, the CRM ontology is very complicated and requires significant expertise to understand and use. Third, the pool of students that we had available to work on this project were skilled undergraduate and masters students in computer science, but they were not experts in the Semantic Web, cultural heritage data, or the CRM ontology.

In previous work, we developed the Karma information integration system, a semi-automated tool for mapping data sources to a domain ontology [2,3]. Karma supports a wide variety of source types, has a machine learning capability to provide recommendations on the mappings to an ontology, and has an intuitive graphical interface for visualizing and refining mappings. Figure 1 provides a fragment of a screen shot of the use of Karma to map one of the datasets to the CRM ontology. In the screenshot, the graph showing the mapping is shown at the top of the figure, the attribute names and an analysis of the distribution of the data for that attribution are shown in the blue and green rectangles, and the data is shown at the bottom.

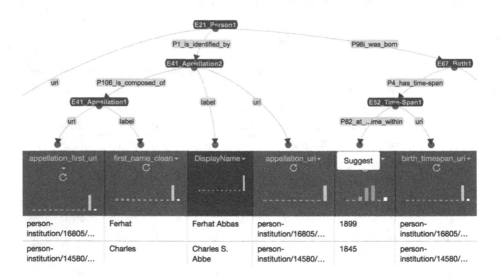

Fig. 1. Screen shot of Karma building a mapping of the National Portrait Gallery data

After completing a mapping or updating it to address an issue, users can publish the mapping (R2RML file) and associated resources (report of all data transformations and visualization of the mapping) to GitHub using Karma. Figure 2 shows a visualization of a mapping. In addition, the R2RML mapping is applied to the raw data to create RDF triples, which are subsequently loaded into the triplestore and posted on GitHub.

We started the mapping process with a team of USC computer science students in January 2016. The students quickly became proficient in Karma and worked closely with a local CRM expert to begin the mapping process for the data from the National Portrait Gallery. Because of the complexity of the CRM ontology, it took several iterations to create a mapping that satisfied the expert. Other students worked on mapping the data from other museums and by the end of the spring semester 2016, we had built mappings for a half a dozen museums.

Review by a different CRM expert revealed many issues with the mappings. Some issues resulted from inconsistencies in the mappings produced by different students. Interestingly, some issues revealed disagreements among CRM experts who had previously worked together. Students updated the mappings according to guidance provided in the discussion forum associated with each issue. The process was slowed-down by lengthy discussions among the experts on the correct way to map various attributes (e.g., several issues had over 20 replies by different CRM experts). After a significant number of weeks spent on numerous revisions of the mappings and lack of convergence, we decided to suspend the mapping process until the CRM experts could provide clear and consistent guidance.

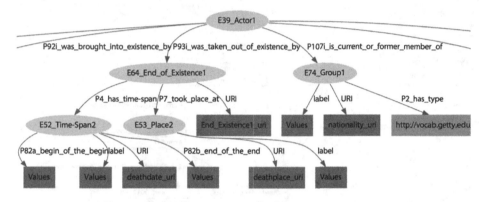

Fig. 2. Mapping of artist data from the Amon Carter Museum to the CRM ontology

Validating the Mappings: To address the challenges in creating consistent and correct mappings, we developed the AAC Mapping Validator,[5] (Fig. 3). In this tool, two of our Semantic Web experts defined a target mapping for each of the relevant pieces of information from the museums. The figure shows the target mapping for Classification. The Mapping Validator implements this target mapping as a query, which can then be run against any one of several SPARQL Endpoints. The upper half of the figure shows that the AAC Endpoint has been selected, and a specific object from the National Portrait Gallery is specified. The tool runs that SPARQL query for the target mapping against the AAC triplestore and displays the result for the specified object (#49748).

The validation tool led to a dramatic improvement in the efficiency of the mapping process. The validation tool diagram showed students how to map the data, and the query enabled students to test their mappings after loading the RDF in the triplestore.

---

[5] http://review.americanartcollaborative.org.

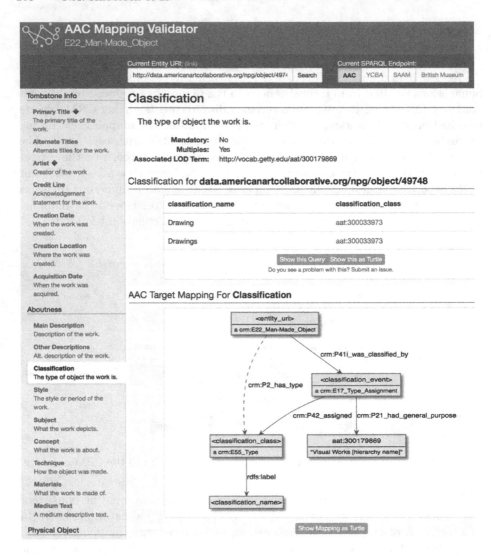

Fig. 3. The Mapping Validator specifies the target mapping and queries the triplestore based on the mapping to verify that the mapping is done correctly

At this point, a year into the project, more than half of the datasets had been mapped twice. For many attributes, the templates defined in the validation tool required mapping the data a third time. In order to meet the project deadlines, we recruited a team of 6 M.S. students to participate in an intense 2-week "Karma-fest" after their final exams. Using the validation tool for guidance, and Karma to build the mappings, the students re-mapped the datasets for 12 of the 13 AAC museums. The two museums that were left out were the Archives of American Art, whose data was very different from the other museums since it is an archive, and the Yale Center for British Art, which had already mapped their data to the CRM. Then in the spring 2017 we had one student refine the mappings based on a new review, complete some missing pieces, and map the Archives data. Table 2 shows the details of mappings created for each museum, including the number of data transformations, structure transformations, classes, semantic types, and links between classes. Table 3 provides details of the data produced by the mappings, including the number of constituents (e.g., artists), object, events, places, and the total number of triples.

Table 2. The AAC mappings

Museum	Data trans.	Structure trans.	Classes	Semantic types	Links
Archives of American Art	46	0	30	65	43
Amon Carter Museum	13	3	13	26	14
Autry Museum	76	0	46	87	49
Crystal Bridges Museum	112	6	74	132	89
Colby College Museum of Art	52	0	36	69	52
Dallas Museum of Art	46	0	27	55	39
Gilcrease Museum	105	5	75	132	109
Indianapolis Museum of Art	87	2	55	101	75
National Museum of Wildlife Art	37	0	24	47	34
National Portrait Gallery	112	2	64	118	69
Princeton University Art Museum	116	5	95	153	115
Smithsonian American Art Museum	88	4	67	114	95
Walters Art Museum	78	8	56	99	71
Total	968	35	662	1,198	854

In this process, we learned a number of important lessons:

Lesson 1 - Reproducible Workflows: To enable construction of reproducible workflows, allow museums to submit the raw data exported from their collection management systems, and implement the necessary data cleaning as part of the mapping workflows. We found line-based data formats, such as JSON Lines, CSV, or XLS, to be much easier to work with compared to large document formats, such as XML or JSON dictionaries.

Lesson 2 - Shared Repository: GitHub proved invaluable for managing multiple data submissions from museums, multiple versions of the mappings and associated resources, and the issues raised during the mapping process. Karma was extended to support the GitHub-based workflow, providing a one-click *publish mapping* command to publish into Github the R2RML file along with a visualization of the mapping, which is automatically created using Graphviz.[6]

---

[6] http://www.graphviz.org.

Table 3. The results of applying the mappings

Museum	Constituents	Objects	Events	Places	Triples
Archives of American Art	6,944	15,025	7,301	1,592	210,360
Amon Carter Museum	806	6,421	13,164	532	225,528
Autry Museum	148	193	558	0	14,639
Crystal Bridges Museum	514	1,691	3,384	0	96,533
Colby College Museum of Art	2,210	8,217	18,905	0	456,711
Dallas Museum of Art	1,299	2,229	5,639	0	114,184
Gilcrease Museum	1,578	20,904	83,603	4,159	1,851,246
Indianapolis Museum of Art	2,131	22,314	34,560	432	846,952
National Museum of Wildlife Art	376	2,208	2,226	0	83,486
National Portrait Gallery	12,553	16,829	54,097	5,713	1,902,699
Princeton University Art Museum	2,899	13,314	43,828	881	1,253,239
Smithsonian American Art Museum	20,490	43,038	106,534	3,042	2,597,938
Walters Art Museum	182	801	1722	159	60,136
Total	52,130	153,184	375,521	16,510	9,713,651

Lesson 3 - Data Cleaning: The data submitted was of varied quality because most museum data has legacy data issues that have not been resolved for decades. For example, museums do not consistently record dates, dimensions, or have consistent ways of referring to an "unknown" work of art. A significant amount of data cleaning is necessary to produce high quality RDF. Karma supports arbitrary data transformations as part of the mapping process (using Python scripts), which made it possible to address an open-ended set of data cleaning scenarios.

Lesson 4 - Mapping Inconsistencies: Even though the CRM is a very prescriptive ontology, different CRM experts may map the same data differently, making it difficult to write reliable SPARQL queries. A template-based validation tool makes it easy to enforce consistency.

Lesson 5 - Expert Review: A formal review process by an outside consultant was very effective in identifying and resolving problems and inconsistencies in the mapping of the data. The USC students conducting the mapping were not art experts or CRM experts and at times made assumptions that did not work for the museums or were incorrect mappings, but were not identified by the validation tool.

3   Linking and Reviewing the Data

An important aspect of producing high quality Linked Data is to link subjects to external datasets. In the cultural heritage community, the Getty Union List of Artist Names (ULAN) is an authoritative reference dataset, containing over 650,000 names for over 160,000 artists. The goal of our linking effort was to discover links to ULAN for artists in the museum datasets.

Museums take enormous pride on the quality of their data, so they want 100% correct links. They were willing to manually review *every* link before publication, so we developed a workflow where an automated algorithm first proposes links (pairs of museum actors and ULAN artists), and a human curator verifies each link. Given the large number of artists (52,130), the review effort is significant, so it was important to use a high precision algorithm to propose candidate links for review. A natural approach was to use existing tools, as the students working on the project are not experts in entity resolution algorithms.

We explored several different approaches to generate candidate links. We first assigned a student to work with Dedupe,[7] a popular entity resolution library based on Bilenko's work [4]. Initial results with a subset of the data were good, but then we ran into problems getting the algorithm to scale to the full ULAN dataset, running out of memory. Next we assigned a student to use SILK [5], a popular entity resolution tool. But the student struggled to configure the software to generate good results and we decided to abandon this approach after several weeks of effort.

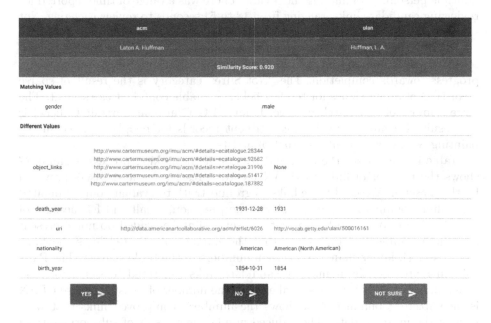

Fig. 4. Screenshot of the link review tool

We then assigned a student to implement a simple blocking scheme using birth year and the first two characters of the names (for records that didn't

---

[7] https://github.com/dedupeio/dedupe.

include birth year). He compared the names using Hybrid Jaccard with Jaro Winkler string similarity. Reusing software found on GitHub, he was able to implement this simple algorithm in a couple of weeks and tune the similarity thresholds in a few more weeks. The final algorithm uses different thresholds for records where birth or death dates are available, using a stricter string comparison threshold for records without birth or death years. Although not efficient, the algorithm produces links for the entire dataset in 20 hours running on a laptop.

The automated algorithm produced 24,733 links that needed to be reviewed by museum personnel. Some museums wanted links to be independently reviewed by more than one person and published if at least two reviewers approved them. We developed a generic link review tool optimized to support efficient and accurate comparison of pairs of records. The tool (Fig. 4) requires the two datasets to be represented in the same schema to enable building a simple card that shows values side by side. Each row shows the values of one record field, placing the values side-by-side to support rapid assessment. The card segregates fields with identical values from fields with different values so users can quickly see the differences. When multiple candidates exist for a single record, the tool shows all cards for the record in a single page. Even though the number of links is large, all museums reviewed their links in a week or two, sometimes with multiple personnel conducting the review. There was a range of time reported for reviewing candidate links, ranging from 18 to 51 seconds to review each one. Not surprisingly, museums with fewer candidates spent more time on each candidate.

Figure 5 shows the statistics chart present in the home page of the link review tool. For each museum it shows the total number of links in need of review, and progress towards completion. The "Not Sure" category is the result of sparse records, containing values for too few fields to enable confident assessment. The large number of "Unmatched" records for NPG (National Portrait Gallery) is the result of a large number of constituent records for people depicted in the painting with names similar to that of artists.

Table 4 summarizes the data and results of the linking process. Column G shows the number of links to ULAN records present in the datasets provided by the museum. We used these links as ground-truth to evaluate our automated algorithm: columns P, R and F shows the precision, recall and F1-measure of our algorithm. We hypothesize that the set of links provided do not represent a random sample of artists given that the number of rejected links shown in Fig. 5 is much larger than the precision numbers in the table suggest. The Pairs column represents the number of candidate links generated by our algorithm. The number of pairs is always smaller than the number of artists because ULAN is incomplete. Column $G \cap A$ shows the number of approved links that were part of the museum data. The reduced number is a result of sub-optimality of the blocking algorithms and recall failures of the matching algorithm. Column G^* shows the count of incorrect ULAN links present in the museum dataset. We identified the links where the museum and our review tool disagree, and we evaluated the links by looking at the Web pages in the museum and Getty websites. Similarly, A^* shows the count of incorrect links produced by our review

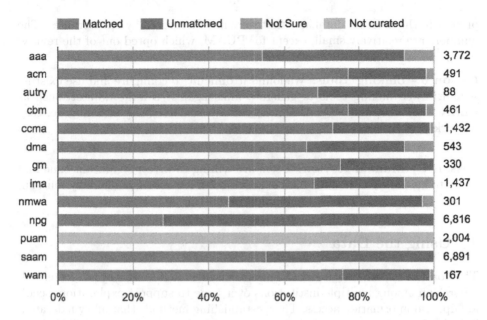

Fig. 5. Status chart from the link review tool showing the work completed for each museum

Table 4. Statistics on the linking process.

Museum	|Artists|	|G|	P	R	F	|Pairs|	|G∩A|	|G*|	|A\G|	|A*|	|G\A|
AAA	6,944	0	-	-	-	3,772	-	-	2,038	-	-
ACM	772	0	-	-	-	491	-	-	377	-	-
AM	114	73	.93	.75	.83	88	55	0	6	0	18
CBM	513	0	-	-	-	461	-	-	354	-	-
CCMA	2,005	1,060	.96	.85	.90	1,432	1,043	1	0	0	17
DMA	649	0	-	-	-	543	-	-	358	-	-
GM	1,198	266	1.0	.94	.97	330	229	0	16	1	37
IMA	2,077	671	.96	.92	.94	1,437	596	17	359	1	58
NMWA	375	0	-	-	-	301	-	-	135	-	-
NPG	12,552	0	-	-	-	6,816	-	-	1,919	-	-
PUAM	2,866	1,174	.95	.90	.93	2004	-	-	-	-	1,174
SAAM	12,439	0	-	-	-	6,891	-	-	3,769	-	-
WAM	181	105	.98	.95	.97	167	99	1	26	0	6
Total	42,685	3,349	.96	.88	.92	24,733	2,022	19	9,357	2	1,310

tool. Column $A\backslash G$ contains the counts of new links produced with our linking workflow. The number of new links is more than double the number of links present in the museum databases. The last column shows the counts of links present in the museum databases that were not discovered by our workflow. The numbers are relatively small, except for PUAM, which opted out of the review.

Lesson 6 - Linking Tools: We found it difficult to configure and use existing semantic web linking tools to generate links against a large dataset, such as ULAN, DBPedia, and VIAF. We need to have scalable, easy-to-configure, easy to work with libraries for creating the links.

Lesson 7 - Manual Review: Users are willing to invest significant time and effort to ensure that the final data is accurate (a few weeks of effort by museum personnel more than tripled the number of existing links).

4   Using the Data

The goals of the American Art Collaborative include finding ways to foster collaboration among multiple institutions over time to support exploration, scholarship, and information access. Thus, establishing methods that allow federated, linked information to grow over time along with the commitment of all the people who use and manage the information within institutions is critical to success. The development of the prototype Browse Application described in this section is important to make Linked Data real to museum users.

The project established a Browse Working Group, involving 6 of the 14 institutions, to design and develop a usable application for exploring the AAC data. The group began the process by identifying the goals of the partner institutions, as well as gathering ideas for the types of explorations that were difficult to do currently on the web. An analysis survey was developed to gather qualitative input from curators, registrars, educators, and outside researchers. One finding from this analysis was, as expected, that people find it easy to identify barriers in their existing work processes, yet struggle to imagine alternative approaches. This validated the project's commitment to a browse application that would present information in new ways.

The Mapping Validator and the Browse application (Fig. 6) were designed and developed in parallel, making sure that the data to be displayed was valuable and available. Iterative design focused on both presenting the primary entities from the data (people, artworks, museums, and possibly also locations and subjects) and exposing relationships between the entities. Pages for artworks and artists feature a small panel on the right side that provides links to related objects and are described with short phrases that describes the relationships.

To help with search and to improve performance across the growing collection of data, the browse application is populated by querying the triplestore and generating JSON-LD documents for each primary entity. These documents include all the associated link references for the entity, to allow rich cross-referencing within the browse application and to allow populating dynamic JavaScript features that need rich data. The JSON-LD documents are stored in Elasticsearch

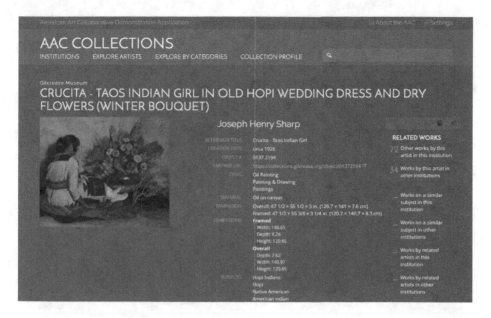

Fig. 6. Screenshot from the Browse application, which allows museums to review their data and access relationships

so that they are easily searchable by the application, which is useful when generating lists of related artworks based on specific parameters. The triplestore remains available for more complex and ad hoc queries.

Each page was designed to incorporate small visualizations, aggregations, and tools that help expose interesting aspects of the data about the page's artwork or artist. These tools were nicknamed "toys in the toybox" and presented below the artwork's data on the page (Fig. 7).[8] Each individual toy has its own horizontal row, and has a profile that expresses what data it needs from the linked data to be able to present a usable representation. As the entity loads into the page, the available data is checked against the profiles, and each toy is shown or hidden accordingly. This allows developers from different institutions to create toys over time and for each institution to decide what toys they think are useful to present with their entity data. The toybox approach extends the capabilities that are available as the data contributions from partner museums grows.

Even in its early stages as a prototype, the browse application is proving useful to all the partner institutions when reviewing the data that has been generated. This clear, human-readable presentation helps museum data managers check that the full pipeline from export of their initial data, through mapping and conversion to RDF, through querying and populating the browse application, produces the high quality and accuracy they expect.

---

[8] The depicted screen is under development.

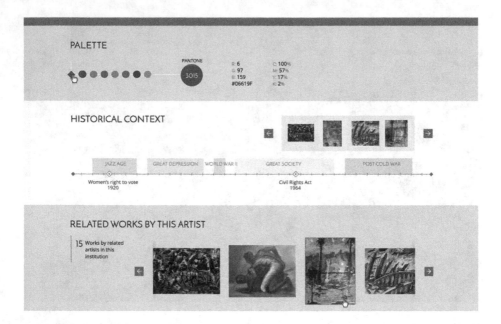

Fig. 7. The artwork and artist pages allow small independent tools to be incorporated, so scholars can discover patterns and have different ways to explore the available data

Lesson 8 - Data Visualization: An easy to understand visualization is needed for non-technical users to review the linked data. With a complicated ontology, existing Linked Data interfaces, such as Pubby,[9] are not useful for users to view their data.

Lesson 9 - Simple Schema: We needed a simple schema rather than the complicated one provided by the CRM, so we created SPARQL queries to map subjects, persons, and objects into JSON and then used Elasticsearch to analyze the interconnections to build the interface.

5   Related Work

There is a great deal of interest in publishing museum data as Linked Data. Europeana [6], one of the most ambitious efforts, published the metadata on 17 million items from 1,500 cultural institutions. The Canadian Heritage Information Network (CHIN), published the data on 85,000 items from 8 Canadian museums.[10] For both Europeana and CHIN, they integrate the data by publishing a fixed schema and requiring all of the participating institutions to transform their data into the required format (in a few cases CHIN mapped the data for

---

[9] https://github.com/cygri/pubby.
[10] http://chin-rcip.canadiana.ca/aclod/about.

the museums). The MuseumFinland published the metadata on 4,000 cultural artifacts from museums and sites in Finland [7] and the Amsterdam Museum [8] published the metadata on 73,000 objects. In both of these efforts the data is first mapped directly from the raw source into RDF and then complex mapping rules transform the RDF into an RDF expressed in terms of their chosen ontology. The LODAC Museum published metadata from 114 museums and research institutes in Japan [9]. They defined a relatively simple ontology that consists of objects, artists, and institutions to simplify the mapping process.

Research Space is a large effort to create the infrastructure for conducting research on cultural heritage data. A number of institutions participate in research space and have mapped their collections to the CRM ontology and published their data as Linked Data. These include the British Museum[11] and the Yale Center for British Art.[12] There are also consortiums that are participating in Research Space, such as the PHAROS project, a consortium of fourteen historical photo archives that are in the process of publishing their data as Linked Data using the CRM ontology.[13] In all these projects, the individual institutions are responsible for publishing their own data to the CRM ontology and these are multi-year projects with experienced technical staff that have a strong working knowledge of both the Semantic Web and the CRM ontology.

In a precursor to this project, we collaborated with the Smithsonian American Art Museum to publish their data as Linked Data [10]. In that project we also mapped the data to both the EDM and CRM ontologies using Karma, linked the artists to other sources (DBPedia), and created an initial link review tool. The AAC project forced us to address the issues of how to do all this work in a consistent fashion across multiple museums and to do so at scale, such as the mapping validation tool, the browse application, and a link review tool that supports crowd sourcing.

In this project we go beyond earlier work in several important ways. First, we developed a workflow that transforms and maps the data using Karma, and then validates the mappings using the Mapping Validation tool. Other approaches first map data directly into RDF [11] and then aligns the RDF with the domain ontology [12]. There is also work on specifically mapping to CRM using X3ML [13], a system that requires mapping data into XML and writing rules to map the XML to the corresponding CRM terms. For the AAC that would require manually writing a prohibitive number of such rules. These other approaches automate less of the mapping task and all of the data cleaning, mapping validation, and data verification would need to be done by hand.

Second, in order to provide an integrated view of artists across museums, we developed a crowd-sourcing link review tool. There is a great deal of work on linking data, such as the work on Silk [5], but very limited work on how to review the proposed links. Museums want to publish high-quality data, so verifying the links is critical part of the linked data creation process. There are several other

---

[11] http://collection.britishmuseum.org/.
[12] http://britishart.yale.edu/collections/using-collections/technology.
[13] http://pharosartresearch.org.

tools for solving this problem. Mix'n'match[14] is a tool for importing and linking new data into Wikidata.[15] The tool runs a fuzzy name match to generate a set of candidate entities in Wikidata and then allows the user to confirm or remove the matches. OpenRefine [14] provides a reconciliation capability that allows users to link a dataset to another one using specified fields and then interactively disambiguate the links. Both of these tools provide a link review capability, but they are targeted to highly technical users and are not well suited to experts in other fields.

6 Discussion

In this project we collaborated with 14 American art museums to build high-quality linked data about their artwork. We also created a set of tools that allowed a team of USC students to map the data without being experts in the CRM ontology and allowed the staff of the museums to review links to other resources. These tools, which are all available as open source, include: (1) the Karma data integration tool,[16] which cleans and maps the data, and has been extended for this project to store all of the associated mappings and data directly in Github, (2) a Mapping Validation tool[17] that provides both a specification of the precise ontology mapping and corresponding query that returns the data only if it has been correctly mapped, (3) a data generation tool (available as part of Karma), which applies the Karma mappings to the datasets to create the RDF data and load it directly into a triplestore, (4) a general link review tool[18] that allows non-technical users to quickly and easily review the links to other resources, and (5) a browse application[19] that allows both the museum staff, art historians, and the general public to review and explore the resulting Linked Data. All of these tools are being released as open source. The mapping tools were used extensively by the students that worked on the project (with limited background in the Semantic Web) and the link review and browsing tools were used extensively by the museum staff (who had limited technical background).

In future work we plan to explore techniques to simplify the task of publishing Linked Data so additional museums can easily join the AAC. Since many museums already publish their data on the web, we would like to gather, map, and link their data directly from the content they already make available online. We also want to extend the types of information supported and to link the existing data to other resources, such as VIAF,[20] Geonames, and DBpedia.

---

[14] https://tools.wmflabs.org/mix-n-match/.
[15] http://www.wikidata.org.
[16] http://karma.isi.edu.
[17] http://review.americanartcollaborative.org.
[18] https://github.com/american-art/linking.
[19] http://browse.americanartcollaborative.org.
[20] https://viaf.org/.

Acknowledgements. The American Art Collaborative was made possible by grants from the Andrew W. Mellon Foundation and the Institute of Museum and Library Services. We thank Eleanor Fink for leading the AAC project and all of the USC students and museum personnel who helped with all aspects of the project.

References

1. Hyvönen, E., Tuominen, J., Alonen, M., Mäkelä, E.: Linked data Finland: a 7-star model and platform for publishing and re-using linked datasets. In: Presutti, V., Blomqvist, E., Troncy, R., Sack, H., Papadakis, I., Tordai, A. (eds.) ESWC 2014. LNCS, vol. 8798, pp. 226–230. Springer, Cham (2014). doi:10.1007/978-3-319-11955-7_24

2. Knoblock, C.A., et al.: Semi-automatically mapping structured sources into the semantic web. In: Simperl, E., Cimiano, P., Polleres, A., Corcho, O., Presutti, V. (eds.) ESWC 2012. LNCS, vol. 7295, pp. 375–390. Springer, Heidelberg (2012). doi:10.1007/978-3-642-30284-8_32

3. Taheriyan, M., Knoblock, C.A., Szekely, P., Ambite, J.L.: Learning the semantics of structured data sources. J. Web Semant. **37–38**, 152–169 (2016)

4. Bilenko, M., Mooney, R.J.: Adaptive duplicate detection using learnable string similarity measures. In: Proceedings of ACM SIGKDD, pp. 39–48 (2003)

5. Volz, J., Bizer, C., Gaedke, M., Kobilarov, G.: Silk-a link discovery framework for the web of data. In: Proceedings of the 2nd Linked Data on the Web (2009)

6. Haslhofer, B., Isaac, A.: data.europeana.eu: The Europeana linked open data pilot. In: International Conference on Dublin Core and Metadata Applications (2011)

7. Hyvonen, E., Makela, E., Salminen, M., Valo, A., Viljanen, K., Saarela, S., Junnila, M., Kettula, S.: MuseumFinland - finnish museums on the semantic web. Web Semant. **3**(2–3), 224–241 (2005)

8. de Boer, V., Wielemaker, J., van Gent, J., Hildebrand, M., Isaac, A., van Ossenbruggen, J., Schreiber, G.: Supporting linked data production for cultural heritage institutes: the amsterdam museum case study. In: Simperl, E., Cimiano, P., Polleres, A., Corcho, O., Presutti, V. (eds.) ESWC 2012. LNCS, vol. 7295, pp. 733–747. Springer, Heidelberg (2012). doi:10.1007/978-3-642-30284-8_56

9. Matsumura, F., Kobayashi, I., Kato, F., Kamura, T., Ohmukai, I., Takeda, H.: Producing and consuming linked open data on art with a local community. In: Proceedings of the COLD Workshop, vol. 905, pp. 51–62 (2012). http://CEUR-WS.org

10. Szekely, P., Knoblock, C.A., Yang, F., Zhu, X., Fink, E., Allen, R., Goodlander, G.: Publishing the data of the Smithsonian American Art Museum to the linked data cloud. Int. J. Humanit. Art Comput. **8**, 152–166 (2014)

11. Cyganiak, R., Bizer, C.: D2R Server: a semantic web front-end to existing relational databases. XML Tage **2006**, 171–173 (2006)

12. Bizer, C., Schultz, A.: The R2R framework: publishing and discovering mappings on the web. In: 1st International Workshop on Consuming Linked Data (2010)

13. Marketakis, Y., Minadakis, N., et al.: X3ML mapping framework for information integration in cultural heritage and beyond. Digital Libr. **18**, 1–19 (2016)

14. Verborgh, R., De Wilde, M.: Using OpenRefine. Packt Publishing Ltd., Birmingham (2013)

Modeling and Using an Actor Ontology of Second World War Military Units and Personnel

Petri Leskinen[1]([⊠]), Mikko Koho[1], Erkki Heino[1,2], Minna Tamper[1,2], Esko Ikkala[1], Jouni Tuominen[1,2], Eetu Mäkelä[1,2], and Eero Hyvönen[1,2]

[1] Semantic Computing Research Group (SeCo), Aalto University, Espoo, Finland
{petri.leskinen,mikko.koho,erkki.heino,minna.tamper,esko.ikkala,
jouni.tuominen,eetu.makela,eero.hyvonen}@aalto.fi
[2] HELDIG – Helsinki Centre for Digital Humanities,
University of Helsinki, Helsinki, Finland
http://seco.cs.aalto.fi, http://heldig.fi

Abstract. This paper presents a model for representing historical military personnel and army units, based on large datasets about World War II in Finland. The model is in use in WarSampo data service and semantic portal, which has had tens of thousands of distinct visitors. A key challenge is how to represent ontological changes, since the ranks and units of military personnel, as well as the names and structures of army units change rapidly in wars. This leads to serious problems in both search as well as data linking due to ambiguity and homonymy of names. In our solution, actors are represented in terms of the events they participated in, which facilitates disambiguation of personnel and units in different spatio-temporal contexts. The linked data in the WarSampo Linked Open Data cloud and service has ca. 9 million triples, including actor datasets of ca. 100 000 soldiers and ca. 16 100 army units. To test the model in practice, an application for semantic search and recommending based on data linking was created, where the spatio-temporal life stories of individual soldiers can be reassembled dynamically by linking data from different datasets. An evaluation is presented showing promising results in terms of linking precision.

Keywords: Semantic web · Linked open data · Actor ontology · Digital humanities · Biographic representation

1 Introduction

Authority files [18], vocabularies (e.g., ULAN[1]), and actor ontologies (e.g. FOAF[2], REL[3], BIO[4], schema.org [5]) are used for (1) identifying people, groups,

---

[1] http://www.getty.edu/research/tools/vocabularies/ulan/about.html.
[2] http://xmlns.com/foaf/spec/.
[3] http://vocab.org/relationship/.
[4] http://vocab.org/bio/.

© Springer International Publishing AG 2017
C. d'Amato et al. (Eds.): ISWC 2017, Part II, LNCS 10588, pp. 280–296, 2017.
DOI: 10.1007/978-3-319-68204-4_27

and organizations and (2) for representing data about them. They constitute a central resource for cataloging and information management in museums, libraries, and archives, but also a challenge for data linking due to alternative names, homonyms, spelling variations, different languages, transliteration rules, and changes in time. Although actor ontologies play an essential part in modeling historical information, there are still very few published scientific articles about the subject.

Historical military units and personnel is a particularly challenging domain for creating an actor ontology: the structures of units are large and change rapidly, different codes can be used for actors in order to confuse the enemies, and people come and go due to the violent actions of war. For example, during the phases of WW2 in Finland (The Winter War, The Continuation War, and The Lapland War) different units have used the same name, and during Winter War in Finland the names of major units were changed just to bluff the enemy. Furthermore, the data about the actors is often incomplete and uncertain, involving lots of "unknown soldiers" of whom little is known.

From a Linked Data viewpoint this poses two major problems: (1) Data linking (based on named entity linking [2,6]) is difficult, because it has to be done in a changing and vague domain specific contexts [7]. For example, to tell whether a mention *captain Smith* and *colonel Smith* can refer to the same person, and to which *Smith* in the first place, data about different Smiths and their ranking history in time is needed. (2) It is difficult to aggregate and enrich data about actors that come from different sources and in different documentary forms, such as death records, diaries, magazine articles, or photographs, and to compile the global biographical history of the actors to the end users [9].

We argue that to address the problems above, a semantically rich spatio-temporal model for representing actors in relation to the events of the war is needed. This paper contributes to the state-of-the-art by presenting such an ontological actor model for historical military units and personnel. The model is in use in end-use application perspectives of the semantic portal WarSampo[5], where the idea is to reassemble automatically the biographical war history of individual soldiers and units. The model enables disambiguation of names in spatio-temporal contexts as well as combining contents from various sources, and publishing them in a harmonized format. The ontology and related data has been published as a Linked Open Data service[6] that can and has been used in digital humanities research and as well for developing online portals. For example, the community portal Sotapolku[7], provided by a commercial company, makes use of the WarSampo actor data.

The work is done as part of the WarSampo project[8], and builds upon our previous publications [7,9,11,12], which focus on the architecture, named entity

---

[5] Sotasampo in Finnish; available with an English GUI at http://www.sotasampo.fi/en, but the content is in Finnish.
[6] http://www.ldf.fi/dataset/warsa.
[7] http://sotapolku.fi.
[8] http://seco.cs.aalto.fi/projects/sotasampo/en/.

linking, and end-user views of the application. In contrast, this paper represents the underlying ontology model and dataset regarding army units and people in detail, as well as the actor related application perspectives in use.

The paper is structured as follows: First, ontology model for representing army units, and military personnel, is presented. After this the collecting of WarSampo actor dataset is represented, and a brief look on person and unit perspectives at WarSampo portal is taken. In conclusion, contributions of the work are summarized and some directions for further research are suggested.

2   Use Case and Datasets

The use case for our work is the WarSampo semantic portal[9] [9]. It provides the end user with richly interlinked data about the WW2 in Finland via application perspectives in the Sampo model [8]. An illustration of the WarSampo datasets is represented in Fig. 1. In total, the WarSampo data cloud contains data of more than a dozen different types (e.g. casualty data, photographs, events, war diaries, and historical maps) from an even larger pool of sources (e.g. the National Archives, the Defense Forces, and scanned books, from which part of the data has been extracted semi-automatically).

The actor dataset contains ca. 100 000 soldiers, and ca. 16 100 army units. The data is enriched with ca. 488 000 links from events to actors. Actors have furthermore been linked to external resources in the LOD cloud databases on the Web.

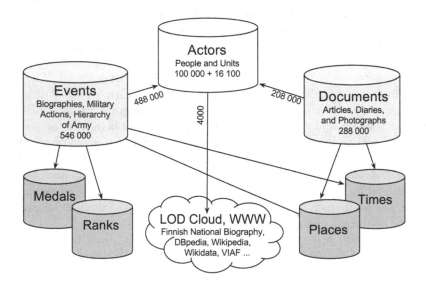

Fig. 1. Linkage in the actor-event based dataset

---

[9] http://sotasampo.fi/en/.

3   Actor Ontology Model

The ontology of actors is based on the CIDOC CRM[10] [4] model, where the resources of actors are essentially described in terms of the spatio-temporal events they participate in. An event represents any change of status that divides the timeline into periods before and after the event. Using the actor-event-model facilitates reconstructing the status of an actor at a specified moment. One main reason for adapting the model is that the information regarding a single actor varies a lot in both form and amount; in some cases we may have access to a very detailed description of the actor's biography, in some other cases only sparse pieces of information exist. All this data can be harmonized into a sequence of events. The applied actor-event-model also allows us to easily add new event types to the schema and new events the to database.

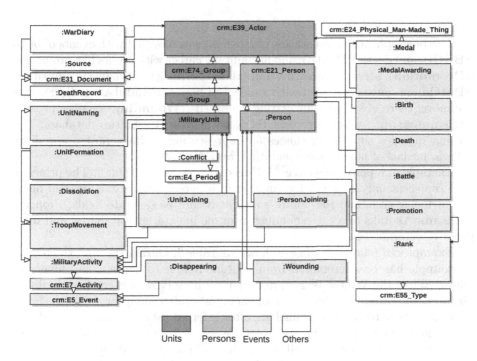

Fig. 2. Ontology schema of actors and events

Schema of the ontology is illustrated in Fig. 2. The schema is available at http://ldf.fi/schema/warsa, the namespaces and prefixes in use are listed in Table 1. The actor superclass **crm:E39_Actor**[11] is shown at center on the top. There is one subclass for people, and two for groups. For various types of events there are 19 classes with superclass **:Event**[12].

---
[10] http://cidoc-crm.org/.

[11] http://www.cidoc-crm.org/Entity/e39-actor/version-6.2.

[12] http://www.cidoc-crm.org/Entity/e5-event/version-6.2.

Table 1. Namespaces and prefixes used in actor ontologies

Namespace	Prefix
http://ldf.fi/schema/warsa/	:
http://www.cidoc-crm.org/cidoc-crm/	crm:
http://purl.org/dc/elements/1.1/	dc:
http://purl.org/dc/terms/	dct:
http://xmlns.com/foaf/0.1/	foaf:
http://rdf.muninn-project.org/ontologies/organization#	mil:
http://www.w3.org/2002/07/owl#	owl:
http://www.w3.org/1999/02/22-rdf-syntax-ns#	rdf:
http://www.w3.org/2004/02/skos/core#	skos:

The biographical representation of a person was modeled with events of birth
(**:Birth**), and death (**:Death**), and his military career with events like promotion
(**:Promotion**), serving in an army unit (**:UnitJoining**), participating in battles
(**:Battle**), or getting awarded with a medal of honor (**:MedalAwarding**). Fur-
thermore, there are classes for getting wounded (**:Wounding**) or disappearing
(**:Disappearing**), which represent the data fields in Casualties database. The
schema includes supporting classes for representing military ranks, war diary
entries, medals of honor, documentation, and data sources.

Example of a person resource[13] (**:Person**) is shown in Table 2. The principle
is to represent only constant information in a person resource; it has full name
as a primary title, and the family and first names as separate fields. Property
owl:sameAs links to a corresponding resource in external databases, and **foaf:
page** to external web pages.

Examples of related events are shown in Table 3. During the war, the person
in example has been promoted from lieutenant first to captain and finally to
major. When the Winter War started in 1939 he served as a commander in an
air force squadron, and shot down an enemy aircraft soon after.

In literature military personnel are ofter referred using a combination of current military rank and family name (e.g. *Captain Karhunen* or *Colonel Talvela*).
So, to describe a person in detail, an ontology of military ranks was needed. The
rank ontology is based on Muninn Military Ontology [19]. The hierarchy of
ranks was constructed by interlinking the instances to equal and lower ranks.
The **:Rank** instances in the datasets were enriched with additional information
(e.g. countries or service branches in which the rank has been used, or categories
like officer or non-commissioned officer). Event **:Promotion** was used to attach
a rank to a person. Due to the variations in the amount of available data, a
promotion event was created in all cases, even if a person is known to have only
a single rank with no specific date of promotion.

---

[13] http://ldf.fi/warsa/actors/person_294.ttl.

Table 2. Properties of a resource describing pilot Jorma Karhunen

Property	RDF identifier	Value
Primary title	skos:prefLabel	"Jorma (Joppe) Karhunen"
Family Name	foaf:familyName	"Karhunen"
First name (Nickname)	foaf:firstName	"Jorma (Joppe)"
Text description	dc:description	"Jorma Karhunen was a Finnish Air ..."@en
External LOD-links	owl:sameAs	http://dbpedia.org/resource/Jorma_Karhunen http://wikidata.org/entity/Q5482501
Related websites	foaf:page	https://en.wikipedia.org/wiki/Jorma_Karhunen www.mannerheim-ristinritarit.fi/ritarit?xmid=38

Table 3. Examples of events describing pilot Jorma Karhunen

Event description/resource URI	RDF class	Date
Born at Pyhäjärvi http://ldf.fi/warsa/events/birth_294.ttl	:Birth	1913-03-17
Serving as a squadron commander in 24th Fighter Squadron http://ldf.fi/warsa/events/joining_294_459.ttl	:PersonJoining	1939-11-30
Aerial victory in Tainionkoski: enemy SB-2 shot down http://ldf.fi/warsa/events/event_lv2408.ttl	:Battle	1939-12-01
Promotion to captain http://ldf.fi/warsa/events/kapteeni_294.ttl	:Promotion	1941-08-04
Photograph of capt. Karhunen with his dog Becky Brown http://ldf.fi/warsa/photographs/sakuva_7265.ttl	:Photography	1942-06-01
Awarded with the Mannerheim Cross of Liberty http://ldf.fi/warsa/medals/medal_83_294.ttl	:MedalAwarding	1942-09-08
Died at Tampere http://ldf.fi/warsa/events/death_294.ttl	:Death	2002-01-18

An example of RDF resource of a military unit is shown in Table 4, the resource is also available in Turtle format[14]. Just like in the case of a person, the properties describe only constant information like unit's preferable name and abbreviation, description, conflicts participated in, and links to LOD cloud resources. The events (Table 5) describe the unit's position in the army hierarchy and the involved military activities. The lifespan of a unit spans from its formation **:UnitFormation** to dissolution **:Dissolution**. The changes of the unit

---

[14] http://ldf.fi/warsa/actors/actor_459.

Table 4. Properties of a resource describing 24th Fighter Squadron

Property	RDF identifier	Value
Preferred label	skos:prefLabel	"Lentolaivue 24"
Preferred abbreviation	skos:altLabel	"LLv 24"
Description	dc:description	"No. 24 Squadron was a fighter ..."@en
Conflict	:hasConflict	wcf:WinterWar, wcf:ContinuationWar, ...
Army postal code	:covernumber	"8523", "8524", "8567"
Unit category	:hasUnitCategory	"Flying Regiments and Squadrons"
External LOD-links	owl:sameAs	https://www.wikidata.org/wiki/Q4356342
Related websites	foaf:page	https://fi.wikipedia.org/wiki/Lentolaivue_24

Table 5. Examples of events describing 24th Fighter Squadron

Event description/resource URI	RDF class	date
Troop founded as 24th Squadron (abbrev. LLv 24) http://ldf.fi/warsa/events/formation_971.ttl	:Formation	1934-10-10
Troop Movement to Immola Air Base http://ldf.fi/warsa/events/concentration_491.ttl	:TroopMovement	1939-10-12
Aerial victory in Tainionkoski: enemy SB-2 shot down http://ldf.fi/warsa/events/event_lv2408.ttl	:Battle	1939-12-01
Being part of Flying Regiment 2 http://ldf.fi/warsa/events/joining_458.ttl	:UnitJoining	1940-01-10
Written War Diary document http://ldf.fi/warsa/diaries/diary_c26701.ttl	:WarDiary	1941-06-19–1941-09-02
Changing the name to 24th Fighter Squadron (HLeLv 24) http://ldf.fi/warsa/events/form_459.ttl	:UnitNaming	1944-02-14

name were modeled as **:UnitNaming** events. Also the army hierarchy, including the temporal changes made in it, was modeled using the event schema: the hierarchy was represented as a tree graph where the army units are the nodes and the events of joining into a superior unit **:UnitJoining** form the edges. The events also included the military activities taken (e.g. movements **:TroopMovement** and battles **:Battle**). The event **:PersonJoining** was used to combine a person to the unit, in which he has served. The event could also announce a role in the unit (e.g. being a commander or a squadron pilot).

4   Warsampo Actor Data

Currently the actor dataset contains ca. 100 000 people. The data has been collected from various sources: lists of generals and commanders, lists of recipients of honorary medals, the Casualties database[15], Finnish National Biography[16], photographers mentioned in Finnish Wartime Photograph Archive[17], Wikidata[18], and Wikipedia. Besides military personnel, an extract of 580 Finnish or foreign civilians from the National Biography database and Wikidata was included. This set consisted of people with political or cultural significance.

The unit dataset consists of over 16 100 Finnish wartime units, including Land Forces, Air Forces, Navy, Medical Corps, stations of Anti-Aircraft Warfare and Airwarning, Finnish White Guard, and Foreign Volunteer Corps. At this stage Soviet and German troops were excluded. The main sources of information have been the War Diaries, Army Postal Code list[19], and Organization Cards, all of which provided the information as datasheets in CSV format.

In general, the method to produce the data depended on the format of data source. The biographies of the National Biography and the Casualties Database had been transformed into LOD in our earlier projects, and therefore the information extraction process was to convert the existing data into new actor entries and relating events. Transformation was mostly done by using specific SPARQL construct queries. More than 95 000 entries were generated from the Casualty Database to actor dataset [12].

The organization cards (Fig. 3) were written by Finnish Defense Forces shortly after the WW2. The cards contain the major part of units in Finnish Army, unfortunately not those of Navy and Air Force. An example of organization card is shown in Fig. 3. The proper name and abbreviation of the unit is shown at the upper left corner (a), in this case *Jalkaväkirykmentti 7* (7th Infantry Regiment), abbreviated as *JR 7*. The regiment has been part of *3. divisioona* (3rd Division), which is told at the upper right corner (b). The card provides further information about the foundation (c) and the military district (d) of the unit. Changes considering the unit, like different names, are shown at part (e). During the Winter War *JR 7* participated in four battles (f). The three columns on each line show the location or a short description of the battle, battle's duration, and the name of the commanding officer.

The organization cards were provided as scanned booklets in PDF format, and converting to RDF had several steps. Firstly each page in PDF booklet

---

[15] http://kronos.narc.fi/menehtyneet/.
[16] http://www.kansallisbiografia.fi/english/.
[17] http://sa-kuva.fi/neo?tem=webneoeng.
[18] https://www.wikidata.org/.
[19] http://www.arkisto.fi/uploads/Aineistot/kopsa[1].pdf.

was written as an individual PNG image. Images were preprocessed by adjusting the contrast and image rotation, and removing the compression artifacts. Next an *Optical character recognition (OCR)* process was applied. The resulting text was however very erroneous, and plenty of post-processing was required. The structured format of the cards, and the recurring use of military terms in the vocabulary however eased the automated error fixing. From the resulting text, the fields a-f (in Fig. 3) were extracted, and converted into RDF. The produced resources consisted of military units (:**MilitaryUnit**), their commanders (:**Person**) with ranks (:**Promotion**), and events like unit formations (:**UnitFormation**), joinings of units (:**UnitJoining**), movements (:**TroopMovement**), renamings (:**UnitNaming**), and battles (:**Battle**).

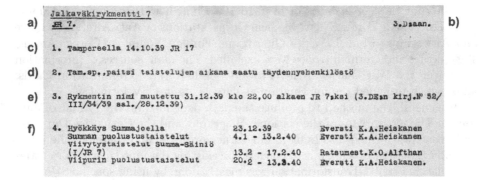

Fig. 3. Information on an organization card

Although the Wikipedia may not be considered as the most reliable source of information, it provided a way to connect data with external LOD cloud databases Wikidata, DBpedia[20], and VIAF[21]. The material regarding personnel was widely available, but for units, specially those of Finnish Army during the WW2, the information was sparse. Information was extracted from Wikipedia pages of e.g. Finnish high-ranking officers, politicians, wartime casualties, and foreign volunteers. The pages of Wikipedia follow a structured layout which facilitated extracting the information. In case of military units, detailed information for events like unit foundation, troop movements, battles, and for names of commanding officers were available. In total 2500 people and 480 units with 5000 events were generated from corresponding Wikipedia pages.

Characteristic sentences picked from Wikipedia were descriptions like "*1st Artillery Group was founded in Pori with Captain Paavo Suominen as the first commander*", "*10th July 1941 Regiment was moved to Kitee, from where it begun attacking towards Lake Ladoga*", or "*Regiment participated in the occupation of Prääsä September 7–8, 1941*". Each sentence was converted to an event, and

---

[20] http://wiki.dbpedia.org/.
[21] https://viaf.org/.

the named entities of personnel, places and dates were recognized and linked to database resources. The data retrieval was done using Python scripts utilizing MediaWiki API[22], and Wikipedia API for Python[23]. Entity linking was done with ARPA service [13].

The datasets of conflicts, war diaries, medals, and ranks are in separate graphs. Conflicts[24] contain four main periods of WW2 in Finland. The War Diary graph[25] has 26 400 entries. There are 200 medal types[26] and 200 rank entries[27]. The data includes ranks used by the Finnish Military with most common German and Soviet ranks, among with some civil titles (e.g. the ones used by women's voluntary association *Lotta Svärd*) [9].

5   The WarSampo Portal

The perspectives at WarSampo portal[28] visualize the linkage between the various datasets (e.g. military unit, personnel, casualties, events, places) etc [9,11]. WarSampo portal is a Rich Internet Application (RIA), where all functionality is implemented on the client side using JavaScript with AngularJS framework, only data is fetched from the server side SPARQL endpoints.

5.1   The Person Perspective

The WarSampo person perspective application[29] is illustrated in Fig. 4. A typical use case is someone searching for information about a relative who served in the army. On the left, the page has an input field (a) for a search by person's name. The matching query results are shown in the text field (b) below the input. After making a selection, information about the person is shown at the center top of the page (c). The tabs (d) allow the user to switch between this information page or a map-timeline application. In the example case, the page shows description of the person (e), photograph gallery (f), lists linking to related events (g), military units (h), battles (i), ranks (j), medals (k), related people (l), places (m), Wikipedia page (n), related Kansa Taisteli magazine articles (o), and a Finnish National Biography widget (p).

As an example of SPARQL query, the query fetching related people[30] defines a similarity measure between two people. The more events, medals, units, and the higher ranks the two share in common, the higher the similarity gets. The list of related people (l) shows the results sorted in descending order.

---

[22] https://en.wikipedia.org/w/api.php.
[23] https://pypi.python.org/pypi/wikipedia.
[24] See, e.g., http://ldf.fi/warsa/conflicts/LaplandWar.
[25] See, e.g., http://digi.narc.fi/digi/hae_ay.ka?sartun=319.SARK.
[26] See, e.g., http://ldf.fi/warsa/medals/medal_83.
[27] See, e.g., http://ldf.fi/warsa/actors/ranks/Majuri.
[28] http://www.sotasampo.fi/en/.
[29] http://www.sotasampo.fi/en/persons.
[30] http://yasgui.org/short/B1w2O71gb.

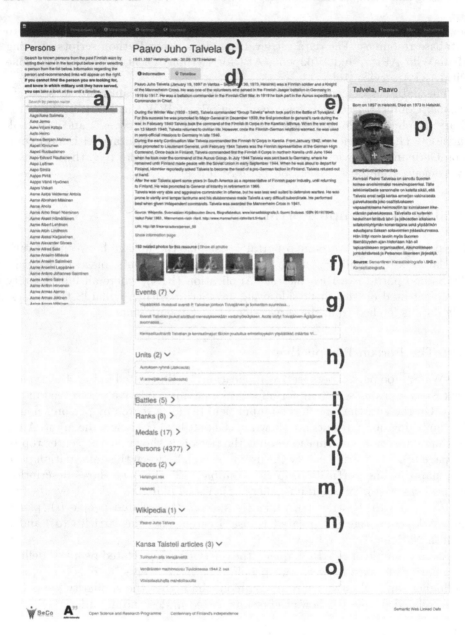

Fig. 4. Information on person perspective

WarSampo military unit perspective application[31] is illustrated in Fig. 5. In a typical use case someone searches for information about an army unit, where perhaps an elder relative has served during the wartime. On the left

[31] http://sotasampo.fi/en/units.

there is an input field (a) for a search by unit's name. The matching results are shown in the text field (b) below the input. The map (c) depicts the known locations of the unit. The heatmap shows the casualties of the unit, and the timeline (d) the events (e), e.g. dates of unit foundations, troop movements, and durations of fought battles. On the right there are unit names and abbreviations (f), description (g), and a collection of related photographs (h). Three lists of related units are shown: larger groups in which the unit has been as a member (i), subdivisions being parts of the unit (j), and units at the same hierarchical level (k). Below there are fields for related battles (l), links to Kansa Taisteli magazine articles (m), Wikipedia page (n), and War Diaries (o). The number of casualties during the specified time is shown at the bottom of page (p).

5.2   The Military Unit Perspective

See Fig. 5.

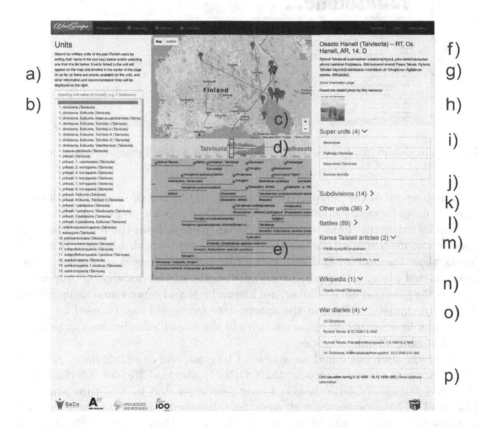

Fig. 5. Information on unit Perspective

5.3   The Kansa Taisteli Magazine Perspective

Kansa Taisteli is a magazine published by Sanoma Ltd and Sotamuisto association between 1957 and 1986. The magazine articles cover the memoirs of WW2 from the point of view of Finnish military personnel and civilians. The articles contain mentions of people, military units, and places. From these the military units and personnel have been linked to Actor ontology. The magazine perspective[32] can be used for searching and browsing articles relating to WW2. Military units and personnel are used as separate facets to search for articles. In addition, writers have been linked to Actor ontology as well.

Fig. 6. The Contextual Reader interface targeting the Kansa Taisteli magazine articles

The purpose of the perspective is two-fold: (1) to help a user find articles of interest using faceted semantic search and, (2) to provide context to the found articles by extracting links to related WarSampo data from the texts. The start page of the magazine article perspective is a faceted search browser. Here, the facets allow the user to find articles by filtering them based on author, issue, year, related place, army unit, or keyword. Some of the underlying properties, such as the year and issue number, are hierarchical and represented using SKOS. The hierarchy is visualized in the appropriate facet, and can be used for query expansion: by selecting an upper category in the facet hierarchy one can perform a search using all subcategories.

After the user has found an article of interest, she can click on it, and the article appears on the screen in the CORE Contextual Reader interface [14]. Depicted in Fig. 6, CORE is able to automatically and in real time annotate PDF and HTML documents with recognized keywords and named entities, such as army units, places, and person names. These are then encircled with colored boxes indicating the linked data source. By hovering the mouse over a box, data is shown to the user, providing contextual information for an enhanced read-

---

32 http://sotasampo.fi/en/articles.

ing experience. In Fig. 6, for example, detailed data are shown about *Raymond August Ericsson*, one of the battalion commanders discussed in the article.

Solving the technical issues, however still left the problem of semantic disambiguation; in this case this concerned named entity recognition of correct people and military units. The identification was made by customizing the SPARQL queries, the order of the queries, and the article metadata. Each magazine article was identified and firstly references to people were searched from the text. The identification of people was done by using name and possibly a rank. Secondly the linking of the military units was performed from the remaining text. The article metadata was also used to identify the war to which the events of the article are related to. Afterwards the military units were linked based on the war into the corresponding units. A detailed description and evaluation of the process is available at [17].

5.4 Photographs

WarSampo contains a dataset of the metadata of ca. 160 000 historical photographs taken by Finnish soldiers during WWII. The data contains e.g. captions of the photographs. The actor ontology was used to automatically disambiguate and link people and military units mentioned in the metadata. Information in the actor ontology was used extensively in linking: For example, when disambiguating people, names, ranks, promotion dates, military units, sources, medals, and death dates were used to rank otherwise ambiguous mentions in the photograph captions [7].

The results of the linking can be seen in the person and unit perspectives of the WarSampo portal, as well as in the photograph perspective itself[33] which provides a faceted search interface for the photographs.

6 Related Work, and Discussion

There are several projects publishing linked data about the World War I on the web, such as Europeana Collections 1914-1918[34], 1914-1918 Online[35], WW1 Discovery[36], Out of the Trenches[37], Muninn [19], and WW1LOD [15]. There are few works that use the Linked Data approach to World War II, such as [1,3], Defence of Britain[38], and Open Memory Project[39]. The main focus on our work

---

[33] http://www.sotasampo.fi/en/photographs.
[34] http://www.europeana-collections-1914-1918.eu.
[35] http://www.1914-1918-online.net.
[36] http://ww1.discovery.ac.uk.
[37] http://www.canadiana.ca/en/pcdhn-lod/.
[38] http://thesaurus.historicengland.org.uk/thesaurus.asp?thes_no=305&thes_name=Defence%20of%20Britain%20Thesaurus.
[39] http://www.bygle.net/wp-content/uploads/2015/04/Open-Memory-Project_3-1.pdf.

is on representing an actor as a biographical life story, unlike databases like Getty ULAN or Smithsonian American Art Museum [16] that have actor vocabularies.

Our research group, Semantic Computing Research Group (SeCo), has produced several projects with highly interlinked actor ontologies: The National Biography, CultureSampo[40], BookSampo[41], and Norssit—High School Alumni [10] datasets. Bio CRM model[42] is developed to facilitate and harmonize the representation of an actor in semantic web, and therefore deals with the same problematics as the WarSampo actor ontology.

We have considered combining the different datasets like articles and photographs to actor ontology as one of the use-cases of the actor ontology. The evaluation of the ontology and actor dataset, has been work- and data-driven e.g. it has developed to the needs of semantically representing the data and of rendering the data at the end-user portal. 94% of users come from Finland and 25% of them are returning visitors. We have received feedback via the user interface, and we have considered their comments e.g. on misidentified people.

Main requirement for the ontology was to represent changes in spatio-temporal context as described in Introduction. Constant actor resources are enriched with events marking the changes in spatio-temporal continuity, adding details to the semantic biographical representation, and connecting the otherwise separate datasets of personnel, units, places, articles, photographs etc. The unit model had to be capable of representing even more dynamical changes than with people; identifiers like name and abbreviation may change in the time domain. The army hierarchy is represented as a tree graph where the groups are connected by the events of joining.

The actor ontology is based on CIDOC CRM standard which provides a clear framework and basis for actor-event schema. The Muninn Military Ontology offered an example of modeling military concepts semantically. In conclusion, there was no obvious basis for the ontology. On the contrary, it was constructed by combining principles of several solutions all serving different needs.

In a similar way Warsampo project has collected historical, wartime information from Finland. There is abundance of information about the WW2 in different countries, written in local languages, and published in various formats; often even having divergent points of view. Collecting the data and publishing it as LOD forms a tremendous field of work, but aims at constructing a comprehensive, worldwide database. In the events of history, individual people and groups are at the focal center; it is from their point of view that we build our notion of history.

The ontology model represented in this article may not be all-purpose suitable, but we encourage and hope to inspire the researchers to develop the ideas further.

---

[40] http://seco.cs.aalto.fi/applications/kulttuurisampo/.

[41] http://seco.cs.aalto.fi/applications/kirjasampo/.

[42] http://seco.cs.aalto.fi/projects/biographies/.

Acknowledgements. Our work is funded by the Open Science and Research Initiative (http://openscience.fi/) of the Finnish Ministry of Education and Culture, the Finnish Cultural Foundation, and the Academy of Finland.

References

1. de Boer, V., van Doornik, J., Buitinck, L., Marx, M., Veken, T.: Linking the kingdom: enriched access to a historiographical text. In: Proceedings of the 7th International Conference on Knowledge Capture (KCAP 2013), pp. 17–24. ACM, June 2013
2. Bunescu, R.C., Pasca, M.: Using encyclopedic knowledge for named entity disambiguation. In: EACL, vol. 6, pp. 9–16 (2006)
3. Collins, T., Mulholland, P., Zdrahal, Z.: Semantic browsing of digital collections. In: Gil, Y., Motta, E., Benjamins, V.R., Musen, M.A. (eds.) ISWC 2005. LNCS, vol. 3729, pp. 127–141. Springer, Heidelberg (2005). doi:10.1007/11574620_12
4. Doerr, M.: The CIDOC CRM - an ontological approach to semantic interoperability of metadata. AI Mag. **24**(3), 75–92 (2003)
5. Guha, R.V., Brickley, D., Macbeth, S.: Schema.org: evolution of structured data on the web. Commun. ACM **59**(2), 44–51 (2016)
6. Hachey, B., Radford, W., Nothman, J., Honnibal, M., Curran, J.R.: Evaluating entity linking with Wikipedia. Artif. Intell. **194**, 130–150. http://dx.doi.org/10.1016/j.artint.2012.04.005
7. Heino, E., Tamper, M., Mäkelä, E., Leskinen, P., Ikkala, E., Tuominen, J., Koho, M., Hyvönen, E.: Named entity linking in a complex domain: case second world war history. In: Gracia, J., Bond, F., McCrae, J.P., Buitelaar, P., Chiarcos, C., Hellmann, S. (eds.) LDK 2017. LNCS, vol. 10318, pp. 120–133. Springer, Cham (2017). doi:10.1007/978-3-319-59888-8_10
8. Hyvönen, E.: Cultural heritage linked data on the semantic web: Three case studies using the sampo model (2017). http://seco.cs.aalto.fi/publications/submitted/hyvonen-vitoria-2017.pdf. Invited talk, Proceedings of the VIII Encounter of Documentation Centres of Contemporary Art: Open Linked Data and Integral Management of Information in Cultural Centres Artium, Vitoria-Gasteiz, Spain, 2016. Forth-coming
9. Hyvönen, E., Heino, E., Leskinen, P., Ikkala, E., Koho, M., Tamper, M., Tuominen, J., Mäkelä, E.: WarSampo data service and semantic portal for publishing linked open data about the second world war history. In: Sack, H., Blomqvist, E., d'Aquin, M., Ghidini, C., Ponzetto, S.P., Lange, C. (eds.) ESWC 2016. LNCS, vol. 9678, pp. 758–773. Springer, Cham (2016). doi:10.1007/978-3-319-34129-3_46
10. Hyvönen, E., Leskinen, P., Heino, E., Tuominen, J., Sirola, L.: Reassembling and enriching the life stories in printed biographical registers: Norssi high school alumni on the semantic web. In: Gracia, J., Bond, F., McCrae, J.P., Buitelaar, P., Chiarcos, C., Hellmann, S. (eds.) LDK 2017. LNCS, vol. 10318, pp. 113–119. Springer, Cham (2017). doi:10.1007/978-3-319-59888-8_9. http://ldk2017.org/
11. Hyvönen, E., Ikkala, E., Tuominen, J.: Linked data brokering service for historical places and maps. In: Proceedings of the 1st Workshop on Humanities in the Semantic Web (WHiSe), CEUR Workshop Proceedings, vol. 1608, pp. 39–52 (2016). http://ceur-ws.org/Vol-1608/#paper-06
12. Koho, M., Hyvönen, E., Heino, E., Tuominen, J., Leskinen, P., Mäkelä, E.: Linked death - representing, publishing, and using second world war death records as linked open data. In: WHiSe@ ESWC, pp. 3–14 (2016)

13. Mäkelä, E.: Combining a REST lexical analysis web service with SPARQL for mashup semantic annotation from text. In: Presutti, V., Blomqvist, E., Troncy, R., Sack, H., Papadakis, I., Tordai, A. (eds.) ESWC 2014. LNCS, vol. 8798, pp. 424–428. Springer, Cham (2014). doi:10.1007/978-3-319-11955-7_60

14. Mäkelä, E., Lindquist, T., Hyvönen, E.: CORE - a contextual reader based on linked data. In: Proceedings of Digital Humanities 2016, long papers, July 2016

15. Mäkelä, E., Törnroos, J., Lindquist, T., Hyvönen, E.: WW1LOD - an application of CIDOC-CRM to World War 1 linked data. Int. J. Digital Libr. **2016**, 1–11 (2016)

16. Szekely, P., Knoblock, C.A., Yang, F., Zhu, X., Fink, E.E., Allen, R., Goodlander, G.: Connecting the Smithsonian American art museum to the linked data cloud. In: Cimiano, P., Corcho, O., Presutti, V., Hollink, L., Rudolph, S. (eds.) ESWC 2013. LNCS, vol. 7882, pp. 593–607. Springer, Heidelberg (2013). doi:10.1007/978-3-642-38288-8_40

17. Tamper, M., et al.: AATOS – a configurable tool for automatic annotation. In: Gracia, J., Bond, F., McCrae, J.P., Buitelaar, P., Chiarcos, C., Hellmann, S. (eds.) LDK 2017. LNCS, vol. 10318, pp. 276–289. Springer, Cham (2017). doi:10.1007/978-3-319-59888-8_24

18. Taylor, A.: Introduction to cataloging and classification. Library and Information Science Text Series, Libraries Unlimited (2006)

19. Warren, R.: Creating specialized ontologies using Wikipedia: the Muninn experience. In: Proceedings of Wikipedia Academy: Research and Free Knowledge (WPAC2012), Berlin, DE (2012). http://hangingtogether.org

Sustainable Linked Data Generation: The Case of DBpedia

Wouter Maroy[1], Anastasia Dimou[1(✉)], Dimitris Kontokostas[2],
Ben De Meester[1], Ruben Verborgh[1], Jens Lehmann[3,4], Erik Mannens[1],
and Sebastian Hellmann[2]

[1] imec – IDLab, Department of Electronics and Information Systems,
Ghent University, Ghent, Belgium
{wouter.maroy,anastasia.dimou,ben.demeester,ruben.verborgh,
erik.mannens}@ugent.be
[2] Leipzig University – AKSW/KILT, Leipzig, Germany
{Kontokostas,Hellmann}@informatik.uni-leipzig.de
[3] University of Bonn, Smart Data Analytics Group, Bonn, Germany
jens.lehmann@cs.uni-bonn.de, jens.lehmann@iais.fraunhofer.de
[4] Fraunhofer IAIS, Sankt Augustin, Germany

Abstract. DBpedia EF, the generation framework behind one of the
Linked Open Data cloud's central interlinking hubs, has limitations with
regard to quality, coverage and sustainability of the generated dataset.
DBpedia can be further improved both on *schema* and *data* level. Errors
and inconsistencies can be addressed by amending (i) the DBpedia EF;
(ii) the DBpedia mapping rules; or (iii) Wikipedia itself from which it
extracts information. However, even though the DBpedia EF and mapping rules are continuously evolving and several changes were applied
to both of them, there are no significant improvements on the DBpedia
dataset since its limitations were identified. To address these shortcomings, we propose adapting a different semantic-driven approach that
decouples, in a declarative manner, the *extraction, transformation* and
mapping rules *execution*. In this paper, we provide details regarding the
new DBpedia EF, its architecture, technical implementation and extraction results. This way, we achieve an enhanced data generation process,
which can be broadly adopted, and that improves its quality, coverage
and sustainability.

1 Introduction

The *DBpedia Extraction Framework* (DBpedia EF) [12] extracts raw data from
Wikipedia and makes it available as Linked Data, forming the well-known and
broadly used DBpedia dataset. The majority of the DBpedia dataset is derived
through *Wikipedia infobox templates*, after being annotated by the *DBpedia*

The described research activities were funded by Ghent University, imec, Flanders
Innovation and Entrepreneurship (AIO), the Fund for Scientific Research Flanders
(FWO Flanders), and the EU's H2020 program for ALIGNED (GA 644055).

ontology[1] [12]. The DBpedia dataset is further enriched with additional information derived from the articles such as free text, abstracts, images, links to other Web pages, and tables. *Mapping Templates*, i.e., *rules* generating most of the DBpedia dataset from Wikipedia are executed by the DBpedia EF, defined by a world-wide crowd-sourcing effort, and maintained via the *DBpedia mappings wiki*[2].

Even though DBpedia is one of the central interlinking hubs in the Linked Open Data (LOD) cloud [16], its generation framework has limitations that reflect on the generated dataset [14,18]. We distinguish two types of issues with DBpedia:

schema-level rules that define *how* to apply vocabularies to raw data [6, 10,14], e.g., the `dbo:militaryBranch` property is used for entities of `dbo:MilitaryUnit` type, but it should only be used with entities of `dbo:Person` type [13].

data-level *extracted, or processed and transformed data values*. The former includes incorrect, incomplete or irrelevant extracted values and datatypes, or not (well-)recognized templates [18]; the latter issues with parsing values [17], interpreting/converting units [17], or transforming cardinal direction [15].

Errors or inconsistencies in DBpedia can be addressed by amending the DBpedia EF, mapping rules, or Wikipedia itself [18]. However, even though several changes were applied to both the DBpedia EF and mapping rules [12], quality issues still persist. For instance, 32% of its mapping rules are involved in at least one inconsistency [13], and more than half of all cardinal direction relations are still invalid or incorrect [15]. These issues challenge DBpedia dataset's usage, hence the demands for DBpedia EF to improve in terms of *expressivity*, i.e., level of details that a user can specify in mapping rules, *semantic flexibility*, i.e., possibility to interchange among different schemas, and *modularity*, i.e., declarative rules and modular components for extraction, transformation and mapping. Given that quality issues persist over a long period of time [13,15], the custom DBpedia EF appears to not meet the above and more foundational changes are required.

In this work, we show that the coupling among *extraction*, i.e., retrieving data from Wikipedia, *transformation*, i.e., processing the extracted data values, and *mapping rules execution*, i.e., applying semantic annotations to the retrieved and transformed data values, contributes to DBpedia EF's inadequacy to cope with the increasing demands for high quality Linked Data. While just decoupling these processes and keeping them hard-coded is just (re-)engineering, we look into a radical solution that turns the DBpedia EF more semantic rather than just a black-box. The goal is to adjust the current DBpedia EF and provide a general-purpose and more sustainable framework that enables more added value. For instance, in terms of semantic flexibility, interchanging among different schema

---

[1] http://dbpedia.org/ontology/.
[2] http://mappings.dbpedia.org/index.php/Main_Page.

annotations should be supported, instead of e.g., being coupled to a certain ontology as it is now, and allowing only certain semantic representation.

In this paper, we show how we incorporate in the existing DBpedia EF a general-purpose semantic-driven Linked Data generation approach, based on RML [7]. It replaces the current solution, decouples extraction, transformations and conditions from DBpedia EF, and enables generating high quality Linked Data for DBpedia. The activities to achieve this solution started as a GSoC2016 project[3,4] and continue till nowdays. Our contribution is three-fold: we (i) outline the limitations of the current DBpedia EF; (ii) identify the requirements for a more sustainable approach; and (iii) incorporate a generic approach that fulfills those requirements to the current DBpedia EF and compare the two approaches.

The paper is organized as follows: after outlining the state of the art (Sect. 2), we detail the current DBpedia EF limitations and requirements for a sustainable framework (Sect. 3). In Sect. 4, we introduce our approach, and provide a corresponding implementation. In Sect. 5, we provide the results of our approach's evaluation. Finally, we summarize our conclusions in Sect. 6.

2   Background and Related Work

In this section, we discuss related work in Linked Data generation (Sect. 2.1) and we outline the current DBpedia EF functionality (Sect. 2.2).

2.1   State of the Art

In the past, *case-specific solutions* were established for Linked Data generation, which couple schema and data transformations. XSLT- or XPath-based approaches were established for generating Linked Data from data originally in XML format, e.g., AstroGrid-D[5]. There are also *query-oriented* languages that combine SPARQL with other languages or custom alignments to the underlying data structure. For instance, XSPARQL [1] maps data in XML format and Tarql[6] data in CSV. Nevertheless, those approaches cannot be extended to cover other data sources.

Different approaches emerged to define data transformations declaratively, such as VOLT [15] for SPARQL, Hydra [11] for Web Services, or FnO [4]. Hydra or VOLT depend on the underlying system (Web Services and SPARQL, respectively), thus their use is inherently limited to it. Using Hydra descriptions for executing transformations only works online, whereas VOLT only works for data already existing in a SPARQL endpoint. Describing the transformations using FnO does not include this dependency, thus allows for reuse in other use cases and technologies.

---

[3] www.mail-archive.com/dbpedia-discussion@lists.sourceforge.net/msg07837.html.
[4] https://summerofcode.withgoogle.com/projects/#6213126861094912.
[5] http://www.gac-grid.de/project-products/Software/XML2RDF.html.
[6] https://tarql.github.io/.

2.2 DBpedia Extraction Framework

The DBpedia Extraction Framework (DBpedia EF) generates the DBpedia dataset [12]. It extracts data from Wikipedia, such as infobox templates or abstracts. The DBpedia EF consumes a *source*, i.e., an abstraction of a set of Wiki pages in wikitext syntax, parses it with a Wiki parser, and transforms it in an Abstract Syntax Tree (AST). To process the page's content, several AST-processing components, called *extractors* (e.g., Mapping Extractor, Geo Extractor), traverse a Wiki page's AST and generate RDF triples. Eventually the DBpedia EF forwards them to a sink that outputs them to different datasets based on their properties.

Extractors. The core DBpedia EF components are the *extractors*, whose common main functionality is to traverse the AST-representation of a Wiki page and generate RDF triples based on the syntax tree and other heuristics. Many extractors contribute in forming the DBpedia dataset [12, Sect. 2.2]. A prominent one is the *Mapping-Based Infobox Extractor*, which uses manually written mapping rules that relate infoboxes in Wikipedia to terms in DBpedia ontology, and generates RDF triples. It is the most important extractor, as the most valuable content of DBpedia dataset is derived from infoboxes [12], and covers the greatest part of the DBpedia ontology. Infobox templates are defined in wiki syntax and summarize information related to a page's article in a structured, consistent format which is presented on the article's page as a table with attribute-value pairs.

Mapping-Based Infobox Extractor. It uses community-provided, but manually written mapping rules, which are available at the DBpedia Mappings Wiki.[7] The mappings wiki enables users to collaboratively create and edit mapping rules, specified in the custom DBpedia Mapping Language. The DBpedia Mapping Language relies on MediaWiki templates to define the DBpedia ontology classes and properties and align them with the corresponding template elements [12]. A mapping rule assigns a type from the DBpedia ontology to entities that are described by the corresponding infobox and the infobox's attributes are mapped to DBpedia ontology properties. This extractor traverses the AST and finds infoboxes for which user-defined mapping rules were created. The infoboxes' attribute-value pairs are extracted and RDF triples are generated.

DBpedia Mapping Language. The custom DBpedia mapping language is in wikitext syntax and is used to define how RDF triples are generated from infobox. Each mapping template contains mapping rules for a certain infobox template, such as geocoordinates and date intervals. The mapping rules might specify another mapping template for an infobox property to help the DBpedia

---

[7] http://mappings.dbpedia.org.

EF produce high quality Linked Data [12]. The following exemplary mapping document contains three different mapping templates: (i) a class mapping (Listing 1, line 2) that maps articles that use that template to the DBpedia Automobile class, (ii) a property mapping template (line 4), which maps the name attribute in the infobox to `foaf:name` and, (iii) a date interval mapping template (line 7), which splits the production attribute (which should be a start and end date) and semantically annotates each part with different ontology terms.

```
1    {{TemplateMapping
2    | mapToClass = Automobile
3    | mappings =
4        {{PropertyMapping
5            | templateProperty = name
6            | ontologyProperty = foaf:name }}
7    {{DateIntervalMapping
8        | templateProperty = production
9        | startDateOntologyProperty = productionStartDate
10       | endDateOntologyProperty = productionEndDate }} }}
```

Listing 1. Extract of a DBpedia mapping templates in wikitext syntax

3   Limitations and Requirements

To address DBpedia dataset quality issues, the current DBpedia EF limitations need to be addressed by adopting a more sustainable approach. In this section, we discuss the current limitations (Sect. 3.1) and requirements for a sustainable framework (Sect. 3.2) that enables higher quality Linked Data generation.

3.1   Limitations

The current DBpedia EF has the following limitations:

mapping rules and implementation coupling Although a set of DBpedia *Mapping Templates* (DMT) is available, the DBpedia community is limited to this set only and cannot easily introduce new ones. The reason is that the DMTs translation happens directly inside the DBpedia EF. Thus, different mapping rules that are defined in each DMT are coupled to their implementation. Some rules, such as transformation of values are, in some case, more flexible to change. For example, changing the `language` value from 'de' to 'el', or converting a string to an IRI by appending a namespace, can be done directly from the mapping rules. However, there are still many useful mapping rules that are not supported without adjusting the DBpedia EF. For instance, combining different values of an infobox is not supported.

Any community member who would like to adjust the mapping rules should be aware of how to develop the DBpedia EF and Linked Data principles. Extending, adjusting or adding a new template, requires (i) extending the current custom DBpedia mapping language, by specifying and documenting the new constructs, and (ii) providing the corresponding implementation to extract these constructs to generate the corresponding RDF triples.

Extending the language is not straightforward and is performed in an ad-hoc manner, while the corresponding implementation is developed as custom solutions, hampering the DBpedia EF maintenance.

transformations and implementation coupling The DBpedia community can neither adjust nor add new transformations because the mapping rules only refer to schema transformations. Transformations over extracted data values are hard-coded and executed at different places within the DBpedia EF, from *extraction* to *mapping* and RDF *generation*. For instance, the actual value for the birth_date property of Person infobox is {{*Birth date and age|yyyy|mm|dd*}}. The DBpedia EF, parses and extracts this to a valid XSD date value, i.e., "yyy-mm-dd". If another date format is desired, it is required to be implemented within the DBpedia EF. Similarly, for the mapping rules that use the DBpedia ontology, DBpedia EF retrieves the DBpedia ontology predicates ranges and uses the defined range to transform the values accordingly. For example, for object properties, the DBpedia EF tries to extract only links and for datatype properties, custom parsers for numbers, floats, dates etc. are applied. Nonetheless, there are cases where the values can be of different types and the users cannot override this behavior without extending the DBpedia EF. Another limitation is the hard-coded unit measurements calculations which, when combined with not consistently formatted input, can lead to wrong values [17]. Overall, the DBpedia dataset is restricted to certain transformations which cannot be easily amended, unless the DBpedia EF is amended, which on its own turn, is not so trivial. Even reusing existing transformation functions requires adjusting the DBpedia EF.

hard-coded mapping rules The DBpedia community cannot adjust all RDF triples which form the DBpedia dataset, because not all of them are generated based on mapping rules. Certain RDF terms and triples are generated without mapping rules being defined, but the DBpedia EF generates them based on hard-coded mapping rules. Adjusting such mapping rules requires adjusting the DBpedia EF. For instance, each RDF triples's subject is dependent on the context of the extraction's execution. Entities in localized datasets (a DBpedia dataset within a certain language) are identified with a subject that is a language specific IRI, e.g., the http://{lang}.dbpedia.org/resource/{resource} namespace is used in the different DBpedia language editions. Generating RDF terms that represent entities with other identifiers or adding new entities cannot be expressed with a mapping rule. For instance, adjusting the aforementioned IRI template to http://{lang}.dbpedia.org/example/{resource} or generating another entity with a different IRI, such as http://example.com/{resource}, requires adjusting the implementation. Overall, configuring current mapping rules has limited influence on most RDF terms and triples generation.

restricted to the DBpedia ontology The DBpedia community cannot use other schema(s) to annotate the Wikipedia pages, than the DBpedia ontology. The current mapping extractor functions only with DBpedia ontology, e.g., the predicate depends on the ontology term used for a certain attribute of an infobox. This occurs because the DBpedia EF interprets the context and selects the corresponding parser based on where the mapping template is used and which ontology term is selected. For instance, the `dbo:date` triggers the `Data parser`. If an ontology term is not added to the DBpedia ontology, it cannot be used, e.g., only the `dbo:location` may be used to indicate an entity's location. Other vocabularies, such as *geo*[8] vocabulary, cannot be used unless imported into the DBpedia ontology. Incorporating any other vocabulary requires adjusting the DBpedia EF, because the *extractor* will not recognize its properties, namely it will not generate RDF triples if `geo:location` is provided. Only certain vocabularies, such as `dcterms`[9] or `foaf`[10], are supported. Similarly, the assigned data type is also dependent on the mapping template and ontology term, e.g., the area in square kms generates an `xsd:double` but also a DBpedia datatype (`dbo:areaTotal`) that depends on the used predicate.

domain validation If the DBpedia community uses ontology terms which cause violations, there is no support for schema validation. Domain validation of the mapping templates defined in the custom DBpedia mapping language can not be supported [6]. Nevertheless, the DBpedia dataset quality would significantly improve if schema violations is applied to the mapping templates [6,13,18]. Currently custom DBpedia mapping templates are only validated for syntax violations (using the Mapping Syntax Validator[11] [12]).

3.2 Requirements

Adjusting the DBpedia EF with a general-purpose Linked Data generation tool allows to adopt a more sustainable solution and enables generating higher quality Linked Data. Such a sustainable approach has the following requirements:

1. **declarative mapping rules** The DBpedia community needs to be able to directly edit, adjust, and define mapping rules for all RDF triples which are generated, while the underlying implementation should be able to interpret them in each case. Hence, a declarative language is required which is able to express all mapping rules. A corresponding underlying implementation should generate all RDF triples relying on declaratively defined mapping rules, either they refer to *schema* or *data* transformations [5]. If the DBpedia mapping rules are formalized in a generic and complete approach, the DBpedia EF mapping process and maintenance will be improved, and, thus, the DBpedia dataset quality will improve too, as it is already indicated by e.g., [6,13].

2. **modular and decoupled implementation** The DBpedia community should be able to add new mapping rules for schema annotations, and alternate or add new transformation rules, as well as data transformation libraries, without requiring to adjust the underlying implementation. The *extraction*,

---

[8] http://www.w3.org/2003/01/geo/wgs84_pos#.

[9] http://purl.org/dc/terms/.

[10] http://xmlns.com/foaf/0.1/.

[11] http://mappings.dbpedia.org/server/mappings/en/validate/.

transformation, mapping and RDF *generation* should be decoupled from each other, but aligned as modular components which can be extended or replaced, if e.g., other or new transformations are desired [5].

3. **machine-processable mapping rules** The DBpedia community should be able to build applications which can automatically process the mapping rules. To achieve this, mapping rules should be processable by both humans and machines [7]. For instance, machine processable mapping rules can be assessed not only for syntax but also for schema validation. More, the results of the validation might be automatically processed, as it occurs e.g., with [6,13], or automated mapping rules generation might occur as indicated by [8,9].

4. **vocabulary-independent** The DBpedia community should be able to generate each time any data model is desired, uniquely identify entities as it is desired, as well as annotate data values derived from Wikipedia pages relying on any vocabulary. Mapping rules should be defined and executed, and RDF terms and triples should be generated, independently of the vocabulary used to annotate the extracted data values.

4   Sustainable DBpedia EF with RML

To overcome the current DBpedia EF limitations, we developed a solution that fulfills the aforementioned requirements. R2RML [2] is a W3C standardized language for defining mapping rules to generate Linked Data from data residing in relational databases. The RDF Mapping Language (RML) [7] extends R2RML [2] to enable specifying how Linked Data is generated from sources in different (semi-)structured formats, such as CSV, XML, and JSON. Mapping rules in RML are expressed as RDF triples *(Requirement 3)* and any vocabulary can be used to annotate the data *(Requirement 4)*. Thanks to its extensibility [7], RML can also cover wikitext syntax to generate Linked Data from Wikipedia *(Requirement 1)*. Moreover, RML is aligned with FnO [4], an ontology to define data transformations declaratively *(Requirement 1)*. The RMLMapper executes mapping rules expressed in RML, while the FnO Processor interprets data transformation expressed in FnO and discovers corresponding libraries that execute them *(Requirement 2)*.

In this section, we discuss how we replaced the existing *Infobox based Mapping Extractor*, which is custom for DBpedia EF, with the RMLMapper[12] and challenges we faced. The transition to the new solution was fulfilled in three steps:

1. **mapping rules translation** The DBpedia mapping rules were translated in RML (schema) and FnO (data transformation) statements (Sect. 4.1);
2. **transformations decoupling** The DBpedia Parsing Functions were decoupled from the DBpedia EF and aggregated in a distinct module (Sect. 4.2);
3. **mapping rules execution** The RMLMapper was integrated as extractor (the RMLExtractor) in the DBpedia EF (Sect. 4.3) to execute the mapping rules.

---

[12] https://github.com/RMLio/RML-Mapper.

```
1   <#infobox_country_mapping_en> rr:subjectMap <subject_mapping_1>;
2     rml:predicateObjectMap <pom_mapping_1>.
3
4   <subject_map_1> rr:template "http://en.dbpedia.org/resource/{wikititle}".
5   <pom_mapping_1> rr:predicateMap [ rr:constant dbo:name. ];
6     rr:objectMap [ rml:reference "common_name"; rr:datatype xsd:string ].
7
8   dbf:extract-entity a fno:Function ;
9     fno:name     "generates a DBpedia IRI" ;
10    dcterms:description "returns an entity" ;
11    fno:expects ( [ fno:predicate dbf:property ] ) ;
12    fno:output  ( [ fno:predicate dbf:entity ] ) .
13
14  :exe a fno:Execution ;
15    fno:executes dbf:extractEntity ;
16    dbf:property  "Bill Gates";
17    dbf:entity dbr:Bill_Gates .
```

Listing 2. RML mapping rules and FnO data transformations

4.1 Mapping Rules Translation

To take advantage of the RML-based solution, we needed to translate the custom DBpedia mapping rules into RML statements. This was one of the most labor-intensive tasks of the integration process and it was performed in two phases, firstly the translation and, then, the decoupling. In more details:

1. The custom mapping templates in wikitext syntax were translated in RML statements. The RML mapping rules after the first phase can be found at http://mappings.dbpedia.org/server/mappings/en/pages/rdf/.
2. The mapping rules which were embedded in the DBpedia EF were expressed as RML statements and the data transformations as FnO statements. Every mapping template was assigned its own function, e.g., the *DateInterval Template* was assigned the *DateInterval Function* with same parameters. Moreover, we added basic functions like *ExtractDate*, which extracts and processes dates from a value. The RML mapping rules after this phase can be found at http://mappings.dbpedia.org/rml_mappings-201705.zip.

Manually translating all mapping rules in RML would have been difficult, hence, a temporary extension in the DBpedia EF was built to automate the translation[13]. This extension builds on top of the RMLModel [14], and can be run both within the DBpedia EF and standalone. To generate the new RML mapping rules, the original custom DBpedia mapping rules are loaded by the DBpedia EF. Once loaded, the mapping rules are represented in the DBpedia EF data structures and based on these, RML mapping rules are automatically generated. Each template is translated into RML statements and are dumped to a file.

The RML building blocks are *Triples Maps* (Listing 2: line 1) which define how RDF triples are generated. A *Triples Map* consists of three main parts: the

---

[13] https://github.com/dbpedia/extraction-framework/tree/rml/server/src/main/scala/org/dbpedia/extraction/server/resources/rml.
[14] https://github.com/RMLio/RML-Model.

Logical Source, the *Subject Map* and zero or more *Predicate-Object Maps*. The *Subject Map* (line 4) defines how unique identifiers (URIs) are generated for the mapped resources and is used as the subject of all RDF triples generated from this *Triples Map*. A *Predicate-Object Map* (line 2) consists of *Predicate Maps*, which define the rule that generates the triple's predicate (line 2) and *Object Maps* (line 6) or *Referencing Object Maps*, which define how the triple's object is generated. The *Subject Map*, the *Predicate Map* and the *Object Map* are *Term Maps*, namely rules that generate an RDF term (an IRI, a blank node or a literal).

The Function Ontology (FnO) [3,4] allows to declare and describe functions uniformly, unambiguously, and independently of their implementation technology. A *function* (`fno:Function`, Listing 2: line 8) is an activity which has input parameters (line 11), output (line 12), and implements certain algorithm(s). A *parameter* is the description of a function's input value. An *output* is the description of its output value. An *execution* (`fno:Execution`, line 14) assigns values to the function's parameters for a certain execution. For instance, `dbf:extractEntity` (line 8) is a function extracted from DBpedia EF and generates a DBpedia IRI (line 17) for a given Wikipedia title (line 16) which is passed as parameter. An *Execution* (line 14) can be instantiated to bind a value to the parameter. The result is then bound to that *Execution* via the `dbf:entity` property (line 17).

Addressed Challenges. While the original DBpedia mapping templates mainly build on top of a core template, different templates emerged to cover specific cases, such as templates for geocoordinates and date intervals. Therefore, we had to make sure that each extension and each edge case is covered and RML mapping rules are automatically generated. Nevertheless, a few cases were deliberately excluded because they were not used or they were introduced only for very rare or specific cases; others were omitted because they did not produce sustainable IRIs (see Sect. 5.1 for details). For the latter, the community still needs to agree on a more sustainable modeling. Moreover, we had to interpret each parameter's underlying functionality and to describe it declaratively. Last, the mapping rules and data transformations which were embedded in the DBpedia EF should also be declaratively described and this required to manually define additional RML mapping rules. Refining and extending the mapping rules required several iterations before we reach to a version that generates the same RDF triples as the current DBpedia EF. Moreover, even though it is convenient that certain RDF statements are generated without the community being involved, the complete lack of control over what is generated or how the data values are transformed, it is often the cause for deteriorating DBpedia dataset quality [17,18]. Then again, declaratively defining everything causes an overhead when editing the mapping rules. Nevertheless, it is not expected that the DBpedia community will directly edit the mapping rules, as a corresponding interface is foreseen (GSoC2017[15]).

---

[15] https://summerofcode.withgoogle.com/projects/#6205485112885248.

4.2   Transformations Decoupling

The custom DBpedia mapping rules allow the DBpedia community to partially define how Linked Data is generated from Wikipedia (schema transformations), without allowing though to customize how the extracted data values can be transformed (data transformations) to form the desired Linked Data. The data transformations are hard-coded in DBpedia EF and restricted to what is implemented. To this end, after formally describing all DBpedia mapping rules and transformations, we decoupled their implementation from the DBpedia EF.

All template functionalities were extracted and gathered into an independent module which can be found at https://github.com/FnOio/ dbpedia-parsing-functions-scala/. The FnO Processor is integrated as an independent module in the RMLMapper. It uses the DBpedia data transformation declarations in FnO to retrieve and execute the corresponding implementation each time.

A function might disclose the functionality of a certain mapping template, e.g., the *Property Mapping Template*[16] becames *Simple Property Function*[17] Moreover, other functions were isolated from the DBpedia EF which performed data transformations without a mapping template being involved. There were three major cases: (i) the *extract-entity* function[18] which takes a value of an infobox and creates a DBpedia IRI from it. For instance, it takes '*Melinda gates*' and returns <http://dbpedia.org/Melinda_Gates>; (ii) the *dates* function which takes a date and generates a valid XSD date; and (iii) the *string* function which removes the wikitext syntax and returns the actual data value. All of these functions my be reused beyond the DBpedia EF scope.

Besides data transformations, there were mapping rules which were embedded in the DBpedia EF and they generated automatically RDF triples, without having corresponding mapping rules, such as the datatype annotations, i.e., http://www.w3.org/2001/XMLSchema#double, as well as the custom DBpedia datatypes, e.g., https://dbpedia.org/ontology/PopulatedPlace/areaTotal.

Addressed Challenges. It was challenging to identify each single transformation that the current DBpedia EF has for transformations, as they were spread all over the implementation. The mapping rules only provide a very abstract and high level idea (e.g., dates or coordinates). Moreover, extracting those transformations and gathering them as an independent module for reuse beyond the scope of DBpedia required thorough analysis of the DBpedia EF implementation. The heuristics of these functions are optimized for a large number of

---

[16] https://github.com/dbpedia/extraction-framework/blob/ 0496309a0e142b27d940e9d8baa25446b1da4ccb/core/src/main/scala/org/dbpedia/ extraction/mappings/SimplePropertyMapping.scala.

[17] https://github.com/FnOio/dbpedia-parsing-functions-scala/blob/development/ src/main/scala/functions/implementations/SimplePropertyFunction.scala.

[18] https://github.com/FnOio/dbpedia-parsing-functions-scala/blob/development/ src/main/scala/functions/implementations/core/ExtractEntityFunction.scala.

cases and their reuse would contribute on improving the quality of datasets beyond DBpedia.

4.3   Mapping Rules Execution

The generation procedure of DBpedia EF is *data-driven*. Namely, the Linked Data generation is driven by the data sources and an extract of data is considered each time to perform the applicable mapping rules; in contrast to *mapping-driven* where the mapping rules request for the applicable data.

To make sure that the performance remains good, the mapping rules are pre-loaded. This offers faster lookups among the mapping rules, compared to re-loading them every time from the hard-disk. The RML mapping rules are executed by triggering the RMLExtractor. In the beginning of each generation process, the RML-MapDocHandler[19] loads all RML mapping rules which are considered for generating DBpedia in memory. Once all RML mapping templates are loaded, the DBpedia dataset generation is initiated. The data is extracted from all Wikipedia pages and the Extraction Manager forwards the incoming AST to all configured extractors, including the RMLExtractor. The RMLExtractor runs over the data to identify the infobox templates which are included in a certain Wiki page. When an infobox template is found, the corresponding RML mapping rules are identified and once all relevant ones are gathered, the RMLMapper is triggered with the AST and mapping rules as input. For instance, when the RMLExtractor finds an infobox, e.g., Infobox_person, the RMLExtractor will load the corresponding RML mapping rules, e.g., Mapping_en:Infobox_person.rml.ttl. The infobox associated with each set of RML mapping rules are provided to the RMLMapper which processes these inputs and returns RDF triples. Eventually, the RMLExtractor forwards all generated RDF triples to an output sink.

Addressed Challenges. Developing an RMLExtractor that performs large extractions from a Wikipedia dataset within an acceptable time frame had some complexities. The RMLMapper was not designed for being used as an external module, adaptations had to be made to make the integration with DBpedia EF possible. Additionally, the RMLMapper does not process datasets in parallel, since the DBpedia EF does exploit parallel processing. These obstacles have been addressed, but there is still room for more improvement. Besides performance, there were issues with processing steps (e.g., storing triples in specific datasets) during mapping rules executions. These processing steps were initially executed by the DBpedia EF but were adapted because, with the new approach, the RMLMapper handles the mapping execution, instead of the DBpedia EF.

4.4   New DBpedia Architecture

The DBpedia EF allows adding different extractors to fulfill different Linked Data generation processes. Taking advantage of its modularity, a new extractor was

---

[19] https://github.com/RMLio/RML-MapDocHandler.

built, called the RMLExtractor. The DBpedia EF with the RMLExtractor can be found at https://github.com/dbpedia/extraction-framework/tree/rml.

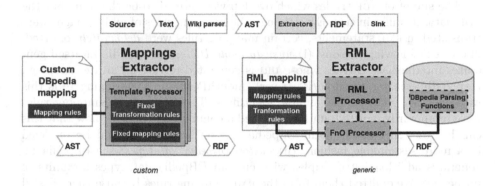

Fig. 1. To the left the Mappings Extractor, to the right the new RML Extractor:

The RMLExtractor, as every other extractor, is available to be used when a user triggers DBpedia's generation. It is independent of other extractors and runs over each AST to generate RDF triples for the infobox values that are contained in the AST based on the loaded RML mapping templates. The RMLExtractor wraps up the RMLMapper which is used as a library (Fig. 1). Each infobox together with the associated mapping template are given as input to RMLMapper, to generate the corresponding RDF triples. The RMLMapper depends on the Function Processor (FnO Processor)[20] which, depends on the DBpedia Parsing Functions[21]. The FnO Processor parses the FnO statements [3] which are included in the DBpedia mapping rules. Afterwards, it fetches the functions and executes them, using values derived from each extraction as parameters. The DBpedia Parsing Functions were extracted from the DBpedia data parsers and were put in an independent module which can be reused beyond the DBpedia EF scope.

5 Evaluation

The new approach was compared with the existing DBpedia EF with respect to *coverage* (Sect. 5.1), *performance* (Sect. 5.2), and *flexibility* (Sect. 5.3).

5.1 Coverage

We generated RDF triples for 16,244,162 pages of the English Wikipedia (version 20170501[22]), both with the current Mapping Extractor and new RMLExtractor.

---

[20] https://github.com/FnOio/function-processor-java.

[21] https://github.com/FnOio/dbpedia-parsing-functions-fno.

[22] https://dumps.wikimedia.org/enwiki/20170501/enwiki-20170501-pages-articles.xml.bz2.

The former extraction yielded 62,474,123 RDF triples in total, the latter 52,887,156. In terms of entities, 4,747,597 are extracted with the current, whereas 4,683,709 entities are extracted with RMLExtractor, offering 98% coverage.

The subset of RDF triples which overlap was verified to be the same but the RDF datasets differ in size. Even though the mapping rules of all languages were translated in RML statements, certain mapping rules were *deliberately* omitted, due to the following reasons: (i) *unsustainable URIs*; the DBpedia EF itself generates intermediate entities whose URI is generated relying on an iterator, e.g., http://dbpedia.org/resource/Po_(river)_mouthPosition__1. Assigning URIs this way does not generate sustainable identifiers. Therefore, those mapping rules were temporarily omitted, until the DBpedia community decides – now that this can be resolved outside of the DBpedia EF– on how they should be modeled in a more sustainable fashion. (ii) *custom DBpedia datatypes*; the DBpedia EF generates additional RDF triples with custom DBpedia datatypes for units of properties. We omitted them from the RML mapping rules because there is still discussion on whether these should be included in the dataset or not. (iii) *RDF triples added by the DBpedia EF;* These are RDF triples generated from a value of an infobox, if the article's text contains a URI with this value. Currently the RMLMapper does not support referencing the articles text, thus generating those RDF triples is temporarily omitted, until the RMLMapper is configured to work with data from Wikipedia beyond infoboxes.

5.2 Performance

The prototype RMLExtractor generates the DBpedia dataset on reasonable time. Currently, performance is put aside for more sustainable mapping rules and data transformations, as achieving sustainability is much more important than speed which may be optimized in the future. The RMLExtractor is still on average 0.46 ms slower per page than the original framework. Namely the RMLExtractor requires 1.31 ms/page, compared to the original DBpedia EF which requires 0.85 ms/page. On a larger scale the RMLExtractor generates Linked Data from 16,244,162 pages in 5 h and 56 min, compared to the current DBpedia EF which requires 3 h and 50 min (35% slower than the DBpedia EF, Fig. 2).

5.3 Flexibility

The mapping rules, being RDF triples, can be (automatically) updated and other semantic annotations can be applied or other datasets can be generated from Wikipedia. For instance, relying on the DBpedia mapping rules and the alignment of DBpedia with schema.org[23], we translated the RML mapping rules for DBpedia, but any other vocabulary may be used too. This way, we can generate a DBpedia dataset with *schema.org* annotations, instead of only using the DBpedia ontology. This was accomplished by generating a new RML mapping file with *schema.org*

---

[23] http://schema.org.

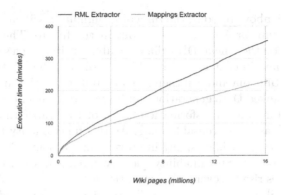

Fig. 2. Performance comparison: Mappings Extractor vs RML Extractor

annotations, based on the mapping rules with the DBpedia ontology annotations. The extracted data values are transformed to a clean format by relying on the same FnO functions which are specified in the RML mapping rules. In our exemplary case, we based on *Infobox_person* mapping template that generates RDF triples for entities of person type. An extraction was done over 16,244,162 pages, 191,288 Infobox_persons were found. 1,026,143 RDF triples were generated. Indicatively, 179,037 RDF triples were generated with `schema:name` property, 54,664 with `schema:jobTitle`, 23,751 with `schema.org:nationality`, 144,907 with `schema.org:birthPlace`, and 139,488 with `schema.org:birthDate`. The dataset is available at http://mappings.dbpedia.org/person_schema.dataset.ttl. bz2.

6   Conclusions and Future Work

In this paper, we presented a generic and semantics-driven approach to replace the Mapping Extractor in DBpedia EF which contributes in the adoption of Semantic Web technologies and Linked Data principles. Thereby, we address several major challenges that currently exist in the DBpedia generation process. We show that our solution can cover same Linked Data output with a more sustainable and reusable process, without prohibitively increasing the execution time.

The resulting new DBpedia EF is easier to maintain, as changes are limited to declarative mapping and transformation rules. We moved from a tightly coupled architecture to a sustainable Linked Data generation approach, as the code of the extractor does not require modifications anymore to improve the Linked Data generation. This better prepares DBpedia for changes, and thereby also facilitates quality improvements to the output. Indeed, many errors and inconsistencies in DBpedia are either due to the old DBpedia EF [18]—which our solution succeeds— and due to the DBpedia ontology [13]—which can more easily be adjusted [13] or replaced thanks to our solution. More, we can apply validation on the mappings themselves, catching potential inconsistencies even before they are generated [6].

Because of the above reasons, the DBpedia community will apply our solution as the default setup for generating DBpedia in the future. The source code is already available on the official DBpedia GitHub repository in a separate branch.

Importantly, and in contrast to the old DBpedia EF, the solution we propose is not specific to DBpedia and can therefore be applied to other use cases as well. Any part of the Linked Data generation can be reused to generate other datasets, such as the mapping and transformation rules; or the transformation functions that were written as small, reusable units. As this functionality becomes shared with other generation workflows, any improvement to them will directly lead to improvements in others. Sustainability thereby spreads beyond just DBpedia.

This work gives rise to several opportunities for future work. A user interface is planned and will enable people to collaboratively create, update, and manage DBpedia generation, while assessing the impact of new ontologies becomes straightforward. By improving the DBpedia generation sustainability, we not only improve DBpedia today, but enable continuous advancements in the future.

References

1. Bischof, S., Decker, S., Krennwallner, T., Lopes, N., Polleres, A.: Mapping between RDF and XML with XSPARQL. J. Data Semant. **1**(3), 147–185 (2012)
2. Das, S., Sundara, S., Cyganiak, R.: R2RML: RDB to RDF mapping language. Working group recommendation, W3C, September 2012. http://www.w3.org/TR/r2rml/
3. De Meester, B., Dimou, A.: The Function Ontology. Unofficial Draft (2016). https://w3id.org/function/spec
4. De Meester, B., Dimou, A., Verborgh, R., Mannens, E.: An ontology to semantically declare and describe functions. In: Sack, H., Rizzo, G., Steinmetz, N., Mladenić, D., Auer, S., Lange, C. (eds.) ESWC 2016. LNCS, vol. 9989, pp. 46–49. Springer, Cham (2016). doi:10.1007/978-3-319-47602-5_10
5. De Meester, B., Maroy, W., Dimou, A., Verborgh, R., Mannens, E.: Declarative data transformations for linked data generation: the case of DBpedia. In: Blomqvist, E., Maynard, D., Gangemi, A., Hoekstra, R., Hitzler, P., Hartig, O. (eds.) ESWC 2017. LNCS, vol. 10250, pp. 33–48. Springer, Cham (2017). doi:10.1007/978-3-319-58451-5_3
6. Dimou, A., Kontokostas, D., Freudenberg, M., Verborgh, R., Lehmann, J., Mannens, E., Hellmann, S., Van de Walle, R.: Assessing and refining mappings to RDF to improve dataset quality. In: Arenas, M., et al. (eds.) ISWC 2015. LNCS, vol. 9367, pp. 133–149. Springer, Cham (2015). doi:10.1007/978-3-319-25010-6_8
7. Dimou, A., Vander Sande, M., Colpaert, P., Verborgh, R., Mannens, E., Van de Walle, R.: RML: a generic language for integrated RDF mappings of heterogeneous data. In: Proceedings of the 7th Workshop on Linked Data on the Web, CEUR Workshop Proceedings, vol. 1184 (2014)
8. Heyvaert, P., Dimou, A., Verborgh, R., Mannens, E.: Ontology-based data access mapping generation using data, schema, query, and mapping knowledge. In: Blomqvist, E., Maynard, D., Gangemi, A., Hoekstra, R., Hitzler, P., Hartig, O. (eds.) ESWC 2017. LNCS, vol. 10250, pp. 205–215. Springer, Cham (2017). doi:10.1007/978-3-319-58451-5_15

9. Heyvaert, P., Dimou, A., Herregodts, A.-L., Verborgh, R., Schuurman, D., Mannens, E., Van de Walle, R.: RMLEditor: a graph-based mapping editor for linked data mappings. In: Sack, H., Blomqvist, E., d'Aquin, M., Ghidini, C., Ponzetto, S.P., Lange, C. (eds.) ESWC 2016. LNCS, vol. 9678, pp. 709–723. Springer, Cham (2016). doi:10.1007/978-3-319-34129-3_43

10. Kontokostas, D., Westphal, P., Auer, S., Hellmann, S., Lehmann, J., Cornelissen, R., Zaveri, A.: Test-driven evaluation of linked data quality. In: Proceedings of the 23rd International Conference on World Wide Web, pp. 747–758. ACM (2014)

11. Lanthaler, M.: Hydra core vocabulary. Unofficial Draft, June 2014. http://www.hydra-cg.com/spec/latest/core/

12. Lehmann, J., Isele, R., Jakob, M., Jentzsch, A., Kontokostas, D., Mendes, P.N., Hellmann, S., Morsey, M., Van Kleef, P., Auer, S., Bizer, C.: DBpedia – a large-scale, multilingual knowledge base extracted from Wikipedia. Semant. Web (2015)

13. Paulheim, H.: Data-driven joint debugging of the DBpedia mappings and ontology. In: Blomqvist, E., Maynard, D., Gangemi, A., Hoekstra, R., Hitzler, P., Hartig, O. (eds.) ESWC 2017. LNCS, vol. 10249, pp. 404–418. Springer, Cham (2017). doi:10.1007/978-3-319-58068-5_25

14. Paulheim, H., Gangemi, A.: Serving DBpedia with DOLCE – more than just adding a cherry on top. In: Arenas, M., et al. (eds.) ISWC 2015. LNCS, vol. 9366, pp. 180–196. Springer, Cham (2015). doi:10.1007/978-3-319-25007-6_11

15. Regalia, B., Janowicz, K., Gao, S.: VOLT: a provenance-producing, transparent SPARQL proxy for the on-demand computation of linked data and its application to spatiotemporally dependent data. In: Sack, H., Blomqvist, E., d'Aquin, M., Ghidini, C., Ponzetto, S.P., Lange, C. (eds.) ESWC 2016. LNCS, vol. 9678, pp. 523–538. Springer, Cham (2016). doi:10.1007/978-3-319-34129-3_32

16. Schmachtenberg, M., Bizer, C., Paulheim, H.: Adoption of the linked data best practices in different topical domains. In: Mika, P., et al. (eds.) ISWC 2014. LNCS, vol. 8796, pp. 245–260. Springer, Cham (2014). doi:10.1007/978-3-319-11964-9_16

17. Wienand, D., Paulheim, H.: Detecting incorrect numerical data in DBpedia. In: Presutti, V., d'Amato, C., Gandon, F., d'Aquin, M., Staab, S., Tordai, A. (eds.) ESWC 2014. LNCS, vol. 8465, pp. 504–518. Springer, Cham (2014). doi:10.1007/978-3-319-07443-6_34

18. Zaveri, A., Kontokostas, D., Sherif, M.A., Bühmann, L., Morsey, M., Auer, S., Lehmann, J.: User-driven quality evaluation of DBpedia. In: Proceedings of the 9th International Conference on Semantic Systems, pp. 97–104. ACM (2013)

Semantic Rule-Based Equipment Diagnostics

Gulnar Mehdi[1,2(✉)], E. Kharlamov[3], Ognjen Savković[4], G. Xiao[4],
E. Güzel Kalaycı[4], S. Brandt[1], I. Horrocks[3], Mikhail Roshchin[1],
and Thomas Runkler[1,2]

[1] Siemens CT, Munich, Germany
gulnar.mehdi@siemens.com
[2] Technical University of Munich, Munich, Germany
[3] University of Oxford, Oxford, UK
[4] Free University of Bozen-Bolzano, Bolzano, Italy

Abstract. Industrial rule-based diagnostic systems are often data-dependant in the sense that they rely on specific characteristics of individual pieces of equipment. This dependence poses significant challenges in rule authoring, reuse, and maintenance by engineers. In this work we address these problems by relying on Ontology-Based Data Access: we use ontologies to mediate the equipment and the rules. We propose a semantic rule language, *sigRL*, where sensor signals are first class citizens. Our language offers a balance of expressive power, usability, and efficiency: it captures most of Siemens data-driven diagnostic rules, significantly simplifies authoring of diagnostic tasks, and allows to efficiently rewrite semantic rules from ontologies to data and execute over data. We implemented our approach in a semantic diagnostic system, deployed it in Siemens, and conducted experiments to demonstrate both usability and efficiency.

1 Introduction

Intelligent *diagnostic systems* play an important role in industry since they help to maximise equipment's up-time and minimise its maintenance and operating costs [29]. In energy sector companies like Siemens often rely on *rule-based* diagnostics systems to analyse power generating equipment by, e.g., testing newly deployed electricity generating gas turbines [24], or checking vibration instrumentation [26], performance degradation [27], and faults in operating turbines. For this purpose diagnostic engineers create and use complex diagnostic rule-sets to detect abnormalities during equipment run time and sophisticated analytical models to combine these abnormalities with models of physical aspects of equipment such as thermodynamics and energy efficacy.

An important class of rules that are commonly used in Siemens for rule-based turbines diagnostics are *signal processing rules* (SPRs). SPRs allow to filter, aggregate, combine, and compare *signals*, that are time stamped measurement values, coming from sensors installed in equipment and trigger error or notification messages when a certain criterion has been met. Thus, sensors report

© Springer International Publishing AG 2017
C. d'Amato et al. (Eds.): ISWC 2017, Part II, LNCS 10588, pp. 314–333, 2017.
DOI: 10.1007/978-3-319-68204-4_29

temperature, pressure, vibration and other relevant parameters of equipment and SPRs process this data and alert whenever a certain pattern is detected. Rule-based diagnostics with SPRs can be summarises as in Fig. 1 (left), where the data consists of signals coming from sensors of turbines, and the diagnostic layer consists of SPRs and analytical models.

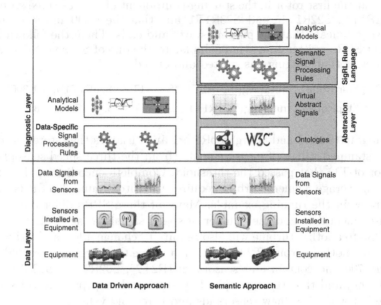

Fig. 1. General scheme of diagnostics with signal-processing rules. Left: data driven approach. Right: semantic approach.

SPRs that are currently offered in most of existing diagnostic systems and used in Siemens are highly *data dependent* in the sense that specific characteristic of individual sensors and pieces of equipment are explicitly encoded in SPRs. As the result for a typical turbine diagnostic task an engineer has to write from dozens to hundreds of SPRs that involve hundreds of sensor tags, component codes, sensor and threshold values as well as equipment configuration and design data. For example, a typical Siemens gas turbine has about 2,000 sensors and a diagnostic task to detect whether the purging[1] in over can be captured with 300 SPRs. We now illustrate diagnostic tasks and corresponding SPRs on a running example.

Example 1 (Purging Running Example). Consider the purging diagnostic task:

> *Verify that the purging is over in the main flame component of the turbine T1.*

---

[1] Purging is the process of flushing out liquid fuel nozzles or other parts which may contain undesirable residues.

Intuitively this task requires to check in the turbine T1 that: *(i)* the main flame was on for at least 10 s and then stopped, *(ii)* 15 s after this, the purging of rotors in the starting-component of T1 started, *(iii)* 20 s after this, the purging stopped. The fact that the purging of a rotor started or ended can be detected by analysing its speed, that it, by comparing the average speed of its speed sensors with purging thresholds that are specific for individual rotors. Let us assume that the first rotor in the starting-component of T1 has three speed sensors 'S21R1T1', 'S22R1T1', and 'S23R1T1' and that the 1.300 and 800 rotations respectively indicate that the purging starts and ends. Then, the following data dependent SPRs written in a syntax similar to the one of Siemens SPRs can be used to detect that purging has started and ended:

$$\$PurgStartRotor1 : truth(avg(\text{'S21R1T1'}, \text{'S22R1T1'}, \text{'S23R1T1'}), > 1.300). \qquad (1)$$

$$\$PurgStopRotor1 : truth(avg(\text{'S21R1T1'}, \text{'S22R1T1'}, \text{'S23R1T1'}), < 800). \qquad (2)$$

Here \$PurgStartRotor1 and \$PurgStopRotor1 are variables that store those average time stamped values of measurements (from the three speed sensors in the first rotor of T1) that passed the threshold. Complete encoding of the purging task for an average Siemens turbine requires to write around 300 SPRs some of which are as in the running example. Many of these SPRs differ only on specific sensor identifiers and the number of speed signals to aggregate. Adapting these SPRs to another turbine will also require to change a lot of identifiers. For example, in another turbine T2 the rotor may have the purging threshold values 1.000 and 700 and contain four sensors 'S01R2T2', 'S02R2T2', 'S03R2T2', and 'S04R2T2 mrq and thus the corresponding start and stop purging rules will be as above but with these new sensors ids and threshold values.   □

Data dependence of SPRs poses three significant challenges for diagnostic engineers in *(i)* authoring, *(ii)* reuse, and *(iii)* maintenance of SPRs. Indeed, authoring such rules is time consuming and error prone, e.g., while aggregating the speed signals from a given rotor one has ensure that all the relevant speed signals are included in the aggregation and that other signals, e.g., temperature signals, are not included. As the result, in the overall time that a Siemens engineer spends on diagnostics up to 80% is devoted to rule authoring where the major part of this time is devoted to data access and integration [19]. Reuse of such rules is limited since they are too specific to concrete equipment and in many cases it is easier to write a new rule set than to understand and adapt an existing one. As the result, over the years Siemens has acquired a huge library of SPRs with more than 200,000 rules and it constantly grows. Maintenance of such SPRs is also challenging and require significant manual work since there is limited semantics behind them.

Adding Semantics to SPRs. Semantic technologies can help in addressing these three challenges. An *ontology* can be used to abstractly represent sensors and background knowledge about turbines including locations of sensors, structure and characteristics of turbines. Then, in the spirit of *Ontology Based Data Access* (OBDA) [25], the ontology can be 'connected' to the data about the actual turbines, their sensors and signals with the help of declarative *mapping specifications*. OBDA has recently attracted a lot of attention by the research community: a solid theory has been developed, e.g. [7,28], and a number of mature systems have been implemented, e.g. [5,6]. Moreover, OBDA has been successfully applied in several industrial applications, e.g. [8,14,15,17].

Adopting OBDA for rule-based diagnostics in Siemens, however, requires a rule based language for SPRs that enjoys the following features:

(i) Signals orientation: The language should treat signals as first class citizens and allow for their manipulation: to filter, aggregate, combine, and compare signals;

(ii) Expressiveness: The language should capture most of the features of the Siemens rule language used for diagnostics;

(iii) Usability: The language should be simple and concise enough so that the engineers can significantly save time in specifying diagnostic tasks;

(iv) Efficiency: The language should allow for efficient execution of diagnostic tasks.

To the best of our knowledge no rule language exists that fulfills all these requirements (see related work in Sect. 5 for more details).

Contributions. In this work we propose to extend the traditional data driven approach to diagnostics with an OBDA layer and a new rule language to what we call *Semantic Rule-based Diagnostics*. Our approach is schematically depicted in Fig. 1 (right). To this end we propose a language *sigRL* for SPRs that enjoys the four requirements above. Our language allows to write SPRs and complex diagnostic tasks in an abstract fashion and to exploit both ontological vocabulary and queries over ontologies to identify relevant sensors and data values. We designed the language in such a way that, on the one hand, it captures the main signal processing features required by Siemens turbine diagnostic engineers and, on the other hand, it has good computational properties. In particular, *sigRL* allows for rewriting [7] of diagnostic rule-sets written over OWL 2 QL ontologies [2] into multiple data-dependent rule-sets with the help of ontologies and OBDA mappings. This rewriting allows to exploit standard infrastructure, including the one used in Siemens, for processing data-dependent SPRs.

We implemented *sigRL* and a prototypical Semantic Rule-based Diagnostic system. We deployed our implementation in Siemens over 50 Siemens gas turbines and evaluated the deployment with encouraging results. We evaluated usability of our solution with Siemens engineers by checking how fast they are in formulating diagnostic tasks in *sigRL*. We also evaluated the efficiency of our solution in processing diagnostic tasks over turbine signals in a controlled environment. Currently, our deployment is not included in the production processes, it is a prototype that we plan to evaluate and improve further before it can be used in production.

---

[2] OWL 2 QL is the W3C standardised ontology language that is intended for OBDA.

2   Signal Processing Language *sigRL*

In this section we introduce our signal processing language *sigRL*. It has three components: *(i)* Basic signals that come from sensors; *(ii)* Knowledge Bases (KBs) that capture background knowledge of equipment and signals as well as concrete characteristics of the equipment that undergoing diagnostics, and *(iii)* Signal processing expressions that manipulate basic signals using mathematical functions and queries over KBs.

Signals. In our setting, a *signal* is a first-class citizen. A signal s is a pair (o_s, f_s) where o_s is *sensor id* and *signal function* f_s defined on $\mathbb{R}$ to $\mathbb{R} \cup \{\bot\}$, where $\bot$ denotes the absence of a value. A *basic signal* is a signal which reading is obtained from a single sensor (e.g., in a turbine) for different time points. In practice, it may happen that a signal have periods without identified values. Also, such periods are obtained when combining and manipulating basic signals. We say that a signal s is *defined* on a real interval I if it has a value for each point of the interval, $\bot \notin f_s(I)$. For technical reasons we introduce *undefined* signal function $f_\bot$ that maps all reals into $\bot$. In practice signals are typically step functions over time intervals since they correspond to sensor values delivered with some frequency. In our model, we assume that we are given a finite set of basic signals $\mathcal{S} = \{s_1, \ldots, s_n\}$.

Knowledge Bases and Queries. A Knowledge Base $\mathcal{K}$ is a pair of an *ontology* $\mathcal{O}$ and a *data set* $\mathcal{A}$. An *ontology* describes background knowledge of an application domain in a formal language. We refer the reader to [7] for detailed definitions of ontologies. In our setting we consider ontologies that describe general characteristics of power generating equipment which includes partonomy of its components, characteristics and locations of its sensors, etc. As an example consider the following ontological expression that says that RotorSensor is a kind of SpeedSensor:

$$\mathsf{SubClassOf(RotorSensor \ \ SpeedSensor)}. \tag{3}$$

Data sets of KBs consist of *data assertions* enumerating concrete sensors, turbines, and their components. The following assertions says that sensors 'S21R1T1', 'S22R1T1' and 'S23R1T1' are all rotor sensors:

$$\mathsf{ClassAssertion(RotorSensor \ 'S21R1T1'), ClassAssertion(RotorSensor \ 'S22R1T1'),}$$
$$\mathsf{ClassAssertion(RotorSensor \ 'S23R1T1').} \tag{4}$$

In order to enjoy favorable semantic and computational characteristics of OBDA, we consider well-studied ontology language OWL 2 QL that allows to express subclass (resp. sub-property) axioms between classes and projections of properties (resp. corollary between properties). We refer the reader to [7] for details on OWL 2 QL.

To query KBs we rely on conjunctive queries (CQs) and certain answer semantics that have been extensively studied for OWL 2 QL KBs and proved to be tractable [7]. For example, the following CQ returns all rotor sensors from start component:

$$\text{rotorStart}(x) \leftarrow \text{rotorSensor}(x) \wedge \text{locatedIn}(x, y) \wedge \text{startComponent}(y). \qquad (5)$$

Signals Processing Expressions. Now we introduce signal expressions that filter and manipulate basic signals and create new complex signals. Intuitively, in our language we group signals into ontological concepts and signal expression are defined on the level of concepts. Then, a *signal processing expression* is recursively defined as follows:

$$
\begin{aligned}
C \;=\; & Q && |\; C_1 : value(\odot, \alpha) && |\; \{s_1, \ldots, s_m\} && |\; \text{agg } C_1 && | \\
& \alpha \circ C && |\; C_1 : duration(\odot, t) && |\; C_1 : \; align \; C_2
\end{aligned}
$$

where C is a concept, Q is a CQ, $\circ$ is in $\{+, -, \times, /\}$, agg is in $\{\min, \max,$ avg, sum$\}$, $\alpha \in \mathbb{R}$, $\odot \in \{<, >, \leq, \geq\}$ and $align \in \{within, after[t], before[t]\}$ where t is a period.

Table 1. Meaning of signal processing expressions. For the interval I, size(I) is its size. For intervals I_1, I_2 the *alignment* is: "I_1 *within* I_2" if $I_1 \subseteq I_2$; "I_1 *after*[t] I_2" if all points of I_2 are after I_1 and the start of I_2 is within the end of I_1 plus period t; "I_1 *before*[t] I_2" if "I_2 *start*[t] I_1".

$C =$	Concept C contains
Q	All signal ids return by Q evaluated over the KB
$\alpha \circ C_1$	One signal s' for each signal s in C_1 with $f_{s'} = \alpha \circ f_s$
$C_1 : value(\odot, \alpha)$	One signal s' for each signal s in C_1 with $f_{s'}(t) = \alpha \odot f_s(t)$ if $f_s(t) \odot \alpha$ at time point t; otherwise $f_{s'}(t) = \bot$
$C_1 : duration(\odot, t')$	One signal s' for each signal s in C_1 with $f_{s'}(t) = f_s(t)$ if exists an interval I such that: f_s is defined I, $t \in I$ and size$(I) \odot t'$; otherwise $f_{s'}(t) = \bot$
$\{s_1, \ldots, s_m\}$	All enumerated signal $\{s_1, \ldots, s_m\}$
$C = \text{agg } C_1$	One signal s' with $f_{s'}(t) = \text{agg}_{s \in C_1} f_s(t)$, that is, s' is obtained from all signals in C_1 by applying the aggregate agg at each time point t
$C_1 : \; align \; C_2$	A signal s_1 from C_1 if: there exists a signal s_2 from C_2 that is *aligned* with s_1, i.e., for each time interval I_1 where f_{s_1} is defined there is an interval I_2 where f_{s_2} is defined s.t. I_1 *aligns* with I_2

The formal meaning of signal processing expressions is defined in Table 1. In order to make the mathematics right, we assume that $c \circ \bot = \bot \circ c = \bot$ and

$c \odot \bot = \bot \odot c = \mathit{false}$ for $c \in \mathbb{R}$, and analogously we assume for aggregate functions. If the value of a signal function at a time point is not defined with these rules, then we define it as $\bot$.

Example 2. The start and end of a purging process data-driven rules as in Eqs. (1) and (2) from the running example can be expressed in *sigRL* as follows:

$$\mathsf{PurgingStart} = \mathit{avg}\ \mathsf{rotorStart} : \mathsf{value}(>, \mathit{purgingSpeed}), \tag{6}$$

$$\mathsf{PurgingStop} = \mathit{avg}\ \mathsf{rotorStart} : \mathsf{value}(<, \mathit{nonPurgingSpeed}). \tag{7}$$

Here, rotorStart is the CQ defined in Eq. (5). For brevity we do not introduce a new concept for each expression but we just join them with symbol ":". Constants *purgingSpeed* and *nonPurgingSpeed* are parameters of an analysed turbine, and they are instantiated from the turbine configuration when the expressions are evaluated.   □

Diagnostic Programs and Messages. We now show how to use signal expressions to compose diagnostic programs and to alert messages. In the following we will consider *well formed* sets of signal expressions, that is, sets where each concept is defined at most once and where definitions of new concepts are assumed to be acyclic: if C_1 is used to define C_2 (directly or indirectly) then C_1 cannot be defined (directly or indirectly) using C_1.

A *diagnostic program* (or simply *program*) $\varPi$ is a tuple $(\mathcal{S}, \mathcal{K}, \mathcal{M})$ where $\mathcal{S}$ is a set of basic signals, $\mathcal{K}$ is a KB, $\mathcal{M}$ is a set of well formed signal processing expressions such that each concept that is defined in $\mathcal{M}$ does not appear in $\mathcal{K}$.

Example 3. The running example program $\varPi = (\mathcal{S}, \mathcal{K}, \mathcal{M})$ has the following components: sensors $\mathcal{S} = \{`\mathsf{S21R1T1}', `\mathsf{S22R1T1}', `\mathsf{S23R1T1}'\}$, KB $\mathcal{K}$ that consists of axioms from Eqs. (3)–(4), and $\mathcal{M}$ that consists of expressions from Eqs. (6)–(7).   □

A *message rule* is a rule of the form, where C is a concept and m is a (text) message:

$$message(m) = C.$$

Example 4. Using expressions (6) and (7) we define the following message:

$$\mathsf{message}(\textit{``Purging over''}) = \mathsf{FlameSensor} : \mathsf{duration}(>, 10s) :$$
$$\mathit{after}[15s]\ \mathsf{PurgingStart} : \mathit{after}[20s]\ \mathsf{PurgingStop} \quad (8)$$

The message intuitively indicates that the purging is over.   □

Now we are ready to define the semantics of the rules, expression and programs.

Semantics of *sigRL*. We now define how to determine whether a program Π fires a rule r. To this end, we extend first-order interpretations that are used to define semantics of OWL 2 KBs. In OWL 2 a first class citizen is an object o and interpretation is defining whether $C(o)$ is true or not for particular concept C. In our scenario, domain of objects is a domain of sensor ids (basic or ones defined by expressions). Thus each object o is also having assigned function f_o that represents the signal value of that object. Obviously, an identifier o can also be an id of a turbine component that does not have signal function. At the moment, (since it is not crucial for this study and it simplifies the formalism) we also assign undefined signal $f_\perp$ to such (non-signal) objects.

Formally, our *interpretation* $\mathcal{I}$ is a pair $(\mathcal{I}_{FOL}, \mathcal{I}_S)$ where $\mathcal{I}_{FOL}$ interprets objects and their relationships (like in OWL 2) and $\mathcal{I}_S$ interprets signals. First, we define how $\mathcal{I}$ interprets basic signals. Given a set of signals for an interpretation $\mathcal{I}$: $\mathcal{S}^{\mathcal{I}} = \{s_1^{\mathcal{I}}, \ldots, s_n^{\mathcal{I}}\}$ s.t. $\mathcal{I}_{FOL}$ 'returns' the signal id, $s^{\mathcal{I}_{FOL}} = o_s$ and $\mathcal{I}_S$ 'returns' the signal itself, $s^{\mathcal{I}_S} = s$.

Now we can define how $\mathcal{I}$ interprets KBs. Interpretation of a KB $\mathcal{K}^{\mathcal{I}}$ extends the notion of first-order logics interpretation as follows: $\mathcal{K}^{\mathcal{I}_{FOL}}$ is a first-order logics interpretation $\mathcal{K}$ and $\mathcal{K}^{\mathcal{I}_S}$ is defined for objects, concepts, roles and attributes following $S^{\mathcal{I}}$. That is, for each object o we define $o^{\mathcal{I}_S}$ as s if o is the id of s from $\mathcal{S}$; otherwise $(o, f_\perp)$. Then, for a concept A we define $A^{\mathcal{I}_S} = \{s^{\mathcal{I}_S} \mid o_s^{\mathcal{I}_{FOL}} \in A^{\mathcal{I}_{FOL}}\}$. Similarly, we define $\cdot^{\mathcal{I}_S}$ for roles and attributes.

Finally, we are ready to define $\mathcal{I}$ for signal expressions and we do it recursively following the definitions in Table 1. We now illustrate some of them. For example, if $C = \{s_1, \ldots, s_m\}$, then $C^{\mathcal{I}} = \{s_1^{\mathcal{I}}, \ldots, s_m^{\mathcal{I}}\}$; if $C = Q$ then $C^{\mathcal{I}_{FOL}} = Q^{\mathcal{I}_{FOL}}$ where $Q^{\mathcal{I}_{FOL}}$ is the evaluation of Q over $\mathcal{I}_{FOL}$ and $C^{\mathcal{I}_S} = \{s \mid o_s^{\mathcal{I}_{FOL}} \in Q^{\mathcal{I}_{FOL}}\}$, provided that $\mathcal{I}_{FOL}$ is a model of $\mathcal{K}$. Otherwise we define $C^{\mathcal{I}} = \emptyset$. Similarly, we define interpretation of the other expressions.

Firing a Message. Let Π be a program and '$r : message(m) = C$' a message rule. We say that Π *fires* message r if *for each* interpretation $\mathcal{I} = (\mathcal{I}_{FOL}, \mathcal{I}_S)$ of Π it holds $C^{\mathcal{I}_{FOL}} \neq \emptyset$, that is, the concept that fires r is not empty. Our programs and rules enjoy the *canonical* model property, that is, each program has a unique (Hilbert) interpretation [3] which is minimal and can be constructed starting from basic signals and ontology by following signal expressions. Thus, one can verify $C^{\mathcal{I}_{FOL}} \neq \emptyset$ only on the canonical model. This implies that one can evaluate *sigRL* programs and expressions in a bottom-up fashion. We now illustrate this approach on our running example.

Example 5. Consider our running program Π from Example 3 and its canonical interpretation $\mathcal{I}_\Pi$. First, for each query Q in $\mathcal{M}$ we evaluate Q over KB $\mathcal{K}$ by computing $Q^{\mathcal{I}_\Pi}$. In our case, the only query is rotorStart that collects all sensor ids for a particular turbine. Then, we evaluate the expressions in $\mathcal{M}$ following the dependency graph of definitions. We start by evaluation the expression from Eq. (6), again in a bottom-up fashion. Concept rotorStart$^{\perp_\Pi}$ contains sensor ids: 'S21R1T1', 'S22R1T1' and 'S23R1T1'. At the same time, those sensors have signal functions assigned from $\mathcal{S}^{\mathcal{I}_\Pi}$. Let us call them f_1, f_2 and f_3. Expression

322   G. Mehdi et al.

avg rotorStart computes a new signal, say s_4, by taking average of f_1, f_2 and f_3 at each time point. After this, value($>$, $purgingSpeed$) eliminates all values of s_4 that are not $> purgingSpeed$. Similarly, we compute signal transformations for the expression from Eq. (6). Finally, we use those two expressions to evaluate the message rule from Eq. (8). If there exists at least one FlameSensor that aligns with one signal in evaluated expressions corresponding to Eqs. (6) and (7), then the message is fired.   □

3   System Implementation and Deployment in Siemens

System Implementation. The main functionality of our Semantic Rule-based Diagnostics system is to author *sigRL* diagnostic programs, to deploy them in turbines, to execute the programs, and to visualise the results of execution. We now give details of our system by following its architecture in Fig. 2. There are four essential layers in the architecture: application, OBDA, rule execution, and data. Our system is mostly implemented in Java. We now discuss the system layer by layer.

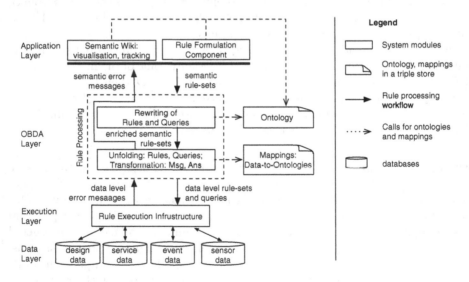

Fig. 2. Architecture of our Semantic Rule-based Diagnostics system.

On the *application layer*, the system offers two user-oriented modules. The first module allows engineers to author, store, and load diagnostic programs by formulating sets of SPRs in *sigRL* and sensor retrieving queries. Such formulation is guided by the domain ontology stored in the system. In Fig. 3 (top) one can observe a screenshot of the SPR editor which is embedded in the Siemens analytical toolkit. Another module is the semantic Wiki that allows among other features to visualize signals and messages (triggered by programs), and to track deployment of SPRs in equipment. In Fig. 3 (center) one can see visualization of signals from two components of one turbine. Diagnostic programs formulated in the application layer are converted into XML-based specifications and sent to the OBDA layer, which returns back the messages and materialized semantic signals, that is, signals over the ontological terms. In Fig. 3 (bottom) one can see an excerpt from an XML-based specification. We rely on REST API to communicate between the application layer and the OBDA layer of our system and OWL API to deal with ontologies.

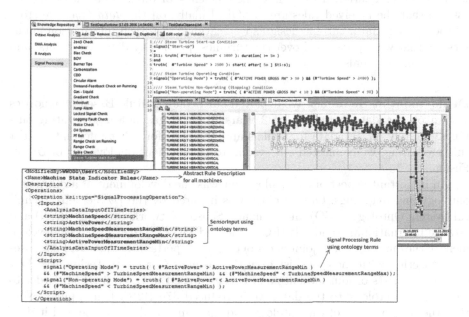

Fig. 3. Screenshots: SPR editor (top), Wiki-based visualisation monitor for semantic signals (centre), and a fragment of an XML-based specification of an SPR (bottom).

Note that during the course of the project we have developed an extension to the existing Siemens rule editor and a dedicated wiki-based visualisation monitor for semantic signals. Note that we use the latter for visualising query answers and messages formatted according to the Siemens OWL 2 ontology and stored as RDF.

The *OBDA layer* takes care of transforming SPRs written in *sigRL* into either SPRs written in the Siemens data-driven rule language (in order to support the existing Siemens IT infrastructure) or SQL. This transformation has two steps: rewriting of programs and queries with the help of ontologies (at this step both programs and queries are enriched with the implicit information from the ontology), and then unfolding them with the help of mappings. For this purpose we extended the query transformation module of the Optique platform [11–13,15,19] which we were developing earlier within the Optique project [10].

The OBDA layer also transforms signals, query answers, and messages from the data to semantic representation.[3]

The *rule execution layer* takes care of planning and executing data-driven rules and queries received from the OBDA layer. If the received rules are in the Siemens SPR language then the rule executor instantiates them with concrete sensors extracted with queries and passes them to the Drools Fusion (drools.jboss.org/drools-fusion.html) the engine used by Siemens. If the received rules are in SQL then it plans the execution order and executes them together with the other queries. To evaluate the efficiency of our system in Sect. 4 we assume that the received rules are in SQL. Finally, on the *data layer* we store all the relevant data: turbine design specifications, historical information about services that were performed over the turbines, previously detected events, and the raw sensor signals.

Deployment at Siemens. We deployed our Semantic Rule-Based Diagnostics system on the data gathered for 2 years from 50 gas power generating turbines. We rely on Teradata for signals and MS SQL for other information. For rule processing, we connected our system to the Siemens deployment of Drools Fusion.

An important aspect of the deployment was the development of a diagnostic ontology and mappings. Our ontology was inspired by the *(i)* Siemens Technical System Ontology (TSO) and Semantic Sensor Network Ontology (SSN) and *(ii)* the international standards IEC 81346 and ISO/TS 16952-10. The development of the ontology was a joint effort of domain experts from Siemens businesses units together with the specialist from the Siemens Corporate Technology. Our ontology consists of four modules and it is expressed in OWL 2 QL. In order to connect the ontology to the data, we introduced 376 R2RML mappings. Note that the development of the ontology and mappings is done offline and it does not affect the time the engineers spend to author rules when they do turbine diagnostics. We now go through the ontology modules in more detail.

The main module of our ontology in partially depicted in Fig. 4 where in grey we present SSN and with white TSO terms. This module has 48 classes and 32 object and data properties. The other three modules are respectively about equipment, sensing devices, and diagnostic rules. They provide detailed information about the machines, their deployment profiles, sensor configurations, component hierarchies, functional profiles and logical bindings to the analytical rule definitions. More precisely:

– *The Equipment module* describes the internal structure of an industrial system. The main classes of the module are *DeploymentSite* and *Equipment* and they describe the whole facility of system and machines that have been physically deployed and monitored. It also defines the system boundaries, substantial descriptions of the system environment, set of components it operates

---

[3] In this work we assume that RDF is the semantic data representation.

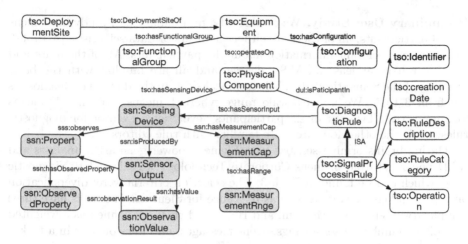

Fig. 4. A fragment of the Siemens ontology that we developed to support turbine diagnostic SPRs.

on, part-of relations, system configurations and functional grouping of components. For example, it encodes that every *Equipment* should have an *ID*, *Configuration* and at least one *Component* to operate on, and an optional property *hasProductLine*.

- *The Sensing Device module* is inspired by the SSN ontology. In particular, we reuse and extend the class *SensingDevice*. The module describes sensors, their properties, outputs, and observations. One of our extensions comparing to SSN is that the measurement capabilities can now include measurement property range i.e. maximum and minimum values (which we encode with annotations in order to keep the ontology in OWL 2 QL). For example, *VibrationSensor* is a sensing device that observes *Vibration* property and measures e.g. *BearingVibrations*.
- *The Diagnostic Rules module* introduces rules and relate them to e.g., *Description*, *Category*, and *Operation* classes. For example, using this module one can say that *SignalProcessingRule* is of a type *DiagnosticRule*, that it has certain *Operation* and it may have different sensor data input associated with its operation.

4 Siemens Experiments

In this section, we present two experiments. The first experiment is to verify whether writing diagnostic programs in *sigRL* offers a considerable time saving comparing to writing the programs in the Siemens data dependent rule language. The second experiment is to evaluate the efficiency of the SQL code generated by our OBDA component (see Sect. 3 for details on our OBDA component).

Preliminary User Study. We conducted a preliminary user study in Siemens with 6 participants, all of them are either engineers or data scientists. In Table 2 we summarise relevant information about the participants. All of them are mid age, most have at least an M.Sc. degree, and all are familiar with the basic concepts of the Semantic Web. Their technical skills in the domain of diagnostics are from 3 to 5. We use a 5-scale range where 1 means 'no' and '5' means 'definitely yes'. Two out of six participants never saw an editor for diagnostic rules, while the other four are quite familiar with rule editors.

During brainstorming sessions with Siemens power generation analysts and R&D personnel from Siemens Corporate Technology we selected 10 diagnostic tasks which can be found in Table 3. The selection criteria were: diversification on topics and complexity, as well as relevance for Siemens. The tasks have three complexity levels (Low, Medium, and High) and they are defined as a weighted sum of the number of sensor tags, event messages, and lines of code in a task.

Table 2. Profile information of participants.

#	Age	Occupation	Education	Tech. skills	Similar tools	Sem. web
P1	43	Design Engineer	Ph.D.	3	3	Yes
P2	46	Senior Diagnostic Engineer	Ph.D.	4	1	Yes
P3	37	Diagnostic Engineer	M.Sc.	5	4	Yes
P4	45	R& D Engineer	M.Sc.	4	4	Yes
P5	34	Software Engineer	B.Sc.	3	3	Yes
P6	33	Data Scientist	Ph.D.	3	1	Yes

Before the study we gave the participants a short introduction with examples about diagnostic programs and message rules in both Siemens and *sigRL* languages. We also explained them the constructs of *sigRL*, presented them our diagnostic ontology, and explained them the data. The data was from 50 Siemens gas turbines and included sensor measurement, that is, temperature, pressure, rotor speed, and positioning, and associated configuration data, that is, types of turbines and threshold values. During the study participants were authoring diagnostic programs for the tasks T1 to T10 from Table 3 using both existing Siemens rule language (as the baseline) and *sigRL*; while we were recording the authoring time. Note that all participants managed to write the diagnostic tasks correctly and the study was conducted on a standard laptop.

Figure 5 summarises the results of the user study. The four left figures present the average time that the six participants took to formulate the 10 tasks over respectively 1, 5, 10, and 50 turbines. We now first discuss how the authoring time changes within each of the four figures, that is, when moving from simple to complex tasks, and then across the four figures, that is, when moving from 1 to 50 turbines.

Observe that in each figure one can see that in the baseline case the authoring time is higher than in the semantic case, i.e., when *sigRL* is used. Moreover, in the

Table 3. Diagnostic tasks for Siemens gas turbines that were used in the user study, where complexity is defined using the number of sensor tags, event messages, and lines of code.

	Complexity	# sensor tags	# event msg	# code lines	Monitoring task
T1	Low	4	2	102	Variable guided vanes analyses
T2	Low	6	5	133	Multiple start attempts
T3	Low	6	3	149	Lube oil system analyses
T4	Medium	6	2	231	Monitoring turbine states
T5	Medium	18	0	282	Interduct thermocouple analyses
T6	Medium	16	2	287	Igniter failure detection
T7	High	17	3	311	Bearing carbonisation
T8	High	19	2	335	Combustion chamber dynamics
T9	High	15	4	376	Gearbox Unit Shutdown
T10	High	12	8	401	Surge detection

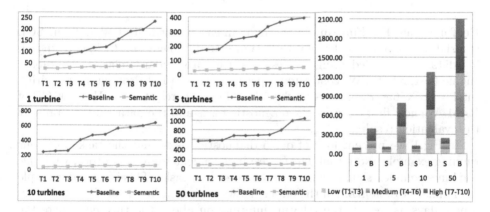

Fig. 5. Results of the user study. Left four figures: the average time in second that the users took to express the tasks T1–T10 for 1, 5, 10, and 50 turbines using existing Siemens rule language (Baseline or B) and our semantic rule language *sigRL* (Semantic or S). Right figure: the total time in seconds the user took to express the tasks grouped according to their complexity.

semantic case the time only slightly increases when moving from simple (T1–T3) to complex (T7–T10) tasks, while in the baseline case it increases significantly: from 2 to 4 times. The reason is that in the baseline case the number of sensor tags makes a significant impact on the authoring time: each of this tags has to be found in the database and included in the rule, while in the semantic case the number of tags does not make any impact since all relevant tags can be specified using queries. The number of event messages and the structure of rules affects both the baseline and the semantic case, and this is the reason why the authoring time grows in the semantic case when going from rules with low to high complexity.

Now consider how the authoring time changes for a given tasks when moving from 1 to 50 turbines. In the baseline case, moving to a higher number of turbines requires to duplicate and modify the rules by first slightly modifying the rule structure (to adapt the rules to turbine variations) and then replacing concrete sensors tags, threshold values, etc. In the semantic case, moving to a higher number of turbines requires only to modify the rule structure. As the result, one can see that in the semantic case all four semantic plots are very similar: the one for 50 turbines is only about twice higher than for 1 turbine. Indeed, to adapt the semantic diagnostic task T4 from 1 to 50 turbines the participants in average spent 50 s, while formulating the original task for 1 turbine took them about 30 s.

Finally, let us consider how the total time for all 10 tasks changes when moving from 1 to 50 turbines. This information is in Fig. 5 (right). One can see that in the baseline case the time goes from 400 to 2.100 s, while in the semantic case it goes from 90 to 240. Thus, for 10 tasks the semantic approach allows to save about 1.900 s and it is more than 4 times faster than the baseline approach.

Performance Evaluation. In this experiment, we evaluate how well our SQL translation approach scales. For this we prepared 5 diagnostic task, corresponding data, and verified firing of messages using a standard relational database engine PostgreSQL. We conducted experiments on an HP Proliant server with 2 Intel Xeon X5690 Processors (each with 12 logical cores at 3.47 GHz), 106 GB of RAM. We now first describe the diagnostic tasks and the data, and then report the evaluation results.

In Fig. 6 we present four of our 5 diagnostic tasks, and the task D_2 is our running example. Note that D_1–D_4 are independent from each other, while D_5 combines complex signals defined in the other four tasks. This is a good example of modularity of *sigRL*. On the data side, we took measurements from 2 sensors over 6 days as well as the relevant information about the turbines where the sensors were installed. Then, we scaled the original data to 2000 sensors; our scaling respect the structure of the original data. The largest raw data for 2000 sensors took 5.1 GB on disk in a PostgreSQL database engine.

During the experiments our system did two steps: translation of semantic diagnostic programs into SQL code and then execution of this SQL. During the first step our system generated SQL code that ranging from 109 to 568 lines depending on the diagnostic task and the code is of a relatively complex structure, e.g., for each diagnostic task the corresponding SQL contains at least 10 joins. The results of the second step are presented in Fig. 7. We observe that

Diagnostics Task D_1: "Is there a ramp change after 6 min in the turbine T100?":

$$\text{SlowRotor} = \min \text{RotorSensor} : \text{value}(<, slowSpeed) : \text{duration}(>, 30s).$$
$$\text{FastRotor} = \max \text{RotorSensor} : \text{value}(>, fastSpeed) : \text{duration}(>, 30s).$$
$$\text{RampChange} = \text{FastRotor} : after[6m] \text{ SlowRotor}.$$
$$\text{message}(\text{``Ramp change''}) = \text{RampChange}.$$

Diagnostic Task D_3: "Does the turbine T100 reach purging and ignition speed for 30 sec?":

$$\text{Ignition} = avg \text{ RotorSensor} : \text{value}(<, ignitionSpeed).$$
$$\text{PurgeAndIgnition} = \text{PurgingStart} : \text{duration}(>, 30s) :$$
$$after[2m] \text{ Ignition} : \text{duration}(>, 30s).$$
$$\text{message}(\text{``Purging and Ignition''}) = \text{PurgeAndIgnition}.$$

Diagnostics Task D_4: "Does the turbine T100 go from ignition to stand still within 1min and then stand still for 30 sec?":

$$\text{StandStill} = avg \text{ RotorSensor} : \text{value}(<, standStillSpeed).$$
$$\text{IgnitionToStand} = \text{Ignition} : \text{duration}(>, 1m) :$$
$$after[1.5m] \text{ StandStill} : \text{duration}(>, 30s).$$
$$\text{message}(\text{``Ignition to Stand''}) = \text{IgnitionToStand}.$$

Diagnostics Task D_5: "Is the turbine T100 ready to start?":

$$\text{message}(\text{``Ready to Start''}) = \text{RampChange} : after[5m] \text{ PurgingOver} :$$
$$after[11m] \text{ PurgingAndIgnition} :$$
$$after[15s] \text{ IgnitionToStand}.$$

Fig. 6. Signal processing rules that we used for performance evaluation.

query evaluation scales well. Specifically, the running time grows sublinearly with respect to the number of sensors. The most challenging query D_5 can be answered in 2 min over 2000 sensors.

5   Related Work

The authors in [19] introduce temporal streaming language STARQL that extends SPARQL with aim to facilitate data analysis directly in queries. This and other similar semantic streaming languages, e.g., SPARQL$_{stream}$ [9], are different from our work, since we propose *(i)* a rule diagnostic language and *(ii)* focus on temporal properties of signals which are not naturally representable in those languages.

A preliminary idea on how to use semantic technologies in abstracting details of machines was presented in [21,22] where the authors use KBs to abstract away details of particular turbines in Siemens. Data about turbines is retrieved using OBDA and send to further analytical analysis (e.g., using KNIME system (www.knime.com)). This line of work does aims at using off-the-shelf analytical software instead of diagnostic rules.

Recent efforts have been made to extend ontologies with analytical and temporal concepts. Authors in [1,2] allow for temporal operators in queries and ontologies. Still, such approach use temporal logics (e.g., LTL) which in not adequate for our case since sensor data are organized based on intervals, e.g. [0s,10s].

Work in [16,19] introduces analytical operations directly into ontological rules in such a way that OBDA scenario is preserved. This line of work, we use an inspiration on how to define analytical functions on concepts, e.g. avg C, in OBDA setting. However, the authors do not consider temporal dimension of the rules.

Finally, our work is related to a well-studied Metric Temporal Logic [20]. One can show that $sigRL$ is a non-trivial extension of the non-recursive Datalog language $Datalog_{nr}MTL$ that has been introduced in [4]. Our rewriting techniques from $sigRL$ rules into SQL follow similar principles as the ones for $Datalog_{nr}MTL$.

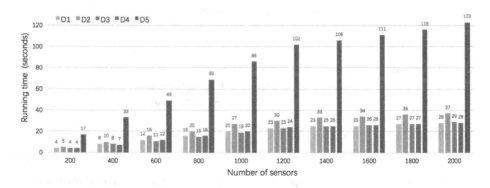

Fig. 7. Performance evaluation results for the Siemens use case.

6   Lessons Learned and Future Work

In this paper we showcase an application of semantic technologies for diagnostics of power generating turbines. We focused on the advantages and feasibility of the ontology-based solution for diagnostic rule formulation and execution. To this end we studied and described a Siemens diagnostic use-case. Based on the insights gained, we reported limitations of existing Siemens and ontology based solutions to turbine diagnostics. In order to address the limitations we proposed a signal processing rule language $sigRL$, studied its formal properties, implemented, and integrated it in an ontology-based system which we deployed at Siemens.

The main lesson learned is the effectiveness of our semantic rule language in dealing with the complexity of the rules and the number of turbines and sensors for rule deployment. The evaluation shows up to 66% of engineers time saving when employing ontologies. Thus, our semantic solution allows diagnostic engineers to focus more on analyses the diagnostic output rather than on data understanding and gathering that they have to do nowadays for authoring data-driven diagnostic rules. Following these experiments, we are in the process of setting up a deployment of our system into the Siemens remote diagnostic system to further evaluate the usability and impact. Second important learned lesson is that execution of semantic rules is efficient and scales well to thousands of sensors which corresponds to real-world complex diagnostic tasks.

Finally, note that our system is not included in the production processes. There are several important steps that we have to do before it can be included. First, it has to become much more mature and improve from the university-driven prototype to a stable system. Second, we have to develop an infrastructure for rule management, in particular, for rule maintenance and reuse—some of this work has already be done and one can our preliminary ideas in [18,23]. Third, we need more optimisations and evaluations that will include a performance comparison of our solution with the Siemens solutions that are based on the Siemens data-driven rule language. Moreover, we need techniques for abstracting (at lease some of) the existing 200k SPRs from the data driven rules into a much smaller number of sigRL. All of these is our future work.

Acknowledgements. This research is supported: EPSRC projects MaSI[3], DBOnto, ED[3]; and the Free University of Bozen-Bolzano project QUEST.

References

1. Artale, A., Kontchakov, R., Ryzhikov, V., Zakharyaschev, M.: The complexity of clausal fragments of LTL. In: McMillan, K., Middeldorp, A., Voronkov, A. (eds.) LPAR 2013. LNCS, vol. 8312, pp. 35–52. Springer, Heidelberg (2013). doi:10.1007/978-3-642-45221-5_3

2. Artale, A., Kontchakov, R., Wolter, F., Zakharyaschev, M.: Temporal description logic for ontology-based data access. IJCAI **2013**, 711–717 (2013)

3. Baader, F., Calvanese, D., McGuinness, D.L., Nardi, D., Patel-Schneider, P.F. (eds.): The Description Logic Handbook: Theory, Implementation, and Applications. Cambridge University Press, New York (2003)

4. Brandt, S., Kalaycı, E.G., Kontchakov, R., Ryzhikov, V., Xiao, G., Zakharyaschev, M.: Ontology-based data access with a horn fragment of metric temporal logic. In: AAAI (2017)

5. Calvanese, D., Cogrel, B., Komla-Ebri, S., Kontchakov, R., Lanti, D., Rezk, M., Rodriguez-Muro, M., Xiao, G.: Ontop: answering SPARQL queries over relational databases. Semant. Web **8**(3), 471–487 (2017)

6. Calvanese, D., De Giacomo, G., Lembo, D., Lenzerini, M., Poggi, A., Rodriguez-Muro, M., Rosati, R., Ruzzi, M., Savo, D.F.: The MASTRO system for ontology-based data access. Semant. Web **2**(1), 43–53 (2011)

7. Calvanese, D., De Giacomo, G., Lembo, D., Lenzerini, M., Rosati, R.: Tractable reasoning and efficient query answering in description logics: the DL-Lite family. JAR **39**(3), 385–429 (2007)

8. Charron, B., Hirate, Y., Purcell, D., Rezk, M.: Extracting semantic information for e-Commerce. In: Groth, P., Simperl, E., Gray, A., Sabou, M., Krötzsch, M., Lecue, F., Flöck, F., Gil, Y. (eds.) ISWC 2016. LNCS, vol. 9982, pp. 273–290. Springer, Cham (2016). doi:10.1007/978-3-319-46547-0_27

9. Corcho, O., Calbimonte, J.-P., Jeung, H., Aberer, K.: Enabling query technologies for the semantic sensor web. Int. J. Semant. Web Inf. Syst. **8**(1), 43–63 (2012)

10. Horrocks, I., Giese, M., Kharlamov, E., Waaler, A.: Using semantic technology to tame the data variety challenge. IEEE Internet Comput. **20**(6), 62–66 (2016)

11. Jiménez-Ruiz, E., Kharlamov, E., Zheleznyakov, D., Horrocks, I., Pinkel, C., Skjæveland, M.G., Thorstensen, E., Mora, J.: BootOX: practical mapping of RDBs to OWL 2. In: Arenas, M., et al. (eds.) ISWC 2015. LNCS, vol. 9367, pp. 113–132. Springer, Cham (2015). doi:10.1007/978-3-319-25010-6_7

12. Kharlamov, E., Brandt, S., Giese, M., Jiménez-Ruiz, E., Kotidis, Y., Lamparter, S., Mailis, T., Neuenstadt, C., Özçep, Ö.L., Pinkel, C., Soylu, A., Svingos, C., Zheleznyakov, D., Horrocks, I., Ioannidis, Y.E., Möller, R., Waaler, A.: Enabling semantic access to static and streaming distributed data with optique: demo. In: DEBS (2016)

13. Kharlamov, E., Brandt, S., Jiménez-Ruiz, E., Kotidis, Y., Lamparter, S., Mailis, T., Neuenstadt, C., Özçep, Ö.L., Pinkel, C., Svingos, C., Zheleznyakov, D., Horrocks, I., Ioannidis, Y.E., Möller, R.: Ontology-based integration of streaming and static relational data with optique. In: SIGMOD (2016)

14. Kharlamov, E., et al.: Capturing industrial information models with ontologies and constraints. In: Groth, P., Simperl, E., Gray, A., Sabou, M., Krötzsch, M., Lecue, F., Flöck, F., Gil, Y. (eds.) ISWC 2016. LNCS, vol. 9982, pp. 325–343. Springer, Cham (2016). doi:10.1007/978-3-319-46547-0_30

15. Kharlamov, E., et al.: Ontology based access to exploration data at statoil. In: Arenas, M., et al. (eds.) ISWC 2015. LNCS, vol. 9367, pp. 93–112. Springer, Cham (2015). doi:10.1007/978-3-319-25010-6_6

16. Kharlamov, E., et al.: Optique: towards OBDA systems for industry. In: Cimiano, P., Fernández, M., Lopez, V., Schlobach, S., Völker, J. (eds.) ESWC 2013. LNCS, vol. 7955, pp. 125–140. Springer, Heidelberg (2013). doi:10.1007/978-3-642-41242-4_11

17. Kharlamov, E., et al.: Towards analytics aware ontology based access to static and streaming data. In: Groth, P., Simperl, E., Gray, A., Sabou, M., Krötzsch, M., Lecue, F., Flöck, F., Gil, Y. (eds.) ISWC 2016. LNCS, vol. 9982, pp. 344–362. Springer, Cham (2016). doi:10.1007/978-3-319-46547-0_31

18. Kharlamov, E., Savković, O., Xiao, G., Mehdi, G., Penaloza, R., Roshchin, M., Horrocks, I.: Semantic rules for machine diagnostics: execution and management. In: CIKM (2017)

19. Kharlamov, E., et al.: How semantic technologies can enhance data access at siemens energy. In: Mika, P., et al. (eds.) ISWC 2014. LNCS, vol. 8796, pp. 601–619. Springer, Cham (2014). doi:10.1007/978-3-319-11964-9_38

20. Koymans, R.: Specifying real-time properties with metric temporal logic. Real-Time Syst. **2**(4), 255–299 (1990)

21. Mehdi, G., Brandt, S., Roshchin, M., Runkler, T.A.: Semantic framework for industrial analytics and diagnostics. In: IJCAI, pp. 4016–4017 (2016)

22. Mehdi, G., Brandt, S., Roshchin, M., Runkler, T.A.: Towards semantic reasoning in knowledge management systems. In: AI for Knowledge Management Workshop at IJCAI (2016)
23. Mehdi, G., Kharlamov, E., Savković, O., Xiao, G., Kalaycı, E.G., Brandt, S., Horrocks, I., Roshchin, M., Runkler, T.: SemDia: semantic rule-based equipment diagnostics tool. In: CIKM (demo) (2017)
24. Mitchell, J.S.: An Introduction to Machinery Analysis and Monitoring. Pennwell Books, Tulsa (1993)
25. Poggi, A., Lembo, D., Calvanese, D., De Giacomo, G., Lenzerini, M., Rosati, R.: Linking data to ontologies. J. Data Semant. **10**, 133–173 (2008)
26. Randall, R.B.: Vibration-Based Condition Monitoring: Industrial, Aerospace and Automotive Applications. Wiley, Hoboken (2011)
27. Rao, B.K.N.: Handbook of Condition Monitoring. Elsevier, Amsterdam (1996)
28. Savković, O., Calvanese, D.: Introducing datatypes in DL-Lite. In: ECAI (2012)
29. Vachtsevanos, G., Lewis, F.L., Roemer, M., Hess, A., Wu, B.: Intelligent Fault Diagnosis and Prognosis for Engineering Systems. Wiley, Hoboken (2006)

Automatic Query-Centric API for Routine Access to Linked Data

Albert Meroño-Peñuela[1]([✉]) and Rinke Hoekstra[1,2]

[1] Computer Science Department, Vrije Universiteit Amsterdam, Amsterdam, Netherlands
{albert.merono,rinke.hoekstra}@vu.nl
[2] Faculty of Law, University of Amsterdam, Amsterdam, Netherlands

Abstract. Despite the advatages of Linked Data as a data integration paradigm, *accessing* and consuming Linked Data is still a cumbersome task. Linked Data applications need to use technologies such as RDF and SPARQL that, despite their expressive power, belong to the data *integration* stack. As a result, applications and data cannot be cleanly separated: SPARQL queries, endpoint addresses, namespaces, and URIs end up as part of the application code. Many publishers address these problems by building RESTful APIs around their Linked Data. However, this solution has two pitfalls: these APIs are costly to maintain; and they blackbox functionality by hiding the queries they use. In this paper we describe grlc, a gateway between Linked Data applications and the LOD cloud that offers a RESTful, reusable and uniform means to routinely access *any* Linked Data. It generates an OpenAPI compatible API by using parametrized queries shared on the Web. The resulting APIs require no coding, rely on low-cost external query storage and versioning services, contain abundant provenance information, and integrate access to different publishing paradigms into a single API. We evaluate grlc qualitatively, by describing its reported value by current users; and quantitatively, by measuring the added overhead at generating API specifications and answering to calls.

Keywords: Linked Data · API · REST · SPARQL · Data access · OpenAPI

1 Introduction

Data integration across multiple sources is an important challenge in the development of information systems [2]. The Linked Data [9] publishing paradigm is designed to make the Web evolve into a global *dataspace* [1] through syntaxes for data standardization and linkage, and query languages (RDF, SPARQL). These technologies have steep learning curves and limited adoption [24], which

---

This paper is a significantly revised and extended version of a paper about an earlier version of grlc presented at the SALAD 2016 workshop [16].

C. d'Amato et al. (Eds.): ISWC 2017, Part II, LNCS 10588, pp. 334–349, 2017.
DOI: 10.1007/978-3-319-68204-4_30

has resulted in a dataspace that is quite *heterogeneous* compared to, and *distinct* from, more mainstream Web-based architectures that use RESTful Application Programming Interfaces (APIs) to mediate between the application and the underlying data. This heterogeneity is very tangible when we *access* Linked Data, which can be done in multiple ways: by submitting SPARQL queries to endpoints, downloading RDF dumps, parsing RDFa in HTML pages, or as Linked Data Fragments; to name a few. Different requirements drive the choice for each of these methods, but it is the *publisher* who is in control. Client applications need to be specifically tailored to each of these methods to consume Linked Data. This creates two problems. First, the data models easily become intertwined with application code, generating hard-coded queries that are difficult to maintain and share. Second, the disconnect with mainstream remote data access in Web development (which simply requires HTTP and JSON) undermines the adoption of Semantic Web technology, decreasing the "market value" of published Linked Data.

A number of solutions have been proposed to overcome these problems. Work such as [23] and the smartAPI [26] propose to expose REST APIs as Linked Data. Despite the value of this for clients with high expressivity requirements, these solutions pose an additional (API) integration problem for clients that need to query Linked Data without having to learn complex query languages, with low expressivity requirements, and in conjunction with other non-Semantic Web data sources. We aim at this specific target user community. Accordingly, we build from existing work targeting this community, such as the OpenPHACTS platform [6], LDtogo [18] and the BASIL server [3], which deploy APIs on top of their internal Semantic Web stacks, functioning as wrappers around their Linked Data endpoints. However, these solutions have two pitfalls. First, the APIs need to be routinely written and maintained by (costly) developers. Second, they typically blackbox the queries they use under the hood, offering a mutually exclusive solution of either using queries *or* API calls, but not both.

Publishing an API that simply executes Semantic Web queries *should be as easy as sharing these queries*. This is the basic idea of grlc [16], which clearly separates the workflows of *query maintenance* and *API construction*. As a result, it allows for a neat, open and collaborative management of queries (typically via GitHub repositories), and uses the logic of this management to build equivalent Linked Data APIs automatically on demand. In this paper, we extend grlc turning it into a generic Linked Data gateway that provides uniform API access to *any* Linked Data published in SPARQL endpoints, Linked Data Fragments servers, RDF dumps, or RDFa embedded in HTML pages. Its added values are the clear decoupling between different Linked Data access requirements; the zero-effort of coding APIs for accessing Linked Data; and the non-blackboxing of queries, which remain always available. Concretely, the contributions of this paper are:

- Architectural guidelines for decoupling semantic queries from application code (Sect. 2);
- A system architecture that generates OpenAPI specifications and enables API call name executions using remote Git repositories containing SPARQL, triple pattern fragments, dump, or RDFa queries (Sects. 2 and 2.3);
- Rich features that such guidelines and architecture enable, like zero-effort versioning and API provenance (Sects. 2.5 and 2.6)
- A qualitative evaluation (Sect. 3.1) providing evidence of use and fulfillment of requirements by users;
- A quantitative evaluation (Sect. 3.2) measuring grlc's overhead.

2   System Architecture

grlc[1] is a lightweight middleware that automatically builds complete, well documented, and neatly organized Linked Data APIs on the fly in a query-centric way, effectively allowing client applications to access any Linked Data via RESTful APIs. This includes Linked Data exposed in SPARQL endpoints, but also in Linked Data Fragments servers [25], RDF dumps, and HTML pages enriched with RDFa (see Sect. 2.3). grlc provides three basic operations: (1) it generates the OpenAPI specification for the queries contained in a given repository; (2) it forwards browsers to the Swagger UI[2] to provide an interactive user-facing frontend of the API contents; and (3) it translates http requests to call the operations of the API against a SPARQL endpoint with several parameters. A docker bundle for easy deployment is available in Docker Hub via docker pull clariah/grlc.

grlc's system architecture is shown in Fig. 1. The basic idea behind grlc is depicted at the bottom: an external *query provider* (typically GitHub or GitLab) is responsible for storing, versioning and exposing semantic queries via Git and http. This decouples these queries, and their curation workflows, from applications using them; and in particular, from applications generating APIs on top of them. The typical use cases start when a client application wants to generate an *OpenAPI spec* or *execute a call name*. When generating an OpenAPI spec, grlc retrieves metadata from the query provider (query names, descriptions, versions, endpoints, etc.) and uses them to build a valid API specification that mimics the organization of the query repository. To extract these metadata, grlc uses a *YAML parser* for enriched query decorators (see Sect. 2.1) and a *parameter parser* for mapping API parameters with query variables (see Sect. 2.2). When executing a call name, grlc retrieves the original content from the query provider, and uses the *query rewriter* to replace query variables with parameter values. Next, it sends the rewritten query to its corresponding endpoint, gets the results, and passes them on to the client application.

---

[1] Source code at https://github.com/CLARIAH/grlc; public instance at http://grlc.io/.

[2] See https://github.com/swagger-api/swagger-ui.

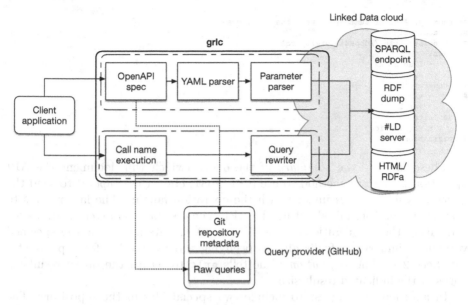

Fig. 1. Architecture of `grlc`. Linked Data sources and query providers are external to the system, and used to access and build Linked Data APIs.

To run these workflows, `grlc` uses a simple API that allows client applications to express what APIs (call names) to generate (execute). Let us assume that our query provider is GitHub, and that we are using the public instance of `grlc` at http://grlc.io/.[3] If the GitHub repository containing queries is at https://github.com/:owner/:repo, then the `grlc` API provides the following routes:

- http://grlc.io/api/:owner/:repo/spec: JSON OpenAPI-compliant specification for the queries of `:owner` at `:repo`.
- http://grlc.io/api/:owner/:repo/api-docs: Swagger-UI, rendered using the previous JSON spec, as shown in Fig. 1.
- http://grlc.io/api/:owner/:repo/: Same as previous.
- http://grlc.io/api/:owner/:repo/:operation?p_1=v_1...p_n=v_n: `http GET` request to `:operation` with parameters $p_1, ..., p_n$ taking values $v_1, ..., v_n$.

2.1 Query Decorators

To generate rich, accurate and descriptive OpenAPI specifications, we use *SPARQL decorators* to add metadata in queries at the query provider. These metadata do not pollute the query contents, since we implement them as comments before the query. Each query translates into an API operation. The syntax is depicted in the following example[4]:

---

[3] These are the defaults, but can be customized in different configuration files.

[4] Additional examples can be found at http://grlc.io.

```
#+ summary: A brief summary of what the query does
#+ method: GET
#+ endpoint: http://dbpedia.org/sparql
#+ tags:
#+     - I am a tag
#+     - Awesomeness
#+ enumerate:
#+     - var_1
#+     - var_2
#+ defaults:
#+     - var_1 :"foo"
#+ pagination: 100
```

These indicate the *summary* of the query (which will document the API operation), the `http` method to use (`GET`, `POST`, etc.), the *endpoint* to send the query to, and the *tags* under which the operation falls in. The latter helps to keep operations organized within the API. The decorator *enumerate* allows for generating the enumerations (possible values) of parameters for the specified variables; similarly, *defaults* allows specifying a default value for a parameter (see Sect. 2.2). The *pagination* value tells `grlc` to return the query results in pages of the indicated result size.

In addition, we suggest to include two special files in the repository. The first is a `LICENSE` file containing the license for the SPARQL queries and the API. The second is the `endpoint.txt` file, with the URI of a default endpoint to direct all queries of the repository; this allows for fast endpoint switching and enables an easier query reuse. `grlc` gives preference to the endpoint at the `#+` `endpoint` decorator, then the `endpoint.txt` file, and finally a default one[5].

2.2   Parameter Mapping

It is often useful for SPARQL queries to be parameterized. This happens when a resource in a basic graph pattern (BGP) can take specific values that affect the result of the query. Previous work has investigated how to map these values to parameters provided by the API operations [3,6].

`grlc` follows BASIL's convention for mapping HTTP parameters to SPARQL[6], by interpreting some "parameter-declared" SPARQL variables as parameter placeholders. An example parametrized query[7] is shown in Listing 1.1. SPARQL variable names staring with `?_` and `?__` indicate mandatory and optional parameters. If they end with `_iri` or `_integer`, they are expected to be mapped to IRIs and literal (integer) values. API operations of the form http:// grlc.io/:owner/:repo/:operation?p_1=v_1...p_n=v_n using these queries are executed as follows: `grlc` first retrieves the raw SPARQL query from the query provider (see Fig. 1); and secondly it replaces the placeholders by the parameter values $v_1, \ldots, v_n$ supplied in the API request. After this, the query is submitted to the endpoint (see Sect. 2.1) and results are forwarded to the client.

---

[5] In http://grlc.io/ this is DBpedia's endpoint.

[6] See https://goo.gl/K0YQDK.

[7] The original query can be found at https://goo.gl/P5nvml.

```
1   SELECT (SUM(?pop) AS ?tot) FROM <urn:graph:cedar-mini:release> WHERE {
2       ?obs a qb:Observation.
3       ?obs sdmx-dimension:refArea ?_location_iri.
4       ?obs cedarterms:Kom ?_kom_iri.
5       ?obs cedarterms:population ?pop.
6       ?slice a qb:Slice.
7       ?slice qb:observation ?obs.
8       ?slice sdmx-dimension:refPeriod ?_year_integer.
9       ?obs sdmx-dimension:sex ?_sex_iri.
10      ?obs cedarterms:residenceStatus ?_residenceStatus_iri.
11      FILTER (NOT EXISTS {?obs cedarterms:isTotal ?total }) }
```

Listing 1.1. Example of a parametrized SPARQL query (prefixes have been omitted).

Parameter Enumerations. To guide users at providing valid parameter values, grlc tries to fill the enumeration `get->parameters->enum` of the OpenAPI specification, which (optionally) lists available parameter values. To generate it, grlc sends an additional SPARQL query to the endpoint, using the original BGP but projecting all parameter variables to obtain their bindings. Figure 2 shows an example of how the Swagger UI displays parameter enumerations.

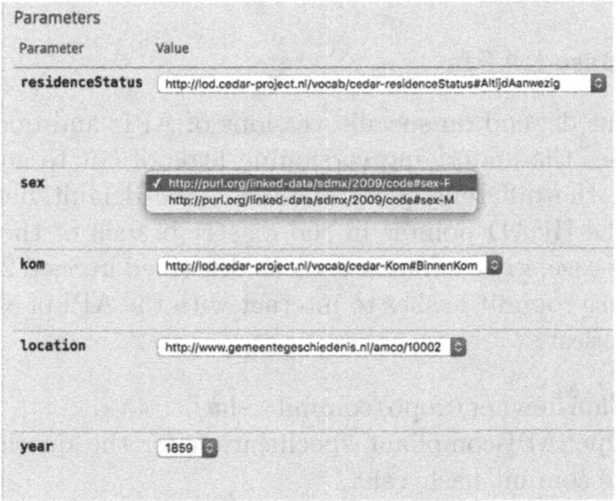

Fig. 2. Screenshot of the Swagger user interface rendering parameter enumerations generated by grlc.

2.3   Access to Any Linked Data

grlc acts as a multiplexer between the different Linked Data access methods. The currently supported access methods include SPARQL endpoints, Linked Data Fragments servers, RDF dumps, and HTML pages with RDFa markup. SPARQL queries are detected as files with the extensions .rq and .sparql in the remote repository (.tpf for triple pattern fragments). Queries against RDF dumps and HTML embedded RDFa are detected by the decorators #+

mime: turtle[8] and #+ mime: rdfa; in such cases the endpoint must point to RDF/RDFa resources. This provides three advantages for Linked Data consumers. First, it hides from them the specific Linked Data access method used by publishers, offering a universal Web API that operates over these methods and only demands HTTP requests. Second, it integrates Linked Data sources independently of these publication methods into a standard Web API. And third, it allows for quickly and effectively switching the queries targets if needed.

2.4 Content Negotiation

grlc supports content negotiation at two different levels: by *request*, and by *URL*. By request, grlc checks the value of the Accept header in incoming http requests. By URL, grlc checks whether a route calling an API operation ends with a trailing .csv, .json or .html. In both cases, the corresponding Accept http header is used in the request to the SPARQL endpoint, delegating support of specific content types to each endpoint. When the response from the server is received, grlc sets the Content-Type header of the client response to match that received by the endpoint, and therefore it only proxies both requests and responses.

2.5 Commit-Based APIs

Often, applications depend on specific versions of APIs and queries to function properly. grlc uses the underlying versioning logic of Git to generate API versions that match the different query versions. The default behavior is to use the contents of the HEAD pointer in the master branch of the query provider repository. In this case, grlc's routes work as described in Sect. 2. Otherwise, the following routes use commit hashes to interact with the API of a commit-specific version of the queries:

- http://grlc.io/api/:owner/:repo/commit/:sha/
  spec: JSON OpenAPI-compliant specification for the queries of :owner at :repo with the commit hash :sha.
- http://grlc.io/api/:owner/:repo/commit/:sha/api-docs: Swagger-UI for the commit hash :sha, rendered using the previous JSON spec, as shown in Fig. 1.
- http://grlc.io/api/:owner/:repo/commit/:sha/: Same as previous.
- http://grlc.io/api/:owner/:repo/commit/:sha/:operation?
  p_1=v_1...p_n=v_n: http GET request to commit hash :sha of :operation with parameters $p_1, ..., p_n$ taking values $v_1, ..., v_n$.

In these cases, the OpenAPI specification will be generated on the basis of what that specific commit contains; calls to commit-specific operations work likewise. To ease user interaction and browsing across versions, we add links to

---

[8] The xml, n3, nt, trix and nquads syntaxes are also supported.

the generated OpenAPI spec and Swagger-UI to the next and previous versions (i.e. commit), if available. All APIs generated by `grlc` are versioned using their corresponding commit hashes.

2.6 Provenance

One advantage of `grlc` over other Linked Data API methods is that it does not use APIs to blackbox queries, allowing both queries and APIs to be used simultaneously. To further enhance its transparency and explainability, `grlc` generates provenance using the W3C PROV [7] standard in two different ways. First, it generates a graph representing the workflow of creating the OpenAPI specification by reusing externally retrieved queries. Second, it adds to this graph the PROV representation of the Git history behind all queries reused, by calling Git2PROV [4]. To allow the exploration of all this provenance information, we integrate the visualizations of PROV-O-Viz [10], accessible via an *Oh yeah?* button in the Swagger-UI page of the API specification.

2.7 SPARQL2Git

Interacting with languages like SPARQL and technologies like Git can be tedious for some users. To alleviate this, `grlc` works in conjunction with another tool: SPARQL2Git[9] [17]. SPARQL2Git combines a user interface for comfortably editing and trying SPARQL queries and their decorators (see Sect. 2.1), with a transparent use of the GitHub API. Users can "save" versions of their queries and the system deals with managing commits on their Git repositories. A `grlc` button is always accessible to try out the APIs generated from their committed queries.

3 Evaluation

We evaluate `grlc` in two different ways: qualitatively, and quantitatively. In the qualitative evaluation, we provide testimonies of the utility of `grlc` for (third party) organizations and projects. In the quantitative evaluation, we study the performance of `grlc`. First, we investigate its overhead over direct SPARQL queries (Sect. 3.2). Secondly, we benchmark the speed in which it generates OpenAPI specifications (Sect. 3.2).

3.1 Qualitative Evaluation

From the start of its operation in July 2016, the public instance of `grlc` has attracted 646 unique visitors, 46.4% of return rate, and generating 1,205 sessions. `grlc` has also attracted the attention of external developers, who have sent 13 pull requests that have been integrated into the master branch. A list of community maintained queries and matching APIs is available at http://grlc.io.

---

[9] See http://sparql2git.com.

In this section we evaluate the requirements satisfied by `grlc` in a number of external institutions in 6 different domains where `grlc` is being currently used. We asked members of these institutions to describe their use cases, the advantages and disadvantages of addressing them by using `grlc`, and their motivation for choosing it over other solutions.

DANS: Historical Statistics. The Netherlands Institute for Permanent Access to Digital Research Resources (DANS) publishes the Dutch historical censuses (1795–1971) as Linked Data [15].[10] Queries across this data are maintained on GitHub. These queries are used across various client applications,[11] and other organizations (Statistics Netherlands, a.o.) inspiring the need for a shared API. The then existing lightweight solutions, such as BASIL[12] and implementations of the Linked Data API created a maintenance problem as they require one to keep multiple copies of the same queries in different places. Given the frequency of mutations in the queries, this was problematic. The `grlc` system allows queries to be maintained in a single location, and offers an ecosystem where SPARQL and non-SPARQL savvy applications coexist.

IISH: Social History. The International Institute for Social History partners in the CLARIAH[13] project for digital humanities. Typical social history research requires querying across combined, structured humanities data, and performing statistical analysis in e.g. R [11]. Given that there are potentially infinitely many such research queries, building a one-size-fits all API is not feasible. The R SPARQL package [8] allows one to use SPARQL queries directly from R. However, this results in hard-coded, non reusable, and difficult to maintain queries. As shown in Fig. 3, with `grlc` the R code becomes *clearer* due to the decoupling

```
46  ## using grlc API call
47  library(RCurl)
48  canada <- getURL("http://grlc.clariah-sdh.eculture.labs.vu.nl/clariah/wp4~
49  canada <- read.csv(textConnection(canada))
50  sweden <- getURL("http://grlc.clariah-sdh.eculture.labs.vu.nl/clariah/wp4~
51  sweden <- read.csv(textConnection(sweden))
52
53  fit_canada_base <- lm(log(hiscam) ~ log(gdppc), data=canada)
54  fit_canada <- lm(log(hiscam) ~ log(gdppc) + I(age^2) + age, data=canada)
55  fit_sweden_base <- lm(log(hiscam) ~ log(gdppc), data=sweden)
56  fit_sweden <- lm(log(hiscam) ~ log(gdppc) + I(age^2) + age, data=sweden)
```

Fig. 3. The use of `grlc` makes Linked Data accessible from any `http` compatible application.

---

[10] This was done through the CEDAR project, see http://www.cedar-project.nl/ and https://github.com/CEDAR-project/Queries.

[11] YASGUI-based browsing: http://lod.cedar-project.nl/cedar/data.html, drawing historical maps with census data: http://lod.cedar-project.nl/maps/map_CEDAR_women_1899.html.

[12] https://github.com/the-open-university/BASIL.

[13] http://clariah.nl/.

with SPARQL; and *shorter*, since a `curl` one-liner calling a `grlc` enabled API operation suffices to retrieve the data. Furthermore, the exact query feeding the research results can be stored, and shared with fellow scholars and in papers.

National eScience Center: Cultural Heritage. The National eScience Center uses `grlc` in a tool for Linked Data exploration of cultural heritage data (Dive+). The Dive+ UI calls the `grlc`-generated API to access underlying data. The `grlc` code is included as a library to augment parts of the Dive+ API that are not Linked Data data-access related (e.g. search, legacy data). The advantage of using `grlc` is that it allows NLeSC to manage SPARQL queries separate from the rest of the API – this enables, for instance, to have different queries without having to deploy a new version of the API. NLeSC used `grlc` instead of other solutions because it was easy to deploy and open source.

TNO: FoodCube. The Netherlands Organisation for Applied Scientific Research (TNO) uses `grlc` in a food related project for the municipality of Almere. Food-Cube aims to provide an integrated view to all kinds of datasets related to the food supply chain; domain knowledge and interesting domain questions are the core focus. FoodCube uses `grlc` to provide 'FAQ' (Frequently Asked SPARQL Questions) for those who would prefer REST over SPARQL, but also to explore the data. This is made possible by the ability to annotate the SPARQL queries with keywords and a description.

NewGen Chennai: Conference Proceedings. NewGen uses `grlc` to build the IOS Press ECAI API. Their goal is to expose the ECAI conference proceedings not only as Linked Data that can be used by Semantic Web practitioners, but also as a Web API that web developers can consume. This is useful for bringing together and bridging the two communities and rich ecosystems of software. Key features of `grlc` for this use case are query curation, sharing and dissemination. For this last point, being able to provide metadata to individual queries is reportedly very useful. NewGen finds easy to use and document the API, and to set-up. Similarly, the use of Git as a backend is an advantage, and they consider the `grlc` development community helpful. SPARQL2Git (see Sect. 2.7) emerged as a requirement for a query curation frontend. Other alternatives[14] were considered, but the two advantages of `grlc` were its use of GitHub for ingesting community curated queries, and the minimum infrastructure/resources needed for building APIs.

EU RISIS: Science, Technology and Innovation. `grlc` is currently used within the Semantically Mapping Science (SMS) platform[15] for sharing of SPARQL queries and thereby their results among multiple researchers. As technical core within the RISIS EU project[16], SMS aims to provide a data integration platform

---

[14] Reportedly   https://github.com/danistrebel/SemanticGraphQL,   https://github.com/nelson-ai/semantic-graphql   and   https://github.com/ColinMaudry/sparql-router/wiki/Using-SPARQL-router.

[15] http://sms.risis.eu.

[16] http://risis.eu.

where researchers from science, technology and innovation (STI) can find answers to their research questions. The SMS platform provides a faceted data browser where interactions of non-linked-data expert users are translated into a set of complex SPARQL queries, which are then run to aggregate data from relevant SPARQL endpoints. One of the challenges within the platform was how to share, extend and repurpose user-generated queries in a flexible way. `grlc` helps to address this issue by providing a URI for the resulted queries and by supporting collaborative update of those queries. Furthermore, creating Linked Data APIs on top of `grlc` enables external applications to reuse and exploit some of the features of the SMS platform, e.g. SMS geo-services to annotate addresses within a spreadsheet document.

3.2 Quantitative

Call Execution Overhead. Here, we quantify the added overhead of `grlc` as a middleware between Web clients and Linked Data providers. To do so, we compare the execution times of sending SPARQL queries directly to a SPARQL endpoint over HTTP, and calling the equivalent service names containing such SPARQL queries using `grlc`.

We use the SPARQL queries of the SP²Bench SPARQL Performance Benchmark[17] (SP2B) [22]. All runs in one single node inside a `lxc` container running Linux Ubuntu 14.04.4 LTS, an Intel(R) Xeon(R) E5645 CPU at 2.40GHz, and 98GB of memory. As a backend triplestore we use a Virtuoso Open Source Edition 6.1.6. To avoid the influence of network traffic on our tests, we configure `grlc` to use local namespaces to resolve API calls and dereferencing query contents.[18] To make comparisons fair, both systems are queried using `curl`, making HTTP GET requests, and requesting the query results as CSV by setting the HTTP header `Accept: text/csv`. We disable all `grlc`'s caching mechanisms.[19]

Figure 4 shows the results of executing the SP2B queries on datasets of 50K, 500K, and 5M triples, sending HTTP requests to (a) directly to the SPARQL endpoint (submitting the query as a parameter of the request); and (b) using `grlc` (calling the equivalent call name in a Linked Data API generated using such queries[20]). We observe that, in queries that Virtuoso takes a considerable time (above 100 ms), `grlc` only adds a marginal overhead (e.g. *q2*, *q7*, *q9*, *11*); contrarily, the impact of `grlc` is higher in fast queries below that threshold. We calculate the *relative overhead* of `grlc` with $\frac{t_g - t_v}{t_g}$, where t_g is the time consumed by `grlc`, and t_v is the time consumed by the SPARQL endpoint. Figure 5a shows the dependency of this ratio with the total execution time t_g. We observe that,

---

[17] See http://dbis.informatik.uni-freiburg.de/index.php?project=SP2B.

[18] For this, we implement a basic GitHub-like API, see https://github.com/albertmer onyo/dummyhub.

[19] All measurements in this section apply to the first execfution only; subsequent executions are immediate due to caching.

[20] See https://github.com/albertmeronyo/sp2b-queries and http://grlc.io/api/albert meronyo/sp2b-queries.

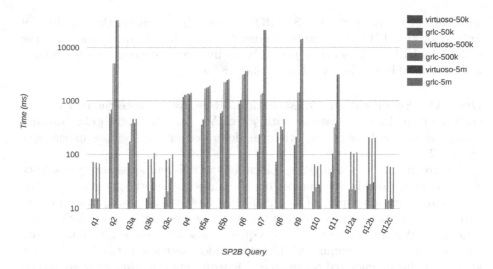

Fig. 4. Execution time of SP2B queries on 50K, 500K and 5M triple datasets, using: (a) Virtuoso alone; and (b) an instance of `grlc` that exposes the same queries as an API.

for queries that SPARQL endpoints can solve very quickly (e.g. less than 200 ms), more than 50% of the time is spent in `grlc` rather than at the endpoint. In even faster queries (e.g. below 100 ms), the ratio taken by `grlc` is even larger (above 75% of the time). Nonetheless, in queries that take more than 400 ms `grlc`'s impact is more limited (less than 25%).

The *absolute overhead* of `grlc` is given by $t_g - t_v$, and equals on average over all queries 96.86 ± 46.83, 77.18 ± 46.48, and 80.87 ± 48.14 for the three dataset sizes. We observe here that, as expected, the cost of `grlc` is independent of the dataset size. However, there are some fluctuations in this cost that make it non-constant. A cause for the variability in `grlc`'s absolute cost can be observed in Fig. 5b, which shows a linear relationship between `grlc`'s absolute overhead

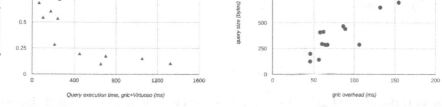

(a) Execution time of a callname in `grlc` (x-axis), and share of this time taken by `grlc` (y-axis).

(b) `grlc` absolute overhead (y-axis) depending on the total size of a callname's query (x-axis).

Fig. 5. Breakdown of `grlc`'s overhead, and its dependency with total execution times and query size.

with respect to the size of the SPARQL queries. In summary, the penalties of `grlc`'s additional HTTP requests (needed for retrieving the query contents, the endpoint's URI, etc.) and their payloads are important contributors to its cost. In our tests, this cost is never higher than 187.9 ms.

OpenAPI Specification Construction. Here, we evaluate the cost of generating OpenAPI specifications with `grlc`. We use the same `grlc` instance (i.e. local API and query resolution) as described in the previous experiment (Sect. 3.2).

We create various OpenAPI specifications of different sizes and types. Spec sizes are determined by the number of call names (i.e. queries) contained in the spec, and we generate specs of 1, 10, 100 and 1000 call names. Query types are determined by the features typed in the query: we generate *plain* queries, containing only the query itself; *decorators* queries, also containing YAML metadata (endpoint URI, query summary, HTTP method, pagination, tags); and *enum*, also containing enumerated parameters. Figure 6 shows the time `grlc` spends on creating these specifications. We observe that in all cases this cost is linear with respect to the spec sizes (the time axis is in log scale). For APIs of conventional size (i.e. between 10 and 100 call names) containing only plain queries, `grlc` can generate specs between 335.4 ± 12.43 and $3,026.7 \pm 41.28$ ms. The cost of adding useful decorators is only relatively more expensive for small APIs of 10 call names (510.8 ± 27.70 ms), converging to the cost of plain queries ($3,388.5 \pm 27.72$ ms) for larger 100 call name APIs. APIs containing many enumerated parameters are very expensive to generate ($34,658.7 \pm 70.21$ ms for 10 call names), but single queries are more affordable ($3,487 \pm 18.32$ ms).

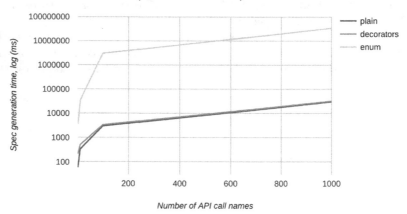

Fig. 6. Performance of `grlc` at creating OpenAPI specifications of different sizes and types.

4   Related Work

Decoupling Linked Data queries from the applications that use them follows principles of encapsulation and abstraction. There is abundant work in so-called

SPARQL query repositories, which are fundamental to study the efficiency and reusability of methods querying Linked Data. SPARQL query logs, for instance, have been used to study differences between queries by humans and machines [20], and to understand how queried entities are semantically related [12]. Saleem et al. [21] propose to "create a Linked Dataset describing the SPARQL queries issued to various public SPARQL endpoints". Loizou et al. [14] identify (combinations of) SPARQL constructs that constitute a performance hit, and formulate heuristics for writing optimized queries.

The Semantic Web has developed a large body of work on the relationship between Linked Data and Web Services [5,19]. In [23], authors propose to expose REST APIs as Linked Data. These approaches suggest the use of Linked Data technology on top of Web services. Recently, the smartAPI [26] has proposed API building blocks for clients with with high expressivity requirements. Our work is related to results in the opposite direction, concretely the Linked Data API specification[21] and the W3C Linked Data Platform 1.0 specification, which "describes the use of HTTP for accessing, updating, creating and deleting resources from servers that expose their resources as Linked Data"[22]. Kopecký et al. [13] address the specific issue of writing (updating, creating, deleting) these Linked Data resources via Web APIs. However, our work is more related to providing APIs that facilitate Linked Data access to a variety of publishing mechanisms. SPARQL is the most popular among such supported mechanisms in the OpenPHACTS Discovery Platform for pharmacological data [6], LDtogo [18] and the BASIL server [3]. These approaches build Linked Data APIs compliant with the Swagger RESTful API specification[23] that function as wrappers around SPARQL endpoints. Inspired by this, our work contributes additional: *(a)* decoupling with respect to the query storage and maintenance infrastructure, which we outsource to code repository providers; *(b)* abstraction over various Linked Data access methods (Linked Data Fragments, RDF dumps, HTML+RDFa) besides SPARQL; and *(c)* tools for automatically building well-documented API specifications.

5 Conclusions and Future Work

We have presented `grlc`, an automatic and query-centric method for enabling routine access to any Linked Data. `grlc` leverages the decoupling of semantic queries from applications, allowing query-based and API-based access simultaneously. It generates uniform and universal Web APIs irrespective of the Linked Data publishing method, making these Linked Data consumable and accessible to the mainstream Web community. It uses Git features to transparently provide versioning and provenance. In the future, we plan on extending this work in multiple ways. First, we will enlarge our current supported infrastructures (GitHub, GitLab, SPARQL, dumps, etc.) to cover increasing requirements demanded by users. Secondly, we devise a JSON transformation language for customizing the struc-

---

[21] https://github.com/UKGovLD/linked-data-api.
[22] https://www.w3.org/TR/2015/REC-ldp-20150226/.
[23] https://github.com/OAI/OpenAPI-Specification.

ture of API results. Finally, we intend to investigate the reusability, exchangeability, and linkability of semantic query catalogs created by users of `grlc`.

Acknowledgements. This work was funded by the CLARIAH project of the Dutch Science Foundation (NWO). We want to thank all external users and contributors to this work, especially Carlos Marínez Ortiz, Ali Khalili, Barry Nouwt, and Trevor Lazarus. We also want to thank Laurens Rietveld for his technical suggestions, and Richard Zijdeman and Auke Rijpma for their testing.

References

1. Halevy, A.Y., Franklin, M.J., Maier, D.: Principles of dataspace systems. In: Proceedings of 25th Symposium on Principles of Database Systems (PODS 2006), pp. 1–9. ACM (2006)
2. Bernstein, P.A., Haas, L.M.: Information integration in the enterprise. Commun. ACM **51**(9), 72–79 (2008)
3. Daga, E., Panziera, L., Pedrinaci, C.: A BASILar approach for building web APIs on top of SPARQL endpoints. In: Services and Applications over Linked APIs and Data – SALAD 2015 (ISWC 2015), vol. 1359. CEUR Workshop Proceedings (2015). http://ceur-ws.org/Vol-1359/
4. De Nies, T., Magliacane, S., Verborgh, R., Coppens, S., Groth, P., Mannens, E., Van de Walle, R.: Git2PROV: exposing version control system content as W3C PROV. In: Poster and Demo Proceedings of 12th International Semantic Web Conference, October 2013. http://www.iswc2013.semanticweb.org/sites/default/files/iswc_demo_32_0.pdf
5. Fielding, R.T.: Architectural styles and the design of network-based software architectures (2000)
6. Groth, P., Loizou, A., Gray, A.J., Goble, C., Harland, L., Pettifer, S.: API-centric Linked Data integration: the Open PHACTS Discovery Platform case study. Web Semant.: Sci. Serv. Agents World Wide Web **29**, 12–18 (2014). lifeScienceandeScience. http://www.sciencedirect.com/science/article/pii/S1570826814000195
7. Groth, P., Moreau, L.: PROV-overview. An overview of the PROV family of documents. Technical report, World Wide Web Consortium (W3C) (2013). http://www.w3.org/TR/prov-overview/
8. van Hage, W.R., with contributions from: Kauppinen, T., Graeler, B., Davis, C., Hoeksema, J., Ruttenberg, A., Bahls., D.: SPARQL: SPARQL client, R package version 1.15 (2013). http://CRAN.R-project.org/package=SPARQL
9. Heath, T., Bizer, C.: Linked Data: Evolving the Web into a Global Data Space, 1st edn. Morgan and Claypool, San Rafael (2011)
10. Hoekstra, R., Groth, P.: PROV-O-Viz - understanding the role of activities in provenance. In: Ludäscher, B., Plale, B. (eds.) IPAW 2014. LNCS, vol. 8628, pp. 215–220. Springer, Cham (2015). doi:10.1007/978-3-319-16462-5_18
11. Hoekstra, R., Meroño-Peñuela, A., Dentler, K., Rijpma, A., Zijdeman, R., Zandhuis, I.: An ecosystem for linked humanities data. In: Sack, H., Rizzo, G., Steinmetz, N., Mladenić, D., Auer, S., Lange, C. (eds.) ESWC 2016. LNCS, vol. 9989, pp. 425–440. Springer, Cham (2016). doi:10.1007/978-3-319-47602-5_54
12. Huelss, J., Paulheim, H.: What SPARQL query logs tell and do not tell about semantic relatedness in LOD. In: Gandon, F., Guéret, C., Villata, S., Breslin, J., Faron-Zucker, C., Zimmermann, A. (eds.) ESWC 2015. LNCS, vol. 9341, pp. 297–308. Springer, Cham (2015). doi:10.1007/978-3-319-25639-9_44

13. Kopecký, J., Pedrinaci, C., Duke, A.: Restful write-oriented API for hyperdata in custom RDF knowledge bases. In: 2011 7th International Conference on Next Generation Web Services Practices (NWeSP), pp. 199–204, October 2011

14. Loizou, A., Angles, R., Groth, P.: On the formulation of performant SPARQL queries. Web Semant.: Sci. Serv. Agents World Wide Web **31**, 1–26 (2015). http://www.sciencedirect.com/science/article/pii/S1570826814001061

15. Meroño-Peñuela, A., Guéret, C., Ashkpour, A., Schlobach, S.: CEDAR: The Dutch Historical Censuses as Linked Open Data. Semant. Web – Interoper. Usability Appl. (2015, in press)

16. Meroño-Peñuela, A., Hoekstra, R.: grlc Makes GitHub taste like linked data APIs. In: Sack, H., Rizzo, G., Steinmetz, N., Mladenić, D., Auer, S., Lange, C. (eds.) ESWC 2016. LNCS, vol. 9989, pp. 342–353. Springer, Cham (2016). doi:10.1007/978-3-319-47602-5_48

17. Meroño-Peñuela, A., Hoekstra, R.: SPARQL2Git: transparent SPARQL and linked data API curation via Git. In: Proceedings of 14th Extended Semantic Web Conference (ESWC 2017), Poster and Demo Track, Portoroz, Slovenia, 28th May – 1st June, Springer, Cham (2017, in print)

18. Ockeloen, N., de Boer, V., Aroyo, L.: LDtogo: a data querying and mapping frameworkfor linked data applications. In: Cimiano, P., Fernández, M., Lopez, V., Schlobach, S., Völker, J. (eds.) ESWC 2013. LNCS, vol. 7955, pp. 199–203. Springer, Heidelberg (2013). doi:10.1007/978-3-642-41242-4_24

19. Pedrinaci, C., Domingue, J.: Toward the next wave of services: linked services for the Web of data. J. Univers. Comput. Sci. **16**(13), 1694–1719 (2010)

20. Rietveld, L., Hoekstra, R.: Man vs. machine: differences in SPARQL queries. In: Proceedings of 4th USEWOD Workshop on Usage Analysis and the Web of of Data, ESWC 2014 (2014). http://usewod.org/files/workshops/2014/papers/rietveld_hoekstra_usewod2014.pdf

21. Saleem, M., Ali, M.I., Hogan, A., Mehmood, Q., Ngomo, A.-C.N.: LSQ: the linked SPARQL queries dataset. In: Arenas, M., et al. (eds.) ISWC 2015. LNCS, vol. 9367, pp. 261–269. Springer, Cham (2015). doi:10.1007/978-3-319-25010-6_15

22. Schmidt, M., Hornung, T., Küchlin, N., Lausen, G., Pinkel, C.: An experimental comparison of RDF data management approaches in a SPARQL benchmark scenario. In: Sheth, A., Staab, S., Dean, M., Paolucci, M., Maynard, D., Finin, T., Thirunarayan, K. (eds.) ISWC 2008. LNCS, vol. 5318, pp. 82–97. Springer, Heidelberg (2008). doi:10.1007/978-3-540-88564-1_6

23. Speiser, S., Harth, A.: Integrating linked data and services with linked data services. In: Antoniou, G., Grobelnik, M., Simperl, E., Parsia, B., Plexousakis, D., De Leenheer, P., Pan, J. (eds.) ESWC 2011. LNCS, vol. 6643, pp. 170–184. Springer, Heidelberg (2011). doi:10.1007/978-3-642-21034-1_12

24. Vandenbussche, P.Y., Aranda, C.B., Hogan, A., Umbrich, J.: Monitoring the status of SPARQL endpoints. In: Proceedings of 12th International Semantic Web Conference ISWC 2013 Posters and Demonstrations Track (ISWC 2013), pp. 81–84. CEUR-WS (2013)

25. Verborgh, R., Hartig, O., Meester, B.D., Haesendonck, G., de Vocht, L., Sande, M.V., Cyganiak, R., Colpaert, P., Mannens, E., van de Walle, R.: Querying datasets on the web with high availability. In: Proceedings of 13th International Semantic Web Conference, ISWC 2014 (2014)

26. Zaveri, A., Dastghcib, S., Whetzel, T., Verborgh, R., Avillach, P., Korodi, G., Terryn, R., Jagodnik, K., Assis, P., Wu, C., Dumontier, M.: smartAPI: Towards a more intelligent network of web APIs (2017, in print)

Realizing an RDF-Based Information Model for a Manufacturing Company – A Case Study

Niklas Petersen[1,2]($\boxtimes$), Lavdim Halilaj[1,2], Irlán Grangel-González[1,2],
Steffen Lohmann[2], Christoph Lange[1,2], and Sören Auer[3,4]

[1] Enterprise Information Systems (EIS), University of Bonn, Bonn, Germany
{petersen,halilaj,grangel,langec}@cs.uni-bonn.de
[2] Fraunhofer Institute for Intelligent Analysis and Information Systems (IAIS),
Sankt Augustin, Germany
steffen.lohmann@iais.fraunhofer.de
[3] Computer Science, Leibniz University of Hannover, Hannover, Germany
soeren.auer@tib.eu
[4] TIB Leibniz Information Center for Science and Technology, Hannover, Germany

Abstract. The digitization of the industry requires information models describing assets and information sources of companies to enable the semantic integration and interoperable exchange of data. We report on a case study in which we realized such an information model for a global manufacturing company using semantic technologies. The information model is centered around machine data and describes all relevant assets, key terms and relations in a structured way, making use of existing as well as newly developed RDF vocabularies. In addition, it comprises numerous RML mappings that link different data sources required for integrated data access and querying via SPARQL. The technical infrastructure and methodology used to develop and maintain the information model is based on a Git repository and utilizes the development environment VoCol as well as the Ontop framework for Ontology Based Data Access. Two use cases demonstrate the benefits and opportunities provided by the information model. We evaluated the approach with stakeholders and report on lessons learned from the case study.

1 Introduction

Although the vision of digitizing production and manufacturing has gained much traction lately (viz. Industry 4.0), it is still not clear how it can actually be *implemented* in an interoperable way using concrete standards and technologies [4]. A key challenge is to enable industrial devices to communicate and to *understand* each other as a prerequisite for cooperation scenarios [13]. Different standards, such as those from the ISO and IEC series, are used to describe information about manufacturing, security, identification and communication, among other areas.

This work has been supported by BMBF (German Federal Ministry of Education and Research) grants 01IS15035C (SDI-X) and 01IS15054 (Industrial Data Space).

C. d'Amato et al. (Eds.): ISWC 2017, Part II, LNCS 10588, pp. 350–366, 2017.
DOI: 10.1007/978-3-319-68204-4_31

Integrating all relevant information and automating as many production steps as possible is the central goal of the Industry 4.0 vision [11]. Instead of envisioning one monolithic system or database, we pursue a decentral semantic integration, i.e., the formal description and linking of all relevant assets and data sources based on an aligned set of RDF vocabularies – the *information model*. This avoids unnecessary data redundancy and allows for structured querying and analyses across individual assets and data sources based on SPARQL. The information model serves as a crystallization point and reference for data structures and semantics emerging from the data sources and value chains. Furthermore, it is aligned to important industry standards, such as *RAMI* [2] and *IEC 62264* [1], to additionally foster data exchange and semantic interoperability.

The information model is more than a set of aligned RDF vocabularies. It comprises (i) a methodology for the development, curation and integration of vocabularies for the domain in focus; (ii) a technical infrastructure for following the methodology; (iii) governance procedures, which are aligned with the corporate organizational structure.

In this paper, we report on a case study in which we realized such an information model for a global manufacturing company, and discuss findings and lessons learned derived from the case study. In Sect. 2, we describe the context, requirements and motivating scenario of this work. The core contributions—the information model and its implementation—are presented in Sects. 3 and 4. In Sect. 5, we apply the information model to two use cases demonstrating its benefits and opportunities. Section 6 reports on stakeholder feedback and summarizes the lessons learned. Section 7 reviews related work, and Sect. 8 concludes with an outlook to future work.

2 Motivating Scenario

The information modeling project involved employees from different departments and hierarchical levels of the manufacturing company, external consultants and a third party IT provider. The company itself realized that their IT infrastructure has reached a level of complexity making difficult to manage and effectively use their existing systems and data. While adding new sensors to production lines is straightforward, using the sensor data effectively to improve the production process and decision-making can be cumbersome. The need to share production data with clients led them to evaluate the fitness of semantic technologies. For example, the production of bearing tools is fairly quality-driven depending on the customer specifications. Sharing the production details in a more processable format (compared to non-machine-comprehensible formats) aroused interest. Further goals were to gain a *bigger picture of the company's assets* (physical and non-physical) and to capture as much expert knowledge as possible.

2.1 Use Cases

The concrete use cases are based upon a machine newly introduced into the production lines of the company, a so-called *machine tool*. This is a machine that requires the mounting of tools to assemble specific metal or rigid products. Compared to older generations, the new machine features more than 100 embedded sensors that monitor the production.

Tool Management. Possible tools to be mounted into the machine are cutters, drillers or polishers. A tool usually consists of multiple parts. The number of parts depends on the manufacturer of the tool, which is not necessarily the same as the manufacturer of the machine. Mounting tools into a machine is a time-consuming task for the machine operator. Uncertain variables of the tools, such as location, availability and utilization rate, play a major role in the efficiency of a work shift and of a machine in particular. The production of certain goods may wear a tool out quickly, thus decreasing its overall lifetime and forcing the machine operator to stop the machine and replace it with a new tool. Reducing the idle time for remounting the machine by clearly describing its configuration, location and weariness was therefore one concrete goal to be addressed by the information model.

Energy Consumption. Producing goods with the machine tool is an energy-intensive process. Before we started the information modeling project, only the energy costs per factory were known. Sensors were added to track the energy consumption per machine and processed work order. For the cost calculation, data from the added sensors and the work orders, which resides in different data sources, needs to be linked and jointly queried. Therefore, integrating this data to be able to retrieve the information at run-time was another concrete goal addressed by the information modeling project.

2.2   Data Sources

Three types of data were of particular interest in the project: (i) Sensor Data (SD), (ii) the Bill of Materials (BOM), and (iii) data from the Manufacturing Execution System (MES). The SD comprises sensor measurements of the machine tool. These measurements record parameters needed for the continuous monitoring of the machine, such as energy, power, temperature, force, vibration, etc. The MES contains information about work orders, shifts, material numbers, etc. The machine produces assets based on the work order details, which provide the necessary information for the production of a given asset. The BOM contains information about the general structure of the company, such as work centers, work units, associated production processes, as well as information related to the work orders and the materials needed for a specific production.

3   Realizing the RDF-Based Information Model

The information model aims at a holistic description of the company, its assets and information sources. The core of the model is based on a factory ontology we developed in a previous project [18], which describes real world objects from the factory domain, including factories, employees, machines, their locations and relations to each other, etc. In addition, the information model comprises the mappings between ontologies that represent the data sources (i.e., SD, BOM, MES) and their corresponding schemes.

3.1 Development Methodology

Our development methodology was based on the approach proposed by Uschold and Gruninger [22]. We first defined the purpose and scope of the information model; then, we captured the domain knowledge, conceptualized and formalized the ontologies and aligned them with existing ontologies, vocabularies and standards. Finally, we created the mappings between the data sources and ontological entities. In line with best practices, we followed an iterative and incremental development process, i.e., with an increased understanding of the domain, the information model was continuously improved.

All artifacts were hosted and maintained by VoCol [10], a collaborative vocabulary development environment which we adapted for the purpose of this project. VoCol supports the requirements of the stakeholders: (i) version-control of the ontology; (ii) online and offline editing; and (iii) support for different ontology editors (by generating a unique serialization before changes are merged to avoid false-positive conflicts [9]). In addition, it offers different web-based views on the ontology, including a human-readable documentation, a visualization and charts generated from queries applied to the ontology and instance data. These views are designated to ease the collaboration of domain experts in the development process, i.e., enabling them to participate without having to set up and maintain a proper infrastructure themselves.

Purpose and Scope. The information model comprises (i) a formal description of the physical assets of the company, (ii) mappings to database schemas of existing production systems, and (iii) a formalization of domain-related knowledge of experienced employees about certain tasks and processes within the company.

The heart of the information model represents the aforementioned *machine tool*, including its sensor data, usage processes and human interaction. Therefore, the majority of concepts are defined by their relation to this machine.

The scope is set by the motivating examples *energy consumption* and *tool management* introduced in Sect. 2.1. Nevertheless, the management considered it also *nice to have* to gain a clearer picture of all assets of the company. For example: What local knowledge exists in the factory? What kind of data exists for which machine? Where is that data? Who has access to it? Discussions on fully automated order-driven production sites are ongoing. The management hopes for this to be supported by the information model, and we aim to provide the basis for that goal.

Capturing Domain Knowledge. We captured the domain knowledge in different ways:

1. The company provided descriptive material of the domain, including maps of factories, descriptions of machines and work orders, information about processes, sensor data and tool knowledge. The types of input material ranged from formatted and unformatted text documents to spreadsheets and SQL dumps.
2. An on-site demonstration of the machine within the factory was given during the project kick-off, including a discussion of further contextual information missing in the material. In subsequent meetings, open questions were clarified and concrete use cases for the information model were discussed.
3. We reviewed relevant existing ontologies and industry standards, intending to build on available domain conceptualizations and formalizations.
4. We created customized document templates to enable easy participation of domain experts by collecting input on the ontology classes and properties in a structured way. We collected names and descriptions of all properties having a given class as their domain in one table with one row per property; additional details about the domains and ranges of properties were collected in a separate table. These documents were handed over to the domain experts to be reviewed and completed.
5. We trained IT-affine employees of the company on modeling ontologies using editors such as Protégé, TopBraid Composer and the Turtle editor integrated into the VoCol environment.[1]

Conceptualizing and Formalizing. Figure 1 shows the core concepts of the developed information model. The colors group the different subdomains and reused vocabularies. Since `Machine`(s) are the main assets of the manufacturing company, they have been used as a starting point for creating the ontology. Each machine contains a geo-location (property with range `Geometry`) and is part of a certain `Section`, which is in a certain `Hall`. Each `Hall` can contain multiple sections and also has a geo-location (inherited from `Building`). `Plant`, `OfficeLocation` and `DistributionCenter` are different types of `Site`(s), each serving a specific purpose. The `MachineTool` comprises domain-related properties to describe its `AVO` (operation status). Next, it is connected with `WorkOrder`(s) to be processed. Each `WorkOrder` defines the required `Material` and `Tool`(s), as well as which machine should be used by which operator to execute a particular task.

Figure 2 provides a more detailed view on the `Tool`-related concepts. Machines have different interfaces, called `ToolStore`(s). Tool stores can be equipped with different `BasicHolder`(s). There exist three kinds of basic holders: `SingleHolder`(s), `DoubleHolder`(s) and `TripleHolder`(s). The name indicates the number of tools a holder can be assembled with. A `CombinationHolder` is a special kind of `SingleHolder` that can only be combined with a specific tool. The majority of holders are to be combined with a `ToolAdapter`, on which the actual `Tool` is mounted. Certain tools can be mounted directly onto the holder.

---

[1] http://protege.stanford.edu/,   http://www.topquadrant.com/tools/ modeling-topbraid-composer-standard-edition/, https://github.com/vocol/vocol.

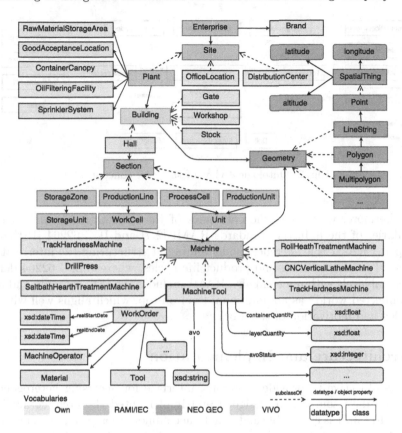

Fig. 1. Core concepts of the information model

Tools are the parts that wear out over time and need to be replaced. As with machines, their geo-location is defined, such that their position can be shown on a map. The tool ontology part reflects the configuration options for tools of multiple tool manufacturers.

In total, the developed ontologies comprise of 148 classes, 4662 instances, 89 object and 207 datatype properties. We focused on the description of the core concepts here that are needed to understand this work; a description of all ontology concepts would be out of the scope of this paper.

Aligning with Existing Ontologies and Standards. The developed information model consists of concepts from existing vocabularies and industrial standards that we formalized during the project. In particular, concepts from the VIVO (`vivo:Building`), NeoGeo (`ngeo:Geometry`), FOAF (`foaf:Person`) and Semantic Sensor Network `ssn:Sensor`) vocabularies and ontologies are reused.[2]

---

[2] http://vivoweb.org/,   http://geovocab.org/doc/neogeo.html,   http://xmlns.com/ foaf/spec/, https://www.w3.org/TR/vocab-ssn/.

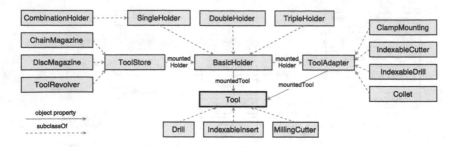

Fig. 2. Ontological view of the *Tool* concept

Furthermore, we aligned the ontologies of the information model to RDF vocabularies of the industry standards RAMI [2,7] and IEC 62264 [1] that we developed.[3] RAMI is a reference model aiming at structuring the interrelations between IT, manufacturing and product life cycles, whereas IEC 62264 defines hierarchical levels within a company. RAMI includes the IEC concepts and adds the "connected world" as an additional level on top, which aligns well with the basic idea and motivation of this work.

4   Architecture and Implementation

With the objective to provide a uniform interface for accessing heterogeneous distributed data sources, we designed and implemented the architecture illustrated in Fig. 3. It is extensible and able to accommodate additional components for accessing other types of data sources as well as supporting federated query engines. The architecture distinguishes the following four main layers, some of which are orthogonally located across different components:

The **ontology layer** consists of several ontologies that have been created to conceptualize a unified view of the data (cf. Sect. 3). Wache et al. distinguish three main approaches of using ontologies to explicitly describe data sources [23]: (i) *Global Ontology Approach*—all data sources are described in an integrated, global ontology; (ii) *Multiple Ontology Approach*—separate local ontologies represent the respective data sources, and mappings between them are established; the (iii) *Hybrid Ontology Approach*—a combination of the two previous approaches with the aim to overcome the drawbacks of maintaining a global shared ontology and mappings between local ontologies.

We followed the third approach, which enables new data sources to be added easily, avoiding the need for modifying the mappings or the shared ontology. Accordingly, our ontologies are organized in two groups: (i) a shared ontology to represent the highest level of abstraction of concepts and mappings with external ontologies; and (ii) local ontologies representing the schemas of the respective data sources. This makes our architecture quite flexible with respect to the addition of diverse types of data sources [3].

---

[3] https://w3id.org/i40/rami/, https://w3id.org/i40/iec/62264.

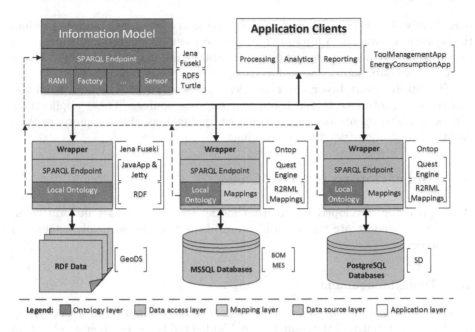

Fig. 3. The implemented architecture comprised of different layers

The **data access layer** consists of various wrappers acting as bridges between client applications and heterogeneous data sources. It receives user requests in the form of SPARQL queries, which are translated into the query languages of the respective data sources, and returns the results after query execution. Accessing relational databases is realized using the *Ontology-Based Data Access* (OBDA) paradigm, where ontologies are used as a conceptualization of the unified view of the data, and mappings to connect the defined ontology with the data sources [19]. In particular, the Ontop [5] framework is used to access the data sources, i.e., the BOM, MES, and SD data, which exposes the relational databases as virtual RDF graphs, thus eliminating the requirement to materialize data into RDF triples. Additionally, Jena Fuseki is used as in-memory triple store for loading GeoDS, since the information about the geo-locations of the machines are less than 20,000 RDF triples.

The **mapping layer** deals with the mappings between the data stored in the data sources and the local ontologies. For the definition of the mappings, we used $R2RML$[4], the W3C standard RDB-to-RDF mapping language. As a result, it is possible to view and access the existing relational databases in the RDF data model.

The **data source layer** comprises the external data sources, i.e. databases and RDF datasets as described in Sect. 2.2. Due to the high dynamicity and the great amount of incoming data, the data sources are replicated and synchronized

---

[4] http://www.w3.org/TR/r2rml/.

periodically. As a result, any performance and safety degradation of the production systems is avoided. Additional types of data sources can be easily integrated in the overall architecture by defining local ontologies, mappings with the global ontology and data sources as well as choosing an appropriate wrapper.

The **application layer** contains client applications that benefit from the unified access interface to the heterogeneous data sources. These applications can be machine agents or human interface applications able to query, explore and produce human-friendly presentations.

5   Application to the Use Cases

We applied the developed information model to the use cases introduced in Sect. 2.1 to demonstrate the possibilities resulting from semantically integrated data access.

5.1   Tool Management

Figure 4 displays different views on the assets of the company. On a world map (see Fig. 4a), the sites of the company are highlighted based on their geo-location given in the information model. By zooming in, the different locations can be investigated w.r.t. their functionality, address, on-site buildings up to the level of machines, etc. By clicking on the objects on the map, static and live production data is displayed. As an example, Fig. 4b shows all tools stored in a certain paternoster system, grouped by drawer. Figure 4c provides an example of a machine with its properties: production name, current status, self-visualization, mounted basic holder, tool with its diameter, etc. Further, it contains links to existing external analytical web pages. A "Determine Tool Availability" function is offered for locating the tools to be assembled in the closest paternoster storage system based on the location of the machines.

Each time a certain view is opened, a SPARQL query is executed to retrieve the required data in the information model. Geo-locations are drawn to the world map view using the Leaflet JavaScript library[5].

```
1   @prefix rr: <http://www.w3.org/ns/r2rml#> .
2   @prefix im: <http://iais.fraunhofer.de/vocabs/infomodel#> .
3   <WorkOrderMap> a rr:TriplesMap ;
4       rr:logicalTable [ rr:tableName"WorkOrders"];
5       rr:subjectMap    [ rr:template
6       "http://.../infomodel/WorkOrder/{WorkOrderId}"; rr:class im:WorkOrder];
7       rr:predicateObjectMap
8           [rr:predicate im:workOrderId;      rr:objectMap [rr:column"WorkdOrderId"]],
9           [rr:predicate im:beginWorkOrder;   rr:objectMap [rr:column"BeginWorkOrder"]],
10          [rr:predicate im:targetAmount;     rr:objectMap [rr:column"TargetAmount"]],
11          [rr:predicate im:totalExecTime;    rr:objectMap [rr:column"TotalExecTime"]],
12          [rr:predicate im:matDesc;          rr:objectMap [rr:column"MatDesc"]].
13          ...
```

Listing 1.1. R2RML mapping for work orders

---

[5] http://leafletjs.com/.

5.2   Energy Consumption

Information about the energy, power or temperature are critical for the company to forecast the production process, expenses and maintenance. In the second use case, we asked the following question: what is the *energy consumption* of a given machine for a given day for a particular *work order*? To answer this question, data from sources introduced in Sect. 2.2 (SD, MES, BOM) needs to be taken into account. Since the SD lacks work order definitions, we used time intervals to access the required energy stream data. Next, we linked the work order IDs in the BOM and MES databases. Listing 1.1 displays an excerpt of the R2RML mappings for the relational database table `WorkOrders`. Among others, it includes its material number, total execution time and target production amount.

Based on these mappings, we defined two queries: The first one retrieves information about work orders (cf. Listing 1.2); the second one retrieves the energy consumption values for a work order in a specific time interval (cf. Listing 5.2).

(a) Global view of the company sites

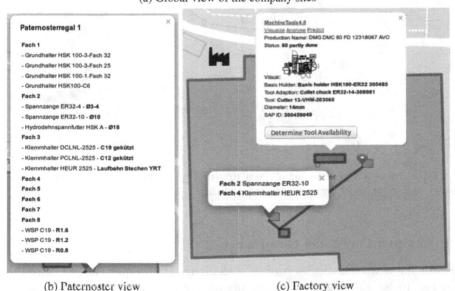

(b) Paternoster view   (c) Factory view

Fig. 4. Various views of the tool management application

```
 1  PREFIX im: <http://iais.fraunhofer.de/vocabs/infomodel#>
 2  SELECT DISTINCT  ?workOrderId ?materialDesc ?materialNumber
 3     ?beginTime ?dateFrom ?dateTo ?totalExecTime ?targetAmount
 4  WHERE {
 5     ?o a im:workOrder;              im:workOrderId ?workOrderId ;
 6        im:beginWorkOrder ?beginTime;  im:dateFrom ?dateFrom;
 7        im:dateTo ?dateTo;            im:targetAmount ?targetAmount;
 8        im:totalExecTime ?totalExecTime;  im:matNr ?materialNumber;
 9        im:matDesc ?materialDesc.
10  FILTER (?dateFrom >= dateFrom && ?dateTo <= dateTo)}
```

Listing 1.2. Query to retrieve information about work orders for a time interval

```
   caption
 1  PREFIX im: <http://iais.fraunhofer.de/vocabs/infomodel#>
 2  SELECT ?hour ((?latest - ?earliest) AS ?measurementByHour) {
 3    { SELECT ?hour (MIN(?measurement) AS ?earliest)
 4      WHERE { ?machineSensor im:energyTime ?time; im:energyValue ?measurement.
 5      } GROUP BY (HOURS(?time) AS ?hour) }
 6    { SELECT ?hour (MAX(?measurement) AS ?latest)
 7      WHERE { ?machineSensor im:energyTime ?time; im:energyValue ?measurement.
 8      } GROUP BY (HOURS(?time) AS ?hour) }
 9    FILTER (?hour>= timeFrom && ?hour <= timeTo) } ORDER BY ?hour
```

This allowed us to integrate the information from the three data sources using the information model and SPARQL queries. Figure 5a depicts the integrated information of work orders for a given machine, and Fig. 5b shows the energy consumption per hour for that machine for a given day. Overall the performance of the implemented solution was satisfactory, i.e., time to retrieve the information for energy consumption of particular work order was less than five seconds.

(a)   (b)

Fig. 5. (a) Work order data for a given machine in a time interval of one day, (b) Energy consumption of a given work order within a day

5.3 Information Model Governance

Introducing new technologies is often a challenge for companies. The introduction has to be well-aligned with the organizational structure of the company to balance the added value produced for the information model to the business and the maintenance costs of the technology. Thus, in parallel with the introduction of the information model, we defined a procedure to support the *governance* of information to ensure the maintenance of the model and uniform decision-making processes.

Since the core of the information model is a network of ontologies and vocabularies with a clear hierarchical and modular structure, there are boards of experts assigned to each part, which are responsible for its maintenance. Decisions cover, for instance, new terms to be included or existing ones to be removed, external vocabularies to be reused and aligned, and the continuous alignment with industry standards implementing the Industry 4.0 vision, e.g., RAMI, IEC, ISO. Additionally, we provided concrete guidelines for maintaining the information model along with the use of VoCol, for example[6]

- detailed documentation of all terms defined in the vocabulary by `skos:prefLabel`, `skos:altLabel`, and `skos:definition`;
- multilingual definition of labels, i.e., in English and German;
- definition of `rdfs:domain` and `rdfs:range` for all properties;
- inclusion of provenance metadata, licenses, attributions, etc.

6   Evaluation and Lessons Learned

To gain feedback from the stakeholders involved in the information modeling project, we designed a questionnaire and sent it to the stakeholders, asking for anonymous feedback. Table 1 lists the questions and results of the questionnaire. We were interested in how the stakeholders evaluate the developed information model and semantic technologies in general, based on the experience they gained in the project.

6.1   Stakeholder Feedback

Five employees of the manufacturing company (three IT experts, one analyst, and one consultant) who were actively involved in the project answered the questionnaire. The results varied across the stakeholders: While some regarded the information model and future potential of semantic technologies as promising, others remained skeptical about its impact within the company. Question 6 asking for the expectations towards semantic technologies (cf. Table 1) was answered by nearly all as an "enabler for autonomous systems" and by one as a "potential technology to reduce the number of interfaces". One stakeholder praised the "integration and adaption" capabilities of semantic technologies. Question 7 asking for the biggest bottleneck yielded the following subjective answers: "lack of standardized upper ontologies", "lack of field-proven commercial products", "lack of support for M2M communication standards", "skepticism of the existing IT personnel". While the stakeholders find the advantages of semantic technologies appealing, the lack of ready-to-use business solutions, industrial ontologies

---

[6] These are based on the W3C "Data on the Web Best Practices" Recommendation, https://www.w3.org/TR/dwbp/.

and available IT personnel is halting their efforts to move forward. As a result of the project, the company is actively seeking IT personnel with a background in semantic technologies.

Table 1. Questions of the questionnaire and answers of the stakeholders

Question (with Likert scale of 1 to 5, 1 = not at all, 5 = very much; M = mean value, SD = standard deviation)	M	SD
1. Did the developed RDF-based information model meet your expectations?	2.4	0.9
2. Do you think investing in semantic technologies can result in a fast ROI?	3.0	1.4
3. Do you consider semantic technologies fit for usage in the manufacturing domain?	3.6	0.9
4. Are you satisfied with the software for semantic technologies available on the market?	2.8	1.3
5. Is it easy to hire personnel with knowledge in semantic technologies?	1.8	0.4
Free-text questions:		
6. What do you expect from semantic technologies in manufacturing contexts?		
7. What is the biggest bottleneck in using semantic technologies in manufacturing contexts?		

6.2   Lessons Learned

Technology Awareness within the Company. After all, the majority of the stakeholders were enthusiastic and committed to developing an integrated information model and applications on top of it. Nevertheless, reservations on the fitness of the technology and methodology existed from the start. A few stakeholders preferred a bottom-up approach of first gathering and generating internally an overview of the existing schemas and models before involving external parties (such as our research institute). However, the management preferred an *outside view* and put a focus on quick results. Instead of spending time on finding an agreement on how to proceed, speed was the major driving force. Thus, they preferred to try out a (for them) "new" technology and methodology, which does not yet have the reputation of strong industrial maturity.

Perceived Maturity of Semantic Technologies. While semantic technologies are already widely used in some domains (e.g., life sciences, e-commerce or cultural heritage), there is a lack of success stories, technology readiness and show-case applications in most industrial areas. With regard to smaller and innovative products, the penetration of semantic technologies is still relatively small. A typical question when pitching semantic technologies within companies is "Who else in our domain is using them already?". Therefore, it is important to point to successful business projects, even if details on them are usually rare.

Lack of Semantic Web Professionals on the Job Market. Enabling the employees of the manufacturer to extend the information model by themselves is crucial for the success of the project. Consequently, it is necessary to teach selected stakeholders the relevant concepts and semantic technologies. Hiring new staff experienced with semantic technologies is not necessarily an easy alternative. Compared to relational data management and XML technologies, there is still a gap between the supply of skilled semantic technology staff and the demand of the market.[7]

Importance of Information Model Governance. Of major importance for the company is a clear governance concept around the information model, answering questions such as who or which department is allowed to access, modify and delete parts of the information model. An RDF-based information model has advantages in this regard: (i) it enables people across all sites of the company to obtain a holistic view of company data; (ii) current data source schemes are enriched with further semantic information, enabling the creation of mappings between similar concepts; and (iii) developers can follow a defined and documented process for further evolving and maintaining the information model.

Building on Top of Existing Systems. Accessing data from the existing infrastructure as a virtual RDF graph was an important requirement of the manufacturing company. It avoids the costs of materializing the data into RDF triples and maintaining them redundantly in a triple store, and at the same time, benefits from mature mechanisms for querying, transaction processing, security, etc. of the relational database systems. Three different data access strategies were considered:

DB in Dumps Relational data to be analyzed is dumped in an isolated place away from the production systems, as not to affect their safety and performance. This strategy is used in cases where the amount of data is small and most likely to be static or updated very rarely.

DB in Replication All data is replicated, allowing direct access from both production systems and new analytic platforms. This solution was considered in cases where data changes frequently and the amount of data is relatively high. It requires allocation of additional resources to achieve a "real-time" synchronization and to avoid performance degradation of the systems in production. We used this strategy to implement our solution, since it allows accessing the data sources as a virtual RDF graph and benefit from the maturity of relational database systems.

DB in Production The strategy of accessing data in real-time systems does not require allocating additional resources, such as investment in new hardware or software. Since this strategy exposes a high risk for performance degradation of the real-time systems, whereas sensitive information requires high availability and not providing it on time can have hazardous consequences, we did not apply it in our scenario.

---

[7] For the related field of data science, the European Data Science Academy has conducted extensive studies highlighting such a skill/demand gap all over Europe; cf. Deliverables D1.2 and D1.4 ("Study Evaluation Report 1/2") downloadable from http://edsa-project.eu.

7 Related Work

In this section, we give an overview on the development and usage of semantic models in related industrial scenarios: Siemens developed an *ontology-based access* to their wind turbine stream data [12,15]. The ontology serves as a global view over databases with different schemata. It thus enables SPARQL queries to be executed on different databases without having to take the different schemas into account. Statoil ASA also established a "single point of semantic data access" through an ontology-based data integration for oil and gas well exploration and production data [14]. They thus reduced the time-consuming data gathering task for their analysts by hiding the schema-level complexity of their databases. Ford Motor Company captures knowledge about manufacturing processes in an ontology such that their own developed AI system is able to "manage process planning for vehicle assembly" [21]. Furthermore, Ford examined the potential of federated ontologies to support reasoning in industry [17] as well as detecting supply chain risks [16]. Volkswagen developed a *Volkswagen Sales Ontology*[8] to provide the basis for a contextual search engine [8]. Renault developed an ontology to capture the performance of automotive design projects [6]. With regard to Ontology-Based Data Access (OBDA), Statoil chose the *Ontop* [20] framework because of its efficient query processing. While Siemens initially favored Ontop as well, they developed their own system in the end to further optimize stream data processing. Based on these experiences and our own tests of OBDA tools (mainly Ontop and *D2RQ*[9]), we chose Ontop as well. Regarding semantic models for companies, none of the existing works has specifically addressed machine tools and factory infrastructures. While it is understandable that companies prefer not to share internal details of their methodologies and infrastructure, there is nevertheless very limited evidence of semantic technologies being deployed in the manufacturing industry.

8 Conclusion and Future Work

We have presented a case study on realizing an RDF-based information model for a global manufacturing company using semantic technologies. The information model is centered around machine data and describes all relevant assets, concepts and relations in a structured way, making use of existing as well as specifically developed ontologies. Furthermore, it contains a set of RML mappings that link different data sources required for integrated data access and SPARQL querying. Finally, it is aligned to relevant industry standards, such as *RAMI* [2] and *IEC 62264* [1], to additionally foster data exchange and semantic interoperability. We described the used methodology to develop the information model, its technical implementation and reported on the gained results and feedback. Additionally, we reflected on the lessons learned from the case study.

---

[8] http://www.volkswagen.co.uk/vocabularies/vvo/ns.
[9] http://d2rq.org.

As for the enterprise, a high-level ontology is under development to extend the existing information model with our guidance. Its goal is to describe entire business units, their processes and assets for the entire organization.

The use of data-centric approaches in engineering, manufacturing and production is currently a widely discussed topic (cf. the related initiatives concerning Industry 4.0, the Industrial Internet or Smart Manufacturing). The challenges and complexity of data integration are perceived as a major bottleneck for the comprehensive digitization and automation in these domains. A key issue is to efficiently and effectively integrate data from different sources to ease the management of individual factories and production processes up to complete companies. The presented information model is envisioned to serve as a crystallization point and semantic reference in this context.

Future work concerns the continuous translation of relevant industry concepts and standards into RDF as well as their integration and alignment with existing ontologies and vocabularies. In addition, further ontologies for different industry domains need to be developed to enable data integration and semantic interoperability within and between companies. There is also a lack of related business processes and governance models, as it was shown by the case study.

From a technical point of view, further support for ontology-based data access would be needed to achieve the envisioned scalability. While we had good experiences with Ontop as an OBDA framework, complete coverage of SPARQL 1.1 is not yet given and challenging to achieve [5]. Further, R2RML supports only RDB-to-RDF mappings, while other types of data sources are not covered. Although there exist first proposals to extend R2RML beyond relational databases (e.g., RML[10]), tool support for these extensions is limited and not yet on the same maturity level as for R2RML.

References

1. IEC 62264–1: Enterprise-control system integration part 1: models and terminology. Standard, IEC (2013)
2. Adolphs, P., et al.: Reference Architecture Model Industrie 4.0 (RAMI4.0). Status report, ZVEI and VDI (2015)
3. Bellatreche, L., Pierra, G.: OntoAPI: an ontology-based data integration approach by an a priori articulation of ontologies. In: DEXA (2007)
4. Brettel, M., Friederichsen, N., Keller, M., Rosenberg, M.: How virtualization, decentralization and network building change the manufacturing landscape: an industry 4.0 perspective. Int. J. Mech. Aerosp. Ind. Mechatron. Eng. 8(1), 37–44 (2014)
5. Calvanese, D., Cogrel, B., Komla-Ebri, S., Kontchakov, R., Lanti, D., Rezk, M., Rodriguez-Muro, M., Xiao, G.: Ontop: answering SPARQL queries over relational databases. Semant. Web 8(3), 471–487 (2017)
6. Golebiowska, J., Dieng-Kuntz, R., Corby, O., Mousseau, D.: Building and exploiting ontologies for an automobile project memory. In: K-CAP (2001)
7. Grangel-González, I., Halilaj, L., Auer, S., Lohmann, S., Lange, C., Collarana, D.: An RDF-based approach for implementing industry 4.0 components with administration shells. In: ETFA (2016)

---

[10] http://rml.io/spec.html.

8. Greenly, W., Sandeman-Craik, C., Otero, Y., Streit, J.: Case study: contextual search for Volkswagen and the automotive industry (2011). https://www.w3.org/2001/sw/sweo/public/UseCases/Volkswagen/

9. Halilaj, L., Grangel-González, I., Vidal, M., Lohmann, S., Auer, S.: Proactive prevention of false-positive conflicts in distributed ontology development. In: KEOD (2016)

10. Halilaj, L., Petersen, N., Grangel-González, I., Lange, C., Auer, S., Coskun, G., Lohmann, S.: VoCol: an integrated environment to support version-controlled vocabulary development. In: Blomqvist, E., Ciancarini, P., Poggi, F., Vitali, F. (eds.) EKAW 2016. LNCS (LNAI), vol. 10024, pp. 303–319. Springer, Cham (2016). doi:10.1007/978-3-319-49004-5_20

11. Hermann, M., Pentek, T., Otto, B.: Design principles for industrie 4.0 scenarios. In: 49th Hawaii International Conference on System Sciences (HICSS), pp. 3928–3937. IEEE (2016)

12. Kharlamov, E., Brandt, S., Jimenez-Ruiz, E., Kotidis, Y., Lamparter, S., Mailis, T., Neuenstadt, C., Özçep, Ö., Pinkel, C., Svingos, C., et al.: Ontology-based integration of streaming and static relational data with OPTIQUE. In: SIGMOD (2016)

13. Kharlamov, E.: Capturing industrial information models with ontologies and constraints. In: Groth, P., Simperl, E., Gray, A., Sabou, M., Krötzsch, M., Lecue, F., Flöck, F., Gil, Y. (eds.) ISWC 2016. LNCS, vol. 9982, pp. 325–343. Springer, Cham (2016). doi:10.1007/978-3-319-46547-0_30

14. Kharlamov, E., et al.: Ontology based access to exploration data at statoil. In: Arenas, M., et al. (eds.) ISWC 2015. LNCS, vol. 9367, pp. 93–112. Springer, Cham (2015). doi:10.1007/978-3-319-25010-6_6

15. Kharlamov, E., Mailis, T., Mehdi, G., Neuenstadt, C., Özçep, Ö., Roshchin, M., Solomakhina, N., Soylu, A., Svingos, C., Brandt, S., et al.: Semantic access to streaming and static data at Siemens. Web Semant. (2017, in press)

16. Kim, M., Wang, S.T., Ostrowski, D., Rychtyckyj, N., Macneille, P.: Technology outlook: federated ontologies and industrial applications. Semant. Comput. **10**(1), 101–120 (2016)

17. Ostrowski, D., Rychtyckyj, N., MacNeille, P., Kim, M.: Integration of big data using semantic web technologies. In: ICSC (2016)

18. Petersen, N., Galkin, M., Lange, C., Lohmann, S., Auer, S.: Monitoring and automating factories using semantic models. In: Li, Y.-F., Hu, W., Dong, J.S., Antoniou, G., Wang, Z., Sun, J., Liu, Y. (eds.) JIST 2016. LNCS, vol. 10055, pp. 315–330. Springer, Cham (2016). doi:10.1007/978-3-319-50112-3_24

19. Poggi, A., Lembo, D., Calvanese, D., De Giacomo, G., Lenzerini, M., Rosati, R.: Linking data to ontologies. J. Data Semant. **10**, 133–173 (2008)

20. Rodríguez-Muro, M., Kontchakov, R., Zakharyaschev, M.: Ontology-based data access: *Ontop* of databases. In: Alani, H., et al. (eds.) ISWC 2013. LNCS, vol. 8218, pp. 558–573. Springer, Heidelberg (2013). doi:10.1007/978-3-642-41335-3_35

21. Rychtyckyj, N., Raman, V., Sankaranarayanan, B., Kumar, P.S., Khemani, D.: Ontology re-engineering: a case study from the automotive industry. In: AAAI (2016)

22. Uschold, M., Gruninger, M.: Ontologies: principles, methods and applications. Knowl. Eng. Rev. **11**(2), 93–155 (1996)

23. Wache, H., Voegele, T., Visser, T., Stuckenschmidt, H., Schuster, H., Neumann, G., Huebner, S.: Ontology-based integration of information - a survey of existing approaches. In: IJCAI-01 Workshop: Ontologies and Information (2001)

Personalizing Actions in Context for Risk Management Using Semantic Web Technologies

Jiewen Wu[1], Freddy Lécué[1,4(✉)], Christophe Gueret[1], Jer Hayes[1],
Sara van de Moosdijk[1], Gemma Gallagher[3], Peter McCanney[2],
and Eugene Eichelberger[2]

[1] Accenture Labs, Dublin, Ireland
freddy.lecue@gmail.com
[2] Accenture The Dock, Dublin, Ireland
[3] FJORD, Dublin, Ireland
[4] Inria, Sophia Antipolis, France

Abstract. The process of managing risks of client contracts is manual and resource-consuming, particularly so for Fortune 500 companies. As an example, Accenture assesses the risk of eighty thousand contracts every year. For each contract, different types of data will be consolidated from many sources and used to compute its risk tier. For high-risk tier contracts, a Quality Assurance Director (QAD) is assigned to mitigate or even prevent the risk. The QAD gathers and selects the recommended actions during regular portfolio review meetings to enable leadership to take the appropriate actions. In this paper, we propose to automatically personalize and contextualize actions to improve the efficacy. Our approach integrates enterprise and external data into a knowledge graph and interprets actions based on QADs' profiles through semantic reasoning over this knowledge graph. User studies showed that QADs could efficiently select actions that better mitigate the risk than the existing approach.

1 Introduction and Related Work

Risk is pervasive in every complex business, and businesses must manage risks in the sense that after identifying and externalizing risks they should take appropriate actions to mitigate risks, rather than eliminating risks [1]. Such practices are essential for large enterprises because of the promised quality outcomes to be delivered to clients, stakeholder or collaborators. With proper risk management, businesses can improve predictability of financial variance [2], be more flexible [3], enhance their competitiveness in the market, and develop growth through increased client satisfaction [4] by delivering what is promised and beyond.

Project risk management has been studied for more than half a century with a different focus e.g., risk identification, estimation, response and monitoring and control [5]. Various approaches have been suggested to address such problems with more and more roots in Artificial Intelligence and Machine Learning given the recent access to large amount of digitalized projects monitoring data.

© Springer International Publishing AG 2017
C. d'Amato et al. (Eds.): ISWC 2017, Part II, LNCS 10588, pp. 367–383, 2017.
DOI: 10.1007/978-3-319-68204-4_32

For instance risks of software-related projects can be predicted using ensemble learning of Artificial Neural Networks and Support Vector Machine [6]. Other approaches such as [7] presented a framework based on a risk ontology to monitor and identify risks through the project life cycle. Most of the work has been focusing on risk prediction and monitoring and less on mitigation, although mitigation processes have been largely curated by in-house quality assurance experts of most companies to limit revenue loss. Indeed mitigation actions are usually discussed among senior experts, and often subject to non consensus given the complex nature of contracts, and their complex environments and contexts e.g., contract type, industry group, geography delivery centre, client lead among others. In this respect the identification of relevant and impactful actions for the right contracts is a challenging task.

In Accenture an Intelligent Risk Management tool (IRM) has been developed to provide leadership with a holistic view of project risks. The tool consolidates data from multiple systems and predicts the risk tier of ongoing Accenture projects. Based on the computed risk tier, a project will be assigned a corresponding Quality Assurance Director (QAD), who oversees the project to identify and mitigate its risk(s). The sources of the risk can be manifold, such as the dependencies of the clients, the terms and conditions stipulated in the contract, or the capability of the company to staff the project with the right people, among others. Once the risk is identified for a contract, the task of the risk management team is to determine what is *actionable*, in other words which parameters can be controlled to reach positive outcome. In general, a QAD works with the project team (and leadership team if necessary) to determine the right actions that need to be taken to mitigate the risk. These actions, usually specific to the project, are documented in meeting minutes during portfolio review meetings.

The purpose of risk management is to mitigate risk and recover the losses as much as possible and in the most efficient way. One critical responsibility of QADs is to ensure the actions proposed by project personnel and leadership team are well understood and executed, as they might have very negative outcome if wrongly applied. Documented in meeting minutes, actions need to be reviewed and well understood by QADs before they can be executed. On average, a QAD can be assigned to oversee a few dozen contracts, each of which has a number of tasks that demand different levels of attention according to the risk tier of the contract. To help our 3,000+ QADs streamline this process, we designed a solution that customizes the actions recommended for the contracts based on the context the actions were proposed in, with the aid of semantic technologies from both an integration and reasoning perspective. QADs are empowered to explore actions in relevant context more quickly and to prioritize actions more confidently.

1.1   Motivation

The process of monitoring review meetings and tracking actions is laborious, in particular for QADs who are newly assigned to oversee the contracts. With the popular adoption of Artificial Intelligence practices in enterprises, Accenture has been phasing in machine learning to aid in its business processes, among which is risk management. Once a contract has been identified to have above normal risk, an action recommender automatically proposes a list of actions based on past five years' records, which would have required numerous portfolio review meetings involving various resources without the recommender.

Some challenges that QADs face in this process, with or without the aid of an action recommender, have been identified: (1) A QAD needs an efficient way to read the relevant meeting documents, e.g., to identify the list of actions when no recommender is used, or to understand the context of these actions. (2) QADs who are new to a contract or business may have difficulty in understanding the terms used in actions. They want to understand the actions and associated context accurately and effectively. For QADs, the purpose of reviewing actions is to ensure a correct understanding of the actions in context and prioritize the actions to be taken, e.g., actions that demand immediate attentions or that have a greater impact on the outcome. To help our leadership team manage risk-mitigation actions more efficaciously, we build a solution, deployed at validated by Accenture risk officer, to improve the understanding of actions, which in turn leads to better prioritization of actions for execution.

1.2   Problem Statement

To ensure a quicker and effective understanding of the actions, we find the following tends to help our users: (1) salient terms are highlighted, especially if the descriptions of actions are lengthy, and (2) terms are put into context, preferably customized for each individual user, so that confusion is minimized and minimum efforts are required from QADs to read relevant passages in meeting minutes. Personalization is important to our users due to the various levels of background knowledge they possess about actions in different contracts. To help readers understand our approach, Example 1 shows a typical action documented in a review meeting.

Example 1 (Actions). Action 1 reads *Meet with John Doe re the role requirements that the team has identified and notify the group when the next MLR should be scheduled.* Action 2 reads *Adjust time and material for delivery center in Chicago.* Without proper context, a QAD may, for instance, have difficulty in understanding the specific employee *John Doe* or the term *MLR* mentioned in the action.

Formally, the problem to be dealt with in this paper is stated as follows. Let a term T be a sequence of (at least one) words. An action, denoted A, is a sequence of n terms ($n \geq 1$). A user (a QAD in our business case) is denoted U, and her profile is encoded in a knowledge base (a.k.a. ontology) $\mathcal{K}$. Without loss of generality, we can assume all facts in $\mathcal{K}$ are represented by triples $\langle s, p, o \rangle$. Given an action $A = (T_1, \ldots, T_n)$, the problem is to generate a *personalized* action for U: $\overline{A} = \overline{A_a} \cup \overline{A_e}$ such that:

- $\overline{A_a} = (T_1, \ldots, T_m)$, where $m \leq n$, represents the key terms that carry the essential information of the raw action.

- $\overline{A_e} = (G_1, \ldots, G_m)$, where $G_i \subseteq \mathcal{K}$, $1 \le i \le m$. The context of each key term is represented separately by a graph consisting of a set of semantic entities and binary relations between entities, all associated with the given knowledge bases. Note that a graph can be empty, in which case there is no additional context available for the corresponding term.
- $\overline{A}$ is sufficiently small in size for users to understand the action A.

Our solution aims to provide proper context of each action so that a user can easily understand the actions and better prioritize the actions to be executed.

The paper is organized as follows: Section 2 gives an overview of the system architecture, as well as high level descriptions of the miscellaneous data sources and the applications. Following the system description, Sect. 3 details the three applications as a pipeline that ingests user profiles and raw actions to generate personalized action context. An empirical evaluation is provided in Sect. 4 to validate the efficacy of the system, which also includes a discussion on the learned lessons. Section 5 summarizes the paper and presents some extensions that we plan to build on the existing solution.

2   System Architecture

Figure 2 depicts the architecture of the solution we built to contextualize actions. Below is a detailed, bottom-up description of the architecture, in which Sect. 2.1 gives an overview of the data sources. Section 2.2 describes the functionality of system applications, and Sect. 2.3 describes the data flow and how users interact with the system.

2.1   Data Sources and Integration

Enterprise data provides information on the business context, for instance, actions usually mention specific business entities, Accenture acronyms, or employees names. Most internal datasets we used are structured, while some of them are unstructured, such as the dataset for actions, which is a set of meeting minutes notes. External data includes some standard RDF datasets, namely, DBpedia and Wikidata.

Accenture Business Schema describes the organization structure of Accenture and attributes of several types of objects, such as employees information, contracts, among others.

Accenture Data Lake is the internal Accenture data lake that serves as a hub for accessing key business data sourced from a variety of systems, ranging from SAP to MS SQL Server to documents. We have access to data about human resources (e.g., employees), financial outcomes (e.g., contract economics), and risk assessment (e.g., review meeting minutes and notes).

When both internal and external datasets are identified, we need to align their entities so semantic contextualization becomes possible on enterprise data

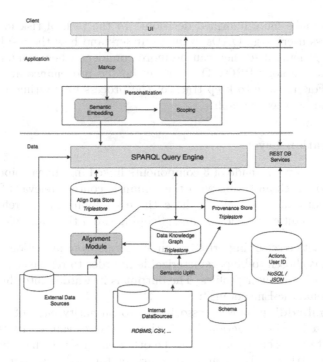

Fig. 1. The architecture

e.g., actions. The first step is to uplift internal data into semantic knowledge, which leads to an enterprise Knowledge Graph (KG) that captures the semantic information of relevant enterprise data. The next step is to align the enterprise KG with external data sources.

Semantic Uplift. The relational data and unstructured data used in the system is converted explicitly into RDF triples[1], with the latter given as the file paths referencing the actual unstructured content.

Alignment leverages both syntactic keyword searches and SPARQL queries and it enables us to interface the enterprise data with the external linked dataset via a uniform query engine.

Provenance Store records two types of data: (1) the source graph of RDF statements and (2) the source application or data unit of the resulting statements. The former is used to differentiate different types of application data, for instance, the user profile of a given user has to be separated from the actions' data during personalization. The latter is for end users to understand the details of computation. In our business environment, it is important to keep track of data flow in any process. In addition to compliance and regulation requirements due to data confidences, a more compelling reason is to

---

[1] https://www.w3.org/TR/rdb-direct-mapping/, last accessed 15 May 2017.

help users make more informed decisions. In the task of risk management, our business users, e.g., QADs, want to understand how the resulting action context is generated so they can be more confident when making decisions. We use the ontology PROV-O[2] to describe the provenance at the level of datasets. For instance to keep track of the process integrating a given CSV file into the knowledge graph.

2.2   Application Layer

The application layer is made of 3 components linked in a linear pipeline. Their objective is to enrich an action with the semantic context relevant for the user currently looking at this action. Those three components are referred to as "Markup", "Semantic Embedding" and "Scoping" after the main role they fulfill.

Markup extracts a set of important complex terms from an action. The implementation is chosen to be parameterizable in order to return sets of different sizes depending on user profiles. The output is forwarded into the next component "Semantic Embedding";

Semantic Embedding aims at associating to an entity each of the complex terms marked up in the action. In addition to the relevant entity the immediate context of this entity, that is all the other entities it is directly connected to, is also retrieved. The component further taps into the data store containing the provenance data in order to make this information available to the next component ("Scoping"). Finally, the graph describing the user currently using the system is also retrieved. This combined large graph (entities + embedding entities + provenance + profile) is passed as NQuads to the next component in the pipeline for scoping;

Scoping the large graph resulting from the embedding is important in order to avoid an information overload. Any given user need to be presented with the only data (s)he needs to understand a particular action, no more no less, as stated in the problem definition on the size of A in Sect. 1.2. The graph thus needs to be scoped to remove superfluous nodes and edges. The outcome of this process is sent back to the user interface for rendering.

2.3   Application, Data, and User Interfacing

The data layer provides a uniform access interface through SPARQL query engine (i.e., StarDog[3] in our implementation). As can be seen from Fig. 2, applications can query external KGs directly, or a combination of alignment data, provenance data, with enterprise and external KGs when needed (e.g., for semantic embedding). To our end users (QADs), the interaction with the system applications is a series of steps.

---

[2] https://www.w3.org/TR/prov-o/, last accessed 15 May 2017.
[3] http://www.stardog.com/.

User Login and Contract Selection. A QAD must be logged onto the system to see the assigned portfolio of contracts. She can then select a particular contract for review. To this end, two types of data items have been requested by the User Interface through some REST services: the user's unique identifier and, with the newly introduced action recommender, an automatically populated list of recommended actions if the contract is considered to be risky.

Application Processing. Once the input is identified, appropriate applications will be triggered, with access to the relevant data via the query engine. Any action in the recommended list will go through the full computation cycle in order: markup, semantic embedding, and scoping. An action, as defined in Sect. 1.2, is simply a list of complex terms. After processing, it will be enriched with proper context in the form of knowledge graphs (triples).

Output Rendering. The final output consists of 2 parts: one is the personalized context of this action, while the other is the provenance information associated with the computation, which users can choose to be presented.

3   Semantic Approach Towards Project Risk Management

This section describes the techniques of the three applications given in Fig. 2.

3.1   Markup

The markup functionality is leveraging [8] to identify the most important terms in any action. To this end [8] retrieves the key terms of an action that make this action in a particular class: documentation, financial, resources, capability, delivery, meeting, contract.

Example 2 (Markups of Actions). Consider the actions in Example 1. Action 1 has been marked with two key terms: "*John Doe*" and "*MLR*", while Action 2 has also two term highlighted: "*time and material*", "*delivery center in Chicago*".

3.2   Semantic Embedding

The objective of Semantic Embedding functionality is to embed the action into its global, semantically rich, context. This context is defined by the set of complex terms associated to the action (computed from the Markup functionality) and the concepts from the knowledge graph $\mathcal{K}$ they relate to. To this end we start by extracting some key terms $(T_1, \ldots, T_m)$ from the textual description of the action using both *part-of-speech (POS) tagging* and *named entity recognition (NER)*. For each key term, a matching for some concept, as well as the triples that have this concept as a topic, is performed in the given $\mathcal{K}$.

Once the extracted terms are mapped into concepts in the knowledge graph, an additional step is to obtain more relevant concepts through graph traversal. For example, in Example 2, the two concepts *Delivery Centre* and *Chicago* initially extracted from Action 2's text *Delivery Centre in Chicago* will get replaced by the concept *Delivery Centre in Chicago*, which is defined to be related to both *Delivery Centre* and *Chicago*.

Example 3 (Semantic Embedding of Actions). Consider the actions in Example 2. Semantic embedding matches key terms with these entities:

>   Action 1:   `http://accenture.com/people/irm#john.doe`
>
>   `http://accenture.com/irm#ManagementLevelReview`
>
>   Action 2:   `http://accenture.com/irm#TimeAndMaterial`
>
>   `http://accenture.com/irm#DeliveryCenterChicago`.

Additional concepts within certain distances of the key terms in the KG are also obtained, which result in more statements. Some sample statements are given below, where entities are denoted by local names instead of URIs for readability (the Accenture name spaces are omitted).

Action 1 has part of its context being:

$$\langle john.doe, gender, male\rangle, \langle john.doe, hireDate, \text{``}2009.04.19\text{''}\rangle,$$
$$\langle john.doe, hasSkill, MDM\rangle, \langle MDM, a, SAP\_Skills\rangle,$$
$$\langle john.doe, hasSupervisor, jane.roe\rangle,$$
$$\langle ManagementLevelReview, a, AccentureProjectReview\rangle.$$

Action 2 has part of its context being:

$$\langle DeliveryCenterChicago, inCity, wikidata : Q1297\rangle,$$
$$\langle DeliveryCenterChicago, a, DeliveryCenter\rangle,$$
$$\langle wikidata : Q1297, a, wikidata : Q515\rangle,$$
$$\langle TimeAndMaterial, partOf, Time\rangle, \langle TimeAndMaterial, partOf, Material\rangle.$$

3.3   Scoping

After semantic embedding, the context of an action consists of user-specific context, enterprise context, as well as general knowledge. This also means the generated context is potentially large, which may overload the users with excessive contextual information. To this end, we developed an algorithm to reduce the contextual information (represented as a knowledge graph w.l.o.g.) based on the user-specific context. Algorithm 1 shows how a given user profile is used to scope the action context (in the form of triples). Given a user profile G_u, Algorithm 1 decides if a statement from an action context can be filtered. We first collect all the entities that are *known* to the user on lines 1–2. On line 3, the subject s of the contextual statement is tested: if it is a known entity to the user, the algorithm considers if the statement is a description of some attribute of s (line 4), if the predicate or object is a known entity in general (the set *StandardVocab* denotes the set of entities defined in standard vocabularies such as RDF/S, OWL, SKOS, among others. An example of generally known entity is `skos:Concept`.), or if both the object and the predicate are also known to the user (line 6).

Input : $\langle s, p, o \rangle$, G_u
Output: true/false
1 $UC \leftarrow \{s' \mid \langle s', p', o' \rangle \in \mathsf{G}_u\} \cup \{o' \mid \langle s', p', o' \rangle \in \mathsf{G}_u\}$;
2 $UP \leftarrow \{p' \mid \langle s', p', o' \rangle \in \mathsf{G}_u\}\}$;
3 **if** $s \in UC$ **then**
4 $\quad$ **if** $o \in Literal$ **then return** true;
5 $\quad$ **if** $\{p, o\} \cap StandardVocab \neq \emptyset$ **then return** true;
6 $\quad$ **if** $o \in UC$ and $(p \in UP$ or $p \in StandardVocab)$ **then return** true;
7 **end**
8 **if** $s \in StandardVocab$ **then return** true;
9 **return** false;

Algorithm 1: Statement Test

Example 4 (Scoping of Actions Context). Continue the examples given in Example 3. Assume a QAD, $user_1$, logs onto the system and scoping takes place by looking at the user context of $user_1$, with a small part shown below:

$$\langle user_1, knows, john.doe \rangle, \langle user_1, hasSkill, SAPNetWeaver \rangle,$$
$$\langle SAPNetWeaver, owl:sameAs, MDM \rangle.$$

Finally, scoping reduces Action 1 context to the following:

$$\langle john.doe, hasSupervisor, jane.roe \rangle,$$
$$\langle ManagementLevelReview, a, AccentureProjectReview \rangle.$$

For Action 2, the user context does not reduce the action context due to limited user context on the key terms such as *TimeAndMaterial*. Thus, Action 2's context remains the same.

4 Validation

We discuss our asset in use by senior Accenture QADs. We review the main functionality exposing contexts of actions for risk management mitigation (Sect. 4.1). Then, we present an end-user validation on the fit-for-purpose of the contextualization asset (Sect. 4.2). Section 4.3 evaluates the scalability of components involved in our main architecture (Fig. 1). Finally, we review lessons learnt from the deployment of the asset in an industrial context (Sect. 4.4).

4.1 Actions in Context Asset

• **Broader Asset:** Figure 2 presents the Intelligent Risk Management (IRM) asset (and its 5 main functionalities) we deployed at Accenture. It represents the general user interface, in which our *"action in context"* asset has been integrated, tested and validated by QADs. A QAD connects to the IRM tool on a daily basis to assess a portfolio of projects that she is responsible for. She aimed at evaluating the level of risk predicted by the system (details of the prediction component is beyond the scope of this paper), investigating the root causes of the risk tiers, potentially requesting support from other QADs, exploring inconsistencies in the project and finally selecting relevant actions to be applied for mitigating financial risks, and limiting any revenue loss. The remaining part of this section emphasises on the latter functionality, captured in ⑦ through "*Action Explanations*" of Fig. 2. This particular component is selected when the project is at high risk (cf. upper part of risk scale ② in Fig. 2).

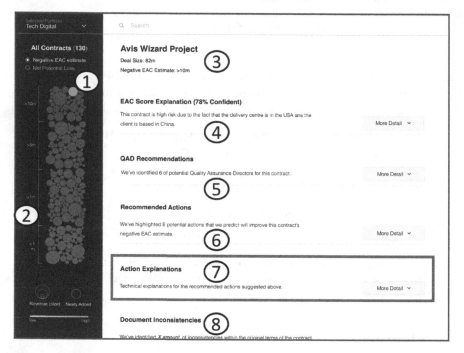

Fig. 2. fig:IRM-Action fig:IRM IRM - Intelligent Risk Management - Asset. ①: Project (represented as a yellow circle) selected (the larger the bubble the greater the target revenue). ②: Risk scale of the project (the higher the circle / project the riskier). ③: Summary of project details with expected revenue and risk tier. ④: Functionality for explaining risk tier prediction. ⑤: Functionality for recommending additional QADs for this particular project. ⑥: Functionality for recommending actions to QAD. ⑦: Functionality for explaining the context of actions to QAD (focus of the paper). ⑧: Functionality for flagging inconsistencies in projects (Color print).

• **"Action in Context" Asset:** Figure 3 provides a detailed description of functionality ⑦ of Fig. 2. QADs are shown a list of potential actions in ① of Fig. 3 which have been applied to projects with similar risk tier, and under similar conditions (industry e.g., resources, client classification e.g., diamond client). Each action is represented by its category ② e.g., Documentation, Financial and

Resourcing for general context, and its intent ③ e.g., "*Adjust Time and Material for Delivery Centre in Chicago*". The DBpedia and wikidata vocabularies have been used for cross-referencing categories using syntactic mapping e.g., http:// dbpedia.org/resource/Category:Financeforfinancial. Each action is broken-down in important complex terms (as opposed to entities) in Fig. 4 e.g., "*Time and Material*" and "*Delivery Centre in Chicago*" for action in ③. Then a graph, capturing the context and provenance of each important complex term, is displayed for action contextualization (cf. Fig. 4 for zoomed-in version of graphs ⑤–⑧ in Fig. 3). For instance the "*Pricing structure*" of selected project is "Time and Materials" ⑤, which is inconsistent with "*Fixed Price*", and "*Contract Price*" can be adjusted for a short "*Duration*" of "*6 months*". Some similar contexts are retrieved for complex term "*Delivery Centre in Chicago*" ⑥. ⑦ connects our enterprise knowledge graph with external resources such as SKOS, DBpedia, and Wikidata concepts. Item ⑧ provides context using our enterprise knowledge graph, for instance

- http://accenture.com/labs/people/irm#Person for Person or
- http://accenture.com/labs/people/irm#PCrossWorkForceCareerLevel   for career level.

A sample of our enterprise knowledge graph is available[4]. The latter context is crucial for QAD to understand how the action can be applied, and more importantly what is the rational of the context. In addition the context brings general information which is somehow discarded from initial information by the traditional approach e.g., Chicago is a city in North America region. This has been possible only because we initially mapped the enterprise data with external vocabularies such as DBpedia and wikidata.

4.2   Experimental Results: User Satisfaction

The evaluation of personalization and contextualization systems remains a challenge due to the lack of understanding of what factors affect user satisfaction [9]. Towards this issue, the applicability and usability of our approach has been tested in real world scenarios with users. In particular we evaluate the relevance and usefulness of the context of action selection.

• **Users:** To test the proposed approach, we have conducted a focus group study with 20 senior QADs at Accenture, aiming to explore the degree to which they understand, accept, and make use of the provided context for deciding on which actions to recommend. We split directors among 4 groups depending on their level of experience with the QAD role: (G1) [0–3) months, (G2) [3–6) months, (G3) [6,12) months and (G4) over 12 months of experience.

• **Tasks:** The participants were asked to interact with the action explanation component (Fig. 3) of the Integrated Risk Management tool (Fig. 2) to select action to be escalated for execution. First of all they have been requested to select

---

[4] Ontology sample available: https://goo.gl/uAQOD7.

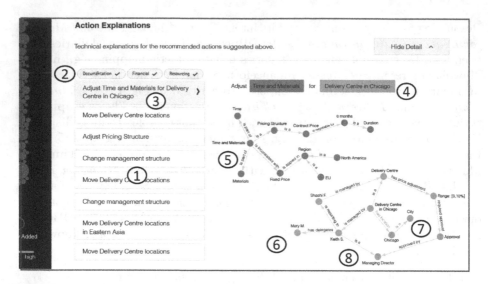

Fig. 3. "Action in Context" Functionality of IRM Asset. ①: List of recommended actions. ②: Categories of actions. ③: Action: "Adjust Time and Material for Delivery Center in Chicago" selected by QAD. ④: Breakdown of terms uplifted by our semantic embedding approach. ⑤: Contextualization of term: "Time and Material". ⑥: Contextualization of term: "Delivery Centre in Chicago". ⑦: Knowledge context of city Chicago captured from external sources: SKOS concept, DBpedia city, wikidata Q515. ⑧: Knowledge context of person Keith S. captured from internal enterprise knowledge graph: Work Force Career Level Managing Director, Delegates. (Color print).

actions using the traditional approach i.e., neither semantic uplift of actions nor context. Then they were asked to interact with our semantic-based model. Finally they were asked to rate the perceived usability of both approaches i.e., without and with semantic context and answer three open-ended questions: (1) the merits of contextualisation, (2) problems arising from contextualisation, and (3) possible ways to overcome these issues.

• **Results:** Selection of actions using the traditional approach has been a very difficult task to achieve by most of the least experienced participants (i.e., 77% for G1 and G2). 63% of the most experienced directors identify this particular task as difficult. Overall, our users' interest in contextualization and personalization (using semantics) is rooted in the hope that it will empower them to perform tasks more effectively, save time, and expose details according to their own needs and experience.

Table 1 shows that all groups of users were highly satisfied with the approach (an average rating 4.04 on a 5-point Likert scale where 1 = disagree and 5 = agree) and also demonstrates benefits against an approach without contextualization activated: Overall, Convenient to use and Engaging. Although all groups consider contextualization to be engaging, the less experienced is the director the more useful is the contextualization for their day to day work (G1: 4.55, G2: 4.12, G3: 3.85, G4: 3.65).

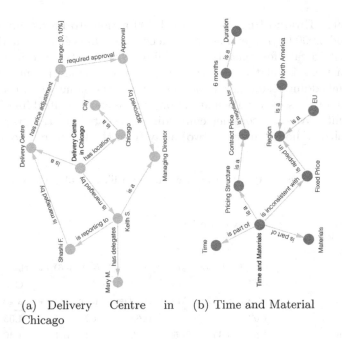

(a) Delivery Centre in Chicago   (b) Time and Material

Fig. 4. Semantics-driven representation of context for complex terms of action: "Adjust time and material for delivery centre in Chicago".

Usability measures, such as easy to use, efficient to use and easy to learn, all received high ratings, particularly for the least experienced directors. The more experienced group had more difficulties navigating through the graph representation and its context. More surprisingly experienced users are more optimistic regarding the quality of the outcome (Makes no mistake), and tend to trust the system more easily (G1: 3.55, G2: 3.75, G3: 4.35, G4: 4.75). This is due to the fact that more senior users already know about the context, and therefore trust a system that is giving information they already know. Junior users are less exposed and then tend to be more cautious about the outcome.

4.3   Experimental Results: System Evaluation

The system is tested on: 16 Intel(R) Xeon(R) CPU E5-2680, 2.80 GHz cores, 32 GB RAM.

On Markup. The markup functionality requires to have a classification model ready to be used for important terms identification. Classification is performed off-line with an average computation time of 65 seconds for 1, 200 actions and 5 classes. Once the model is computed the identification of terms is done action by action, which takes on average 18 seconds. The latter is also computed off-line for scalability reasons.

On Semantic Embedding. There are 1,200 actions to be recommended for contracts and 3,000 QADs (end users) in Accenture. On average an action would require about 15 calls for semantic embedding, which costs up to 500 ms. Since the set of actions is relatively static, we performed semantic embedding and cache the embedding results for all actions. We do the same on all user profiles. When a given user sees a particular action, the semantic embedding is a union of both results. We only consider embedding concepts over the graph up to a certain number of hops (currently two) away from the key terms' concepts.

Table 1. Perceived usability rating by users using a likert scale, where $1 =$ Disagree, $5 =$ Agree.

Interacting with contextualization (OFF/ON) is ...	Contextualization							
	G1 ([0–3) months)				(G2) [3–6) months			
	OFF		ON		OFF		ON	
	Mean	St. Dev	Mean	St. Dev	Mean	St. Dev	Mean	St. Dev
Easy to use	1.02	0.25	4.10	0.62	1.62	.25	4.05	0.05
Efficient to use	1.82	0.35	4.50	0.25	2.04	0.45	4.40	0.25
Makes no mistakes	1.15	0.25	3.55	0.45	1.15	0.15	3.75	0.14
Easy to learn	1.15	0.45	4.90	0.15	1.65	0.15	4.75	0.15
Convenient to use	1.25	0.55	4.15	0.65	1.25	0.25	4.05	0.45
Reliable	2.55	0.85	3.85	1.05	2.65	0.65	4.05	0.32
Engaging	0.77	0.25	4.85	0.25	0.99	0.10	4.75	0.21
Overall, I am satisfied	1.15	0.55	4.55	.55	1.95	0.15	4.12	0.15
Interacting with contextualization (OFF/ON) is ...	Contextualization							
	G3 ([6–12) months)				(G4) over 12 months			
	OFF		ON		OFF		ON	
	Mean	St. Dev	Mean	St. Dev	Mean	St. Dev	Mean	St. Dev
Easy to use	2.02	0.15	3.85	0.42	3.22	.36	3.45	0.33
Efficient to use	1.95	0.35	4.00	0.45	2.45	0.66	3.95	0.52
Makes no mistakes	0.95	0.35	4.35	0.15	1.55	0.33	4.75	0.41
Easy to learn	3.15	0.35	3.95	0.85	3.05	0.25	3.85	0.51
Convenient to use	2.55	0.45	4.05	0.25	2.25	0.42	3.85	0.99
Reliable	3.05	0.45	4.35	0.95	3.05	0.31	4.15	0.21
Engaging	2.85	0.15	4.35	0.15	1.49	0.23	4.45	0.14
Overall, I am satisfied	1.15	0.55	3.85	0.25	2.45	0.12	3.65	0.11

On Scoping. Scoping is not resource-consuming as the processing is done locally in memory (requiring no querying). On average, a user has about 100 statements to describe the user context, while an action has generally fewer statements as the action context. Scoping on a single action's context w.r.t. the user context in most cases requires less than 15 milliseconds. Caching is possible: the combination of frequently recommended actions and most active users can be pre-computed.

4.4 Lessons Learnt

• **Context Importance:** Although directors are senior, they do not have necessarily all the same deep and long experience in selecting actions for mitigating risks of projects. Indeed the turnover of QAD within the company i.e., 24% is very high for such roles. The latter is one of the strongest motivation to get context for non-experienced directors, specially for projects which may be out of their industry, geography or scope.

• **Context Navigation:** Our focus group user study emphasizes the advantage of using semantic Web technologies for bringing contextualization and personalization to the tasks of actions selection. In particular the least experienced directors benefit the semantic context the most. Although the most experienced group also benefits from the contextualization, deeper contexts were expected in some cases for this group. More detailed context would require more information on a graph, which we limited to 11 nodes. Handling larger knowledge graphs might be challenging from a user perspective. Towards this issue we have been requested by quality assurance directors to handle graph summarization [10] for capturing the essence of some information to understand actions.

• **Context Display:** As emphasized in Table 1, the usability of the context, and in particular the graph part of the personalization, has been questioned by the most experienced user groups. Some of the users had difficulties navigating the concepts in the graph, which emphasizes the common usability issues in knowledge representation systems [11]. Towards this issue it has been recommended to expose narrative-like sentences rather than tree or graph structures, which are less of use by financial experts.

• **Context Trust:** As mentioned in Sect. 4.2 context trust might be an issue for some users. Indeed they needed evidence the systems is displaying correct context, which not all users have knowledge to assess its veracity. This is true for more junior users, who tend to verify the facts. Although we integrated PROV-O for provenance, but more from a debugging perspective, it turns out that we should have communicated this information more explicitly to our users.

• **Vocabulary Alignment:** The OWL/RDF (concept) linking (alignment) process has been performed manually between our enterprise context and external vocabularies, but only once. However the latter needs to be replicated for each new data source or schema we might need to integrate. The automation of this process is a complex task as it required to align descriptions from very dedicated enterprise vocabularies with concepts from broad and sometimes inexpressive models such as DBpedia or wikidata.

• **Markup Scalability:** The Markup functionality, ensuring the detection of important terms to be contextualized, has shown some scalability, in particular for real-time processing. The identification of terms using [8] requires complex and time-consuming similarity functions to evaluate which terms are representative in an action with respect to a give class. Given that pair-wise similarity is performed, on-time processing is limited. Therefore our current implementation does not consider incremental adds-on of new actions in the system. The task of classification needs to be re-activated each time a new action and its class are added. Senior QADs questioned about the end-to-end automation of the risk management chain i.e., from minutes meeting ingestion to real-time suggestion of new actions (when available). This is a clear limitation of our asset.

5 Conclusions

Daily tasks of quality assurance directors range from: evaluating the level of risk of projects, investigating its root causes, requesting support from other QADs, exploring inconsistencies and selecting relevant actions to be applied for mitigating financial risks, and limiting any revenue loss. This work addresses the problem of understanding complex and sometimes generic and broad actions together with the rational of their context. Our approach integrates enterprise and external data into a knowledge graph and interprets actions based on QADs' profiles through semantic reasoning over this enterprise KG. User studies have shown that QADs, and particularly more junior directors, could more efficiently select actions that better mitigate the risk than the existing approach.

In future work, we will consider interactive learning to facilitate the on-the-fly integration of user feedback. We also expect to expand linkage of our enterprise knowledge graph with more LOD entities.

References

1. Cooper, D.F.: Project Risk Management Guidelines: Managing Risk in Large Projects and Complex Procurements. Wiley, Hoboken (2005)
2. Mustafa, M.A., Al-Bahar, J.F.: Project risk assessment using the analytic hierarchy process. IEEE Trans. Eng. Manage. **38**(1), 46–52 (1991)
3. Huchzermeier, A., Loch, C.H.: Project management under risk: using the real options approach to evaluate flexibility in R&D. Manage. Sci. **47**(1), 85–101 (2001)
4. Raz, T., Michael, E.: Use and benefits of tools for project risk management. Int. J. Project Manage. **19**(1), 9–17 (2001)
5. Chapman, C.: Project risk analysis and managementpram the generic process. Int. J. Project Manage. **15**(5), 273–281 (1997)
6. Hu, Y., Zhang, X., Sun, X., Liu, M., Du, J.: An intelligent model for software project risk prediction. In: 2009 International Conference on Information Management, Innovation Management and Industrial Engineering, vol. 1, pp. 629–632. IEEE (2009)
7. Tserng, H.P., Yin, S.Y., Dzeng, R., Wou, B., Tsai, M., Chen, W.: A study of ontology-based risk management framework of construction projects through project life cycle. Autom. Constr. **18**(7), 994–1008 (2009)

8. Ribeiro, M.T., Singh, S., Guestrin, C.: Why should i trust you?: explaining the predictions of any classifier, pp. 1135–1144 (2016)
9. Anand, S.S., Mobasher, B.: Introduction to intelligent techniques for web personalization. ACM Trans. Internet Technol. **7**(4), 18 (2007)
10. Gunaratna, K., Thirunarayan, K., Sheth, A.P.: FACES: diversity-aware entity summarization using incremental hierarchical conceptual clustering, pp. 116–122 (2015)
11. McGuinness, D.L., Patel-Schneider, P.F.: Usability issues in knowledge representation systems. In: AAAI, pp. 608–614 (1998)

Author Index